COVERT CADRE

Covert Cadre

INSIDE THE INSTITUTE
FOR POLICY STUDIES

S. Steven Powell

Introduction by David Horowitz

Green Hill Publishers, Inc.
Ottawa, Illinois

Distributed by Kampmann & Co., New York

Green Hill books are available at special discounts for bulk purchases for
sales promotions, premiums, fund-raising, or educational use. Special
editions or excerpts can also be created to specification.

For details contact:

Special Sales Director
Green Hill Publishers, Inc.
P.O. Box 738
Ottawa, IL. 61350
(815) 434-7905

10 9 8 7 6 5 4 3 2 1

Printed in the United States of America

Library of Congress Cataloging-in-Publication Data
Powell, S. Steven, 1951-
Covert cadre.

Includes bibliographies and index.
1. Institute for Policy Studies. I. Title.
H97.P69 1987   361.6′1′06073   87-6095
ISBN 0-915463-39-3

ACKNOWLEDGMENTS

I am deeply indebted to the people who contributed both in large and small ways to the research and writing of this book. First, I would like to thank those who provided financial assistance for the research and secretarial assistance, traveling expenses, and legal counsel that were required by the protracted project manifest in this book. Special thanks go to Virginia Armat, whose encouragement and contributions on so many levels at often critical times were so valuable that the book may have been impossible without her.

Among those institutions and organizations that provided access to specialized collections, papers and libraries I would like to thank the American Enterprise Institute, the Education and Research Institute, the Ethics and Public Policy Center, the Foundation Center, the Foundation for Public Affairs, the Heritage Foundation, *Human Events,* the National Journalism Center, the Media Institute, Accuracy in Media, and The Northcote Parkinson Fund. This book began as a research project at the National Journalism Center in 1981 and resumed the following summer at the NJC with assistance from the Fund for Objective News Reporting.

I am deeply indebted to many individuals who helped in a host of ways: research, translation, note-taking and tape transcription of the proceedings at countless public meetings held at or sponsored by the various organizations described herein. Jacob Van Rossum, a Columbia graduate, scholar of Soviet studies and the Russian language, was particularly helpful in assembling the material in chapters sixteen, seventeen and eighteen on the World Peacemakers and the Riverside Church.

In the spring and summer of 1984, Laurel Suomisto, a resourceful investigative journalist, provided critical assistance in the area of economic democracy and the U.S. Congress. Andrew Hruska, an extremely talented student from Yale, came to my rescue in the summer of 1985, and helped with major revisions of the entire work and contributed in a very significant way to chapters six and twenty. I am also grateful to my good friend Michael Hayes, who put me up in San Francisco during a difficult period in his own life. Thanks also to Steve Baldwin, Eugenia Benoit, Carol Chandler, Charles Dickens, Steve Edelen, Mark Falcoff, Samuel Francis, Lisa Frieman, Willa Johnson, James Hackett, Sandra Harton-McCluskey, Karen Hayes, Joyce Hemenway, Judith Hydes, Cliff Kincaid, Debra Krauss, Sayoko Kuwahara, Karen Lehrman, Wilson Lucom, Dan McCardle, Amy Moritz, Andrea Musacchio, John O'Hara, Ivan Pereira, Juliana Pilon, William Poole, Virginia Prewitt, Karen Rosedale, David Spray, Michael Tisdale, Ileana Urcayo, Michael Waller, Dierdre Weber and Tina Westby.

In a world where time is a precious commodity, thanks also must be given to those who were able to read and comment on parts of the manuscript. My thanks go to Richard Araujo, Louis Barron, Ladislav Bittman, Patricia Bozell, Walter Connor, Lee Edwards, M. Stanton Evans, David Horowitz, Rael Jean Isaac, Joachim Maitre, Vojtech Mastny, Joshua Muravchik, Richard Neuhaus, William Schulz, Candace Strother, James Tyson.

I would also like to thank various people at the Institute for Policy Studies and related organizations who shared so many valuable insights over many months. It was often their leads and firsthand knowledge that proved to be so fruitful. I also appreciated the opportunity to photograph some of the colorful personalities described in these pages, for pictures have a way of bringing life to a story that the written word can never quite do justice to.

To those others I may not have mentioned who helped facilitate this project in any number of ways, I offer my thanks. Everyone involved was thorough, fair and accurate; however, the responsibility for what errors may remain in the book rests with the author.

Contents

To my mother and father
and
Lubosh Hale

*A section of photographs can be found
between Part III and Part IV*

INTRODUCTION

After the 1960s, when people referred to the Institute for Policy Studies as "the only surviving institution of the New Left," that description was only a slight exaggeration. The radical decade had indeed left few institutional traces. But the remark also revealed a misperception of the nature of both IPS and the sixties revolt.

It was no accident the New Left established little permanent institutional presence. From the beginning, it had proclaimed itself a rebellion against institutions and traditional orders—not only those of "the system," but even of the left itself. The oppressive bureaucracies of the international Communist movement and its manipulative "progressive" fronts were as significant as targets of the New Left rebellion as were America's big-business bureaucracies.

The old left previously had masked its subversive intentions with liberal slogans, identifying itself as "progressive" and then infiltrating the Democratic Party and other mainstream institutions. The New Left regarded this deception with open contempt. Condemning the old left's elitist bureaucracies and conspiratorial vanguards, it styled itself a rejectionist force *outside* electoral politics. The New Left had no intention of entering the system to influence its direction. Its goal was to *end* the system. Through a "revolution in the streets."

But IPS was never really a part of this New Left revolution, although at times it served as a haven for New Left activists while pursuing its own strategy of infiltrating and influencing the political establishment. IPS's founders, Marcus Raskin and Richard Barnet, were former government bureaucrats, Democrats from the New Frontier—the very "corporate liberals" the New Left had identified as political enemies. However, Barnet and Raskin had abandoned a central tenet of cold war liberalism: anti-Communism. It was this abandonment of anti-Communist politics that allowed them to chart IPS's distinctive path to success.

IPS defined itself in terms that were characteristic not of the New Left, but of the old left. For this reason, and no other, at the end of the decade, when the

xi

battalions of the New Left rebellion disintegrated in exhaustion and defeat, the Institute for Policy Studies survived.

The New Left was born in 1956, the year Russian tanks invaded Hungary and reclaimed it as a captive nation of the Soviet empire. Communists who endorsed the invasion confirmed that their loyalty was not to progressive social revolution *per se* but to a totalitarian power. The New Left rejected this loyalty of the old left that made it a fifth column servant of the Soviet state.

The old leftists had been comfortable posing as "progressives" and infiltrating liberal institutions, because their purpose was not to overthrow the system themselves, but to weaken its defenses against Soviet power. The New Left despised this duplicity, calling the Communist progressives "gravediggers of the revolution." To distance itself, the New Left adopted an outrageous political style that drew attention to its "subversive" agenda and, in so doing, established its identity as an indigenous and independent "revolutionary" force.

This independence made New Leftists anathema to the old left. As the Vietnam War progressed during the sixties decade, the old left veterans positioned themselves in the peace movement, the most venerable popular front cause. But whenever a public demonstration was held, the New Left's political candor unmasked the peace fronts the old left contrived. With the burning of American flags and chants of "victory to the Vietcong," the New Left publicly revealed their real agenda, an agenda the old left wanted to conceal.

However, in all the areas the New Left caused distress for the old left survivors, the IPS founders put the latter at ease. In IPS's "progressive" politics and bureaucratic style, the old left saw a mirror of its political past. And since the Communist Party was in a state of organizational decline, it was only natural that old left stalwarts, faithful to the fifth column vision, would turn to the Institute for Policy Studies as a political base. If IPS owed its origins to Richard Barnet and Marcus Raskin, it owed its continuing existence to the old left diehards. And to three in particular: Peter and Cora Weiss and her father, Samuel Rubin, a Communist Party member of the Stalin epoch, whose fortune provided IPS with its chief source of financial support.

At Sam Rubin's funeral in 1978, IPS cofounder Marc Raskin eulogized Rubin as one of those "who dare call themselves revolutionary." His words were a revealing commentary on IPS's roots in the old left paradigm, which the New Left had tried, but failed to change. By 1978 IPS had become the institutional base of another generation of political survivors: the New Leftists who personified this failure, who even before the decade was out had returned to their political roots, as fifth columnists for totalitarians in power.

The IPS style has aspects that are flexible and disarming, in New Left fashion—for example, a tolerance for surfaces that appear chaotic, suggesting an element of spontaneity and political innocence. But its substance is defined by the covert agendas that shape its attitudes of unrelenting hostility toward the United States, and solidarity with Soviet-backed regimes.

Now Steven Powell's exhaustive investigation has stripped away IPS's ingenuous political façade and unveiled its hidden agendas for all to see. His portraits of the Institute's principals and analyses of its programs show clearly how IPS presents its purposes as one thing in order to accomplish another.

Although Powell's study, that tells the IPS story up through 1986, leaves little room for uncertainty, there is one element in the IPS character that remains opaque, as it would to any external observer of the Left. For only those who have lived inside its illusions can fully understand the destructive dimensions of the radical passion, and the true extent of its political deceit. What follow, by way of an introduction to this important book, are observations by one who lived this illusion for a quarter of century, from the late forties until the end of the Vietnam War.

I was born in 1939 into the same "progressive" generation as the architects of IPS, and in particular, Saul Landau and Cora Weiss, two of its guiding influences who typify the links between the radical generations. My parents (like those of Landau and Weiss) were members of the Communist Party, together with all of our family friends. The same deceptive exterior that hides the political agendas of IPS hid theirs as well. Outwardly, my parents were high school teachers, middle class in their habits, scrupulous in their respect for the community's mores and unfailing in their obedience to its laws. Like their friends, they always identified themselves publicly as progessives, espousing views that were liberal and democratic. They thought of themselves (and were perceived by others) as socially conscious, idealistic and concerned; they were active in unions and civil rights groups and in the left wing of the Democratic Party. The world of progressive and liberal politics was the world in which outsiders perceived them.

But like all their friends and political associates, my parents inhabited another, secret world as soldiers in the Third International, founded by Lenin. In their eyes, the first socialist triumph had taken place in Russia, establishing the Communists as humanity's vanguard in the global conflict that would bring about universal justice and peace.

This clandestine membership in the international revolutionary army was what really mattered to them and to all their political friends: it was the world that gave significance and meaning to otherwise modest and unassuming lives.

In their own minds my parents and their friends were secret agents. When they joined the Communist Party, they had even been given code names—for the time when their revolutionary objectives would require them to abandon the façade of progressive politics and go "underground" to lead the revolutionary struggle.

All their legitimate political activities were merely ruses and stratagems to camouflage the real tasks of their political commitment (which they could discuss only with other secret agents like themselves). Their activities in all the democratic organizations they entered, and all their liberal campaigns, were part of their secret service. The long-range purpose in all these activities was not to promote liberal or democratic values but to serve the interests of the Soviet Union. For them, the Soviet Union was the forward base of revolutionary power that would change the world.

To most Americans the revolutionary's apocalypse seems like an exotic fantasy, but for the left the fantasy is real. So real, in fact, that in 1949 the Communist Party decided that its time had come. Announcing that America was on the verge of fascism, the Party cast off its liberal mask and took its entire apparatus underground. My parents were still school teachers and registered Democrats. But the organization which absorbed their lives and to which they had pledged their political faith was now wholly clandestine, preparing as a secret conspiracy to war against the fascist state. In 1949 America the situation was farcical, but the intentions and capabilities it demonstrated were real.

The same intentions and capabilities characterize all those who have truly pledged themselves to the leftist faith. For the faithful, duplicity becomes a political virtue, and betrayal a political way of life. This reality is seldom understood by Americans guided by liberal values. Just as my parents' generation of fifth column Communists were generally misperceived as well-meaning but misguided idealists, so the covert agendas of the IPS activists have implications that are rarely acknowledged: "Amid . . . persistent accusations that the institute is a conspiratorial nest of Marxist-Leninists [a *Washington Post* profile recently concluded], the place more nearly resembles the stateroom scene in the Marx Brothers' 'A Night at the Opera,' in which the purposeful, the alienated, and the merely curious crowd themselves into a small cubicle.''

Powell's carefully documented account of IPS's words and deeds, and the trails connecting IPS personalities with the shadowy agencies of the East bloc, should suffice to dispel such illusions of comic innocence. It dramatizes how coherent forces may indeed operate behind a façade of political chaos, if the political context is right. (And in the left tradition to which IPS belongs that political context is right from the start.)

What those who mistake the left's idealism for innocence fail to understand is this: an international movement that mobilizes social idealists and commands their faith *can* commit acts of enduring evil without causing so much as a ripple on the comforting surface. For me, this truth is etched in a personal memory concerning the mother of a childhood friend.

This woman was a high school teacher, like my parents; like them, her only flirtation with an existence beyond the bounds of middle-class prudence was her membership in the Communist Party. Despite its Bolshevik rituals and conspiratorial fantasies, her Party life was mainly confined to quite ordinary activities like raising funds for the volunteers in Spain and playing the part of a cadre in a New York City teacher's union the Party controlled. But on one occasion she was chosen for a task unlike the rest, a deed that would burden her with guilt for the rest of her life.

When she was still the mother of an infant son, the Party selected her for a "special mission." The nature of the mission required that its purpose not be revealed to her and that its details not be discussed with anyone, not even her Party comrades. Normally the illegality and danger implied in such a proposal would have provoked intolerable anxieties in a person of her temperament and sheltered experience. But it was the Party that had made the request. And because it was the Party, these elements had the opposite effect. Fear was there, but the cause was greater. The aura of illegality and the prospect of danger only heightened the honor the Revolution had bestowed on her. It was the Party that spoke, but it was History that called. She had been given a chance to prove herself on a stage grander than any other she might imagine.

The mother of my childhood friend agreed to undertake the Party's mission. She left her infant son with her husband in New York, and took a plane to Mexico. There she delivered a sealed envelope to a contact the Party had designated. After making the delivery she flew back to New York and resumed the life she had lived before. It was as simple as that. Later she realized it was not so simple. The year was 1940. My friend's mother had become a link in the chain by which Joseph Stalin was able to reach all the way from the Kremlin in Moscow to Coyoacán in Mexico and put an ice pick in Leon Trotsky's head.

While not apparent to them, the political fantasy my parents and their comrades lived was a dangerous and destructive one. As secret agents of a cause that would bring justice to the world, they felt innocent and noble. But in their fantasy the revolution had already taken root in Soviet Russia. Thus, my parents and their friends also became secret agents of a foreign power—not in an official sense perhaps, but, more important, in their hearts.

As American Communists, the first principle of their politics was to serve and defend the Soviet power. This same principle defined their political loyalties and guided their political deeds. For my parents to betray these loyalties, to break faith with the Soviet rulers, or to weaken the instruments of the Soviet power, would be to betray everything important to them in their lives. They would rather have betrayed their country, or their friends.

Until 1956, Cora Weiss, Saul Landau, and I all shared this political fantasy, and inhabited its secret world. But in 1956 this world was shattered by the *Khrushchev Report* and the Soviet invasion of Hungary. The fantasy was exposed as a lie: the revolutionary cause the left had served was not social justice at all, but mass murder, slavery, and empire.

The old left was divided in its response to the *Khrushchev Report*. To the loyalists the epic crimes that socialism had committed were regrettable "mistakes" from which it had already begun to recover; the invasion of Hungary was necessary to secure the ramparts of the socialist world against the continuing threat from the capitalist West. To the loyalists, like Sam Rubin, Cora Weiss and Saul Landau the Soviet Union was still the mother of the revolution, the cradle of progressive hope.

Others rejected the loyalist compromise. A New Left generation emerged, whose battle cry was loyalty to revolutionary principle, not to totalitarian states with a revolutionary name. The New Left welcomed Castro's revolution in Cuba when he described it as "bread without terror" and "neither red nor black, but Cuban olive green." But even at the beginning, differences began to appear among us, between those who were really committed to the New Left idea and those who were already returning to the fifth column loyalties of the Communist past.

Those of us who were committed New Leftists could be identified by our readiness to criticize the revolution. Our loyalty was to the principles the Cubans were trying to put into practice, not to the revolutionary state itself. We would not repeat the disasters of the past by becoming servile supporters and secret agents of totalitarian states.

Many New Leftists made pilgrimages to Cuba. Some began to endorse the revolution's course without reserve. A few, like Saul Landau, established connections with various officials of the Havana regime.

I had met Saul when we were both members of the Communist Party's youth organization years before. That he was now willing to befriend Cuban officials disturbed me. What if Cuba became a police state like other leftist revolutions of the recent past? Who would Saul's friends be then? By forming loyalties to Cuban officials, he was ignoring the political lesson of 1956: loyalty to the revolutionary state had led a whole generation down the path of moral and political betrayal—of country, of friends, of political allies, and of the revolutionary principle itself.

In fact, Cuba soon followed the pattern of the left's revolutionary past. Castro, who had been a secret Communist before, now declared himself a Communist to the world at large. He began turning Cuba into a Soviet-style totalitarian state. In 1968, Soviet troops marched into Czechoslovakia to crush the Czech "New Left," and Castro gave them his support. The "revolution" he now championed was the Soviet empire. It was a rerun of the very same nightmare from which we'd awakened in 1956.

Just as Castro completed his betrayal of the principles he had once seemed to revere and by which we defined our own political vision, Saul Landau appeared as his New Left apologist, celebrating the Communist *caudillo* in the propaganda "documentary" *Fidel*. To anyone with our bitter memories of the time when the left's propagandists had made a paradise of the Soviet hell, the significance of Saul's act could not be mistaken. It was a declaration of political identity, a repudiation of what we had all begun. Landau's loyalty was not to revolutionary principles, but to powers that appropriated the revolutionary name. His duty to the revolutionary cause would be fulfilled in service to the totalitarian state. Saul had once again become a "secret agent." He had joined the old left loyalists, like Sam Rubin and Cora Weiss, and had found his Stalin in Fidel.

The Institute for Policy Studies provides the perfect institutional base for Saul Landau and his fellow radicals to play the roles of "secret agents." A bureaucratic public policy institution with a liberal ambience and Washington connections suits their purposes well. As an IPS senior fellow, Landau can pass as an "expert" commentator on Latin American affairs among the editors of the establishment press. In early 1986, for example, a crucial vote was scheduled in Congress on whether or not aid should be given to the anti-Communist guerrillas in Nicaragua. On the eve of the vote, an article by Landau (identified simply as "an analyst for the Washington-based Institute for Policy Studies") appeared on the op-ed page of the *Los Angeles Times*.

Saul Landau had begun his political life in the Communist movement and for nearly thirty years had been a collaborator and a supporter of the totalitarian regime in Communist Cuba. He had recently made a propaganda film for the Sandinistas with the cooperation of their security police. But there was no hint of these political commitments in the article he wrote for the *Los Angeles Times*. Instead, Landau submerged his lifetime commitment to socialism and posed instead as a mere taxpayer outraged by alleged corruption among the contra leaders, and their alleged misuse of public funds.

Landau's article never indicated that he might oppose aid to anti-Communist forces for political reasons. On the contrary, his article was written to appeal to readers for whom anti-Communism was a worthy cause. Aid to the contras should be denied, he argued, because the funds would not be used for their intended purpose, but be diverted to the pockets of corrupt and greedy contra leaders. Not once did Landau's article hint of his support of the Sandinista regime, or his personal friendship with its patron, Fidel. For Landau to own up to his actual political commitments and beliefs would have damaged his credibility—and his true ideological cause.

How can being truthful about one's real commitments damage one's political cause? Only if the cause is secret. Only if one's loyalties are not what they appear to be.

Today Saul Landau and the IPS "progressives" are heard criticizing Soviet society in ways they would not have done publicly in an earlier phase of the cold war. But their attitude toward Soviet *power* is exactly the same. For example, in April 1987, Landau addressed an audience of leftists gathered in Washington, D.C. to protest U.S. anti-Communist policy in Central America in the name of "justice and peace."

Landau urged the crowd not to pay heed to cold war myths of a Soviet threat, adding, "The Soviet Union is the mother of revolutions everywhere" and the United States is the patron of its "counterrevolutionary" enemies.

The dead man, Trotsky, had a phrase with which he expressed his contempt for the progressive vanguards which operated in the democracies of the West. He called them "frontier guards" for the Stalinist state. Their devotion to the revolutionary cause had degenerated into loyalty to a foreign, totalitarian power. They thought of themselves, secretly, as a revolutionary cadre; but the politics they actually espoused were pacifism and liberal reform, because their real role was as Soviet fifth columnists, and their real objective was to weaken adversaries of Communist power.

The IPS leftists are "frontier guards" in the same tradition, having long ago betrayed their revolutionary principles for privileged relationships with revolutionary power. Publicly they claim to be progressive participants in the democratic process. But like the leftist progressives of the past, their liberalism and pacifism are not political commitments. They are deadly weapons with which to lay siege to democracy's defenses, to cripple its resistance to the totalitarian advance.

This new generation, of the same old covert cadre I grew up with, fend off inquiries about their real agenda by accusing their questioners of "Red-baiting." But our democratic tolerance for unpopular ideas does not mean ignoring political commitments that undermine our republic and strengthen its enemies. The time has come in the life of this nation to name these attitudes for what they are, and to eliminate the taboos that inhibit discussion and recognition of the dangers they pose.

David Horowitz

Los Angeles
August 1987

Part I

The People, Ideas, and
Controversy Behind the
Institute for Policy Studies

CHAPTER 1

East Meets West at IPS

The late-model white Chevrolet sedan barreled around the corner onto Corcoran Street in the Northwest section of Washington, D.C., a quiet tree-lined street with brick sidewalks. The driver abruptly pulled the car next to a fire hydrant, the diplomatic plates flouting local parking regulations.

A thick-set man of medium height in a tweed jacket jumped out of the car. Scowling, he flicked away his cigarette as he locked the car door. He moved brusquely, as if late for an important meeting, and hurried down Nineteenth Street. I lost sight of him as he turned right on Que Street, the corner where the Institute for Policy Studies building stood, my own destination.

The institute was hosting a public discussion on the Soviet Union, a subject of more than usual news coverage in recent days. It was October 12, 1983, and the shock and confusion of the recent Korean Airlines flight 007 tragedy lingered in the minds of many. Although I had attended several public lectures at the institute and walked by it countless times on my way to and from the Dupont Circle subway station, I took particular note of the building that day.

The structure is seedy and peculiar, with portholes for windows whose cracked and half-puttied panes complement the stained deteriorating concrete walls. The sullied outside—five stories with chipped black trim, streaked green at the top from copper roofing—echoes the dark interior with its dirty gray carpeting, and dingy off-white paint. In the meeting room, where visitors attend lectures and discussions, just left of the entrance, there are benches along the walls and twenty or thirty chairs.

3

Associate fellow Michael Parenti, who has been published widely in Communist Party publications, had already begun his lecture, "From the Heart of the 'Evil Empire.' " There was a good crowd. I glimpsed a few familiar faces in the motley crowd that regularly attended the brown-bag lunch series. Young professionals and jacketed interns mingled with scraggly bearded men and testy-looking women in blue jeans and T-shirts.

Parenti was explaining why there were lines at stores in the Soviet Union and not in the United States.

"So what the Soviets do have is what economists call a very high percentage of disposable income, discretionary income," he said. "What is missing from Soviet consumerism is the rationing of the free market. Bloomingdale's is less crowded than GUM because millions of persons in the New York metropolitan area who might otherwise choose to shop there cannot afford to—either because they are unemployed or because they expend the bulk of their income on food, housing, fuel, medical care, tuition, and transportation."

Having just returned from a trip to Russia, Parenti expressed enthusiasm about other aspects of the Soviet system.

"In the USSR there has been no unemployment problem since the mid-1930s; everyone is guaranteed a job; rents can never be more than 3 or 4 percent of one's wages; medical care is free; education is free to the highest level of one's ability; utility services are inexpensive; bread prices have remained the same since 1928; most other food staples are subsidized; and it costs only seven cents to ride the subway. Small wonder Soviet citizens have a good deal of what economists call 'discretionary income'—which explains the crowded shops."

Parenti then talked about politics.

"Well, in fact there are elections in the Soviet Union," said Parenti. "There are elections in Cuba."

At this, some listeners couldn't contain themselves. A few snickers could be heard around the room.

Indignant, Parenti continued, "Cuba elects their apparat. The Soviet Union elects their deputies and whatnot, but you also think of a democracy as really to what extent do the democratic forces of society, that is the ordinary workers, minorities, people, women, and the people who are starving, to what extent do they get an outcome."

Now, Parenti discussed food in the Soviet Union.

"Our breakfast table was a veritable cholesterol city, with eggs, buttermilk, butter, cream, sour cream, yogurt, and lots of cheese." More restrained laughter erupted, but it was impossible to tell whether it was caused by Parenti's content or style. "And this tasty dark bread, which is really great bread," he continued, "hell, I must have gained five pounds."

I wondered why I'd never heard any kudos for the Soviet cuisine.

Next Parenti tackled housing.

"You get back to the U.S. and you run into people wondering about these things, you know, 'Where can I get a job?' and 'Where can I get a better place to live?' and apartments and this and that and the other thing. And you've got to wonder, 'Hey, we've got it so good, how come other people don't have it?' But it's not that way in the Soviet Union. Where does Yuri Andropov live? He lives in a housing project in the Kremlin in a five-room apartment. Most of the dachas, most of them are summer cottages and shacks. Not everybody wants a dacha by the way . . .

"And there's this myth that goes up about this class that rips off the lion's share of the surplus value for its own self-interests. So what? What exactly do they do with all that money?"

Antisemitism followed.

"The official policy of antisemitism is illegal in the Soviet Union," Parenti insisted. "One of the bus drivers I'd met, he was a Jew also, but he'd never received any antisemitism. Jews are statistically overrepresented in the party, in the professions, in the managerial positions. So if there's any antisemitism it's not represented in terms of career opportunities."

He did not explain why so many Jews want to get out of the Soviet Union.

The seminar was nearing its end. But Parenti had one last word of advice: "I beg you to do just one thing with the media, one thing. Always, always ask: 'Is it really true?' even if it looks so self-evident, so obvious. This plane, KAL flight 007, just strayed into that territory, got shot down by these guys who knew there were 269 civilian passengers on it, I guess, or something, and always ask yourself, 'Is it really true?' "

People began filing out of the room, past the receptionist's cubicle, out into the street. Parenti stood next to the large semicircular table of chipped formica, from which he had delivered his address. He was conversing animatedly with a tall man wearing wire-rimmed glasses and a backpack sporting a red and white "No Nukes in Seattle" button beside an "Impeach Reagan" pin. I walked up and tried to enter the conversation.

"I found your presentation very interesting. I was wondering whether I could get a copy of your speech."

Parenti didn't respond; he was talking while trying to get the attention of a dark-haired man in a tweed jacket leaning against the far wall near the blinded windows. Looking more closely, I recognized him as the driver of the white Chevy with diplomatic plates.

"How was it? How did I do?" Parenti called over. The man lit another cigarette, intently examining the departing audience. There was no answer.

"Mr. Parenti," I said, finally getting his attention, "I thought your presentation was very interesting. Do you think I could get a copy of the speech?"

"Sure." Parenti's face lit up. "You know, I'm writing a book on that now. About American political disinformation and about how it is that you can't get any reliable information about the Soviet Union."

"You know what they're going to say about that, don't you? The media I mean," interjected the backpacker from Seattle.

"Of course I know. You can't even debate it or question it at all without being typed as a Soviet apologist or a knee-jerk Moscow puppet or something like that. You tend to forget how knee-jerk and puppeted and strung up our conceptions might be here in the West," Parenti complained.

"How do you mean exactly?" I ventured.

"Oh, it's all over the place. Even on the Left the anti-Soviet bias is so incredible it's hard to have an intelligent conversation . . . . You start reading things closely, and you start going a little bonkers at the outrageous omissions and lies. I mean just the task of trying to find . . ." Parenti broke off as he observed the silent man in the tweed jacket approaching our group.

"Valeriy, how did I do?" Parenti asked the man, who now stood next to us. "You're from over there, what did you think?"

He smiled, nodded, and took another drag, inhaling some of the smoke through his nostrils. He was a heavy smoker, and obviously intense.

Parenti turned to me, "Oh, by the way, this is a friend of mine, Valeriy Lekarev. He works at the Soviet embassy."

"Pleased to meet you, Mr. Lekarev," I said as we shook hands. He smiled, but did not return the salutation. "What is your responsibility over at the embassy?"

"I am third secretary of the Department for Cultural Exchange," he answered readily.

"Well, Mr. Lekarev, what *did* you think of Michael's talk?" I asked.

With a wave of his cigarette he answered, "It was a fair presentation."

"And the Korean Airlines incident?" Only six weeks earlier, the Soviets had shot down flight 007 on its way from Anchorage to Seoul, killing 269 civilians aboard. "What do you think of the American press coverage?"

Another wave of the cigarette was his only answer. He seemed reluctant to comment. Instead he asked, "You, as an American, what did you think of it?"

"Well," I replied, "I mean everyone knows it was a mistake; your pilots or commanders just made a mistake."

Parenti and the tall man were engaged in a discussion of their own. Lekarev stubbed out the butt of his cigarette in a styrofoam cup and searched his pockets for another.

"There was," he pronounced each word deliberately, "no mistake."

"But, everyone recognizes the tragic mistake the Soviet government made," I countered. "You know, the incident has done more to hurt peace efforts and the nuclear freeze than anything else." I had spoken without a hint of reproach, yet Lekarev's face soured as he opened a new pack of Lucky Strikes.

"I mean, I just don't understand it," I went on. "It's hard to believe that your government is sincere about peace when they go around shooting down civilian planes and then harass the search efforts in the Sea of Japan." Lekarev cleared his throat as if about to speak. I realized I was probably making him uncomfortable.

"I'm sorry you feel it has hurt the cause of peace," Lekarev said placidly between puffs.

"Even if there are unanswered questions that justify what your government did, the least they could do is apologize. After all, there were innocent people on board. How does it advance the cause of peace when your government threatens to do it again?" I waited expectantly.

"As I said, there was no mistake," Lekarev answered. "Our air defense force responded to a real danger to Soviet security."

Sensing that I was about to get the same Soviet line heard countless times in news accounts, I decided to phrase the problem differently. "What do the Russian people think about this incident? What do you think?"

"It was no accident that the KAL plane flew directly over sensitive Soviet military installations," Lekarev replied with smug confidence. He looked me in the eye. "As is well known, the 747 had turned off its navigation lights and ignored all signals to land. In fact, the pilot took evasive action when he saw our interceptors. It is not the Soviet Union that hurts the cause of peace, but the United States which endangers the lives of civilians with its territorial violations and espionage activities."

"Do you mean that the Korean Airlines plane was on a spy mission for the U.S.?" I asked.

"Let us say that it was not by chance the 747 crossed the path of an American RC-135 spy plane just before it 'strayed' off course . . ."

I cut in. "That's what your government says, but what do you think? As a Russian citizen you must have opinions of your own. What did the Russian people think when they heard about the incident?"

"Our understanding is different from that of you Americans," Lekarev said in precise English. "You see, the will of the party is the will of the people."

"Are you a member of the Communist party?" I asked.

"Yes. It is not like here in the United States where you have a struggle of class against class and people against government. In our system, there is harmony between our people and our government. The people trust the decisions of the party. You might say the will of the people and the will of the party are one.

"Think about it," Lekarev insisted, as if in response to my unasked questions. "The Korean plane could not have strayed that far into Soviet territory by accident with all the advanced American technology and navigation equipment that it had on board. It could only have been on a planned intelligence-gathering mission."

Lekarev showed no signs of stopping, but Parenti interrupted him. "I've got to run. Give me a call and I'll send you a copy of the paper," he assured me. "See you later, Valeriy."

Lekarev waved goodbye to him.

I posed what I thought might be a neutral question. "How long have you been in the United States? Do you have family here?"

"About three years. My wife and son are here."

"How do you all like it? The United States I mean?"

"Of course I miss the Soviet Union. It is home. I do, however, enjoy much of what is in your country," Lekarev said. "The food, the movies, the climate. At home in Moscow soon the snow will fall. My one regret, perhaps, is that while the climate is warm here, Americans are themselves sometimes cold. It is not easy to get to know Americans. People do not want to talk to me once they learn that I work for the Soviet government."

"I would think that most people would like to talk with someone from the Soviet Union," I ventured. "I'd certainly like to get to know more about the Soviet Union. I've even been thinking of visiting your country if I can get enough money together. Some years ago, my parents went and really enjoyed themselves. They got separated from the tour guide, and rode the subway around Moscow all night. As Michael said, I have to wonder about what I read in the press about the Soviet Union."

At this Lekarev smiled broadly, without exposing his teeth. His wide Slavic face and somewhat greasy hair looked slightly out of place with the smartly tailored jacket and Oxford shirt. He offered me his hand. "Here is my card. Let me have your number and I'll give you a call, or you can give me a call anytime. Perhaps we can have lunch some time. I'm sorry but now I must leave. I have another engagement." I had no intention of meeting Lekarev again, but out of courtesy I gave him the name and address of the friend with whom I was staying.

We were both ready to leave. We made our way to the vestibule and the door leading to Que Street. Stepping outside, I was struck by the brightness and warmth of the Indian summer day after nearly two and a half hours in the dark IPS meeting room. It had been a bizarre encounter.

I had almost forgotten the incident when about three weeks later, on the morning of November 1, I was struck by a letter to the editor in the *New York Times* by Michael Parenti, associate fellow of the Institute for Policy Studies. Parenti was concerned that when Sen. Jesse Helms contended that Martin Luther King had communist associations, Helms's charges had been labeled "slanderous" by King's liberal defenders. Parenti's letter to the editor posed this question, "But what is obscene about associating with communists?" In fact, wrote Parenti, "there may be an element of truth in Helms's contention. . . . The three areas in which King was most active—civil rights, peace, and the labor struggle—are also areas in which U.S. communists have worked long and devoutly. It is possible then that King unknowingly or even knowingly associated with the American Communist party or with other leftist organizations. My question is, so what?"

Reading Parenti's letter instantly took me back to that meeting at the Institute for Policy Studies. I remembered the encounter with Lekarev, his hardened, yet sophisticated, character; his unquestioning support of the Soviet government's action that had outraged the world. I recalled Parenti's talk on the Soviet Union, a rather disingenuous account of Soviet socialism. Sipping coffee, staring at the paper in front of me, I pondered the familiarity between Lekarev and Parenti.

"So what?" I asked myself.

I decided to look through the IPS Washington School course catalogue. A course titled "Talking with the Russians" caught my attention as an interesting subject for a freelance article. That IPS was conducting "alternative arms-control talks" with high-level Soviet officials, while the U.S. government was being snubbed, held out the prospect of some interesting ironies and twists, the vital raw material for any article to be submitted to a popular journal. I called the institute and enthusiastically explained my idea to write an article. To my delight, the Washington School director waived the tuition fee, apparently expecting that I would write an article reflecting favorably on the institute.

Two or three weeks later I was having a cup of coffee at the Café Rondo across from IPS before a session of "Talking with the Russians." Gazing out the window, I recognized Valeriy Lekarev, the Soviet official. He crossed the street and went into IPS.

Since attending the first class I had wondered if he or another Soviet official might participate in the Washington School "Talking with the Russians" program. I had also thought of Lekarev's friend Michael Parenti. Parenti's enthusiasm about life in the Soviet Union and his suggestion in a letter to the editor in the *New York Times* that communism was a force for good seemed to me a curious anomaly in light of recent events. The shooting down of Korean Airlines flight 007 was but a harsh manifestation of the Soviet political posture expressed throughout 1983. The Soviets had walked out of the arms-control talks in Geneva while inflating the fear of nuclear war in a clumsy attempt to divide the NATO alliance. When Prime Minister Nakasone of Japan expressed his commitment to stand firm with the United States in defending the Far East, Soviet boss Yuri Andropov threatened Japan with nuclear annihilation.

I sat at the Café Rondo musing. Then, I had no idea that my article was to plunge me into a tangled world of political intrigue and intellectual duplicity, and consequently the writing of this book.

CHAPTER 2

In Washington but Not of It
Profile of a Revolutionary Think Tank

"The Institute is a Washington fixture," boasts Director Robert Borosage of the Institute for Policy Studies in an annual report, "sharing the travails of those who choose to tell truth to power."[1] "Our job," Borosage explains, "is to expose the moral and political bankruptcy of the ideas and assumptions now governing America. . . ."[2] Members of the IPS community are committed to being "public scholars," he adds.

According to *First Harvest*, IPS's twenty-year anniversary compendium published in 1983, "the philosophy that has most strongly shaped the Institute for Policy Studies . . . is perhaps best expressed in the introduction to *Being and Doing*,"[3] written by IPS cofounder Marcus Raskin. "Although hardly visible, the operation of the Violence Colony is the central fact of human relations in American society," argues Raskin. "Ultimately, the violence specialists tear all mediating influence away and the nation-state stands exposed for all to see, its rulers using the rest of the society as their hostage." Americans are in fact "hostages" or "prisoners," Raskin contends.[4] The mission of the Institute for Policy Studies, commonly known as IPS, is to "liberate" people from their colonized status and to "reconstruct" society—an ambitious if rather vague undertaking. But then IPS is not the usual sort of institution.

On Que Street just off Dupont Circle, a depressing dilapidated five-story building hosts IPS, self-styled as being "in Washington, but not of it."[5] IPS is "a center of scholarship and education . . . a new form of public university,

10

teaching formally through the Washington School, the Ph.D. Program, the intern and guest scholars programs; and indirectly through writing, conferences, seminars, lecture projects and social investigations."[6]

But it is by no means a detached institution of policy analysis. IPS has a sweeping political agenda, described in its latest annual report:

> The Institute's contribution to the public dialogue cannot be measured within the short-term boundaries of legislative calendars and presidential terms. IPS is engaged in a longer and deeper struggle, a struggle over the underlying principles and future direction of the political culture itself.[7]

Although IPS is ostensibly an educational enterprise, one of its founding fellows, Arthur Waskow, admits that "the Institute stands on the bare edge of custom in the United States as to what an educational institution is, as against what a political institution is."[8] IPS's first annual report, published three years after its founding, offers a glimpse behind its public posture. What is unique about IPS, it says, is the "'backstage' where participants may interact in spontaneous ways: pursuing hunches, sharing fantasies, exchanging scraps of potentially useful information, revealing ignorances, or exposing intellectual or personal antipathies and sympathies that would be deemed inappropriate by the conventional canons of the craft or be discrepant with the desired public image."[9]

But who are the public scholars who share fantasies and so on? IPS's latest annual report lists twenty-three trustees, twenty-five fellows, seven visiting fellows, and fifty-eight associate fellows. These titles lend the appearance of organization to the institute, but at no point elucidate their functions or their interrelationship. Interestingly, some who have worked at the institute for years never have risen above the rank of research associate, whereas others who have spent virtually no time there have been accorded fellowships.

Quite a few in the IPS community and among its alumni have led notable lives in politics, both domestic and foreign. Peter Weiss, chairman of the board of trustees, has been prominent in the National Lawyers Guild and National Emergency Civil Liberties Committee (both cited as Communist party front organizations by congressional committees in the sixties). Although Weiss specializes in patent and trademark law, he petitioned the West German government to help defend the Baader-Meinhoff terrorists on trial for bombing and kidnaping. IPS trustee Terry Herndon gained notoriety when, as executive director of the National Education Association, he backed a public school curriculum that instilled fear of nuclear war. Fellow Eqbal Ahmad endorses the Palestine Liberation Organization and Libyan dictator Moammar Qaddafi.[10] Fellow Saul Landau is a personal friend of Fidel Castro and has produced several documentaries lionizing the Cuban dictator.[11] Fellow Fred Halliday is one of the few Western journalists the Soviets have seen fit to let into Afghanistan to report on the war. The list goes on, and the activities of various members of the IPS community are detailed in later chapters.

Educational Outreach

The institute has disseminated its publications to thousands of institutions of higher education. According to the 1980 annual report, "Institute publications are carried in over 1,500 libraries," and "2,300 colleges and universities have now purchased one or more Institute titles."[12]

Besides this success, the institute has been able to establish relationships with numerous colleges and universities. The IPS "Project on Reconstructive Knowledge" is described in the institute's 1982–83 prospectus as a "network of study groups at Harvard, MIT, Hampshire College, Princeton, and IPS exploring . . . alternatives."[13] It has organized or cosponsored academic programs at colleges and universities nationwide and also cosponsors a clinical law program to help those who "blow the whistle" on the U.S. government.

In 1985 IPS fellow Michael Klare received a three-year Ford Foundation grant to become a "Five College Professor of Peace and World Security Studies" at Amherst, Hampshire, Mt. Holyoke, Smith, and the University of Massachusetts, despite Dr. Klare's questionable academic credentials. The school from which Klare says he received a Ph. D., Union Graduate School, had a joint "doctoral" program with IPS, but no accreditation. Klare directs the Peace and World Security Studies program to "enrich the faculty in the area of peace, security and disarmament."

Typically, the institute's "Ph.D." students do research and write political analyses to advance IPS activism. For instance, one doctoral candidate, David Cortright, wrote a dissertation that became the basis for *Soldiers in Revolt*. The book advocated "undermining discipline" in the armed services and argued that "democratization and resistance inside the army represent our best hope for preventing war and restraining state aggressive power" and "crippling military effectiveness."[14] Patrick Esmond-White, a 1983–84 Ph.D. student, has been developing strategies involving the Public Broadcasting System and cable and satellite technology to "bring pressure to bear on the system" so as to force the major media to adopt a more progressive agenda.[15] Noting "the growing availability of cable television," IPS fellow Sue Goodwin invites media-activists to "join us [the institute] as we get ready for the video revolution."[16]

To influence the Washington community more directly, IPS established the Washington School in 1978, which, it boasts, is attended by "over 450 students from Capitol Hill, the public-interest community, the federal bureaucracy and the Washington community in the fall and spring term courses."[17] The Washington School and informal noontime and evening seminars on a variety of topics serve two purposes. First, they provide a forum at which the leftist community can meet on a regular basis, allowing the American Left to network with the foreign Left. Second, because the programs are attended by congressional staff members and lobbyists, they influence government policymaking. As a tactical alternative to having congressmen and staffers attend classes, IPS often asks them to teach. The radicals in the audience then ask questions, and our policymakers presumably learn through the Socratic method.

Dozens of U.S. government officials have taught and participated in its programs. Many hold or have held national security-related positions, such as Richard Kaufman, chief counsel of the Joint Economic Committee, who informs Congress on Soviet military capability; Chris Clarke, research analyst for the Bureau of Research and Intelligence, Department of State; Larry Forest, staff member of the National Security and International Affairs Division of the Congressional Budget Office; Paul Warnke, former SALT II negotiator and director of the Arms Control and Disarmament Agency; Morton Halperin, former deputy assistant secretary of defense and staff member of the National Security Council; W. Anthony Lake, former director of the State Department policy-planning staff; and David MacMichaels, former CIA analyst.

Senators and congressmen who have also participated in Washington School programs include: Sens. Mark Hatfield (R–Oreg.) and Tom Harkin (D–Iowa); former Sens. James Abourezk (D–S.Dak.), Paul Tsongas (D–Mass.), and J. William Fulbright (D–Ark.); and Reps. John Conyers (D–Mich.), Ronald Dellums (D–Calif.), Henry Reuss (D–Wis.), and George Miller (D–Calif.).

The Washington School offers courses like "Investigating the Government," "Managing the Bureaucracy," "The Limits and Possibilities of Congress," and "Lobbying: Concepts and Techniques." While such titles lend a certain respectability, the course content derives from IPS ideology.

Course titles and faculty vary from year to year, but themes remain fairly consistent. In foreign policy and national security, IPS encourages students to criticize U.S. foreign policy rigorously and take a more accommodating and enlightened approach to Soviet foreign policy. The United States is described as having an "interventionist" foreign policy, whereas the Soviet Union is "involved" in the third world. Some in the IPS community applaud Soviet foreign policy to the extent that it helps Marxist revolutionary movements in Central America, Africa, and the Middle East. In the area of third-world development and modernization, IPS is enthusiastic about socialist alternatives despite socialism's record of perpetuating poverty and underdevelopment, as demonstrated by every third-world country embracing that ism. In the areas of U.S. public policy and economics, IPS classes emphasize the need for more regulation and more labor organizing, even though the progressive trend in the service economy is one of deregulation, and free and mobile labor.

Relations with Organized Labor

IPS enjoys close ties with several large labor unions involved in government, public education, and the defense industry. In 1980 the executive council of the

American Federation of Government Employees (AFGE) adopted a resolution stating that "AFGE will establish liaison with progressive research and development organizations, such as the Institute for Policy Studies, to assist AFGE in developing detailed, specific, reasonable alternatives to administration and congressional tax, budget, organizational and contracting-out proposals."[18]

The American Federation of State, County, and Municipal Employees (AFSCME) supports the nation's largest "independent socialist" newsweekly, *In These Times*, a magazine that serves as a mouthpiece of IPS. Not only do IPS staffers regularly contribute to *In These Times*, but its editor and associate editor, James Weinstein and John Judis, are both associate fellows of IPS. For many years IPS published the magazine.

Officials of the United Auto Workers (UAW) have taught at IPS and served on its board. UAW advertised that it "joins other progressive Americans in congratulating *In These Times* on its fifth anniversary of providing an outstanding alternative voice for America."[19]

Two former IPS fellows, Stephen Daggett and Cynthia Washington, joined forces with the International Association of Machinists and Aerospace Workers (IAMAW) to produce a slick study, *The Costs and Consequences of Reagan's Military Buildup*, which it opposed. IAMAW leaders stated that "we wish for *In These Times* success, perseverance, and long life in the pursuit of vital common goals."[20] But seeing that the majority of IAMAW's members work in defense-related industries, one may question what "vital goals" the rank and file share with *In These Times*, which seeks to dismantle the defense establishment.

Around the World

IPS fellows write position papers and organize conferences to support the new international economic order, a hot topic at the United Nations. In a paper published by the U.N. Commission on Trade and Development, IPS fellow John Cavanagh argues that transnational corporations serve as instruments of "repression" and that "such repression is mandatory since historically its explicit class function has been to act as a disciplinary force on the labor process; and to arrest change, notably from national liberation movements."[21] In fact, IPS has the unique privilege among think tanks of holding consultative status at the U.N. Economic and Social Council (ECOSAC).

IPS has associates in both the National Council of Churches (NCC) and the World Council of Churches (WCC), and has contributed to their anticorporate activism, their promotion of socialism, and the political and financial backing of third-world "liberation" movements.[22] Prexy Nesbitt, an IPS associate fellow, was one of the executive officers of the Program to Combat Racism, a project of the WCC that was discredited after CBS's "60 Minutes" and the *Reader's*

Digest exposed its support of Marxist liberation movements and terrorists to the tune of millions of dollars collected from unwitting churchgoers. Cora Weiss (wife of the IPS chairman of the board of trustees), though admittedly not a Christian, worked in a subsidiary program of the NCC, the Church World Service.[23] The highlight of her career there was the founding of "Friendshipment" in 1977, which subsidized the economic disasters brought on by the Vietnamese communist government.

Bread and Butter

No political institution can remain ideologically independent of its financial backers, and IPS is no exception. As an "educational organization," registered with the IRS as a 501(c)(3) organization, IPS can receive tax-free contributions. According to its annual report, "the Institute endorses no institutional causes; it enforces no institutional political line; it serves no specific interest and no political line."[24] However, if IPS has no institutional political line and serves no specific interest, its general activities consistently emphasize two overriding goals: dismantling the capitalist economic order and reshaping public-sector institutions in ways that give the Left political power thus far denied by the electoral process.

At the 1985 IPS trustees meeting, the board decided to undertake a fundraising drive to establish a $10 million endowment by 1988, the twenty-fifth anniversary of the institute. But what motivates those who have benefited most from our capitalist economic system to seek its destruction? There are no easy answers, but a brief look at the background of those who fund IPS offers some clues.

In 1963 Richard Barnet and Marcus Raskin incorporated the Institute for Policy Studies with grants from such sources as the Stern Family Fund and the Samuel Rubin Foundation. By the early 1970s the Rubin Foundation—founded by Samuel Rubin, a Russian émigré—was providing the bulk of IPS funding.

Samuel Rubin was a registered member of the Communist party and made his fortune in the cosmetic business of Fabergé, Inc., which he founded in 1936.[25] Rubin sold the lucrative family business for some $25 million in 1963, the same year that IPS was founded.

According to A. C. Fabergé, a descendant of Carl G. Fabergé, who served as "Jeweler of the Imperial Russian Romanov Court" (famous for crafting some of the most exquisite jewelry in the world, such as the Fabergé eggs, before his business was expropriated by the Bolsheviks), Samuel Rubin chose the name Fabergé for his cosmetic firm on the recommendation of his friend Armand Hammer.[26] Hammer was familiar with the allure associated with the Fabergé jewelry from his dealings with Lenin. To obtain hard currency and bankroll their New Economic Policy, Lenin and Bolshevik functionaries sold various objects of art and Fabergé jewelry to Armand and Victor Hammer, which they in turn sold through the Hammer galleries in New York.[27]

In 1920 the Carl Fabergé family fled the Soviet Union, after an heroic escape from Bolshevik prisons by two of the sons. Resettling in France, they set up a modest new jewelry house in Paris and a smaller craftshop in Geneva. After World War II the Fabergés discovered, to their surprise, that Samuel Rubin had stolen their trade name. They sued and initially got an injunction against Rubin, but, according to A. C. Fabergé, "Rubin was prepared to spend lavishly, and it later became reasonably clear that bribery of legal advisers had occurred. . . . Eventually an agreement was signed in 1951, [lifting] the injunction that had been issued against Rubin, who paid $25,000 to use the name for perfumery and toiletries"[28]—a name that had already earned Rubin millions.

The Fabergés were justifiably upset that their stolen name was used to bankroll IPS and other left-wing causes. A. C. Fabergé explained, "My family took part in the fight against the Bolshevik takeover. My father Alexander Fabergé participated in the so-called officer's revolt of Moscow in the early days of the revolution, while two of Agathon Fabergé's sons fought with Yudenich's White Army."[29]

Cora Rubin Weiss, the daughter of Samuel Rubin, and her husband, Peter Weiss, IPS chairman of the board of trustees, carry on the international socialist tradition through the Rubin Foundation, which is located in New York City across from the United Nations building in an unmarked office at 777 U.N. Plaza. They also administer a Rubin Foundation spinoff, the Fund for Tomorrow, which supports many of the same groups as the Rubin Foundation itself.

Philip Stern, an IPS trustee, is the president of the Stern Fund and provided much of the seed money that launched IPS in 1963. IPS has continued to receive support from the Stern Fund, which derived much of its original endowment from the estate of Julius Rosenwald, the late Sears, Roebuck magnate. Stern has remained a committed friend of the institute over the years. While traveling overseas recently, Stern wrote his colleagues, "Dear IPSers . . . it's so good to be outside of that psycho-*meshuga* country of yours."[30] Stern's uncle, Alfred K. Stern, also deemed it good to get free of the United States. In 1958, when a grand jury indicted him on three counts of spying for the Soviet Union, he decided to flee to Czechoslovakia.

The executive director of the Stern Fund, David R. Hunter, doubles as the executive director for the Ottinger Charitable Trust, another source of funding for IPS. Previously Hunter was an official of the National and the World Council of Churches, organizations which, since the 1960s, have been providing support for communist causes.

IPS has also received financial support from the Rabinowitz Foundation, originally founded by Louis Rabinowitz to promote Jewish culture. After the founder's death, the foundation fell under control of his nephew Victor Rabinowitz, a member of the Rabinowitz, Boudin & Standard partnership, a law firm which has represented the Castro government since 1960 and defended Soviet spy Judith Coplon and Alger Hiss. Victor Rabinowitz has also served as president of the National Lawyers Guild, cited by Congress as a front and "the chief legal bulwark of the Communist Party."

The Youth Project also provides support for IPS, but mainly it serves as a clearinghouse for funding IPS spinoffs and other groups that mobilize political action to implement many of the ideas and policy proposals popular with IPS. It receives funding from IPS backers such as the Stern Fund, the Ottinger Trust, the Rubin Foundation, and others, notably the C. S. Mott Foundation. That the Youth Project has located its Washington office in the IPS building off Dupont Circle also suggests close cooperation between the two organizations.

Another donor is the Funding Exchange, which channels money from nine of the most extreme foundations in the United States—1960s radical heirs of such fortunes as IBM, Pillsbury, Gulf and Western, and DuPont.

The web of funding becomes yet more complex for IPS works closely with three projects of the Fund for Peace, which receives considerable sums from the Stern Fund, Mott Foundation, and Rubin Foundation. The projects are the Center for Defense Information, the Center for International Policy, and the Center for National Security Studies, the last being an IPS spinoff. Interlocking directorates between the Fund for Peace and IPS's chief sponsor, the Samuel Rubin Foundation, presumably facilitate the cooperation between the two. Peter Weiss, IPS chairman of the board and vice president of the Rubin Foundation, has served on the executive committee of the board of trustees of the Fund for Peace, and J. Sinclair Armstrong has served as chairman of the board for both the Fund for Peace and the Samuel Rubin Foundation.

In addition to receiving funding from other large foundations like the J. Roderick MacArthur Foundation, the Ford Foundation, and the Mary Reynolds Babcock Foundation, IPS receives money from smaller ones: the Janss Foundation, DJB Foundation, ARCA Foundation, Bydale Foundation, W. Alton Jones Foundation, Playboy Foundation, Shalan Foundation, San Francisco Foundation, and New World Foundation; as well as from the World Council of Churches. (See Appendix 1 for listing of IPS's financial backers.) Although it is impossible to know precisely what motivates some of these donors, they clearly feel a certain antipathy toward the political and economic institutions of the United States. Daniel J. Bernstein, who founded the DJB Foundation and whose will bequeathed IPS a million dollars upon his death, was quoted as saying that "the chief enemy of mankind" is "the injustice of governments and of the United States in particular."[31] Edwin Janss, founder of the Janss Foundation, said that "when the revolution came, the houses of his neighbors would be people's palaces."[32] The Haymarket People's Fund, one of the nine backers of the Funding Exchange, states that it is "dedicated to eliminating rich people" and to remaking "a sexist and racist system that puts profits before the needs of the majority."

IPS says it operates on an annual budget of $1.7 million, which somehow allows it to operate three office buildings, hire over fifty full-time employees, issue an endless stream of publications, and shuttle people all over the world. Though the institute's annual report states that a certified public audit is open for public inspection (as required by law), IPS's accountant, Larry Stokes, resisted every attempt made by the author and research assistants to obtain one.[33]

A Wilderness of Mirrors: The Spinoffs of IPS

Alone, IPS could never have enjoyed its present power and influence. According to IPS's 1980 annual report, "the Institute community of scholars and activists includes networks of individuals and organizations in the United States and abroad . . . the Institute's programs now work with transnational networks of scholars and activists."[34] These "continuing relationships with others are *central to the Institute's work*," the IPS report explains, adding that "*no manageable list can encompass these associations*" (emphasis added).[35]

Because of the fellows' desire to be "actively engaged in creating change," says Borosage, "they merged theory and practice by developing experimental 'social inventions' "[36] In fact, IPS fellows have become champions at "spinning off" organizations born of these social inventions. To this end, IPS has been able to harness human attributes of competitiveness that undermine many other political organizations. It encourages these factions to split up, that is, spin off, rather than languish from ego and personality conflicts, a problem characteristic of conservative organizations.

The proliferation of spinoffs has given IPS influence a multiplier effect. Its themes are reinforced by ostensibly separate groups, but in fact little diversity exists. The spinoff strategy has also helped to diversify funding sources and to build networks. This gives IPS a central role in coalition building, which is increasingly important in this era of special-interest politics.

In 1968 two IPS fellows, Gar Alperovitz and Christopher Jencks, left Washington to establish a sister organization, the Cambridge Institute in Massachusetts, which founded the influential "alternative" periodical *Working Papers for a New Society*. The following year IPS helped establish the Bay Area Institute in San Francisco, which in turn created the Pacific News Service, to which more than three hundred major newspapers in the United States now subscribe.

During the 1970s IPS was the springboard for the creation of a range of left-wing organizations—the Institute for Southern Studies, the Institute for Women's Studies, the Institute for Neighborhood Studies, the National Conference on Alternative State and Local Policies, the Exploratory Project on Economic Alternatives, the Foundation for National Progress (which in turn founded *Mother Jones* magazine and the Center for Investigative Reporting), the Public Resource

Center, and the Institute for Food and Development Policy. In 1983 IPS established Policy Alternatives for the Caribbean and Central America, which led the fight against the Reagan administration's Central America policy. And in 1985 Saul Landau established ''IPS West'' in Santa Cruz, California, as ''an official outreach branch of IPS.''

The institute's annual report for 1980 elaborates on its pervasive influence, noting that IPS ''fellows have been instrumental in organizing the Committee on National Security and the Progressive Alliance, and have been active organizers in the World Peacemakers, the Chile Committee for Human Rights, the Coalition for a New Foreign and Military Policy, Americans for Democratic Action, the New Democratic Coalition, Mobilization for Survival, the Riverside Church Disarmament Program, the Urban Bishops of the Episcopal Church, and many more organizations.''[37]

IPS also founded the Center for National Security Studies, and has worked closely with the Center for Defense Information and the Center for International Policy—three groups sponsored by the Fund for Peace, which, as noted above, shares an interlocking directorate with IPS's chief sponsor, the Samuel Rubin Foundation. In addition, Paul Warnke, former Arms Control and Disarmament Agency director who headed the SALT II talks, serves as a trustee for both IPS and the Fund for Peace.[38]

One of the more sophisticated and influential IPS spinoff ventures of Warnke and Barnet has been the Committee on National Security, founded in 1980 to challenge ''those who exaggerate American military weakness and call for excessive military spending.''[39] According to the committee's promotional literature, ''recent events in Afghanistan, Iran and Latin America . . . illustrate a single simple truth—our world is changing and we must adapt to that change . . . through a new, wider definition of national security.''[40] Even though its appeasement and disarmament positions differ little from those of IPS, the committee has won prestige by recruiting former disaffected government officials. Some of these are Townsend Hoopes, former assistant secretary for the air force; William Colby, former CIA director; Admiral Tom Davies, former assistant director of the Arms Control and Disarmament Agency; James Leonard and Don McHenry, former U.N. ambassadors; Clark Clifford, former secretary of defense; William Kaufmann, former assistant secretary of defense; and Stanley Resor, former secretary of the army.

Because IPS provides training for radical activists, many of its fellows have become leaders in other organizations, which, though not technically spinoffs, add to the network seeking radical changes in U.S. domestic and foreign policy.

For instance, IPS fellow Joe Stork founded the Middle East Research and Information Project (MERIP), which supports radical Arab factions that are openly committed to the destruction of the state of Israel.

The Council on Economic Priorities (CEP), backed by the Rubin Foundation, has developed multiple strategies to oppose and restrict U.S. and multinational corporations. Complementing these efforts, IPS fellow Chester Hartman has taken over Planners Network and now operates it out of the IPS Washington headquarters. The Planners Network readily admits that its purpose is to "promote fundamental change in our political and economic system,"[41] for, among other ills, "the private market has proven incapable . . . because it values property rights over human rights."[42]

The activities of IPS and its network are most controversial with regard to Western defense policy and East-West relations. Two lobbying groups prominent on Capitol Hill and headed by former IPS fellows, the Coalition for a New Foreign and Military Policy (CNFMP) and the Committee for a Sane Nuclear Policy (SANE), have opposed every weapons system/defense program initiated by any legislator, Democratic or Republican.

The Riverside Church Disarmament Program and World Peacemakers target religious bodies to train antidefense activists. Rubin Foundation executor and Riverside Church Disarmament Program director Cora Weiss told a 1979 IPS conference, "As long as *we* give the meetings and people come to hear us, we will not see the essence of the fear of the Soviets in this country."[43] Even while Weiss boasted, the Soviet Union was deploying five new generations of nuclear missiles (the SS-16, SS-17, SS-18, SS-19, SS-20) and financing the Sandinistas' power grab in Nicaragua and the Vietnamese invasion of Cambodia, and Cuba, with forty thousand troops, was fighting to consolidate Marxist rule in four African nations.

In 1982, after two million refugees had been driven from Afghanistan, an IPS senior fellow and cofounder of World Peacemakers, Richard Barnet, assured us that "the Soviet threat is the big lie of the arms race."[44]

The above is but a sampling. The disarmament network associated with IPS includes numerous other groups, such as the Council for a Livable World, the Arms Control Association, American Friends Service Committee, Mobilization for Survival, Women Strike for Peace, War Resisters League, the Institute for Defense and Disarmament Studies, Physicians for Social Responsibility, Citizens Against Nuclear War, Peace Links, the Women's International League for Peace and Freedom, and Common Cause.

Beyond ignoring the Soviet military buildup, the disarmament network often falls in line with Soviet propaganda campaigns like those against the Trident submarine, the M-1 Abrams tank, the neutron bomb, the STEALTH and B-1 bombers, the Cruise, Pershing II, MX, and A-Sat missile systems. It cannot be denied that these groups contributed to the cancellation of the neutron bomb and delayed the B-1 bomber and the MX missile—all of which were designed to redress the imbalance of power, which developed during the years that détente gave the Soviets their advantage.

The network is now gearing for a major campaign against the Strategic Defense Initiative (SDI), which it prefers to call Star Wars.

But the network doesn't stop at lobbying against weapons systems. In 1974, IPS spun off the Center for National Security Studies (CNSS), which lobbied Congress to suspend domestic intelligence gathering and overseas covert operations, fed the press negative data on U.S. intelligence agencies, offered instruction on how to take advantage of the Freedom of Information Act to obtain national security information, assisted CIA defector Philip Agee, and lobbied against the Intelligence Agents Identities Protection Act. CNSS enjoys virtually unlimited access to lawmakers and congressional aides. According to CNSS promotional literature, "The CNSS staff are widely regarded as the nation's leading experts on matters affecting national security and civil liberties. They are consulted regularly by administration officials, members of Congress and their staffs, journalists and scholars, and other public-interest groups."[45] (See Appendix 2 for listing of organizations supported by the Samuel Rubin Foundation.)

On the Hill: IPS Influence in Congress

Because of its many affiliated lobbying groups, IPS has considerable influence on Congress. With a plethora of ostensibly independent groups all lobbying for identical goals, IPS can sway legislators to conform to what appears to be the going position. Then too, certain senators and representatives—IPS "point men on the Hill"—do their own lobbying and open up the legislative infrastructure to IPS.

In 1975, at the request of one such point man, Rep. John Conyers (D–Mich.), forty-seven members of Congress asked IPS to prepare an alternative budget study to that of President Ford. The request was repeated the following year, this time from fifty-five legislators, and again in 1978, when fifty-six members commissioned a study, which resulted in a 470-page report edited by Marcus Raskin. The report proposed "a socialist housing program which would compete with and steadily replace the private housing and mortgage markets," "a publicly controlled and operated health service," "a strategy for organizing for radical social change in the educational system" that "would disrupt capitalist control over the distribution of knowledge," "a 50 percent cut in the defense budget," and "disengagement" from America's overseas commitments.[46] Although such recommendations have little support among the vast majority of Americans, liberal congressmen keep looking to the Left. In 1983 sixty congressmen signed a letter requesting IPS to undertake yet another "alternative" budget study.

Founded in 1966, the Arms Control and Foreign Policy Caucus (originally called Members of Congress for Peace Through Law) has become a powerful *in-House* lobby for "greater arms limitation, the development of a global economy, strengthening of the United Nations, and abolition of war."[47] Though

ACFPC professes to run an educational, nonpartisan information service, it has had ties to IPS from the start. Three founders of the caucus participated in a 1966 IPS seminar entitled "New Era of American Policy and Statecraft." By 1985 ACFPC's membership included some one hundred twenty representatives and fifteen senators. Rep. George Miller (D–Calif.), who chairs the caucus's task force on Latin America, has as his legislative aide IPS associate fellow Cynthia Arnson, who does much of the legwork and position-paper writing. In addition, the ACFPC's executive director, Edith Wilkie, coordinates the caucus's activities and legislative strategies with those of key IPS affiliates, the Coalition for a New Foreign and Military Policy and SANE.

In addition to George Miller, other lawmakers, notably Reps. Don Edwards (D–Calif.) and Ted Weiss (D–N.Y.), and Sens. Tom Harkin (D–Iowa), Mark Hatfield (R–Oreg.), and John Kerry (D–Mass.), are staunch IPS partisans.

Congressman Edwards married Edith Wilkie in 1981 and was a member of the IPS Twentieth Anniversary Committee. In a "dear colleague" letter he exhorted his fellow congressmen and their staff members to attend courses at IPS.[48]

Congressman Weiss, for his part, admitted to an audience at the Riverside Church convened under Cora Weiss's Disarmament Program, a mouthpiece for IPS views, that "I spend more time at this institution than almost any other one. . . . You provide leadership and substance to people throughout the district."[49]

Senator Hatfield showed up at IPS's twentieth-anniversary celebration, and offered a warm endorsement: "I respect the often thoughtful and scholarly work of these individuals. I have no doubt that theirs is a legitimate and useful role in the formulation of national policy."[50]

And Senator Harkin heartily supports IPS. At an IPS reception in February 1984 he said, "I want to thank the Institute for Policy Studies and the people who worked so hard . . . [and] . . . have been in my office a lot."[51]

Sen. John Kerry has hired a former IPS fellow, Gary Porter, to be his legislative aide. IPS staffer Peter Kornbluh helped arrange an April 1984 trip to Nicaragua for Senators Kerry and Harkin on the eve of the vote on the contra-aid bill. Their celebrated meetings with Sandinista junta leaders captured headlines and helped sway the vote against the contras.

Key actors in the Congressional Black Caucus, such as Ron Dellums (D–Calif.), John Conyers (D–Mich.), and George Crockett (D–Mich.), have close ties to IPS. They also cohost delegations from the World Peace Council, the notorious Soviet front. After Congressman Crockett returned from a trip to Cuba in September 1981 where, according to *Prensa Latina*, he had "expressed approval of [Castro's] statements on the situation in Central America, and the U.S responsibility for the current crisis in El Salvador,"[52] he joined with Richard Barnet, Robert Pastor, and others in a Capitol Hill symposium, "The U.S. and

Cuba: Prospects for the 80's," sponsored by the Center for Cuban Studies, yet another organization backed by the Rubin Foundation. The seminar was convened to drum up support for normalizing relations with Cuba.

"They Must Be the Good Guys": *IPS and the Major Media*

By carefully selected euphemisms, such as *progressive* and *alternative*, IPS has successfully marketed its Marxist and radical views to the mass media. And the media in turn have softened up Congress.

The 1980 IPS report says that "Institute Fellows have appeared on the 'Today Show,' 'McNeil-Lehrer Report,' 'Good Morning America,' 'Bill Moyers Presents,' and a range of national television documentaries, not to mention all three network nightly news shows. Their commentaries are heard regularly over National Public Radio, and through local radio interviews and broadcasts."[53] In addition to Pacific News Service, the IPS spinoff that reaches some three hundred newspapers nationwide, "IPS Features," a weekly op-ed news service, now goes to two hundred newspapers across the country. Roger Wilkins, an IPS fellow since 1983, "credits his involvement with IPS with 'greatly enriching' the contribution he makes to the national political dialogue through his daily broadcasts over the Mutual Radio Network and his frequent articles in the *New York Times, Village Voice*, and other major publications."[54] That Wilkins was formerly an editorial board member of both the *New York Times* and the *Washington Post* has certainly not hurt IPS's access to these newspapers. In fact, IPS's success can be gauged by its uncritical acceptance by the nation's two most influential newspapers on foreign affairs, the *Post* and the *Times*.

The *Washington Post* describes IPS as "the first respectable offspring of the New Left."[55] The *Post*'s senior foreign editor, Karen DeYoung, so admires IPS that she joined the institute's faculty. Her comment at one class—"most journalists now, most Western journalists at least, are very eager to seek out guerrilla groups, leftist groups, because you assume they must be the good guys"[56]—offered a fascinating view into the political culture of the media. In fact, DeYoung's comment created such a flap that the *Post* barred her further participation at IPS functions. But DeYoung's colleague John Dinges, associate editor at the *Post*'s foreign desk, is an IPS associate fellow and continues to teach at the institute. Robert Kaiser, *Washington Post* national news editor, has also taught at the Washington School, as has the *Post*'s Moscow bureau chief, Dusko Doder.

A survey of the *New York Times* for 1980 and 1981 found that its op-ed page carried twice as many articles from IPS as from other policy research institutions.[57] The *Times* lends IPS credibility by identifying IPS as independent or liberal rather than as leftist or radical, which IPS proudly admits to being.

One of the *Times*'s most respected authorities on foreign affairs and national security issues, Leslie Gelb, asserts that IPS is "one of three preeminent centers for foreign policy perspectives."[58] In February 1985 Gelb accepted classified information on U.S. nuclear defense contingency plans from IPS fellow William Arkin and wrote a front-page story that severely damaged America's relations with her NATO allies.[59]

IPS Establishes an International Arm: The Transnational Institute

In 1973 IPS founded the Transnational Institute (TNI) to serve as its international arm with major centers in Amsterdam, London, and Washington. TNI in turn formed the Transnational Information Exchange (TIE), which established affiliations with organizations in France, Germany, Belgium, Denmark, Sweden, Switzerland, Spain, Italy, Australia, the Far East, and Latin America.

The core aim of TNI's work is to amass a data base on multinational corporations and to develop ties with unions and research/action groups to thwart corporate expansion. Through its subsidiary, TIE, TNI organizes anticorporate activities worldwide, even to the extent of reaching out to terrorists and revolutionaries.

Eqbal Ahmad, a supporter of radical Arabs from Qaddafi to Arafat, became TNI's first director in 1973. In 1976 TNI made news when its director, Orlando Letelier, was assassinated. The FBI recovered Letelier's briefcase from the wreckage of his bombed-out car and found evidence indicating that Letelier was acting as an "agent of influence" for the Cuban intelligence agency, the DGI, and the Chilean Socialist party apparatus exiled in East Germany.[60] Basker Vashee, a native of Rhodesia deported in 1966 with links to the Marxist ZAPU, became director of TNI in 1977.[61]

Although in practice there is little, if any, division between IPS and TNI, TNI protects IPS's respectability by providing a cover for IPS's relations with the international communist movement. One of TNI's 1980 Samuel Rubin seminar participants, Ruth First, a South African Communist party member and leader of the outlawed African National Congress (ANC), was the wife of Joseph Slovo, second in command of the KGB's Mozambique operations.[62] Other participants in TNI's programs include Victor Husbands, Gardenia Lewis, and Bernard Coard of the Peoples' Revolutionary Government of Grenada (the last was charged with the murder of Maurice Bishop in the October 1983 coup); Rene Mujica and Jose S. Delgado, first and third secretaries respectively of the Cuban Interest Section; Lea Guide, Rosario Murillo, Magda Enriquez, and Roberto Vargas of the Sandinista government in Nicaragua; members of Zimbabwe's Marxist parties, ZAPU and ZANU; representatives of the Soviet/Libyan-backed Western Saharan POLISARIO Liberation Front; ministers of the Marxist regimes in Angola and Mozambique; and representatives of the Communist parties of Spain and Italy.[63]

The activities of IPS and TNI go beyond mere ideological solidarity. TNI also helps raise money to bolster fledgling communist regimes in the third world. In July 1982 TNI arranged for representatives from the Marxist governments of Zimbabwe, Mozambique, and Angola to brief selected parliamentarians from West Germany, England, Holland, Austria, Spain, and Greece on the need for "support against South Africa's destabilizing efforts."[64] Six months later TNI facilitated a meeting between the Mozambican foreign minister and selected European parliamentarians who agreed to give Mozambique $20 million in aid. At yet another 1982 conference, in November, held at its center in Amsterdam, TNI arranged for the Sandinista vice minister of finance, William Huper, to petition European parliamentarians for support for Nicaragua.[65]

IPS and TNI play no small role internationally in bankrolling the Sandinistas. Upon their return from Nicaragua and Cuba, where they were hosted by Tomas Borge, the Cuban-trained internal security minister, IPS director Robert Borosage and senior fellow Saul Landau addressed a gathering at IPS in December 1983. Borosage explained their purpose:

> We were there [in Nicaragua] for a whole series of purposes. One was to work on a project we have going in Europe which was to encourage European support for aid to Nicaragua to keep it from being isolated economically and politically. The other was to work with the eight ministries down there to make sure they had their projects in order so that the Europeans could operate effectively.[66]

Bolstering International Socialist Solidarity: The Institute for Food and Development Policy

Other IPS spinoffs associate freely with communist governments. The Institute for Food and Development Policy (IFDP), headed by Joseph Collins and Frances Moore Lappé, has established close relations with the communist governments of Mozambique, Vietnam, Nicaragua, and Cuba.[67]

While ostensibly providing consulting services on alternative "collectivist" models of agricultural development, IFDP has concentrated on discrediting U.S. private-sector initiatives by attacking the practices of corporations and financial institutions. To "make America safe for the world," IFDP's first book, *Food First,* recommends that we should

> Outlaw government assistance through AID [Agency for International Development] and OPIC [Overseas Private Investment Corporation] and indirectly through the World Bank to U.S. private corporations investing in foreign countries . . . and promote economic assistance, not as loans but as grants untied to purchases in the United States, to countries where steps are being taken to democratize control over agricultural resources, such as Vietnam and Mozambique.[68]

It would block loans to the private sector and give unconditional grants to communist countries. The *Washington Post* called *Food First* "a major achievement!" The *New York Times* viewed the book as "full of intriguing perceptions," and the *Los Angeles Times* thought it "a clear-headed explanation of a complex and important subject."[69]

IFDP, itself a child of IPS, has sired various organizations to join the voices echoing the IPS agenda. For instance, in 1986 IFDP formed Neighbor to Neighbor, with the help of the Rubin Foundation, to organize a nationwide lobbying effort to "counter the lies of the Reagan administration" and sway uncommitted congressmen to vote against aid to the contras. On a more global scale, the formation of the Pesticide Action Network provides another case in point. An IFDP progress report notes that "we had little idea at the beginning of this year, when representatives of the Institute met with colleagues in Malaysia to form the Pesticide Action Network (PAN), that one year later PAN would have grown to include hundreds of active organizations in Africa, Asia, Europe, and both Latin and North America."[70]

Administrations Come and Go, but IPS Remains

The Institute for Policy Studies is not a run-of-the-mill think tank or a detached policy research center. IPS's policy prescriptions not only diverge radically from America's political heritage but seek to change it. In the political arena, IPS hopes to "move the Democratic party's debate internally to the left by creating an invisible presence in the party,"[71] to which end Director Borosage praised the Jesse Jackson 1984 presidential campaign. In point of fact, Borosage was the foreign affairs adviser to Jackson, and IPS senior fellow Roger Wilkins was one of Jackson's key speechwriters.

In economic policy, IPS has launched a many-tiered campaign to foster socialism in the United States, headed by such as Lee Webb, Gar Alperovitz, Derek Shearer, and Chester Hartman. Since socialism is anathema to Americans, the campaign speaks instead of "economic democracy"—stage one in IPS's revolution.

On foreign policy, IPS opposes efforts of the United States to halt the growth of Soviet power. "They may be a lot more democratic in certain features than we think we are," says IPS associate fellow Michael Parenti, "because the Soviet Union has class democratic features."[72] Insisting that the Soviet threat is but a myth, IPS advocates such deep cuts in the military budget that it comes down to unilateral disarmament. Closer to home, the institute lauds Fidel Castro, and helps raise funds for the Sandinistas to consolidate their power in Nicaragua, while, at the same time, attacking Central American allies of the United States for their imperfect human rights record.

To what end all these IPS activities?

The institute's publications and activities make it clear that the direction IPS would have our country follow is toward an isolated, defenseless, and socialized political and economic system, a future the American people firmly reject.

How is it, then, that IPS has been so successful in selling its radical views and sweeping agenda to the elites in academe, mainstream religious institutions, the media, and even Congress itself?

CHAPTER 3

Political Pilgrims Turn Militant
Hub of Activism at Home and
Links with Revolutionaries Abroad

In the Beginning: Cleansing the Haze from Liberalism

The roots of the Institute for Policy Studies extend back to the Liberal Project of 1959, undertaken by ten Democratic congressmen and forty-six intellectuals, scientists, and scholars for the avowed purpose of "cleansing the haze from the word 'liberalism' so as to allow its development into a truly effective political force."

The book that emerged, the *Liberal Papers*, urged the United States to allow the Soviet Union to plug into its early-warning defense system, unilaterally abandon nuclear testing, dismantle the NATO alliance, withdraw from Berlin, and neutralize Central Europe under terms proposed by the Soviet satellite Poland. But the Liberal Project really became a viable political force only when its major contributors—Marcus Raskin, Arthur Waskow, David Riesman, Michael Maccoby, and James Warburg—joined forces with Richard Barnet in founding the Institute for Policy Studies.

It all started when Barnet met Raskin at a White House/State Department conference in 1961. Barnet was deputy director for political research of the U.S. Arms Control and Disarmament Agency, and Raskin was an aide to McGeorge Bundy and staff member of the National Security Council. At the time, neither realized how fateful that meeting would be, but later Barnet recalled how he had noticed Raskin's alienation and contempt for "the whole military-industrial es-

28

tablishment sitting there at one table." "Marc and I both grimaced at the same moment," said Barnet, "and knew we didn't belong here."[1] Two years later, in 1963, Barnet and Raskin incorporated the Institute for Policy Studies with the help of an initial major grant from the Stern Family Fund and other sources, notably the Samuel Rubin Foundation. In addition to drawing from the ideas and people of the Liberal Project, IPS used the resources and experience of Arthur Waskow's Peace Research Institute, established several years earlier.

From its beginning, the institute made no pretense about its radical views. The first major book published by Barnet and Raskin, *After Twenty Years: The Decline of NATO and the Search for a New Policy in Europe*, declared that the U.S. effort to "build an Atlantic Community" was "obsolete and dangerous."[2]

Scholarly Research or Militant Activism?

Doubts soon began to surface about the "scholarly activities" going on at IPS. Karl Hess, an IPS fellow, supported the Black Panther party, whose members carried shotguns in public and were advocates of violence.[3] Hess said that he saw "no alternative but to use violent tactics to destroy the U.S. government."[4] Robert (Bo) Burlingham, an associate fellow of IPS and its spinoff the Cambridge Institute, agreed: "I do not believe that an equitable, just, free, democratic world order can be achieved in any other way but through violence."[5] Burlingham had been a member of the Weather Underground. And Paul Jacobs, another associate fellow, said he was "dissatisfied with the present form of government and was in favor of its violent overthrow."[6] A Washington weekly newspaper, the *Examiner*, summed it up by describing IPS as a "center which helped train extremists who incite violence in American cities," where "educational research serves as a cover for intrigue and political agitation."[7]

In 1964, less than a year after its founding, IPS brought Stokely Carmichael to its Washington headquarters for a conference series. A little later, Carmichael joined Fidel Castro in Havana, where he declared that "we are moving toward urban guerrilla warfare within the United States." Carmichael added, "We have to fight in the United States in order to change the structure of that capitalist society" and, he insisted, "we have no alternative but to use aggressive armed violence."[8]

By 1965 IPS had become a hub of revolutionary activism, having brought together such militants as Tom Hayden of the Newark Community Union Project, Jerry Rubin of the Vietnam Day Committee, and representatives from the Student National Coordinating Committee (SNCC), SDS, the Mississippi Freedom Democratic party, and the Congress of Racial Equality.

Seven black militant groups, among them the Black Panther party (BPP) of

New York, met in December 1966 at IPS to form a black power alliance.[9] Later, Emory Douglas, BPP minister of culture, said, "The only way to make this racist U.S. government administer justice to the people it is oppressing, is . . . by taking up arms against this government, killing the officials, until the reactionary forces . . . are dead, and those that are left turn their weapons on their superiors, thereby passing revolutionary judgment against the number one enemy of all mankind, the racist U.S. government."[10] Waskow and Hess also contributed to Black Panther activities—for instance, in a demonstration at George Washington University, the purpose of which was to demand release of the "New Haven Nine," the Black Panthers being held on murder charges.[11] In addition to supporting the BPP and outfits like the Black Belt Liberation Project—an advocate of violence to destroy the "repressive" United States government—the institute employed James Garrett, a former leader in the Black Panther party.

Garrett's main responsibility centered around directing a spinoff organization known as the Center for Black Education (CBE), which for a time operated out of IPS headquarters. The CBE described itself as "an educational institution independent of and opposed to the objectives of the American nation . . ." and had among its objectives the "training of technicians who will work to liberate the African people."[12]

Frankie Clark Cox, the wife of Courtland Cox, a self-styled revolutionary who claimed solidarity with the PLO, was a staff member at IPS. Jean Wiley, the former coordinator of the Student National Coordinating Committee (SNCC) and personal secretary to Stokely Carmichael and H. Rap Brown, also found full-time employment at IPS. Even as her former boss, H. Rap Brown, was awaiting trial for robbery and assault, she was hired by the institute as the first black female visiting fellow. But Wiley couldn't shake her connections with the revolutionary underworld. On March 11, 1970, while working at the institute, she lent her car, a 1964 Dodge Dart, to Ralph Featherstone, a well-known black militant associated with Brown and Carmichael. Apparently she was unaware that the car was to be used to transport explosives. Near Bel Air, Maryland, the bomb's timing device malfunctioned and detonated the dynamite. The blast killed Featherstone and his companion, William Payne, and destroyed Wiley's car.[13]

Black militants associated with IPS were among the prime suspects in the Washington, D.C., police investigation of two bombings later that year—one at the Rhodesian embassy and the other at the Portuguese embassy.

Near midnight on August 30, 1970, two district policemen, on their way to answer a complaint, saw two people running out of the shadows and across the grass by the Portuguese embassy. As the two jumped into a parked Volkswagen, one of them said, "Quick, let's get out of here." Having noted the Volkswagen's license plate, the police officers put a tracer on the car; less than a half hour later, an explosion ripped through the embassy annex. The vehicle belonged to a Julie Richardson, employed at IPS, who denied any knowledge of the matter when the police questioned her the following day.[14]

Arthur Waskow in particular was known for his rationalizations to justify violence. ''Creative disorder'' was a term he coined to describe the use of illegal or nearly illegal techniques to force revolutionary changes on society. At an antiwar demonstration outside the Internal Revenue Service on April 15, 1970, for instance, Waskow told the crowd that chanting was futile: ''Revolution must be planned, organized and then pulled off . . . not through the courts, but through methods that put lives on the line.''[15] After urging the demonstrators not to pay taxes, Waskow acclaimed the postal strike he had helped organize as coming ''closest to bringing the system down because of the potential of mass action by workers.''[16]

Waskow was himself arrested numerous times for disorderly conduct and obstructing justice at various New Left demonstrations. And he often criticized the antiwar New Mobe leaders, many of whom were Socialist Workers party Trotskyists and members of the Communist party, for not being aggressive enough.

IPS, the WEB DuBois School of Marxist Studies, the Venceremos Brigade, and Women Strike for Peace

During this period, IPS sponsored the educational program of the WEB DuBois School of Marxist Studies, holding weekly classes with lecturers such as fellow Karl Hess and Alfred Henley, the director of the DuBois School. The DuBois School was a Communist party front which openly professed its approach in its promotional brochures:

> Many activists do not relate to or comprehend the social forces, the mass movements, and the quality of organization needed for revolutionary struggle. Therefore, the most urgent requirement at the present time . . . is to organize the people and to spread as widely as possible a knowledge of Marxism as the Science of Social Change.[17]

IPS associates were also among those who participated in the Venceremos Brigade, which defied a 1961 State Department ban on travel to Cuba. The ostensible purpose of the visit was to help harvest sugar cane. However, Gerardo Peraza, a high-ranking Cuban DGI intelligence officer who defected, said the Venceremos Brigade was formed by the Castro regime to recruit Americans for intelligence purposes.[18]

Cora Weiss, the daughter of IPS's chief funder, Samuel Rubin, a Communist party member and former Fabergé cosmetics magnate, had her own ideas about violence in the service of revolution. She helped lead Women Strike for Peace (WSP), which mobilized some four thousand women from thirty-five states in a March on the Pentagon on February 15, 1967. After the demonstration the group attended a rally in a nearby church, where Cora declared that "the next time WSP should storm the doors of the White House."[19]

The 1968 Democratic Convention and the "Days of Rage"

Along with Rennie Davis, Dave Dellinger, and Tom Hayden, Cora Weiss was a member of an interim committee planning activities for the 1968 Democratic National Convention in Chicago. In June, Dellinger and Hayden told a press conference in New York that "we are planning tactics of prolonged direct action to put the heat on the government and its political party . . . and responsibility for any violence that develops lies with the authorities, not the demonstrators."[20] While Yippie leaders Abbie Hoffman and Jerry Rubin were proclaiming to the mass media that the Chicago convention demonstrations were to be a Festival of Life, other movement insiders were privately convinced that violence would erupt. One of Rubin's personal friends, journalist Michael Rossman, broke ranks and wrote a column in the *San Francisco Express Times* to warn the naive and idealistic would-be demonstrators that potential danger awaited them in Chicago:

> This style of organizing was dangerously irresponsible. For the formless publicity building the magical beckoning symbol of music projects an image that is recklessly and inescapably slanted. It promises grooving and warmth, and does not warn that joy there must be won from within—not absorbed from others—in a landscape of total hostility whose ground conditions may well be the terror and death of one's brothers . . . and once triggered, the energies there may not soon subside.[21]

Rossman's warning was picked up by other underground papers and put a chill on the demonstrations. But neither Waskow nor the Weisses were deterred from marching with the diehard revolutionaries. In the end, the Chicago demonstration resulted in violence and the arrest of 686 persons, including Peter Weiss, who was charged with disorderly conduct.[22] Seven of the leaders were charged with "conspiring to cross state lines to incite a riot and inciting to riot as individuals." In the next four days Cora Weiss helped form the Committee to Defend the Conspiracy, which hired defense lawyers William Kunstler and Leonard Weinglass, members of the National Lawyers Guild.

In defending the accused, William Kunstler flouted legal protocol and was found guilty of "contempt of court."

But the violence was not over for Chicago. The Weathermen, a newly formed SDS offshoot, were already planning the "Days of Rage." They were responsible for directing the group that ran amuck in downtown Chicago, burning and overturning cars and smashing windows on October 9 and 10, 1968. Their rampage resulted in hundreds of thousands of dollars of property damage and the arrest of 284 people. Arthur Waskow from IPS wired $500 to Neil Burnham, in charge of coordinating efforts, to bail out the prisoners.[23] Ignoring the evidence that the violence was premeditated, Waskow went to the Justice Department in Washington, demanding that the government indict Illinois State Attorney Edward Hanrahan for prosecuting the 284 rioters.

IPS and the Weathermen

Weathermen took credit for over two dozen bombings in Washington—at the Capitol, the Pentagon, the State Department, and other government buildings.[24] IPS's relationship with the Weathermen dates back to the Weathermen's founding in 1969, when Bill Ayers participated in an IPS seminar. Ayers later became one of the Weathermen's chief bomb and demolition engineers. In the early 1970s two other Weathermen, Mike Spiegel and Cathy Wilkerson, were known to have frequented IPS.

Reflecting on these controversial associations, IPS trustee Garry Wills commented:

> Wherever things were happening on the Left throughout the sixties, the Institute was bound to be represented by one or more of its Fellows. Civil rights, the Mississippi Freedom Democratic party, Black Power, campus reform, antiwar demonstration, teach-ins, free universities, draft resistance, the Spock trial, the Chicago Convention, the New Party, Mobe marches, the Chicago trial, campus strikes—one way or another, it was involved in them all.[25]

Earl Ravenal, a former IPS fellow, concurs with Wills, describing IPS as a place where "there was an infusion . . . of revolutionary activists . . . people who didn't like to write and didn't want to think very much, and spent most of their time demonstrating and just using the IPS building more or less as a headquarters."[26]

To give strength and direction to the growing antiwar movement, Marc Raskin collaborated with Bernard Fall in 1966 to write *The Vietnam Reader*, which became the basic text for the teach-in movement that followed. The following year Raskin and Waskow wrote *Call to Resist*, which was the primary document used to encourage draft dodging. Later this document led to Raskin's indictment as a "conspirator," along with William Sloane Coffin and Dr. Benjamin Spock.

Influencing the Media on Vietnam

To mobilize public opinion against the Vietnam War IPS collaborated with the North Vietnamese and Vietcong. IPS officials were involved in establishing a "message network" that linked them with the North Vietnamese and Vietcong delegations in Paris and with the Hanoi government,[27] which eased the flow of propaganda from the communists to the radical underground press—soon to surface in the mainstream press. Using the media to undermine the American peoples' support for the war was, of course, part of the overall North Vietnamese/Vietcong strategy.

Two antiwar activists, Raymond Mungo and Marshall Bloom, decided to establish a news service in Washington, D.C., to feed the underground press. IPS, because of its contacts with various third-world revolutionaries, guerrilla movements, and national liberation fronts, was an invaluable asset.

Mungo traveled to Czechoslovakia with IPS fellow Christopher Jencks and others in September 1967 to meet with representatives of North Vietnam and the Vietcong.[28] Mungo received strong encouragement from the North Vietnamese and Vietcong who, in Mungo's words, became "old friends" within a few days. In his memoirs, *Famous Long Ago*, Mungo recalls some of details of that experience:

> And I had a very high time with Madame Binh, who later went to the negotiations in Paris, and with a smiling lawyer from Hanoi named Le Duy Van, who absolutely convinced me that the forthcoming news service must become strong and soon speak to all the people of America . . .
> When I finally did reach Marshall [Bloom], he was in Denver and I was standing near a Vietcong friend and we talked about the news service now in very positive terms, like a fait accompli . . .[29]

Mungo and Bloom decided to name their operation Liberation News Service (LNS) to honor the Vietcong's impending "liberation" of their homeland. "Bloom and I," writes Mungo, ". . . had for weeks been planning and advertising such a gathering, to be held at the Institute for Policy Studies, the sugar daddy of New Left operations. . . ."[30]

LNS was to be the underground's UPI or AP and it was the first media organization to have "worldwide contacts among Western radical groups and third-world guerrilla forces."[31] In his definitive account of the alternative media, *A Trumpet to Arms*, David Armstrong describes LNS:

> The news service was financed by hook and by crook. According to Mungo, some of LNS's equipment was "liberated," and many of LNS's bills went unpaid. Friends at the *Washington Post* helped develop LNS photographs on the sly, while typesetting equipment at the Institute for Policy Studies—Washington's leftist think tank—was commandeered for setting copy.[32]

Two years later after an internal power struggle, according to Armstrong, "the surviving branch of LNS in New York continued under the de facto leadership of Allen Young, a *Washington Post* dropout, who made it clear that LNS's job was to make the news as well as report it."[33] By 1969 LNS had become the major conduit of news and views from a Marxist perspective for the burgeoning underground media, distributing propaganda from Fidel Castro's *Prensa Latina* on a regular basis.[34] At its peak, LNS claimed a thousand alternative subscribers. A report of the Senate Subcommittee on Internal Security described LNS material as "Marxist-Leninist, anti-capitalist, anti-military, pro-Vietcong, and pro-Black Panther."[35]

Key people at IPS also collaborated in establishing Dispatch News Service, a wire service to feed antiwar stories to the mainstream media. Philip Stern, chairman of the board of IPS, funded Dispatch, and Richard Barnet served on its board of advisers. A curious organization that seems to have been created for the explicit purpose of discrediting U.S. policies, Dispatch News Service disappeared as mysteriously as it had appeared once the U.S. was pulling out of Vietnam.[36] Gary Porter, Dispatch bureau chief, then became a fellow at IPS and then the director of the Indochina Project under the auspices of the Center for International Policy, a Fund for Peace affiliate. Derek Shearer, a correspondent for Dispatch, emerged as a founding member of IPS's National Conference on Alternative State and Local Public Policies.[37]

Wilfred Burchett, an Australian journalist and colleague of Richard Barnet, also wrote for Dispatch. According to Armstrong, the alternative media authority, "Burchett was the only full-time correspondent in Vietnam for the American radical media."[38] Burchett's most acclaimed stories were based on disinformation and accused the United States of willfully killing and maiming civilians in bombing runs over North Vietnam and the "systematic bombing of dams and flood control dikes in an attempt to produce famine."[39] In truth, U.S. policies proscribed any offensives on civilians and specifically prohibited bombing the dams and dikes.

Wilfred Burchett was, as it turned out, more than just some left-leaning journalist from Australia. In 1969 Yuri Krotkov, a defector from the KGB, testified before the U.S. Senate Subcommittee on Internal Security about his years of experience as Burchett's "control officer." Originally an Australian Communist party member, Burchett was recruited by the Soviets after his pro-Soviet performance during the Korean War. In the 1950s the Soviets agreed to give Burchett a steady income (dispersed through the Communist party, instead of the KGB, to protect Burchett from being accused of spying).[40]

After Australia revoked his passport on grounds of treason during the Korean War, Burchett was pampered by the Kremlin, which furnished him with a large luxury apartment in Moscow and a Cuban passport for future journalistic endeavors. By the time Burchett left to cover Vietnam, he had been in the employ of the Soviet Union for many years.[41] When Dispatch News carried stories by Burchett—"the only full-time correspondent in Vietnam for the American radical media''—it was assisting, however unwittingly, in the disinformation efforts of the KGB. (More on Wilfred Burchett appears in Chapter 9.)

Meeting with the World Peace Council in East Berlin

The 1967 meeting of Jencks, Bloom, and other antiwar activists in Czechoslovakia marked the beginning of an increased effort by the Soviets and the North Vietnamese to push anti-American activism on a worldwide scale.[42]

In May 1969 a liaison meeting with the National Mobilization Committee to End the War in Vietnam (MOBE) was called in Stockholm, under the auspices of the Soviet front World Peace Council (WPC) to plan antiwar activities for the autumn in Washington, D.C. Nguyen Thi Binh headed the Vietcong delegation (NLF) and Nguyen Minh Vy represented North Vietnam. The American representatives included Dr. Carlton Goodlett, a WPC member and leader of MOBE; and members of the Student National Coordinating Committee (SNCC), which included IPS fellow John Wilson.[43] The seeds were planted for an antiwar offensive on Washington that autumn.

Subsequent planning was undertaken at an East Berlin WPC meeting in June, attended by Irving Sarnoff and, again, Carlton Goodlett.

The assembly received formal greetings from both Leonid Brezhnev and Aleksei Kosygin, who emphasized the importance of ''mass actions of peace supporters and participants of various antiwar movements.''[44] In closing, Irving Sarnoff described how the antiwar effort in the U.S. should be linked to special-interest advocate groups:*

> Our task is to broaden the base and understanding of our movement to include the many organized groups who are in motion around specific issues—wages, welfare, prices, taxes, racism, repression, housing—and to make them understand that there can be no improvement until the war in Vietnam is ended and the national priorities are reordered.[45]

At the time, IPS and its spinoff groups were deeply involved in all of these areas. In fact, the comprehensive agenda developed by the institute was specifically referred to as ''reordering the national priorities.''

---

*In *What Is to Be Done?* Lenin said, ''We must go among all classes of the people as theoreticians, as propagandists, as agitators, and as organizers.'' He advocated the infiltration of established organizations from the outside, and where there was none, to create one. As grease for infiltration, Lenin developed the formula of the united front. One type was the specific-issue front, whose purpose was to organize those who might side with the communists on a particular issue, though otherwise oppose them. While the front groups appear heroic for championing specific-issue ''good causes,'' they also reap a secondary benefit because their propaganda is often designed to represent each fear, each discontent, and complaint as merely one aspect of a general rejection of the entire society, thus exacerbating citizens' discontent with their own institutions.

Less than a month later—over the July 4 weekend in Cleveland—the New Mobilization Committee to End the War in Vietnam (New Mobe) was formed to plan antiwar activities for the summer and to make final plans for the offensive on Washington in the autumn after Congress and the universities were back in session. New Mobe was organized by Sidney Peck, a former member of the Communist party, and drew much of its leadership from those in the vanguard of the National Mobilization to End the War in Vietnam. Peck made sure that the "call" went out to other old left veterans, such as Irving Sarnoff, Arnold Johnson, and Carlton Goodlett, as well as to IPS associates, among them Cora Weiss, Arthur Waskow, Sidney Lens, Rennie Davis, and Dave Dellinger.[46] New Mobe's plans crystallized in a two-pronged offensive: a national moratorium scheduled for October 15, and the culminating event—the biggest march on Washington ever—scheduled for November 15.[47]

The communist prime minister of North Vietnam, Pham Van Dong, cabled a message to the American antiwar movement after the moratorium:

> We are firmly confident that with the solidarity and courage of our two peoples, with the sympathy and support of the peace-loving peoples in the world, the struggle of the Vietnamese people and of progressive people in the United States against U.S. aggressions will end in total victory. I wish your "Fall Offensive" a brilliant success.[48]

Barnet Travels to Hanoi, Dispatch News Breaks My Lai

On November 13, 1969, two days before the November 15 march on Washington, D.C., Dispatch News provided the *New York Times* with one of its biggest scoops to date, Seymour Hersh's My Lai massacre story. Hersh's research of My Lai was made possible by the newly created Fund for Investigative Journalism (FIJ), which, like Dispatch, was launched and backed by money provided by IPS's board chairman, Philip Stern.

In Washington, as the huge crowds were assembling for the march, it was Cora Weiss who coordinated the logistics of many of the activities. William Sloane Coffin recounts those experiences in his memoirs, *Once to Every Man*. "Late the night before in the Mobilization command post, I had watched her issue last-minute instructions concerning portable outhouses, aid stations, walkie-talkies and the positioning of marshals, with a calm and efficiency one associates with wartime commanders."[49]

While Cora was taking care of Washington activities, her close associate Richard Barnet was "in Hanoi with Premier Van Dong [who only two weeks previously had sent the telegram to New Mobe] and other leaders" for "a week of intensive discussions" on how best to exploit the rising opposition to the war.[50] Barnet claimed that he had been invited to Hanoi as a result of his affiliation with the Lawyers Committee on American Policy Toward Vietnam, of which Peter Weiss, Cora's husband, was also a member. The Lawyers Committee was largely composed of members of the National Lawyers Guild, cited in congressional reports as "the chief legal bulwark for the Communist party." Stating that he was "absolutely certain that the speech would be used, be broadcast" [for the propaganda purposes],[51] Barnet told the North Vietnamese that they were fighting "against the same aggressors that we will continue to fight in our country."[52]

In retrospect, it is interesting to ponder that at the exact time that Richard Barnet was in Hanoi and Cora Weiss in Washington, organizing the biggest antiwar crowds to date, the My Lai massacre story splashed onto the front page of the *New York Times*. Although the story had been floating in the underground press for months, Dispatch News Service's timely circulation apparently made the difference, facilitating its appearance just two days before hundreds of thousands of protesters were to appear on nationwide television, to give another surge to the rising tide of antiwar sentiment.

Saigon news reporters were outraged by Seymour Hersh's My Lai story in the face of the savage and unending atrocities committed by the communists which went unreported, such as the mass executions at Hue, where some thirty-five hundred civilians were murdered or buried alive by the Vietcong and North Vietnamese. (According to Hersh, the American platoon under Lieutenant Calley killed 109 at My Lai.) Disgusted not only by My Lai, but by the general American news coverage of the entire war, one South Vietnamese reporter declared:

> The Indochina conflict could have been terminated years ago had it not been for public opinion at home and abroad, supported by a largely negative and often hostile American press, exemplified by such dailies as the *New York Times* and weekly magazines like *Newsweek* . . . if Hanoi ever gets around to issuing its version of the Pulitzer Prize, *Newsweek* correspondents are sure to receive theirs.[53]

The communist government in Vietnam later admitted that "it could not have won the war without the Western press."[54]

Cora Weiss: Collaborating with Hanoi

A few weeks after the My Lai scoop, Cora Weiss took off for North Vietnam at the invitation of the Hanoi government, which apparently was impressed by her organizing ability. The strategy was to release the names of American POWs for her use in influencing public opinion to give in to Hanoi's demands.

Weiss returned to the U.S. two days before Christmas and held a major press conference. She reported that American POWs were well treated and housed in "immaculate" facilities. The implied message: families could once again share holidays if the American government could be persuaded to bring the boys home. Weiss emphasized that any negotiations by the North Vietnamese concerning the treatment of POWs would depend upon a complete withdrawal of all American forces and the recognition by the United States of a coalition government in South Vietnam.

Some weeks later, on January 27, 1970, when Cora Weiss held a news conference in the Cannon House Office Building in Washington, D.C., she began by criticizing the U.S. government for alleged atrocities committed in Vietnam, giving as her source for these allegations a communist document. At this press conference, according to the *Annual Report for the Year 1970* of the U.S. House Committee on Internal Security, Weiss made light of the testimony of two navy men, Lieutenant Robert Frishman and Seaman Douglas Hegdahl, both of whom had testified before the committee in December 1969 about the inhumane treatment they had received at the hands of their North Vietnamese captors. Weiss flippantly dismissed Frishman's arm injury with the comment that "since he was captured as a 'war criminal,' he was lucky to have an arm at all."[55]

Two weeks later Weiss officially formed the Committee of Liaison with Families of Servicemen Detained in North Vietnam (COL). According to a COL information sheet, Weiss took this step "at the request of the North Vietnamese." Indeed, she proceeded to use the North Vietnamese information on POWs to encourage the prisoners' families to join in the antiwar movement. According to North Vietnamese propaganda, "The success of the movement [COL] would be the first step toward the release of the pilots."[56]

The Hanoi government's strategy in establishing COL was to circumvent the U.S. government by setting up Cora Weiss as the sole conduit for mail and messages between the POWs and their families. The House Committee on Internal Security declared that COL was "a propaganda tool of the North Vietnamese government, and appeared to be acting as an agent for a foreign power." Mrs. Sue Allen Schuman, the wife of an American POW, testified before the House Committee on Internal Security that "one of the cruelest activities of the Committee of Liaison was the group's habit of releasing a handful of names of POWs they claimed they had learned were still alive. They never put out full lists, just a trickle of information, to increase the anguish of the families of those POWs not so named."[57]

Disrupting and Liberating Washington

While Cora Weiss was collaborating with the Hanoi government through COL, she was also participating in strategy with the New Mobe leadership. On April

29, 1970, when news broke that U.S. military forces were intervening in Cambodia, Weiss called a meeting of New Mobe leadership at her house in New York.[58] There a decision was made to organize a mass demonstration at the White House scheduled for May 9. Logistical planning and stategizing for the May 9 action in Washington took place at the apartment of Barbra Bick, a staff member of IPS.[59] Although many, such as Arthur Waskow, Rennie Davis and Dave Dellinger, thought that May 9 would be a repeat of Chicago 1968, the violence turned out to be minimal, with only about four hundred arrests. However, the May 9 rally did provide a catalyst for a whole wave of demonstrations that swept the country and forced the closing of hundreds of colleges and universities.

IPS activists were also trying to keep the heat on in Washington beyond May 9 and were busy circulating a document written by Arthur Waskow and SDS leader Rennie Davis, "A Proposal for the Formation of Liberation Collectives and Brigades for the Disruption and Liberation of Washington." The proposal urged radical groups throughout the country to "descend on Washington" with a sixfold strategy: (1) hold "teach-ins" for federal employees; (2) meet with the staffs of the "genocidal agencies"—the army, the CIA, and even the Department of Health, Education and Welfare—and force their closure if necessary; (3) hold public hearings televised upon the Capitol lawn and force members of Congress to explain their support of "genocide," with possible sit-ins in the Capitol; (4) block the highways and bridges to the Pentagon and CIA buildings in Virginia; (5) stop armed forces conscription and enlistment; and (6) open government hospitals and cafeterias to "all people" and turn military reservations over to people who need housing.[60]

Another plan entailing "creating chaos and upheaval" was being considered by the Strategy Action Conference convened by the Communist party on June 26–28, 1970, which was attended by over eight hundred delegates from the major antiwar groups, including New Mobe. In the name of one of those groups, the Women Strike for Peace, Cora Weiss issued a "call for chaos" to bring new enthusiasm to a burned-out antiwar movement.[61]

Building Bridges to the Liberal Establishment

While in many respects IPS and its personnel were at the eye of the storm, supporting many of the activists and their calls for confrontation and chaos, Marc Raskin and Richard Barnet never lost sight of the importance of cultivating the elite. Although many of the New Left activists who hung their hats at IPS spoke of the establishment as the enemy, Barnet and Raskin were busy building bridges to liberal congressmen and Washington bureaucrats. The emerging genius of the institute was manifest in its ability to infuse mainstream liberalism with its radical ideology.

In 1964 and 1965 forty-six congressional legislative aides participated in for-eign-policy-related seminars at IPS, and from 1965 to 1967 some eighteen congressmen participated in IPS seminars. Richard Kaufman, senior staff member of the Joint Economic Committee, had become an associate fellow at IPS and chaired two seminars, "The Impact of the Vietnam War on American Society" and "Military Procurement." Dr. William Kissick, an assistant to the surgeon general of the United States, was an associate fellow and chaired an IPS seminar: "Dimensions and Determinants of Health Policy." Stephen Hess, a former assistant to President Eisenhower, also became an associate fellow and chaired several IPS seminars on "New Trends in Public Policy." In effect, IPS had managed to cloak itself with a degree of respectability, and thus became more effective in pushing legislators and federal bureaucrats to the left.

In the latter 1960s, IPS held a series of seminars for members of Congress titled "The New Era of American Policy and Statecraft," which proved seminal in the formation of the Members of Congress for Peace Through Law (MCPL), informally known as "The Group." By 1969 MCPL had become an in-house lobby for senators and congressmen opposed to the war. Said the *Washington Post*: "IPS itself became the site of a perpetual teach-in with congressmen and their aides bustling in and out of countless seminars. In the House of Representatives, the antiwar caucus organized informally as The Group; at every twist and turn in the legislative battle, The Group, assisted by IPS, forwarded resolutions, designed amendments, and monitored appropriations."[62]

When MCPL member John Dow (D–N.Y.), a regular participant in the IPS seminars, addressed the House Committee on Foreign Affairs, he asserted: "History will never charge those Vietnamese who came from the north into South Vietnam in the early '60s—many of them were born in the south—with committing aggression, while at the same time saying our American forces, coming 10,000 miles from home, were not aggressors."[63]

In mid-September 1969 twenty-four congressmen and senators, many of them friendly to IPS, met in secret caucus on Capitol Hill and decided to express their solidarity with the New Mobe October 15 moratorium. In May 1970 Sens. George McGovern (D–S.Dak.) and Mark Hatfield (R–Oreg.), MCPL members associated with IPS,[64] introduced an amendment to the defense procurement bill that became known as the McGovern-Hatfield, or "end-the-war," amendment. Although the bill was defeated fifty-five to thirty-nine, it set in motion a movement to end the war by withholding funding for American troops still engaged in Vietnam.[65] Constant attacks on the president's war policies by MCPL congressmen demonstrated to Hanoi that the United States was hopelessly divided. Even as early as 1968, when he was eschewing renomination, President Johnson said that "as in times before, it is true that a house divided against itself by the spirit of faction, of party, of religion, of race, is a house that cannot stand." When he left office in 1969 Lyndon Johnson said that "dissension prolonged the war, prevented a peaceful settlement on reasonable terms, encouraged our enemies, disheartened our friends, and weakened us as a nation."[66]

Leonid Brezhnev noted, "In the United States the anti-war movement is assuming an increasingly mass scale and is bringing strong pressure to bear on the government. Resistance to the increase in military spending is growing in other NATO countries too."[67]

The next year the North Vietnamese government broke off talks with American representatives in Paris. Hanoi's terms for the resumption of negotiations included setting a withdrawal date for American troops in South Vietnam. While Cora Weiss pressured Congress to accept Hanoi's terms through the Committee of Liaison's monopoly of information concerning American POWs and MIAs, her colleague Richard Falk, who had accompanied her to Hanoi, was testifying before Congress to the same effect. Later that year members of MCPL drew up the Vietnam Disengagement Act of 1971, which set December 31 as the date for final withdrawal.

The Final Assault: Shutting Down the Operations of the U.S. Government

By 1971 the United States was deescalating its activities in Vietnam, withdrawing troops on schedule, but the leaders of the antiwar movement were still trying to rally demonstrators to take further mass actions in Washington. Sidney Peck, then leader of the People's Coalition for Peace and Justice (PCPJ), insisted that the time for peaceful demonstrations had ended. He advocated "massive civil disobedience and direct action in order to shut down the operations of the government."[68] But PCPJ was having difficulty with other antiwar factions in agreeing on a date to demonstrate.

Following an urgent plea from Hanoi's ambassador, Xuan Thuy, for "the progressive American people and all antiwar organizations in the United States to unite closely,"[69] Sidney Lens, a Trotskyist active with the Chicago Peace Council and an IPS associate fellow, took the initiative to reconcile the Communist party and Trotskyist factions within the newly formed PCPJ. April 24 was set as the date for mass mobilization on Washington, and kicked off a week of activities intended to "close down the government."[70] IPS played a major role in helping PCPJ's organizing efforts, arranging financial backing and offering its own facilities for organizational meetings and telecommunications.[71]

Four days before the April 24 March Against the War, Hanoi sent another message to the antiwar movement. Addressed to "all American friends of all social positions, political tendencies, and religious beliefs participating in the spring offensive," it reminded them that the political message of the rally must be to get President Nixon to "set a reasonable date for the total withdrawal of American troops so we may have a cease-fire between the Liberation armed forces and the U.S. forces. . . ."[72]

On April 24 March Against the War crowds paraded down Pennsylvania Avenue in Washington, D.C., waving Vietcong flags and burning American flags. Arriving at the Capitol, they held a five-hour rally, at which PCPJ leader Dave Dellinger and IPS honorary fellow I. F. Stone spoke, along with eight MCPL congressmen.[73]

The demands that PCPJ put before the government were almost identical to those planned the previous year by IPS fellow Arthur Waskow when he proposed that brigades converge on Washington. Like Waskow's brigade strategy, the demonstrators' instructions were to block the entrances to government buildings and paralyze key traffic arteries, in order to close down the U.S. government. In response, President Nixon was forced to move military units into the city, which subsequently arrested some seven thousand demonstrators, thus confirming for many the charges that the U.S. government was as repressive at home as it was in Vietnam.

Conclusion

By this time, what support there was for the Nixon administration's "peace-with-honor" strategy was clearly dying. It is a moot question whether this traced to the mismanagement of the American war effort, the mass actions and demonstrations against the war, division in Congress precipitated by MCPL, or the preponderance of negative media coverage. It was certainly a combination of them all. What is also clear is that IPS was itself a key figure on almost every level of the antiwar activity. Not only did IPS make an unceasing effort to undermine U.S. policies, but a number of its fellows and associates worked in league with the communist regime in Hanoi, even as American soldiers were dying in the rice paddies and jungles.

But the turmoil was not yet over; it took the publication of the Pentagon Papers two months later for the final blow to fall on America's commitment to the freedom of South Vietnam. Coming after the news of My Lai, the dramatized media reports of civilian deaths in North Vietnam, and the news of incursions into Laos and Cambodia, the publication of the Pentagon Papers sealed a communist fate for the region. Strangely, IPS had possession of the stolen top-secret U.S. government documents, known as the Pentagon Papers, for nearly a year and a half before their publication.

Part II

Weakening American
National Security

CHAPTER 4

Machinations Behind the Scoop
IPS and the Pentagon Papers

Seldom has a leak damaged security—or shocked the American public—as when the *New York Times* published the Pentagon Papers, a collection of top-secret documents about the Vietnam War, on June 13, 1971. In the words of former Defense Secretary Clark Clifford, it was "an event of outstanding significance . . . I had never seen anything like it in twenty-six years."[1] It triggered a landmark Supreme Court decision on the First Amendment rights of a free press, and moved the media from a supportive, albeit critical, role to that of antagonist of the executive branch of our government. It resulted in the first military defeat of the United States and the eventual resignation of a president.

But there was another side to the controversy. The circumstances leading up to the publication of the Pentagon Papers raise as many questions about government officials in the national security establishment and their relations with the Institute for Policy Studies as they do about Vietnam.

The Pentagon Papers study was commissioned by Defense Secretary Robert S. McNamara in 1967 to assemble the official documents on the history of U.S. involvement in Vietnam. McNamara's commission, the Vietnam Task Force, pledged not to divulge any information dealing with the confidential and often top-secret documents.

McNamara exercised poor judgment from the outset. He assigned Leslie Gelb, a newcomer to the International Security Affairs (ISA) section of the Defense Department, to direct the project. And despite the importance of the project,

McNamara never met Gelb personally until after he had left office. Gelb had to communicate through Paul C. Warnke, assistant secretary of defense for ISA. This was particularly striking considering that, as Gelb noted, "the task force had 'unprecedented access' for an internal study group to the raw materials of foreign policy."[2]

About nine months into the project, Daniel Ellsberg of the Rand Corporation climbed aboard. Even though Ellsberg behaved erratically throughout and repeatedly failed to meet deadlines, Gelb and Warnke agreed to give him "personal access to the entire study."[3] Ellsberg's "top-secret clearance" at Rand no doubt helped. The Task Force leaders' oversight and the maneuverings of Ellsberg himself combined to allow him eventually to become the custodian of the classified documents when they were transferred from Washington to the Rand Corporation in Santa Monica, California.[4]

Sometime in early autumn 1969, after receiving the documents from the Defense Department, but before turning them over to Rand, Ellsberg copied them to make them public and undermine the American war effort. For this purpose, Ellsberg's first choice was none other than IPS, which was deeply embroiled in antiwar activism. The institute leaders jumped at the offer—they were already working on various projects to discredit U.S. policy in Vietnam. But it was not quite so simple. Both Ellsberg and IPS were leery of the potentially grave consequences of disclosing classified information stolen from the government. Their lawyers advised them to seek a member of Congress—protected by legislative immunity—to disclose the papers.[5]

Ironically, while Ellsberg worried away, IPS kept the stolen government documents with no apparent liability. In fact, in September 1970, nearly a year after receiving the documents, IPS held a conference, "U.S. Strategy in Asia," featuring Daniel Ellsberg, Morton Halperin, Leslie Gelb, and a number of other high-level government officials, such as the director of International Security Policy and Planning of the Department of State, Leon Sloss; a special assistant to the secretary of defense, Pierre M. Sprey; National Security Council staff member Andrew Hamilton; senior counsel to the Joint Economic Committee, Richard Kaufman; and the director of Asian Communist Affairs of the State Department, Alfred Jenkins.

As IPS fellows were rather open about their study project, which hinged on nonpublic source information, it must have been common knowledge among some of the attendees at the conference that IPS had at least some classified information on hand. If Halperin and Gelb had known about Ellsberg's theft of the Pentagon Papers, it is understandable that they didn't talk because of their mutual friendship. No one did raise any questions about IPS's possession of the papers. Disclosure of IPS's involvement would have probably led straight to Ellsberg.

However, handling the hot documents was not without problems. As Harrison

Salisbury puts it in *Without Fear or Favor*, "there had been a disagreement between Ellsberg and his friends at the Institute for Policy Studies because of what Ellsberg thought was their carelessness in allowing access to the papers that he had given them."[6] Says Salisbury, "Ellsberg was concerned lest the FBI get on the track and he finally compelled Raskin to return the documents."[7] But the IPS fellows could play the copying game too, and they retained a copy for their own use.

Two other explanations for the silence about IPS's illegal possession of the papers come to mind: (1) certain people may have been compromised and were thus unwilling to blow the whistle on IPS; (2) certain government officials or ex-officials were aware of the disposition of the documents but did nothing because of their opposition to the war. Like Ellsberg, both Gelb and Halperin had grown alienated from the defense establishment and become strong critics of the war. In fact, Halperin was suspected of being a source of leaks. Secretary of State Kissinger was sufficiently suspicious of Halperin to have his phone tapped, to which Halperin responded by launching a suit against Kissinger, and getting in more deeply with IPS and the Left.

Meanwhile, Ellsberg's search for a congressman willing to publish the papers proved fruitless. After being refused even by Sen. George McGovern, the "peace candidate," Ellsberg decided to approach the press directly. (Ellsberg may have already leaked bits of the papers for he asked *Washington Post* assistant managing editor Ben Bagdikian which reporters would be appropriate to approach.)[8]

"Neil Sheehan [the *New York Times* Washington bureau chief]," writes Harrison Salisbury in *Without Fear or Favor*, "had already learned of the Pentagon study in earlier talks with Raskin, Barnet and Ralph Stavins, all associated with the Institute for Policy Studies to which Ellsberg had given a selection of the most important papers." Salisbury further notes that "Sheehan had seen some of the documents, and the idea of publishing them was in his mind although he did not yet clearly know the scope of the Pentagon study."[9] Sheehan had written an essay on Vietnam War crimes which caught the attention of Raskin and Barnet. As a result, they strongly urged Ellsberg to approach Sheehan directly to discuss the possibility of the *Times*'s publishing the papers.[10]

Ellsberg had known Sheehan in Vietnam some years earlier. When Sheehan was in Saigon covering the war for the *Times* in the mid-1960s, he received leaks from Ellsberg, who was privy to U.S. embassy cable traffic as a member of Major General Edward Lansdale's staff overseeing the State Department's AID Vietnam program.[11] Leaking sensitive information through the press seemed not to bother those men at all.

Once Sheehan realized the scope of the Pentagon Papers, after discussions with Ellsberg, he decided to check with his superiors at the *Times*. On receiving the go-ahead, he began, in March 1971, to receive the documents from Ellsberg. FBI records note that Ellsberg was staying at the Hotel Dupont Plaza right around the corner from IPS at the time, and that Ellsberg may have been there "to obtain the remainder of the study from IPS for Sheehan to Xerox in the early part of April 1971."[12]

But why would IPS want to be scooped by the *New York Times* after working for some twenty months on its own book, *Washington Plans an Aggressive War*, a project IPS hoped would be a monumental exposé? The answer is all but self-evident. Like Ellsberg, IPS leaders worried about the legal implications of publishing a book with references to stolen classified documents. But once a major newspaper like the *New York Times* had absorbed the legal repercussions, IPS could safely spread the material.

In any case, IPS wasted no time in approaching the *Washington Post*. On Sunday morning, June 13, 1971, the day of the *Times* extravaganza, IPS directors Barnet and Raskin called on *Washington Post* executive editor Ben Bradlee with a proposal that the *Post* serialize *Washington Plans an Aggressive War* and thus prevent its being scooped by the *Times*. After several days of consideration, during which a federal injunction halted the presses of the *New York Times*. Bradlee declined the IPS offer. The *Post*'s Ben Bagdikian had already made contact with Daniel Ellsberg, who was in hiding, and was negotiating for a copy of the original documents. Furthermore, Chal Roberts, who had been covering diplomatic stories for the *Post* for decades and was assigned to review the IPS book, steered Bradlee away from it, with the comment,

> It was infuriating because [IPS] kept paraphrasing things, or they'd take one sentence out of quotes, and you never knew what the rest of [a document] said. It smelled like they'd grabbed out what they wanted to prove their own case . . . I told Ben I wouldn't touch it with a ten foot pole.[13]

After Bagdikian secured copies of the originals from Ellsberg, the race was on—the *Washington Post* carried on where the *New York Times* ended. But no sooner did the *Post* begin to print the story than a federal injunction closed down its presses too. But immediately the documents mysteriously appeared in other big dailies, notably the *Boston Globe* and the *St. Louis Dispatch*. Federal injunctions were invoked against them too.

After a preliminary investigation the FBI suspected that Ellsberg, IPS, and its related spinoff group the Cambridge Institute were responsible for the mischief.[14] And for two likely reasons. First, each newspaper was adding to the public source material, thus paving the way for the IPS publication. Second, as the story gained exposure, the government would have greater difficulty prevailing against the press. For "freedom of the press" is both revered and manipulable, and the government's case invited charges of "repression."

When the *Washington Post* and the *New York Times* challenged their injunctions, a number of advocate groups with interlocking directorates or close relations with IPS, such as the National Emergency Civil Liberties Committee (NECLC), took up the cause. The NECLC was headed by members of the National Lawyers Guild, such as Leonard Boudin and his partner Victor Rabinowitz,[15] William Kunstler, and Peter Weiss, chairman of the board of IPS.

Almost as peculiar as the events leading up to the publication of the Pentagon Papers were the circumstances surrounding the appeal of the *New York Times* and the *Washington Post* against the government's injunctions. It so happened that Judge David Bazelon, hearing the *Post* case in the U.S. Court of Appeals for the District of Columbia, communicated closely with Chief Judge Henry J. Friendly, presiding over the *New York Times*'s appeal. They concurred in their decisions to lift the injunctions and agreed to release their decisions simultaneously. David Bazelon had been a fellow at IPS a few years earlier and had just participated in a major IPS seminar.[16]

At the recommendation of IPS and others, Daniel Ellsberg hired Leonard Boudin as his legal counsel. Boudin's advice was similar to that offered previously: Ellsberg's best defense would be through the legislative immunity of a congressman's disclosing the papers. IPS felt that Mike Gravel (D–Alaska) was a likely candidate, for he was a cosponsor of the McGovern-Hatfield "end-the-war" amendment. Ellsberg contacted Senator Gravel and offered him the Pentagon Papers for the antidraft filibuster he planned for June 30, 1971. After some consternation—his own staff recommended "nearly unanimously that he abandon his plan to disclose the Pentagon Papers"[17]—Senator Gravel agreed to read from the documents during his proposed thirty-hour monologue.

Feeling the need for support as well as for a chronicler to record the momentous occasion that could turn the course of history, Gravel turned to Paul Jacobs, a radical television commentator on the West Coast who was associated with IPS. (Jacobs had told the *San Francisco Examiner*, "I am for the military defeat of the United States in Vietnam.")[18] Jacobs recommended to Gravel that he contact "Leonard Rodberg, a fellow at the Institute for Policy Studies in Washington and a Ph.D. physicist who was formerly chief of science policy research for the U.S. Arms Control and Disarmament Agency."[19]

As it turned out, IPS fellow Rodberg did more than just chronicle Senator Gravel. After the filibuster, Rodberg contacted David Obst, an IPS associate and agent for IPS's Dispatch News Service, the syndicate that landed Seymour Hersh's My Lai massacre story in the *New York Times*. Together, Rodberg and Obst dashed off to New York to close a deal with Simon and Schuster, which was interested in publishing the papers. But by midnight the following day the deal was off. Bantam had just released the paperback edition of the *New York Times* Pentagon Papers story. Off again in pursuit of a publisher, Rodberg and Obst approached the nonprofit Beacon Press of Boston and negotiated a contract for the Gravel edition.

The case against Daniel Ellsberg consisted of an indictment for "conspiracy against the United States and eleven charges of stealing, concealing, obtaining, retaining, and conveying classified government property.'' In the course of the grand-jury investigation, subpoenas were issued to IPS fellows Ralph Stavins and Leonard Rodberg and associate Richard Falk, all of whom were involved with the IPS Pentagon Papers bookwriting project, *Washington Plans an Aggressive War*. Although they refused to testify, they weren't cited for contempt of court because the investigation of Ellsberg ran aground on technicalities, and concern about IPS impropriety became irrelevant once the case against Ellsberg had bogged down.

The Pentagon Papers case won landmark status in constitutional history for the court's ruling on prior restraint pertaining to the First Amendment and national security interests. Those who support the Ellsberg position most often base their arguments on the merit of disclosure and the First Amendment rights of a free press. The critics of the Pentagon Papers outcome assert that the nation's security should not be jeopardized by irresponsible media. The tension between national security and freedom of the press has continued to plague the conduct of American foreign policy.

IPS's possession of the stolen classified documents for nearly a year and a half before their publication drew little attention. The institute was never made to answer for its violation of national security, neither legally nor by public reproach. And this though many of its fellows and associates—like Peter and Cora Weiss, Marc Raskin, Richard Barnet, Arthur Waskow—had not only traveled to Hanoi, but had assisted the North Vietnamese government. Given the direction of their political sympathies, IPS leaders may have wanted to share the Pentagon Papers—which included classified information from the CIA and the National Security Council and texts of cables and communications transmitted in secret diplomatic code—with the North Vietnamese.

Some conservatives even suggested that IPS may have passed the Pentagon Papers on to the Soviet Union. But the revelations following the exposure of ''Fedora,'' the Soviet double agent, cast doubt on this allegation. Fedora had told the FBI that the Pentagon Papers had been smuggled to Moscow, but apparently this was a ploy to provoke President Nixon into a series of rash and unnecessary actions.[20] Although the Kremlin had no way of knowing what would follow from Fedora's disinformation, history took a sharp turn in the unfolding course of events. Nixon became so alarmed at the news of Moscow's supposed possession of the Pentagon study—an unprecedented security breach—that he took extreme action to get to the bottom of the Ellsberg case and prevent further leaks. He formed his own investigative unit, ''the plumbers.'' The plumbers led to Watergate and Watergate led to Nixon's downfall. As Gay Talese put it, ''The *New York Times*' publication of the Pentagon Papers not only made journalism history, but reverberated far beyond the Fourth Estate, leading to the fall of a president.''[21]

Belated concern about impropriety associated with the Pentagon Papers was again raised, in 1977, when Paul Warnke was nominated for director of the Arms Control and Disarmament Agency. In a letter from ten Democratic congressmen urging his rejection for the post, Warnke is charged with "a lack of concern for the protection of highly classified government documents," and having "set in motion the chain of events that allowed Daniel Ellsberg to steal the Pentagon Papers." While pointing out that top-secret cable traffic was indeed published, the letter quotes from the *New York Times*, June 24, 1971: "In his [Warnke's] view, none of the material published so far could endanger the national security." Interestingly, the letter goes on to observe, "On May 16, 1973, while testifying before the United States Senate, Ellsberg, before taking the oath, stated that Warnke, Halperin and Gelb were not involved in his theft of the Papers. No one had asked him the question . . . but later, after Sen. Strom Thurmond insisted that he be put under oath, he did not discuss this matter."[22]

Were Ellsberg and IPS motivated to get the Pentagon Papers published only for high-minded reasons to end the war? Ellsberg said he wanted to preempt what he believed was a plan by Nixon and Kissinger to escalate the war. But at the time Ellsberg copied the papers, Nixon was already reducing troop strength, of which fact Ellsberg was well aware. By the time he passed the papers on to the *Times*, 250,000 troops remained in Vietnam, down from Johnson's high of 541,000. Twelve months later, in June 1972 only 69,000 troops remained, and eighteen months later the entire force had been recalled. Ironically, the publication of the Pentagon Papers may have actually prolonged the war and raised the toll of American soldiers for it exacerbated the division in the U.S. and this encouraged Hanoi to launch another offensive, thus postponing the final American withdrawal.

But possession of the Pentagon Papers during 1970 and 1971, before they were made public, was only the beginning of IPS's determination to transform America's political culture, and restructure its institutions. From further studies of the Pentagon Papers and other documents obtained while pressing suit against the federal government, IPS, with its entourage of National Lawyers Guild activists and friends in the media, attempted to scandalize and discredit the U.S. intelligence agencies. Henceforth, a great portion of IPS energies would be devoted to an antiintelligence campaign, the power of which was fully felt some years later, in the guilt-ridden and myopic political climate following Vietnam and Watergate.

CHAPTER 5

Blinding America
IPS and the Campaign Against the Intelligence Agencies

In 1970 Marc Raskin came right out with it. He told the Federal Employees for Peace convention that "government agencies such as the FBI, Secret Service, intelligence services of other government agencies, and the military should be done away with in that order."[1]

Several years later IPS initiated a project which became the hub of a remarkably successful campaign against the intelligence agencies, and integral to what co-directors Richard Barnet and Marcus Raskin called "dismantling the national security state." But Raskin and Barnet also had a vested interest in thwarting U.S. intelligence. IPS personnel had relations with hostile foreign powers, such as the Cuban and North Vietnamese governments, and IPS itself was in the midst of myriad activities and projects directed against U.S. government policies and multinational corporate businesses. Naturally, IPS leadership wanted to prevent any monitoring of its activities. And there was concern that if the real IPS agenda were made public, it would jeopardize its credibility with the liberal establishment and perhaps invite legal action against the institute.

Communist Revolution Is Inevitable and Desirable

Given that most IPS fellows believe that revolution in the third world is not only inevitable but desirable, they naturally view the CIA's activities with a jaundiced eye. In 1969 Richard Barnet wrote in his book *The Economy of Death*:

. . . the U.S. has no alternative to offer the poor nations which is any better than revolution, which, for all its brutality, has had some spectacular successes. The rapid modernization of backward Russia and her transformation into the world's second power, the end of massive starvation in China, and the great progress in literacy in Cuba are a few examples of what regimentation and the shake up of an old corrupt order can do. We may not like it. . . . But what about the status quo in many backward countries of the "Free World" where thousands starve. . . . It may be that revolution is the only answer to the physical survival of these societies.[2]

Apparently serious, Barnet, while asserting that the U.S. has "no alternative to offer" the developing nations, points to none other than the Soviet Union, Red China, and Cuba as "spectacular successes."

For Barnet and IPS in general, U.S. measures to contain communist insurgencies are generally considered "counterrevolutionary" or "reactionary." Barnet insists that it is undesirable and futile for the United States to counter expanding Soviet influence even though he acknowledges that the Soviets "support liberation movements" and make "efforts to exploit opportunities in the third world." In short, for Barnet and Raskin, U.S. intelligence agencies were all part of the American "national security apparatus," which, like the capitalist system—incapable of reform—had to be dismantled.

The CIA: Dirty Tricks Department or Criminal Enterprise?

Richard Barnet contends that the "United States' covert action and clandestine intelligence collection could be abandoned unilaterally with a net gain in security for the American people."[3] He focuses his indignation on the CIA's covert action and clandestine intelligence gathering, referring to it as a "dirty tricks department" and "a criminal enterprise which must be dismantled," and notes only as an afterthought the "unmatched record of the KGB for murder, theft, torture and forgery."[4]

IPS's campaign against the intelligence agencies, like many of its other activities, sought to "work within the system" and force Congress to enact new legislation restricting intelligence gathering. At the same time, IPS quietly helped others—notably Philip Agee, who defected from the CIA and sought the help of the Cubans and ultimately the Soviets to expose and undermine CIA personnel and operations.

Richard Barnet: Foreseeing the Future in the Economy of Death

It's interesting that the congressional action, namely the Hughes-Ryan Amendment of 1974, which significantly rewrote the CIA guidelines, and the expanded oversight resulting from congressional investigations in 1975 and 1976, had been articulated in 1969 in Richard Barnet's book *The Economy of Death*. There Barnet recommended:

> Congressmen should demand far greater access to information than they now have, and should regard it as their responsibility to pass information on to their constituents. Secrecy should be constantly challenged in Congress, for it is used more often to protect reputations than vital interests. There should be a standing congressional committee to review the classification system and to monitor secret activities of the government such as the CIA.[5]

Despite the ravages caused by leaks of sensitive information, Barnet asserted that "the risk to the nation of compromising classified information is far less than the risk of an invisible government. . . ."[6]

During the years following the publication of *Economy of Death* IPS associates and trustees were deep in activities directed at changing U.S. foreign policy, from collaborating with Vietnamese communist leaders, such as Cora Weiss's Committee of Liaison, to establishing an information and news network designed to manipulate public opinion. Media sensationalism was used to focus attention on stories like the My Lai massacre and the Pentagon Papers, which thoroughly demoralized the American public.

IPS Institutionalizes the Campaign Against Intelligence Agencies

No sooner had the Pentagon Papers controversy settled than IPS concentrated its energies on exposing wrongdoing in the national security agencies. In 1972, with funds provided by the Field Foundation, IPS set up the Project on National Security, directed by Marc Raskin, Ralph Stavins, Robert Borosage, and George Pipkin, to conduct studies on the intelligence agencies—the CIA, FBI and NSA. IPS also gathered information on corporate and private security programs,[7] which so alarmed a number of corporate executives that they filed complaints against IPS with the FBI.[8] After all, terrorist attacks on corporate facilities and kidnapings of executives and their family members had by this time become commonplace in Europe and Latin America.

In 1974, as Senator Church's Subcommittee on Multinational Corporations began holding hearings on ITT and CIA operations in Chile, a decision was made at IPS to move the Project on National Security out of the institute.

Thereafter, the project became a separate operation, a spinoff called the Center for National Security Studies (CNSS), directed by fellow Robert Borosage, and a separate legal entity, operating under the aegis of the Fund for Peace—a foundation closely linked to IPS and its financial backers.

The Center for National Security Studies Kicks Off

CNSS launched its activities with a two-day conference on September 12 and 13, 1974, in the Russell Senate Office Building. Sens. Edward Brooke (R–Mass.), Philip Hart (D–Mich.), and James Abourezk (D–S.Dak.), and Rep. Michael Harrington (D–Mass.) lent credibility to the proceedings and papers presented by chairing various panels during the two-day conference. Thus from its inception CNSS was accorded serious attention on Capitol Hill. Senator Hart personally welcomed some three hundred participants, many of them legislative aides, saying that Congress should be "indebted to them . . . for their serious efforts to unravel problems."[9] That these efforts to unravel problems were limited to an agenda that stacked the deck against the intelligence community seemed to bother no one.

The proceedings amounted to a trial of the CIA, which was assumed guilty of various crimes; the embattled CIA director, William Colby, faced nearly two dozen accusers, critics, and witnesses. The first day's panel discussions were chaired by people almost entirely hostile to the CIA: "The Structure and Function of the Intelligence Community" was chaired by Victor Marchetti and John Marks; "Covert Actions Abroad" by David Wise; "Surreptitious Entry" by David Ross; and "The CIA and Watergate" by Walter Pincus. The next day's offerings were: "Covert Operations and Decision Making," chaired by Morton Halperin and Anthony Lake, Sen. Frank Church's legislative aide; "Technology of Intelligence," led by Herbert Scoville, the director of the Arms Control Association, Jeremy Stone of the Federation of American Scientists, and Nancy Stein of NACLA; and "The CIA and the Constitution," chaired by Robert Borosage, director of CNSS, and Melvin Wulf, general counsel to the ACLU.

The hostility of the conference reached its height that afternoon when William Colby was subjected to a twenty-five-minute harangue by Pentagon Papers thief Daniel Ellsberg. The conference ended with a panel, "The Dirty Tricks Gap," chaired by Richard Barnet, Paul Warnke, and Neil Sheehan, the *New York Times* Pentagon Papers reporter. Barnet's paper, "Dirty Tricks and the Intelligence Underworld," embodied the sentiments of most of those present. He recommended the complete dismantling of the "covert intelligence arm," explaining that spies in the Kremlin were "unlikely to produce reliable information," and tended to jeopardize détente.[10] Barnet also rejected covert monitoring of international terrorist groups on the ground that people's privacy and civil liberties would be violated.[11] Driving his points home, Barnet asserted:

> It is not possible to maintain a bureaucracy of hired killers, thieves, and con men for use against foreigners who get in our way without soon feeling the effects at home. . . . The fundamental reason why the secret war bureaucracy threatens the rule of law is that by all democratic norms it is inherently a criminal enterprise.[12]

The media were to be enlisted to make public either real or alleged intelligence-agency abuse and wrongdoing, which in turn would provoke investigation and congressional oversight—the very recommendations Barnet had made in the *Economy of Death*. Such action would necessarily politicize the intelligence agencies and erode trust, increasing the likelihood of leaks.

Most of the CNSS staff came from IPS. The IPS chairman of the board, Peter Weiss, served on its advisory board from the start. The CNSS staff included David Cortright, whose IPS research applauded "crippling military effectiveness" and concluded that "resistance inside the army represents our best hope for preventing war and restraining aggressive state power";[13] George Pipkin, who worked at IPS with Barnet, Raskin, Borosage, and Ralph Stavins on the Pentagon Papers research and the ensuing national security investigations at IPS; and Mark Ryter, a member of the IPS Government Accountability Project.

Peter Weiss and IPS Personnel Form Backbone of Antiintelligence Lobby

Peter Weiss had already been involved in antiintelligence activities in conjunction with the National Lawyers Guild* and two affiliated groups—the National Emergency Civil Liberties Committee and the Center for Constitutional Rights. Although mainly concerned with patent law, Weiss offers legal counsel in cases against the intelligence agencies and in defense of terrorists. For example, in 1975 he filed suit against the CIA in the Federal District Court in Manhattan on behalf of Grove Press, a publisher of leftist and pornographic literature.[14] Several years later Weiss petitioned the West German court to allow him to assist Kurt Grunewald in the defense of the Baader-Meinhoff gang, charged with multiple counts of bombings and kidnapings.[15] In 1981–82 Weiss contributed his services to two cases, *Sanchez* v. *Reagan* and *Dellums* v. *Smith*, both of which sought to curtail military and intelligence-agency efforts to forestall Marxist revolution in Central America. In these cases, and in others, the discovery process often provided information which sometimes reflected negatively on the intelligence agencies, and which was leaked to the press.

*Since the 1960s the National Lawyers Guild (NLG) has grown from an association of some five hundred "Old Left" lawyers to an organization claiming some five thousand law students, paralegals, and lawyers as active members. Despite the influx of new blood, the policy positions remain basically unchanged from the 1950s, when the NLG was cited as a communist front. NLG's International Committee remains aligned with Cuba and Vietnam, and affiliated with the International Association for Democratic Lawyers, a Soviet front organization.

At the close of an NLG convention in Austin, Texas, in the 1970s delegates sang the "Internationale," which includes: " 'Tis the final conflict, let each stand his place. The International Soviet shall be the Human Race!"

According to the *Congressional Record* of March 3, 1978, pp. E1021–27, the Democratic Caucus, an organization within NLG, accused the NLG leadership of conducting "Guild affairs as though we were a committed Marxist-Leninist entity," and the NLG International Committee of identifying NLG "with the positions of the 'socialist' countries on every major international issue."

A number of organizations with interlocking directorates or close affiliation with IPS—such as the National Lawyers Guild, the Center for Constitutional Rights, the National Emergency Civil Liberties Committee, the American Civil Liberties Union, and the Committee for Public Justice—were working in collusion, as a sort of antiintelligence lobby, even before the Center for National Security Studies added its muscle to the campaign.[16] Some of these groups had tried with limited success, through civil suits and the Freedom of Information Act, to gain access to CIA, Defense Department, State Department, and Justice Department documents. But it was CNSS, under the directorship of IPS fellow Robert Borosage, that, in late 1975, began orchestrating the process and making the campaign against the intelligence agencies a political force with which Congress would have to reckon.

The Hughes-Ryan Act Institutionalizes Leaks to the Press

In 1974 the National Emergency Civil Liberties Committee filed suit for Michael Harrington (D–Mass.) against the CIA director, William Colby. Congressman Harrington's suit precipitated congressional action, and shortly thereafter the House Intelligence Committee forced Colby to testify in closed session. With the privileges associated with being a House member, Harrington demanded—and received—the transcript of Colby's testimony, which he then leaked to Seymour Hersh of the *New York Times*. That action cost Harrington dearly, for he was severely reprimanded by his fellow congressmen.*

Although the Senate Foreign Relations Subcommittee on Multinational Corporations, headed by Frank Church (D–Idaho), had been holding hearings on ITT, the CIA, and Chile for over a year, the hullabaloo over CIA impropriety didn't begin until Hersh's sensational story broke on the front page of the *New York Times*, September 20, 1974, a week after the CNSS conference on the CIA and covert operations had primed the congressional pump for investigating intelligence-agency abuse.

Hersh alleged in the cleverly written article that the CIA engaged in large-scale covert actions against Salvador Allende in Chile. Buried in the back pages was the fact that the CIA was not involved in the Chilean military coup.[17] But in the inflammable atmosphere carried over from the Vietnam War and Watergate, the public was ripe for outrage. Hersh's story helped nudge the Hughes-Ryan bill into law the following month, and precipitated Senate hearings on establishing a committee to investigate CIA activities.

The Hughes-Ryan Act was designed to subject covert operations to congres-

---

*Harrington was one of the contacts of Orlando Letelier, TNI director and "agent of influence" for the Cuban DGI. Letelier arranged and paid for the travel of Michael Harrington to a conference on Chile in Mexico City, February 1975, sponsored by the Soviet front World Peace Council.

sional oversight. It specifically stipulated that no funds could be expended by the CIA for any covert action "until the President finds that each such operation is important to the national security of the U.S. and reports in a timely fashion, a description and scope of such operation to the appropriate committees of the Congress, including the Committee on Foreign Relations of the Senate and the Committee on Foreign Affairs of the House of Representatives." Because covert operations require secrecy, the policy continually undermined the CIA. For all intents and purposes, a "leak mechanism" was now in place.

The storm swirling around the CIA became a hurricane a few months later. Starting on December 22, 1974, Hersh broke another headline-making series of articles alleging that "the CIA had directly violated its charter, conducted a massive, illegal domestic intelligence operation . . . against the anti-war movement and other dissident groups in the U.S."[18] The Senate was urged to vote affirmatively on January 27, 1975, to establish the Select Committee to Study Government Operations with Respect to Intelligence Activities, chaired by Frank Church (henceforth referred to as the Church committee).

Not to be outdone, the House established the Select Committee on Intelligence (henceforth referred to as the Pike committee). The ensuing investigations by the Church and Pike committees were unprecedented and attracted wide media coverage. Although the Pike committee's report was leaked to the press and created a scandal, the Church committee's investigation had more impact because of the Senate's greater responsibility in foreign affairs. The committee's investigation involved fifteen senators, required a staff of one hundred, including sixty professionals, and lasted for about fifteen months. There were eight hundred interviews and two hundred fifty executive hearings, and the paperwork exceeded a hundred ten thousand pages.[19]

The Church Committee Hearings

Although the Church committee was not given blanket permission to examine the files of the CIA and FBI, it did request a mass of documents. To contend with the congressional investigations, William Colby hired Mitchell Rogovin of the prestigious Arnold and Porter law firm, who had in fact been awarded stature as a fellow by IPS while serving as its chief attorney—the same Rogovin who, just a year earlier, filed a lawsuit by IPS against the FBI. Given Rogovin's controversial background and involvement with IPS, his hiring by the CIA as chief legal counsel and liaison was seen as being equivalent to enlisting a fox to guard the chicken coop.

Not surprisingly, committee investigators thereafter had easy access to the most sensitive material. As Roy Godson points out in his book, *The CIA and the American Ethic*, this was "the first such study of U.S. intelligence, and, in

all likelihood, the first of any government's intelligence service by its legisla-
ture.''[20] According to the Church committee's concluding report, there were
"no classes of documents which the Committee has not obtained.''[21]

IPS's cultivation of big names on Capitol Hill, which began in the 1960s,
paid off now. Richard Barnet, who thought CIA covert operations a "criminal
enterprise," had a personal rapport with Frank Church, who, just before the
formation of the Church committee, reviewed Barnet's book *Global Reach* for
the *Washington Post*.[22] Church concluded that "Barnet and Muller had struck
a vital theme" and, indeed, the "world-view in which American military and
corporate expansion [is] deemed a prerequisite of the Cold War imperative of
stopping communism" should be reevaluated.[23]

When Senator Church formed his committee, he placed a number of people
from the Center for International Policy (CIP) in key staff positions. CIP was
formed with the help of Orlando Letelier, and Richard Barnet was a consulant.
Like the IPS spinoff CNSS, CIP operated under the aegis of the Fund for Peace.
William Miller and David Aaron, both from CIP, became the Church committee's
staff director and task force leader respectively. Like IPS, CIP backed the "human rights" approach to foreign policy, with its one demand—criticize only
noncommunist countries allied with the United States. Marxist leaders and terrorist movements—like Castro, the Colombian M-19, the Puerto Rican FALN,
the Nicaraguan FSLN—were never reproached for human rights violations.

The Pike Committee Hearings

Even though most of the Pike committee hearings in the House were closed,
a great deal of sensitive material leaked to the press, augmenting the whirlwind
of controversy over the CIA. So much so that the House voted 246 to 124 to
block the release of the committee's final report. But a draft of the report was
surreptitiously obtained by CBS reporter Daniel Schorr, a friend of Seymour
Hersh who shared his antipathy toward the CIA. Schorr felt that it was his
"journalistic duty" to get the report published, but, to his chagrin, his CBS
editors not only turned down the report but decided to fire him for his unbecoming
efforts.

Schorr finally succeeded with the *Village Voice*, which ran a feature article,
and the story was picked up by the media nationwide.[24] CIA Director William
Colby called the Pike committee report "biased, pejorative, and inaccurate,"
and Henry Kissinger told the Senate that the committee members had "used
classified information in a reckless way, and the version of covert operations
they have leaked to the press has the cumulative effect of being totally untrue
and damaging to the nation.''[25] Schorr was subpoenaed by the House committee
and there was a move to have him declared in contempt of the House, but the

matter was finally dropped when Schorr refused to disclose the source of the leak, invoking his First Amendment rights.

By the new rules on oversight of the Hughes-Ryan Act, the director of the CIA would have to report the CIA's activities, covert and all, to no fewer than eight congressional committees. In 1976 Colby reported that secrecy had been entirely lost, for "every" CIA operation subjected to the procedure of the Hughes-Ryan Act had been leaked to the press.[26] For instance, the cover was blown off CIA support of anticommunist forces in Angola fighting against the Soviet- and Cuban-backed MPLA, as well as of the anti-Soviet Kurds in Iraq.[27] These leaks fueled sensational stories for reporters, who were quick to find parallels with Vietnam.

Congress also passed the Clark Amendment in 1975, which forbade funding Savimbi's anticommunist freedom fighters in Angola.

What went almost unreported was the chilling effect the new oversight structures had on U.S. intelligence gathering around the world. Sources on every continent dried up as it became obvious that secrecy in the United States was a thing of the past. The devastating blow to the quality and quantity of U.S. intelligence was fully felt during the Iranian hostage crisis of 1979 and again with the Shi'ite and Syrian- and Libyan-backed atrocities of 1983–86.

The Interlocking Directorates Behind the Antiintelligence Lobby

The ACLU is known as one of the foremost champions of First Amendment rights. In the 1950s the ACLU purged its ranks of Communist party members, but a decade later it faced the same problem. Some of its members were actively opposing foreign and domestic intelligence gathering, a pet project of the Communist party. And many of the more energetic were also members of the National Lawyers Guild and the National Emergency Civil Liberties Committee, both cited by congressional committees as Communist party fronts. Roy Godson comments on this in his book, *The CIA and the American Ethic*:

> After a gradual shift in the ACLU leadership in the late 1960s and early 1970s . . . the organization was drawn into anti-police surveillance work and its inhibitions about cooperation waned, so much so that many of its projects and personnel became all but indistinguishable from those of the other organizations. In 1971 the ACLU, making no distinction between domestic and foreign intelligence, declared that one of its top priorities was "the dissolution of the nation's vast surveillance network."[28]

The ACLU's legal support of Marks' and Marchetti's flouting of CIA security guidelines gave birth to a new project, the Citizen's Project on National Security (CPNS), which it cosponsored with CNSS. The authors of the CIA exposé also acknowledge that their work might never have gotten off the ground without the support of IPS trustee Philip Stern's Fund for Investigative Journalism. Working in tandem with the ACLU, CNSS, and CPNS was ACLU's Political Surveillance Project, headed by Frank J. Donner, identified by three sworn witnesses as a Communist party member during the 1950s.[29] Two other ACLU lawyers working on the Political Surveillance Project, Arthur Kinoy and William Kunstler, were officers or members of the Center for Constitutional Rights (CCR) and the National Emergency Civil Liberties Committee (NECLC).[30]

So by 1974 there were interlocking directorates and advisory boards between the chief groups behind the antiintelligence lobby. Leading figures moved relatively freely between the IPS, CNSS, NECLC, CCR, and ACLU. They sat on one another's advisory boards, participated in one another's conferences, and wrote for one another's journals. The different arguments being made by apparently separate groups which reinforced one another were at the core basically a single argument being repeated over and over again.[31] This is a basic tactic of successful propaganda campaigns, for as a given line is repeated over and over by ostensibly different sources, it assumes the appearance of truth. (See Appendix 3 for organizational chart of the antiintelligence lobby.)

The Tangled Course of Philip Agee

By far the most controversial figure in the campaign against the U.S. intelligence was Philip Agee, a central figure in the development of the Organizing Committee for a Fifth Estate (OC-5) and its publication, *CounterSpy* magazine. But Agee was not just another disgruntled intelligence agent who wanted to get back at the CIA.

Agee's tangled course, which ultimately led to his defection from the CIA, may have begun in October 1964 when he first met Vassily Semenov, a high-ranking KGB officer in Montevideo, Uruguay.[32] Four years later Agee was in Mexico City on a CIA assignment concerning Soviet involvement in the Olympic Organizing Committee. CIA officers remember Agee during these years as an increasingly unstable man with serious personal problems. Finally, late in 1968 the CIA forced Agee to resign for reasons including alcohol abuse and misbehavior with American embassy wives. Agee states that he quit the CIA. Whatever the case, Agee refused a ticket back to the United States from Latin America.

For the next several years, his whereabouts were vague. He did make at least five clandestine trips to Cuba—one of which lasted six months—for help with research for a CIA exposé.[33] By this time, Vassily Semenov had moved to Havana, where, as the chief KGB officer, he oversaw the Cuban DGI.[34] Semenov took great interest in Agee's project, and at one point carried a copy of his manuscript to Moscow to see about a Russian edition of the book.[35] Although

Agee's apologists argue that neither his meetings with East bloc intelligence agents nor his trips to Cuba prove that he "went over to the other side," his cozy relationship with the KGB and the DGI surely suggests one of two things: they either thought pretty highly of him or wanted to use him.

The acknowledgments section of Agee's book *Inside the Company: A CIA Diary*, reads:

> In Havana, the Biblioteca Nacional Jose Marte and the Casa de los Americas provided special assistance for research and helped find data available only from government documentation. Representatives of the Communist Party of Cuba also gave me important encouragement . . . .
>
> Among the people who especially helped, I wish to mention Robin Blackburn and his colleagues at the *New Left Review*, London . . . John Gerassi, Nicki Szulc and Michael Locker of the North American Congress on Latin America (NACLA) . . . .
>
> Without these people and institutions this diary would be far more incomplete than the present form and probably still unwritten.[36]

There is, however, only one institution in Cuba that could provide Agee with research material on the Central Intelligence Agency—the Cuban DGI intelligence service.

The background of Agee's girlfriend, Angela Camargo Seixas, to whom he dedicated *A CIA Diary*, is also revealing. Seixas had been a member of the Revolutionary Communist party of Brazil (PCBR), which she joined in 1970 in Rio de Janeiro at Catholic University. When PCBR and the National Liberation Action (ALN) joined together with three other Castroite terrorist groups to form a "revolutionary front," Angela Seixas was forced to go underground. She was wounded in a shootout with the police and spent two and a half years in jail before she was able to join Agee in Paris in 1977. When Agee was deported from France for security reasons, Angela Seixas told the *London Guardian*, "Now we know there will have to be an armed struggle. This has happened in every country where there has been a revolution."[37]

Of those who helped the project from outside Cuba, Agee neglected to mention that Robin Blackburn, an associate of IPS's Counter-Information Services in London, was also an intellectual associated with the International Majority Tendency (IMT) faction of the Trotskyite Fourth International, a proterrorist organization with close ties with Cuba.[38] Nicole Szulc, whom Agee also credited, was a member of the Center for National Security Studies (CNSS) just as Agee's book was going to press. Michael Locker established the Corporate Data Exchange in 1974 with the help of the Rubin Foundation and support from IPS to facilitate the Left's anticorporate activism.

Robert Moss, a British intelligence expert, believes that though the KGB contacted Agee through Semenov, it probably hesitated to work directly with him so as to avoid jeopardizing Agee's credibility in the campaign against the

CIA. And although Agee was sighted in Moscow during this period,[39] the Soviets chose to maintain liaison with Agee through the Cuban DGI. According to Moss, Agee "had not fewer than 30 meetings with the chief of the DGI network in Britain."[40]

In an interview in 1975, Agee proudly told the Intercontinental Press that "it's much more worrying [to the CIA] that I've done this [expose CIA agents and operations] than if I had become another defector to the KGB. It's been much more important making this information available to the people of the Third World and to the revolutionary movement."[41] His primary objective, he went on, was to "work for the eventual abolition of the CIA as part of the overall process of weakening and finally defeating the ruling capitalist minority in the United States."[42]

Organizing Committee for a Fifth Estate, and CounterSpy

Philip Agee and Victor Marchetti, along with members of the Vietnam Veterans Against the War, launched the journal *CounterSpy*, under the aegis of the Organizing Committee for a Fifth Estate (OC-5). OC-5 stated that its purpose was to develop an "alternative intelligence community . . . with the flexibility of employing both revolutionary and reformist methods."[43] In an early *CounterSpy* article, "Exposing the CIA," Agee spelled out the OC-5 program:

> The most effective and important systematic efforts to combat the CIA that can be undertaken right now are, I think, the identification, exposure, and neutralization of its people working abroad . . . we know enough of what the CIA does to resolve to oppose it. What we should do now is to identify and expose each of the people who instruments and executes the CIA's programs.[44]

OC-5's Annual Report, published in the winter 1975 edition of *CounterSpy*, describes its connections with other members of the antiintelligence lobby, all of them working within the system:

> The Fifth Estate also sought to establish liaison with organizations and individuals in other localities whose work is related to the focus of the Fifth Estate. Among the many conferences attended by the Fifth Estate were: the National Committee Against Repressive Legislation (NCARL) conference [NCARL was originally formed as a communist front to oppose congressional investigation of subversive organizations]; the National Lawyers Guild conference (with whom we work closely); . . . and a conference on covert action sponsored by the Center for National Security Studies.[45]

In the first few years IPS played an important if quiet role in helping OC-5, mostly with the publication of *CounterSpy*, whose editorial board included IPS trustee Edgar Lockwood. On the OC-5 *CounterSpy* advisory board were Marcus Raskin, Victor Marchetti, Dave Dellinger of Chicago Seven fame, and several others, like Frank Donner and Sylvia Crane, both former members of the Communist party. *CounterSpy*'s attorney was Alan Dranitzke, who was a leader of the Cuba Subcommittee of the National Lawyers Guild International Committee, and whose senior law partners include David Rein, a Communist party member, and Joseph Forer, a counsel for the Communist party, USA.

CounterSpy and the Murder of Richard Welch

But all this changed after Richard Welch, the CIA bureau chief in Athens, Greece, was gunned down outside his home after his identity and his residence appeared in Agee's *CounterSpy*, and were picked up by the *Athens Daily News*. After William Colby charged *CounterSpy* with the murder of Welch and a *Washington Post* editorial asked, "What other result than killing did Mr. Butz and his colleagues at *CounterSpy* expect when they fingered Mr. Welch?"[46] IPS prudently distanced itself from *CounterSpy*. But even as Raskin removed his name from the advisory board, others in the IPS community offered some interesting comments.

After dutifully noting that "the assassination was, of course, tragic and inexcusable," Morton Halperin of CNSS made the point in the *Washington Post* that "the Welch murder has become part of CIA mythology." Referring to the CIA reaction to Welch's assassination as "a disinformation campaign," Halperin writes:

> The point here is not whether the assassins learned of Welch's identity because of the *CounterSpy* article or his choice of residence—it is well known that in most capitals, particularly in Western countries, anyone who really wants to learn the CIA chief's name can do so. The point is rather that the CIA engaged in news management immediately after his death to make a political point.[47]

Associate fellow Paul Jacobs compared the murder of Welch with that of a Black Panther in Los Angeles. Of the Panther, Jacobs writes, "with his murder, the Panthers lost, the black community lost—the whole country lost."[48] For Jacobs, the Black Panther party member, dedicated to violence, was a "victim of truly sinister government activity, who goes unhonored."[49] Jacobs continues:

> For Richard Welch, the CIA agent, I cannot mourn. After all, no one has to work for the CIA or FBI. It seems inevitable that the CIA's political murders should be followed by reprisals against its agents. It should come as no real surprise, nor cause for grief, when a CIA agent gets killed in the line of "duty." When you

work for the CIA you make enemies. And when you make enemies you may get killed—it is as simple as that.[50]

Unabashed, a *CounterSpy* article, "Who Is Richard Welch?" stated that the furor should not "have been over the naming of names," but have been "over the propriety of illicit political activity by federal agencies."[51] An editorial in the same issue, written only a month after the murder, reasserts the mission of OC-5:

The Organizing Committee demands the CIA and covert action be abolished not only because we recognize that the CIA serves only the multinational corporate empire, which is thoroughly anti-democratic and unAmerican, but also because the CIA is a criminal organization and covert actions are criminal actions. . . . To support the CIA covert action is to support this thirty year world history of mass murder, torture and high crimes against humanity.[52]

Philip Agee Aspires to Be a Communist and a Revolutionary

Whether or not Agee is a full-fledged agent of the Soviets or the Cubans is really a moot point—his words and actions speak for themselves. Agee, for example, told *Esquire* magazine in June 1975 that "I aspire to be a communist and a revolutionary."[53] And when Swiss journalist Peter Studer interviewed Agee and asked him to compare U.S. and Soviet intelligence operations, Agee said:

The CIA is plainly on the wrong side, that is, the capitalistic side. I approve KGB activities, communist activities in general, when they are to the advantage of the oppressed. In fact, the KGB is not doing enough in this regard, because the USSR depends upon the people to free themselves. Between the overdone activities that the CIA initiates and the more modest activities of the KGB, there is absolutely no comparison.[54]

In another interview, Agee told the Intercontinental Press that he wanted "to contribute to the growing campaign in the United States to call into question [CIA] activities, and to work for the eventual abolition of the CIA as part of the overall process of weakening and finally defeating the ruling capitalist minority in the United States."[55] When questioned about his meetings with Cuban intelligence personnel, Agee responded, "Quite frankly, I don't care whether they're intelligence officers or not."[56] Agee said that his concern was that "disclosures will provide first steps toward abolition of the CIA."[57] On another occasion Agee said, "The only real solutions are those advocated by the communists and the others of the extreme left."[58] As pointed out by former Czechoslovak intelligence officer Ladislav Bittman, "Unlike numerous disillusioned CIA operatives who left the agency and, for some reason or another, wanted to expose and correct past CIA mistakes, Philip Agee became an ideological defector who willingly cooperated with Soviet-bloc intelligence in the anti-CIA campaign."[59]

Deported from Great Britain as Security Risk, Agee Helped by IPS

When Agee's "counterspy" sprees were suspected of precipitating the exposure and subsequent murder of two British intelligence agents in Poland, the British government decided it had had enough. It served a deportation order on Agee, charging him with:

1. maintaining regular contacts harmful to the security of the United Kingdom with foreign intelligence agents;
2. continuing involvement in disseminating information harmful to the security of the United Kingdom;
3. aiding and counseling others in obtaining information for publication which could be harmful to the security of the United Kingdom.

Morton Halperin, assistant to CNSS director Robert Borosage, flew to London to testify for Agee. After the court upheld the deportation, IPS went to some lengths to facilitate Agee's entry into Holland. Through Amsterdam-based TNI, IPS had connections in the Dutch government, and the Labor party's secretary for foreign affairs, Harry van den Bergh, petitioned the deputy secretary of justice, H. J. Zeevalking, to grant Agee a permit of entry.[60] In due course Agee was secure in the TNI center at Paulus Potterstraat 20 in Amsterdam.

IPS never reneged on its moral support for Agee. For though Robert Borosage says that he was an opponent of "naming names" of CIA agents, it was under his direction in 1981 that the institute stated that it "would make the same decision again" to give support and open up the institute's Amsterdam facility to Agee.[61]

In 1985 IPS fellow John Cavanagh and staff member Joy Hackel found positions on CounterSpy's advisory board. In fact, Hackel, serving as its production manager, has helped "face-lift" the magazine, which is now called the National Reporter. Continuing the tradition of its predecessor, the National Reporter attacks every major U.S. foreign policy initiative and promotes many Soviet propaganda themes.

Son of CounterSpy: Agee Initiates Covert Action Information Bulletin from Cuba

By the time IPS issued its statement endorsing Agee in 1981, Agee's U.S. passport had been revoked and he had been barred from nearly every NATO country as a security risk because of his collaboration with East bloc intelligence agents. Agee had also taken the campaign to destroy the CIA to a new level by going to Cuba in July 1978 to be a witness against the CIA at the Youth Accuse Imperialism International Tribunal, an extravaganza of the Soviet-sponsored World Youth Festival.[62]

Among the other honored guests who shared the podium with Fidel Castro were Yassar Arafat of the PLO, Communist party functionary Angela Davis, World Peace Council delegate and African National Congress leader Oliver Tambo, and IPS fellow Saul Landau. The tribunal was patterned after the Stalinist show trials of the 1930s and 1940s and praised the like of Pedro Albizu Campos, the terrorist who stormed the U.S. Congress, shot several congressmen, and attempted to assassinate President Truman. In his closing speech, Castro said that "capitalist nations will pass into the trashcan of history which awaits them."

Agee took the occasion to announce the formation of a new group, Counter-Watch, and a new publication, *Covert Action Information Bulletin*, both dedicated to carrying out *CounterSpy*'s crusade. The editorial of the premier issue of *Covert Action Information Bulletin* boasted:

> We are confident that there will be sufficient subscribers to make this publication a permanent weapon in the fight against the CIA, the FBI, military intelligence, and all the other instruments of US imperialist oppression throughout the world. . . . Most especially, we will never stop exposing CIA personnel and operations whenever and wherever we find them.[63]

Nobody disputes that the CIA, like other institutions, has blundered from time to time. But in many instances the CIA offered the only channel for people in Soviet bloc and other countries throughout the world to advance their struggle for freedom and to work with the United States. Agee and company's success in blowing CIA operations and naming names stunted the CIA's relations worldwide. Many foreigners simply could no longer afford to risk passing information to the CIA for fear of exposure by Agee's network. Not only did intelligence contacts dry up, but the morale of the CIA was severely damaged, particularly after the Welch assassination.

Agee managed to continue his subversive operations from his new privileged sanctuary in West Germany, even after the NATO countries' ban. Through an arranged marriage and the help of Kurt Grunewald, the German lawyer who was convicted by the German court, fined over $50,000, and disbarred for "giving support to a terrorist organization [the Red Army Faction]," Agee secured residency in Hamburg.[64] Meanwhile, back in the United States, IPS and the antiintelligence lobby never let up fighting the legislative battle in Washington.

Throughout 1975 and 1976, the Church and Pike committees were influenced by a report, *The Abuses of the Intelligence Agencies*, published by CNSS and widely circulated on Capitol Hill. The report was a mixture of fact and fiction, with documentation ranging from KGB agent Wilfred Burchett and Philip Agee to government reports. CNSS was also friendly with a number of congressmen and congressional staffs. In the end, media sensationalism, lengthy congressional investigations, and unrelenting lobbying resulted in new intelligence oversight committees and a major reorganization of the intelligence agencies.

U.S. Officials Also to Blame

Government officials, from CIA Director Colby to President Ford, were also to blame for the troubles plaguing the intelligence community. Colby thought that he could appease the antiintelligence groups and their sycophantic colleagues in the media by giving interviews and appearing in conferences, such as CNSS's opening affair held in the Russell Senate Office Building in 1974. His efforts served only to brush the dubious proceedings with some respectability.

Colby's nod to the media also backfired. Reporters like Hersh and Schorr almost invariably quoted him out of context. And if Colby had to be discreet in answering the critics' charges in order to protect intelligence operations, the press pounced on his evasiveness as confirmation of its worst charges.

Still another of Colby's errors was to fire James Angleton as chief of the counterintelligence staff when he did. The timing had the inevitable effect of implying that Angleton was involved in the impropriety that the critics had heaped on the CIA.[65] President Ford himself was the one responsible for the initial leak on assassinations. When in January 1975 Ford hosted a White House luncheon for Arthur Sulzberger and top editors of the *New York Times* in hopes of assuaging their attacks on the CIA, the result was disastrous. President Ford commented that it was best that his newly established Rockefeller Commission not delve too deeply into secrets that might "blacken the reputation of every U.S. president since Truman." The *Times* managing editor, Abe Rosenthal, asked, "Like what secrets?" Ford, assuming his comments were off the record, responded, "Like assassinations." The media had a heyday.[66] In fact, the comment forced the Church committee to launch a special investigation, and the Rockefeller Commission was then obliged to widen its mandate to include assassinations.

Although the CIA had attempted to eliminate only two foreign leaders—Fidel Castro and Patrice Lumumba, both unsuccessfully—the subject monopolized media headlines, further staining the reputation of the CIA and the U.S. government in general. While "assassinations" and "dirty tricks" made sensational copy, the fact that since 1972 CIA directors (Helms, Schlesinger, and Colby) had issued directives specifically prohibiting assassinations hardly caused a ripple.

On balance, the House committee report was more irresponsible than that of the Senate's Church committee, which in its final report rejected Senator Church's comment that the CIA was a "rogue elephant . . . out of control" and affirmed that American intelligence agencies "have made important contributions to the nation's security, and generally have performed their missions with dedication and distinction."[67] But the media preferred to play up those aspects of both committees' reports that focused on impropriety and questionable behavior.

Soviet Propaganda, CounterSpy, and Covert Action Information Bulletin

The Soviets had a field day using these accusations to discredit the United States in the eyes of the world. Moreover, the Kremlin's vilification of the U.S. in Latin America, Africa, and Asia was embarrassingly easy; the Soviets simply quoted from American sources—titillating copy like "CIA Assassination Teams."[68]

In the same way, publications printed in the United States—*Covert Action Information Bulletin* and *CounterSpy*—became domestic organs of Soviet propaganda, to the extent of publishing and defending Soviet forgeries. The spring 1983 issue of *CounterSpy*, for instance, defended printing one Soviet forgery, "U.S. Nuclear War Plans for Europe":

> The CIA and FBI are presenting no documentation to back up their "forgery" charges, while the evidence indicating that the documents are authentic is strong. Moreover, the war plans are consistent with other publicly available U.S. government documents which demonstrate the offensive character of U.S. nuclear policy.[69]

Covert Action Information Bulletin (CAIB) accused the United States, not the Soviet Union, of engaging in disinformation. As an example, *CAIB* asserted that the U.S. government falsely "accuses the Soviet Union of disseminating the phony documents it has itself produced."[70] As for U.S. government officials and agencies, *CAIB* charged:

> The country is being run by people who lie unashamedly; yet most of the media wag their tails and accept everything. Cabinet officers who assert that Grenada is a threat to national security of the United States should be laughed off the podium. . . . In spite of the long history of U.S. government propaganda, disinformation, and lying . . . the State Department has fostered the myth that disinformation is a Russian word.[71]

Morton Halperin, the Campaign for Political Rights, and the Freedom of Information Act

The campaign against the intelligence agencies did not stop when the congressional investigations ended and the intelligence oversight committees began. The antiintelligence lobby kept right on, publishing more books, producing more films, initiating more lawsuits. Several new groups were formed, drawing personnel from the others, giving the appearance of new blood and greater strength.

Among these, the Campaign to Stop Government Spying was founded in 1977 with the help of Morton Halperin, Robert Borosage, and the National Lawyers Guild. Changing its name to the Campaign for Political Rights (CPR) in 1978, it became the chief generator of grassroots support. CPR served as an umbrella for mobilizing dozens of other groups. According to its promotional literature, CPR "served a national network of committed people and organizations—religious, civil liberties, environmental, academic, foreign policy, disarmament, press, women's, native American, black and Latino groups."[72] And, of course, some of the veterans—the Center for Constitutional Rights, the Center for National Security Studies, the National Lawyers Guild, the National Emergency Civil Liberties Committee, *CounterSpy*, and various Communist party front organizations. CPR received its funding through the Youth Project, which supports IPS.

Under the leadership of Morton Halperin, CPR became the workhorse in the campaign against the CIA, FBI, and local law-enforcement agencies. CPR's work was made easier by the Freedom of Information Act, which was by now recognized as a good wrench to throw at the intelligence agencies. CPR was assiduous in instructing its affiliates on strategies to file FOIA requests and lawsuits, and thus tie up CIA and FBI personnel and resources.

From 1975 to 1983 over twenty thousand individuals and groups filed FOIA requests with the CIA.[73] Actually the figure was considerably higher, because nearly half of these were multiple requests. By 1984 the CIA was expending over two hundred fifty thousand man-hours a year at a cost of $3 million to taxpayers in processing and following up on FOIA requests and lawsuits.[74] Philip Agee's suit, which he initiated from exile in West Germany in 1979, had cost the CIA twenty-five thousand man-hours and over $400,000 in taxpayers' money by 1981.[75] In upholding the CIA's position to refuse Agee's demand for CIA documents, the district court judge, Gerhard Gessel, said, "It is amazing that a rational society tolerates the expense, the waste of resources, the potential injury to its own security which this process necessarily entails."[76]

The burden on the FBI is even greater. Since 1975 the bureau has spent $55 million on processing FOIA requests.[77] By 1984 its annual costs were running about $12 million a year for processing some twenty thousand FOIA requests.[78]

Francis J. McNamara, the former staff and research director of the House Committee on Internal Security, points out that not only is FOIA costly and burdensome to the overworked and understaffed intelligence agencies, but it has also severely damaged intelligence gathering. In a study, *U.S. Counterintelligence Today*, published in 1985, McNamara writes:

Officials of both the CIA and FBI have been testifying for years about the difficulties the FOIA poses to the recruitment of sources of all types in the intelligence field—not only informants as such, but police, government officials here and abroad, intelligence agencies, businessmen, academics, etc. In all areas, those who have cooperated with U.S. intelligence agencies in the past have either reduced cooperation or stopped it entirely because they fear exposure of their roles through the FOIA.[79]

Morton Halperin, as director of CPR, and director of CNSS after Robert Borosage returned to IPS to become its director in 1978, emerged as one of the "leading experts" on intelligence matters. He testified at almost every hearing of the House and Senate Intelligence Committees during their investigations and deliberations regarding oversight. But Halperin's expertise on intelligence is dubious. A balance-sheet analysis of Halperin's writings and testimonies reveals a continuing advocacy of weakening U.S. intelligence capabilities and ignoring the vast intelligence, espionage, and intrigues of the KGB.

For Halperin there are, it seems, "no enemies on the Left." One of his CPR assistants, Esther Herst, was national director for the National Committee Against Repressive Legislation (NCARL), a Communist party front; and he helped Frank Donner, an identified member of the Communist party, who openly advocated the dissolution of all U.S. intelligence agencies. Halperin flew to London in 1977 for the defense of Philip Agee, who was being deported from Great Britain as a security risk after his continuing collaboration with Cuban intelligence.

Recruiting the Disgruntled and Harnessing the Media

Central to the antiintelligence campaign is the work being done by IPS and the antiintelligence lobby with disaffected officials and former officials. Some of these included Robert Wall, former FBI agent; John Marks, former intelligence analyst for the State Department; Victor Marchetti and John Stockwell, former CIA agents; and the most notorious CIA defector, Philip Agee. Working with the disaffected, starting with the like of Daniel Ellsberg of Pentagon Papers fame and David Cortright, a leader of GIs United Against the Vietnam War, became an IPS specialty. In 1972 Victor Marchetti collaborated with John Marks to write a CIA exposé. But after bumping up against the new statutes requiring agency review of all writings intended for publication by present or retired intelligence employees, they turned to the IPS spinoff project, the Center for National Security Studies (CNSS), which, by this time, was working with the ACLU on the Project on National Security and Civil Liberties, which brought suit against the CIA.

In 1973 IPS recruited Robert Wall to make a film about his disenchantment with the FBI. Produced by Saul Landau, the film went on to become an Ann Arbor film festival prize winner.

In 1976 the IPS Government Accountability Project (GAP), directed by NLG member Ralph Stavins, collaborated with Robert Borosage and Morton Halperin of CNSS to recruit John Stockwell, former head of the CIA task force in Africa, to produce a movie, *The CIA Case Officer*, which revealed, according to IPS, "heretofore unknown information about CIA practices and policies."[80] Produced by Stavins, directed by Saul Landau, and photographed by IPS associate fellow Haskell Wexler, the film attacks the CIA's role in Angola.

Two years later, Stockwell's book, *In Search of Enemies*, appeared with the acknowledged help of Stavins, Landau, Wexler, and IPS board chairman Peter Weiss. Seymour Hersh heralded the release of the book in a two-column front-page article in the *New York Times*.

The taxpayer-funded Public Broadcasting System (PBS) on May 9, 16, and 23, 1980, aired the three-hour anti-CIA documentary "On Company Business," focusing on Philip Agee, John Stockwell, Victor Marchetti, and *Covert Action Information Bulletin* editors Jim and Elsie Wilcott. In a PBS interview, Howard Dratch, coproducer and production manager of the film, emphasized that "part of what we were trying to show in the film is that covert action has been continuing . . . that these covert actions continue and they continue to be very dangerous. . . ."[81] Film director Allan Francovich said, "You have to realize that . . . the CIA is not the problem. The problem is the foreign policy of this country."[82] That is, the fight to contain communism.

In 1984 the IPS spinoff Committee for National Security succeeded in wooing the former CIA director William Colby to join its ranks in criticizing CIA operations in Central America.

Attorney General Edward Levi Draws Up New FBI Guidelines

Though the campaign to destroy the CIA got more publicity, the one against the FBI was rough. In the aftermath of Watergate and the sensation caused by Seymour Hersh's allegations that the CIA and FBI were acting as some sort of domestic Gestapo "collecting files on at least 10,000 American citizens,"[83] President Ford initiated changes in the Justice Department, which oversees the FBI. Edward Levi was appointed U.S. attorney general on February 7, 1975, and in his first year began drawing up guidelines governing FBI domestic intelligence operations.

The Levi guidelines stated in essence that advocacy of radical ideas—even criminal activity—is protected by the First Amendment and that FBI investigations could be conducted only "where such advocacy is directed at inciting or producing imminent lawless action and is likely to produce such action."[84] In the two and a half years following the implementation of the guidelines, the FBI terminated almost all of its domestic intelligence investigations. The case load plummeted from nearly five thousand to under sixty, and the number of sources of information in the field of domestic internal security also declined radically from some twelve hundred to less than a hundred.[85] Furthermore, restrictions on the use of informants and electronic surveillance made it nearly impossible for the FBI to gather preliminary evidence to justify a more complete investigation. Thus groups with violent or subversive tendencies could carry out their activities with relative ease and confidence.

Edward Levi's reforms elated IPS and the New Left because they guaranteed immunity for any activities short of terrorism or other overtly criminal behavior. And, closer to home, the activities of IPS and its network—undermining American political and economic institutions and fostering foreign powers hostile to the U.S.—could be neither exposed nor interfered with, except by a few journalists and writers who could be easily discredited or ignored.

Intelligence Reform Under the Carter Administration

When Jimmy Carter took office in January 1977 he gave his vice president, Walter Mondale, most of the responsibility for overseeing the reform of the CIA. As a senator, Mondale had been one of the CIA's chief critics; as a member of Frank Church's Senate Intelligence Committee, his assistant had been David Aaron of the Center for International Policy. Mondale now entrusted Aaron, who was appointed to the National Security Council, with pushing reorganization of the CIA. Aaron was aided by two of his colleagues from the Church committee, Rick Inderfurth and Gregory Treverton, contacts of the late Orlando Letelier and both strongly critical of the CIA.[86] Under their guidance, further dismantling of the CIA continued—over eight hundred people were fired, mainly in the covert operations and counterintelligence branches. Still not satisfied, the Carter administration introduced the Foreign Intelligence Surveillance Act (FISA), which was signed into law in 1978.

Akin to the Levi guidelines, FISA prohibited U.S. intelligence agencies from conducting surveillance on visiting foreigners unless they were about to violate a federal law. It also required the destruction of all electronic intercepts not clearly related to a violation of the law. This totally confused the intelligence process with law enforcement because seemingly innocuous statements between foreign agents and Americans often contribute to significant intelligence findings later.

The drafting of FISA came about through the congruence of efforts by the Senate Select Committee on Intelligence, the CIA and FBI, CNSS and the ACLU. Moreover, CNSS and ACLU were deeply involved in drafting a new intelligence charter to establish a new basis for the U.S. intelligence system. That CNSS and ACLU were perceived to have sufficient competence and objectivity to participate in these legal processes is astonishing, given that both groups were dedicated, as an ACLU annual report states, to making "the dissolution of the nation's vast surveillance network a top priority."[87] Whereas government officials would not have considered consulting with Philip Agee or the editors of *CounterSpy*, they might as well have. For there were identity of goals, interlocking personnel, and near agreement on methods between ACLU, CNSS, and *CounterSpy/Covert Action Information Bulletin*. This was demonstrated again in 1982, when the CNSS annual report boasted of having thus far stopped the passage of the Intelligence Agents Identities Protection Act (commonly referred to as the "Anti-Agee Act").[88]

Agee's Friends on Capitol Hill

While congressional oversight of the FBI was being revised, IPS connections on Capitol Hill produced even more dividends. A majority of the members of the Subcommittee on Civil and Constitutional Rights—the House subcommittee responsible for oversight of the FBI—endorsed IPS projects such as the Alternative Study of the Federal Budget, which was initiated in 1977.[89] Don Edwards (D–Calif.), chairman of this subcommittee on the FBI, has been very receptive to the ideas of his committee colleague, John Conyers (D–Mich.), one of IPS's strongest supporters in Congress. Perhaps more telling were Edwards's close relations with Morton Halperin of CNSS and Sylvia Crane of *CounterSpy*. Whatever the cause, in a congressional memo, Edwards said that he opposed FBI intelligence gathering on any radical groups whether they "advocate resistance to the draft, spout Marxist slogans, or say that [they are] against nuclear weapons and will blockade a missile factory."[90]

But the controversy goes deeper. Don Edwards and his colleagues on the subcommittee—Conyers, Robert Kastenmeier (D–Wis.), Pat Schroeder (D–Colo.), and Charles Schumer (D–N.Y.)—advocate policies that defy common sense and are probably contrary to the interests of most of their constituents. They were, for instance, part of a tiny minority who voted against the Intelligence Agents Identities Protection Act, designed to prevent "Philip Agee types" from publicizing the names of CIA officers and imperiling their lives in the process. Just a year earlier, Sen. John Chafee (R–R.I.), a ranking member of the Select Committee on Intelligence, had grimly pointed out in the *Congressional Record*:

> At the time of the Welch assassination, *CounterSpy* magazine claimed they had leaked the names of 225 alleged CIA agents. Now, five years later, Louis Wolf of *Covert Action Information Bulletin* can boast that he has helped to disclose the names of more than 2,000 American intelligence officers stationed around the world.[91]

Even as Congress was debating the protection bill, other tragedies took place.

Terrorists emptied their machine guns into the home of Richard Kinsman, an American diplomat in Kingston, Jamaica, just forty-eight hours after he was named, along with fourteen others, as a CIA agent by Louis Wolf in the second Agee publication, *Covert Action Information Bulletin*.[92] And shortly after Agee traveled to Nicaragua in 1981, the pro-Sandinista newspaper *El Nuevo Diario* published the names of thirteen alleged CIA officers assigned to the U.S. embassy in Nicaragua. U.S. officials there believed "the publication of those names was linked with Agee's visit. Several of the individuals named in the list soon received death threats, and the families of all these American officials were evacuated for their personal safety."[93] For Edwards and his colleagues voting against the bill, tenuous civil liberties and an unfettered press outweighed the risks to American public servants and their country's vital protection.

Don Edwards was at the fore of those congressmen who ridiculed President Reagan for asserting on November 11, 1982, that the "freeze movement" is largely influenced by "those who want the weakening of America." Edwards was particularly infuriated by the president's comment, "There is no question about foreign agents that were sent to help instigate and help keep such movements [as the freeze movement] going."[94] When Roger Young, FBI assistant director, publicly confirmed the president's assertions, Edwards lashed back: "[I]t is particularly unseemly for the FBI to appear to be taking sides in the nuclear freeze debate by providing secret information untested by any of the safeguards that constitute due process. . . ."[95] Edwards further accused the FBI of making "ambiguous half truths and innuendo" that "poison the public debate on this important national issue," which he compared to Vietnam.[96]

William Webster, director of the FBI, responded on December 9, 1982, stating that he did "not view Mr. Young's response to a legitimate press inquiry as violative of [the FBI's] policies."[97] Webster noted that the FBI had recently presented public testimony on Soviet active measures relative to the peace movement, and offered to present further testimony before Edwards's subcommittee in either closed or open session on the same subject. Edwards was intent on keeping the FBI quiet, but quite uninterested in any discussion of communist involvement in the freeze movement by those best qualified.

Edwards responded,

> In my mind, this is no different from the . . . practices of the House Un-American Activities Committee and Director Hoover of labeling civil rights, anti-war and student organizations as being communist-controlled or influenced. . . . Neither an organ of Congress nor the FBI should cast itself in the role of an arbiter of facts that are being discussed in the context of political debate . . . This is a lesson I thought we had learned.[98]

In view of his previous activities, Edwards's invective against the FBI is not surprising. A year previously, in May 1981, Edwards joined two subcommittee colleagues, Pat Schroeder and John Conyers, in hosting a delegation from the Soviet front World Peace Council (WPC). Providing the WPC a forum in the halls of Congress,[99] Edwards and Conyers invited fellow congressmen and staffers "to meet members of an international delegation . . . led by Romesh Chandra, president of the World Peace Council, to discuss the global impact of arms spending . . . the worldwide campaign against South Africa and Southwest Africa . . . and developments in Central and South America."[100]

Congressman Edwards and the WPC go back a long way. In 1978 he addressed a WPC meeting on Capitol Hill. "WPC Call from Washington," a report published by the World Peace Council in Helsinki in 1978, documents Don Edwards's participation at that meeting:

> The wide interest in the work of the Bureau [WPC] and the Dialogue was indicated by the participation in the sessions, and also in special meetings inside the U. S. Congress itself of Bureau members with several Congressmen among which were Congressmen John Burton, Ted Weiss, Ronald Dellums, John Conyers, Jr., Don Edwards, Charles Rangel and others.[101]

In 1979 Congressman Edwards interceded in behalf of Alfred and Martha Dodd Stern, who had been convicted of espionage for the Soviet Union. As a token of their appreciation—and after an absence of twenty years of self-imposed exile in Czechoslovakia to avoid prison sentences in the U.S.—the Sterns contributed $500 to the Edwards Congressional Campaign Fund.[102] In apparent agreement with IPS and CNSS that there are "no enemies on the left," Edwards believed the World Peace Council and a pair of Soviet spies worthy of endorsement and exoneration.

Edwards has constantly opposed any measures to improve the FBI's task of monitoring domestic internal security. During the Carter years, Edwards consulted with Morton Halperin and CNSS. He was a driving force behind a new FBI charter, the language of which echoed the input of ACLU and CNSS.[103] This would have barred the use of informants and manacled the FBI in its investigation of revolutionary or subversive organizations (until they were about to commit a crime or until after a crime had been committed). Debate on the bill lasted for nearly four sessions of Congress, but was finally dropped in the midst of the Iranian hostage crisis, which demonstrated the humiliating results of intelligence failure.

Revolutionary Solidarity Networks and the Intelligence Crisis

While domestic intelligence was being muzzled, the spectacle of American confusion in the face of repeated terrorist attacks on citizens of the U.S. and its allies spotlighted the impotence of foreign intelligence operations. A substantial precedent was also set in 1979, when IPS won its lawsuit against the FBI, thus *ipso facto* allowing IPS to provide a "safe house" for revolutionary activists at its headquarters in Washington, D.C. Paragraph 3 of the stipulated settlement states:

> The Federal Bureau of Investigation shall not collect, gather, index, file, maintain, store or disseminate any information regarding the plaintiffs [IPS], their associations, speech or activities except in accordance with Federal statute, executive order or regulation in connection with the authorized investigative or administrative functions of the Federal Bureau of Investigation.[104]

Pro-Western leaders around the world had meanwhile fathomed what was going on in the growing networks of revolutionary solidarity. For all his failures and shortcomings, the shah of Iran was no fool. According to an IPS annual report, he pointed the finger directly at the Washington-based IPS as playing an important role in his downfall and in the triumph of anti-Western fanatics.[105] Latin American revolutionaries have long recognized the importance of IPS.

Isabel Letelier, an IPS senior fellow, was involved with the formation of the Committee in Solidarity with the People of El Salvador (CISPES) and the U.S. Peace Council, two communist front organizations which have taken leading roles in protesting U.S. policies toward Central America. CISPES, the U.S. Peace Council, and other groups in the Latin American network work closely with IPS to further the revolutionary cause in various ways, such as lobbying Congress and organizing speaking tours in the U.S. for Latin American revolutionaries.

When Robert Borosage, Saul Landau, Richard Barnet, Peter Kornbluh and Cora Weiss—all associated with IPS—traveled to Nicaragua in 1983, 1984 and 1985, they were warmly embraced by the top Sandinista leadership—Tomas Borge, Daniel Ortega, and Sergio Ramirez. And no wonder. For after returning to the United States Borosage and Landau reported that they had gone there to "make sure that the eight ministries [of the Sandinistas] had their projects in order" so that European support, which IPS was also organizing, would continue "to keep Nicaragua from being isolated politically and economically."[106] When the Sandinista president, Daniel Ortega, came to New York in November 1985 and in July 1986 to address the U.N., he paid a personal visit to Rev. William Sloane Coffin, and Cora and Peter Weiss at the Riverside Church. Coffin and Cora have been instrumental in generating propaganda and American support for the Sandinistas, and Peter has helped spearhead a lawsuit against the Reagan administration and the CIA for their "illegal campaign of destabilization against the government and people of Nicaragua."

IPS fellow Fred Halliday and *CounterSpy* reporter Konrad Ege are two of the very few journalists the Soviet Union has permitted to enter Afghanistan. Both attribute Soviet intransigence there to CIA support for the resistance.

Today, despite the revolutionary activism that immensely complicates the conduct of U.S. foreign policy, the Levi guidelines remain in effect, with only the marginal modifications introduced by Attorney General William French Smith in March 1983. Short of major terrorist actions in the United States, new internal security guidelines will meet stiff opposition from Edwards's subcommittee and the antiintelligence lobby—which can still count on the media. For as late as 1982 the editors of *Covert Action Information Bulletin* stated that "journalists from virtually all the major printed and electronic media in the country . . . call upon us daily for help, research, and of all things, names of intelligence operatives in connection with articles they are writing."[107]

Today, in addition to *CounterSpy* and *Covert Action Information Bulletin*, there are no fewer than eight publications devoted exclusively to campaigns against American intelligence and law-enforcement agencies.[108] The Privacy Act of 1974 prohibits the FBI from keeping records on any of these publications or the activities of people involved in them.

Conclusion

The campaign against the intelligence agencies, begun in the 1960s by a few fringe groups associated with the National Lawyers Guild, took off when it was adopted by IPS. Richard Barnet's assertion that the "secret war bureaucracy"—the intelligence agencies—was "inherently a criminal enterprise" was sold to the media, which in turn swayed the public and forced legislative action.

Within two years of its founding, IPS's Project on National Security was spun off as a separate entity to wage its own war against the intelligence agencies. According to its literature, CNSS recognized that "the scandals of the 1970's provided a unique opportunity to seek genuine reform."[109] "Reform" in the Orwellian sense perhaps. For if a "dirty tricks department must be recognized for what it is, a criminal enterprise,"[110] as Barnet contends, then "dismantle" is the correct word.

Under the direction of Robert Borosage and Morton Halperin, CNSS carried the ball downfield for the antiintelligence lobby. According to a recent CNSS report:

In a few short years the Center has more than fulfilled its original aspirations. The CNSS staff are widely regarded as the nation's leading experts on matters affecting national security and civil liberties. They are consulted regularly by administration officials, members of Congress and their staffs, journalists and scholars, and other public interest groups. Through the Center's efforts important changes have been made by legislation and executive order as well as by court order.[111]

Although CNSS remains at the center, its personnel—notably Morton Halperin—have created even larger lobbying groups. The Campaign for Political Rights, established in 1978 and directed by Halperin until 1983, became an umbrella group coordinating the efforts of over fifty grassroots organizations. Ironically, in the name of the Bill of Rights, CPR works with and defends a number of communist front organizations.

The Iranian hostage crisis, the Soviet invasion of Afghanistan, and the discovery of a Soviet combat brigade in Cuba, spurred American citizens and their government to call a halt to further "intelligence reform." But nothing much has changed except for an increase in recruitments to the intelligence agencies, and the Intelligence Agents Identities Protection Act of 1982.

As for the FBI, its internal security capabilities remain largely confined to criminal activity, and many intelligence terms have been stripped of their meaning and application—there is no language in the current FBI guidelines to deal with revolutionary or subversive political activity short of its becoming criminal. When William French Smith revised the Levi guidelines in March 1983, Don Edwards swiftly responded, insisting that the legal language should emphasize that "the FBI has no investigative interest in constitutionally protected advocacy of unpopular ideologies or political dissent."[112] And although the new Smith guidelines ban intelligence gathering on individuals and focus on organizations, the number of cases on domestic organizations has, in fact, continued to decline. As of 1985 there were only fifteen active investigations being conducted by the FBI on domestic political revolutionary organizations.[113] FBI Director William Webster stated that the result of the 1970s reform meant that "we're practically out of the domestic security field."[114] Francis J. McNamara, a respected intelligence authority, declared in his 1985 study, *U.S. Counterintelligence Today*: "The United States today has no domestic intelligence agency. There is a huge hole in its national security and counterintelligence capabilities."[115]

By their own admission, CPR and CNSS did much to block repeal of the Clark Amendment, which prohibited the CIA from aiding Savimbi's UNITA in fighting the Soviet-backed MPLA in Angola. And CPR boasts that its "special assistance with press, organizing and publicity" were responsible for overturning the Blitz Amendment, which would have kept persons who advocated revolutionary change from participating in federal job-training (CETA) programs.[116]

Although oversight of the CIA has been reduced from eight to the two Permanent Select Intelligence Committees, the leaks and security breaches have not changed, as graphically demonstrated by Nicaragua operations. Nor is the problem of leaks limited to oversight. The Freedom of Information Act has become not only a tool for the antiintelligence lobby, but an expensive and time-consuming burden to the country. Adversaries of U.S. policies have increased their demands on the intelligence agencies through the Freedom of Information Act—the new sacred cow of the Left—and forced compliance through lawsuits.

FBI chief William Webster spoke of the difficulties in 1983 when he told Congress:

My problem today is not unleashing the FBI; my problem is convincing those in the FBI that they can work up to the level of our authority. Too many people have been sued, too many people have been harassed and their families and life savings tied up in litigation and the threat of prosecution. So that we and others like us run the risk that we will not do our full duty in order to protect our individual selves.[117]

Foreign intelligence gathering has also suffered. In 1980 CIA Deputy Director Frank Carlucci testified that "the chief of a major foreign intelligence service sat in my office and flatly stated he could no longer fully cooperate as long as the CIA is subject to the Freedom of Information Act."[118] The following year CIA Director William Casey testified that fifteen friendly foreign intelligence services had taken the same position.[119] Many nations can no longer believe that information they might share with the U.S. will be kept secret. Some U.S. allies have expressed the concern that some Americans would turn their Constitution into a suicide pact. The terrorist bombings and kidnapings of American servicemen and civilians in Beirut, Athens, Rome, and Vienna during 1983–86 were a tragic illustration of our inadequate intelligence.

Even so, the antiintelligence groups show no signs of relenting. Quite the opposite. CNSS asserts that "much remains to be done," and that its "staff must be ready to exploit new opportunities and meet new challenges."[120]

At an IPS seminar in February 1984 on the "increasing FBI domestic activities," fellow Michael Parenti actually accused the FBI of being "primarily an instrument of class control." "The FBI does its job," said Parenti, "but it cannot quite do its job in the way that it would want—which by the way explains why it turns to Nazis and Klansmen to do its dirty work. The Freedom of Information Act is the only thing we have left to keep them from rounding us up."[121]

Dan Schernber of the National Lawyers Guild presented material at an IPS seminar that stated that the first line of defense was the legal arena. "To give civil liberties lobbyists the muscle," Schernber said, "we must effectively develop public opinion and action."[122] Schernber's literature advocated "preventing the intelligence agents from persevering in their work . . . and . . . bringing the agents to court to stop intelligence activity."[123] Summing up the opposition on three fronts, one brochure claimed:

> Tactically the civil liberties community is in a good position to work with groups and organizations in the legal, legislative, and investigative fields. But, the tactics which the various movements use to combat government repression must be unified and we must hammer out how we are going to struggle. I think that this has to start by all people demanding that civil libertarians serve the ongoing work of the movements for social change, and by organizations taking up the fight in their own back yard. We have to meet the agents in the field and prevent them from carrying out their mission.[124]

The success of the campaign cannot be laid solely on the doorstep of IPS and its allies. The naiveté of Congress and the media's appetite for sensationalism can claim their fair share.

CHAPTER 6

Dividing American Alliances

The system of American alliances which spans the globe was intended to give substance to the post–World War II policy of containment of Soviet and communist expansion. As the former U.N. ambassador Jeane Kirkpatrick recognized, "The Atlantic Alliance was forged as a direct response to the actual, imminent danger to Western Europe of Soviet subversion and aggression. No amount of historical revisionism can explain away the facts of Soviet expansion into Europe."[1]

Since its very inception, IPS has sought to disparage in every way possible the alliance system and regional security treaties. In one of the institute's earliest publications, *After Twenty Years: The Decline of NATO and the Search for a New Policy in Europe*, founders Richard Barnet and Marcus Raskin called the philosophy of the alliance system into question. Some eighteen years later, Barnet expresses essentially the same in his book *The Alliance*, while Raskin says that the United States should seek "neither friends nor enemies in terms of other nations," for, he reasons, "once you develop a notion of passionate attachments to a particular group of nations around the world, you're in trouble. . . ."[2]

The American alliances do not receive the same intense attention from IPS as do so many of its other objects of attack. Rather, the alliance system suffers a prolonged and subtle erosion from a number of simultaneous assaults.

In a study requested by fifty-four congressmen of the Ninety-sixth Congress, *The Federal Budget and Social Reconstruction*, IPS recommends "in all three

84

major areas of American commitment—Europe, Asia, and the Middle East—a policy of disengagement.''[3] The imperative to dismantle the alliances springs directly from the IPS worldview, and *all* IPS campaigns can be viewed as a part of it. Barnet and Raskin stand out most prominently in this particular IPS cause.

Making a Myth of the Soviet Threat

All IPS analysis of the alliance system rests on one incredible assertion. And this assertion, as Barnet puts it in his article "Lies Clearer Than Truth," is that "the Soviet threat is the big lie of the arms race."[4] Moreover, Barnet insists, the threat of communism is "a myth." Western leaders share this view, Barnet asserts, calling the threat "the war that no one quite believed in."[5]

Not only is the Soviet Union a much maligned nation, but Russian conduct in its own sphere is equally harmless. In regard to the December 1981 crackdown on Lech Walesa's Solidarity labor union, Barnet theorizes that it "may have been a purely Polish initiative to forestall a Soviet intervention."[6] As for the invasion of Afghanistan, the Soviets engaged in a purely "defensive" action. "A credible theory for what happened in Afghanistan," says Barnet, "is that the breakdown of order in the region was perceived by the Soviets as a threat rather than an opportunity. The Soviets moved in a spirit of insecurity and panic rather than overconfidence."[7]

With Soviet military aggression ruled out, Barnet and Raskin labor long and hard to fabricate involved, and often amusing, explanations for the why and how of the alliance system. Barnet claims that NATO serves "as a leash for the Germans," who would otherwise reassert the nationalism which "the U.S. government . . . had gone to war twice in the last century to combat."[8] Barnet also suggests that NATO's real purpose is to repress internal dissent within member states.

Raskin laid the philosophical groundwork for these explanations with his critiques of the American political and economic system.

Political Paranoia: Conspiracy Theory of National Security

In *The Politics of National Security*, Raskin explains that the essence of the problem lies in what he calls the "national security state." This state is "the means by which the dominant and achieving groups in American society organize taxation, bureaucratic, technical, and military power to support the U.S. imperial system."[9] Raskin identifies these groups as "a conglomerate of great corporations, police and military agencies, and technical and labor elites tied [to] their world empire, making and preparing for war, and transforming nature into material processes for domination while parading these processes as social development."[10]

In other words, the American political system is basically run to perpetuate the power of the corporations and repress internal dissent. As Raskin puts it in *Being and Doing*, "The idea of America as a colonized society is neither impertinent nor metaphorical. It is closer to a realistic description of what the American body politic is than can otherwise be imagined."[11] America may be viewed, Raskin argues, as a "violence colony" where "specialists in the techniques of violence" govern "using the rest of society as their hostage."[12] The colonizers, that is, the corporations that secretly control the American government, must also colonize other societies—become imperialists—to satiate their lust for wealth and power. Thus the "national security state" must become the international security state, repressing dissent on a global scale.

Myth of Moral Relativism

Believing that the United States is a coercive and "colonized" society and the Soviet Union is a status quo power whose expansionism is best understood as defensive behavior, IPS fellows find the two superpowers morally equivalent. As Raskin succinctly puts it, "The Soviet Union and the United States organize their technical, strategic, and bureaucratic ideologies along the same lines."[13]

Barnet's tactics in proving the moral equivalency of the U.S. and the USSR follow a similar line. For example, Barnet notes in his 1977 book, *The Giants*:

> The intelligence services in both the United States and the Soviet Union function in remarkably similar ways. . . . Scholars at the Institute for the Study of the United States are in much the same position as scholars at the Harvard Russian Research Center or at the Columbia Institute of Russian Studies. The Soviet scholars are of course part of the Soviet Government, which funds their institute, and the American scholars do not normally receive funds from the U.S. Government. But the difference is less than one might think.[14]

Nothing could be further from the truth. The Institute for the Study of the United States and Canada takes its cues from the International Department of the Soviet Communist party and often works closely with the KGB to gather useful information for "active measures" against the U.S. The main task of the KGB—the Committee for State Security—is to repress internal dissent as the "sword and shield" of the Communist party. As military intelligence analyst Harry Rositzke describes it, "The broad task of the KGB is to monitor the daily lives of the Soviet citizenry and to detect and investigate any 'anti-Soviet' actions or words. Its main function is that of a political police controlling the 'political' actions, and guaranteeing the loyalty of the Soviet citizenry."[15]

To equate the Soviet Institute for the Study of the U.S. and Canada (IUSAC) with the independent American centers for academic study does our universities a grave disservice. Whereas Columbia University's Institute for Russian Studies and the Harvard Russian Research Center often criticize official U.S. policy, no such discord is allowed to exist between the Kremlin and IUSAC. For that matter, no analog to IPS exists in the Soviet Union. The mere existence of Barnet's book denies his conclusions.

If Barnet should concede a minor Soviet wrongdoing, such as the repression of Soviet dissidents, an inevitable "but" tags the statement. Next in line, Barnet invariably accuses the U.S. of equal or greater malfeasance. "Compared with many military dictatorships around the world with which the United States has close friendly relations," Barnet asserts, in the Soviet Union "the treatment of dissent is lenient."[16] Barnet does not bother to cite any source for his comparison. In fact, *The Giants* has no footnotes at all.

This "equivalence" absolves the Soviets in Barnet's eyes and demonstrates that they are just like us, that neither side is right, and if one is, it's probably the Soviet Union. On the face of it, the argument is preposterous. Barnet and his IPS colleagues ignore the litany of continuing Soviet atrocities, treating communism as if it were just another homespun ideology which we must accept in good faith.

Fears, Jealousies, and Isolationism

With these three propositions in hand—there is no threat from the Soviet Union, America is a repressive state, the two superpowers are morally equivalent—IPS goes on to question the basis of the alliance system.

Barnet exploits the natural weak points in the alliance: economic rivalries, nationalism, and the controversy over defense expenditures. Such disagreements are natural, even healthy, in an organization of sovereign states and do not, as Barnet would have it, presage the impending demise of the alliance. But, in the absence of a Soviet threat, Barnet latches onto these quarrels to cast doubt on the stability of the alliance system. He aims his attacks on two distinct targets. One preys on the fears and jealousies of the Europeans and Japanese. The other, more subtle, nurtures the isolationist tendencies within the United States.

Describing the American occupation of Germany following World War II, Barnet attempts to sow seeds of discord between the U.S. and West Germany. Whereas among the Americans "there was little sympathy to waste on the Germans,"[17] who were therefore brought to the brink of starvation, "the Russians tried to make it clear that they wished to win over, not reform, the Germans who had fallen into their power."[18] In fact, says Barnet, "in some respects . . . the Soviet authorities ruled with a lighter touch than did the American authorities."[19]

And "what ultimate fate the Russians had in mind for their zone in the early postwar months is not clear."[20] It was not conquest, Barnet implies.

Referring quite obviously to the United States, Barnet contends that "it is questionable whether a Great Power can ever participate in a regional organization without subverting it. A powerful state cannot form a community with a group of clients."[21]

Barnet argues that American defense would be useless, even if there were an external threat, because the U.S. will not sacrifice itself to save its "allies." As Barnet describes the Japanese-American alliance, "America's nuclear bombs could not 'defend' Japan in the literal sense, and no one believed that the United States was going to court its own nuclear destruction just because Japan was threatened."[22]

Barnet's argument to Americans, though somewhat veiled, is potentially damaging to the alliance because it plays on the fears and distrust that plague even the best of accords. "If Europeans did not wish to be protected, if they saw the Soviet Union more as a customer than as an adversary . . . perhaps the alliance was over,"[23] Barnet exhorts his American audience to believe. To this end, Barnet repeatedly refers to the "acrimonious split in the alliance" and the "end to friendship and partnership," observing that "the military, economic and political underpinnings of America's Atlantic and Pacific alliances had come loose."[24] Barnet glides by the fact that European and Japanese elections continually reaffirm their commitment to an alliance with the United States.

Marcus Raskin is much less guarded in his analysis of the American alliances. In a 1983 interview he roundly condemned NATO:

It is a military alliance; I argue that this is one of its greatest problems, that it has to transform itself, because as long as it stays a military alliance, in relation to the kinds of weapons they now have, the very object they are trying to protect, which is themselves, is going to be destroyed by the military weapons they're going to employ. So in that sense there's a fundamental defect in this entire operation.[25]

Since *After 20 Years*, Barnet and Raskin have jumped on the alliance for the expense entailed in maintaining troops overseas. They complain that the Atlantic alliance "has exacted staggering costs and commitments from the people of the United States in return for a vision resting on the premise that there is, or should be, a separately organized sub-world of white, wealthy, Western nations."[26]

Since Barnet chooses to dismiss the military necessity for the NATO alliance, he can easily lash out at the economic and political tensions which, though of some importance, pale in comparison with the consequences of Soviet aggression should deterrence break down. Fortunately, Barnet's insistence that "no one really believes" in the Soviet threat is so patently fraudulent as to undermine his other arguments.

Playing the Politics of Nuclear Fear to Divide U.S. Alliances

Fears associated with nuclear defense have handed IPS another weapon with which to assail the alliance system. Over and beyond supporting "peace" movements, IPS fellows have gone on several missions overseas to dissuade American allies from cooperating in their defense. In November 1979 Richard Barnet, Herbert Scoville (executive director of the Arms Control Association), and Arthur Macy Cox (an IPS Washington School faculty member) traveled to Denmark to persuade the government that American missiles in Europe would threaten Danish security. According to the *Washington Post*, "the three Americans had a significant impact on the political debate in Denmark," and "further complicated" the situation by persuading several Danish parliamentarians to reverse their pro-missile stands. "Washington officials dealing with the sensitive NATO missile issue were 'burned up' over the trio's activities," noted the *Post*.[27]

As Marc Raskin puts it, "I don't see how it [American missile deployment in Europe] improves American national security one bit. My concern is a much more parochial one. I think that it's stupid for the Europeans; the fact of the matter is it would make them that much more of a sitting duck."[28] Raskin expresses no concern about the Soviet Union's destabilizing action of deploying hundreds of mobile SS-20s, which fact precipitated the NATO response in the first place.

The furor over the deployment of the Pershing and Cruise missiles spurred IPS to expand its activities in Europe.

In April 1981 IPS fellow Wendy Chapkis and Cynthia Enloe organized a meeting of feminist activists at the Transnational Institute in Amsterdam to discuss strategies to "restructure" NATO and organize against the deployment of U.S. Cruise and Pershing missiles. "If women start paying attention to NATO and treating it as more than simply an association for men-in-brass-and-khaki, NATO will be revealed as the socio-economic-ideological tool that indeed it is," said Enloe, and "it is important that women 'blow its cover' and even more starkly reveal NATO to open public debate and scrutiny . . . ."[29]

The next month IPS fellow Mary Kaldor and associate fellow Dan Smith organized a conference at the Transnational Institute in Amsterdam along with END, one of the largest disarmament groups in Europe, to oppose the NATO alliance and promote "non-alignment and new forms of defense." This was the beginning of what became TNI's New Europe Project, headed up by Kaldor and Fred Halliday, whose stated purpose was "to explore the potential for greater independence" for European nations, "especially on such questions as the deployment of nuclear weapons."[30] When NATO reaffirmed its commitment to deploy the missiles in December 1983, IPS undertook another initiative to complement TNI's New Europe Project and organized a conference to come up with new disengagement strategies.

Alongside its work in Europe, the institute undertook to intrude on the other side of the globe. The South Pacific Study Project of 1983 set out to undermine the trust between the United States and Micronesia embodied in the Compact of Free Association; specifically, it fomented independence movements on the islands so as to deny access to U.S. military bases. Testifying before a House subcommittee, IPS research associate David Chappell said, "If we leave the Compact as it stands, though, our relationship with them will remain distorted and unequal and will remain so only on the basis of rather incoherent incantations about strategic importance which have ceased to have any meaning in the real military world of today."[31]

IPS has taken the lead in pinpointing American nuclear weapons deployment in allied countries, and that in turn aids home-grown activists to raise the populace against the United States. This puts stress on the alliance and threatens to decouple those countries from the U.S. Typically, IPS charges that the alliance is dangerous for the people of the allied country because it is likely to involve them in a nuclear war that is really none of their business. As Barnet argues, "The danger of war came from America, not Russia. . . ."[32] The U.S. would use the lands of its allies as nuclear battlefields in a war against a nonexistent enemy born out of cold-war hysteria and the archdemonic profit motive.

On February 14, 1985, Leslie Gelb broke a front-page story in the *New York Times* titled "U.S. Tries to Fight Allied Resistance to Nuclear Arms." In it Gelb revealed that the United States had drawn up contingency plans to deploy nuclear depth charges in Canada, Iceland, Bermuda, Puerto Rico, the Azores, the Philippines, Spain, and Diego Garcia in time of war. Gelb's source for this classified information? William Arkin, fellow at the Institute for Policy Studies.

Arkin had done more than just distribute classified information injurious to national security. The previous December (1984) Arkin traveled to Iceland to deliver to the prime minister, Steingrimur Hermannson, a classified 1975 nuclear weapons deployment report, which prompted angry demands for an explanation. Quick to take advantage, the Soviet news agency TASS reported that "such a development of events testifies to U.S. dangerous intentions toward Iceland."[33]

After his Icelandic junket, Arkin journeyed to Canada. There a spate of news articles describing nuclear contingency plans followed in his wake.[34] Anti-American fallout proliferated wherever Arkin or his press releases went. Relations between the U.S. and Canada, Spain, and Portugal became increasingly strained. Dr. William Steerman, a senior-level White House adviser, commented, "William Arkin had to know that his so-called revelations about secret plans to deploy nuclear weapons abroad would create problems for the United States in several friendly countries and would provide grist for the Soviet propaganda mill."[35]

These stories struck a raw nerve in the alliance in the aftermath of the March 1985 action of David Lange, the prime minister of New Zealand, who prohibited

American warships carrying nuclear weapons from entering New Zealand's waters. As the navy refuses to comment on which of its ships carry atomic devices, the sanction effectively excluded all U.S. ships from the harbors of New Zealand, and subsequently led to the demise of the ANZUS alliance.

In June 1985 Arkin and IPS colleague Richard Fieldhouse appeared on all three networks to promote their new book, *Nuclear Battlefields: Global Links in the Arms Race*. The book catalogues in excruciating detail the location and description of what the authors believe are *all* American and allied nuclear weapons installations. Though Arkin and Fieldhouse got much of the information through public sources, they make a point of thanking in the acknowledgments the "conscientious officers" who helped them obtain classified material. The Department of Defense issued an immediate response: "What we have concern about is that all of Mr. Arkin's data may not have come from open sources."[36] *Nuclear Battlefields* put DOD in a "catch-22" situation; as spokesman Michael I. Burch explained it, "The figures are not accurate, but I'm not in a position of being able to straighten them out . . . since I can neither confirm nor deny the presence of nuclear weapons at any given location in the world."[37]

The stated purpose of the IPS study, "exposing and explaining how the entire [nuclear] infrastructure works in unprecedented detail, by demonstrating how that structure is out of control, and by showing that a different concept—'denuclearization'—is necessary to reestablish control over the system,"[38] leaves little doubt of the conclusions reached. The study concludes, "Denuclearization can only be achieved by worldwide action to check the nuclear system."[39] In light of the fact that no significant antinuclear activism is permitted in the communist world, IPS's invocation for "worldwide action" comes down to unilateral action.

Besides providing a "boon to the KGB," as the *Economist*'s *Foreign Report* put it, the details of the book aid nuclear protesters and provide the groundwork for potential nuclear terrorists.

Questionable Intentions, Unquestionable Effects

It is odd that IPS, its founders Richard Barnet and Marcus Raskin, and fellow William Arkin profess only the best of intentions concerning the United States. One has to wonder how much their work has damaged the system of American alliances and consequently weakened the security of the free world, and why they are so oblivious to the Soviet Union's nuclear buildup and its projection of military power globally.

If the ordinary people of foreign countries are led to believe, however erroneously, that the protection afforded them endangers rather than ensures their security, they cannot be blamed for demanding that their treaties of mutual security with the United States be abrogated. The activities and publications promoted by IPS all suggest it would be far better to maintain a wholly independent foreign policy and leave the "cold war" to the Americans who are obsessed with the Soviet threat.

If the ordinary people of the United States are led to believe, however erroneously, that their interest does not lie in defending foreign countries from Soviet communism, then they can hardly be blamed for demanding that their government withdraw its military to fortress America.

A Warsaw Pact invasion of Europe confronted only by the West German army would be like a small boat confronting a tidal wave. Soviet leaders have made much of their desire to disband all military blocs, that is, NATO and the Warsaw Pact, so as to leave the superpowers alone to slug it out. But as a high-ranking defector from the Soviet military officer corps, Victor Suvorov, points out:

> If NATO is disbanded, the West will have been neutralised once and for all. The system of collective self-defence of the free countries will have ceased to exist. If the Warsaw Treaty Organization is disbanded at the same time, the U.S.S.R. loses nothing except a cumbersome publicity machine. . . . Let us suppose, for example, that France should suddenly return to NATO. Would this be a change? Certainly—one of almost global significance. Next, let us suppose that Cuba drops its "non-alignment" and joins the Warsaw Treaty Organization. What would change? Absolutely nothing. Cuba would remain as aggressive a pilot fish of the great shark as she is today.[40]

An age-old military strategy is divide and conquer. The question in this case is not of IPS intentions, but of the effect of IPS activities on American security. Were the United States to withdraw from overseas commitments to its allies, would the cause of peace be better served?

CHAPTER 7

From the Lawsuit Against the FBI
to the Government Accountability Project

At 1:30 A.M. on May 25, 1973, Marc Raskin dialed the Washington, D.C., Metropolitan police to report that the Institute for Policy Studies building had just been broken into. Raskin said that an anonymous phone call had alerted him to the break-in. But when he and the police arrived at the scene minutes later, they could find no evidence of any illegal entry. Despite this and Raskin's later admission that "there was nothing mentioned around IPS the following day indicating that anyone had discovered anything missing or having information concerning the alleged burglary,"[1] he instructed the institute's attorney, Mitchell Rogovin, to file a complaint with the FBI. Addressed to the acting FBI director, William Ruckelshaus, Rogovin's letter specifically requested

> an investigation to be conducted—not simply into an alleged burglary—but rather into what appears to be a pattern of illegal surveillance including illegal entry by law enforcement agencies. We would also appreciate information regarding any electronic surveillance. Such an investigation should also include any evidence of electronic surveillance of the Institute, its officers, or employees or those associated with the organization.[2]

Rogovin's letter was written on the same day as the alleged break-in. That, combined with the insinuation that the break-in had been a "black-bag job" conducted as part of a pattern of FBI surveillance, seems to suggest that the incident was a frame-up, premeditated to provide an excuse to sue the FBI. Why?

93

The FBI did in fact have IPS under surveillance at the time—it was routine for the FBI to investigate individuals or groups advocating the violent overthrow of the government. And IPS had, after all, employed people associated with the Black Panthers and the Weathermen and had sponsored the Communist party front WEB DuBois School of Marxist Studies. The FBI was particularly interested in the connections between IPS and the mass demonstrations against the Vietnam War, which, largely organized by Communist party members, resulted in trash-ins, arson, and the obstruction of government affairs. IPS directors Richard Barnet and Marcus Raskin, various fellows, and principal financial backer Cora Weiss had collaborated with the North Vietnamese and the Vietcong hoping to undermine U.S. policies.

It was no secret that curtailing the FBI was only part of it: the institute wanted to do away with the FBI altogether. As noted in Chapter 5, much IPS literature advocated the dismantling of the American "national security state," of which the FBI is an integral part. In short, to acquire evidence of FBI wrongdoing as a basis for a legal case against the FBI, IPS needed to obtain the FBI files.

The FBI routed Rogovin's inquiry to its Intelligence Division, which instructed the Washington field office to determine if there had been any impropriety or illegality in regard to its investigation of IPS. None was found, and Rogovin's allegations remained unsubstantiated—the bureau investigation had been conducted within FBI guidelines. The only electronic surveillance of IPS that could be attributed to the FBI was coincidental to other investigations. For instance, conversations of IPS employees were overheard when they talked by phone, as they often did, to people associated with the Black Panthers, the Communist party, and others who were being monitored under Justice Department authorization.

The FBI concluded that "Rogovin's allegations were probably provocative actions in an attempt to gain access to FBI files."[3] Getting nowhere with the FBI, Rogovin turned to the Civil Rights Division of the U.S. attorney general's office and put his case to Assistant Attorney General Stanley Pottinger. Rogovin couched his charges in carefully phrased language.[4] "The purpose of this letter," he wrote, "is to merely indicate our willingness to cooperate in this investigation and secure your office's guidance with respect to the conduct of the inquiry currently underway."[5]

The assistant attorney general's office, under pressure from Rogovin and some of the institute's friends on Capitol Hill, questioned the results of the FBI's review, which had turned up no evidence of wrongdoing. To allay any doubt, the bureau undertook yet a more minute review of the whole investigation, cross-checking all files with those of the Washington, D.C., Metropolitan Police Department investigative division.

Nothing really new turned up. One FBI officer was driven to state that IPS attorney Rogovin was "engaged in accusative speculation, approaching paranoia by way of imputation of wrongdoing to the Bureau without factual basis."[6] In an interdepartmental memo, another senior FBI officer said, "having bent over backwards, and 'walked the extra mile' as it were, I feel it intolerable that the Civil Rights Division of the Attorney General's Office should consider attempting to test the Bureau's credibility by a review of raw field office files instead of telling Rogovin to 'put up or shut up' with regard to furnishing specifics." He added, "I am sure the Bureau also regards Rogovin's position as only a thinly veiled attempt to learn whatever the FBI knows concerning IPS."[7]

But Rogovin did not stop. He began to press the case with Special Prosecutor Archibald Cox. A better political strategy could hardly have been conceived, for in the charged atmosphere of Watergate the move was brilliant. IPS and Rogovin alleged the same basic charges as those regarding Watergate—there had been a burglary and a coverup.

Shortly thereafter, in early 1974, IPS brought civil suit against multiple parties—FBI Director Clarence Kelly, Attorney General John Mitchell, Assistant Attorney General Robert Mardian, presidential aides John Ehrlichman, E. Howard Hunt, and G. Gordon Liddy, a number of FBI agents, and Washington, D.C., police investigators. Mitchell, Mardian, Ehrlichman, Hunt, and Liddy had not the slightest connection with the IPS investigation, but their names evoked the Watergate scandal and seasoned the ensuing prosecutorial hysteria. That, plus the threat of scandalous publicity, was sure to intimidate the opposition. This shotgun approach—naming multiple defendants in a lawsuit—would also protract the litigation process, tie up the government's manpower and resources, and improve the prospects for a favorable settlement.

There were some who believed that IPS was using the lawsuit as a ploy to discredit the FBI and discover the inner workings of the intelligence agencies. For instance, through the ensuing discovery process, depositions made by IPS attorneys went off on tangents completely unrelated to the case—such as methods used in FBI counterintelligence operations. Also, according to FBI files, IPS used the depositions of FBI personnel as "opportunities to harass the Bureau by photographing agents, recording comments, attempting to draw them into arguments, and subsequently alleging misconduct on the part of the agents."[8]

In 1976 Mitchell Rogovin stepped down as IPS's attorney to take a full-time position offered by CIA Director William Colby, who was being questioned about CIA conduct before the Church and Pike committees. Ironically, Colby was hiring the very man who had just distinguished himself by attacking the intelligence agencies for IPS. Later, Colby would join the Committee for National Security, founded by Richard Barnet and IPS trustee Paul Warnke.

IPS replaced Rogovin with David Rudovsky, a prominent attorney with the National Lawyers Guild, who continued to press the FBI to release its files on IPS. Rudovsky's strategy was different, perhaps in anticipation of a new administration, which could be naive about national security issues and amenable to a favorable settlement.[9] Between 1976 and 1979, he took only five depositions on FBI agents and informants, and introduced a second amended complaint before getting a settlement favorable to IPS.

Although the whole thing may have been a ploy, it worked. IPS gained access to the entire FBI file on the institute, and obtained a favorable out-of-court settlement. After five years of litigation, in 1979, under the Carter administration, all parties signed a stipulated settlement providing immunity from past or present FBI monitoring and, most important, a blanket prohibition of any future intelligence gathering on IPS by the FBI or by any other government agency. Paragraph 3 of the settlement reads:

> The Federal Bureau of Investigation shall not collect, gather, index, file, maintain, store or disseminate any information regarding the plaintiffs, their associations, speech or activities except in accordance with Federal statute, executive order or regulation in connection with the authorized investigative or administrative functions of the Federal Bureau of Investigation.[10]

In effect, IPS was given carte blanche to support domestic and foreign parties, movements, and governments hostile to the United States. The institute's activities to socialize American society, divide and weaken American alliances, and generally frustrate U.S. foreign policy efforts to contain communism would not be disturbed.

Through the litigation, the institute learned a great deal about the vulnerabilities of the intelligence agencies, just as it had during the Pentagon Papers windfall some years earlier. IPS institutionalized a research project on U.S. military and intelligence agencies in conjunction with their study of the Pentagon Papers. Founded in 1972, the Project on National Security, as it was called, was directed by Marc Raskin, Ralph Stavins, Robert Borosage, and George Pipkin.[11] Information that IPS gained from its experience with the Pentagon Papers, the lawsuit against the FBI, and Freedom of Information Act lawsuits all became part of the Project on National Security. In addition, Marc Raskin had begun a program to probe the private sector, requesting each Fortune 500 company to describe its security system.[12]

Two spinoffs came out of the Project on National Security. The first (described at length in Chapter 5), known as Center for National Security Studies and directed by Robert Borosage, operated outside the institute and developed legal strategies against the intelligence agencies. A related research effort, the Project on Official Illegality (POI), remained in the institute and was directed by Ralph Stavins. Although there was some overlap between the two (Robert Borosage directed the Center for National Security Studies until 1978, when he came back to direct IPS), POI was concerned with "national security whistleblowers"—Daniel Ellsberg of Pentagon Papers fame, Victor Marchetti, CIA renegade, and Robert Wall, disaffected FBI agent. POI was originally busy ferreting out and publicizing controversies aimed at the intelligence agencies, but in 1975 it broadened to include other branches of the U.S. government and changed its name to the Government Accountability Project (GAP).

GAP became one of IPS's most innovative programs. While operating under the cover of "a public interest group formed to help restore confidence in the federal system by making public officials responsible . . . and promoting accountability throughout the government,"[13] GAP was ideally set up to embarrass and harass government officials and create media scandals.

Although it can be argued that GAP did (and does) help legitimate whistle-blowers, the institute is openly contemptuous of American political, military, and intelligence institutions, which collectively it dubs the "national security state." Marc Raskin told the 1970 Washington Convention of Federal Employees for Peace, Equality, and Priorities that because "the capitalistic system in the United States is causing imperialism and aggression in other parts of the world . . . the FBI, Secret Service, intelligence services of other government agencies, and the military should be done away with. . . ."[14] GAP's director, Ralph Stavins, was a member of the National Lawyers Guild, known for its legal support of and involvement with the Communist party in the United States.

The average government employee had no real reason to suspect that GAP was a radical antiestablishment organization. GAP's red, white, and blue star-spangled promotional literature, widely distributed throughout Washington's bureaucracies, represented the program as providing a great service to the country. The caption of one GAP brochure reads: "How Federal Employees Can Help America." GAP's literature neither identifies the program as a project of IPS nor mentions that the "whistleblower hotline" phone rings in the IPS building.

GAP is an ideal tool to gather sensitive information that can be easily leaked to the media. The Vietnam War demonstrated that political war in Washington was as important as what happened on the battlefield. According to its own literature, "GAP works directly with journalists,"[15] and because GAP has been so successful in making contact with various disaffected government employees it has become a source of leaks for media pundits hungry for sensation. Indeed, at a Conference on Whistleblowing in 1977, GAP staffers admitted that they were primarily concerned with getting information from the Department of Defense, the largest bureaucracy in Washington.

The problem of press leaks versus national security has been an ongoing problem since the Vietnam War. It was highlighted during the Grenada operation in October 1983 when the Reagan administration decided that the political cost of excluding the media was worth ensuring the security of the military operation. In November 1984 a reporter associated with an IPS spinoff, the Pacific News Service, helped undermine CIA efforts to support the contra freedom fighters by publicizing a CIA manual on guerrilla warfare. In February 1985 IPS fellow

William Arkin leaked classified information on U.S. naval nuclear contingency plans to Leslie Gelb, who went public with the information on the front page of the *New York Times*, causing considerable fallout within the NATO alliance.

Obviously, IPS benefits from the fact that it "works directly with journalists." Since IPS and GAP feed so much information to the news media, the media undoubtedly owe favors in return. This helps explain why leading media institutions enjoy cozy relations with the left-wing Institute for Policy Studies, the subject of the following chapter.

Part III

IPS and the Media

CHAPTER 8

Fourth-Estate Interface
IPS, the *Washington Post*, and the *New York Times*

While IPS enjoys good relations with a number of newspapers nationwide, its greatest success has been with the nation's two most influential newspapers, the *Washington Post* and the *New York Times*. These set the tone and agenda for news coverage in most of the country's print and electronic media.

When FBI agents retrieved IPS/TNI director Orlando Letelier's briefcase from the shattered wreckage of his bombed-out car, they found evidence that indicated Letelier had been serving as an "agent of influence" for hostile foreign powers—the Cuban DGI and the Chilean Socialist party in exile, headquartered in East Germany.[1] According to FBI records, Letelier had relations with twenty-seven reporters and editors in major U.S. media institutions, many with the *Post* and *Times*.[2]

Media Coverup: Spiking the Letelier Story

The strange silence of the press, despite all the evidence against Letelier, suggests ignorance or bias in the media, or great success by Letelier and IPS in cultivating their favor. With the exception of several conservative columnists, like William F. Buckley and Evans and Novak, the major media, notably the *Washington Post* and the *New York Times*, ignored or covered up the data pointing to Letelier's connections with the East bloc. Karen DeYoung of the *Post* called Letelier "a tall, charming redhead" who "lived a quiet life in the Maryland suburbs, studying how the world's wealth could be more equitably distributed."[3] Evans and Novak's second column on Letelier, which contained information just released by the FBI that shed further light on Letelier's activities, was suppressed altogether. In its place the *Post* ran a coverup story by Lee Lescaze, followed the next day by an op-ed piece by IPS fellow Saul Landau.[4] One *Post* editorial stated, "Orlando Letelier was a rare individual, as patient in argument as he was passionate in conviction, the model of the private man prepared to act on his beliefs and to accept their public consequences."[5]

In a 1975 letter to Cuban colleague Pablo Armando Fernandez, Saul Landau, a personal friend of Castro and successor to Letelier as director of the Transnational Institute, wrote that "the time has come to dedicate myself to narrower pursuits, namely making propaganda for American socialism."[6] He also stated that he intended to make socialism a "serious political movement in the United States."[7] Producing political propaganda was, however, not new to Landau. In the late sixties and early seventies he had devoted considerable time and effort to producing propaganda movies extolling Marxist regimes such as Castro's in Cuba and Allende's in Chile.[8]

If a healthy democracy requires an informed electorate, the attention the media grant IPS is startling. When the most powerful arbiters of public opinion, the media, smile on the admitted propagandists at IPS, public opinion may be misled.

Three Factors Predispose the Media to Favor IPS

IPS influence in the mainstream media is aided by three factors. First, a preponderance of liberal attitudes dominates the major media institutions in the United States. Robert Lichter and Stanley Rothman conducted scientific surveys during 1981–84 and found that across the board, in voting behavior and on most issues, the media elite were considerably more liberal than the population at large. In 1972, the year of the "Nixon landslide," when McGovern, the "peace candidate," received only 38 percent of the popular vote, the media elite gave him 81 percent of their votes. In 1976 Ford received 49 percent of the popular vote, but only 19 percent of the media elite voted for him.[9]

Second, since the early 1970s, after the Vietnam War and Watergate brought discredit to the U.S. government and particularly the executive branch, the media began actively to assume the role of a fourth branch of government. Stepping beyond their traditional role of holding the government accountable through criticism, they took an adversarial position regarding the government.

Third, the media's reporting of the "truths" about politics and world affairs has become increasingly bound by symbols and fashion—akin more to the values of the entertainment industry than to rigorous, objective analysis.

As a result of the first factor, a great part of the big media is dominated by persons who filter the news through a liberal screen. Irving Kristol notes that "the national networks and national newspapers are sincerely convinced that a liberal bias is proof of journalistic integrity."[10] Because liberals are often proud of being progressive and look to the Left for insight, they will accept IPS views more readily than those of moderate or conservative institutions like the American Enterprise Institute, the Hoover Institution, and the Heritage Foundation.

The genius of IPS, remember, has largely been in grafting radicalism onto the liberal tradition. That IPS views have found acceptance in the media is readily admitted by a number of leading publications. The *New Republic* calls IPS "a national resource," the *Washington Post* says it is the "first respectable offspring of the New Left," and Leslie Gelb, of the *New York Times*, described the institute as "one of three preeminent centers for foreign policy perspectives."[11]

The second trend—that the media often see their role as an adversary to the U.S. government[12]—plays right into the hands of IPS, which has a remarkably consistent record of opposing government policies, no matter what party is in power. Reporters can turn to IPS, knowing that it will reliably attack almost any aspect of the U.S. government, its personnel or policies, domestic or foreign.

As for the third factor—the increasing trendy orientation of the media—since the debacle of a failed Vietnam policy and the emergence of détente, it became unfashionable to think of using military force to contain communism or protect U.S. interests overseas. Increasingly, academics and the media have been inclined to accept communism as though it were just another political system—the Soviet Union a superpower that would yield to the rules governing Western democracies, if given a chance. Indeed, the press often labels fringe right-wing those who soberly address the need for firmness in dealing with communism and the Soviet Union. Worse, it has grown cavalier in exposing U.S. national security secrets.

After the idea of a "military industrial complex" had been accepted by the media, along with an optimism over an expanding welfare state and the "détente process," they came to regard any political regression or return to the cold-war or containment mentality as hopelessly conservative and quite beyond the pale of intellectual respectability. IPS was one think tank that built its entire worldview on these new premises, unabashedly advocating more demilitarization and more socialism. Many among the media elite were charmed by this "fashionable" think tank whose very appearance embodied the third world. Its appeal was reflected in the institute's 1973 annual report:

> The new body of knowledge is knowledge for liberation, for reconstruction. We need it to analyze the new economic and productive forces; to understand and build on them. We need it to insure that the new forces serve to free all people. Lack of such knowledge has betrayed social transformation in the past. Without such knowledge, we shall simply reinstitute hierarchical structures and oppression. . . .[13]

IPS analyses brim with sensational and utopian nostrums in contrast to the dry academic research of other think tanks, which is not as easily read or tailored into articles for mass consumption. IPS is entirely different from traditional research institutes which emphasize objectivity. IPS recognizes that news cannot be reported just as it happens. Passionately involved with issues, IPS fellows are activists who exploit and create issues that divide and agitate society. And they recognize the importance of the mass media, whose reporters have increasingly stepped off the sidelines and begun to create news.[14]

Enlisting the Mass Media to Pave Way for New Social Order

To prepare society for the radical change that IPS explicitly seeks, it is imperative to create news showing that the institutions of American society are faulty, inadequate, and corrupt. For this, IPS has created unique counterinstitutions, like the Government Accountability Project (GAP). GAP attacks and discredits both public and private institutions. The strategy usually involves pressing legal suits along with publicity campaigns. GAP's promotional literature states that the "Government Accountability Project works directly with journalists" and "initiates a variety of public education activities . . . to inform the public and the media about the problem of government wrongdoing."[15] GAP's annual report for 1982–83 speaks for itself about its ability to harass and cripple:

> We at GAP were able to halt construction at two nuclear power plants, keep another one from starting up, expose massive toxic contamination of a city, stop Three Mile Island's (TMI) clean up operation, push out the top management at TMI and the Zimmer Nuclear Power Plant, disclose numerous illegal practices of government and corporate bodies . . . and maintain a national leadership position on nuclear, environmental and federal employee rights issues.[16]

Taking credit for stopping the cleanup operation at Three Mile Island, GAP reveals it is interested not so much in safe nuclear power as in closing down the entire industry. There are, in fairness, some who believe that there is no such thing as safe nuclear power, but IPS activities show a consistent pattern of using the cover of "reform" to prepare the way for radical change.

Major Media "Call Upon Us Daily for Help"

In creating scandals and gaining leads on real and potential impropriety, public and private, through programs like GAP, IPS has been remarkably successful in currying favor with the press—a press which becomes more and more vulnerable to manipulation as it thirsts for sensation. In this regard IPS and GAP offer easy access to the public as well as the private sector.

This was alluded to when *Covert Action Information Bulletin (CAIB)*, the publication started by IPS colleague Philip Agee to undermine the CIA,[17] lashed back at the editors of the *Washington Post* for their criticism:

> Your diatribe only highlights the gap between the editorial offices and the reporters, for your people are among the large number of working journalists from virtually all the major printed and electronic media in the country who call upon us daily for help, research, and of all things, names of intelligence operatives in connection with articles they are writing.[18]

Reporters are likely to use the institute as a resource of information more frequently than they use Philip Agee's anti-CIA networks, since IPS has greater credibility in establishment circles. And the payoff is significant, for as one favor deserves another, the media reciprocate by running IPS articles and book reviews. But IPS has other means of cultivating the media. Every semester, IPS invites big-name journalists, particularly from the *New York Times* and the *Washington Post*, to teach its Washington School courses "Investigative Journalism" and "Foreign Reporting."

Karen DeYoung, Senior Editor at the *Washington Post*

Karen DeYoung, for instance, now a senior foreign editor at the *Washington Post*, taught at the IPS Washington School. In one summer course in 1980, entitled "Foreign Reporting," she revealed an insight into the liberal media's tendency to see "no enemies on the Left." DeYoung told the class of up and coming Woodward and Bernstein types that "most journalists now, most Western journalists at least, are very eager to seek out guerrilla groups, leftist groups, because you assume they must be the good guys."[19] DeYoung's comment caused such a flap in Washington that the *Post* stopped her further participation in IPS programs.

Actually, DeYoung was speaking from her own experience. In autumn 1978 the Sandinistas allowed her to visit and live at their guerrilla training center in the mountains of Costa Rica, from which they made raids into Nicaragua. Appropriately titled "At a Sandinista Training Camp," DeYoung's series of articles were run on the front page of the *Post*, and one appeared nearly always on the same day, or the day before, Congress debated whether or not to continue American aid to the Somoza government in Nicaragua, under siege by the Sandinistas.

In a period of heightened anti-Somoza sentiment, DeYoung's stories did a great deal to dispel the public perception that the Sandinistas were Marxist-oriented, a fact well known in Nicaragua. Her articles painted the Sandinistas as romantic revolutionaries, inspired by a noble mission to "liberate" the oppressed. In one article DeYoung denied that the Sandinistas were Marxists,[20] and in another she even described Daniel Ortega as a member of "the most moderate faction which advocates pluralistic democracy,"[21] though it was commonly known that Ortega was a long-time Marxist ideologue who received training in Cuba and worshipped Fidel Castro.

After the Sandinistas had toppled Somoza, DeYoung continued to reassure her readers that all was well with the revolution. On July 23, 1979, for example, she wrote that the Sandinistas were "courteous and unfailingly cheerful . . ."[22] and a week later she described the smiling soldiers who "waxed poetic" and addressed their fellow countrymen as "dear comrades." "The credo in Nicaragua these days," she wrote, "is: You will be nice to each other, you will share for the good of all, and the Sandinistas are here to make certain you do."[23] At the very time that DeYoung was painting this idyllic picture of "liberated" Nicaragua, the "courteous" Sandinistas were executing prisoners, a fact which she conceded nearly three years later when the OAS publicized it.

A former officer in the Sandinistas' elite security forces who defected to the United States, Miguel Bolanos Hunter, says that the Sandinista leaders viewed Karen DeYoung as one of their most important allies in the American media.[24] When DeYoung confronted Bolanos in June 1983 during an exclusive interview with the *Washington Post*, she appeared visibly shaken by the things he had to say. At one point, DeYoung asked Bolanos in Spanish, "Why did you come back to the underbelly of the country that is trying to eat your country?"[25]

Shortly after the Sandinistas had come to power in 1979, DeYoung began to write articles critical of the Salvadoran government and sympathetic to the Marxist FMLN guerrillas. In a cover story for *Mother Jones*, the radical "alternative" journal published by the Foundation for National Progress, which was "created to carry out the work of IPS," DeYoung argues that "what happened in Nicaragua is key to understanding El Salvador and our posture toward it. . . ."[26] Noting that El Salvador's "principal guerrilla groups had formed a unified command following a meeting in Havana, Cuba," she concludes that "there is little reason to expect the killing in El Salvador will soon stop, or the battle be won by one side or the other, with or without U.S. advisors."[27] In other words, U.S. efforts to resist Soviet- and Cuban-backed insurgencies are futile, whether in Nicaragua or El Salvador.

Les Whitten, Jack Anderson, Pat Tyler, Alma Guillermoprieto, and Joanne Omang

Jack Anderson is another important columnist who helped shape public opinion in favor of the Sandinistas without alluding to the Marxist character of its leadership and by making unrelenting attacks on Somoza. Les Whitten, Anderson's righthand man, was well connected to IPS and the Washington Office on Latin America (WOLA), both of which did their best for the Sandinistas. Whitten, who has taught at the Washington School, helped provide Anderson with enough material to fill twenty-five columns of bitter attacks on Somoza from 1977 to 1979.

Pat Tyler appeared at John Dinges's class on investigative reporting at IPS in fall 1983. A member of Bob Woodward's investigative team at the *Washington Post*, Tyler was the first reporter to expose President Reagan's classified authorization of covert operations by the CIA to put the brakes on the Sandinistas and cut off the arms flow into El Salvador. Presidential counselor Edwin Meese was quick to denounce these reports, saying they compromised the legitimate authority of the executive branch and gave the enemy food for propaganda. But the damage could not be undone; Tyler's exposé was picked up by the media nationwide.

Two other reporters specializing in Latin American affairs, Alma Guillermoprieto and Joanne Omang, have good relations with IPS. Guillermoprieto feels strongly enough to have paid to attend IPS's Letelier-Moffitt Memorial Human Rights Award ceremony in September 1984.[28] Omang has taught at the IPS Washington School on several occasions. In the spring 1984 session, when asked whether she ever found the line between objective and advocacy reporting blurred, she responded: "Well sure, sure, but that's because you're a human being, you know; you're going to end up caring about things . . . So when you write a story you can't help but become an advocate for basic human rights, against murders or things like this."[29]

Some reporters from the *Washington Post* are in close touch with IPS for ideological reasons, but others perhaps because IPS offers them a reliable contact with foreign powers and revolutionary movements otherwise beyond reach.

Elizabeth Becker and Roger Wilkins: From the *Post* to Fellowship at IPS

Despite considerable evidence of the brutality of Pol Pot's Khmer Rouge regime, which had destroyed some two million of its own people by 1977, Elizabeth Becker's *Post* stories belittled the Cambodian genocide. Writing in the *Post*, she tacitly supported the Pol Pot regime by referring to the visit of Lon Nol, the anticommunist Cambodian leader who came to Washington, D.C., in October 1978, as "an embarrassment."[30] She called his appeal for aid to his suffering people "hopeless."[31]

Not surprisingly, less than two months later, Becker was one of the first reporters invited into Cambodia after a three-year moratorium on foreign journalists, during which blackout Pol Pot conducted the genocide. Becker's eye-

witness stories offered little explanation of Cambodia's desolation, even going
so far as to claim that the Pol Pot "system was working."[32] After returning to
the U.S., Becker left the *Post* to join IPS as a visiting fellow.

Roger Wilkins, an editorial board member at the *Washington Post* and the
New York Times, also joined IPS, where he was named senior fellow in 1983.
An op-ed piece that appeared in the *New York Times* in summer 1983 offers a
glimpse of Wilkins' views. He suggests that in light of the "nuclear future,"
it is necessary to "reinvent politics," for the "concept of national sovereignty
may be obsolete"[33]—a view long held by Richard Barnet and Marcus Raskin.
The addition of Wilkins to the staff has undoubtedly helped the institute's relations with both the *Post* and the *Times*.

"I am from Cuba . . . Larry Stern Was One of My Best Friends"

Another former editor of the *Post*, Larry Stern, was a close colleague of IPS
until his fatal heart attack in 1979. While Stern was serving as the *Post*'s national
news editor, media critics accused him of "suppressing stories that were embarrassing to the Communist cause."[34] The *Post*'s chairman of the board, Kath-
erine Graham, and executive editor, Benjamin Bradlee, angrily denied such
allegations. But what people more intimate with Stern said about him at his
memorial service lends credibility to these charges.

One such noteworthy person was Teofilo Acosta, identified as a Cuban DGI
agent, who served as first secretary of the Cuban Interest Section in Washington.
Introducing himself to Ben Bradlee and others at the service, Acosta said, "I
am from Cuba, I am Marxist-Leninist . . . Larry Stern was one of my friends,
one of my best friends. I loved him."[35] Veteran leftist and IPS honorary fellow
I. F. Stone eulogized Stern saying, "Larry was one of us, one of the best of
us."[36] Stone also said that "there is no doubt where Larry's sympathies
lay . . . he hated those huge mindless institutions that devour our substance and
corrupt our fundamental ideals, like the Pentagon and the CIA."[37]

In the *Village Voice* Alexander Cockburn wrote that Stern had been "a Trotskyite in his hot youth" and that "Larry knew what the facts were going to tell
him before he discovered what they actually were. . . ."[38] Cockburn also noted
the power Stern held as the national news editor at the *Post*. Stern, he lauded,
"could write the important stories, broker the important stories, which would
start in the *Washington Post* and filter into the *New York Times*, out-of-town
newspapers, wire services, and TV newscasts across the country."[39]

Peter Osnos and Dusko Doder in Moscow and Havana

In summer 1980 Peter Osnos, the *Post*'s former Moscow correspondent, appeared as a guest lecturer at IPS. Although Osnos, unlike IPS, was not one to

apologize for the Soviet Union, still, after three years behind the Iron Curtain, his analysis of the Soviet system is less than incisive. "I've given up trying to decide why they do what they do—because they're aggressive or because they're scared," said Osnos to the gathering at IPS.[40]

After Osnos left Moscow, one of his new assignments was to Havana in March 1979. Despite Cuba's economic dependence on Moscow—to the tune of $8 million a day—Osnos could find little evidence of Soviet influence and reported that there was "apparently genuine rapport" between Castro and the Cuban people.[41] There was no reported comment from Osnos a year later when some one hundred twenty-five thousand Cubans flocked to the United States during the Mariel boatlift.

A participant in IPS's Washington School, Dusko Doder, the *Post*'s Moscow bureau chief from 1982 to 1985, had remarkable access to high-level Soviet officials, including an exclusive interview with Secretary General Chernenko in 1984. Doder also played an important role in arranging meetings between IPS representatives and Soviet officials in preparation for their "alternative arms control talks," which began in Moscow in 1982 and have been held in the United States every other year since.

Robert Kaiser and Philip Agee's Disinformation Effort

In spring 1981 Osnos, as a foreign news editor, was involved in the disinformation controversy at the *Post* which resulted in a front-page story undermining the Reagan administration's policy on El Salvador. The story alleged that the State Department's white paper "Communist Interference in El Salvador" did not prove Soviet and Cuban involvement in El Salvador.[42]

When asked how the story originated, Osnos said he had received a call from Jeffrey Stein, a former IPS fellow, who urged him to challenge the report. Osnos decided to assign Robert Kaiser, a *Post* staff reporter who had been Moscow bureau chief from 1971 to 1974, to look into the matter. Apparently in good standing with IPS and other elements on the Left (he had taught at the IPS Washington School), Kaiser had no difficulty finding fault with the State Department's arguments. As it turned out, Kaiser's primary source was Philip Agee.[43] Kaiser also made use of two stories written by John Dinges, which did their best to discredit the white paper. Dinges's stories, circulated by Pacific News Service (an IPS spinoff), appeared in a number of major newspapers, including the *Los Angeles Times*. After the State Department made a telling rebuttal, the *Post* reluctantly—and belatedly—apologized for the Kaiser-Agee story in a back page of the paper. But the damage had already been done.

When Howard Simon, managing editor for the *Post*, was asked what the management was doing to guard against incidents like the Kaiser-Agee story, he said, "This disinformation thing has been highly overblown. We take information from all sources . . . we publish what the administration's views are, we publish what the Soviet Union says. Look, I know Bob Kaiser and he's a nice guy."[44]

Just months before, this same Howard Simon ignored the warnings of two of his subordinates who doubted the authenticity of the Janet Cooke story of an eight-year-old heroine addict, a story that ended up bringing disgrace to the *Washington Post*. Cooke's story was awarded the Pulitzer Prize, which had to be forfeited when an outsider pointed out that she had lied about her Vasser academic credentials, which subsequently led to the discovery that she had fabricated the story itself.

Bob Kaiser was a participant in IPS's alternative arms control talks with the Soviet Union held in Minneapolis in May 1983 and San Francisco in September 1985. These events brought together key people in the American peace movement and Soviet officials—all party members, some intelligence agents.[45] Kaiser's commentary in the *Post* on the conference did not offer many critical observations. Most notably he failed to point out that two of the main objectives of the IPS agenda—disengagement from Europe (the dissolution of NATO) and cancellation of NATO's deployment of Pershing and Cruise missiles—were (and are) exactly those of the Soviet Union.

John Dinges: *Washington Post Assistant Editor and IPS Associate Fellow*

John Dinges has been on the payroll as an assistant editor at the *Post* and is simultaneously a correspondent for the Pacific News Service, an IPS spinoff. Dinges is, moreover, an associate fellow at IPS. In all these capacities Dinges has been busily engaged discrediting the elected government of El Salvador. Championing the cause of human rights in his *Post* articles and those syndicated nationally by Pacific News Service, Dinges accuses the Salvadoran government of collusion with "death squads," which, he asserts, are exclusively responsible for civilian killings.[46]

But, when Dinges writes to his leftist audience, he lets his hair down. In the *Progressive* magazine, for instance, Dinges exhibits the classic "no enemies on the Left" perspective:

> The programs sponsored by opposition movements in El Salvador and Guatemala, and already instituted in Nicaragua, contain no element that is incompatible with US interests, and it is the height of arrogance for the Reagan Administration . . . to question the sincerity of these programs.[47]

Like his colleagues at IPS, when they wrote about the Vietcong fifteen years before, Dinges insists that the guerrilla movements in Central America are good because they are led rather by peasants and agrarian reformers than by Marxists, who find their military hardware through Managua and Havana.

Leading an IPS class discussion on "Foreign Reporting" with regard to third-world revolution, Dinges stated, "The whole tone of the reporting assumes that right and justice is on one side and evil is on the other."[48] He followed that by stating that "almost all journalists are liberals,"[49] a fact demonstrated by random survey analysis. Dinges's two comments help account for the patterned behavior of the American media since Vietnam, which caused Secretary of State George Shultz to remark during the Grenada mission: "It seems as though reporters are always against us. . . ."[50]

Continuing his "revolution and U.S. agenda" stories in his IPS class, Dinges got around to Latin America, where he saw himself as getting in on the ground floor. "The human rights stories in the mid-70s in Latin America I'm familiar with because I was writing a lot of those stories," said Dinges. "I was down there talking to human rights officials in the first human rights organization ever set up probably any place in the world in the middle of a dictatorship, set up by the church inside of Chile . . . I kept [wondering] whether I should use the term 'human rights' or 'civil rights,' " Dinges told the class. "I started using the word 'human rights' [when] the vocabulary was not even there."[51]

Chile was only the beginning for Dinges and his fellow "liberal" journalists imbued with the "human rights" emphasis. By the time revolution had swept through Nicaragua and threatened El Salvador, Guatemala, and Honduras, the issue of human rights was so dominating news analysis on Latin American affairs that traditional American security interests often played second fiddle. When Joanne Omang, who taught the IPS session after Dinges, was asked how it was that criticism for human rights violations was leveled against governments, but almost never against national "liberation" movements or guerrilla groups, she replied, "We can't expect the indigenous groups to be concerned with human rights . . . we expect the government to protect human rights. It is the responsibility of government to comply with human rights standards."[52] This pattern predictably changed in early 1985 when the pro–U.S. contra rebels came under attack for violating the human rights of Nicaraguan civilians. The American media picked up the anticontra stories from a well-orchestrated campaign conducted by IPS, the Washington Office on Latin America, Americas Watch, and the Council on Hemispheric Affairs. (More on this in Chapter 14.)

Ben Bagdikian, Scott Armstrong, Sidney Blumenthal, and Sally Quinn Bradlee

A number of other important people at the *Washington Post* have had close relations with IPS. Ben Bagdikian, former assistant managing editor for national affairs, cooperated with IPS contacts—"operating cloak and dagger fashion"[53]—in securing a copy of the Pentagon Papers for the *Washington Post*. After leaving the paper, Bagdikian revealed his own leftist sympathies in his book *Media Monopoly*, and in his foreword to David Armstrong's *A Trumpet to Arms*, which glorified the "alternative media" for their radical chic and nihilism.

Scott Armstrong, another *Post* reporter, taught at the IPS Washington School and assisted John Dinges and Saul Landau in writing *Assassination on Embassy Row*, a book about the murder of Orlando Letelier. Armstrong is famous for his own book, *The Brethren*, a muckraking exposé of the Supreme Court that was accused of "violating the confidentiality of court proceedings and inhibiting the free exchange among the justices."[54] Armstrong wrote a front-page story on May 22, 1981, entitled "State Reviewing Lefever's Role in Policy on Formula Sales," which alleged collusion between Ernest Lefever's Ethics and Public Policy Center and the Nestlé Corporation. Although it was largely a mélange of misquotations and distortions, Armstrong's story helped the campaign to block the nomination of Lefever for assistant secretary of state for human rights—a campaign led by IPS, the Washington Office on Latin America (WOLA), the Council on Hemispheric Affairs (COHA), and the National Council of Churches (NCC). Armstrong also contributed to IPS's *Nuclear Battlefields*, a book that published classified information on the U.S. nuclear defense forces, and strained relations with America's allies.

Sidney Blumenthal was hired by the *Post* in 1984 after beginning his journalistic career writing for various liberal and left-wing publications. His friendship with IPS was well established in the late 1970s when he served as the Boston correspondent for *In These Times*, the socialist newspaper published by IPS. Since coming to the *Post* he has mainly written for the "Style" section, where his talents have been employed in colorful investigative articles discrediting conservatives and the people and policies of the Reagan administration. But as a designated "national correspondent" he has also written a number of influential news stories. For instance, the day before the House was to vote on aid to the contras in the spring of 1986 Blumenthal wrote a front-page story in the *Post* alleging that the National Endowment for Democracy had misused funds in conjunction with grants issued to the democratic opposition in Nicaragua. An eleventh-hour effort to influence Congress to vote against aid to the contras, his story backfired. The House voted for the $100 million aid package after an emergency congressional investigation found Blumenthal's charges baseless.

Any documentation of IPS connections with the *Washington Post* would be incomplete without mentioning that Sally Quinn, wife of the *Post*'s executive editor, Benjamin Bradlee, was employed as a secretary at IPS in the mid-70s. In 1977 the Bradlees visited Cuba, where they were given a seven-hour audience with Fidel Castro. Upon their return to Washington, Sally Quinn wrote a lengthy story in the *Post* about the visit with Castro. It offers a fascinating look at the naiveté of the media elite. "Part of Castro's charm," she wrote, "exasperating as it is at times, is that he can convince someone, at least for the moment, of something they do not believe in. In fact, he can actually make it sound logical when he says that the press should be a tool of the state and party."[55]

T.D. Allman and the New York Times

IPS influence at the *New York Times* has been firmly established for nearly a decade and a half. T. D. Allman, for one; a writer currently associated with the Pacific News Service, he got an antiwar scoop onto the front page of the *New York Times* on September 18, 1969, charging that the U.S. had violated the Geneva Accords by taking the war into Laos.[56] According to his "reliable" and "informed" sources, Allman wrote that "as many as 500 sorties a day were being flown over Laos."[57] "So far there has been at least one confirmed battle death in Laos," Allman continued; "it occurred last week when an American CIA agent was killed by gunfire at an advanced post." The story created an uproar not only because of the supposed death of a U.S. government official, but because the U.S. was bound to respect the neutrality of Laos under the Geneva agreement.

As it happened, the story was fabricated. The death certificate belonged to the infant of an Air America employee, and was unrelated to any combat.[58] Whether Allman wrote this for political reasons or whether it was just accidental misinformation we may never know. But it certainly had a negative impact on the American war effort. In either case, Allman may have felt morally justified and compelled to write the story because of his opposition to the Vietnam War. The *Times* never printed a retraction.

IPS, Seymour Hersh, and the Times

In 1969, the year before IPS got Pacific News Service off the ground, Philip Stern, IPS chairman of the board, funded Dispatch News Service, another "alternative" news agency dedicated to rousing public opposition to the Vietnam War.[59] The *New York Times* picked up Seymour Hersh's "My Lai Massacre" story only after Dispatch News Service had brought it to the *Times*'s attention.[60]

The scoop, splashed onto the front page of the *Times* on November 13, 1969, sent shockwaves across the nation just two days before the November 15 antiwar march on Washington. As a result, Seymour Hersh, virtually unknown, became a journalistic star almost overnight. Hersh's research for the My Lai story was also funded by Philip Stern under the auspices of the newly created Fund for Investigative Journalism.

Hersh's story ran for several weeks and was picked up by every major media outlet in the United States. In the end, it was instrumental in turning the tide of American public opinion against the war.

Hersh's next major exposé was a devastating blow to the CIA. In blazing front-page stories in the *Times* in September 1974 Hersh charged that the CIA was directly involved in ousting Allende in Chile.[61] A few months later, in another front-page series, Hersh charged that the CIA "had violated its charter, and conducted a massive illegal domestic intelligence operation during the Nixon administration against the antiwar movement and other dissident groups in the United States."[62] (See Chapter 5.) The gist of Hersh's stories—that the CIA was out of control abroad and acting like the Gestapo at home—severely undermined the CIA. During an era of all-time low trust in the government because of Vietnam and Watergate, Hersh's stories were swallowed whole. In reality, they were exaggerated and misleading, as Senator Church's committee, formed to investigate intelligence-agency abuse, discovered some eighteen months later.

Like Elizabeth Becker of the *Washington Post*, who was one of the first Western journalists allowed into Pol Pot's Cambodia in 1978, Hersh was one of the two American journalists permitted into Vietnam after the communists took over the south in 1975. Following his visit, Hersh wrote a series of six articles which were published in the *New York Times* starting August 3, 1979. Ironically, despite his talents as an investigative journalist, Hersh painted a positive picture of "liberated" Vietnam, and probed not at all such phenomena as the "reeducation centers," the treatment of POWs, religious persecution, or the Soviet's use of Camranh Bay's naval base.

Hersh continues his close relations with the institute, contributing his talents to the Washington School faculty. In December 1983 IPS presented Hersh in its "Other Side of Town Lecture Series" to a standing-room-only crowd at the National Education Association auditorium.

Hersh's 1986 book on Korean Airlines flight 007, *The Target Is Destroyed*, offers some telling insights into Soviet disinformation efforts. Shortly after Hersh let it be known that he was writing a story on KAL flight 007, the Soviet government invited him to Moscow, apparently confident that, given his political predilections and connections with IPS, Hersh would be receptive to disinformation against the CIA. Hersh notes that "[Marshal] Ogarkov agreed to my visa in the hope that they could persuade me, as a journalist, to investigate the CIA's role in the shootdown."[63] Upon Hersh's arrival in Moscow, the deputy foreign minister, Georgi M. Kornienko, told Hersh flat out that "your assignment is to find that [flight 007] was an intruder."[64]

To his credit as a journalist, Hersh pursued his work with rigor and found, after two years of investigation—during which the Soviets tried to persuade him otherwise—that "flight 007 was not on an intelligence gathering mission for the CIA or any other agency of the United States or South Korea."[65] Although

Hersh's research did not, in the end, buttress Soviet disinformation attempts to accuse the CIA, it did assist the Soviets in other ways. Hersh certainly helped dispel Soviet blame for the tragedy by focusing on the Reagan administration's alleged overreaction and political use of raw intelligence data. But much more significant for the Soviets was the fact that Hersh exposed new information about the organization and operation of U.S. technical intelligence gathering. In fact, CIA Director William Casey charged that "Hersh was perilously close to prosecution for revealing so much about important intelligence secrets."[66]

In the book's acknowledgments, Hersh credits William Arkin and others at the Arms Race and Nuclear Weapons Research Project with whom "he worked closely . . . in shaping . . . requests for documents under the Freedom of Information Act."[67] Hersh neglects to mention that the Arms Race and Nuclear Research Project to which he owes this gratitude is an entity within the Institute for Policy Studies.

Neil Sheehan, the Pentagon Papers, and IPS

Neil Sheehan, like his colleague Seymour Hersh, was a *New York Times* reporter made famous by his reporting on Vietnam. And like Hersh's My Lai scoop, Sheehan's Pentagon Papers stories had a huge negative impact on public support for the American war effort. Recall (Chapter 4) that, according to FBI records, Sheehan apparently cooperated with IPS in getting a copy of the classified documents, originally stolen by Daniel Ellsberg.[68] Again like Hersh, Sheehan continued his relationship with IPS after the war by participating in the Washington School, where he taught a course on investigative reporting.

Harrison Salisbury and Wilfred Burchett

Western reporters in Saigon were dumfounded when in early 1967 Harrison Salisbury of the *New York Times* was allowed behind enemy lines to report on the war. His passage to North Vietnam had been facilitated by friend and colleague Wilfred Burchett, a Communist party member who wrote for the Marxist weekly *Guardian* while doubling as an intelligence agent for the KGB.[69]

The circumstances surrounding Harrison Salisbury's professional life are particularly revealing and offer a good look at the problems the Western media face in reporting on the Soviet Union, or any totalitarian society. The way in which Salisbury became the *Times* reporter in Moscow demonstrates with what simplicity the Soviets can exercise real influence over the world's free press.

In 1948 the *Times* Moscow bureau chief, Drew Middleton, was expelled by the Kremlin for "excessive anti-Soviet" reporting. *Times* management needed official Soviet approval to fill the vacancy. But the Kremlin rejected one proposal after another. Finally, at a diplomatic cocktail party, a Soviet official suggested to an American official that Harrison Salisbury, who was then on assignment in Moscow for UPI, would be viewed favorably by the Soviet government. Salisbury had a record of relatively sympathetic reporting on Soviet affairs. Within a few weeks, the *Times* hired Salisbury as its Moscow bureau chief.

That experience sent a message to all the Western media: "Don't make waves, if you want to continue to operate your Moscow news bureau."[70] That message has been recently driven home again by *Newsweek* reporter Andrew Nagorski and *U.S. News & World Report* reporter Nick Daniloff, both of whom were incarcerated and expelled for anti-Soviet reporting. Because the Western media operate as commercial enterprises with a bottom line—minimize inconvenience and expense—they naturally tend to avoid alienating the Soviets.

In Salisbury's case, two decades after he was recognized as a sympathetic reporter by the Soviets in Moscow, he was again helping the communist cause in North Vietnam. Shortly thereafter he became one of the first Western journalists to be invited into Red China, and one of the few ever allowed into North Korea.[71]

As for Wilfred Burchett, although he gained a reputation for spreading disinformation during the Korean War and collaborated with the Soviets thereafter, this didn't stop the Associated Press and the *New York Times* from working with him and using his material. In his study on the alternative media in America, *A Trumpet to Arms*, David Armstrong inadvertently acknowledges how they were taken in by Burchett:

> He did, however, have the satisfaction of being solicited to write a series for the Associated Press in January 1967, in which he outlined North Vietnam's outlook toward the peace negotiations that always seemed to be pending. Burchett was chosen because of his excellent contacts with communist leaders. His pieces for the AP were widely read in official Washington, where they arrived on diplomats' desks in the pages of the *New York Times*, which had finally chosen to print his work.[72]

When Salisbury was finally admitted to North Vietnam, it was Burchett who was at his side to guide his tour and to serve as liaison for Salisbury when his North Vietnamese hosts offered him material for his news stories. Not surprisingly, when Salisbury's stories appeared as a front-page exclusive series in the *New York Times*, their perspective resonated with Burchett's line—namely, that the U.S. was purposely bombing civilian targets.[73] The *Washington Star* reacted on its editorial page: "To suggest, as some appear to be doing, that the civilian casualties amount to a systematic slaughter of the innocents by the barbarous United States government, is to abandon fact and good faith and to embrace Hanoi's propaganda line with a passion that defies reason."[74] *U.S. News &*

World Report of February 27, 1967, noted the more unsavory side of Burchett's record:

> Mr. Burchett, who long maintained an apartment in Moscow, does not have an Australian passport any more. At the time of the Korean peace talks, Australian counterintelligence officials said he would be arrested as a traitor if he ever returned to his homeland. . . . Among their charges against him then: trying to convert Australian prisoners of war to the communist cause while acting as a bona fide war correspondent.[75]

Wilfred Burchett's stories were carried by Dispatch News Service, an IPS spinoff. Burchett then made his way to Washington in fall 1971 to talk to Henry Kissinger, who hoped to communicate to Hanoi through him when the Paris peace talks broke down.[76] After the war Burchett broke with the radical newspaper *Guardian*, for which he had been writing for twenty-two years (1957–79), when it refused to endorse the Soviet-backed Vietnamese invasion of Cambodia. Subsequently a number of Burchett's articles appeared in the IPS newspaper, *In These Times*.

By the close of the Vietnam War, IPS influence at the editorial level of the *New York Times* had become more evident. In 1972 Salisbury initiated the op-ed page at the *Times*, which increasingly became a sounding board for the New Left. Within a few years IPS articles were found on the *Times* op-ed page more frequently than those of any other policy research institution. The preference was continued under Charlotte Curtis, known for her left-leaning politics, after she became the *Times* op-ed-page editor following Salisbury's retirement.[77] In 1979 and 1980 Curtis authorized the publication of two articles by Wilfred Burchett. In 1981 Times Books, a *New York Times* subsidiary, published *At the Barricades* by Burchett. One of the Times Books' editors responsible for Burchett's book, John Simon, said he had heard that Burchett was a KGB agent, but he didn't bother to investigate because he didn't take the charges seriously. Besides, Simon went on, Burchett's memoirs were a contribution to history and so what if he were KGB.

IPS and *New York Times* Op-Ed Page

In 1980 and 1981, under the direction of Curtis, the op-ed pages of the *New York Times* printed more than twice as many IPS articles than it did of any other policy research institution. In 1980, for example, the *Times* carried twenty articles by IPS fellows, compared with nine by persons from the American Enterprise Institute, and seven from Brookings Institution.[78] In 1981 the number of pieces by IPS fellows and associates increased to thirty-seven, over three times more than those of the next policy research center,[79] even though Curtis received upwards of twenty thousand articles per year from diverse policy research centers. The changing of the guard on the *Times* op-ed page from Curtis to Robert Semple in 1981 brought some change. But Semple continues to publish commentary from IPS and its spinoffs. And the *Times* insists on identifying IPS as a "liberal institution," instead of giving it its proper designation—radical, left-wing, or Marxist.

Raymond Bonner on El Salvador

Raymond Bonner, another *New York Times* reporter with connections to IPS, greatly assisted the revolutionary cause in El Salvador. Like Seymour Hersh, who was picked up by the *Times* after his My Lai scoop was pushed by Dispatch News Service, Raymond Bonner was abruptly hired by the *Times* after working as director of the Consumers Union, a left-wing group founded by Ralph Nader. Bonner was hired despite having had no previous experience in journalism, a rather unusual move, given that the *New York Times*'s chairman and president, Arthur Ochs Sulzberger, says his policy is to hire only journalists with prior newspaper experience.

Bonner says that he left Nader's organization for Latin America because of a need for "a change in lifestyle . . . about five years ago I just took off . . . with no idea what I was going to do."[80] Yet almost in the same breath he admits calling John Dinges, Joanne Omang, and a string of other media people:

> Joanne I had met ten years earlier when I was in Washington, and I was working for Nader at the time, and she was covering some of the stuff I was doing. When I got ready to go down to Latin America . . . I called her and she gave me all kinds of names . . . and before I went I made contact with *Newsweek*, ABC Radio, NPR, the *Wall Street Journal*, all kinds of different places.[81]

Although Bonner says he "had no idea what [he] was going to do," he certainly concentrated his efforts on the media. On another occasion, when Bonner was featured at an IPS seminar in June 1984 he showed up with John Dinges. Being introduced, he frankly said, "It was John Dinges [who] gave me my start."[82]

Bonner readily admits, "I come from an advocacy background, which makes it easy for . . . people out there to say that I'm an advocate journalist . . ." He adds, "There is no such thing as an objective journalist."[83]

Bonner also personifies the criticism that American reporters are often ill equipped to cover foreign affairs because of their lack of historical understanding of the countries they are assigned to cover. Bonner himself says,

> Like most Americans, I didn't know El Salvador from San Salvador . . . I think

back to my first questions—it took me a year to understand what they [the Salvadoran FMLN guerrillas] were fighting for. And I really had no sense of it at all. . . . To understand a revolution . . . we're not objective, come on! I'm not going to admit to being—I mean, I try, I mean, I try to be balanced and I try to be fair, but look, I've got twenty-four hours a day. I've probably got sixteen to work. Now look—I'm going to pick and choose what I do during those sixteen hours. You cannot do it all.[84]

Discussing his journalistic experience in Latin America, Bonner relates:

I went to Guatemala for a week and then I went to Salvador, and two days after I got there they killed the nuns and two days after that was the funeral for the FDR leaders who'd just been killed and then after that, they restructured the junta and Duarte became president, and it was just a cascading of front-page events after front-page events.[85]

For someone who didn't know El Salvador from San Salvador, who "had no sense of it all," and who "took a year to understand what the Salvadoran guerrillas were fighting for," Bonner didn't hesitate to become an instant expert.

In 1981 and 1982 Bonner's reporting, often featured as front-page stories for the *Times* and picked up by other major media outlets across the country, pushed the theme that the Salvadoran government was primarily responsible for the killings and turmoil in El Salvador. Like Harrison Salisbury, T. D. Allman, and Neil Sheehan, who asserted a decade and a half earlier that the South Vietnamese government was corrupt and unworthy of American support, Bonner wrote story after story that undermined U.S. support for the fledgling Salvadoran government struggling to prevent a communist takeover. Bonner's sixty-odd stories written in 1981 on El Salvador were so tilted, his sources so questionable, his sympathy for the Marxist guerrillas so obvious, that he was publicly denounced by the moderate U.S. ambassador to El Salvador, Deane Hinton.

Bonner relied heavily for his stories on the Human Rights Commission of El Salvador and the Legal Aid Office of the Catholic Archdiocese of El Salvador. Both of these sources Bonner portrayed as being connected with the Roman Catholic church. But Bonner's claims were as spurious as they were misleading.

The Human Rights Commission of El Salvador is a front organization headed by Marxists. Its director, Marianela Garcia Villas, openly supports the revolutionary Left. The HRC has neither the support nor the sanction of the Roman Catholic church.

The Legal Aid Office was disavowed by Bishop Arturo y Damas as early as May 31, 1981. In July, a member of LAO was arrested in Texas on charges of smuggling arms. On November 15, 1981, the bishop again denounced LAO, charging that its publications "create confusion." He also pointed out that LAO never attributed any deaths to the guerrilla forces, even though the guerrillas themselves had claimed responsibility on numerous occasions for taking lives.[86] On December 2, 1981, the Episcopal Conference charged that LAO spread "confusing information . . . abroad."[87] On January 6, 1982, the four Roman Catholic bishops in El Salvador issued a formal declaration denouncing *any* statement by the Legal Aid Office that "has been made or will be made in the future in the name of the Church or the Archbishopric . . . ."[88] Finally, the Catholic church evicted LAO from the small office it occupied in a church-owned building. Not one of these developments was reported by Bonner, who blithely continued to cite Legal Aid Office information as though it had the ecclesiastical blessing of Rome itself.

Like Karen DeYoung of the *Washington Post*, Bonner traveled with the FMLN guerrillas and expressed sympathy for their cause. In fact, when given in early January 1982 a guided tour of the guerrilla-controlled province of Morazan—in which Bonner saw only what the guerrillas wanted him to see—he never questioned the accounts of the guerrillas and the "facts and figures" of the Marxist-controlled Human Rights Commission. Accordingly, Bonner's stories accused the Salvadoran army of killing 926 civilians in El Mozote, although as the assistant secretary of state for inter-American affairs, Thomas Enders, noted, the total population of El Mozote was only about 300.[89] Also like DeYoung—who, it may be recalled, told her IPS class that "most journalists . . . are very eager to seek out guerrilla groups, leftist groups, because you assume they must be the good guys"[90]—Ray Bonner preferred believing the Marxist guerrillas and their support apparatus to believing the U.S. government. Bonner noted that "the guerrillas treated us well."[91]

Shortly after, Bonner wrote a story (January 11, 1982) suggesting that American advisers condoned the torture by the Salvadoran army of suspected guerrillas. The American embassy had to cable Washington to clear up Bonner's "totally false" charges. On February 19 Deputy Secretary of Defense Frank C. Carlucci sent a letter to A. M. Rosenthal, executive editor of the *Times*, informing him that the story was "based on erroneous information" and that it did "a disservice to our men in uniform." Carlucci added that the *Times*'s Washington bureau had been "warned" before publication that the story was false.[92]

A curious aspect of Bonner's torture stories—and similar ones by Alma Guillermoprieto of the *Washington Post*—is that their publication was delayed for two weeks, appearing just as President Reagan was certifying El Salvador for its human rights progress.

Bonner was also prominent among those who questioned the Salvadoran elections. The seventeen articles Bonner wrote on the topic seemed to impugn the electoral process itself. After the election—in which the FMLN guerrillas and the FDR support group refused to participate—Bonner was one of the first journalists to assert that the elections were "massively fraudulent."[93]

A survey of the sixty or so stories Bonner wrote in 1982 raises serious doubt about his objectivity. For example, even though the rebels' Radio Venceremos broadcast repeatedly that the FMLN/FDR were Marxist-led, Bonner never labeled them so in the *New York Times*. Bonner told a group of Americans, "I have always stayed away from calling groups Marxist-led, because I don't know exactly what that means."[94] Bonner usually used the term "rebels" or "guerrillas," but, he said, "even calling them 'guerrillas' has negative connotations." For that matter, he added, "calling them 'leftists' . . . has negative connotations."[95]

Appearing at a July 4 reception at the American embassy in the company of his colleague John Dinges, Ray Bonner was ill received, for he was looked upon as being closer to the Marxist guerrillas than to his own government.[96] But to Bonner, the snub was a privilege. "Obviously there's a certain badge of honor," he said to a class at IPS's Washington School, ". . . that goes with being attacked by the U.S. embassy, and being attacked by the State Department, and being attacked by the U.S. government."[97]

Numerous complaints about Bonner's reporting were brought to the attention of the *Times* management. Sydney Gruson, *Times* vice chairman, had to admit that Bonner had reported irresponsibly, and in September 1982 had Bonner recalled and reassigned.

One of Bonner's first public appearances after returning to the United States was at IPS, where he was honored as a keynote speaker. In spring 1984 Bonner joined the Washington School faculty alongside John Dinges in teaching a class at IPS on foreign reporting. True to the course description—to "examine the role of foreign journalism in our perceptions of the world, and in the formation of foreign policy"[98]—Bonner proudly recounted how his reporting helped shape U.S. foreign policy toward El Salvador.

David Burnham and IPS's Government Accountability Project

Another *New York Times* reporter and frequent participant in IPS programs is David Burnham. Burnham teaches courses on investigative journalism and the information revolution at the Washington School, and has worked closely with the Government Accountability Project in his antinuclear advocacy reporting. Burnham was one of the first reporters to hype the fears of a nuclear meltdown at Three Mile Island (TMI) in Middletown, Pennsylvania. His first story on the TMI accident stated that "the Nuclear Regulatory Commission told Congress . . . that the risk of a reactor core meltdown had arisen at the crippled Three Mile Island atomic power plant . . . an event that could necessitate the evacuation of the immediate area."[99]

In fact, Dudley Thompson, the official press spokesman for the Nuclear Regulatory Commission, emphasized that there was no real hazard of nuclear contamination outside the plant, and that real risk was limited to the reactor container. But with the help of IPS's GAP, Burnham and most of the media plowed ahead, misinforming the public and making Three Mile Island a symbol of death for the nuclear industry in the United States.

Times **Columnist Anthony Lewis Becomes Samuel Rubin Fellow**

Cora and Peter Weiss have exerted their influence on the *Times* in other ways as well. For instance, in 1982 they endowed Columbia University with $1 million to establish the "Samuel Rubin Program for the Advancement of Liberty and Equality Through Law," and encouraged the appointment of Anthony Lewis, veteran columnist of the *Times*, as Samuel Rubin fellow for the 1982–83 academic year.[100]

Pulitzer Prize winner Anthony Lewis projects in his columns a worldview that generally reflects that of IPS. A fairly typical example is an op-ed piece of October 10, 1983, asserting that resisting communist revolution is futile for the United States:

> The point is not that revolutionary governments are angels. Far from it. The point, rather, is the futility of resisting reality. American interests would have been far better served in Vietnam and China by living with those Communist governments from the start. There is still time, barely, to understand that change in Central America need not threaten U.S. security—unless we go on blindly resisting it.[101]

Also noteworthy, Anthony Lewis was one of the first among American media personalities to apologize for the Soviet Union on the tragedy of Korean Airlines flight 007. Echoing a Soviet line, Lewis wrote, "Conceivably Soviet radar technicians could have mistaken it as an intelligence-gathering aircraft."[102]

Times **Columnist Tom Wicker Appears at Riverside Church**

New York Times associate editor and columnist Tom Wicker has also been courted by the Weisses. On October 1, 1983, Wicker gave a keynote address to a gathering of radical organizers sponsored by the Riverside Church Disarmament Program under the auspices of Rev. William Sloane Coffin, Riverside Church's senior minister; Cora Weiss, director of the church's disarmament program; and her husband, Peter Weiss, IPS chairman of the board. Like all the other media representatives present, including Igor Ignatiev of TASS,[103] Wicker was courted by Coffin and Weiss. The day after the meeting, which brought him together with the Sandinista foreign minister, Miguel D'Escoto, Wicker wrote in the *Times* that in regard to American relations with Latin America, "the trouble was the Administration's fixed ideological position that looks on a revolution as necessarily bad."[104]

The Soviet Union, which openly supports numerous "liberation movements," certainly must take note of such commentary in the *Times*. This was the indirect observation of Herman Dinsmore, who left the *New York Times* after thirty-four years, including a long stint as associate foreign editor and nine years as editor of its international edition. In his 1969 book, *All the News That Fits*, Dinsmore wrote:

> The *New York Times* took no really effective steps to counter these Communist thrusts and all too frequently appeared to back them, as if to play the Soviet regime off against the United States and other democratic nations of the West. The *New York Times* in more recent years has stated that it wants a balance of power in the world—as if it were possible to maintain such a thing. Editorially, it has freely criticized the United States while but sparingly finding fault with Communist actions. . . .
>
> That attitude of the *New York Times* toward the Soviet Union has resulted in remarkable distortions in its news columns and in its editorial judgments . . . .[105]

Times Columnist Flora Lewis Falls for Soviet Disinformation

Flora Lewis, a colleague of both Tom Wicker and Anthony Lewis, was taken in by a KGB forgery in early 1981. Called "Dissent Paper on El Salvador and Central America," the forgery circulated among a number of groups associated with IPS—such as the Committee in Solidarity with the People of El Salvador (CISPES) and the Council on Hemispheric Affairs (COHA). After Karen DeYoung of the *Washington Post*, Thomas Brom of the Pacific News Service, and John Clements of *In These Times* wrote stories critical of U.S. policy based on this document, Flora Lewis picked up the story. Writing in her *Times* column on March 6, 1981, that the document, "drawn up by people from the National Security Council, the State and Defense Departments, and the CIA," was based on "solid facts and cool analysis," Lewis counseled that the Reagan administration would "do well to listen to the paper's authors before the chance for talks is lost."[106] When the State Department came out with a detailed report on the forgery the next day, she admitted to having been taken in. But her colleague, Anthony Lewis, continued to plug the document—without calling it official—and his column was convincing enough for Sen. Edward Kennedy to insert it into the *Congressional Record*.

Conclusion

IPS enjoys considerable influence with many at the *Washington Post* and the *New York Times*. And these are the two most influential papers in the United

States. The *Post* and particularly the *Times* select the daily diet of news for the major American media. As ABC White House correspondent Sam Donaldson noted, "The print media such as the *New York Times*, the *Washington Post*, the *Los Angeles Times*, and the *Boston Globe* are my best sources." Putting the *Times* and the *Post* at the top of the list, Donaldson said, "These newspapers set the agenda for the stories which those of us in television then follow up on. The stories you see us do at night at 6:30 or 7:00 are because we read them that morning in the newspaper."[107]

The *New York Times* slogan, "All the News That's Fit to Print," is apparently taken seriously by many news editors. There are currently 511 subscribers to the *New York Times* syndicated wire and news service worldwide, three quarters of which are in the United States. A cliché in journalistic circles has it that "if it isn't in the *New York Times* it isn't worth reporting." Commenting on the "multiplier effect" of the *Times*, columnist James Reston points out that "what appears in the *Times* automatically appears later in other places." And Alice Widener, a columnist for *Barron's*, asserts that "most editors and newsmen on the staffs of *Life, Time, Newsweek*, etc., and most editors, reporters, and commentators at NBC, CBS, and ABC take their news and editorial cues from the *New York Times*. Technically, it is a great newspaper; but it reports much of the news in conformity with its editorial policies."[108]

In the nation's capital the *Washington Post* has equal footing with the *Times*. And like that of the *Times*, the reach of the *Post* is great, with some three hundred fifty daily newspapers in the United States and Canada subscribing to its syndicated wire service.

Most congressmen and senators treat the *Times* and the *Post* as their bibles, and more than fifty copies of both papers go to the White House daily. According to the Library of Congress, the two most frequently cited sources in congressional debate are the *Post* and the *Times*. The *Times* and, to a lesser extent, the *Post* are found in virtually every academic library. There are over three thousand subscribers to the *New York Times* microfilm service, and the *Times* is read by more than half the presidents of our nation's colleges.[109]

While modern technology has made its impact on the media, it seems to have fostered greater homogenization rather than improved the quality of news reporting. Columnist Robert Novak, of the Evans and Novak team, has called the media "the setting where journalists are welded into one homogenous ideological mold."[110] Major U.S. media institutions tend to parrot one another, and they tend to filter out what is not in keeping with the liberal attachments of the *Washington Post* and the *New York Times*. The fact that the *Post* and the *Times* are out of touch with the political attitudes of the majority of the American people was pathetically demonstrated in the 1984 presidential election—both endorsed Mondale, who suffered the biggest electoral defeat in American history.

It goes without saying, of course, that there are many qualities that make the

Times and the *Post* great newspapers and there are people at various levels who recognize the need for more balanced news reporting. And although we have seen that the institute has commanded respect and influence at both papers, they have not always been receptive to IPS's views. Because of this, the IPS entourage has tried to influence the media in other ways. It has created, funded, and in other ways supported a whole series of left-wing "transmission belts," to bring its ideas to mainstream media outlets nationwide. Some of these are wire services and radio broadcast syndicates, the subject of Chapter 9. Other efforts have been manifest in alternative journals and investigative research centers, the subject of Chapter 10.

CHAPTER 9

Transmission Belts to the Media
IPS over the Airwaves and Wire Services

Although IPS has aggressively pushed its views on the media, newspaper, radio, and television reporters have not always been receptive. To compensate, the institute entourage began separate news services and radio commentary syndicates—"alternative media"—to serve as transmission belts to the mainstream media. Although the institute does promote its views openly through its own "IPS Features" and "IPS Air Express"—the weekly op-ed, commentary and news services—which go to some two hundred newspapers and radio stations nationwide, its real success has come from the multiplier effect of the alternative services. Because they appear as a multiplicity of voices speaking for a particular policy or viewpoint, the alternative networks lend legitimacy to that view by creating the appearance of widespread support.

Pacific News Service: History and Organizational Structure

Pacific News Service (PNS) was established in 1970 as a nonprofit organization by the Bay Area Institute (BAI), the West Coast affiliate of IPS, under the direction of Franz Schurmann. At first, PNS had limited appeal because, like its predecessor, Liberation News Service (LNS), also founded with the help of IPS, its radicalism was strident. But PNS's fortunes began changing after Schurmann hired Alexandra Close, previously writer for the *Far East Economic Re-*

view, as managing editor in 1974. Close helped Schurmann to tone down PNS's rhetoric, and later she married him.

Although PNS was largely successful in erasing the signs of Marxist political counterculture from which it was born, the changes may have been only cosmetic. Schurmann states in the introduction to his book, *Logic of World Power:*

> Nothing has influenced my political thinking so much as years of immersion in the writings of the Chinese Communists, both formal, like the canonical works of Mao Tse-tung, and the hundreds of mundane pieces in the daily newspapers. Their notions of class struggle, of ideology, and of contradictions have fed into my thinking. Unlike much Western political thinking that is becoming increasingly techno-bureaucratic, that of the Chinese remains absolutely democratic—people shape politics, not the other way around.[1]

Conceding that there may be some practical problems, Schurmann says, "Yet I find myself again and again drawn to the Marxian vision which still captures the minds of millions of people."[2] He expands on the possibilities of his convictions:

> But visions have ebbs and flows, and Marx's vision always returns to life when a social system, particularly in an advanced capitalist country, begins to crack. The secret of Marxism's resilience is what Marx thought it was: a vision or theory grounded on human reason and not divine revelation that teaches there is moral purpose and inevitability to history.[3]

Notwithstanding the political predilections of its guiding light, PNS has been "circulating material with a left-liberal slant to daily newspapers."[4] David Armstrong describes the PNS success story in *A Trumpet to Arms:*

> Pacific News Service, by way of contrast [with LNS], managed to do what no other alternative news service has done: have its material accepted for publication by daily newspapers, including the *Los Angeles Times* and the *Boston Globe.* Branching out from its base of alternative periodicals, PNS more than doubled its number of subscribers (to 250) between 1977 and 1979.[5]

The managing editor of the *Boston Sunday Globe* pointed out that "when PNS was an alternative kind of thing that was heavily into Vietnam, there were some editors at the *Globe* who grew rather nervous about it as an objective, dispassionate service."[6] Mike Cooper, editor of the *Fairbault* (Minn.) *Daily News,* uses PNS material, but only on his op-ed pages. As he put it, "I see them as having a bias. It's not exactly a political bias; it's more in their choice of topics."[7] Harvey Myam, editor of the *North East Bay Independent and Gazette* in Berkeley, California, agrees: "PNS's bias shows in their selection of stories."[8]

Other editors find PNS's bias a plus. For instance, Ed Orloff, the assistant managing editor of the *San Francisco Examiner,* says, "Pacific News Service represents . . . a rare and useful alternative to the sop that floods American newsrooms . . . PNS gives us substantial material for the op-ed page and its pieces usually come with insight and background we can't get anywhere else."[9] Robert Maynard of the *Oakland Tribune* believes that "the value of PNS to American journalism lies in its willingness to explore subjects more conventional media rarely approach."[10]

But what are the subjects that PNS explores? PNS has broadened its appeal beyond foreign policy by focusing on seemingly nonpartisan domestic issues like crime, housing, youth, and immigration. Naturally, this enhanced its appeal to liberal mainstream newspapers.

Take environmental problems, a nonpartisan issue, for instance. In the ordinary way, one would assume that PNS would run a series of environmental stories for general interest. But a close reading suggests that PNS could be manipulating environmental issues much as IPS does—to convey a deep distrust of the American private enterprise system. For after PNS recounts story after story of corporate neglect of the environment, the reader subconsciously arrives at this conclusion. On foreign policy issues, PNS is cautious with its sympathies for America's adversaries, but unrelenting in its criticisms of U.S. allies, particularly their shortcomings on human rights. After all, human rights, like the environment, is a nonpartisan issue. But the net effect is to undermine those allies.

An interesting sidelight to PNS history emerged when the FBI asked PNS about its association with IPS back in the early 1970s. PNS/BAI spokesmen flatly denied that there had been any such thing. But Schurmann, the founder of BAI/PNS, wrote in the foreword to *Logic of World Power:*

> I owe much to periodic visits I made to the Institute for Policy Studies in Washington. . . . My debts, personal and intellectual, to Richard J. Barnet are particularly great. Stimulated and supported by IPS, I became a participant in setting up a comparable though much more modest institute in San Francisco, the Bay Area Institute.[11]

Moreover, the PNS promotional prospectus reveals a cast of familiar characters as correspondents—Richard Barnet, Michael Klare, John Dinges, James Ridgeway, T. D. Allman, and Richard Falk. It also lists two other PNS writers, Howard Kohn and David Weir, who are correspondent and executive director respectively for the Center for Investigative Reporting (CIR). And CIR is an organization financed by the Foundation for National Progress, which stated in its 1976 financial report that it was created "to carry out the charitable and educational activities of the Institute for Policy Studies."[12]

The PNS prospectus gives the impression of a structured organization of regular staff writers. In reality, PNS is run much like IPS—as a somewhat loose network of people who wear a number of different hats. The prospectus describes some of the PNS contributors as "academics, missionaries, [and] activists inside and outside the political mainstream."[13] But when PNS executive editor Close was asked who these correspondents were, she said it was hard to name them because they were always changing. "I'm not really interested in the credentials of writers. . . . I'm interested in areas that the information class is not interested in," she said. "I'm concerned with social fabric, human landscapes that are out on the margin."[14] Some of the PNS contributors might also be considered somewhat marginal in their political views.

For instance, one of PNS's specialists on Middle East politics is Mansour Farhang, formerly Bani-Sadr's senior foreign policy adviser under Ayatollah Khomeini. Julia Preston, a former consultant for the pro-Castro North American Congress on Latin America (NACLA), who also writes for the *Boston Globe*, specializes on emigration from the Latin and Caribbean countries. Gary MacEoin, a leader of the sanctuary movement (see Chapter 18), covers third-world development and religion for PNS. Nicole Szulc, another former consultant for NACLA and assistant to CIA defector Philip Agee, has served as a PNS stringer in Portugal and Spain. Abdul Rahman Babu, an African socialist who spent six years in a Tanzanian prison, is a PNS specialist on developing countries.

PNS has also brought on board (or at least its prospectus says so) one or two more credible types, like Robert B. Hawkins, a member of President Reagan's Advisory Commission on Intergovernmental Affairs, apparently to improve its image and marketability. PNS got its biggest break in 1981 when it was spotted by Jim Cooney of the *Des Moines Register and Tribune Syndicate* who was looking for a substitute to fill the vacancy left by the *Christian Science Monitor*. PNS seemed to meet that need—perhaps in part because PNS's nonprofit status meant lower costs—and the marketing-distribution marriage was consummated in 1982.

With the syndicate's computerized distribution service, PNS stories would now get nationwide distribution. Wire-service technology not only helped regularize PNS stories, but also defrayed the expense of mass mailings twice a week. By 1983 PNS was carried by some two hundred fifty newspapers in virtually every geographic region of the United States. Among them are such major dailies as the *Washington Post, Baltimore Sun, Philadelphia Inquirer, Long Island Newsday, Boston Globe, Cleveland Plain Dealer, Chicago Sun-Times, Chicago Tribune, Gary Post-Tribune, St. Louis Globe Democrat, Des Moines Register, Milwaukee Journal, Minneapolis Tribune, Seattle Post-Intelligencer, Sacramento Bee, Daily Californian, San Francisco Examiner, San Francisco Chronicle, Oakland Tribune, San Jose Mercury, Fresno Bee, Los Angeles Times, Long Beach Press-Telegram, Memphis Commercial Appeal, Miami Herald,* and *Atlanta Journal.*

Pacific News Service Covers Korean Airlines Flight 007 and Grenadan Rescue Mission

A few days after the U.S. Marines landed on Grenada on October 25, 1983, IPS fellow and PNS correspondent Mike Klare landed a PNS story in papers across the country. In the *Plain Dealer*, Ohio's largest newspaper, Klare's article was not an op-ed feature, but a front-page splash. Titled "Is World War III Upon Us?" Klare's story concluded by admonishing:

> Finally, and most importantly, we must resist the temptation to intervene whenever Western interests appear threatened by turmoil abroad. We may suffer some losses in the process, but no such setbacks can compare to the steady erosion of our strength and prosperity in a continuing series of local wars.[15]

Writing about the tragedy of Korean Airlines flight 007 in a PNS syndicated article of September 9, 1983, Klare suggested that Soviet behavior was justified:[16]

> Clearly, the Soviet bases could be considered inviting targets for a U.S. attack in response to a superpower clash elsewhere. Such an attack would be in line with the Reagan Administration's concept of "horizontal escalation.". . .
> Although specific moves are shrouded in secrecy, Soviet strategists can have few doubts about U.S. capabilities and intentions. . . . But a careful look at the little-noticed buildup on both sides in this area might allow us to begin to understand the paranoia behind the violent Soviet response to a flight over their facilities.[17]

Although the burden of guilt rested squarely on the Soviets' overreaction and the Koreans' navigational errors, Klare didn't hesitate to turn the incident around to suggest that the U.S. share the blame.

Stating that "PNS has a deliberate global perspective," the PNS prospectus also credits its organization with including "activists" on the roster of its contributors.[18] Does this mean that PNS will engage in "creating news" and "advocacy reporting"? PNS executive editor Close describes her vision of PNS:

> PNS believes that a major change is taking place in the world: People, independent of governments, are acting on their own to secure their survival, to create hope for themselves and their children. Their cumulative decisions are reshaping the world as we all know it—through vast global migrations, religious revolutions, burgeoning alternative economies. To cover these changes, PNS starts at the ground level—the chicken's-eye view—and moves from the bottom up rather than the top down.[19]

When PNS correspondent Paul Geopfert reported from Nicaragua, his chicken's-eye view missed some seven thousand Cubans and hundreds of East bloc officials, and the ever-present Committees for the Defense of the Revolution, a nationwide surveillance system patterned on the Cuban model to monitor and discourage all political opposition. Geopfert did say, however, that "it's exactly that Army which will guarantee the Revolution will not be turned back as it was in Chile."[20]

PNS coverage of the landing on Grenada demonstrates its hypocrisy in claiming to speak from "the people's perspective." Over 90 percent of the Granadans and 70–80 percent of the Americans and virtually all of the American medical students polled supported the rescue mission.

In a PNS news release of November 2, 1983, James Ridgeway argued that "the threat to American medical students was barely credible, and accusations that the island was a secret base for Cuban terrorists were shot through with inconsistencies."[21]

PNS correspondent Nelson Valdes wrote that "the Cubans were defending the integrity as well as the honor of the Grenadan people, even though the Cuban regime had been highly critical of the murders committed October 18 by the government of Hudson Austin."[22] Further, said Valdes, "Cuban defiance of the greatest power in the world may very well capture the imagination of the Third World countries, as the death of Che Guevara did in the 1960s."[23] And he assured us that "Cuban behavior in the Third World is not a response to Soviet designs. The Cuban Revolution has a foreign policy of its own."[24]

Percy Hintzen, another PNS correspondent, believes that "if U.S. aid follows its usual pattern, it might do more harm than good. . . . This is precisely why some governments in the region have been attracted to the 'Cuban package'—medical personnel, education assistance and skilled help on public works projects."[25] Hintzen concludes:

> The United States might wisely consider the possibility that *Havana has a positive role to play in the region, based on its own experience and past relations with other Caribbean states.* As it stands, however, when the euphoria of a quick and easy military victory wears off, the United States may well find itself bogged down in yet another unsuccessful attempt to place its own stamp on countries it neither knows nor understands.[26] [Emphasis added.]

IPS and Television

IPS gets its voice heard on major radio and television news broadcasts. According to an IPS annual report, "Institute Fellows have appeared on the 'Today Show,' 'MacNeil-Lehrer Report,' 'Good Morning America,' 'Bill Moyers Presents,' and a range of national television documentaries. Their commentaries are heard regularly over National Public Radio and through local radio interviews and broadcasts."[27] And as IPS fellows have become celebrities on TV, so a number of TV personalities have worked with IPS.

Washington School courses on "Investigative Reporting" have been taught by such TV news people as Kathy McCampbell, executive producer of newscasts for NBC-TV Washington; her coworker, Jack Cloherty, an investigative reporter for the Washington, D.C., affiliate of NBC (WRC-TV); Jim Polk of the NBC-Washington news bureau; Brian Ross of NBC–New York news; and Howard Rosenberg, a consultant to CBS evening news. Still others affiliated with IPS's West Coast spinoff, the Center for Investigative Reporting, have been hired by CBS's "60 Minutes" and ABC's "20/20" (discussed in the following chapter). And the institute's in-house investigative team, the Government Accountability Project, is a major source for network TV on all manner of sensational "public-interest" stories dealing with nuclear power and toxic waste.

Rose Goldsen, professor of sociology at Cornell University, teaches courses at the Washington School on how television imagery shapes social reality. The focus of these classes is not merely "observing and decoding the medium's distinctive languages, such as imagery, metaphor, drama, music, sound, color, and camera work," as suggested in the IPS catalog.[28] Goldsen told one class that "the power of television can immediately mobilize action," and many of her class discussions centered around how TV can be used to effect political and social change.[29]

Similarly, Patrick Esmond-White, an IPS Ph.D. student, is concerned with ways in which television can have a political impact via satellite, cable, and the Public Broadcasting System.

At two IPS seminars in January 1984 Esmond-White explained how the "ascertainment process" could be used to affect TV programming. Esmond-White told the audience that "pressure on both public and private stations could be brought to bear . . . if the proper grassroots networks were established."[30] Stations would be bound to respond to people petitioning for more progressive programming simply because, as Esmond-White points out, "almost no one else is doing anything."

Arlen Slobodow, the director of the Public Interest Video Network, joined Esmond-White's presentation at IPS. "What we do is come up with strategies to get progressive programs on the air," Slobodow commented, "even in the face of a commercial television system and a public broadcasting system that is not favorable to labor and progressive organizations."[31] Toward this end, Slobodow recommended an end run around the PBS station in Washington, which normally determines national programming:

> What we've been able to do is find ways to bypass the gatekeepers in Washington and use the public television satellite system to feed programs to the 280 affiliate stations out there and let the stations themselves, the station managers, make the decisions. So by strategically looking at opportunities in broadcasting where we have one gatekeeper blocking the entire system we look at ways to avoid that one gatekeeper and distribute the program to a wide variety of stations out there.[32]

Slobodow also reminisced fondly about his experience in organizing an alternative media network at the June 12, 1982, "peace" demonstration in New York City, reportedly the largest ever held. "In New York City we covered the march for disarmament where a million people were gathered." And, he continued, "through a low or nonexistent budget and a lot of independent video producers and people who worked in a variety of capacities, we were able to get the speech out of Central Park, bounce it around on microwaves through New York City, and through the Gulf and Western Union Building, and then to get it up to the PBS satellite."[33]

Said Slobodow, "In terms of news and how news is defined and in terms of the number of players involved and what their definition of the news is, the exciting thing about these new technologies . . . is that we can expand the number of players that are giving their definition as to what is news and what is news value." Enthusiastic about the future, he also pointed out that "the capacity for it to change even further is really great [because] there have been a number of times where we were in a position of telling a mass audience what is news on a particular issue . . . and the potential for doing that on a regular basis and getting new viewpoints on the air is one that's tremendously exciting."[34]

Your Tax Dollars at Work: IPS and National Public Radio

The IPS annual report points out that institute fellows' commentaries "are heard regularly over National Public Radio [NPR] and through local radio interviews and broadcasts."[35] NPR has a regular nationwide audience of about nine million.

NPR's liberal-left bias in its news reporting has been derived in part from the politics of Frank Mankiewicz, NPR president until he left in April 1983. Mankiewicz has been a fairly regular Washington School faculty member and consultant for IPS.

According to FBI records, Mankiewicz was scheduled to meet with Teofilo Acosta, a top-ranking Cuban DGI officer, Orlando Letelier and Kirby Jones at his home in Washington on June 7, 1975.[36] In 1974 and 1975 Mankiewicz traveled to Cuba three times with IPS fellow Saul Landau and Kirby Jones to produce a documentary on Fidel Castro. Like Landau, Mankiewicz found Castro captivating.[37] In the preface of his book, *With Fidel*, coauthored with Jones, Mankiewicz writes:

Comparing notes later, it seemed clear we had been with one of the most charming and entertaining men either of us had ever met. Whether one agrees with him or not, Castro is personally overpowering. U.S. political writers would call it a simple case of charisma, but it is more than that. Political leaders often can be and are charismatic in a public sense, but rather normal in more private moments. Such is not the case with Fidel Castro. He remains one of the few truly electric personalities in a world in which his peers seem dull and pedestrian.[38]

In April 1983 Mankiewicz resigned from NPR amidst charges of gross financial mismanagement—a $7.8 million shortfall, 26 percent of its annual operating budget. But NPR retains its ties with IPS through fellows like Richard Barnet, Ariel Dorfman, Roger Wilkins, Michael Klare, Peter Kornbluh, and Barbara Ehrenreich who offer commentaries or are quoted over NPR. Over the years a number of NPR reporters and employees have also participated in IPS activities.

Jim Angle, editor of "All Things Considered," chaired a workshop, "Public Opinion and the Media," at a Riverside Church Conference on Central America in October 1983. Angle said he didn't mix his politics with his professional work, but the main topics discussed in his workshop were "advocacy reporting" and how media activists could use events "like the human rights certification process of El Salvador" to influence public opinion.[39]

Michele Magar, an assistant producer at NPR, chaired the IPS Washington School's six-week class on foreign reporting in spring 1984—a class that brought in three reporters from the *Washington Post* and one from the *New York Times*. The IPS syllabus called for Magar to be joined by coworker Deborah Amos, a news producer at NPR, for the final session. The IPS agenda billed the class as one that would "examine the role of foreign journalism in our perceptions of the world, and in the formation of foreign policy."[40] Topics discussed included the "Impact of Foreign Reporting: Implications Here and Abroad," "Neutrality vs. Advocacy," "The Politics of Foreign Reporting," "Falling out of Favor with the U.S. Embassy: What Are the Costs?"[41]

On U.S. intervention in Grenada, NPR's polls found that the American public disapproved of our action by a margin of about three to two. This conflicted with *all* respected public opinion polls, which found no less than 65 percent of the public in favor.

After the release of the bipartisan Kissinger Commission Report on Central America in January 1984, NPR got on the bandwagon to discredit its findings. The commission specifically warned of the increasing Soviet and Cuban involvement in the Western Hemisphere, the escalating conflict in Nicaragua and El Salvador, and the general instability in Central America should the United States sit back and do nothing. The week of February 20, 1984—the same week the report was released and distributed to Congress—the "Morning Edition" news program promoted a new IPS publication, *Changing Course: Blueprint for Peace in Central America and the Caribbean*. On February 23 NPR aired a lengthy interview with Richard Barnet, who criticized the Kissinger Commission findings while promoting his institute's alternative study.

NPR sympathy for the Marxist guerrillas in El Salvador continued despite the enthusiasm for democracy demonstrated by the large voter turnouts in the 1982 and 1984 Salvadoran elections. NPR prefers to despair by focusing on "right-wing death squads." Two days after the Salvadoran election of March 1984, the news anchor for "Morning Edition," Bob Edwards, said that "it is likely that the elections will make little difference to the future of El Salvador."[42]

The numerous connections with IPS aside, NPR's failure to uphold rigorous standards of objectivity in news coverage and to comply with the FCC's guidelines on fairness and equal access is not in keeping with its responsibility to the American public, particularly since the American taxpayers foot 95 percent of NPR's budget, which is over $25 million annually.

SANE Radio

SANE, a group closely associated with IPS, has added another leftist voice to the airwaves. David Cortright, a former IPS fellow, is the executive director of SANE and Marcus Raskin is one of SANE's vice chairmen. "Consider the Alternatives," the syndicated radio commentary of the SANE Education Fund, was launched at the end of the Vietnam War and had a very limited audience. But the program has since developed in sophistication and is carried by a hundred fifty radio stations nationwide, with some 1.5 million listeners.[43]

SANE Radio consistently criticizes U.S. foreign policy and advocates unilateral steps toward disarmament, withdrawal from any military commitments in the world, and mandatory unilateral conversion of military industries to peaceful concerns. SANE Radio frequently airs the commentaries of IPS fellows. One such program, besides carrying Michael Klare's warning about the inevitability of nuclear war if the U.S. continued to maintain its overseas defense commitments, aired the propaganda of the Sandinista foreign minister, Miguel D'Escoto. D'Escoto praised his native revolutionary regime, then assailed the United States, whose democracy he called "a farce that pleases so much certain people in Washington but makes absolutely no difference to the people because they continue to play musical chairs allowing an elite of seven percent to give it a shellac of respectability . . . not too much different from that hideous situation in South Africa."[44]

That SANE Radio promotes such views may be attributed in part to the fact that Joseph Miller, chairman of SANE Education Fund, which provides SANE Radio's budget, is a member of the Soviet front World Peace Council.

In the Public Interest

Another radio commentary service, similar to SANE, only much larger, is In the Public Interest (IPI), which also echoes the IPS line. Philip M. Stern became a regular IPI commentator after Peter Weiss took over his position as chairman of the board at IPS in 1973. Weiss also serves on the Executive Committee of the Board of Trustees of the Fund for Peace, which sponsors IPI. And the Fund for Peace's chairman of the board, J. Sinclair Armstrong, has also served as chairman of the board for the Samuel Rubin Foundation with Peter and Cora Weiss serving as vice president and president respectively.[45] Other IPS people, such as Richard Barnet and Robert Borosage, have also served on IPI's advisory board.

Billing itself as "the Voice of the Fund for Peace since 1973," IPI reaches nine million listeners in all fifty states through some four hundred twenty-five participating radio stations. According to the Fund for Peace prospectus, IPI has three main focuses; (1) the violation of human rights by governments throughout the world; (2) the disparity in economic and social welfare between industrialized and developing nations; and (3) the threat of nuclear war and the needless expansion of nuclear and conventional weapons.

For IPI, human rights are never an issue in "people's democracies" or "liberated" countries like Vietnam, Cuba, and Nicaragua. But in countries like El Salvador, Guatemala, Chile, and South Korea, human rights are constantly violated and provide the criteria with which to discredit their governments in the United States.

In spring 1983, Rep. Tom Harkin (D–Iowa), addressing the Salvadoran human rights issue on IPI, said "it was pure baloney" that "the government of El Salvador is making remarkable progress toward greater respect for the basic human rights of its own citizens."[46]

IPS trustee and IPI commentator Philip Stern considers U.S. policies misguided because of their flawed first principles. He argues that if we "wrap" Nicaragua, Guatemala, and El Salvador in the "terms of an East-West struggle . . . as we did with Cuba, our policymakers will surely succeed, once again, in forcing them into the Russian camp."[47] In another commentary, addressing U.S. policy toward Nicaragua, Stern said, "There, as in Cuba twenty-three years ago, the winds of change and reform are blowing. There, as in Cuba, fledgling regimes are struggling to carve out an existence for their country."[48] Although he concedes that the Sandinistas get military backing from the Soviet Union and in turn give aid to the Marxist FMLN insurgents in El Salvador, Stern leads his listeners to believe that the proliferation of communist regimes has to do less with Soviet policies than with those of the United States.[49]

But even though IPI commentaries ridicule the "East-West linkage paradigm" in Central America—notwithstanding heavy Cuban and East bloc involvement in Nicaragua and the solidarity between revolutionaries in Cuba, Nicaragua, and El Salvador—linkage is relevant when it comes to U.S. relations with its allies. For instance, IPI commentator Corinna Gardner broadcast that

> Korea is one of the Cold War's hottest trouble spots, and many analysts say that American military policy there is aggravating the tension. . . .

In spite of the military dictatorship in power in South Korea, opposition to American nuclear weapons there is growing. The Korean National Council of Churches has issued a declaration opposing the weapons, and many Korean dissidents link the American military in Korea with the continuation of their repressive government.[50]

IPI has increasingly focused its programming on what it says are the "threat of nuclear war and the needless expansion of nuclear and conventional weapons."[51] Commentator Stern advocates unilateral actions by the United States, for linking our policy to that of the Soviets "puts our policy in a straitjacket."[52] In stating that "some military experts have suggested, for example, that we unilaterally halt the testing of new weapons," Stern argues that "as long as we insist on limiting our actions to what the Russians will agree to," the United States "deprives [itself] of that sensible policy."[53]

In yet another commentary, "Making the World Safe for Democracy—and Others," Stern argues that "immediate 50 percent reduction of all U.S. nuclear weapons . . . is the one course offering hope, however faint, however mixed with danger."[54] Stern justifies his optimism by ridiculing Eugene Rostow, chief negotiator of the State Department's Arms Control and Disarmament Agency, while assuring his audience that "Russia's behavior toward Poland, Afghanistan, and Cuba has nothing to do with disarmament."[55]

For Anne Cahn—another IPI commentator and also the director of the Committee for National Security, an IPS spinoff founded by Richard Barnet and Paul Warnke—the onus is on the United States, not the Soviet Union, to apologize for the yellow-rain uproar. She said:

> For the American government to assert, as it repeatedly has done, that the Soviet Union is using chemical and toxic weapons on defenseless people is a serious charge and the fact that the charge has been made repeatedly does not necessarily make it true. If yellow rain is indeed bee feces, our government will have a lot of explaining to do. And I, for one, think a straightforward "Oops, we goofed," and apology would be in order.[56]

Another IPI staff member, Edward P. Morgan, blames world conflict on the United States. He asserts, for instance, that "it must be remembered that every single major move to make the nuclear arsenal more deadly came not from the Soviet Union but the United States."[57]

Philip Stern insists that the "control of nuclear weapons is too serious a matter to be left any longer to governments. . . . They are not going to get it for us . . . in fact they are the obstacle."[58]

Similarly, in the commentary "How Much Is Security Worth?" Gene La-Roque, a retired admiral and a regular IPI commentator, argues that "at the highest price in peacetime history, the U.S. government cannot protect the

American people from nuclear war; it cannot guarantee victory in conflicts in foreign countries; and it cannot assure prosperity at home."[59] LaRoque offers an interesting alternative: "I firmly believe that the American people have the power to prevent nuclear war by joining with Musicians Against Nuclear War and thousands of other groups of concerned citizens across the country, to endorse the proposal for a nuclear weapons freeze."[60]

IPI delivers its service free to every subscribing station, some four hundred twenty-five, because its costs are completely underwritten by the Fund for Peace and other contributors. Furthermore, there is a multiplier effect in the print media, for as IPI says, its "transcripts of selected broadcasts are sent monthly to approximately six hundred newspapers and several thousand individuals."[61] The Fund for Peace promotional brochure states: " 'In the Public Interest' has secured free newspaper space and broadcast time worth several million dollars commercially. It is alone in using free public-service air time daily and effectively in all fifty states."[62]

The marketing strategy of IPI is similar to that of Pacific News Service, which rides on the coattails of well-established media outlets. Since mid-1982 IPI has been part of a marketing program with WMCA of New York City, to expand distribution to six hundred key stations, primarily located in urban centers. Robert Maslow, IPI's producer and director, hoped that after the peace mobilization of June 1982 and the growing support for the nuclear freeze, IPI could double its listenership in a short period of time. He said, "It is vital to launch a more concerted and intense marketing effort as the current play list is insufficient compared with the need for arms-control discussion in this time of history."[63]

Inter Press Service, Interlink Press Service, and the New International Information Order

Interlink Press Service, exclusive U.S. distributor of Inter Press Service, the world's sixth largest wire service, was founded in 1981 by Brennon Jones, a former anti–Vietnam War activist with the American Friends Service Committee (AFSC) and the National Council of Churches (NCC). Jones was captivated by Inter Press founder Roberto Savio's concept of creating an alternative to networks like UPI, AP, and Reuters.

Savio's antipathy toward Western capitalism has emerged in some interesting political views. For instance, in a 1980 interview he expressed great optimism for Southeast Asia now that the United States had withdrawn and "liberate[d] the people from all the horrors of capitalism."[64] On Castro's expulsion of the unwanted from Cuba in the Mariel boatlift, Savio said, "I think to send out 200,000 people is a very brilliant solution to the keeping inside of 100,000 opponents."[65] Savio also feels that when conditions require it, "radicalism and extremism become a very valuable way of political commitment for a people who feel politically motivated."[66]

Orlando Letelier, onetime director of the Transnational Institute, was a personal friend of Roberto Savio. Philip Agee was connected with Inter Press through his friend and anti-CIA collaborator Phil Kelly, who served as Inter Press's London bureau chief. Inter Press, like IPS/TNI, is involved in a global effort to create a New International Information Order (NIIO), a sister project to the New International Economic Order (NIEO).

The major step forward for NIIO was undertaken in the late 1970s by the Mexico City–based Latin American Institute for Transnational Studies (ILET—Instituto Latino-America Estudios Transnacionales), an affiliate of the Transnational Institute, which undertook "a three-year project to formulate principles for a New International Information Order." One of ILET's conferences on NIIO, held in September 1977 in the Netherlands, was partially underwritten by the Dutch Ministry of Development Aid. The secretary of the Dutch Ministry of Development Aid is Jan Pronk, who has the honor of being an "Associate Fellow of the Transnational Institute." ILET is directed by Juan Somovia and its board of advisers includes Clodomiro Almeyda. Both Somovia and Almeyda worked in solidarity with the late Orlando Letelier in his efforts to restore Chile to the socialist camp.[67] Following Allende's fall, Almeyda chose to reside in East Germany.

Much like the NIEO, the NIIO encapsulates a series of deliberately ambiguous and vague objectives. For instance, ILET's literature on NIIO refers to the need for "a new scale of values of news reporting."[68] Among topics discussed at the NIIO symposium two were particularly striking: (1) the need for a new juridical charter governing the operation of the media and individual journalists in the third world; and (2) the need for requisite changes in the content and role of the principle of a "free flow of information."[69]

Does the NIIO mean to alienate further and isolate the third world from the West by restricting the Western media? The concluding paragraph of ILET's May 1976 NIIO conference declaration stated: "The principle of free flow of information is being dispensed with, because its application has led to a system of information that maintains the structure of the exercise of power which transgresses borders."[70]

Jim Lobe, Inter Press Washington bureau chief, addressed the question of "a new scale of values for news reporting" at an IPS Washington School class he taught in spring 1984. "It's the use of East-West terms, the politically and culturally loaded terms, like Moslem fundamentalist, fanatic, terrorist . . . those kinds of words we try to stay away from," said Lobe. "We try to make our writing as neutral as we can."[71] Lobe pointed to AP coverage of Nicaragua as exemplifying the value-laden problems of most Western news coverage of the third world:

There's a story about Nicaragua that you're getting from AP and they talk about words like communist, Marxist, radical Sandinista state, and so on. Not only is it distorting and does it give them the sense that Nicaragua is no good, but it also shows no concern for them at all . . . it doesn't treat the Nicaraguans as people. . . . The term Soviet-backed Sandinista government is very distorting at this time, but you see it all the time in the U.S. press.[72]

Summing up the NIIO's "new scale of values for news reporting," Lobe said, "There is some editorial input in our writing. We tend to write more sympathetically of Third World demands or the Third World plight. . . . We don't feel the same compulsion to say you have to balance your stories. . . ."[73]

Savio has sought a key role in the NIIO process. Lobe is frank to say that the position of his boss Savio is that "everything that Inter Press has done is the New International Information Order."[74] Savio has created networks of third-world press agencies which are anti-U.S. and generally critical of the Western world, such as ASIN (Accion de Sistemas Informativos Nacionales) in Latin America and FANA in the Arab world. But he fails to differentiate between news and state-controlled political propaganda. For instance, Inter Press puts JANA of Libya, AIM of Mozambique, INA of Iraq, WAFA of the Palestinians, ANN of Nicaragua, and Prensa Latina of Cuba on an equal footing with privately owned news agencies such as CRI of Costa Rica.

When the United States undertook the Grenada rescue mission, the first stories that came over the Inter Press wire were from Havana. Subsequent stories speak for themselves about the kind of news service Inter Press provides.

Inter Press correspondent Claude Robinson did his best to call into doubt the joint actions in Grenada of the United States and the Organization of Eastern Caribbean States (OECS). Datelined New York, October 28, 1983, Robinson wrote:

[T]he treaty which the United States and its Caribbean allies have been relying on to support the claims of legality did not, in fact, meet the requirements of the U.N. Charter and hence, its validity has been cast into serious doubt.
. . . At a time when the U.S. Congress has begun to raise questions about the way in which President Reagan was using the U.S. War Powers act in the Grenada case, the sponsors of the invasion may be stepping on some slippery legal ground.[75]

Jim Lobe, for his part, ridiculed the legitimacy of the U.S.–OECS action by pointing out that "the invasion was justified at the time through an obscure treaty among eastern Caribbean states and an alleged threat posed by the situation on the island to some 1,000 U.S. citizens."[76] Lobe also charged, erroneously, that President Reagan's assertion that "Grenada was a Soviet-Cuban colony being readied as a major military bastion" was in no way sustained by Grenadan documents.[77]

In fact, all dispatches from Inter Press cast doubt on U.S. statements concerning the geopolitical role of Grenada. Another dispatch, for instance, said, "To the Grenadan People's Revolutionary Government (PRG) the new airport being built at Pointe Salines with Cuban assistance represented a potential economic salvation"—rather than "a potential Cuban base," as the Reagan administration asserted.[78]

In 1982 Inter Press succeeded in placing an article in the *New York Times* by one of its correspondents who used a pseudonym because he "feared being denied readmission to El Salvador for Interlink" (the U.S. branch of Inter Press). The article, based on an interview with Cayetano Carpio, Marxist leader of the Salvadoran FMLN guerrillas, was thinly veiled propaganda:

> One of the biggest dangers of the elections proposed by President Jose Napoleon Duarte and supported by the Reagan Administration is that they will serve as a smokescreen for a stepped-up offensive and for asking for increased logistical support from the Pentagon. . . .
> But weapons are not the only factor in this conflict . . . you can't make such calculations in a popular war that has been going on for over 10 years, pitting the army against the people. . . .[79]

That the guerrillas have never been able to muster support of more than ten thousand from a population of 4.5 million, and that over 80 percent of the population went to the polls, are facts that carried little weight with Inter Press as Carpio touted the guerrillas as representing the "people" in a "popular war."

Inter Press Service Expands Worldwide and Opens Its American Affiliate, Interlink Press Service

As revolutionary fervor has swept through much of the third world in the last two decades, so has Inter Press Service. Originally set up in 1964 as an "information bridge" between Latin America and Europe, Inter Press "developed an extensive network of bureaus and correspondents in 60 countries, primarily in the Third World."[80] According to its literature, it has over a hundred correspondents and "links with some 30 Third World or non-aligned national news agencies."[81] But all has not always gone well for Inter Press, for as Jim Lobe acknowledged to an IPS class on the New International Information Order, Inter Press correspondents have occasionally been deported from countries for their political activism.

Among its four hundred fifty subscribers worldwide, Inter Press feeds major European outlets, including the *Financial Times* and the *Guardian* of Great Britain, *Le Monde Diplomatique* of France, *Neue Zuricher* of Switzerland, *Der Spiegel* and *Die Welt* of West Germany, and *El Pais* of Spain. In North America

Inter Press is carried by *Uno Mas Uno* of Mexico, and the *Globe and Mail* of Canada. And Inter Press has been marketed to the American media since 1981 through its subsidiary Interlink Press Service.

Interlink Press Service is located at 777 U.N. Plaza in New York City, a few floors down from the Rubin Foundation, which funds it.[82] By 1984, under the leadership of Brennon Jones, Interlink had contracts servicing such prestigious media outlets as the *New York Times,* the *Baltimore Sun,* the *Wall Street Journal*'s Los Angeles bureau, the *Atlanta Journal and Constitution,* the *San Francisco Examiner,* the *Christian Science Monitor,* the *Long Island Newsday,* CBS News, National Public Radio, Cable Network News, and Metromedia's Channel 5 in New York City. Jones has also been negotiating with Associated Press a contract that would give it potential access to some five hundred major media outlets by way of AP's Data Feature Wire.

Under a board of directors that includes Peter Weiss of IPS, Richard Falk of Princeton, Sen. Tom Harkin, Herbert Schiller of the University of California and ILET's academic committee, Steve Hayes of the American Field Service, and Dwain Epps of the World Council of Churches, Interlink has developed far beyond merely providing an outlet for Inter Press in the United States. It also services university libraries, businesses, international financial institutions, and foundations such as the World Bank, the Ford Foundation, and the Rockefeller Foundation.

Interlink is making a concerted effort to expand, exploring ways to add material from such publications as the *Nation, Mother Jones,* and the *Progressive.* Looking to the future, Jones is confident that Interlink's market will continue to grow, serving more and more nonprofit organizations, universities, foundations, and financial and business corporations. He also hopes to build Interlink's news staff and operate regional bureaus across the United States. The alternative transmission belts are already beginning to be spliced, with Pacific News Service subscribing to Interlink.[83] (See Appendix 4 for organizational chart of IPS and the media.)

Conclusion

It is, of course, impossible to measure how much the alternative media's airwaves and wire services associated with IPS influence the mainstream media in the United States. Although many of the major media now subscribe to their news and information services, they may use their material only sporadically. But to the degree that the media have allowed the Left to set the agenda of news and commentary, then public opinion, debate, and the legislative process have undoubtedly been affected.

On domestic issues, the alternative media suggest that public-sector institutions and socialist solutions are good, and their private counterparts suspect, if not altogether evil. On foreign policy, they denounce the United States for resisting "inevitable" revolutions in the third world, for which our country is to blame. Third-world use of force is generally condoned, American military action invariably condemned. "Liberation" movements and communist countries are never judged by human rights criteria, but noncommunist third-world countries are berated for every real and imagined violation.

On the question of East-West relations, the arms race, and so on, the alternative media censure the United States—which, they say, is not worth fighting for—and often exonerate the Soviet Union.

The establishment of these alternative transmission belts has helped IPS and the Left infuse liberalism with radicalism and drive the debate on public policy further leftward. Those who argue that this is balanced by right-wing influence would be hard pressed to find a Pacific News Service or Interlink on the Right.

IPS associate Patrick Esmond-White asserts that "the alternative media channels prime the pump so that the major media have to respond and do more." Both Sandy Close of Pacific News Service and Brennon Jones of Interlink candidly admit that they provide a "tip service" to the media.[84] This means that items carried by them can trigger the mainstream media to pursue stories that they would otherwise not carry. In some cases this may be desirable; but in others, particularly those pertaining to national security, it may not be. Most important, it is highly questionable whether the mainstream news media are well served by the alternative media services, which, as their staff members readily admit, are guided by an agenda of advocacy rather than objectivity.

The alternative media industry associated with IPS has had such a significant effect on the mainstream media that the nonpartisan Media Institute in Washington, D.C., described IPS's media operations as a "conglomerate of influence." To understand the full picture of this, the next chapter focuses on the alternative print media associated with IPS and their investigative-reporting support groups.

CHAPTER 10

Bridging the Credibility Gap
From the Underground Press to Alternative Media

IPS and the Underground Media

In the early 1970s IPS directors Marc Raskin and Richard Barnet realized that revolutionary change was not coming to the United States despite the division over Vietnam. There had to be a change in strategy. Hobnobbing with strident protesters and revolutionaries might become a liability if IPS were to maintain credibility with the establishment. So, too, they recognized that they needed to distance themselves from the "underground" press, which clothed its calls for anarchy and revolution in the rhetoric of Marxism.

The underground press flourished in the 1960s because of the Vietnam War and the general rebelliousness of the times. Not only did it celebrate the counterculture—the destruction of government, family, business, schools—but it had its own political replacement. Laurence Leamer, a *Newsweek* writer who traveled around the United States visiting and interviewing staff members of underground papers to write his book, *Paper Revolutionaries,* found that when

> they looked for new tools to end racism in America and bring the GIs home from Vietnam, they were drawn inexorably not toward a revitalized cultural radicalism but to Marxism and political revolution. These ideas could not help but affect the underground press, and by 1971 there were many papers that thought of themselves as propaganda weapons in the struggle for worldwide Marxist revolution.[1]

As noted previously, IPS helped to found the Liberation News Service in 1967

144

(named after the Vietcong National Liberation Front) and Dispatch News Service in 1969. Institute fellows were also involved with the local underground press in Washington—the *Free Press* and *Quicksilver Times*—as well as with major national underground organs such as *Ramparts,* on whose editorial board Raskin served during the sixties.[2]

But by 1972–73, the underground press was suffering. The country was tired of the Vietnam War and sated with the unbridled rhetoric of revolution and violence. Furthermore, many of the underground papers found themselves so saddled with red ink that they were faced with either closing down or adapting their style to attract advertising. By 1973 the *Berkeley Tribe,* the *Chicago Seed,* the *San Francisco Good Times,* New York City's *Rat,* Boston's *Old Mole,* Milwaukee's *Kaleidoscope,* and even *Ramparts*—the national standard-bearer for the New Left—were disbanded or in a state of bankruptcy.[3]

The Alternative Media: Facelifting the Underground

About this time, June 1973, members of the Underground Press Syndicate met in Boulder, Colorado, to work out their collective problems. From it evolved a consensus, which was voiced by Tom Forcade, head of the Underground Press Syndicate. He suggested the underground press assume a new identity, namely, "alternative press." Setting the standard, he announced that henceforth the Underground Press Syndicate would be known as the Alternative Press Syndicate.[4] He later explained: " 'Underground' is a sloppy word and a lot of us are sorry we got stuck with it. 'Underground' is meaningless, ambiguous, irrelevant, wildly imprecise, undefinitive, derivative."[5]

Interestingly, the metamorphosis harmonized with IPS leaders' own shift to greater respectability, manifested in spinoff projects designed to influence the establishment. Only a few years earlier IPS fellows had founded the Pacific News Service and the *Working Papers for a New Society,* whose sophistication set them apart from the underground style. Even the name "alternative" was coined by one of the IPS spinoffs, the Conference on Alternative State and Local Policies—created in 1972 by Lee Webb, former national leader of SDS—which was to provide a mechanism for moving local legislation leftward piecemeal, a kind of creeping socialism.

The Alternative Camouflage to Enhance Credibility

From the beginning, the word *alternative* never really meant option. Rather, it meant the rejection of existing American institutions, "the system," in favor of a system based on radical socialist nostrums that have never had more than marginal appeal in the United States. The Left adopted the term as a rhetorical device to "sweeten" and camouflage its agenda. But the alternative media continued to be as activist as their underground predecessors, while recognizing the need for subtlety and persuasion.[6] "When people [in the United States] opt for socialism," said one figure associated with the alternative media, "it's not necessarily on the basis of having the book-understanding of what socialism means."[7]

Although the transition was basically cosmetic, the alternative media did acquire a greater marketability. In 1970 there were only two hundred underground papers and periodicals, but by 1980 there were some twelve hundred alternative publications, most supported at least in part by advertising revenue from the establishment.[8]

IPS and *Working Papers for a New Society*

Working Papers for a New Society was one of the first alternative journals, and was founded by the IPS spinoff Cambridge Institute in 1973. Unlike the underground media, *Working Papers* presented an upbeat version of the alternative message: reindustrialization, workplace democracy, employment, welfare and social security, reduced crime—popular subjects for a broad readership.

But while diagnosing many of the mainstream problems, *Working Papers* offered a radically different solution, a kind of "revolution-in-stages" approach advocated by IPS. *Working Papers* also suggested that the best way for the Left to seek power was on the grassroots level, another agenda specifically emphasized at the IPS Conference on Alternative State and Local Policies.

Working Papers established itself as a theoretical journal directed at intellectuals concerned with building socialism. It provided a unifying forum for the movement, whose members, factions, and ideas were often isolated and disconnected. To draw on the analysis of David Armstrong in his definitive account of the alternative media, *A Trumpet to Arms,* journals like *Working Papers* provide "heralds that announce new ideas; mirrors that permit activists to see the form their work takes in society; party lines on which members of alternative social movements exchange information and impressions; critics that provide perspectives on grassroots political efforts."[9] Although IPS fellows founded and frequently wrote for *Working Papers* (IPS was also its biggest advertiser), its pages were open to outsiders, thus enticing new people to the elite circles of the Left.

IPS and *Mother Jones*

Of the underground journals trying to make the transition to alternative, the best known was probably *Ramparts*. When Warren Hinkle took over *Ramparts* in 1965, he fully intended to compete with mass-circulation periodicals such as *Time* and *Life*.[10] Successful as it was, *Ramparts* still suffered from staff conflicts and financial difficulties. Three disaffected staff members—IPS associate fellow Paul Jacobs, Adam Hochschild, and Richard Parker—finally left *Ramparts* in 1975 to found a new magazine, *Mother Jones*. They were determined to gain legitimacy within the establishment while simultaneously carrying on *Ramparts'* tradition of muckraking and advocacy journalism to advance the cause of the Left.

Within a few years, *Mother Jones* was the star of the monthly alternative periodicals.[11] Few of its readers, however, would have been aware of its connection to IPS. The *Mother Jones* masthead states that it is published by the Foundation for National Progress. In the February–March 1977 issue, the magazine even raised the question, "Who's Behind *Mother Jones*?" In answer, the editor virtuously asserted that the magazine was not a mouthpiece of the establishment and received no support from "banks or corporations."[12] Nor did the editor mention any connection to IPS, although in 1975 *Mother Jones*'s publisher, the Foundation for National Progress, specifically described its purpose as one "to carry out on the West Coast the charitable and educational activities of the Institute for Policy Studies."[13]

IPS found a way to get around the financial problems that had caused the undoing of *Ramparts* and so many other underground papers. It simply took advantage of the tax-exempt status reserved for nonprofit, nonpartisan, educational organizations. The 501(c)(3) status allowed not only tax advantages but, more important for a mass-market journal, much lower mailing rates than those required of mainstream competitors. By establishing the tax-exempt Foundation for National Progress, which in turn published *Mother Jones*, IPS had persons join the foundation and receive the periodical as part of their membership. Through the foundation, IPS found a quasi-legal way to protect its tax exemption while engaging in political activity. For instance, through the Foundation for National Progress, IPS provided support for the Tom Hayden–Jane Fonda Campaign for Economic Democracy.

Mother Jones has led the alternative monthly journals in circulation, reaching approximately three hundred thousand by 1983.[14] Richard Reynolds, the director of promotion, attributes this success to both management and style. Richard Parker, a cofounder of *Mother Jones*, brought with him marketing, advertising, and direct-mail expertise from the *Santa Barbara News and Review*.[15] Robin Wolaner joined *Mother Jones* in 1980 after six years of marketing and promotion experience at *Penthouse* and *Viva*, and did so well that within two years she became the magazine's chief business officer and publisher.[16]

The second reason for *Mother Jones*'s success, according to Reynolds, was its toning down of the magazine's rhetoric and its focusing on issues of mass appeal, such as feminism, the environment, third worldism, the dangers of nuclear power and nuclear war, and ridicule of conservatism—issues that had appeal to liberal and special-interest constituencies as well as the Left.[17]

Mother Jones established its niche as the preeminent muckraking journal speaking to the burgeoning "protest culture" of the New Left. Like *Working Papers, Mother Jones* has helped to unify the diverse elements of the Left. As its executive editor, Deidre English, pointed out:

> Today, the Left—defined as a broad amalgam, including many feminists, environmentalists, racial and ethnic minorities, progressive labor leaders, community activists, antiwar and antinuclear crusaders and so forth—is reawakening, shaken by the nightmare of the Reagan regime. The rebellious and utopian spirit of the '60s will be a powerful ingredient in the political admixture of the '80s—just watch.[18]

Commenting in a May 1982 editorial that "neoliberals are, today, desperately searching for answers, and it will often prove to be the Left only that has the imagination to provide them,"[19] Deidre English foresaw the Left's takeover of the Democratic party several years before it became apparent in its 1984 platform.

Alternative media analyst David Armstrong saw *Mother Jones* as a "magazine that speaks primarily to readers who may be curious but not committed, people just edging into activism and not yet ready to heed the bugle call to the ramparts of the revolution."[20] While the magazine built much of its reputation on muckraking exposés of alleged corporate crime, exploitation, and government incompetence, these were apparently not the primary concern of the editors, who appeared to revel in the motto of the magazine's heroine (Mother Jones was a socialist union organizer)—Raise Hell! Like *Working Papers, Mother Jones* has advocated, though more subtly, a creeping socialism.

IPS and *In These Times*

In 1976, encouraged by IPS, James Weinstein and some colleagues from the New American Movement established *In These Times (ITT)* in Chicago to go beyond the "left counterculture" that he felt talked mostly to itself. He wanted to build "a sustained mass movement for socialism" in the spirit of the "old Socialist movement of 1900–19, the Communist movement inspired by the example of the Russian Revolution, and the 'New Left' " of the 1960s.[21] Over the years IPS fellows have been major contributors to *In These Times*. Little wonder, for according to its masthead *ITT* was published by IPS until June 1982, when the Mid-America Publishing Company took over (apparently IPS wanted to avoid problems with the IRS, which prohibits 501(c)(3) organizations from engaging in partisan political endorsements or propaganda).

Editor Weinstein said in 1972 that Americans need to "elect new types of representatives to city councils, state legislatures, and Congress—representatives from the ranks of labor, women, blacks, and others who will champion the people's interests and popular sovereignty against corporate power. . . ."[22] *In These Times*'s early promotional literature stated that it intended "to identify and clarify the struggles against corporate power now developing throughout American society, to bring to explicit consciousness their implicit anticapitalism, and to point out that a socialist democracy is the only means of attaining both equality and liberty under modern conditions."[23]

ITT, which bills itself as "an independent socialist newspaper," sees the "socialist movement" as the means for "forging unity against capitalism." The magazine's pages are larded with praise for third-world revolutionary figures, Marxist liberation movements, leftist political figures in the United States, and Eurocommunism abroad.

To a reader's letter questioning whom the paper had in mind when it spoke of the need for "moral authority" over the American socialist movement, the editors responded:

> When we wrote of moral authority we had in mind political leadership based on the public enunciation of principles and program. Like Thomas Jefferson, Fidel Castro, Rosa Luxemburg or maybe Abraham Lincoln, V. I. Lenin, Paul Robeson. More like that. Anyway, *In These Times* is not the American socialist movement, *only a small part of it.*[24] [Emphasis added.]

In These Times became the alternative media's principal draw for labor union leaders and progressive politicians. It has forged links with the left wing of the Democratic party and with union leaders from, among others, the United Auto Workers (UAW), the International Association of Machinists and Aerospace Workers, the American Federation of State, County and Municipal Employees (AFSCME), the Amalgamated Clothing and Textile Workers, and the National Union of Hospital and Health Care Employees. AFSCME promotes *In These Times* to its union members, and the UAW officially endorsed it, stating that it "joins other progressive Americans in congratulating *In These Times* on its fifth anniversary of providing an outstanding alternative voice for America,"[25] and more.

ITT has also served as a conduit of information for other alternative media outlets. For instance, in a letter of thanks, Francisco A. Chateaubriand, director of KAOS Radio News in Olympia, Washington, wrote:

> Our fledgling news department received a gift subscription to *In These Times* for Christmas, and since then it has become an invaluable source of information for us to draw from. Articles from *ITT* have often led us to a story . . . that otherwise would have remained undiscovered, and your news perspective is a successful example of the focus we are trying to achieve in our radiocasts.[26]

IPS and Other Alternative Journals

In addition to *Mother Jones*, *Working Papers*, and *In These Times*, IPS has been instrumental in founding other alternative journals. For instance, *MERIP Reports* (Middle East Research and Information Project), founded in 1971 by IPS's Transnational Institute fellow Joe Stork, operated out of IPS during its first few years. Although neither Joe Stork nor MERIP is today directly affiliated with IPS, IPS fellow Fred Halliday is an editor of *MERIP Reports*, and other fellows such as Michael Klare, Eqbal Ahmad, and Feroz Ahmed contribute to the magazine fairly frequently. *MERIP Reports* has consistently supported anti-Western parties and sided with the many liberation movements of the Middle East–Africa region.

Joe Stork and Fred Halliday have traveled to the Marxist People's Democratic Republic of (South) Yemen and reported favorably on conditions there.[27] As the first Western journalist allowed into Afghanistan after the December 1979 invasion, Fred Halliday wrote several articles in *MERIP*, the *Nation*, and the *New York Times* which rationalized the Soviet aggression.

George Hawatmeh, a leader of the Democratic Popular Front for the Liberation of Palestine (a terrorist organization), candidly admitted that *MERIP* supports the PLO. *MERIP* did suffer some embarrassment from its early enthusiasm for the Iranian revolution after Ayatollah Khomeini bared his reactionary character.

IPS made its facilities available to the founders of *CounterSpy*, a magazine dedicated to emasculating the U.S. intelligence agencies. Although Marcus Raskin withdrew his name from *CounterSpy*'s advisory board after the assassination of CIA officer Richard Welch in 1975, the institute has continued to host *CounterSpy* personnel.[28] And in 1983, IPS fellow John Cavanagh reestablished a formal link by joining *CounterSpy*'s board of advisers. *CounterSpy*'s editor, Konrad Ege, like Fred Halliday, is apparently viewed as a friendly reporter by the Soviet government, which allowed him into Afghanistan in spring 1983. Recounting his "eyewitness account of Afghanistan" at an IPS seminar on July 13, Ege, quoting a source in the puppet government, said that "the problem is with the United States. They are arming the counterrevolutionaries in Pakistan. They have created the problem. . . . For the Reagan administration, it is a cheap way to do damage to the Soviet Union. In Afghanistan, it is costing thousands of lives."[29] *CounterSpy* is now edited by IPS staffer Joy Hackel, who also frequently writes for *In These Times*.

IPS has also directly initiated or supported a number of quarterly journals for the radical highbrow audience. The *Journal of Social Reconstruction* is published jointly by IPS and Hampshire College and edited by Marcus Raskin. The IPS annual report claims that it emphasizes "new ways of knowing" that unite rational and moral inquiry "to affirm the humane purposes of scholarship."[30] The *Journal* editors say that it "will cross the imaginary boundaries between science, social science, and aesthetics," and look "for clues that will help civilization survive and build towards the lived experience of liberation, justice, freedom, dignity, and social equity."[31] In reality, it attempts to reshape people's perceptions of the world by redefining words in an Orwellian fashion.

Race and Class, "a Journal for Black and Third World Liberation," is an unapologetically Marxist journal copublished by IPS's Transnational Institute and the Institute of Race Relations. Typical of many articles is IPS fellow Eqbal Ahmad's piece in the winter 1979 edition, wherein he personally identifies with the PLO. PLO leader Rashed Hassein, says Ahmad, "was clearer than many of us on the dangers Israel represented for our future."[32] As for the U.S. intervention in Grenada, *Race and Class* referred to the United States as "the imperialist enemy" that "has murdered the body of the revolution."[33]

Some years after its establishment, the IPS spinoff Institute for Southern Studies began publishing *Southern Exposure,* a quarterly, later a bimonthly, devoted to the culture and politics of the South, focusing on civil rights, anticorporate concerns, and labor and community organizing, among other issues.

IPS fellows have great input in various other quarterly journals: *New Political Science,* edited by various IPS fellows and associate fellows such as Philip Brenner, Sidney Lens, Frances Fox Piven, and Michael Parenti; *New Left Review,* edited by IPS fellow Fred Halliday and associate fellow Anthony Barnett; *Social Policy,* edited by IPS associate fellows Frances Fox Piven and Alan Wolfe; *World Policy Journal,* edited by IPS fellows Richard Barnet and Mary Kaldor and associate fellow Alan Wolfe.

While it is impossible to measure the assistance that IPS has given the alternative media, it is noteworthy that a majority in the American Left consider IPS the movement's intellectual headquarters. The granddad of the American Left, I. F. Stone, comments that IPS is "the only institute we've got."[34] IPS fellows are widely published in numerous other publications, like the *Nation,* the *Progressive, Sojourners, New Times, Multinational Monitor, NACLA, Inquiry, Dollars and Sense,* and *Intervention.* In this way, IPS has helped create and sustain some of the nation's most influential alternative journals. And reporters for one alternative newspaper contribute to another, reinforcing the illusion of consensus on issues where in fact little may exist. *Village Voice* writer James Ridgeway contributes to the Pacific News Service, the *Nation, Mother Jones* and *In These Times;* John Dinges, an associate editor at the *Washington Post* and reporter for the Pacific News Service, has written for the *Progressive, Mother Jones, In These Times,* and the *Guardian;* Frank Browning, a writer for Pacific News Service, has been a correspondent for National Public Radio and written for *Mother Jones* and the *Progressive;* Frank Viviano, an editor for Pacific News Service, has written for the *Nation* and the *Progressive;* Julia Preston of Pacific News Service has reported for *Mother Jones, NACLA,* National Public Radio, and *Columbia Journalism Review;* John Kelly, editor of *CounterSpy,* has written for the *Nation* and *In These Times.*

IPS and Investigative Journalism

As IPS has helped bring the Left up from the underground, so too the institute has harnessed the techniques of investigative journalism to advance the cause. In 1969 IPS's chairman of the board, Philip Stern, established the Fund for Investigative Journalism (FIJ) to support individuals engaged in this type of research. FIJ's first coup was Seymour Hersh's "My Lai Massacre" in the *New York Times*.

Although it disclaims any philosophical or ideological attachments, virtually all FIJ's projects support the Left's agenda. Not surprisingly, it receives support from the Samuel Rubin Foundation. FIJ's board of directors, holding the sole authority to determine grant recipients, and the FIJ advisory board, which offers editorial consultation to FIJ grantees, include IPS fellows Roger Wilkins and Richard Barnet; IPS trustee Philip Stern; IPS faculty member Seymour Hersh; and IPS associate fellow and Pacific News correspondent James Ridgeway. Over the years the fund has also accumulated a sizable list of publication credits in many mainstream journals and newspapers—the *Times* (London), *New York Times, Washington Post, Boston Globe, St. Louis Post-Dispatch, Chicago Sun-Times, Harper's, Atlantic, Inquiry, Village Voice, Washington Monthly, Federal Times,* and *New Republic,* to name a few.[35]

In 1977 the Stern Fund, under the direction of Philip Stern, helped launch yet another journalistic organization, the Center for Investigative Reporting (CIR), in order to support investigative journalism under a tax-exempt umbrella, the Foundation for National Progress. CIR also receives funding from the ARCA Foundation and the Shalan Foundation, two long-time IPS funders.

At first, the CIR staff wrote chiefly for the alternative media, primarily *Mother Jones* and the Pacific News Service; even today *Mother Jones* accounts for more CIR credits than any other journal.[36] In the past few years, however, the CIR's influence has grown considerably, even branching into television, as noted below. Although CIR stories do involve serious probes, their projects predictably follow the same themes stressed by *Mother Jones*—corporate corruption, the evils of the military, and so on.

A third institution supporting the alternative media and indirectly connected to IPS is the Investigative Resource Center (IRC), founded as a spinoff of the North American Congress on Latin America in 1977. The IRC has two divisions: the Information Service on Latin America, which provides press clippings on a monthly basis for subscribers; and the Data Center, a reference library specializing in individuals, corporations, and organizations active in the political sphere. In addition to its support from the Rubin Foundation, IRC receives support from other IPS backers, such as, once again, the Stern Fund, the Shalan Foundation, and the ARCA Foundation.

It boasts a collection of some thirty-five hundred books, directories, and government documents; four hundred periodicals, including a number of obscure "progressive" journals; propaganda from the communist world; and thousands of press-clipping files. Beyond its general service, the Data Center provides more specific reference and research assistance on contract for interested clients. Of particular interest to investigative researchers are the hundred-plus "Corporate Profiles" giving information on corporate executives, geographic operations, subsidiaries and products, relations with consumer groups and labor unions, and extensive files on "the corporation's social, environmental, and political impact."[37] For more politically concerned clients IRC offers a series of "Press Profiles," a political corollary to the "Corporate Profiles." The Reagan administration's policies and its political power base provide the current focus. IRC published, for example, *The New Right: Issues and Analysis* and *Fundamentalists and Finances*, with the express purpose of "assisting progressive organizations and individuals in developing their own social analysis and political strategy to fight the growing threat of the New Right in communities around the country."[38]

Given the nature of IRC's work and its financial backers, it is not surprising that the Center for Investigative Reporting works with IRC on over 50 percent of its projects.[39] Among the regular subscribers to the Data Center is *Mother Jones*.

Nonprofit, Tax-Exempt Status

Most of the journals and organizations discussed here retain a tax-exempt status with the IRS. This allows them to circumvent market mechanisms, which impose a "bottom-line discipline" on the mainstream news industry, because of the lower mailing costs they enjoy under their tax-exempt status. New subscribers can be solicited at a fraction of the regular cost and contributions are tax-deductible.

Among the alternative journals thus blessed are *Mother Jones, In These Times*, and *Working Papers for a New Society*, as well as the Pacific News Service, the Investigative Research Center, the Center for Investigative Reporting, and IPS itself. The fight put up between 1980 and 1983 by *Mother Jones* and its parent organization, the Foundation for National Progress, when the IRS threatened to revoke their 501(c)(3) tax-exempt classification, is indicative of the importance of that status to their survival. The collapse of one journal could trigger a domino effect on the others. For instance, if *Mother Jones* were to stop publishing, the leading forum for alternative journalism would be gone, thus threatening the Center for Investigative Reporting. To be sure, moderate and conservative publishers such as the Sable Foundation, Reason Foundation, and Fund for Objective News Reporting have discovered the benefits of tax exemption as well, but none of them competes with profit-making organizations on a scale comparable with that of *Mother Jones* or PNS.

According to the IRS code, to qualify for 501(c)(3) status an organization must be a public charity devoted to furthering the public interest above its own. The IRS has further defined *public charity* as prohibiting substantial involvement in partisan politics. But *partisan politics* itself is so narrowly defined that if an organization merely refrains from endorsing specific legislation it is usually safe. The bottom line is: How much political activity can an organization safely get away with? What is the difference, if any, between political advocacy and education? *Education* is so ambiguously defined that virtually any type of journalism could be classified educational.

Lenient as IRS regulations may be, the Institute for Policy Studies nevertheless boasts in its promotional literature that "the Institute stands on the bare edge of custom in the United States as to what an educational institution is, as against what a political institution is."[40] Since the Foundation for National Progress, whose primary activity is publishing *Mother Jones*, says its purpose is to further IPS objectives,[41] the "bare edge" would seem to apply to *Mother Jones* as well. IPS's interpretation of educational versus political material has given editors associated with the institute wide latitude in their publications, but it is education often verging on propaganda.

Uniformity Without Central Control

Even though there is no central control over these different publications, in effect they constitute a network, speaking with a fairly uniform voice. Frequent cross-referencing of articles makes for a consensus of opinion among the different publications. In fact, the alternative journals are rather conformist, not to say hackneyed.

By the 1970s IPS and its financial backers had erected a powerful media network comprising *Mother Jones*, a product of the IPS-sponsored Foundation for National Progress; the Pacific News Service of the Bay Area Institute, an IPS spinoff; the Fund for Investigative Journalism, backed by the Rubin Foundation and the Stern Fund, under the direction of Philip Stern, a former IPS chairman; and the Center for Investigative Reporting and the Investigative Resource Center, both underwritten by the Stern Fund, the Shalan Foundation, and the ARCA Foundation. Taken together one can see how these organizations form a consistent whole: research facility (IRC), a newspaper syndicate (PNS), a team of investigators (CIR), a slick magazine *(Mother Jones)*, and a funding mechanism (FIJ).

As with the alternative journals, they work together as a team, each contributing to the success of the others: the IRC provides research assistance for the CIR, whose articles are then published in journals such as *Mother Jones* with the help of grants from the FIJ. For example, a review of the FIJ List of Grants and Books between 1978 and 1980 shows that in 1978 the FIJ provided grants for T. D. Allman, John Dinges, and Mark Schwarz, all from PNS; and for CIR affiliates Craig Pyes and Suzanne Gordon. In 1979 FIJ underwrote CIR members David Weir and Becky O'Malley, PNS writers Jana Bommersbach and Rasa Gustaitis, three *Mother Jones* articles, and an article for *In These Times*. The following year FIJ supported David Weir's work at CIR, *Circle of Poison*, and Frank Browning, a PNS correspondent working on two books, *Vanishing Land: Corporate Theft of America's Soils* and *The American Way of Crime*. In 1981 FIJ assisted Angus Mackenzie in his work on an article for *Columbia Journalism Review* contesting the IRS's investigation into *Mother Jones*'s tax-exempt status. And in a grant not related to publishable work at all, the FIJ made a donation to a libel defense fund for CIR founder Lowell Bergman.[42]

Further overlap is evident between CIR and *Mother Jones* personnel. Mark Dowie has served as both the publisher of *Mother Jones* and the director of CIR. Becky O'Malley, also a director of CIR, has served as a member of the magazine's editorial staff along with Victoria Dempka, another CIR staff member. Richard Parker of CIR has been listed as a *Mother Jones* publisher and as president of the Foundation for National Progress. Likewise, Dan Noyes, a founder of both CIR and IRC, has been listed on the *Mother Jones* masthead.[43]

Within this amalgamation of influence the Center for Investigative Reporting has surpassed the record of FIJ in contributing to IPS outlets. Between 1978 and 1981 CIR published nine of its thirty-two articles in *Mother Jones*, two through the PNS syndicate, and one in *In These Times*,[44] the total accounting for nearly 40 percent of the center's publications. CIR has also received financial assistance from FIJ, the *Mother Jones* investigative fund,[45] and the Pacific News Service (which mentioned by way of explanation that CIR works closely with the Bay Area Institute on topics of mutual interest).[46] CIR also uses the assistance of the Investigative Resource Center in over 50 percent of its research projects.[47]

Although there is nothing illegal about all this, it does create an illusion of diversity where little exists, and such tight coordination could impair the independent functioning of a free press. Furthermore, the mere number of organizations lacking substantial public support may unduly influence public opinion and policymakers, particularly on emotional issues—nuclear defense policy, nuclear power, human rights, toxic waste, and the like.

Bridging the Credibility Gap: Alternative Media Views Trickle Up

IPS understands that the outcome of ideological and political struggle often depends more on successful propaganda than on facts. The "truth" often emerges as the argument most forcefully hammered home. When ostensibly different publications repeat the same theme again and again, that theme begins to assume the appearance of truth, despite exaggeration, distortion, or falsity. In this regard, the IPS network of alternative publications often helps, however unwittingly, foreign adversaries by frequently repeating a perspective reflecting many of the propaganda lines targeted at the United States.

IPS and the alternative media's efforts to tone down their rhetoric and focus on issues of mass appeal have reaped dramatic benefits. In the 1960s there was a marked distinction between the underground and the mainstream press. Generally the underground was not taken seriously by the mainstream because of its coarse and patently slanted character. But after IPS helped give *Mother Jones* a facelift, the magazine successfully set a new tone and style, and the credibility gap closed. Henceforth, stories and views circulating in the alternative media could more easily trickle up to the major media.

The February–March 1976 issue of *Mother Jones,* for instance, carried a story written by IPS associate fellow Paul Jacobs that purported to document safety failures in an atomic reactor built in India with U.S. aid. The story was picked up by the mass media and precipitated a congressional investigation, which in turn resulted in the revocation of American contracts to supply nuclear fuel.[48] Other stories related to nuclear power have precipitated lawsuits and counterproductive regulations in an industry already mired in red tape.

In the September–October 1977 issue of *Mother Jones,* investigative reporter Mark Dowie broke a story, ''Pinto Madness,'' in which he claimed that ''*Mother Jones* has obtained secret documents showing that for seven years the Ford Motor Company sold cars in which it knew hundreds of people would needlessly burn to death.''[49] Concluded Dowie, ''Ford knows the Pinto is a firetrap, yet it has paid out millions to settle damage suits out of court, and it is prepared to spend millions more lobbying against safety standards.''[50] As a result of the *Mother Jones* story, which won a National Magazine Award in 1978, the government forced Ford Motor Company to make the biggest recall in history—over a million Pintos at the cost of hundreds of millions of dollars.

While many believe it is noble of *Mother Jones* to protect the consumer, a closer look suggests that the people behind the magazine are concerned more with undermining corporations than with the safety of the consumer. *Mother Jones* ran a story in its November–December 1976 edition, ''Bust Your Boss,'' which endorsed Jeremy Rifkin's Peoples' Bicentennial Commission (PBC). PBC sent a form letter to ten thousand secretaries of corporate executives, offering a $25,000 reward to any recipient who could provide ''concrete information that leads directly to the arrest, prosecution, conviction and imprisonment of a chief officer . . . for criminal activity relating to corporate operations.''[51] PBC circulated a similar letter to corporate executives' wives, encouraging them to blow the whistle on their husbands. PBC's letter read, ''We think these corporate scandals put a special responsibility on your family to ask some probing questions of your husband, because it is no longer possible to argue that the rampant corporate criminality represents merely isolated incidents or the aberrational behavior of a few perverted individuals."[52] Like the IPS spinoff Government Accountability Project, which searched out "whistleblowers" in U.S. government agencies, PBC was probing into families, businesses, and the communities to discredit corporations and the American economic system in general.

In 1982 a *Mother Jones* exposé cast a pall over U.S. testing procedures on drugs, chemicals, and pesticides, which among other things caused a falling out with the Canadian government.

Another example of a *Mother Jones* story trickling up into the major media was the exclusive report suggesting that Secretary of Defense Caspar Weinberger and Secretary of State George Shultz were involved in bribing South Korean officials to obtain nuclear power plant construction contracts while they were employed at Bechtel, before their joining the Reagan administration. *Mother Jones* editor Deidre English noted that "when we released this report on April 19, 1984, it was immediately picked up in this country, Korea, Japan, Canada and Western Europe."[53] Noted English, "As we go to press, wire service stories have been carried in newspapers and on radio; the *CBS Evening News* has done two segments, and reporters from *The Washington Post, The Wall Street Journal, The New York Times, The Los Angeles Times* and *The San Francisco Chronicle/Examiner* are on the story."[54]

Propaganda and Disinformation: Undermining National Security Interests

Among the many trickle-up instances, several stand out because of their impact on U.S. national security interests. The campaign originating with Philip Agee to discredit the State Department white paper on El Salvador, February 23, 1981—a document that exposed the trafficking of Soviet bloc arms to the Salvadoran guerrillas—offers an important case study.

Although living in West Germany, Agee got hold of the document and set about to discredit it, in the end charging that it was full of errors and based on fabricated evidence. Agee's colleagues at *CounterSpy* and *Covert Action Information Bulletin (CAIB)* released his critique which the alternative media soon picked up; the first story by John Dinges was carried by Pacific News Service. Pacific News succeeded in promoting the story to about thirty papers nationwide. And the rush was on. The anti-white-paper campaign was joined by James Petras and Ralph McGhee in the *Nation,* Alexander Cockburn and James Ridgeway in the *Village Voice,* Roger Burbach of NACLA in *Mother Jones,* and Jeffrey Stein in the *Progressive.* The alternative media set the stage for the mainstream media to play their role. (See Chapter 8.)

On June 8 the *Wall Street Journal* came out with the front-page article "Tarnished Report?" by Jonathan Kwitny, and the following day the *Washington*

Post ran a front-page story, "White Paper on El Salvador Is Faulty," by Robert Kaiser. Agee proudly took credit for the media coup, claiming that his critique had been the basis for both the *Journal* and the *Post* articles.

As two of the most extreme left publications of the alternative media, *CounterSpy* and *CAIB* reveal some interesting insights into the relationship between the alternative media and their mainstream brethren.

The editors of *CAIB* wrote in an open letter to the *New York Times:*

> Shortly after the Jonestown events in Guyana we received a call from a *New York Times* reporter who wanted to know whatever names we had of CIA officers in Guyana. We constantly receive requests from the "establishment" media in this and many other countries requesting such information and research assistance. We have been hired by some of the most prestigious newspapers in the world to do research for them.[55]

Similarly, after the American embassy in Tehran fell to Iranian fanatics, the editors of *CAIB* wrote:

> We were swamped with calls from reporters with the networks, the wire services, and many major national newspapers and magazines, asking, almost pleading, for the names of CIA personnel in Tehran. "Off the record," they begged. "I promise I won't tell anyone." It was an object lesson all right. Some of the same people who cluck their tongues when we publish our magazines were thirsting for blood, for an international incident, for a page-one byline.[56]

Several years earlier *CAIB* asserted that *Washington Post* reporters "are among the large number of working journalists from virtually all the major print and electronic media in the country who call upon us daily for help, research, information, and, of all things, names of intelligence operatives in connection with articles they are writing."[57]

Walden Bello, a *CounterSpy* advisory board member and frequent participant at IPS functions, admitted that his magazine had supplied the *Wall Street Journal* with critical information for at least fifteen stories having to do with intelligence matters and the strategic concerns of the United States.[58]

Philip Agee, the inspiration behind both *Covert Action Information Bulletin* and *CounterSpy,* attacked in an article in *Nation* those who distinguish between "legitimate" or "straight" reporting and "guerrilla" or "advocacy" journalism. Agee said the distinction was "unashamed hypocrisy [because] mainstream journalists never stop asking me for names of CIA personnel."[59] "They call me at any hour of the day or night for leads and advice," Agee added.[60] Quite a statement from someone who has been stripped of his U.S. citizenship and been barred from all but one NATO country because of his collusion with Soviet and Cuban intelligence agents.

Alternative Media Push the Mainstream Leftward

Not only do the alternative media shower copious questionable stories and disinformation upon the mainstream media, but they force them to adopt the agenda of the Left. At a September 1984 IPS seminar on South Africa, William Minter, an associate editor for *Africa News* (a weekly alternative journal funded in part by the IPS chairman, Peter Weiss), explained that his magazine and other alternatives have to wage a "campaign in order to affect the prestige press in its coverage of South African issues."[61] Just what kind of campaign they should undertake, Minter did not specify. But he did say that if the alternative media expressed solidarity with the African liberation movements, it would help bring the proper perspective to coverage of African news in the mainstream press.[62] Feeling secure in the sanctuary of IPS, Minter reminisced about how he had previously worked for seven years as a teacher for the Marxist FRELIMO liberation movement in Tanzania.[63]

The Center for Investigative Reporting has accomplished considerably more than "priming the pump"; it has had a major impact on one of the nation's major weekly news programs, CBS's "60 Minutes." In 1978, when CIR's director, Lowell Bergman, moved to ABC to work with its "20/20" investigating team, CIR developed an invaluable inside connection with a major network. In a short time CIR was a regularly contracted adjunct of ABC's "20/20" team. The story was repeated when Bergman moved to CBS to take a position as a producer for "60 Minutes."[64]

In each case the CIR's role was to come up with stories for the programs and provide the basic research around which a show could be built. The benefits to CIR, beyond the monetary, were that it not only could direct the focus of the shows, but could imbue its own work with greater credibility by receiving credit from two prestigious news programs. Instead of appearing only in articles of limited circulation of the alternative press, CIR's stories were now conveyed to millions of viewers by the familiar faces of Hugh Downs and Barbara Walters of "20/20" and Mike Wallace and Morley Safer of "60 Minutes." And beyond this, the major networks were also now in effect subsidizing CIR's selected research topics.

Because of the amount of legwork involved, producing a weekly series like "60 Minutes" understandably requires help from the outside. And ABC and CBS have employed CIR repeatedly because they liked the results. In accepting CIR's choice of subjects and its investigations as the basis of their stories, CBS and ABC have allowed outsiders partially to determine what kind of stories should be broadcast. Even if CIR were a purely journalistic operation, with no sign of political bias, this symbiotic relationship with television would raise questions of propriety. But CIR is by no means apolitical and each investigation reflects a distinct outlook. The machinations of the corporate world are fair game, but CIR does not find the schemes of "public-interest" law firms or the waste and fraud in the welfare system suitable topics for investigation.

Conspicuously absent is any reaction by media critics of a network's open support of a political advocacy group. But when "60 Minutes" aired a show disclosing the World Council of Churches' funding of third-world terrorism, for which it consulted the conservative Institute on Religion and Democracy (IRD), it was sharply criticized for propagandizing.[65] In short, the selection of investigative stories on TV over the years confirms the surveys that reveal the liberal slant of the media vis-à-vis mainstream America.

The major media's acceptance of "alternative" sources for news has been manifested in fascinating ways. Prominent figures from leading mainstream media also write for the alternative press. Karen DeYoung, senior foreign editor at the *Washington Post,* wrote a major story for *Mother Jones* in June 1981, "The White Hand of Terror," on death squads in El Salvador. In June 1984 *Mother Jones* carried a piece by *Wall Street Journal* reporter Jonathan Kwitny, "Oh, What a Lovely War." Although the thrust of the article was against the U.S. action in Grenada, Kwitny didn't miss the opportunity to get in some broad sweeps—the world's crises and problems "are the results of misunderstandings and miscalculations by the world's two great imperialist powers, the Soviet Union and the United States."[66] And "instead of teaching liberty, the U.S. foreign relations apparatus has chosen to teach the world coups d'état, assassination, duplicity, torture and state control."[67]

Suffice it to say that the metamorphosis of the underground media into the alternative has had a net effect of blurring the distinction between "objective" and "advocacy" reporting, and between credible sources of information and those so biased as to be unreliable. (See Appendix 4 for organizational chart of IPS and the media.)

The Alternative Media and the Cultural Revolution

The alternative media also play a major role in cultural transformation. Antonio Gramsci, a prominent twentieth-century Marxist theoretician, argued that power is best attained in developed, industrialized countries through a gradual process of radicalization of the cultural institutions (the "superstructure") of bourgeois society, a process that would in turn transform the values and morals of the society. Gramsci believed that as society's morals were softened, so its political and economic foundation would be more easily smashed and restructured.[68]

Even though a steady march of liberalization has marked the twentieth century, much of it good, such as advances in civil rights, changes in the United States were most dramatic in the late 1960s and early 1970s. Then the underground and alternative media were in full cry attacking authority, promoting permissiveness, and unraveling the social fabric of American society.

By the eighties, moral relativism and nihilism had spilled over into the major political parties at home and abroad. The British Labour party and the pacifistic West German Green party embrace a philosophy that ignores what is necessary for a dynamic economy, not to mention political freedom. The Democratic party in the United States has followed in the footsteps of its European counterparts, preaching isolationism, more corporate regulation, and a moral relativism that extends to courting the "homosexual vote." This cultural transformation in the West has contributed to moral confusion and the inability of many political parties to lead, which bodes ill when faced by determined adversaries.

Certainly the election of many conservative governments in Europe and the United States in the early 1980s augured a return to more traditional values. But because culture and fashion are interrelated, the growing cultural influence of the alternative media is bound to have a long-term effect. In a mass society the media tend to reduce issues to a common denominator—a framework of analysis—which can be spoon-fed to the public. Insofar as the mass media are inclined toward sensationalism and "trendiness," especially if seasoned with progressivism, the alternative media provide a natural source for the mainstream media. The alternative media can be counted on to jump at any opportunity to discredit policies, leaders, and institutions they abhor. For instance, they plug peace through negotiations and attack peace through strength, which has historically provided the best approach to defense.

The alternative media's espousal of "no enemies on the Left" also has a considerable impact on the major media's coverage of personalities. The mainstream media like to portray public figures who are anticommunist as part of a right-wing fringe, while bowing before those who advocate détente, pacifism or even appeasement.

The alternative media have successfully molded the cultural and political outlook by coining some popular buzz words. Distorting the language has proved to be one of the Left's most powerful tools. By tampering with words, the alternative media and the Left have infiltrated the liberal mind, sowing seeds of doubt, confusion, guilt. Equally important, they have provided a subliminal means to achieve behavior modification, as, for instance, holding that protest and political activism are more worthy than casting votes at election time.

In a general sense, the alternative media provide a catalyst by introducing new values and concepts which society and the mainstream media may accept or reject. David Armstrong discusses this in *A Trumpet to Arms:*

> Over time, the alternative media and their culture progressively modify society with humanistic reforms. . . . The relationship of alternative media to the dominant society is, of course, two-way. Not only do ideas introduced by alternative media modify society, they are also themselves modified in the course of being absorbed by the mainstream culture. In effect, the mass media, through which the public is introduced directly to those ideas, use the alternative media for research and development.[69]

If the editors of the mainstream media once encouraged their reporters to ferret out the truth and report the facts objectively, they now have become increasingly inclined to accept biased and distorted views from the alternative media. This is advocacy reporting, pure and simple.

Alternative Media: Lifeblood of the Left

In discussing the alternative media, one must address its function in sustaining the New Left political culture. Every philosophy not rooted in common experience and rational consistency requires constant reinforcement, and the alternative media provide this for the Left. In A Trumpet to Arms David Armstrong points out:

> Without media of their own to convey messages that radicals and dissidents themselves select and shape, activists become isolated and weak. If activists supply alternative media with a constituency, alternative media provide activists with a sense of identity and collective purpose. There is a symbiosis between alternative media and alternative culture—an exchange of vital energy that is critical to the health of both.[70]

According to Jacques Ellul's definitive study of modern propaganda, the aim of the alternative media—as institutions whose chief goal is to promote propaganda for the Left—is not just to modify ideas but, more important, to provoke action.

> It is no longer to change adherence to a doctrine, but to make the individual cling irrationally to a process of action. It is no longer to lead to a choice, but to loosen the reflexes. It is no longer to transform an opinion, but to arouse an action and mythical belief.[71]

For the Left, the real power of the alternative media is its capacity to convert individual responses into collective action. In the circles of the Left—IPS and the collective communities of Mother Jones and In These Times—the individual member's attitudes may be so conditioned by ideology that group life becomes the standard by which individuals measure themselves.[72] Eventually, all their behavior reflects politics and emotion subverts reason. The response of leftists to their own ideological propaganda is not, however, passive; that propaganda fulfills psychological needs which engage them actively in political affairs.[73] Insofar as thinking and self-reflection require discipline and honesty, sometimes painful, it is always easier simply to reinforce prior convictions.

For the average person in a pluralistic society who sees the complexities of the world, the questions arise, What sustains the New Left? What enables institutions like IPS and *Mother Jones* to continue? And not just "to continue" but to work long hours for low pay. Ellul has an answer:

> Man, eager for self-justification, throws himself in the direction of a propaganda that justifies him and this eliminates one of the sources of his anxiety. Propaganda dissolves contradictions and restores to man a unitary world in which the demands are in accord with the facts. It gives man a clear and simple call to action that takes precedence over all else. It permits him to participate in the world round him without being in conflict with it, because the action he has been called upon to perform will surely remove all obstacles from the path of realizing the proclaimed ideal.[74]

The price can be high for the individual caught up in the political culture of the Left, for the propaganda he subscribes to drives a wedge between his inner and his outer self, substituting conditioned values and attitudes for what is most needed—a life of reason and self-evaluation. The chief casualty of the Left's alternative media may in the end be independent thought itself.

IPS fellow Saul Landau: "Cuba is the first purposeful society that we have had in the Western Hemisphere for many years . . . "

Richard J. Barnet, IPS cofounder and senior fellow

Marcus G. Raskin, IPS cofounder and senior fellow

Robert Borosage, IPS director

Peter Weiss, IPS chairman of the board

IPS fellows Isabel Letelier and Peter Kornbluh

"The Moorings," IPS headquarters at 1901 Q St, Washington, D.C.

Cafe Rondo and "The Anchorage," IPS's adjacent office building

IPS Fellow Isabel Letelier says about CP leader Sandy Pollack: "As Latin Americans, we know she will always be alive in our struggles, and she will be with us in our victories."

IPS fellow Roger Wilkins

NACLA vice president Janet Shenk and IPS fellow Michael Klare

New York Times reporter and IPS Washington School faculty member Seymour Hersh speaks at IPS program at National Education Association.

Charles Clements, an American M.D. who worked with Salvadoran FMLN guerrillas, shares his experiences at an IPS program at the National Education Association.

Washington Post associate editor John Dinges and *New York Times* reporter Ray Bonner chair an IPS seminar.

IPS fellow Eqbal Ahmad speaks on the "deadly connection" between US military intervention and nuclear war.

IPS graduate and SANE executive director David Cortright

IPS trustee Paul Warnke

Marcus Raskin, Seymour Hersh and Saul Landau confer.

The Eighth Annual Letelier-Moffitt Memorial Human Rights Ceremony; (left to right) Reverend William Wipfler, director of Human Rights Office of the National Council of Churches; Roger Wilkins, IPS fellow; Patricia Derian, Carter administration assistant secretary of state, Ramon Custodio, President of Committee for Human Rights in Honduras and recipient of 1984 Letelier-Moffitt Human Rights Award; Isabel Letelier, IPS fellow.

The Methodist Building, annex and Stewart Mott House, which occupy a city block from 100-122 Maryland Avenue, N.E., is the closest lobbying complex to the U.S.Congress. Housed here are the Center for National Security Studies, the Women's International League for Peace and Freedom, the Coalition for a New Foreign and Military Policy, the Center for International Policy, the Washington Office on Latin America, the Washington Office on Africa, INFACT, Council for a Livable World, and the lobbying offices for the National Council of Churches, the United Church of Christ, and the Unitarian Universalists, among others.

Steward Mott's meeting house at 122 Maryland Avenue, N.E., also provides office space for the IPS spinoff Center for National Security Studies and the Women's International League for Peace and Freedom, an organization with close ties to the Soviet World Peace Council.

Stewart Mott presiding at a "Monday Group" meeting, flanked by Sen. Alan Cranston (D-Cal.) and Rep. Edward Markey (D-Mass.).

Senator Harkin speaks to an IPS reception at the Mott House: "I want to thank the Institute for Policy Studies and the people who have worked so hard [and] have been in my office a lot."

Soviet KGB officer Victor Taltz leaving the same IPS reception at the Mott House at 122 Maryland Ave., Feb. 22, 1984: "I read this book [IPS's *Changing Course*] last night . . . we are very grateful for IPS to be brave enough to tell the truth."

Soviet third secretary and KGB officer Valeriy Lekarev, the chief liaison between the Soviet Institute for Study of USA and Canada and IPS for their "alternative" arms control dialogue.

Soviet agent Taltz (circle) in attendance at Robert Borosage and Saul Landau seminar, "Report from Nicaragua and Cuba," December 12, 1983.

Randall Forsberg, author of the first American nuclear freeze proposal, was a leading participant at the Minneapolis dialogue between IPS and the Soviet Institute for Study of USA and Canada, May 25, 1983.

Georgi Arbatov, head of Soviet Institute for Study of USA and Canada and assistant to Mikhail Gorbachev chats with IPS fellow Saul Landau at San Francisco dialogue, September 6, 1985.

Cora Weiss, Nicaraguan Embassy official Leonor Hupper, and National Lawyers Guild attorney William Kunstler.

Vladimir I. Strokin (circle), a third secretary at the Soviet Embassy, attends an IPS seminar, "South Africa and the Media," September 13, 1984.

Two unidentified representatives from the East bloc visit IPS, August 22, 1984.

Soviet U.N. diplomat, Igor Mishchenko (circle), makes contacts at a "deadly connections" rally April 21, 1984 featuring IPS fellow Eqbal Ahmad and sponsored by Mobilization for Survival and the Riverside Church Disarmament Program.

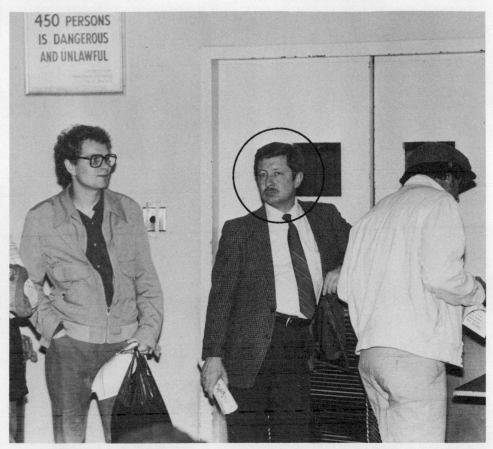

Journalist for the Soviet *Literary Gazette*, Anatoliy Manakov (circle), looks on as IPS fellow Eqbal Ahmad castigates the United States.

Inside the image: 450 PERSONS IS DANGEROUS AND UNLAWFUL

On February 2, 1985 Rene J. Mujica, first secretary of the Cuban Interests Section at the Czechoslovakian Embassy, speaks at the Riverside Church memorial service for Sandy Pollack, an American Communist Party (CP) central committee member who died in a plane crash in Cuba: "Because of her particular love for and identification with the Cuban revolution, and because in so many ways she was indeed one of our own, we feel her loss as also our own."

The Riverside Church and the National Council of Churches office building stand next to each other overlooking the Hudson River.

Reverend Coffin embraces Sandinista President Daniel Ortega, while Sandinista Ambassador Nora Astorga looks on. (Ambassador Astorga was the legendary Sandinista heroine who seduced one of Somoza's generals into bed in order to have him murdered by her waiting compañeros who sprang forth with ice picks.)

D'Escoto confides in Reverend William Sloane Coffin at the Riverside Church.

Cora Weiss and Miguel D'Escoto

Robert Borosage and Saul Landau report on their November 1983 trips to Cuba and Nicaragua: "We were there [in Nicaragua] . . . to work on a project . . . for aid to Nicaragua to keep it from being isolated economically and politically . . . and to work with the eight ministries down there to make sure they had their projects in order so that the Europeans' [funding] could operate effectively."

Introduced as a distinguished scholar of the New Deal, Alger Hiss speaks at IPS March 23, 1984.

Part IV

Restructuring the Economy

CHAPTER 11

Laying Siege to the Corporate Castle

In November 1969 IPS associate fellow Staughton Lynd asked, "Why do we continue to demonstrate in Washington as if the core of the problem lay there? The small group of activists who have burnt corporate records have pointed to the proper target. We need to find ways to lay siege to corporations," Lynd exhorted. "We need to invent anti-corporate actions which involve masses of people, not just a dedicated few."[1]

Since that time, the institute, particularly its Amsterdam branch, has become one of the main centers of anticorporate activism in the Western world. Its efforts have been joined and amplified by other anticorporate organizations that rose amidst the countercultural foment of the 1960s and early 1970s.

The New Class and the Intellectual Roots of Anticapitalism

The crusade against the corporation led by IPS and various other advocacy groups has been fueled by the mainstream intelligentsia—a new class of intellectuals bred on the affluence of capitalism.

The term "New Class" refers to that stratum in contemporary society associated with the knowledge industry, dealing with symbols and values rather than material goods and services.[2] Unlike other sectors of society, the New Class rarely bears responsibility for its actions and is not answerable to the marketplace

167

disciplines, which eliminate products for which there is inadequate demand. In circles where the New Class interests reign supreme—universities, media, publishing houses, foundations—there is little accountability to the practical world. This is why, for instance, socialist theory remains popular among intellectuals, despite its consistent failure to deliver what it promises. The New Class not only fails to appreciate the benefits of capitalism (or perhaps it takes those benefits for granted), but is often hostile to capitalism. Alienated from the mass culture of a consumer society, the New Class is predisposed, however subtly, to critiques of capitalism—notably those from Marxism—and to the politics of the Left.

In this regard, the irony of the modern dilemma is that capitalism has sown the seeds of its own destruction. Its success has created a surplus of wealth and, for many, a surplus of leisure. The surplus of wealth has created foundations, and the leisure time has enabled the alienated, with grants from the foundations, to develop research centers and advocacy groups through which to attack the institutions toward which they feel antipathy—corporate America.

Although many foundations fund legitimate causes, others fuel the Left and New Class intellectuals, who agitate against the very capitalist system that nurtures them. Lenin predicted that capitalists would sell the rope with which they would hang, but Joseph Schumpeter analyzed the ways in which capitalism generated, fostered, and protected its own enemies, this hostile class of intellectuals:

> Intellectuals are people who wield the power of the spoken and written word and one of the touches that distinguish them from other people who do the same is the absence of direct responsibility for practical affairs. The critical attitude arises no less from the intellectual's situation as an onlooker, in most cases also an outsider, than from the fact that his main chance of asserting himself lies in his actual or potential nuisance value.[3]

The assault on the corporation is essentially an assault on capitalism and private enterprise, and has become far more than a nuisance. Although some of these anticorporate research centers and advocacy groups, like the Exploratory Project on Economic Alternatives, were IPS spinoffs, others, such as Ralph Nader's organizations, have had independent beginnings. But almost all the anticorporate groups feel a kinship with IPS and deem it an intellectual center. Joint conferences and media events are frequently held, and coalitions are formed to effect political change.

In the Name of the Public Interest

Many assumed that the anticorporate movement was part of a counterculture fad that would fade with time. Nothing could be further from the truth. Instead, it has evolved into the "public-interest movement," which mushroomed in the latter 1970s as a result of sophisticated public relations and popular phobias—fear of new technology, of environmental disasters, of nuclear accidents, and the like—which fanned the media's lust for sensationalism. By 1980 whole networks of groups were in place. Today, the public-interest movement gnaws away at the free private-enterprise system like a colony of termites, whose activities are often invisible but can bring down seemingly invulnerable structures.

The term "public interest" turns out to be one of those propaganda slogans that have come to figure large in contemporary politics, an attractive encapsulation of deliberately ambiguous objectives; a phrase bursting with moral superiority over the rest of mundane society, busy producing and consuming.

In truth, this movement rests on two questionable assertions: first, the marketplace fails to make producers accountable to consumers; and second, there is a single discernible public interest. Notwithstanding, the movement has hoisted an attractive flag around which to gather the alienated, the idealistic, and the radicals to make the special "private" interests accountable to the "public" good. The image they foster is of a modern-day David standing up to the monstrous Goliath. But the symbol of the British Fabian socialists—the wolf in sheep's clothing—seems more appropriate.

The vast majority of American people do not, in fact, harbor an anticapitalist bias (because, according to IPS fellows, they do not know what is good for them). Thus, the public-interest movement has found that it must create and expose problems and rumors of problems in the corporate world and then attempt to popularize them through the media. As Benjamin J. Lambiotte told a June 1985 IPS seminar on pesticides and toxic waste, "On the pesticide issue there just aren't people dropping dead all over the place, like there were in Vietnam . . . but you can always manufacture crises."[4]

Leaders of the public-interest movement know that if they can weaken people's faith in capitalism, the people will be more inclined to accept regulation and various forms of state intervention, even at the cost of individual freedom. And, as government bureaucracies expand, the vitality of the private sector suffers, thus reinforcing the idea that the free market cannot work and that further tampering and intervention are necessary.

IPS Views on American Economic System

IPS fellows blame private enterprise for most of society's ills. They contend that corporations manipulate foreign policy for their own selfish interests, exploit people for profit, and squander resources in sating their greed. Peter Weiss argues that it is "an imperative" that "we dispense, once and for all, with the utterly foolish notion that capitalism can bring about economic and social justice to the Third World."[5]

Marcus Raskin states in his book *Notes on the Old System* that American capitalism is a system in which "the rich, the quick, the clever, the unseen, set out paths which the wretched and mystified must travel."[6]

Richard Barnet expounds upon the theme in his widely acclaimed 1974 book *Global Reach:*

> Global companies have used their great levers of power—finance capital, technology, organizational skills, and mass communications—to create a Global Shopping Center in which the hungry of the world are invited to buy expensive snacks at a Global Factory in which there are fewer and fewer jobs. The World Manager's vision of One World turns out in fact to be two distinct worlds—one featuring rising affluence for a small transnational middle class, and the other escalating misery for the great bulk of the human family. The dictates of profit and the dictates of survival are in clear conflict.[7]

Barnet concludes that "the myth of the market still forestalls serious public planning, and the market mentality . . . is still a driving force for more mindless accumulation and waste."[8] His solution? Socialism, although he shrinks from calling it that. "If we are to survive as a species, we shall need to cultivate a profusion of alternative assumptions. . . . The United States could use its extraordinary surplus to finance a variety of experiments in public ownership and public planning," says Barnet.[9]

Myth of the Corporation

In a more succinct study, *The Crisis of the Corporation,* Barnet speaks of the "myths which legitimize the role of the corporation in society." He argues that the modern corporation "has weakened the power of the nation-state" because "the excessive power of large corporations over the political and economic life of the country has all but destroyed the system of checks and balances in our society."[10] To begin solving the problem, according to Barnet, we must explode the "Myths of Free Enterprise, Efficiency, Equality, and Democracy."[11]

The "Myth of Free Enterprise" is the "most powerful of the corporate myths" and is, in turn, "based on the exchange transaction." Such free exchange "is the essential legitimizing myth of free enterprise" because it "has put wealth acquired by commerce in a higher moral category than wealth acquired by conquest." "The most important development" challenging this myth, as Barnet sees it, is "the concentration of economic power," which led "to the Age of Oligopoly," in which the United States "operates a dual economy—free enterprise for small business, state welfare for big business." In this age, "products are shaped not to the requirements of public need but to the requirements of corporate growth." This in turn is related to the "Myth of Efficiency," because it "rewards extravagance and punishes thrift." Furthermore, says Barnet, our dependence on "the corporate polluters" has risen while the "Throwaway Society—from disposable bottles to disposable cars—has been successfully marketed as the highest stage of capitalism."

Democracy is threatened in the United States, Barnet believes, because "the concentration of economic power in the hands of a few hundred corporate managers and stockholders is inevitably translated into political power." For Barnet, all of this means that "the redistribution of economic and political power is the price of maintaining democracy in America."[12]

Harnessing the Media

IPS exploits the media to influence the public's view of the corporation, just as it uses them to sway public opinion on foreign policy. Today, the attack on the corporation is not a scholarly debate going on in faraway ivory towers. It is a battle pure and simple, being fought on many levels by many different constituencies. Ambassador Herman Nickel points out that "though the anticorporate movement lacks centralized organization, it functions effectively as a loose coalition" in which "activists for one cause often help campaigners for another."[13]

Because the attack on the corporation has cloaked itself in so many different guises, it has eluded many people. For instance, the divestment movement against South Africa, the opposition to nuclear power, toxic waste, and third-world distribution of infant formula would appear unrelated. Yet they are all manifestations of a common theme—corporations are involved in harmful and unjust enterprises.

The public-interest movement often boasts that it seeks to check the greed of corporate power, which preys on the public good. The problem today for the ordinary citizen is how to discriminate between groups that legitimately want to reform abuses—unsafe products, pollution, antitrust violations, false advertising—and those that wish to do away with private enterprise altogether.

IPS and Ralph Nader

Ralph Nader, probably the most notorious public-interest advocate, goes back to the 1960s when he and a young group of lawyers formed the Project for Corporate Responsibility (PCR). As Nader's colleague Phil Moore, the director of PCR, observed:

Corporate reform today is a natural and appropriate extension of the social and political movement of the 60s. We discovered what we practically knew—that regardless of new laws or consciousness, their objectives would not be accomplished without a commitment of our corporate institutions which have enough power to implement or defy national goals. So now the movement of the 60s is redirecting its energies from institutions of government to institutions of private power.[14]

Although Ralph Nader has become a household name while IPS remains relatively unknown, IPS is busy behind the scenes and has been equally active in providing ideological and institutional support to fight corporate America. In fact, IPS and Nader's umbrella, Public Citizen Inc. (which includes the Public Interest Research Group and the Corporate Accountability Research Group, successors to the Project on Corporate Responsibility), are closely knit. For instance, on September 2 and 3, 1981, Nader joined with Lee Webb, IPS trustee and director of the Conference on Alternative State and Local Policies, an IPS spinoff, and IPS associate fellow Derek Shearer in sponsoring a two-day Washington conference with the theme "Taking Charge: The Next Ten Years."[15]

On January 31, 1983, Nader held a joint news conference with IPS's Government Accountability Project (GAP) to attack President Reagan for understaffing the bureaucracy at the Department of Agriculture. One of Nader's publications, *Multinational Monitor,* offered a free copy of Richard Barnet's book *Global Reach* in one of its early subscription drives.[16]

In a 1982 fundraising letter, Nader praised Barnet as a "leading scholar" on the subject of corporate influence. And Barnet wrote a feature article for the premier issue of Nader's *Multinational Monitor.* In it Barnet said: "The industrialization of the Third World via the multinational has destroyed jobs in the countryside without creating anything approaching equivalent opportunities inside the factory. . . . It is the monumental social problem of the planet, the cause of mass starvation, repression, and crime, petty and cosmic."[17] A more sweeping indictment of the corporation as the root of all evil could hardly be contrived.

IPS fellows John Cavanagh and Michael Goldhaber frequently contribute to Nader's *Multinational Monitor.* In early 1984 Mark Dowie, investigative editor at *Mother Jones,* collaborated with Tim Shorrock, editor of *Multinational Monitor,* on a story to discredit big business and cabinet members in the Reagan administration. The stories, which appeared in both *Mother Jones* and *Multinational Monitor,* suggested that Secretary of State George Shultz and Secretary of Defense Caspar Weinberger were aware of the alleged bribery of South Korean officials to obtain nuclear construction contracts for Bechtel Corporation, for which Shultz and Weinberger had worked. Like so many other stories that trickle up from the alternative media, this one, though unsubstantiated, was picked up by the mainstream media.

Tracing the Roots: The Military Industrial Complex and the Early Days of the Anticorporate Movement

Addressing an angry gathering of the antiwar activists in 1969, IPS associate fellow Staughton Lynd listed the annual meeting dates of twenty-one of the largest defense-related corporations, asserting that "our inevitable enemy in the coming year is the corporation."[18] For the next several years, demonstrating against corporate involvement in the war effort became a major part of the protest. The concept that the "military industrial complex" drove the American war machine in Vietnam gained popularity from the New Left, particularly after the appearance Richard Barnet's book *The Economy of Death*.

Church organizations in the antiwar movement, such as Clergy and Laity Concerned (CALC) and the American Friends Service Committee (AFSC), began to focus on corporations manufacturing war materiel, like Dow Chemical and Honeywell. In 1969 the AFSC formed the National Action/Research on the Military Industrial Complex (NARMIC) and with the help of Michael Klare of NACLA, NARMIC published *Movement Guide to Stockholders Meetings*,[19] which explained the securities laws as they affected public participation at stockholders' meetings and suggested "possible tactics for inside the meetings so that the most effective demonstrations and protests can be conceptualized."[20]

Research Provides Informed Activism

The NARMIC approach was refined by several of Lynd's colleagues at IPS. Fellows Len Rodberg and Lee Webb collaborated with Michael Klare and Michael Locker of NACLA in producing a directory, the *Research and Methodology Guide (RMG)*, which provided specific ways to exploit "the corporation, the universities, churches and the media industry."[21] The purpose of the guide was suggested on its inside cover:

> What if the machinery were reversed? What if the habits, problems, secrets and unconscious motivations of the wealthy and powerful were daily scrutinized by a thousand systematic researchers, published in a hundred inexpensive mass circulation journals and written so that even the fifteen-year-old high school drop-out could understand it and predict the actions of his landlord, manipulate and control him?[22]

The *RMG*, the basis for much of the subsequent anticorporate activism, makes it clear that its goal is revolutionary change and not reform: "In the context of the system of capitalism that brutalizes us, separates us, and forces us to be competitive, power-structure research documents the monopolization of power in a few hands and thus the need for sweeping change."[23] Among strategies for "sweeping change," the *RMG* recommends:

—locating the weak points in the system. Knowledge of such points gives us the leverage to challenge the system effectively with the means at our disposal. Sometimes even an apparently insignificant weakness can be effectively exploited. The public image of a corporation, for instance, can be important to its continued prosperity—investment, government contracts, employee recruiting, etc.

—To move strategically, we must know the opponent. The Army's terminology for such a plan is "order of battle"—we must know what resources the enemy has, what the contingencies are, what countermoves we can expect to our actions. It is necessary, in other words, to take the information available about power in this society, and turn it against that power in ways which weaken its stranglehold upon us. Seen in this light, research is an instrument of our liberation.[24]

The development of power structure research was well suited to the spinoff strategy of IPS. The Bay Area Institute, established in San Francisco with the help of IPS in 1969, agreed to research and compile a data base on the corporate power structures of firms trading between the West Coast and the Far East.[25] Another IPS spinoff, the Institute for Southern Studies (ISS), established in 1970 in Atlanta, compiled a data base on corporate power structures of firms operating in the southern United States.[26] In one brochure, ISS said that it was "systematically collecting, evaluating and disseminating data on the operations of over 400 corporations in the south."[27]

Council on Economic Priorities

During the Vietnam period, church groups began to lobby their national offices to divest all church stock in companies supporting the U.S. war effort. The Council on Economic Priorities (CEP) was formed in 1971 to advise church groups on investments and how to put together "peace portfolios." Edgar Lockwood, a board member of IPS and contributing editor of Phil Agee's *CounterSpy,* donated some of the seed money for CEP. Peter Weiss also gave his support, and by the late 1970s the Rubin Foundation had become one of its chief financial backers. Richard Barnet, Cora Weiss, and Philip Stern, a familiar cast of characters, all served on CEP's board of directors and advisory committee.

Alice Tepper Marlin, the director of CEP, admitted privately that Saul Alinsky, author of *Reveille for Radicals,* had a huge effect on her thinking. "One of the things he stressed was the importance of peer groups and peer pressure," said Marlin.[28] "What we try to do at the Council is to deal with businessmen directly, *to divide the business community* and thus create a setting in which publicity and peer pressure can have a big impact" (emphasis added).[29]

Although CEP started out researching corporations involved in the defense industry, it soon broadened its scope, rating corporations' "social performance" in other ways, such as their environmental impact and overseas operations.

Broadening the Base of Moral Indignation

Those corporations that appeared to be unfair in minority hiring, nonunionization, pollution of the environment, or exporting capital and labor to overseas markets, became the targets of the ballooning anticorporate movement. Corporations operating in South Africa were immediately accused of collusion with the government and tainted with the apartheid brush. This kind of issue had great moral appeal, especially among church groups, already impassioned against and mobilized in opposition to the Vietnam War. And the radical activists knew it. They recognized the potential financial power of the churches, as pointed out in the February 1971 issue of *Grapevine,* an NCC publication:

The corporate responsibility drive has particular significance for the church. First of all, the church is one of this country's foremost financial institutions, with holdings in most major American corporations. It is surpassed only by the federal government in monies received and distributed yearly—more than $22 billion, more than the combined wealth of AT&T plus the five leading American oil companies.[30]

National Council of Churches and the Anticorporate Agenda

In 1971 the National Council of Churches (NCC) formed the Corporate Information Center (CIC) to monitor the "social cost" of corporate activities and to coordinate church campaigns directed at divestment from targeted corporations. In 1974 the NCC decided to merge CIC with the Interfaith Committee on Social Responsibility, naming the new organization the Interfaith Center on Corporate Responsibility (ICCR), and asking Timothy Smith to take charge as director.

Smith had testified in June 1971 before the House Subcommittee on Africa saying, "U.S. companies are a mirror of the racist South African society in almost every way."[31] In early 1972 Smith appeared at the United Nations and testified that companies such as General Motors, IBM, Ford, and Chrysler "never tell the truth about how they are helping to build South Africa's military strength."[32] Taking the floor at an annual stockholders' meeting of Union Carbide in New York a few weeks later, Smith harangued the company for doing business in South Africa. And in June of that year Smith and Carlton Goodlett—

delegate to the Soviet World Peace Council—disrupted the annual stockholders' meeting of Gulf Oil Company, and had to be ejected.[33]

As protests against the Vietnam War waned after 1973, anticorporate activism waxed. By 1975 IPS, NACLA, NARMIC, CEP, ICCR, and Ralph Nader's Corporate Accountability Research Group led the research centers in the growing movement. Ironically, while they decried the concentration of power in the interlocking directorates of oligopolistic corporate structures and conglomerates, the anticorporate groups were mirroring them—sharing information, organizing joint anticorporate ventures, having personnel on each other's boards, and so on. Timothy Smith, the director of ICCR, served on CEP's board of directors and the two organizations joined in some sixty campaigns against different corporations. In like manner, IPS, NACLA, and NARMIC often shared resources and personnel in their anticorporate activities. (See Appendix 5 for organizational chart of major groups cooperating with IPS in anticorporate activism.)

Corporate Data Exchange Feeds the Movement

Strategies most commonly pursued by the anticorporate movement are essentially fivefold: (1) *Petition*—using letters, hearings, and visits to pressure for change in corporate policies; (2) *Divestiture*—selling stock in companies that are "socially offensive," such as those doing business in South Africa; (3) *Proxy Option*—expressing dissent and outrage at stockholders meetings; (4) *Boycott*—leveling economic pressure by organizing campaigns to discourage the purchase of products; and (5) *Stockholder Class-Action Suits*—suing corporations for alleged violations of the law, such as those concerning "human rights" or "environmental damage."

In 1975, in consultation with IPS and NACLA, Michael Locker and Stephen Abrecht founded the Corporate Data Exchange (CDE) to profile selected corporations in great depth. CDE became an information clearinghouse for public-interest groups, labor unions, churches, community activists, and anyone else in the business of baiting corporations. As for CDE's financial backing in the beginning, the Rubin Foundation and the Institute for Policy Studies were prominent.[34]

CDE provided a vital service for the growing anticorporate activist network. By the early 1980s its data base had files on some fifteen hundred corporations. In its second annual report, CDE pointed out:

> Most of the groups were looking for new levers to increase pressure on a corporation to alter specific policies. They often needed a list of company-affiliated targets that local and regional groups could actively challenge to raise the visibility of their

campaign and enlist the support of new forces. For example, a CDE list of the principal stockholders of a company includes institutions located throughout the country. With this information, an organization can ask a group in another part of the country to join the campaign by contacting major local shareholders. We increasingly found ourselves not just supplying this type of data but also offering suggestions on how to actively apply it, based on our knowledge of other people's experience.[35]

CDE published stock-ownership directories covering seven major areas—transportation, agribusiness, banking and finance, energy, defense, communications, and health care—and another one on the Fortune 500 corporations. Invariably, CDE's findings jibed with the Marxist ideological tenets that propel the anticorporate movement, namely, that capitalism is inherently unjust because it concentrates wealth in and is controlled by the few.

CDE has serviced every major public-interest group in the anticorporate network, including the Council on Economic Priorities, the Interfaith Center on Corporate Responsibility, the Transnational Institute, Counter-Information Services, the Institute for Food and Development Policy, the Interreligious Taskforce on U.S. Food Policy, the Institute for Southern Studies, INFACT, the World Council of Churches' Project on Transnational Corporations, and Ralph Nader's ganglia of lobbyists.[36]

The Amalgamated Clothing and Textile Workers used CDE information to carry out its struggle to unionize J. P. Stevens Textile Corporation, mobilizing pension holders, depositors, and insurance policyholders in a coordinated nationwide campaign to isolate J. P. Stevens from its financial network.[37] The textile giant gave in. Much of the grassroots pressure behind the campaign was organized by the Institute for Southern Studies, the IPS spinoff founded in 1970.[38]

The campaign to prohibit infant-formula marketing in the third world was largely spearheaded by ICCR and relied heavily on the Corporate Data Exchange. CDE profiles, identifying over two hundred major institutional stockholders and supporters of the infant-formula industry—banks, insurance companies, mutual funds, educational endowments—were used by ICCR and religious activists to mobilize nationwide protest against third-world distribution of infant formula.[39]

CDE has also devoted a large part of its resources to servicing the political movement against South Africa. Identifying key stockholders of multinationals doing business in South Africa, CDE has been a major contributor to divestment and the isolation of South Africa.

IPS Launches Its International Anticorporate Campaign, the Transnational Institute and Information Exchange

As Richard Barnet was writing *Global Reach,* IPS's backers prepared to launch an unprecedented international campaign against multinational corporations, to be carried out through a new international arm of IPS. Geneva was first considered an appropriate site because the United Nations was located there. But the IPS trustees settled on the permissive political environment of Holland, the home of Europe's largest commercial trading center (Rotterdam) and the headquarters for several of the world's largest multinationals, such as Royal Dutch Shell and Philips Electronics.

In 1973 the Janss Foundation provided the necessary funds (270,000 guilders) to buy the building, located at 20 Paulus Potterstraat, Amsterdam, and IPS launched its ambitious international project, appropriately named the Transnational Institute (TNI)[40]

TNI amassed data on European-based corporations and joined with various unions and research/action groups to force change in targeted businesses. TNI's corporate profiles raised questions in the minds of many dealing with terrorism and internal security. Did European terrorist groups like the Baader-Meinhoff gang, the Red Army Faction, and the Italian Red Brigades use such profiles to identify corporate executives and their families for kidnapings and extortions?

The first director of TNI was Eqbal Ahmad—a Pakistani indicted (and acquitted) in 1971 for conspiring to kidnap Henry Kissinger and blow up federal building heating systems,[41] and a supporter of Qaddafi, the PLO, and other such Arab radicals—which did nothing to assuage suspicions. During TNI's formation, Ahmad announced to the press that he welcomed anyone who wanted to wage war against imperialism.[42] In March 1976 Orlando Letelier became director of TNI. Following his assassination six months later, Basker Vashee, a native of Rhodesia who was a member of the national executive of the Marxist ZAPU, became the third director. Vashee, with a past as dubious as those of his predecessors, had been imprisoned in Rhodesia, and had finally been deported by that government in 1966.[43]

Through its headquarters in Amsterdam, TNI draws on Counter-Information Services in London and IPS in Washington. In 1978 TNI and the World Council of Churches founded the Transnational Information Exchange (TIE), which by 1982 had sprouted into a network of some forty action/research groups and workers' organizations—trade unions, shop stewards' committees, third-world groups, church organizations, labor research centers, and some local government economic planning departments.[44] Today TIE spans the globe, with some one hundred thirty affiliates located throughout Europe, Latin America, and Asia, as well as in Australia and New Zealand.[45] (See Appendix 9 for an overview of TIE's European member organizations.)

New Iron Triangle

Much of IPS/TNI's anticorporate energies are consumed in getting the media to depict corporations as irresponsible toward workers, consumers, and the environment. This harmonizes with the New Class interests in the government's regulatory agencies—Environmental Protection Agency (EPA), Nuclear Regulatory Commission (NRC), Occupational Safety and Health Agency (OSHA), Consumer Product Safety Commission (CPSC)—agencies that look less to performance than to finding potential legal liabilities for the products and industries they are out to regulate.

Unlike the old regulatory agencies—Interstate Commerce Commission (ICC), Federal Communications Commission (FCC), Civil Aeronautics Board (CAB)—which supervised the rates and entry requirements of certain industries, the new regulatory agencies are often adversaries of the interests they regulate. EPA, NRC, OSHA, and CPSC, fueled by the public-interest movement and the media, form what has been referred to as a "new iron triangle."[46]

When *Mother Jones*, the IPS glossy monthly journal, came out with the cover story "The Illusion of Safety," it pictured an obviously distressed-looking housewife carrying a bag of products home from the store. The message could hardly be missed: the regulating agencies are failing to protect the consumer from corporations that willfully endanger the public. After asserting that "our entire regulatory structure is so corporate-dominated, so riddled with incompetence and corruption that it almost completely fails to protect the American people,"[47] the article predictably concluded that "the bright side is this: Dismantling the old structure offers us a golden opportunity to build a new one."[48] The following month, *Mother Jones* recommended: "Bring the entire process of setting safety standards into the public sector and make all safety standards mandatory," and "consolidate all government safety functions in one new cabinet-level office, the Department of Public Safety."[49]

As noted previously, IPS helped launch a whole range of alternative journals that often hounded corporations. By sapping faith in private enterprise, the IPS and the public-interest movement spur the bureaucratic regulatory apparatus to crack down on alleged corporate impropriety. And as these trends damage the performance of many industries, public-sector solutions and planning become more attractive. At the very least, as modern experience demonstrates, regulatory bureaucracies are difficult, perhaps impossible, to eliminate once created.

Glitching High Tech

IPS and TNI have also targeted specific industries. For instance, IPS fellow John Cavanagh, author of *The World in Their Web: The Dynamics of Transnational Fiber and Allied Textile Oligopolies*, writes in Ralph Nader's *Multinational Monitor*:

[W]orkers in both underdeveloped and developed countries also pay a high price for the policies of multinational textile and apparel firms. These firms depend upon and enforce appalling working conditions, long hours, and brutal suppression of what are usually considered trade union rights (such as the right to strike). In developed-country textile and apparel industries, workers face a bleak and uncertain future as their employers liquidate jobs in favor of machines and the lucrative offerings of Third World free trade zones.[50]

In Nader's *Multinational Monitor,* IPS fellow Michael Goldhaber argues against "corporate control of high tech, especially in communications," because it "can often mean cultural domination by developed countries, especially when technology like microelectronics or computer software replaces local methods of communication or indigenous knowledge."[51]

Jeremy Rifkin told an IPS seminar in April 1984 that short of all sorts of new regulations, the biotech industry's research and development should be curtailed because potential risks outweigh the benefits.[52] And in June 1984 IPS fellow Susan George told a TNI conference (its theme was "Meeting the Corporate Challenge") that "the biotech industry should be state-owned" because the funds used for research have come from taxes and excess profits.[53]

But try as it will, IPS has found it difficult to convince. It is, after all, hard to deny that employment has expanded as the high-tech industries fill the void left by the declining smokestack industries. Nonetheless, IPS seems always determined to brandish the negative side, to play on fears for political purposes.

Michael Goldhaber and John Cavanagh lament that "for the present, technology remains firmly in the hands of the multinationals."[54] The solution? Goldhaber doesn't really have one, but he recommends that the public-interest movement take time to regroup. "What is increasingly clear," he points out, "is that these challenges must move beyond simply softening the impact of the new technologies. Instead, they must address the centers of control and decision-making—the multinationals and governments themselves."[55] In other words, high tech is secondary; the real enemy is the American economic and political system.

While the search for a new strategy continues, the institute and its various associates continue their anticorporate activities in four major areas: (1) business operations in South Africa, (2) agribusiness, (3) pesticides and toxic wastes, (4) the nuclear industry.

Marching on Pretoria

The divestment of the assets of American companies from the Republic of South Africa is a tailor-made *cause célèbre*. The issue appears, literally, to be black and white. A white minority, incapable of change, represses a black majority. American direct investment, $2.3 billion, though only 1.5 percent of the foreign investment in the republic, assists the repressive regime. Once again, the U.S. corporations are on the "wrong side of history."

Opponents of divestment say that foreign investment contributes to the dissolution of apartheid by providing opportunities for blacks and nonwhites to improve their lot economically and thus acquire political power as labor union members, entrepreneurs, and consumers. Although there are no easy answers, the problem is best understood by dispassionately evaluating the matter.

There is little doubt that divestment, if it results in terminating businesses, would contribute to black unemployment, and thus add to social turmoil. And any condition that encourages revolution is fair game for the Soviet Union, which has well-armed surrogates in the region. Marxist governments in Angola and Mozambique and the Soviet-backed liberation movements—South West African Peoples' Organization (SWAPO) and the African National Congress (ANC)—dim the prospects for democracy and human rights should revolution sweep South Africa.

There is also the prospect that justice and equity can be won by South Africans through peaceful means. Even if the South African government remains intransigent, multinational corporations can provide a "major agent of liberalization." Unlike politicians whose flexibility is limited by the desire to preserve power and the necessity to balance conflicting interests, pragmatic businessmen understand that the best guarantee of political stability, the necessary condition for long-term economic prosperity, is equal political and economic opportunity and the incentives of upward mobility.

Since 1977 nearly one hundred forty of the three hundred fifty U.S. companies doing business in South Africa have voluntarily implemented a code of conduct called the Sullivan Principles; the code requires desegregation, fair employment practices, equal pay for equal work, job training for advancement, and promotion of nonwhites to management and supervisory positions. Today 70 percent of U.S.–employed South African blacks work under the Sullivan Principles. Progress has been made. Yet IPS associates have done their best to discredit the Sullivan Principles and promote divestment. Indeed, they make no secret of their desire to "break the corporate links" and isolate South Africa from the West.

In the early 1970s, under the directorship of Peter Weiss, the current IPS chairman of the board, the American Committee on Africa (ACOA) began to protest U.S. business ventures in South Africa, and to promote African "liberation" movements, such as the African National Congress (ANC). ACOA was the first organization to bring ANC members to the United States to meet with various radical black activists.[56] In 1980 IPS sponsored Ruth First, a Communist party member and leader of the ANC, to participate in one its Samuel Rubin seminars.[57]

Ruth First was the wife of Joseph Slovo, head of ANC's military forces and the number two man in charge of KGB operations directed at destabilizing South

Africa.[58] Although the *Washington Post* did not identify Slovo's KGB status, it did report in a feature article of July 14, 1985, that he and his wife "helped reconstruct the underground network and cement close ties between the ANC and the Soviet bloc that gradually brought the movement the weapons and training it needed to launch a new sabotage campaign inside South Africa."[59] Slovo told the *Post*—the first interview ever with a Western news organization—that "he has been involved in planning the various bombings of government buildings and strategic installations that have killed more than two dozen persons and shaken South Africa over the last five years."[60] Said the *Post*, "Slovo clings to the idea that a single, well-placed spark—a police murder in Soweto on a hot weekend, for example—could set off the final conflagration."[61] Of Ruth First, the *Post* reported that "there is not a single important decision of the movement in the last 30 years that doesn't bear her imprint in some way."[62]

Timothy Smith, the director of the Interfaith Center on Corporate Responsibility, worked with ACOA and its sister organization, the South African Committee, as did Prexy Nesbitt, an IPS associate fellow and the secretary/treasurer of the WCC Program to Combat Racism.[63] Nesbitt endorses the Marxist liberation movements of ANC and SWAPO, as well as the communist regime in Angola installed and maintained by Cuba and the Soviet Union. And he helped fund them from the coffers of the World Council of Churches.[64]

Another important divestment group, the Campaign to Oppose Bank Loans to South Africa, was headed by IPS associate fellow Carole Collins, who operated the Washington end of the campaign out of IPS until 1983. Collins helped grassroots lobbying efforts, shifting the divestment campaign from the national level to state and local levels, and testifying before state legislatures and city councils throughout the country. Writing in *In These Times,* Collins said that "the divestment movment has achieved more in the past twelve months than in the previous twelve years. One could say it has developed its own brand of 'New Federalism,' by . . . taking its case directly to states, counties and cities."[65]

Since the 1976 Soweto uprising, IPS has generated much of the literature aimed at isolating South Africa. Through its subsidiary, Counter-Information Services, in London, IPS put out *Black South Africa Explodes* (1977) and *Buying Time in South Africa* (1978). In 1979 IPS published *South Africa: Foreign Investment and Apartheid,* and in 1980, *Decoding Corporate Camouflage* by Elizabeth Schmidt, which alleges that "the Sullivan Principles" were "a flimsy camouflage to disguise corporate collaboration with the apartheid regime,"[66] and suggests that violent revolution is the only recourse for South Africa.

For his part, IPS senior fellow Roger Wilkins helped organize the waves of demonstration outside the South African embassy that brought TV news coverage night after night, and helped pressure Congress to pass an economic sanctions bill.

Bitter Harvest—The Campaign Against Agribusiness

IPS has done its best to discredit and undermine transnational agribusiness—"a new form of imperialism, an extension of corporate capitalism"—even though third-world countries, barely able to scratch out a living, can greatly benefit from the agricultural technology that multinationals have to offer.

Richard Barnet's book *Global Reach: The Power of the Multinational Corporations* depicted multinationals as being little more than imperialistic exploiters. Moreover, the book was a catalyst for new spinoff projects, such as the Institute for Food and Development Policy (IFDP) founded by IPS fellow Joseph Collins. IFDP's first project was to put out another book, *Food First: Beyond the Myth of Scarcity,* in which Collins pursued themes he had started while doing research for Barnet's *Global Reach.*

Food First is one of the more clever undertakings of IPS fellows. Because Joe Collins was relatively unknown outside the Left, he enlisted Frances Moore Lappé as his coauthor, capitalizing on her fame from her enormously successful natural-food cookbook, *Diet for a Small Planet.* The difference between the books? The diet book is apolitical. *Food First* is subtly, yet strongly, political, as summed up in its concluding pages, with their straightforward Marxist analysis:

> The struggle is against a system that increasingly concentrates wealth and power. The struggle is against a system profiting on hunger in the Philippines or Brazil just as it is in the United States. The real forces creating hunger span almost all nations in the world. . . . The tragedy is that we have had to reach the point where so many people are hungry and malnourished, including millions here at home, before we could begin to see that our system . . . can never create a humane society.[67]

Hunger—an issue which transcends party politics—is an ideal vehicle to mobilize well-meaning, guilt-ridden Americans. And IFDP does this ingeniously, using hunger as a two-edged sword: Americans should not only feel guilty and donate to IFDP, but also fight against an economic system that, they are told, perpetuates hunger. Off in the wing bides the Marxist alternative.

IFDP charges that multinational corporations are cheating Americans and keeping the rest of the world hungry. All this, IFDP says, "is being cleverly concealed by multinational food conglomerates."[68] And like most all the other organizations in the IPS network, IFDP conceals its socialist agenda by using "popular" jargon. For instance, in its 1983 annual report, IFDP says that it is "dedicated to the premise that there is no true democracy without economic democracy."[69] Economic democracy is a euphemism for the socialist policies of a planned economy, a system with little appeal to most Americans.

Indeed, Collins and Lappé wax romantic about policies in communist countries. Extolling "the actual experience of land reform in countries as different as Vietnam, China, and Cuba," the duo venture that "rather than leading to a drop in production, genuine land reform can be a first step in long-term production advances."[70] In a concluding section of *Food First*, captioned "Make America Safe for the World," Collins and Lappé recommend terminating U.S. aid and loans for private-sector development abroad and giving unrestricted grants to communist governments.[71] At home IFDP advocates an ambitious socialist agenda, couched in seemingly innocuous rhetoric. *Food First* urges the reader to "opt out of the 'food only for profit' system that creates scarcity . . . , work for land reform in the United States, including a ceiling on the amount of land one person or one family can hold . . . , prohibit corporations with significant nonfarm investment from entering agricultural investment . . . , and work to limit the influence of media advertising by a handful of food corporations. . . ."[72]

The fact that IFDP publications are translated into twenty languages and that Marxist governments look to it for assistance betrays its international influence.[73] According to IFDP's 1984 annual report, "In a rare move, eight Cuban ministries and government institutes, as well as the offices of Vice-President Carlos Rafael Rodriguez and President Fidel Castro, have cooperated with the Institute's study."[74] In describing Project Nicaragua, an IFDP funding proposal says that "the Nicaraguan government requested the Institute's help in 1979," and "since that time Joseph Collins, with the assistance of other staff members, has acted as an unpaid advisor on food and agriculture policies in Nicaragua."[75]

In 1983 IFDP published two books praising the accomplishments of the Sandinista revolution, *What Difference Could a Revolution Make?* by Joseph Collins and *Now We Can Speak: A Journey Through the New Nicaragua* by Collins and Lappé. IFDP's promotional material notes, "The Nicaraguan Foreign Ministry was so impressed with these two books that it purchased 100 copies of each to distribute to the American press and members of Congress."[76] IFDP helped the Sandinista government found the Institute for Economic and Social Research (INIES), a research, documentation, and training center for Central America and the Caribbean located in Managua.[77] Collins also helped IPS found Policy Alternatives for the Caribbean and Central America, which in turn works with INIES to influence U.S. foreign policy toward Nicaragua.[78]

Poison Pens: Pesticides and the Toxic Waste Scare

Protesting pesticides and the agrochemical industries generally has become a major platform in the campaign against agribusiness. Similar to so many other issues taken up by the media, the pesticide and toxic waste scare has been greatly exacerbated by the alternative media. After an article on toxic wastes written by David Weir and Mark Schapiro appeared in *Mother Jones*, Collins and Lappé decided to plug the pesticide dumping scare to advance the anticorporate political cause. IFDP hired Weir and Schapiro to write a book, *Circle of Poison,* to elaborate on the theme they began in *Mother Jones.*

Circle of Poison turned out to be a general indictment of the chemical industry involved in the manufacture of pesticides. Weir and Schapiro's corporate conspiracy approach in *Circle of Poison* proved very effective. "While investigating pesticide dumping we have relearned a hard fact," Weir and Schapiro point out. "The problem is not simply unethical corporate executives; the solution is not simply exchanging them for more compassionate, socially responsible types. No, we have concluded that unless all of a society's important decisions—including economic decisions like the development and marketing of agricultural chemicals—are made more democratically, the majority will suffer."[79] By democratically, the authors mean through regulated public ownership. For "the answer is not to make the powerful more responsible, but to redistribute power."[80]

Applying their reasoning to the world situation, Weir and Schapiro state in the conclusion of their book:

> The reality of global corporate power, here reflected in the pesticide trade, forces us to seek solutions involving new ways of working with Third World people for a worldwide redistribution of economic power. We must begin to see Third World people not as a burden or threat, but as allies.[81]

Circle of Poison turned out to be a remarkably successful catalyst. IFDP's 1983 annual report notes that "we had little idea at the beginning of this year, when representatives of the Institute met with colleagues in Malaysia to form the Pesticide Action Network (PAN), that one year later PAN would have grown to include hundreds of active organizations in Africa, Asia, Europe, and both Latin and North America."[82] Mobilizing diverse and seemingly unrelated constituencies in support of a single issue, IFDP helped PAN-USA became a coalition of some fifty church, environmental, labor, farmworker, and consumer organizations.[83]

IPS's Transnational Information Exchange sponsored the Agrochemicals Conference in March 1983, which drew trade unionists, agribusiness researchers, and third-world activists from seven countries. The feature article in the *TIE-Europe Bulletin,* devoted to that conference and other aspects of the agrochemical industry, charged that "unemployment among farm workers, health hazards from pesticide use, and increasing food prices can all be partly traced to the activities of chemical companies."[84] Then the real object surfaced: "Fundamentally we can see the problems associated with agrochemicals as inevitable consequences of an international economic system geared towards the accumulation of private profit. Strategies which expose and explore ways of breaking down the injustices and contradictions of this system must therefore also be international in perspective and scope."[85]

IPS's Government Accountability Project (GAP) joined the toxic waste scare in 1982, and claimed credit for uncovering "that Dow Chemical Company *lied*" about two major styrene spills in Midland, Michigan, its disposal of dioxin and agent orange, and its knowledge about adverse health effects associated with dioxin.[86] GAP's annual report for fiscal 1982 and 1983 states that "GAP's investigations led to national coverage by the *New York Times*, NBC, CBS, ABC, Jack Anderson's television show, and the *Washington Post*."[87]

"Because the problems are so massive," says GAP executive director Louis Clark, "I expect that we'll be there [Midland] for years."[88] Commenting that "the EPA doesn't have the resources to monitor effectively enough," and that "the problems are so massive that the EPA couldn't begin to deal with it," Clark believes that GAP's efforts will result in an "expansion of the regulatory agencies." As a matter of fact, "we hope to work with the bureaucracy along the way. There are a lot of really good people there [at the regulatory agencies]," says Clark.[89]

GAP hopes to make Midland a model case. "Midland is a good example of how we work at GAP," says Clark. "The real key to GAP's success is that we bring local citizen groups . . . together with responsible government officials and national public interest groups, and create a coalition to which the government has to listen."[90]

"Past efforts to solve problems which were made by the industries and the government regulatory agencies are no longer going to be an effective model," says Clark. "In the future, regulation of industries is going to have to take into account the fears, needs, and desires of the community."[91] Industries will then have to deal with the antibusiness activists, like those at GAP, who will speak in the name of the people.

Melting Down the Nuclear Power Industry

IPS's most successful assault on corporate power has been against the nuclear industry, against which the institute has generated both antinuclear studies directed by fellow Mark Hertsgaard and a remarkably effective activist program run by GAP.

In so doing, IPS has also played a key role in building the antinuclear network, helping groups such as the Nuclear Information and Resource Service (NIRS), whose five-member board of directors includes Hertsgaard and IPS trustee Stanley Weiss; *Nuclear Times*, whose board of directors includes Adam Hochschild, a contributing editor of *Mother Jones* and director of the IPS-created Foundation for National Progress; and the World Information Service on Energy (WISE), the Transnational Institute affiliate based in Amsterdam. Like GAP, these groups are committed to dismantling, not reforming, the nuclear industry. "It is not possible to reform an industry which is inherently dangerous and threatening to mankind," said one WISE spokesman.[92] The NIRS annual report for 1982 says that its "imperative" is "to hasten the decline of the nuclear industry."[93] The executive director of NIRS, Betsy Taylor, candidly admitted that "GAP is the leading nuclear legal group in the country."[94]

The scope of GAP's efforts and victories, recounted in its annual reports, includes:

—halting construction at the Zimmer nuclear power plant when it was 97% completed, and forcing Cincinnati Gas and Electric to convert it to a coal fired plant, at a total cost of over $500 million

—halting all construction at the Midland Nuclear Power Plant in Midland, Michigan

—claiming that Bechtel and the utilities mismanaged the entire cleanup operation at Three Mile Island (TMI) nuclear power plant, which resulted in halting the TMI cleanup pending the completion of top to bottom NRC review and the transfer of the two top officials in charge

—alleging that an Arizona utility had submitted a falsified environmental impact statement before it began construction of the Palo Verde nuclear power plant, and subsequently delaying construction and forcing costs higher

—holding up construction at the San Onofre nuclear power plant in California and forcing the NRC to pay $200,000 to check thousands of allegedly faulty welds

—holding up construction at Diablo Canyon and forcing the NRC to devote $18,000 in staff hours to examining faulty construction charges

—holding up construction and/or licensing at Catawba Nuclear Power Plant in North Carolina, Commanche Peak in Texas, Callaway in Missouri, LaSalle and Braidwood in Illinois, and Waterford in Louisiana[95]

GAP's concern for safety, corruption, and fraud appears noble, but its ambitions go well beyond environmental protection. In the conclusion of an internal report, prepared to solicit funding, GAP suggested that its real goal is to halt and dismantle, rather than reform, the nuclear industry: "The 1982–1983 fiscal year was an amazing one," the report begins. "In the year when public interest advocacy was at a low ebb, we at GAP were able to halt construction at two nuclear power plants, keep another one from starting up . . . stop TMI's cleanup operation, and push out the top management at TMI and the Zimmer Nuclear Power Plant. . . ."[96]

GAP's campaign against the nuclear power industry could not have enjoyed such success without the aid of other activist groups and, of course, the media. GAP has worked out a threefold strategy: (1) locating potential "whistleblowers" and allies among the workforce, particularly the disgruntled who may have been fired from power plant construction; (2) working with and helping organize the local antinuclear grassroots efforts against the industry or starting up community action where none previously existed; and (3) fomenting dissension between industry officials, the safety and regulatory agencies, and the community itself. In playing off one side against another, GAP has appeared as being all things to all parties: championing the cause of the worker, the community, the environment—specifically, "the public interest." Moreover, GAP has been remarkably good at winning the confidence of the unsuspecting by providing free legal counsel, a sort of "whistleblowers' protection plan."

The basic strategy of IPS and the antinuclear activists has been "to work both sides of the street," creating scandals by manipulating the disgruntled and the community while at the same time pressing the Nuclear Regulatory Commission to intervene in new ways.

The campaign against nuclear power, of course, hinges on enlisting help from the media. GAP has found it easy to appeal to the media on nuclear power, because of their limitless credulity regarding sensational and emotional issues. Local media are crucial in arousing the public and politicians and forcing the NRC to intervene. Typically, GAP comes up with charges—slipshod workmanship, construction shortcuts, mismanagement, or fraud—which it easily funnels to the media. To answer brand new charges, often at the eleventh hour—just before licensing and preliminary testing and startup—the utilities are forced to undergo an excruciating investigation, which may require them to pay up to $1 million a day in additional interest charges. In holding up plant construction through legal technicalities and delaying tactics, GAP portrays nuclear power as uneconomical because of cost overruns. What GAP conveniently neglects to mention is that GAP itself has been one of the major contributors to the cost overruns—running into hundreds of millions of dollars—that have brought nuclear energy to a standstill in the United States.

Despite the scientific community's strong support for nuclear energy development, the major media have fallen for the sensationalism generated by the antinuclear activists. Conducting a survey to determine why media attitudes and the scientific community's opinions about the peaceful use of nuclear energy so diverge, Stanley Rothman and Robert Lichter found a direct correlation between attitudes toward nuclear energy and political ideology.[97] It is not surprising then that GAP claims, in its annual report, that its efforts precipitated "in depth media coverage of Zimmer by ABC and CBS, national T.V. news, a feature article and a series of articles by Gannett, Scripps-Howard, *Wall Street Journal*, *Cleveland Plain Dealer*, *Dayton Daily News*, *Newsday*, [and] the *Philadelphia Inquirer*."[98]

Conclusion

The professional revolutionaries of today emerged from the street demonstrators of the "protest culture" of the sixties and seventies. IPS fellows Michael

Klare, Lee Webb, and Len Rodberg were instrumental in developing sophisticated power structure research which enabled the movement to go from the street to the corporate boardrooms.

After the Vietnam War, the anticorporate movement gained legitimacy by taking on a new face and calling itself the public interest. And by working with the establishment, anticorporate radicals have made more progress that they did in all their violent protests in the late sixties and early seventies. They have managed to expand the governmental regulatory apparatus, and some have found employment in agencies such as EPA and OSHA.

The term "public interest" is a misnomer; the movement is elitist, not populist. Spokesmen for the public-interest movement, such as Richard Barnet and Ralph Nader, are way out of touch with the American people, whose common sense understands that the benefits of corporate capitalism outweigh the failings. Moreover, the majority of Americans do not embrace the socialist alternative, which is the hidden agenda of IPS and many in the public interest movement.

On the international level, the Transnational Information Exchange is one of IPS's most ambitious undertakings. TIE attacks the "weakest link" in the corporate chain, such as business in South Africa, nuclear power development, agribusiness, and the pesticide-chemical industries. This could have far-reaching geopolitical consequences, particularly on Western energy and strategic needs vis-à-vis those of the Soviet Union.[99]

To complement their efforts against the corporation, IPS fellows have developed and sought to implement a socialist alternative, which they euphemistically call economic democracy. Associate fellows Derek Shearer and Martin Carnoy assert that "dismantling, or at least restricting, the power of these corporations," because "they are the antithesis of democracy," is only the beginning.[100] "It is essential . . . over the next two decades," they say, "to build a mass political movement on the basis of a program such as ours and to win a majority of local, state, and national governing bodies."[101] This program, already established in many localities across the United States, is examined in the next chapter.

CHAPTER 12

IPS and Economic Democracy
Socialist Revolution in Stages

In the 1960s the American Left advocated revolution and militant confrontation. But when it became apparent that the proletariat had no intention of rising, the Left switched to a revolution-in-stages strategy. This amounted to making the public sector the panacea for all modern woes. Under a new name, economic democracy, this revolution was launched at the level of local government.

Appealing as it sounds, "economic democracy" implies the restructuring of American society according to a Marxist model. To rally the people behind them, the collectivists have handed out doses of paranoia through the media, alleging that corporations cause all manner of ills. Indeed, increasingly, hardly a day passes without a report of some new crisis endangering our health, a crisis caused by some corporate enterprise. To counteract the large, evil corporations, the 1980s radicals intend to use the public sector—armed with the powers of regulation, taxation, and eminent domain—to control the economy by driving certain industries under and forcing redistribution and "public control" in the name of the people.

A *New York Times* op-ed article, "Taking over America" (June 1, 1979), by Rep. John Conyers, Jr. (D–Mich.) and Marcus Raskin signaled the new thrust: "Government's responsibility is to revitalize the nation's economy through creative forms of public ownership."[1] The economic-democracy movement gets its leaders from IPS and its progeny: Gar Alperovitz, founder of the tax-exempt

190

Exploratory Project on Economic Alternatives, the National Center for Economic Alternatives (a national planning and policy research center), and its political lobbying arm, the Alliance to Rebuild America, was one of the eight founders of IPS; Lee Webb, formerly a top SDS leader, now an IPS trustee, organized the only national network of left-wing state and local government officials, the Conference on Alternative State and Local Public Policies (CASLP), as an IPS project; and IPS associate fellow Derek Shearer, CASLP cofounder and author of seminal works such as *Economic Democracy* and *A New Social Contract,* is also a leader in left-wing political organizations in California, such as the Tom Hayden–Jane Fonda Campaign for Economic Democracy, and a professor of urban planning at UCLA.

IPS itself is the headquarters for the Planners Network, directed by fellow Chester Hartman, which is described as "an association of professionals, activists, academics, and students involved in physical, social, economic, and environmental planning in urban and rural areas, who promote fundamental change in our political and economic system."[2] Stating that "we oppose the economic structure of our society, which values profit and property rights over human rights and needs [and] advocate public responsibility for meeting those needs, because the private market has proven incapable of doing so,"[3] Hartman's Planners Network makes it clear that radical socialist change, not reform, is the real prize.

Alperovitz has targeted four sectors of the economy for public control: food, housing, energy, and health care. The exponential tax increase necessary to do this in no way deters Alperovitz and his colleagues. For example, Chester Hartman developed a program for public housing supported by direct taxation to replace the private real estate business. Hartman's estimated cost, in 1986 dollars, would add at least $150 billion to the present budget deficit without a tax increase. This is all to the good, because, as Hartman says, his proposal, part of Marcus Raskin's 1978 study of the federal budget prepared at the request of fifty-six members of Congress, "would also further undermine the existing economic system."[4] Inevitably, investment would fall off: "thus the broader issues of public enterprise, economic planning, and control of the economy inevitably would have to be confronted."[5] Hartman did worry that the "elements of the program we have suggested might be picked up and adapted to help rationalize the [present] system, ease some social pressures, prop up the construction industry, bail out mortgage lenders and stave off financial collapse."[6] By implication, Hartman seems to favor financial collapse and the ruination of the U.S. market economy. It is easier to build the new social order on the ruins of the old.

Bringing down American capitalism characterizes economic democracy, as distinct from social democracy, where a welfare state is constructed on top of capitalism. Derek Shearer and Lee Webb wrote in the *Nation:*

The comprehensive economic reform program which we've described will inevitably be labeled socialistic. If socialism is defined as both a democratic government and a democratic economy, accountable to public representatives and not to a rich and powerful elite, then this is democratic socialism.[7]

A Seminal Event

In 1973 IPS organized "the decade's first conference on alternative economic policy from a leftist perspective," according to IPS fellows Derek Shearer and Martin Carnoy in their 1980 manifesto, *Economic Democracy*.[8] The participants included Lee Webb, founder of CASLP; Ed Kirshner, a Berkeley radical who would write *The Cities' Wealth*, a blueprint for power to the people through local government (published and distributed by Webb's organization); Richard Kaufman, an IPS lecturer and assistant director and general counsel of the congressional Joint Economic Committee; Howard Wachtel, professor of economics, American University; Vic Reinemer, assistant to Sen. Lee Metcalf; Chester Hartman, author of a rent-freeze proposal for San Francisco and later an IPS fellow; Bertram Gross, who presented the conference with an outline for a full-employment bill which he had drafted for the Congressional Black Caucus, written into law in 1978 as the Humphrey-Hawkins Full Employment Act;[9] Barry Bluestone and Bennett Harrison, who are cited ad infinitum in Shearer's works and whose books are promoted by CASLP and IPS; and Gar Alperovitz and Jeff Faux, who afterward formed the Exploratory Project on Economic Alternatives.[10] Papers presented at the 1973 IPS conference later appeared as articles in *Working Papers for a New Society*, a journal started by the Cambridge Institute, an IPS spinoff.

IPS continued to work both with the original conferees and on its own domestic policy projects. For example, Len Rodberg and Bluestone contributed chapters to Marcus Raskin's November 1975 budget study, prepared at the request of several members of the House led by John Conyers. Raskin's 1978 budget study included chapters by Bluestone, Hartman, Wachtel, and Shearer. IPS also conducts ongoing projects in each of Alperovitz's strategic sectors—energy, housing, food, and health care.

In lieu of analyzing the entire scope of the economic-democracy agenda, this chapter will focus on the activities and works of four of the most influential theoreticians: Derek Shearer, Martin Carnoy, Gar Alperovitz, and Lee Webb, all associated with IPS. But first a look at the roots of economic democracy aptly expressed by IPS associate fellow Sidney Lens.

Sidney Lens, Unrepentant Radical

Lens explains IPS's battle for public enterprise in America as a "revolution-in-stages" strategy, the seeds of which can be traced to a philosophy evolved from early communist movements in the U.S. It subtly reemerged in the Democratic party—for the first time since the New Deal—in the campaigns of George McGovern and, even more, Jesse Jackson, whose top advisers included Richard Barnet, Marcus Raskin, Robert Borosage and Roger Wilkins—all from IPS.

In 1934 Sidney Lens, long-time activist of the Old Left, joined the Communist League of America, a Trotskyist organization now called the Socialist Workers party.[11] Lens later joined various Marxist groups, including the Workers party and the Revolutionary Workers League, during the tumult of the 1940s.[12] He seems to have removed himself from the organized Left at some point during the 1950s, and gradually to have become convinced that the American revolution would come about in stages by a decentralized coalition rather than by a revolutionary vanguard with a centralized authority, which has generally been an article of faith of the communists.[13]

After a period of relative political inactivity, Lens surfaced in the 1960s peace movement. In 1980 he wrote, "I'm as convinced today as I was in the early 1930s that social revolution is both desirable and all but inevitable."[14] A selection from *Unrepentant Radical*, Lens's autobiography, suggests that the New Left of today is the most promising progeny of the communist movement of the 1930s. He recalls:

> At a meeting and concert of 3,000 people in Madison, Wisconsin, during July 1979, called to protest banning a planned *Progressive* article by Howard Morland on secrecy,* George Wald scanned the crowd silently for a moment, and said slowly: "I think I see a movement again.". . . One can hear it at every rally when someone cries out "no nukes." The trauma of the 1970s, unless I'm mistaken, almost surely will lead to a new New Left in the 1980s. For it is clear that humanity cannot solve its economic problems within this system of capitalism, nor can it prevent a nuclear holocaust. . . . [Capitalism] must give way in the end to a system that is international in character, that divides income and wealth equitably, that plans the conservation and utilization of dwindling resources . . . the struggle against nuclear war is a social revolution in itself. Neither capitalism nor the *present forms* of communism (nationally oriented as they are) can survive the nuclear age.[15] [Emphasis added.]

IPS fellows and most of their offspring endorse an agenda parallel to Lens's strategy for a revolutionary domestic policy. That program, which appears in *Unrepentant Radical*, includes public acquisition of corporations, national indicator planning, nationalization of banks, oil companies, and utilities, a national environmental-ecological plan, and "a dozen forms of neighborhood and regional control of political leaders."[16]

Lens is still waiting for his revolution. He blames the debacle of the 1930s

---

*The subject of Howard Morland's *Progressive* article on secrecy was the publication of the plans of how to build an atomic bomb. The crowd gathered to support publication.

and 1940s on the centralized nature of leftist parties—"borrowed from czarist Russia," not Marxism-Leninism—which blocked any original thinking in the American socialist movement. "Today's socialists must design an organizational form suited to the United States of America—loose and populist. And they must formulate a political program that is at least partially realizable in the near future."[17]

He scoffs at the current economic recovery, and says that in the future millions of people will "become amenable to ideas for basic social change." How?

> At this point no one can describe the exact contours of that change or the precise methods to achieve it, but we can describe many measures toward that end—what might be called a revolution in stages. . . . For instance, it might be possible to mobilize large numbers of Americans to support public ownership of banks and credit institutions, and of the steel and other smokestack industries. A program for government-sponsored jobs could certainly win a constituency. . . . These steps do not constitute a socialist program per se, but they are *part* of a socialist program, and they can be made acceptable to many millions of people.[18]

Lee Webb and the Conference on Alternative State and Local Policies

Lee Webb founded the Conference on Alternative State and Local Public Policies (CASLP), a spinoff project of IPS, as "the only national progressive organization that focuses exclusively on problems faced by state and local governments." An IPS brochure said it was "to strengthen the programmatic work of the Left . . . to enlarge the base committed to policies for a restructured America."

Webb enjoyed the privileges of affluence in private schools and at Harvard and Boston University. In 1963 he became SDS national chairman, and under his leadership SDS chapters increased from ten to one hundred twenty-five in a single year.[19] He served as Washington editor of *Ramparts* and as Washington bureau chief for the *Guardian,* a radical weekly.[20] After receiving his doctorate in economics, he taught economics at Goddard College in Vermont and served as a consultant on energy matters to Sen. Lee Metcalf (D–Mont.).

Before founding the conference, Webb spent considerable effort expounding upon the emerging American police state, providing the Left with intellectual ammunition with which to back up its charges of state repression. "The Vietnamization of the United States is already quite advanced," he wrote in a National Action/Research on the Military-Industrial Complex (NARMIC) study, which received much attention by the Left. "The coordinated national attempt to extinguish the Black Panther Party bears more than a passing resemblance to the CIA Operation Phoenix in Vietnam. . . ."[21]

To Webb, New York City's installation of a central command post to control civil disorders signified the dawn of Orwell's 1984 in America.[22] Webb's founding of the conference only four years after he had identified with the Black Panther party and the Vietcong suggests that he may have rejected violent strategies because they were ineffective. Despite his departure from SDS in 1966 and his credentialed respectability, Webb remains committed to revolutionary socialist change.

The economic-democracy movement has tried to camouflage its origins in violent radicalism. Notwithstanding the movement's roots, it is the ideas of economic democracy themselves that must provide the basis of judgment.

Webb was forced out of the SDS in 1966 during clashes over tactical questions. Some SDS members, like Kathy Boudin, Bernadine Dohrn, and Mike Klonsky, deluded by the prospects of imminent revolution, began to bomb buildings, hoping to incite the proletariat to violent struggle. But others read the handwriting on the wall: The workers were not about to rise. When this became clear, community organizing tactics—door to door, block by block—began to dominate the Left's strategic thinking. Instead of a centralized, disciplined revolutionary organization, neighborhood coalitions were formed which coalesced into statewide coalitions. Webb's conference provided the structure linking them all into national networks, which in time would begin to work within the Democratic party. Years later, this would manifest itself in Jesse Jackson's "Rainbow Coalition."

The conference was founded in 1975 as an IPS project. Martin Carnoy and Derek Shearer have described its beginnings:

In 1974, the Institute for Policy Studies in Washington realized that many 1960s activists were running for and winning public office at the state and local levels. It seemed that substantial political change could occur only if a base of support could be built in local communities where people actually live and work, not in Washington, a town of bureaucrats and lobbyists. A network was formed called the National Conference on Alternative State and Local Public Policy, which publishes a regular newsletter, produces readers on public policy and model legislation, and sponsors annual gatherings where progressive public officials, community organizers, and labor leaders meet to exchange experience and discuss political program [*sic*] and strategy. The conference provides a vital link for reform efforts in different cities and states.[23]

Even back in 1975, when the newly formed conference was ostensibly concerned with local problems, Shearer and Webb dreamed of huge federal holding companies; in fact, they had already picked out a name, the American Enterprise Fund.[24] While most Americans were returning to their traditional suspicion of big government, Webb's passion for "the public," which he wholeheartedly identifies with government, knew no bounds. He and Shearer burned to market a "readable insurance policy, a long-lasting light bulb, or a compact, nonpolluting car,''[25] but they wanted to do it with the taxpayers' capital, far from the distressing disturbances of the marketplace.

Even more can be gleaned from Barbara Bick, the national coordinator of the conference. She was quoted in an interview with a sympathetic magazine as saying the conference was organized by Paul Soglin, an antiwar activist elected mayor of Madison, Wisconsin, who established a city-owned development corporation to help local cooperatives, worker-owned enterprises, and small business; Sam Brown, a leader in the moratorium and the McCarthy campaign in 1968, who was elected state treasurer of Colorado; and Robb Burlage, an IPS fellow who helped initiate the CASLP project. Webb and Burlage traveled the country with a grant from IPS "asking around for these who were populist, progressive, socialist, innovative, open-minded, locally-elected officials.''[26]

The conference was held in Madison. The isolation the Left felt had been acute, so the idea of a network met with enthusiasm. The conference decided to form a continuing organization to provide a forum in which progressives could exchange ideas. Barbara Bick, a former member of the Communist party, USA,[27] became national coordinator of the new organization, headquartered at IPS. She later said, "In many ways, my organizational model was Women Strike for Peace.''[28] Shearer and Webb edited a *Reader on Alternative Public Policies* incorporating the papers, model legislation, and articles contributed by the participants. The *Reader* proposed a sweeping agenda from self-government for prisoners to public ownership of cable, telephones, and utilities.[29] Webb also described sixteen ways for state and local governments to squeeze more money out of citizens.[30] A paper on energy ("Public Energy") was prepared by James Ridgeway and Bettina Conner, both IPS associate fellows who edited the *Elements,* a monthly concerned with energy policy. The authors noted that the plan for nationalization of the energy industry grew out of a seminar held at IPS in 1974.[31] IPS fellows Len Rodberg and Robb Burlage were also there.

Another Madison conferee was Ed Kirshner of the Berkeley-based Community Ownership Organizing Project (COOP), a coalition of "radicals, minorities, students and liberal Democrats working together for popular control of the local economy,''[32] and the "product of radical political activity in Berkeley dating from the late 1960s.''[33]

Kirshner, an Oakland planner and fellow of the Foundation for National Progress (IPS's West Coast arm, publisher of *Mother Jones*), and a participant in the seminal conference at IPS in 1973, wrote a history of COOP in 1976, *The Cities' Wealth: Programs for Community Economic Control in Berkeley, California.*[34] As Lee Webb wrote in the foreword, it was a resource "useful for activist officials, coalitions, and community groups who are struggling to redistribute the benefits of their own cities' resources." CASLP published and distributed *The Cities' Wealth,* and Derek Shearer referred to the book as providing a comprehensive blueprint for urban political action.

The book focused on the "techniques of economic and political policy which lead toward controlling and reallocating a city's wealth."[35] The authors wished to put city government in the front lines of the struggle, "as a feasible alternative to continued corporate dominance of the economy."[36]

The blueprint outlined in the book is not simply a program for reform; it would switch ownership of assets within city limits, with everything pointing to public ownership or control. Rent control, for example, on which more than one leftist coalition has come to power, is used not primarily to prevent landlords from gouging their tenants, but as a ploy to transfer property to the city by driving values down:

> Community ownership of housing and real estate is the ultimate goal of Coalition housing programs. That goal has been approached through tenant unions, rent control, a neighborhood preservation ordinance, rehabilitation and code enforcement programs, and cooperative ownership conversion. Each of these reforms is intended as an interim step towards cooperative and community-owned housing by limiting property speculation and thus deflating or partially expropriating income property values.[37]

Similarly, IPS's housing expert, Chester Hartman, points out that in addition to "the progressive income transfers it effectuates," rent control provides "a gut issue around which people can organize. . . . People begin to see that the notion of a 'free market' in housing is ludicrous."[38]

In addition to rent control, *The Cities' Wealth* advocates expropriation of private utility companies, progressive local taxes, and city- or cooperative-owned banks.

The working class is conspicuously absent from COOP. The authors attempt to explain this: "In a 'liberal' university town with a large white-collar and student population and only light industry, class identifications are often confused. . . . As a result, Berkeley's coalitions have sought to accommodate a wide range of supporters with similar populist and socialist goals."[39] It is highly significant that Berkeley, acknowledged by the authors to be atypical, has been chosen as a blueprint for other towns. No towns with a genuine working class, it seems, were available for such an experiment; the only Americans eager to "build socialism" in America are apparently upper middle-class white intellectuals, who want to control and expropriate other people's money. As one journalist put it:

> Perhaps the biggest reason for the Left's success in both Berkeley and Santa Monica has been its ability to capture the moral advantage, to create the impression that its demands for community control of housing are inspired by selflessness and altruism and that its true and only aim is helping the poor. The poor, as it turns out, are a valuable commodity. They are always trotted out as justification for rent

control, even though the true beneficiaries are political activists and the middle class. "Rent control is a middle-class phenomenon," says UC Riverside economist David Shulman. The two California cities with the strictest rent control laws—Berkeley and Santa Monica—are solidly middle-class, even wealthy in fact.[40]

In addition to being part of the IPS network, the Conference on Alternative State and Local Public Policies (CASLP) is a member of the State Issues Forum, a coalition including Common Cause, National Educational Association, United Auto Workers, People for the American Way, Planned Parenthood, American Nurses Association, and American Public Health Association (headquartered in the same building as CASLP). The State Issues Forum describes itself as having a "close working relationship" with the National Conference of State Legislatures and the National Governors' Association. The forum puts out a hefty monthly report, a loose collection of articles, newsletters, and papers of interest to forum participants.

CASLP drafts legislation, publicizes "progressive" policies in state and local government, publishes and distributes dozens of books to bring "new ideas" to citizens and public officials, and has held national summer conferences since 1975. It advocates a fascinating mix of programs, many of which, like cooperatives, are not specifically associated with a socialist/communist agenda. But underlying everything is the thrust to dismantle capitalism through confiscatory taxation and regulation, and to replace it with "public" control of resources, income, and savings.

> The issue we most want to push is public control of public money. By this we mean city and county and state budgets, which are enormous [and which] are primarily being used for the benefit of corporate interests.[41]

This control, eventually to be implemented at the national level, will ferment in the laboratories of local government. As Lee Webb explained at a conference of IPS, CASLP, and Ralph Nader's Public Interest Research Group:

> It is at [the local] level that progressives can create national models of programs and initiatives. . . . Few people realize that most of the New Deal programs, the ones implemented by Congress in '32, '33 and '34 under Roosevelt's initiative, in fact were programs that had been tried successfully in states like Massachusetts, Wisconsin, Pennsylvania, Illinois and California. Much of the New Deal legislation was developed . . . and political constituencies built around it in battles led by progressives, socialists, the labor movement and others in the nineteen-teens and nineteen-twenties. As Justice Brandeis said, states and cities should operate as the social laboratories of innovation in our federal system of government.[42]

The following are the main points of the conference's agenda for state governments in the 1980s:

Banking: seek to confine capital within state borders

Community Economic Development: pork-barrel program to funnel tax dollars to failing industries

Cooperatives: establish state agencies and public education programs on coops

High Tech: government control of large industrial companies and regulation of technology

Pension Fund Investment: government to decide where private pension funds invest their money; instead of "blue-chip" investments, the money would fund "affordable housing," and small businesses

Plant Closings: establish advance-notice requirement; establish state agencies for job retraining, job placement, modernization of business facilities; subsidize commuters; state banks to finance employee buyouts; require companies to pay a tax equal to 15 percent of payroll "to preserve current jobs, to attract new industry into the community or to maintain the existing tax base if the company closes down any of its plants"; require severance payments to employees equal to one week's pay for each year worked

Small Business: require banks and pension funds to invest in small businesses

Farms: limits to be placed on nonfamily corporate and absentee ownership of land; states to provide financial assistance and loans for small farmers

Housing: encourage affordable housing through rent control and zoning laws

Universities: students to set own fees; reject prohibition of use of student fees for "nonpartisan political education activities," which would allow a university to promote agendas such as the conference's with student money without student consent

Also included in the agenda are proposals for state day-care agencies, higher corporate taxes, progressive income taxes, unisex insurance, extended unemployment benefits, tougher enforcement of minimum-wage laws, and the repeal of right-to-work laws. The conference comes out for abortion, against school prayer, against a balanced budget.

The agenda published for the cities is similarly comprehensive. Numerous ideas for squeezing taxes out of citizens are offered. Rent control, regulations prohibiting condominium conversion, and a high capital-gains tax to discourage buying homes for renovation and resale are emphasized.

Derek Shearer: His Ideas and Connections

Derek Shearer and Gar Alperovitz, both associate fellows of the IPS, are key theorists of the economic-democracy movement. A ubiquitous figure in the loose coalitions characteristic of the American Left in the 1980s, Shearer helped Lee Webb organize the CASLP and serves on its steering committee. He has also been a consultant to Alperovitz's Exploratory Project on Economic Alternatives;[43] West Coast editor of *Working Papers,* a slick progressive magazine; economics consultant with Ralph Nader's California Citizens Action Group in Los Angeles; and member of the boards of directors of the National Consumer Cooperative Bank (which CASLP had a hand in organizing), the New School for Democratic Management (a project of IPS's Foundation for National Progress), the California Public Policy Center (he directed CPPC's IPS-funded Economy Project), and the Popular Economics Press. Shearer edited the readers of the first and second national CASLPs and the bibliographical section in its *Public Policies for the Eighties.* He contributed a chapter ("Public Enterprise") to Marcus Raskin's federal budget study published in 1978 at the request of fifty-six members of Congress.

Shearer has also served on the board of Jane Fonda/Tom Hayden's Campaign for Economic Democracy (CED), a California organization which Shearer says grew out of Hayden's unsuccessful 1976 race for the Democratic nomination for the U.S. Senate, the platform for which race was written by Shearer.[44] Another account reported that CED had its roots in the Conference on Alternative State and Local Public Policies. The article, which appeared in *In These Times,* has a curiously unsympathetic tone:

> The conference looked to Canadian and "Eurocommunist" economic models for inspiration, and was fond of vague phrases like "worker's control." Conference member Derek Shearer, now critical of CED's opportunism, helped write Hayden's campaign platform for his unsuccessful 1976 run for U.S. Senate in California. Written by Shearer . . . the platform . . . is filled with panaceas such as advocacy of state banks, municipally-owned utilities, national health servicie, and direct workers' control of industry.[45]

Shearer frankly says, "Socialism has a bad name in America, and no amount of wishful thinking on the part of the left is going to change that in our lifetimes." Thus, he pleads, "the words economic democracy are an adequate and effective replacement."[46]

Shearer's wife, Ruth Yanatta Goldway, was elected to the Santa Monica city council on a platform of economic democracy, and has headed the California Public Policy Center and the CETA-funded Center for New Corporate Priorities. Two U.S. representatives from California, Ron Dellums and Mervyn Dymally, both Democrats, support "economic democracy."

Shearer embraces "worker controlled enterprises" as practiced in Yugoslavia, China, and Cuba.[47] In the early 1970s he was a special consultant to California's director of employment development; he admitted in *Economic Democracy* that he failed to get unemployment down more than 1 percent or so, but excuses himself by saying nothing could really be done in just one state.[48] He has come out for "planning agreements" among government planners, senior corporate managers, and union representatives, enforced by denial of tax advantages and subsidies, denial of export licenses, and threats of antitrust suits. To implement the agreements government would need its own banks, insurance companies, pension funds, and enterprises.[49]

Martin Carnoy and Derek Shearer: Their Ideas and Strategies as Expressed in Economic Democracy

In his 1980 book *Economic Democracy*, which he coauthored with IPS associate fellow Martin Carnoy, Shearer attacks the Horatio Alger "myth" that "told the poor that the rich had more wealth and power because they worked harder, had greater intelligence, and were more frugal."[50] Americans, the book tells us, are too cynical to believe such lies, because of the "almost daily revelations on TV or in the press of huge corporate bribes to foreign governments, political payoffs, bank manipulations, and tax avoidance by oil companies showing huge profits."[51]

Economic Democracy acknowledges that Americans don't want socialism, but this traces in part to a "false image" of socialist (that is, communist) countries. The authors make no secret of their own predilection for Marxism:

> Ironically, Marxist economic and social philosophy, which—as the basis for a political movement—was and is an attempt to *humanize* economic and social life, is associated with dehumanization. In part this is a false image: American visitors to China and Cuba, for example, will attest to the austerity of life in those countries; yet, they also comment on the spirit of cooperativeness and well-being that pervades Chinese and Cuban life.[52]

Shearer and Carnoy quote Gramsci on strategy:

> The vision of economic democracy must begin to emerge as a *majority* viewpoint. This is what Italian social thinker Antonio Gramsci called "ideological hegemony." People frequently act against their own objective interests: tenants vote against rent control; property owners vote for corporate tax relief and cuts in services they really want. . . .[53]

Gramsci is not just a "social thinker"—he is one of the foremost communist theorists of this century, and is famous for his theory that a communist society is best achieved through cultural transformation.

Economic democracy as explained by Shearer and Carnoy includes workplace democracy on the Yugoslavian model, public enterprise, redistribution of corporate wealth, public control of capital, and alternative technology. Economic democracy would begin at the local level, through policies such as rent control and subsidization of local cooperatives, and progressively move to the national level through taxation, public planning, and regulation of private industry.

Economic Democracy advises readers to work as a "party within [the Democratic] party."[54] After an election is won, leftists are to continue in "action organizations," carrying out "direct action" (one can only speculate what he means), lawsuits, demonstrations, and educational events, and lobbying on economic issues like housing and development. Leftists should take the long view, and never compromise like politicians, who are "building careers, not a movement." They are to run slates, to be bold, to construct community institutions like cooperatives in health care, food, travel agencies, bookstores, movie theaters, and newspapers, to evolve into leaders and make an enjoyable living (directed at sixties types who thought poverty a virtue and dutifully lived miserable lives for the sake of the revolution). "Most of the attention and energy in the decade of the 1980s should go toward building state and local political efforts," advise the authors.[55] But, in the not too distant future, the movement will run a candidate for president—"the one integrating factor in national politics"—in the Democratic party.

Martin Carnoy and Derek Shearer: A New Social Contract: The Economy and Government After Reagan

Carnoy and Shearer are well aware of the difficulty of selling socialism to the American public. Their hopes lie in transferring "the American obsession" with what they elsewhere call the "alleged worldwide Communist revolution"[56] on to a new villain: the large corporation. The reason for poverty in America, they say, is "the anti-Communist ideology pushed so heavily by U.S. private corporations," which have a "direct economic interest in military expansion."[57]

The rhetoric in Shearer and Carnoy's second book, *A New Social Contract: The Economy and Government After Reagan,* proceeds more subtly than that in *Economic Democracy,* without specifically favoring China, Cuba, or Eastern European countries. But the premise remains—"Economic democracy can produce steady, equitable growth without inflation and with far less unemployment."[58]

To Shearer and Carnoy, government spending is a positive force, "not for its economic efficiency but for the democratic vision that it embodies."[59]

> Dominated by giant corporations, the private sector often operates *against* the public interest by dumping waste, building unreliable products, despoiling the wilderness, and providing unsafe jobs.[60]

> The private sector has never been able to provide the social services and equality of economic benefits demanded by the American citizenry.[61]

> We recommend the creation of public corporations that operate under rules whereby public needs dictate investment policy.[62]

The authors have in mind something quite different from Swedish-style socialism, where the private sector is allowed to retain its decision-making power in cooperation with labor: "The private sector can and probably should continue to play an important role in production, but if economic democracy is to be achieved, corporations' autonomy in investment and social decisions must be severely reduced at the same time that efforts are made to democratize these corporations."[63]

In the authors' view, the 1970s inflation stemmed from "attempts by large corporations to recover so-called 'normal' profits and by labor's reaction to falling real wage rates."[64]

They call for "a well-planned expansion of the public sector in nonmilitary areas. The goal is not only jobs per se, but the production of socially desirable goods and services. . . ."[65] By "socially desirable" they mean repair of the infrastructure, support of "public arts," public television and radio, and education.[66]

They criticize the present U.S. policies of supporting authoritarian but anticommunist governments; again, the large corporations are at fault:

> These policies are based on the myth that all Left-populist governments are Soviet stooges and therefore must be opposed as part of the geopolitical struggle against Soviet hegemony. Nothing could be further from the truth. . . . But this mythology is not just plucked out of thin air. It does serve to support the "business climate" that American corporations prefer to have for their investments, the same business climate that they are looking for within the United States—nonunionized, unpoliticized labor; governments that will do anything necessary to bring investments into their country or county; low taxes; and no regulation.[67]

The criticism in *A New Social Contract* of Reagan's New Federalism—returning some power over tax revenues to the states—is revealing:

> The Reagan Administration's talk of local power is essentially a call for reducing overall *democratic* control over the nation's resources. In Reaganomics, local control means that "dynamic," "efficient" private enterprise and the market should decide how communities can best develop and how to provide education and health care, even if those decisions may be inequitable, against the public interest, and interfere with the adequate delivery of human services.[68]

Our version of the New Federalism would use federal funds to improve local publicly controlled programs, not to turn control over public programs and resources to private business.[69]

A New Social Contract recommends that the concept of the municipal planning commission be "reshaped, empowered, and revived" to implement economic democracy.[70] "We advocate a new, positive role for local planning commissions that includes a creative use of zoning, but goes beyond it."[71]

But as Carnoy and Shearer point out, "It is not enough to rely on extracting jobs or public facilities from the private sector." Private corporations should not be allowed to plan strategies in finance, transit, land use, or energy.[72] What, then, is the turf of private business?

> Flea markets, farmers' markets, and the thousands of small businesses that advertise in any city's Yellow Pages are all the proper province of the market. Other human relationships and needs require nonmarket solutions, arrived at through democratic participation and planning. . . . "Government" and "political participation" would have different meanings than they do now. First, the separation between economy and politics would no longer exist, even in theory.[73]

Gar Alperovitz

Gar Alperovitz is one of the principal theorists of the economic-democracy movement. One of IPS's eight founding fellows, Alperovitz is the only progressive economist working with members of Congress to develop a comprehensive national economic plan. In 1984, a surprising 153 members of Congress supported Alperovitz's program, eighteen of whom were on an executive committee: Richard Ottinger (D–N.Y.), Barney Frank (D–Mass.), Mike Lowry (D–Wash.), Richard Gephardt (D–Mo.), Parren Mitchell (D–Md.), Pat Schroeder (D–Colo.), Bruce Vento (DFL–Minn.), Howard Wolpe (D–Mich.), Don Pease (D–Ohio), Stan Lundine (D–N.Y.), Bob Edgar (D–Pa.), Matt McHugh (D–N.Y.), Tim Wirth (D–Colo.), Berkley Bedell (D–Iowa), John Seiberling (D–Ohio), James Oberstar (D–Minn.), Gus Hawkins (D–Calif.), and Bill Richardson (D–N.Mex.).[74] Jesse Jackson, notorious for his admiration of third-world communist dictators and his strident anti-American comments during his 1984 presidential campaign, called *Rebuilding America,* a 1984 book coauthored by Alperovitz and Jeff Faux, "the economic handbook for [my] Rainbow Coalition."[75]

Alperovitz's organization, the Washington-based National Center for Economic Alternatives, grew out of a HUD-funded Alperovitz project to convert a failing steel plant in Youngstown, Ohio, to worker ownership. The project (Exploratory Project on Economic Alternatives) received widespread attention and allowed Alperovitz to marshal troops of congressmen to support legislation for national planning and other socialist derivatives.

Alperovitz's program calls for central planning in four strategic sectors of the economy: energy, food, housing, and health. The government, which he believes is currently "too weak and incompetent,"[76] must be invested with the authority to set investment and production targets in each sector, and to have enough capital to stimulate production through spending. Alperovitz justifies his call for planning by asserting that since government is already involved in planning, it may as well do it competently:

> But the United States cannot recover its economic health unless the federal government becomes a more competent manager of the economy. We have argued that an extension of government is inevitable, irrespective of political ideologies. A worldwide metamorphosis is transforming the broker state into an increasingly complex, if covert, planning system. The difference between liberals and conservatives lies less in their view of the appropriate size of government than in whom government serves.[77]

In a *Washington Post* article published just before the 1984 presidential elections, Alperovitz and Faux implored their readers to "forget today's fleeting fashions—we really need more government, not less. . . . In fact it is almost certain that we will one day look back on the current period of anti-government sentiment in the United States as a brief interlude before a new era of efficient, enlightened and—yes—expanded involvement of federal, state and local government in the economy."[78] They argued with good reason; with 153 congressional endorsements and ever-ballooning federal expenditures (the authors correctly pointed out that federal spending under Reagan averaged 24.2 percent of the GNP whereas under Carter it was 22 percent), Alperovitz and Faux could believe that history was on their side. "There is a worldwide trend toward more government," they wrote, "and not even America under Ronald Reagan has been immune to it."[79] Alperovitz and his colleagues at IPS and its spinoffs uncritically embrace the trend—the revolution-in-stages strategy, or creeping socialism, less obvious to the American people, whose instincts incline them toward less, not more, government.

One of the most disturbing aspects of *Rebuilding America* is its belief that government should inculcate values. If the state does not, the authors say, the "corporate and bureaucratic values of the dominant economic institutions," which make us "materialistic, self-absorbed, greedy and apathetic," will win by default.[80] "Competent economic planning thus requires that we explicitly choose—along with employment levels and housing investment—the values we want to affirm."[81]

The Vision

In short, economic democracy means a bigger and better pork barrel. The system is designed so that public officials would make decisions based on their vision of the common good—government by special interests.

Marx's model of public ownership of the means of production would be unnecessary if there were total public control ("a sensible overall policy would treat both public and private institutions as instruments to implement strategies for a more prosperous and equitable society").[82] Government would compete with the private sector, and with the help of taxation, eminent domain, and the ability to obtain financing at below-market rates, it would, of course, easily take over many private sectors. After the government broke the back of the large corporations and seized their capital, national planning could be implemented to effect full employment. Competition, Alperovitz says, is a principal cause of misery,[83] and without it the economy would stabilize (stagnate?). Government at all levels would grow, but the federal government would rule supreme. Eventually it would completely control housing, energy, food, and health care.

Present Strategy

Economic democrats must become involved in local government so as to build a base to implement their entire agenda. Housing programs are good for expropriating property and they provide a popular issue around which to build a political network and incite class struggle.[84] Local controls over private capital and pension funds, as a result of the public's fears of capital flight, will also weaken the private sector.

Some of the components of economic democracy have already been adopted; for example, the Community Reinvestment Act and Humphrey-Hawkins Full Employment Act. And a National Consumer Cooperative Bank has been established. (See Appendix 6 for organizational chart of key groups working with IPS to implement economic democracy.)

What Is Really at Stake

Economic democracy seriously threatens the American traditions of limited government and private enterprise. Its theorists espouse a conspiratorial worldview which blames all society's ills on large corporations. The public sector is the white knight who will vanquish the evil corporations. The future "public entrepreneurs" will compete without the risks or accountability of private businessmen, and with considerable competitive advantages. But why, the question nags, don't these people associated with IPS and the economic-democracy movement, who all come from privileged backgrounds, simply start their own model banks and cooperatives? They are capable, and—in America—free to run their affairs however they wish. If they were successful, their ideas would soon gain currency. Why can't they be satisfied with what they have accomplished in Berkeley, California, or Madison, Wisconsin?

Something more fundamental than idealism seems to drive them to restructure American society. Far from being populists, they are impelled to *impose* their vision of economic justice on others, willing or not. They see only the vilest of motives in businessmen, and against all evidence charge that private enterprise is inefficient and incapable of meeting the needs of society. They reject careers in business and traditional nonprofit organizations because they know their vision of and faith in socialism have no popular following. Thus their only recourse is to move into government and make it the instrument to engineer social change.

One of the most preposterous assertions of economic democracy is that planning can be at once decentralized and national (that is, centralized). Alperovitz sees the process as slow, evolutionary, and is vague about its operation. "The one certainty is that the process is not predictable," he admits.[85] He also seems to equate "advocacy planning" with democracy, even while stating, absurdly, "Planning skills are no longer simply the province of architects and people who have gone to city-planning schools; the profession's basic function of projecting the future, creating alternatives, estimating costs, integrating social and physical variables, and debating the merits has become accessible to most citizens."[86]

One is reminded of that vague passage to totalitarianism which Marx referred to as "the dictatorship of the proletariat"—theoretically evolving to the "withering away of the state." Empirical evidence increasingly suggests that socialist nostrums fail to deliver. More often, socialist arrangements have created a coercive state, whose regulation and force run contrary to our ideals of freedom and voluntarism. Even though capitalism may have exacerbated the competitive and cold aspects of human nature and contributed to the erosion of community, socialist promises of brotherhood and social solidarity have been worse than illusory.

Undaunted, IPS has continued its fight for national and international socialism. Setting a spark to the dried-out tinder of ideas from the First and Second Internationals, IPS has helped ignite a new intellectual movement whose long-term goal is nothing short of socialism for America.

Part V

Reaching for
Political Power

CHAPTER 13

Orlando Letelier
The Cuban and East German Connections

"I'm sorry, I don't think I'll be able to make it then, I don't expect to be back from Cuba," replied Orlando Letelier regretfully to Ronni Karpen Moffitt's lunch invitation.

The two rode in the front seat of Letelier's Chevelle on their way to the Institute for Policy Studies on the morning of September 21, 1976. In the back, Ronni's husband Michael contemplated the day's busy schedule while flipping through the morning paper.

"I understand," Moffitt chided half mockingly, "the struggle for human rights never takes a break." She was fully aware of the importance that human rights was gaining in the public mind, thanks in large part to the institute's efforts. Letelier had spent much of the past year since coming to IPS, where he had become director of its international arm, the Transnational Institute, working on the human rights campaign against Pinochet in conjunction with various members of the Chilean Socialist party in exile.

"The struggle will not end until Pinochet, that traitor to the true Chile, is brought down and the people once more control the destiny of Chile," said Letelier as he continued driving slowly down Massachusetts Avenue reflecting perhaps on the three whirlwind years since a military coup had plucked him from the Ministry of Defense in Santiago to a Chilean prison on Dawson Island near Cape Horn.

The car rounded Sheridan Circle surrounded by imposing embassy buildings.

Ronni Moffitt hummed a tune, while her husband gazed out the back seat window, absorbed in thought. Suddenly came a hissing sound like a hot branding iron being placed in cold water. Then a flash of light, and a deafening explosion. The Chevelle was thrown off the pavement and careened into a parked Volkswagen. Ronni and Michael Moffitt staggered from the twisted wreckage amidst smoke and splinters of broken glass that sparkled in the early-morning drizzle.

Ronni stumbled onto the lawn of the Romanian embassy, blood gushing from her neck, while Michael ran over to the driver's side to tend to Letelier, still trapped in the wreck. "Orlando," Michael cried, slapping the face of his mentor, "this is Michael, can you hear me?" Letelier moaned, uttered something unintelligible. Moffitt's ears were ringing from the explosion. He tried to free Letelier from the wreck, but the door was jammed. Dazed and confused, he ran over to his wife on the embassy lawn. There, a woman was crouched over his wife, desperately trying to stop the bleeding.

The District Metropolitan police arrived on the scene in less than two minutes, followed by the FBI and an ambulance. Letelier and Ronni Moffitt were dead or dying, victims of a bomb wired to the vehicle's undercarriage.

A preliminary investigation began immediately.[1] Letelier's briefcase was recovered from the vehicle, his former associates interviewed, his files examined. At IPS, Saul Landau, Waldo Fortin, and Juan Gabriel Valdes went into action, cleaning out Letelier's files "to ensure that materials that could compromise the Chilean resistance inside Chile or in exile would not fall into the hands of the FBI."[2] When the FBI arrived at the home of Letelier, they were greeted by Mark Schneider, an aide to Senator Kennedy and a close friend of Letelier.

But IPS fellows and friends could not shield the papers Letelier was carrying in his briefcase, which papers the FBI photocopied to further the investigation before returning the originals to his wife, Isabel Letelier.

The Nature of the Case

The briefcase documents contradicted the image of Letelier leading a "quiet life in the Maryland suburbs, studying how the world's wealth could be distributed more equally,"[3] as *Washington Post* reporter Karen DeYoung described him.

Letelier was receiving financial support from Cuba for his political activism in the United States, and he had extensive contact with the communist world; listed in his address book were eleven Cuban officials, thirteen East German addresses, including Politburo and Central Committee members, and numerous other contacts behind the Iron Curtain. Among his American friends and associates, those in the media composed the largest group. He was in contact with some twenty-seven journalists, reporters, and editors of both the print and the electronic media, seven of whom worked at the *Washington Post*.

Records of Letelier's international communications uncovered a wealth of information regarding the Chilean anti-Pinochet lobby in the United States. He had carried on frequent correspondence with Beatriz (Tati) Allende Ona, daughter of Salvador Allende and wife of high-ranking Cuban intelligence officer Luis Fernandez Ona. In one letter to Havana, Letelier speculates, "Perhaps some day not far distant we can also do [in Chile] what has been done in Cuba."[4]

Letelier was in contact with Clodomiro Almeyda, executive secretary of the Popular Unity coalition, and Carlos Altamirano Orrego, chief of the Chilean Socialist party, both of whom lived in East Berlin and were supported by the East German government. Writing from Cuba, Tati Allende makes two separate references to payments to Letelier, from the party by way of Cuba, in lump sums of $5,000, averaging $1,000 a month for an indefinite period.

Before the Blast

In short, the briefcase papers contradict the image of the quiet and scholarly person Letelier had assiduously constructed since coming to the United States in 1975, when he accepted an invitation to join the Institute for Policy Studies as an associate fellow.

This was not Letelier's first visit to America. A close confidant of Allende, he had been named Chile's ambassador to the United States shortly after the election of Allende, who instructed Letelier to procure sophisticated, concealable automatic weapons with silencers.[5] In May 1975 Allende recalled Letelier to serve, in quick succession, as foreign minister, head of the national police, and finally defense minister. And all this time, Soviet arms were smuggled into Chile aboard Cuban aircraft.[6] Letelier himself conceived a shrewd plan to discredit the CIA while receiving arms: the plan called for an American pilot to agree to being "caught" flying arms into Chile and then to "confessing" that he was a CIA agent under orders to supply the opposition with arms.[7]

But Letelier was more than just a gun runner; he was a consummate politician. And after the coup toppled Allende, he worked tirelessly to restore socialism to Chile. To this end he organized exiled Chilean Marxists and cultivated ties not only with terrorist organizations and communist governments, but also with liberal American congressmen.

The Decline and Fall of Marxist Chile

Allende fell into disfavor in Chile soon after his election in 1970, having received only 36 percent of the vote. The ensuing nationalization of industry and price fixing, aimed at destroying the economic base of the independent middle class, resulted in a severe recession and inflation that provoked massive strikes and calls for his ouster.[8] The Chilean Supreme Court in May 1973 declared Allende's attempts to gag the opposition press illegal, and on August 22 the Chilean Chamber of Deputies (the equivalent of the U.S. Congress) passed a resolution 81–47 condemning Allende's sanctions and his attempts to force a totalitarian order on Chile.[9]

Although Allende was superficially democratic, he had never hidden his affinity with communism. "Cuba in the Caribbean and a Socialist Chile in the Southern Cone will make the revolution in Latin America," he declared during his campaign.[10] Allende's Socialist party, which joined with the Communist party and other leftist parties to form the winning Popular Unity coalition, sent its young activists to Cuba for training.[11] Before his election, Allende had served as vice president of the World Peace Council. And after, in 1971, the Soviets rewarded him with the Joliot Curie Gold Medal.[12]

Letelier accompanied Allende in attending May Day celebrations with Castro in Havana.[13] While there, Letelier received an offer to work for Che Guevara, then head of Cuba's Central Bank, but opted for a position at the new Inter-American Development Bank. "The Cuban Revolution is a fact," Letelier is reported as saying by IPS associate fellow John Dinges and fellow Saul Landau in their account of Letelier's assassination. "It will endure, with or without me."[14]

Allende's Socialist party harbored a large extremist faction, to the left even of the communists, headed by Carlos Altamirano Orrego. On Allende's election, this faction became the dominant force in the party, and Altamirano became the party's secretary general. The day before Allende fell, Altamirano was caught trying to seize control of the navy on Allende's behalf.[15] After the coup, Altamirano fled to East Berlin and from there helped to direct the effort to overthrow Pinochet. He is presently a prominent member of the Soviet World Peace Council, claiming to represent Chile.

While in power Allende imported Cuban intelligence (DGI) officers, including Luis Fernandez Ona, who later became his son-in-law, to train and arm his presidential security guard and to set up a Soviet-style intelligence apparatus complete with informers on each block. Ona was well qualified, having established Committees for the Defense of the Revolution in Cuba. Allende's daughter, Beatriz (Tati), met Ona while serving as Chile's intelligence courier to Havana, and when Ona became the DGI's Santiago station chief, they were married.[16] She and her husband departed for Havana the day after the 1973 coup with one hundred fifty Cubans on an Aeroflot jet.[17]

Back on the Stump: Letelier at the Transnational Institute

Letelier, taken prisoner after the coup, was released a year later when a friend, the governor of Caracas, personally interceded with Pinochet. Upon his release,

Letelier went to Caracas and shortly thereafter received a call from Saul Landau, who, on behalf of Marcus Raskin and Richard Barnet, offered him a fellowship at IPS.[18] Letelier accepted. IPS asked Letelier to develop a study of U.S.–Chilean relations during the Allende years and to organize a major policy conference on U.S.–Latin American affairs.

Although appointed director of the Transnational Institute, which was created to "investigate causes and remedies of the disparities between rich and poor nations,"[19] Letelier seems to have devoted most of his time working to reestablish a Marxist government in Chile through his contacts with exile organizations, terrorist elements and all. While at IPS Letelier became a leader in the World Peace Council's international tribunal, which condemned the Chilean junta.[20]

A Very Busy Man

On the surface, none of this is very interesting or especially noteworthy. But what is revealing is that the briefcase papers showed that Letelier was recruiting American liberals to serve the Marxist cause under the false flag of restoring human rights to the Chilean people.

Letelier's friends tried to camouflage this truth. The day after his assassination, the *Washington Post* described Letelier as living "a quiet life,"[21] and implied that because Letelier had dared criticize the Chilean leaders, "they" had assassinated him. The record does not concur.

It does show that Letelier served as the U.S. head of the Chilean Socialist party in exile, funded from Cuba by the wife of a general in the Cuban DGI intelligence; that he sought to organize the Chilean exiles to stir up political opposition to Pinochet so as to isolate Chile economically; that he interfaced with the media extensively and gave hundreds of interviews, spoke to dozens of universities, and persuaded friends in Congress to strangle U.S. aid to Chile; that he lobbied the U.N. in condemning the Chilean government; and, finally, that at the time of his death he was planning to influence the U.S. presidential campaign and the Human Rights Commission of the OAS.

More specifically, Letelier helped organize exiled members of the Popular Unity coalition and their cohorts into groups across the nation and maintained a national headquarters across the street from the U.N. building in New York. And though he kept in touch with American leftist "solidarity" groups and set up a Washington lobby, the National Legislative Conference on Chile, Letelier was careful that his affiliations with the Soviet bloc not become public lest his cause should be irreparably damaged. One of the unmailed letters to Tati Allende illustrated his caution. His wife Isabel had set up the Chile Committee for Human Rights, and Letelier wanted to make sure Tati understood:

It is incredible that Isabel and a small number of people have already succeeded in setting up an entire *apparat* complete with an office, program of activities, considerable prestige, etc. I think that given the nature of its "sponsors" and of the front which this Committee is serving in the United States, it is preferable that information on it not be broadcast from Havana, because you know how these "liberals" are—it is possible that some of our congressional patrons might be afraid of being linked with Cuba, etc.[22]

The object, he told Tati, was "to mobilize the 'liberals' and other people who, even if they don't identify with us from an ideological view, are with us at least in matters relating to human rights."[23] In the same letter, human rights advocate Letelier told of his good relationship with MIR, the Chilean terrorist group. "MIR is not integrated with the Committee of Chile Democratico," he explained to Tati, "but it functions with NICH [Non-Intervention in Chile, a Berkeley-based organization] in parallel form with a high level of coordination."[24]

The Chile Committee for Human Rights (CCHR) listed among its sponsors seven members of Congress; Richard Barnet, Marcus Raskin, Cora Weiss, and Julian Bond; and CPUSA member Abe Feinglass, who also served on the President's Committee of the World Peace Council. One wonders what was "the nature of" the "sponsors" Letelier referred to in his letter to Tati.

The congressional sponsors of the CCHR were Sen. James Abourezk (an IPS trustee) and Reps. George Brown, Ronald Dellums, Robert Drinan, Don Edwards, Michael Harrington, and Helen Meyner.[25] Under CCHR auspices Tom Harkin, Toby Moffett, and George Miller released a joint statement "denouncing the Pinochet regime . . . and calling for strong sanctions, including the suspension of all bank loans to the Chilean government."[26]

The list of contacts on Capitol Hill goes on and on: Rep. Donald Fraser, who later became mayor of Minneapolis; National Security Council staff members Rick Inderfurth and Gregory Treverton; four members of the Senate Select Committee on Intelligence; Mark Schneider, aide to Senator Kennedy, who later became assistant secretary of state for human rights and humanitarian affairs, working for Patricia Derian in the Carter administration State Department Human Rights Office; and Richard Feinberg, a Treasury Department employee. A letter to Letelier from Elizabeth Farnsworth of the pro-Castro North American Congress on Latin America (NACLA) mentions that Feinberg was assisting in NACLA's work but that Letelier should not mention it as it would hurt his reputation at Treasury. After the briefcase contents were made public, Feinberg resigned. Afterward he found employment at the Policy Planning Staff of the State Department, arranged by its director, Anthony Lake. Lake had been associated with Letelier at the Center for International Policy, a research/advocacy group criticizing human rights violations in countries friendly toward the United States. Letelier had also flown Rep. Michael Harrington to Mexico with World Peace Council money to give the opening remarks at a Popular Unity strategy conference. And Edward Kennedy, not to be outdone, introduced successful amendments in the Senate to halt military and economic aid to Chile in 1975.

The evidence suggests that Letelier was recruiting naive people under a false flag of human rights to serve another cause—inducing an atmosphere conducive to violent revolution through the economic isolation of Chile.

Fidel Gives Thumbs Up to Popular Unity Strategy

A letter dated August 10, 1976, to Letelier from Clodomiro Almeyda, executive secretary of the Popular Unity party, shows the party's ties to Cuba.[27] In it Almeyda counseled Letelier to collaborate with the Havana Solidarity Committee in preparing a speech before the OAS Commission.[28] It also reveals that Almeyda had instructed Luis Maria, a former member of the Chilean Chamber of Deputies, to attend a meeting of the American Secretariat of Solidarity in Havana.[29]

That Moscow itself made efforts to help Letelier's organization is illustrated by Almeyda's reference to some problems the organization was having in getting delegates to a Non-Aligned Nations Conference in Sri Lanka in 1976. Allende's widow, a resident of Mexico, had not been invited, and Almeyda tells Letelier in effect to relax, the Soviets were intervening in her behalf.[30]

A Socialist High Roller: Globetrotter for Socialism

Letelier's financial affairs were interesting, to say the least. His expense accounts submitted to Beatriz Allende in Cuba show that he traveled continually, sometimes visiting New York twice a week. He made a trip to East Germany to visit Altamirano in June 1975, and paid the fares of two "comrades" from Canada to testify before the U.N. Human Rights Commission. "Attentions" in connection with the visits of "comrades," journalists, senators, and representatives of friendly (that is, communist) countries, he notes, are not included in the account as per the instructions of Colonel "L." And, according to instructions, this time of Comrade "OL," the costs incurred by the visits to the U.S. of "Companeros Dirigentes de la Resistencia" (Comrades in Charge of the Resistance) were omitted as well.[31]

Further, the briefcase had a bill from a Maryland hotel for January and February.[32] Why was Letelier, who had a nice house, assuming someone's hotel bills for such a long period? How could he afford it?

A handwritten draft of an expense account for Tati was found among the papers.[33] The June 1975 entry shows expenses for travel to East Germany and Mexico, as well as costs in Paris. The entries obviously do not reflect full costs, so some sort of partial subsidy must necessarily have been worked out.

One explanation is suggested by a handwritten note among the briefcase papers: "CIME—$US 100.000 + 100.000."[34] "CIME" is the acronym for the Venezuelan Labor party. As Letelier had a wealthy mistress in Venezuela who "had offered her resources to the Chilean cause,"[35] she may have supported his activities.

An itinerary in his briefcase shows that he had visited Amsterdam in June and September and planned to return in December. He had traveled to California in July and turned down invitations to Sri Lanka (Non-Aligned Nations Conference) and Pakistan. That fall, 1976, he was to begin a long journey: Mexico from October 11 to 13, Cuba until October 16, the USSR until the 23d, Algeria (Club of Rome meeting) from October 25 to 28. In November it was Iraq, then Amsterdam; and in January he was to have visited India. For the rest of 1977, he had plans to sojourn in Brazil, Australia, and Africa, and Prime Minister Michael Manley had invited him to visit Jamaica.[36]

His upcoming visit to Cuba was probably the reason he was carrying such papers and records in his briefcase the day of the assassination.

Comrades Behind the Iron Curtain

Letelier communicated with Cuba through Julian Rizo, the top official of the DGI's American station, and since 1974 first secretary of the Cuban U.N. Mission.[37] Prior to 1974, Rizo headed Castro's Venceremos Brigade program which was established to facilitate young American leftists' travel to Cuba for the purpose of indoctrination in Marxism-Leninism, which often led to recruitment by Cuban DGI intelligence. IPS fellow Saul Landau, who brought Letelier to IPS, was on board the first Brigade flight to Havana on July 4, 1969. Rizo was also liaison with terrorist organizations in the United States, including the Weathermen, the Puerto Rican FALN, the PLO, and the Chilean MIR,[38] and organized the Puerto Rican Solidarity Committee in New York, a political support group for the pro-Castro Puerto Rican Socialist party.

Letelier had seen Rizo five times in December 1975 alone.[39] He was also in contact with Teofilo Acosta, another high-ranking DGI agent stationed at the Cuban Interests Section at the Czechoslovakian embassy in Washington, D.C., and two top Cuban officials: Raul Roa, the Cuban foreign minister, and Carlos Rafael Rodriguez, the head of the Cuban Communist party.

One of the letters in Letelier's briefcase was to Roa, whom he addressed as "te," a mark of familiarity. In it he asked Roa to grant a visa to a Dutch "comrade," the head of the Dutch Committee of Solidarity with Chile, who wanted to visit Cuba for the twentieth anniversary commemoration of the disembarkation of *Granma*, the boat Castro used for his invasion of Cuba.[40]

Juan Gabriel Valdes, an IPS colleague, had given Letelier a letter to take to

Cuba, a cover letter for a bibliography of the Christian Democratic party, the strongest rival to Allende's Socialist/Communist Popular Unity coalition. The bibliography was destined for the American Department of the Central Committee of Cuba,[41] which specializes in intelligence operations against the United States. It is headed by a former DGI chief.[42] Valdes promised "Comrade Brito," the addressee of the letter, that if he should find any of the books in the bibliography interesting, he, Valdes, would send them "through the [Cuban] Mission."[43] This shows that Valdes, like Letelier, made use of the diplomatic pouch to correspond with top Cuban officials.

Three top leaders of Popular Unity were operating out of East Germany: Carlos Altamirano, Clodomiro Almeyda, and Sergio Insunza.[44] Letelier's address book lists top East German Communist party officials and intelligence officers: Herman Axen, GDR Politburo; Peter Florin, vice minister of GDR; Dr. Sieber, GDR ambassador to the U.S.; Karlheinz Mobus, GDR Foreign Office; Watker Latzsch, GDR second secretary; M. Markiwski, GDR Central Committee; Sergio Politkoff; Osvaldo Puccio; Emilio Rabasa; Walter Hynolosk; and Gerhard Scheumar.[45] Of the intelligence services of the East European nations, it is no secret that East Germany's works the most closely with the KGB.

Among the four Soviet officials listed in Letelier's address book, at least two, Valery Nikolayenko and Victor Degtyor of the Soviet embassy, were believed to be KGB officers.[46]

All the News That Fits: Spiking the Briefcase Papers

The first journalist to view any of the papers was columnist Jack Anderson, who received them several months after the assassination from sources on Capitol Hill. Anderson wrote only one column, which appeared on December 20, 1976, in the *Washington Post,* but which stopped short of pursuing the leads in the leaked documents. In February 1977 Evans and Novak got the papers and wrote a series of three columns. The first was printed by the *Post,* but the others were "spiked." The second appeared in papers outside Washington; and the third was never published.

When the first Evans and Novak column appeared in the *Washington Post,* a furor broke out. Especially controversial was the speculation that the money received from "Helsinki" might have been a secret money drop.[47] Saul Landau responded in the *Post* to the Evans and Novak column saying that the idea for the conference Harrington attended originated in Helsinki.[48] But in fact, "Helsinki" referred to the Soviet front World Peace Council, which is headquartered there.

In their next column, dropped by the *Post,* Evans and Novak said that an antijunta Chilean spokesman told them that the commission was under the World

Peace Council "umbrella." They also noted that in addition to its gold medal to Salvador Allende, the WPC had awarded gold medals in 1976 to Brezhnev and PLO leader Yassar Arafat "for their contributions to peace."[49]

Several years later, 1980, in their account of Letelier's assassination, Saul Landau and John Dinges revealed that the World Peace Council had sponsored an "International Tribunal to Judge the Crimes of the Military Junta" in Mexico City in February 1975 and that Letelier and other Chilean exiles attended.[50]

Letelier had arranged for Michael Harrington to attend the conference. Part of Congressman Harrington's ticket was paid with Soviet bloc funds received from the council, but three months later Letelier was still trying to get the rest reimbursed.[51] He submitted it as an expense to Tati, who received approval for the disbursement of $174 from the Socialist party leadership.[52]

The Jack Anderson and Evans and Novak columns also revealed that Letelier was receiving a $1,000 monthly stipend from Cuba. In his rebuttal, Landau claimed that Letelier's funds came from Western Europe and the United States and were only channeled through Cuba. But the story doesn't wash. Why funnel funds through Cuba, given Cuban restrictions on private monetary transfer and the abysmal relations between the U.S. and Cuba? Why, for that matter, send money from the United States to Cuba merely to have it sent back again? When Evans and Novak and English journalist Robert Moss asked Beatriz Allende where the money came from, she clammed up.[53]

On April 30, 1977, Allende wrote a letter that appeared on the editorial page of the *Post* saying that the money was "collected by Chile support committees throughout the world." She insisted there was nothing "mysterious" about the payments or the fact that they were channeled through her. She went on to make the startling statement, "We will not hide our gratitude for those who give us their generous solidarity in such difficult moments, and especially that given by revolutionary Cuba." Tati also asserted that Letelier "never hid" his Cuba contacts and said that the Chilean resistance would maintain them.[54] This was nonsense. Letelier had *specifically* asked her *not* to "broadcast" his connections with Cuba and his manipulation of American liberals through the false flag of human rights.

That October, Beatriz Allende was reported to have committed suicide in Cuba.[55]

In 1980 the controversy over Letelier's funding was still hot enough for Isabel Letelier to write a letter to the *New York Times* to try to clear her husband's name. She repeated Landau's claim, discredited by Tati Allende's letter, that the money had been raised in the United States and Western Europe.[56]

Among the most controversial briefcase papers leaked to Evans and Novak was a seven-page letter from Letelier to Tati giving a detailed account of his lobbying activities and the state of legislation pertaining to Chile then under consideration in Congress. The letter contained mocking references to the "liberals'' Letelier was recruiting. Also telling was a letter from Tati to Letelier dated August 20, 1976, concerning thousands of propaganda pamphlets she was going to send Letelier to use in his work at the U.N. to get a blockade going against Chile like the one imposed against South Africa. (Tati's title for the pamphlets was ''Pretoria-Santiago.'') Since a problem had developed with the usual channel (Rizo's diplomatic pouch), she was sending the material via the ''comrades'' of the Soviet Union and East Germany.[57]

In his *Post* column, Landau pointed out an error in the Evans and Novak column which confused two Chilean exile conferences held in Mexico. Landau claimed that the conferences were ''unrelated.'' But *Assassination on Embassy Row* by Dinges and Landau says the first conference, sponsored by the WPC and held in Mexico City, was to allow the exiles a chance to plan strategy for the resistance.[58] One of Letelier's papers was a letter from Almeyda indicating that certain strategies planned at Oaxtepec (the second, IPS-sponsored conference) were being put into effect.[59] Therefore, both conferences were strategy sessions for exiled factions of Popular Unity. The only difference was that one was funded by the World Peace Council and the other by IPS.

Other strategy sessions had been held in The Hague, where it was decided to establish Popular Unity operations in Caracas, Mexico, Paris, and Berlin; and in Algeria, where the leaders had discussed positions to be taken at the Non-Aligned Nations Conference. Almeyda told Letelier that the Chilean positions had been discussed with Cuban ''authorities.''[60] The human rights conferences were being used as a cover for strategy sessions for members of Popular Unity. The scale of their efforts was remarkable. In an attempt to explain why Letelier was planning to fly to Cuba for a Popular Unity meeting the day of his assassination, Dinges and Landau say, ''Cuba was one of the few locations where high officials of the Chilean exile movement could safely meet and plan strategy.''[61] Yet Dinges and Landau themselves admit that the Mexico City conference was for strategic planning, and the briefcase papers refer to strategy conferences in Oaxtepec, Mexico; Algeria; and The Hague. Most likely, Letelier and company traveled to Cuba to coordinate better with the Cubans. And this is precisely what Dinges and Landau prefer to slide over.

IPS tried its best to minimize the publicity surrounding the briefcase documents. After the first Evans and Novak column appeared, Saul Landau accused ''organized right-wing elements'' of trying to obfuscate the facts and said Letelier's briefcase, ''which contained no secrets,'' had nothing to do with the case,[62] and never mind that IPS was unwilling to open it to the press. (The FBI had released the briefcase to Isabel Letelier and Saul Landau after photocopying the contents.) Of all the requests from newsmen, only one friendly *Post* reporter, Lee Lescaze, was allowed by IPS to view some of the papers.[63] Since Lescaze did not speak Spanish, IPS kindly provided a translation. Lescaze wrote that there was nothing much unusual about the papers.

This, then, was the man whom Karen DeYoung described as living a quiet life during his two years in the States. He is the same man who was deeply involved in an international activist group dedicated to the overthrow of the Chilean government. And it is his house that his neighbors called a beehive of political activity. Letelier was an important member of a worldwide socialist-communist movement, with ties to terrorists operating from headquarters behind the Iron Curtain.

In the end, the Letelier assassination turned out to be a propaganda windfall for the Left, which made the most of it before any facts could emerge.[64] Senator Abourezk, an IPS trustee, accused Pinochet of the crime from the Senate floor the very day of the assassination,[65] which accusation was duly reported by the *Daily World*, the organ of the U.S. Communist party.[66] Senator Kennedy and Rep. Toby Moffett repeated the charge. As did Sandy Pollack, a member of the Central Committee of the Communist party (USA) and solidarity coordinator of the U.S. Peace Council. Pollack spoke on behalf of the National Coordinating Center in Solidarity with Chile, which Letelier was helping to finance, at a press conference held before a protest at the U.N. two days after Letelier's murder.[67]

A Continuing Legacy

Letelier's work did not die with him; his widow and IPS colleagues carry on. In Letelier's long letter to Tati, he describes a benefit concert for the resistance arranged by Isabel; it filled a large auditorium at George Washington University. No previous solidarity activities had attracted so many people, he wrote Tati. In 1984 the same band was put to work giving benefit concerts for the Sandinista regime in Nicaragua; on the board of the solidarity group which received the funds was Isabel Letelier of IPS. Bear in mind that Letelier was not the head of the Chilean exile organization; the other leaders are still active. In early 1984 Almeyda could be heard on a Radio Havana shortwave broadcast urging Chileans to riot in the streets. Violence inspired by Letelier's colleagues—the Mirista terrorists led by Salvador Allende's nephew, Andres Pascual Allende—increased; the governor of Santiago was machine-gunned to death.[68]

Quite apart from the problems with the Pinochet government, the Letelier case demonstrates how IPS has used fashionable issues, notably human rights, to manipulate liberals into supporting a radical agenda. The Letelier case also highlights the proclivity of IPS to join hands with parties behind the Iron Curtain, parties that, when not denying individual human rights in general, wonder at the incorrigible naiveté of American liberals.

CHAPTER 14

Lobbying
IPS and the Latin Network

By the end of the Carter administration the American electorate was aware that something was seriously wrong with the country's foreign policy. Among other setbacks, the U.S. had suffered humiliation in Iran, the Soviets had invaded Afghanistan, and things were going sour in the new Nicaragua. After the U.S. had handed over some $118 million to the new government, the Sandinistas showed their gratitude by enshrining in Nicaragua's new national anthem their wish to "fight against the Yankee enemy of humanity."

From Utopian Globalism to Revolutionary Socialism

Jimmy Carter's "progressive global" and "human rights" approach to foreign policy had backfired, but it had at least demonstrated what a short distance separated progressive liberalism from revolutionary socialism, the model enthusiastically embraced by IPS and the Latin network.

The philosophical groundwork of Carter's foreign policy was, in part, established by the Nixon-Kissinger policies of détente, Zbigniew Brzezinski's theories expressed in his 1972 book sponsored by the Council on Foreign Relations, *Between Two Ages,* and two reports published by the Linowitz Commission during the Ford administration.

223

The contribution of the Institute for Policy Studies to Carter's foreign policy came out in its report, *The Southern Connection*, which resembled the Brzezinski-Linowitz approach in many ways. For instance, the report suggested that

> the new thrust of U.S. policy in Latin America should be to support the ideologically diverse and experimental approaches to development that are gaining support around the world. Underlying this recognition and response must be the acceptance of ideological pluralism in both economic and political affairs . . . the United States must not intervene to shape governments and societies to our views and preferences.[1]

The Southern Connection thus echoed *Between Two Ages,* which called for abandoning hemispheric continuity—"a more detached attitude toward the revolutionary process"[2]—and the Linowitz Commission recommendation that the U.S. "be less concerned with security in the narrow military sense than with shared interests and values. . . ."[3]

If the Brzezinski-Linowitz philosophy was basically utopian, divorcing morality from national interest, the IPS approach went considerably further by promoting an anti-American "Third Worldism" and the "self-flagellation" characteristic of Carter's foreign policy. For instance, *The Southern Connection* found the "unquestioned presumption of U.S. superiority" and the "official presumption of hegemony" to be "morally unacceptable."[4] In a new application of class analysis, IPS described Latin America's human rights problems as the result of U.S. involvement, "virulent anticommunism," and "national development based on free play of market forces."[5] IPS's solution was to promote human rights and socialism, an agenda whose far-reaching consequences were revealed when the Sandinistas fashioned their new revolutionary society along the lines of Castro's Cuba.

The close correlation between the recommendations of the IPS *Southern Connection* and those of the Linowitz Commission traced in large part to the fact that a number of people—notably Robert Pastor, Abraham F. Lowenthal, Richard Fagen, and Guy F. Erb—who contributed to the IPS project were also members of or consultants to the Linowitz Commission. Robert Pastor was the director of the commission, while Roberta Salper, a member of the Castroite Puerto Rican Socialist party, chaired the IPS project. Years later, when the marines landed on Grenada, letters from Salper to Bishop were found along with various documents, treaties, and military aid agreements between Grenada and the Soviet Union, Cuba, North Korea, East Germany, Bulgaria, and Nicaragua.

In January 1977, when Carter was putting together his foreign policy team, Pastor and Erb were appointed to the National Security Council under Zbigniew Brzezinski, even as their involvement with IPS was becoming well known with the release of *The Southern Connection*. Mark Schneider, a former aide to Sen. Ted Kennedy, who was given credit in *The Southern Connection*, was appointed deputy to Patricia Derian, the assistant secretary of state for human rights. Derian would later become a member of the IPS Washington School. Schneider was also a personal friend of the late Orlando Letelier, who, as noted previously, received payments from Cuba, disbursed by Beatriz Allende Ona, the wife of a high-ranking Cuban DGI intelligence officer, Luis Fernandez Ona.[6]

The Southern Connection approach to Latin America and the third world in general was reinforced by others in the Carter administration, like Brady Tyson, deputy to U.N. Ambassador Andrew Young. Tyson's worldview took shape from his involvement with the pro-Castro North American Congress on Latin America (NACLA).

Ambassador Jeane Kirkpatrick commented on the symbiotic relationship between the policy of the Carter administration and the revolutionary socialism of IPS:

> The ease with which the Linowitz recommendations were incorporated into the IPS analysis and report demonstrated how strong had become the affinity between the views of the foreign policy establishment and the New Left, how readily the categories of the new liberalism could be translated into those of revolutionary socialism, and how short a step it was from utopian globalism and the expectation of change to anti-American perspectives and revolutionary activism.[7]

During the Carter administration the Latin network had Congress and the media convinced that the United States not only should accept responsibility for the problems of poverty and hunger in Latin America, but should also stand idly by while "inevitable," "indigenous" revolutions ran their course.

Latin Network Forestalls a New Foreign Policy Consensus Under the Reagan Administration

Central America's grinding poverty—a breeding ground for communist revolution—and the Sandinistas' boast of "a revolution without borders" posed serious threats to the U.S. when Ronald Reagan took office in January 1981. Secretary of State Alexander Haig warned that Central America was the place where the United States "would draw the line." But drawing the line is difficult when borders are permeable to revolutionary solidarity and transnational ideologies and loyalties. In 1982, Ambassador Jeane Kirkpatrick charged outright that IPS and a "very well-organized lobby work indefatigably to confuse the moral, political and intellectual questions involved in U.S. policy toward Central America."[8]

To galvanize congressional support for his policies, Reagan formed a bipartisan commission under the leadership of Henry Kissinger to undertake a study on

Central America and the Caribbean. But—one step ahead—IPS had already formed its own research/lobbying effort. "Concerned about the Administration's reckless course," IPS said, "a group of scholars founded the Policy Alternatives for the Caribbean and Central America [PACCA]. . . ."[9]

The scholars that IPS brought together were people from the same ideological mold, many of whom were leaders of groups in the Latin network—the North American Congress on Latin America, Washington Office on Latin America, Americas Watch Committee, Center for Development Policy, Center for International Policy, Committee in Solidarity with the People of El Salvador, and Institute for Food and Development Policy. (See Appendix 7 for organizational chart of IPS and the Latin network.)

Noteworthy was the extent to which IPS and PACCA were going to discredit the Reagan administration policy. For no sooner had the Kissinger Commission released its findings than IPS released the PACCA report, *Changing Course: Blueprint for Peace in Central America and the Caribbean*, which said: "We intend this 'Blueprint' to be used as an action and organizing document for Congress."[10] But the activities of IPS go considerably beyond violating IRS guidelines prohibiting partisan political activity.

The Kissinger Commission recommended a two-track approach—economic and military aid for the embattled region. The IPS-PACCA report attacked it as "a disastrous recommendation" and a "misperception of reality."

The IPS-PACCA approach was itself a thinly veiled defense of the Sandinistas. In calling Nicaragua's health and literacy programs "models that work," the PACCA report ignored the fact that the literacy campaign was highly charged with Marxist-Leninist political indoctrination and, together with health programs, provided a pretext for a huge influx of Cuban advisers. Nor did IPS-PACCA criticize Nicaragua's unprecedented military buildup. Indeed, "fear of U.S. intervention," PACCA explained, "often leads radical governments [like Nicaragua] to seek ties with the Soviet Union and Cuba."[11]

IPS-PACCA recommended: for *Nicaragua*—disengagement from the contras and support for Contadora efforts; for *El Salvador*—a way to share power with the Marxist guerrillas; for *Honduras*—the closing down of all U.S. bases; for *Costa Rica*—no military aid; and for *Cuba*—normalization of relations. The PACCA report was circulated on Capitol Hill, received media attention, and helped undercut the Kissinger Commission report. When the $14 million aid package for the contras came up in spring 1985, Congress initially voted it down.

Many congressmen said that, besides the PACCA report, reports of human rights violations had influenced them. Those sources most frequently cited were three Washington-based organizations in the Latin network: the Washington Office on Latin America (WOLA), the Council on Hemispheric Affairs (COHA), and Americas Watch Committee (AWC). Speaker of the House Tip O'Neill (D–Mass.) and Michael Barnes (D–Md.), chairman of the House Subcommittee on Western Hemispheric Affairs, justified their opposition to President Reagan's contra aid bill on the basis of the WOLA report. In fact, that report was written by Reed Brody of the Washington law firm of Reichler and Applebaum, which was paid by the Sandinista government for legal counsel and support. Just forty-eight hours before the vote, Sens. Tom Harkin (D–Iowa) and John Kerry (D–Mass.) traveled to Nicaragua. Their celebrated meetings with Sandinista junta leaders, which captured the headlines and helped sway Congress, were arranged by Peter Kornbluh, a fellow at IPS. Within a week the Sandinista president, Daniel Ortega, flew to Moscow and secured $200 million in Soviet aid. Shocked and embarrassed, Congress reversed gears and granted $27 million in humanitarian aid to the contras.

Latin Network: Political Support for Guerrillas

In guerrilla insurgencies, military factors are important, but rarely decisive. "The battle for Nicaragua is not being waged in Nicaragua," Sandinista leader Tomas Borge told *Newsweek*. "It is being fought in the United States."[12] At a July 5, 1985, press conference called to explain away the guerrillas' murder of four U.S. Marines at a San Salvador café, FMLN guerrilla chief Joaquiń Víllalobos and Salvadoran Communist party chairman Shafik Handal said, "Our strategy has to be based on defeating the resistance and capacity of the Reagan administration to continue supplying the Salvadoran army, for if we succeed on this issue we win the war."[13]

The big battle is in the American media and Congress. And in this struggle, the guerrillas know their chief allies are IPS and other members of the Latin network.

Latin Network: Key Groups and Interrelationships

In addition to the organizations mentioned above, there are dozens of groups that lobby for revolutionary change in Latin America. On the religious side, the National Council of Churches (NCC), the American Friends Service Committee (AFSC), and Clergy and Laity Concerned (CALC) have their own congressional lobbying arms and grassroots networks around the country. Individually, many Protestant missionaries, imbued with the trendy liberation theology, join hands with Marxist revolutionary movements in Latin America. Similarly, the Mary-knoll and Jesuit orders of the Roman Catholic church are deeply involved (about which more later).

Many traditionally nonpartisan humanitarian organizations have become politicized and support revolution in Latin America. Amnesty International (AI) has become increasingly partisan, spending far more of its resources in publicizing human rights violations in friendly Latin American countries (El Salvador, Guatemala, Honduras), than it spends in exposing those in hostile countries (Cuba, Nicaragua). Oxfam-America, which formerly raised millions for food and medicine for Central America, now distributes money to the Sandinistas' "literacy campaign" (political indoctrination) and directly to the FMLN/FDR guerrilla movement in El Salvador.[14]

The ranks of the Latin network have since 1983 been swollen by antinuclear activists, in large measure as a result of the IPS campaigns promoting the "deadly connection" between conventional and nuclear war. As IPS fellow Michael Klare put it, American involvement in a conventional conflict in Central America would likely "leap the firebreak into a nuclear conflagration between the superpowers." The purpose behind the deadly connection theme was to transfer the popularity of the nuclear freeze to the protest movement against U.S. involvement in Central America. This encouraged nuclear freeze proponents like SANE, the Riverside Church Disarmament Program, the Council for a Livable World, and Mobilization for Survival to join forces with the Latin network.

Most of the groups in the Latin network have located their offices in Washington, recognizing that the war over Latin America lies with the U.S. Congress and the media. Each has developed its own niche, for though IPS is often the hub, as in the campaign to discredit the Kissinger Commission, the strength of the campaign for revolutionary socialism in Latin America depends to a great extent on the autonomous activities of the different groups. Political propaganda is most effective when numerous organizations promote variations of the same theme.

Coalition for a New Foreign and Military Policy

The Coalition for a New Foreign and Military Policy, an umbrella organization made up of some fifty-five member groups, was formed in 1976 with the help of IPS. Former IPS fellows like Cynthia Washington and Stephen Daggett are now among the oldest members on the CNFMP staff.[15] The *Congressional Quarterly* describes the coalition as the " 'nerve center' of the liberal grassroots network on Latin America." Today the coalition is a sophisticated lobbying organization complete with computerized communications and congressional hotlines.

Most of the individual organizations in the Latin network described below are members of the coalition and often meet to coordinate lobbying strategies. Located only a five-minute walk from the Capitol, CNFMP tracks legislation, works with congressional staffers, and mobilizes grassroots lobbying efforts.

CNFMP literature contends that it is "working for a peaceful, non-interventionist and demilitarized U.S. foreign policy."[16] In truth, CNFMP advocates abandoning a "balance of power" in foreign policy in favor of a more enlightened approach comprising four basic points: (1) disarming unilaterally; (2) withdrawing the U.S. military from the third world; (3) citing human rights violations only in countries allied with the U.S.; (4) extending aid to "liberated" countries such as Vietnam and Nicaragua.

The bulk of CNFMP's funding comes from individual members, member organizations (like the National Council of Churches), and foundations like the Youth Project (which also funds IPS). The member groups are predominantly New Left organizations, but some—the National Lawyers Guild, the International Longshoremen's Union, the United Electrical, Radio, and Machine Workers—are highly influenced or controlled by the Communist party. Terry Provance, listed as a member of the CNFMP speakers bureau, is a U.S. delegate to the World Peace Council.[17] Although such connections may mean little in and of themselves, there is no distinguishable difference between the foreign policy recommendations of the CNFMP and those of, say, the U.S. Peace Council, a Communist party front.

North American Congress on Latin America

From its founding in 1966, the North American Congress on Latin America has worked closely with IPS. It soon became known as the preeminent American source of solidarity information on guerrilla movements in Latin America.

Although NACLA was originally conceived as the "intelligence-gathering arm of the New Left,"[18] it soon became active. NACLA itself stated:

> The North American Congress on Latin America seeks the participation and support of men and women, from a variety of organizations and movements, who not only favor revolutionary change in Latin America but also take a revolutionary position toward their own society. . . .
>
> In the context of this involvement in the revolutionary struggle at home, NACLA is exploring possibilities for maintaining relationships with Latin American organizations. . . .[19]

John Gerassi, cofounder with Michael Locker and a self-styled Trotskyite,[20] was considerably more candid when he stated that NACLA would support "a 'Revolutionary Peace Corps' . . . to send young Americans to work with leftist Latin American guerrillas." The "Revolutionary Peace Corps," he said, would seek "national liberation forces wherever they are."[21] NACLA's goal, moreover, was "to build a base from which to work for fundamental changes in hemispheric relations."[22]

Although Michael Locker recognized that NACLA's constituency was also composed of the social justice types, he said in a 1981 interview that "those we were working with understood the other position. They knew what Marxism was all about."[23] When asked, "Did the early people in NACLA understand Marxism?" Locker replied:

> How sophisticated were we? We knew what power structures were about, but as a systematic understanding, no. At the beginning, for example, we didn't use the word "imperialism." . . . It was only in the early '70's that people seriously got into studying Marxism.[24]

Many of NACLA's earlier members, such as Michael Klare, Gail Ann Grynbaum, John Frappier, Michael Locker, and Nancy Stein traveled to Cuba with the Venceremos Brigade between 1969 and 1972, some with multiple entries.[25] Stein of NACLA-West was a national committee member for propaganda and communications for the Venceremos Brigade.[26]

While deriving considerable income from its publication *Report on the Americas,* NACLA's funding comes primarily from the National Council of Churches and organizations that also support IPS, such as the ARCA Foundation, the Stern Fund, and the Samuel Rubin Foundation and its subsidiary, the Fund for Tomorrow.

Despite its left-wing bias, NACLA's publications are widely used in U.S. universities. Its members are also active in congressional lobbying campaigns. For instance, in January 1983 NACLA's vice president, Janet Shenk, helped escort to El Salvador a delegation that included two U.S. congressmen on the House Foreign Affairs Committee, Edward F. Feighan (D–Ohio) and Robert G. Torricelli (D–N.J.).[27] NACLA's Roger Burbach sits on PACCA's executive board and Robert Armstrong helped draft the IPS-PACCA publication *Changing Course,* which countered the findings of the Kissinger Commission.

Washington Office on Latin America

General Pinochet's coup in Chile in 1973 and subsequent repressive policies occasioned the creation of a clutch of human rights organizations that became an integral part of the Latin network, among them the Washington Office on Latin America.

WOLA was founded in 1974 by Joseph Eldridge with the help of Joyce Hill of the National Council of Churches and Thomas Quigley of the U.S. Catholic Conference. WOLA's mission was to monitor human rights to help church organizations lobby for political change in Latin American countries. Joyce Hill had worked with the Methodist church in Cuba and was quite taken with Fidel Castro. Likewise, Tom Quigley had traveled to Cuba and was enthusiastic about

Fidel Castro's Marxist "Christianity." And Eldridge had distinguished himself by supporting Allende's Marxist politics during his missionary/social work in Chile.

WOLA and IPS contribute to each other's projects. IPS senior fellow Isabel Letelier is on WOLA's advisory board and WOLA staff members are frequent participants in IPS seminars and studies. But WOLA is an influential organization in its own right. Strategically located in the Methodist building across from the U.S. Capitol, WOLA often arranges for witnesses and speakers from Latin American leftist groups and revolutionary movements to testify at congressional hearings and to address the media.

WOLA's main foundation support comes from many of the same donors that fund IPS—the Ford Foundation, the Bydale Foundation, the Stern Fund, the Ottinger Foundation, and the Fund for Tomorrow (subsidiary of the Rubin Foundation). But the bulk of its contributions comes from religious institutions, such as the WCC, NCC, and Maryknoll order.

From its beginning WOLA has been selective about its human rights analysis, neatly avoiding unpleasant questions about Cuba's role in guerrilla movements hostile to the U.S.

Joe Eldridge's fascination with "liberation" took him on a secret junket to Cuba in 1976,[28] and his experience appeared in a Church of the Brethren publication: "Joe Eldridge . . . shared the excitement of Christians in Cuba . . . and found that many of its prayers for the poor and needy of their society were being answered by Castro's Marxist policies."[29]

In 1979 the Cuban mission to the U.N. invited Eldridge to join in celebrating the twentieth anniversary of the Cuban revolution. Though unable to attend, Eldridge replied, "I hope that at the next opportunity we can be together . . . and that 1979 will be a good year for the continuing struggle of the Cuban regime and its people."[30] Over the years he has worked closely with the Cuban Interests Section to facilitate the travels of numerous American activists to Cuba and hosted a Cuban delegation visiting Washington, D.C.

WOLA's network includes many in the international communist movement. According to Eldridge's personal correspondence, he has worked with James and Margaret Goff of Lima's Latin American Documentation Center; Carlos Tunnerman of the Tercerista faction of the Nicaraguan FSLN; Fabio Castillo, a prominent Salvadoran Marxist; Elice Higgenbotham of the Cuba Resource Center; Patrick Tobin of the International Longshoremen's and Warehousemen's Union; and Phil Wheaton of EPICA. In 1977 Juan Ferreira, a native Uruguayan, became WOLA's associate director. Cuban intelligence recommended Ferreira to Farid Handal when the latter visited the United States to generate solidarity for the Marxist FMLN in El Salvador.[31]

In answering a critic who questioned the nature of Joe Eldridge's work as a "missionary" in charge of WOLA, Joyce Hill, a WOLA founder and a member of its board, said that "back in 1973 the World Division affirmed that one part of our work in bearing witness to the Lordship of Jesus Christ over all of life is in 'participating in God's work of human liberation,' " and that "we see Joe's mission fulfilling this."[32] About Communist party leader Sandy Pollack, Eldridge said he was "enriched by her courage and inspired by her vision."[33]

In the late 1970s WOLA was tireless in publicizing human rights violations in Nicaragua under Somoza. But after the Sandinistas took over in July 1979, WOLA no longer found the issue of much interest. Instead WOLA turned its attention to condemning the governments of El Salvador and Guatemala, and several years later began a campaign against Honduras, charging that it was "a democracy in demise" because of the increased presence of the American military.

In response to the U.S. intervention in Grenada in October 1983, WOLA's *Update* asserted, "Reagan blatantly violated international law, complicated Caribbean politics, alienated allies, humiliated the OAS, and sent shock waves up and down this hemisphere by confirming Latin Americans' worst fears about Washington's intentions."[34]

In addition to joining hands with IPS, WOLA participates in projects of others, such as the Americas Watch Committee and the Lawyers Committee for International Human Rights. Director Eldridge serves on IPS's selection committee for the Letelier-Moffitt Human Rights Award, as does Thomas Quigley. For years WOLA has cochaired the Human Rights Working Group of the Coalition for a New Foreign and Military Policy.

Despite WOLA's open support of Marxism and connections with hostile foreign parties, its reputation remains untarnished in Congress. In 1983 WOLA briefed congressional staff members on El Salvador, and gave testimony on such subjects as human rights conditions in Guatemala and the Reagan administration's record of compliance with existing human rights legislation. WOLA staffers also help congressional offices draft legislation.[35] When the Congressional Research Service was formulating standards for categorizing human rights violations—information vital to policymaking—the CRS division chief of foreign affairs and national defense, Stanley Higinbotham, sought the advice of Joe Eldridge.[36]

In 1983 WOLA sponsored visits to the U.S. from Central America by such leftists as Guillermo Ungo and Ruben Zamora of the FMLN-FDR. Late the following year, WOLA staffer Kay Stubbs decided to leave and take a public-relations position with the Sandinista government. About the same time WOLA sponsored a delegation to observe Nicaragua's November 1984 election.

WOLA had questioned the credibility of the May 1984 Salvadoran elections, in which three different parties vied for power, but its observer, Reggie Norton, fully approved this 1984 Nicaraguan election, in which the Sandinistas had no credible non-Marxist opposition. According to a U.S. embassy cable, Norton said, "Nicaragua has had an exemplary electoral process and from the first results we have seen, it appears that the public has approved the revolution."[37] Congressman James Shannon (D–Mass.), who accompanied Norton, endorsed the delegation's statement, which said, "The Nicaraguan electoral process was meaningful" and "based on our observations today, we are convinced that the procedures provided easy access to the ballot and a secret vote for all Nicaraguans."[38]

Like so many of WOLA's press releases, the Nicaraguan election statement received considerable attention in the American media. And little wonder, for in noting that "the media in the United States plays a powerful role in the formulation of foreign policy," WOLA's annual report also observes:

> Given the spiraling conflict in Central America, WOLA has dedicated increasing energies to sharing with journalists its historical perspective of that region. WOLA serves as an important source of information and analysis for both the print and electronic media. The office maintains working relationships with many domestic and foreign journalists from the wire services, major daily newspapers, radio networks, television and news journals.[39]

Americas Watch Committee

Americas Watch Committee (AWC) was established in 1981 as a human rights watchdog group, adding yet another voice to the Latin network. AWC got off the ground in 1982 when it received funding from Philippe Villers and the Bydale Foundation, the latter sending its largest annual contribution to IPS. AWC's Washington director, Juan Mendez, serves on IPS's selection committee for the Letelier-Moffitt Human Rights Award.

One of the first projects that AWC undertook was to compile data jointly with WOLA, the Center for National Security Studies (CNSS), and the American Civil Liberties Union (ACLU) for a book, *Report on Human Rights in El Salvador*. The book's introduction says it all:

> This report demonstrates, we believe, that the President's January 28 certification is a fraud. . . . It is possible . . . for Congress to demonstrate that it meant what it said in the foreign assistance act by adopting legislation suspending military aid to El Salvador so long as the gross human rights abuses documented in this report persist. That will happen only if Congress is prompted to act by public outrage. In publishing this report, we hope to provoke that outrage.[40]

Widely circulated on Capitol Hill and quoted extensively in the media, *Report on Human Rights in El Salvador* had no small impact on a Congress already deeply divided over Latin American policy.

But this was only the beginning. Throughout 1985 AWC published eight other reports on human rights violations allegedly committed by the Salvadoran government. Fewer than thirty of the nine hundred pages were devoted to human rights violations of the FMLN guerrillas.

After the FMLN machine-gunned four U.S. Marines and nine civilians in a San Salvador café in early summer 1985, AWC finally became aware of human rights violations on the other side, AWC's vice chairman, Aryeh Neier, in a *New York Times* article, concluded that "critics of the Government must not hesitate to condemn the mounting abuses against noncombatants by the Salvadoran guerrillas."[41]

Americas Watch joined WOLA in organizing a trip to Honduras in October 1983 to monitor human rights. The visitors observed, "The human rights situation in Honduras deteriorated in 1983 . . . this trend was directly related to the country's increased militarization and the government's growing preoccupation with national security."[42] Like WOLA, AWC questioned the validity of the 1984 election in El Salvador, yet could find little to criticize in that year's election in Nicaragua. Director Juan Mendez said, "In El Salvador, the choices were not adequate because the Left could not participate [whereas] in the Nicaragua elections the problems appear to have been relatively minor."[43] A subsequent AWC report stated that "the Sandinistas Party obtained a popular mandate."[44]

When Reagan sought support for a $14 million aid package for the contras, AWC helped WOLA to shoot down the aid request.[45] Further, AWC continued its campaign even after President Ortega secured $200 million from the Soviets. In its July 1985 report, *Human Rights in Nicaragua: Reagan, Rhetoric and Reality,* AWC found the U.S. suspect and often deceitful, but trusted in full the statements of the Sandinistas. Some specific findings:

> There is not a policy of torture, political murder, or disappearances in Nicaragua. . .
>
> The Administration has misrepresented the denial of press freedom in Nicaragua. . .
>
> The issue of religious persecution in Nicaragua is without substance. . .
>
> Since then [1981–82], the Government's record of relations with the Miskitos has improved dramatically . . . while the contras' treatment of Miskitos and other Indians has become increasingly violent.[46]

AWC found the contras' record appalling: "In sum, we find that the contras are pursuing their military campaign by systematically violating the basic rights of Nicaraguan civilians."[47] The July 1985 report concludes: "The U.S. has engaged in terrorism against Nicaraguans."[48]

Council on Hemispheric Affairs

The Council on Hemispheric Affairs (COHA) specializes in influencing the media. Its director, Larry Birns, has earned a reputation with Washingtonians, both in Congress and the media, for his tenaciousness in acquiring and brokering leaks—leaks which invariably embarrass the United States. COHA has also helped marshal U.S. labor support for the revolutionary Left in Latin America. Like WOLA, COHA owes its creation to the Chilean coup.

In 1973 Larry Birns traveled to Chile as a representative of the U.N.'s Economic Commission for Latin America. There he met with Orlando Letelier and other members of Allende's Popular Unity coalition. Before this, Birns had edited the monthly magazine *International Documentation on the Contemporary Church*, better known as *IDOC*, founded by a group of Dutch Catholic bishops in the early 1970s, but denounced by the Vatican for its left-wing politics.

COHA became an important part of the Latin network in 1975 after Birns met with Letelier, then working at IPS. Letelier helped pay for Birns and Rep. Michael Harrington (D–Mass.) to travel to a meeting of the International Tribunal to Judge the Crimes of the Chilean Junta in early 1976; sponsored by the World Peace Council, it was being held in Mexico City.[49] In an interview, Birns admitted that COHA emerged as a byproduct of that WPC-sponsored meeting to serve as a vehicle "to manipulate the sophisticated political and academic communities."[50] IPS founder Richard Barnet was a COHA trustee up until 1976, the year of the Letelier scandal. As of 1984, IPS fellow Roger Wilkins and IPS trustee Terry Herndon served on COHA's board along with such people as Thomas Quigley of USCC and WOLA and Brady Tyson, a founding member of NACLA.

COHA has had a consistent record of opposing U.S. policies in Latin America. For instance, regarding U.S.–El Salvador relations in 1981, COHA's Richard Allan White wrote, "Our assistance to the dictatorship there will pale beside the contempt in which the United States will be held if it continues supporting the ever-increasing needs of yet another decaying regime under attack.[51]

As for Nicaragua under the Sandinistas, COHA reported disingenuously at the end of 1983 that "the number of Cuban advisors, including some teachers and military specialists, has been reduced as over 2,000 have returned to Cuba."[52]

Passing judgment on Grenada three months after the U.S. intervention—which met with over 90 percent of the Grenadan peoples' approval—COHA reported:

> . . . The various U.S. actions taken on Grenada after the initial operation have compromised the Grenadan government's authority and the failure to establish high standards for human rights observance and move quickly to hold elections, has made the islanders' constitutional privileges a function of the U.S. government's desire that an acceptable, pro-U.S. candidate win the elections.[53]

COHA pushed its positions on the media, but not all has gone smoothly in this respect. Associated Press correspondent Ary Moleson, who used COHA material, came under sharp criticism from our then ambassador to Nicaragua, James D. Theberge, who wrote A.P.'s management: "While few pay much attention to Mr. Moleson's stories in the U.S., it is regrettable, and should be of concern to you, that he regularly misinforms your Latin American readers by citing this particularly reckless and ill-informed source, COHA."[54]

Assistant Secretary of State Vaky received regular calls from Birns, who threatened to go public with this or that piece of information if Vaky didn't comply with whatever it was Birns wanted. Eventually an exasperated Vaky told his staff, "Ignore him, he's got mental problems."[55]

COHA's credibility also suffered a momentary blow when a document, "Dissent Paper on El Salvador and Central America," which was in fact a Soviet forgery, was traced back to Larry Birns of COHA.[56] Birns said he had circulated it unaware of its true origin. Meanwhile, however, some prominent journalists had swallowed the forged "dissent paper" and concluded that the U.S. should acknowledge that "the FDR/DRU coalition is a legitimate and representative political force in Salvadoran politics."[57] Karen DeYoung of the *Washington Post*, Stephen Kinzer of the *Boston Globe*, Anthony Lewis and Flora Lewis of the *New York Times* were just a few who were taken in. Although the State Department showed it up as a clumsy forgery and Flora Lewis admitted in her *Times* column that she had been duped, the damage was done.

When in 1984 some 80 percent of the Salvadoran people went to the polls in an election in which several parties competed, a COHA press release called it "a downright phony event in a country without a free press and with a downright nasty security force."[58] In sharp contrast, four days before the November 1984 election in Nicaragua, in which the plausible opposition parties refused to participate, COHA announced that "conditions for a credible election are in place in Nicaragua and are better than those that existed in Salvador."[59] Afterward COHA reported that the "Nicaraguan election was qualitatively better than U.S.-sponsored Salvador ballots."[60] "There was definitely much more of an honest effort on behalf of the Sandinistas to present a full-fledged legitimate election," said COHA spokesperson Megan Ballard, who added that the CIA was the principal source of Nicaragua's problems.[61]

Center for International Policy

The Center for International Policy (CIP) was formed in 1975 by Lindsay Mattison, with Orlando Letelier's help, as another "human rights" research/lobbying organization. Like the IPS spinoff Center for National Security Studies, which focused on the intelligence agencies, CIP operates under the aegis of the Fund for Peace, with support from the Rubin Foundation, the Ruth Mott Fund, and the Stern Fund. Donald Ranard, a disaffected State Department official and friend of Orlando Letelier, is CIP's director and William Goodfellow its deputy director.[62] Susan Weber, an early staff member, was previously registered under the Foreign Agents Registration Act as an employee of the Soviet embassy to copyedit *Soviet Life*.

CIP has focused much of its effort on stopping financial institutions, like the World Bank, the Inter-American Development Bank, and the International Monetary Fund, from aiding Latin American countries friendly to the United States.

Although CIP's energies are not exclusively spent on Latin America, it is an important part of the Latin network. CIP's prospectus says that "the Center has been informing the press, the public, and members of Congress about the implications of U.S. foreign policy towards developing countries with special emphasis on the relationship of U.S. economic and military assistance to the status of human rights. . . ."[63]

A theme CIP frequently plays is that Latin America's problems are really the fault of the United States. For instance, the introduction to William Biddle's CIP paper on Nicaragua states that "basic U.S. interests are more threatened by the customary American response to radical governments than by the governments themselves."[64] Likewise, on the Grenadan crisis, CIP fellow W. Frick Curry wrote, "In the final analysis, the greatest threat to American citizens was caused by violence precipitated by the [U.S.] invasion itself."[65] Despite its overt bias, CIP avers that "the press corps and Congressional leaders and staffs have found the Center's bimonthly *International Policy Report* useful in getting a fresh look at the problems of aid and repression."[66]

Center for Development Policy

The Center for Development Policy (CDP), also conceived by Lindsay Mattison, was founded in 1977. CDP and IPS participate fully in each other's activities. CDP has been extremely successful in organizing disaffected U.S. officials and military personnel and arranging opportunities for them to testify before Congress, with full press coverage.

Incorporated as a tax-exempt research and public-interest group, CDP has become a leader in the revolutionary Latin lobby on Capitol Hill, with Congress and the media as its targets. Over the years CDP has been funded by the same sources as IPS—the ARCA Foundation, the Bydale Foundation, the Ottinger Foundation, the Stern Fund, the Youth Project and the Stewart R. Mott Charitable Trust—as well as by a well-known Communist party source, the Bread and Roses Fund of Local 1199, National Health Care and Hospital Workers Union.

The first director of the CDP's Commission on U.S.–Central American Relations was Fred Branfman, former *CounterSpy* editorial board member and colleague of Philip Agee. Members of the commission include IPS fellows Michael Klare, Isabel Letelier, Cynthia Arnson, I. F. Stone, and trustee Philip Stern; *Mother Jones* editor Adam Hochschild; SANE director David Cortright; and WOLA director Joseph Eldridge.

To influence public opinion and policymaking, CDP has sponsored since 1982 over a dozen delegations to Latin America—congressmen, labor union leaders, educators, and clergymen. Invariably their findings contradicted those of the bipartisan Kissinger Commission. One such CDP delegation, led by NACLA staffer Janet Shenk, included Congressman Feighan (D–Ohio), who on returning charged that "the certification statement by President Reagan is a gross misrepresentation to the U.S. Congress [and] an indefensible deceit upon the American people. . . ."[67] CDP credits itself with "the historic shift" of the traditionally anticommunist AFL-CIO, prompting Lane Kirkland to call for an end to U.S. military aid for El Salvador.

CDP's network of former disaffected officials and military officers worked hard to block the Reagan administration's foreign policy initiatives in Latin America. For instance, John Buchanan, a former marine lieutenant colonel, joined CDP in 1981. Thanks to CDP's good connections with the Sandinista government, Buchanan spent a week in Nicaragua inspecting some of its military installations. On Buchanan's return, CDP helped arrange for him to testify before Congress and to have present the requisite press coverage. On September 21, 1982, he told the House Subcommittee on Inter-American Affairs that the United States posed a greater threat to peace in the region than the Soviet-backed military buildup of Nicaragua. "The United States has grossly exaggerated the military potential of Nicaragua as an excuse to fortify Honduras," *USA Today* reported Buchanan as saying.[68]

A more dramatic example is that of the CDP commission director, Robert White. In a 1982 article for the *New York Times Magazine,* White maintained that "Sandinista Nicaragua has been more respectful of human rights than any other Central American republic except Costa Rica."[69] Shortly thereafter, CDP saw to it that White testify before the House Foreign Affairs Committee. There he charged that the source of El Salvador's death-squad activity was none other than one of the country's major political parties headed by Roberto D'Aubuisson, who took his orders from a group of six exiles living in Miami.

A month later, a scandal broke. White's primary source of information was paid $50,000 by CDP. CDP told the press that it was done to provide a " 'security net' to help support him and move his family from El Salvador."[70] However, CDP's executive director, Lindsay Mattison, privately admitted, "We paid him to come forward."[71] Concerning White's specific charges, the first of the Miami six, Viera Altamirano, not only had never been a Miami resident, but had been dead since 1977.[72] The rest of the testimony was equally credible. One of those fingered by White, Arturo Muyshondt, was sufficiently disturbed by the accusations against him that he appeared at White's testimony on March 20, 1984, before the Senate Foreign Affairs Committee, where he served Robert White with a $10 million lawsuit for libel and defamation.

Committee in Solidarity with the People of El Salvador

The Committee in Solidarity with the People of Salvador (CISPES) was formed in 1980 as the U.S. branch of a worldwide apparatus supporting the Marxist FMLN guerrillas in El Salvador. Originally created with the help of Isabel Letelier of IPS and Robert Armstrong of NACLA in 1980, CISPES established some five hundred fifty chapters on college campuses across the United States in five years.

An inside view of CISPES and the Latin network was obtained when the personal papers of FMLN guerrilla leader Farid Handal were captured from a "safe house" in El Salvador in 1981. Among other things, they documented CISPES' connections with member groups of the Latin network and the international communist movement.[73]

CISPES sprang from Farid Handal's February 1980 trip to the United States during which he created a broad-based solidarity network to support the revolutionary movement in El Salvador. After touching down in New York, Handal met Robert Armstrong of NACLA, whom Handal described as a Trotskyite, to discuss propaganda strategy.[74]

When Handal arrived in Washington, D.C., he met first with Chencho Alas, a Jesuit priest attached to Georgetown University who had been expelled from El Salvador for collaborating with the Marxist guerrillas.[75] The next day Handal addressed an IPS seminar, organized by Isabel Letelier. There he met with two other Salvadorans, identified as Andrea and Enrique of the Popular Revolutionary Bloc (PRB), which is linked with the guerrilla faction known as the Popular Forces of Liberation (FPL), itself formerly headed by the late Communist party leader Cayetano Carpio.

That IPS meeting and subsequent ones with Ronald Dellums (D–Calif.) and Communist party members Luis Miguel Vasquez and Arthur Griffiths were seminal in forming CISPES in Washington, D.C.[76] With Congressman Dellums' invitation to return to Washington at a later date to address the Black Caucus, Handal took off for Chicago, San Francisco, and Los Angeles to organize other chapters.

In his itinerary work for CISPES, Handal emphasized that in the United States propaganda should emphasize themes without political labeling—human rights, for instance. He stressed the need for a Leninist popular front strategy. "We cannot speak a different language than those sectors which we hope to incorporate," said Handal. "Our terminology should be acceptable and should not constitute a block to the spirit of solidarity. . . . The problem should be presented with its human features, without political language and, most importantly, without a political label."[77]

In Los Angeles, Handal met with the United Electrical, Radio and Machine Workers of America and the Longshoremen's Union, two unions long dominated by the Communist party. The Longshoremen's Union assured Handal that it would refuse to load ships in Los Angeles with cargos blacklisted by the "comrades" in El Salvador.[78]

Handal then flew back to New York, where he was given practical advice by Alfredo Garcia Almeida and others at the Cuban mission to the U.N. "In order to protect your visa," the Cubans told Handal, "you should give the appearance of providing information on El Salvador to progressive Congressmen and thus make the rest of your work appear more natural."[79] This was no problem for Handal, who had already been invited to address the Black Caucus. The Cuban comrades at the U.N. also recommended that Handal contact Juan Ferreira of WOLA.[80] In New York, Communist party leader Sandy Pollack recommended that "there should be a national conference under the auspices of the U.S. Peace Counscil, the National Council of Churches, Amnesty International, WOLA, and various unions in the U.S. for the purpose of establishing a support mechanism. . . ."[81]

On his return to Washington, Handal met with the Black Caucus. "Monday morning the offices of Congressman Dellums were turned into our offices," Handal reports in the safe-house documents. "Everything was done there," he continued. "The meeting with the Black Caucus took place in the liver of the monster itself, nothing less than in the meeting room of the House Foreign Affairs Committee."[82] Handal also met with Jorge Sol Castellanos of the Inter-American Bank (who would become a fellow at IPS two years later).

As Handal's documents testify, the structure of CISPES reveals a great deal about the nature of the Latin American network. There is collaboration between communists and noncommunists in CISPES as in the other organizations, but in the case of CISPES, the involvement is considerably more overt. CISPES' leadership structure consists of five steering committees: (1) the U.S. Peace Council, then chaired by Communist party leader Sandy Pollack; (2) EPICA, headed by Phil Wheaton; (3) NACLA, led by Robert Armstrong; (4) the Religious Task Force on El Salvador, led by Tom Quigley; and (5) the Inter-Religious Task Force on El Salvador, directed by Beverly Keene.[83]

Groups like WOLA, IPS, CIP, and CDP try to avoid direct affiliation with CISPES because of its communist involvement. But the identity of goals has resulted in extensive behind-the-scenes cooperation. At its first national convention, on May 25, 1985, attended by many in the Latin network, the CISPES program announced:

> What brings us together is clear—U.S. intervention in Central America is destructive and immoral, and must be stopped. As President Reagan and Congress boost aid to El Salvador and Guatemala, and attack Nicaragua, it is more important than ever to build a massive anti-intervention movement here at home. . . . We have to expand our capacity to raise funds, build strong organizations and coalitions, and respond with power and coordination to Reagan's attacks on Central America.[84]

The Central American Historical Institute and the Institute for Food and Development Policy

The Central American Historical Institute (CAHI) and the Institute for Food and Development Policy (IFDP) are based in Washington, D.C., and San Francisco, respectively. Both have sister organizations in Managua. The former is affiliated with the Institute on the History of Central America and the latter with the Institute for Economic and Social Research.

CAHI was established at the behest of Alvaro Arguello, a Jesuit priest who headed the Sandinista-controlled Nicaraguan Council of State. The Jesuits support CAHI by providing the salary of its director, Father Arguello, and defraying the cost of its Washington operations at Georgetown, a Jesuit university. Some support also comes from the Maryknoll order.

CAHI director Betsy Cohn has chaired several seminars at IPS and contributed to the IPS publication *In Contempt of Congress*. According to the *World Council of Churches 1983 Resource Sharing Book*, CAHI intends to provide a telex service to send news to various centers in Europe and America. But the funding request makes it quite clear that CAHI would be little more than a conduit for the official Sandinista line:

> Moreover, an increasing number of organizations in Europe and America in general in addition to cooperating agencies and solidarity committees have drawn attention to the lack of regular, speedy news, above all at the time when Nicaragua is being criticized by conservative circles throughout the world press. The government of Nicaragua does not have necessary resources to meet this challenge.[85]

The Jesuit/Catholic affiliation bestows on CAHI's news analyses a legitimacy that it could not hope otherwise to secure.

When foreign journalists visit Nicaragua, CAHI's Managua staff is often on hand to provide the "correct interpretation" on any given issue. At home, CAHI has joined the fray to influence the U.S. Congress. When Senator Kennedy arranged a forum in July 1984 to air views critical of the contras, CAHI dug up "victims" of abuse—selected by the Sandinista government.

The Institute for Food and Development Policy (IFDP), based in San Francisco, was founded by former IPS fellow Joseph Collins. Like CAHI, IFDP has a sister organization in Managua—the Institute for Economic and Social Research (INIES)—which does research and trains activists in Central America and the Caribbean.[86]

IFDP director Joseph Collins and INIES director Xabier Gorostiaga serve on the PACCA executive board and contributed to IPS's monograph *Changing Course*, which attacked the Kissinger Commission report on Central America.

Not surprisingly, IFDP is largely bankrolled by the same sources that support

IPS—the Rubin Foundation, Stern Fund, Ottinger Foundation, ARCA Foundation, Shalan Foundation, and Ruth Mott Fund.

While attempting to throttle all aid to private-sector development, IFDP rhapsodizes over the economic arrangements in communist countries. "[T]he actual experience of land reform in countries as different as Vietnam, China and Cuba . . . can be a first step in long-term production advances," write Joe Collins and Frances Moore Lappé.[87] In their book, *Food First,* which sold nearly a million copies, they assert that Americans should

> outlaw government assistance through AID and OPIC and indirectly through the World Bank to U.S. private corporations investing in underdeveloped countries . . . and . . . promote economic assistance, not as loans but as grants . . . to countries where steps are being taken to democratize control over agricultural resources, such as Vietnam and Mozambique.[88]

IFDP works directly with the Cuban and Nicaraguan governments. According to IFDP's 1983 annual report, "In a rare move, eight Cuban ministries and government institutes, as well as the offices of Vice-President Carlos Rafael Rodriguez and President Fidel Castro, have cooperated with the Institute's study."[89] According to IFDP's description of its Project Nicaragua, "The Nicaraguan government requested the Institute's help in 1979," and "since that time Joseph Collins, with the assistance of other staff members, has acted as an unpaid advisor on food and agriculture policies in Nicaragua."[90] As for the two books published by IFDP—*What Difference Could a Revolution Make?* and *Now We Can Speak: A Journey Through the New Nicaragua*—IFDP notes in its 1983 progress report, "The Nicaraguan Foreign Ministry was so impressed with these two books that it purchased 100 copies of each to distribute to the American press and members of Congress."[91]

Neighbor to Neighbor, IFDP's latest project undertaken in early 1986, demonstrates yet a new level of sophistication using the power of the media. "We've turned to television to reach the millions of people who don't read our books . . . and . . . we're purchasing air time to put our documentary on U.S. policy in Central America, *Faces of War,* into America's living rooms and fight the contras on national TV," says associate director Kit Miller.[92] IFDP's Neighbor to Neighbor has identified the swing-vote congressional districts nationwide, with the help of WOLA and the Coalition for a New Foreign and Military Policy, and enlisted members of CISPES to organize demonstrations to coincide with its TV show. It proved to be a potent lobbying package. On the first vote in 1986, the House voted down the $100 million aid package to the contras (220–208). "Our efforts paid off in at least four districts in the vote," said Miller.[93]

IPS Serves as Hub of Latin Network

IPS often acts as the ideological center and hub of activism of the autonomous groups in the Latin network. For instance, the year following the IPS-PACCA campaign to discredit the Kissinger Commission, IPS looked for new ways to exacerbate division in the country—within Congress and between Congress and the White House. Thus in early 1985 IPS brought together various players in the Latin network to compile "the Reagan record of deceit and illegality on Central America." *In Contempt of Congress* was a mishmash of contradictory data and not particularly persuasive. But then it was intended not to persuade, but to confuse and sow distrust of the Reagan administration. As with the PACCA report, it got wide circulation in Congress. Sen. Tom Harkin (D–Iowa) offered his praise for it and Sen. John Kerry (D–Mass.) called it "essential reading for every American who remembers Vietnam and Watergate."[94]

In late 1985 IPS produced another study, *Outcast Among Allies,* this time to drive a wedge between the United States and its allies. As IPS founder Richard Barnet put it, "The allies and friends of the United States do not accept as valid the Administration's case for conducting military operations against [Nicaragua], squeezing its economy and seeking to deny legitimacy to its elected government."[95] In respect to this, upon their return from Cuba and Nicaragua, where they were hosted by the internal security minister, Tomas Borge, IPS's Robert Borosage and Saul Landau reported to an IPS gathering:

> We were there [in Nicaragua] for a whole series of purposes. One was to work on a project we have going in Europe which was to encourage European support for aid to Nicaragua to keep it from being isolated economically and politically. The other was to work with the eight ministries down there to make sure they had their projects in order so that the Europeans could operate effectively.[96]

The Latin Network and the International Communist Movement

We have noted the close relations that many leaders of the Latin network in the United States have with officials of the Sandinista and Castro governments. The Institute for Policy Studies itself and its sister organization, the Riverside Church Disarmament Program, have honored prominent Latin American communists. These include Daniel Ortega, Nora Astorga, Carlos Tunnerman, and Miguel D'Escoto, high officials of the Sandinista government; Ramon Sanchez Parodi, chief counselor and identified DGI intelligence officer at the Cuban Interests Section in Washington, D.C.; Rene Mujica, Sergio Martinez, and Jose Delgado, the first, second, and third secretaries respectively at the Cuban Interests Section; Raul Roa Kouri, the Cuban ambassador to the U.N.; and Margaret

Randall, a defector from the U.S. who has worked for both the Castro and Sandinista governments.

The case of Orlando Letelier provided hard evidence of the connection between Cuba and the IPS. As noted in the previous chapter, Letelier worked as an agent of influence under the Cuban DGI while directing IPS's Transnational Institute.[97] Instrumental in the building of the Latin network, Letelier assisted in the establishment of the Council on Hemispheric Affairs (COHA) and the Center for International Policy (CIP). His wife, Isabel Letelier, continued on at IPS after his death, serves on the advisory board of WOLA, and gave the welcoming remarks at the founding conference of the U.S. Peace Council, established by members of the Communist party and spun off from the Soviet front World Peace Council.[98] About Communist party and U.S. Peace Council leader Sandy Pollack, Mrs. Letelier said, "We learned a tremendous amount from Sandy's commitment and the way she worked. [A]s Latin Americanists we know she will always be alive in our struggles and she will be with us in our victories."[99]

Saul Landau, an IPS senior fellow, is a personal friend of Fidel Castro and has access to the top echelon of the Cuban regime. Landau's activities in support of Castro date back to the first few years of the Cuban revolution. In January 1961, the month after Castro proclaimed his communist convictions to the world, Landau spoke at the Cuban American Friendship Rally in New York City, sponsored by the youth wing of the Communist party, USA.

Landau lived in Cuba during the 1960s and worked on a propaganda film praising the Cuban revolution. "Cuba," he wrote, "is the first purposeful society that we have had in the Western Hemisphere for many years."[100] Landau was on the first wave of the Venceremos Brigade, which was formed for the specific purpose of bringing American activists to Cuba for indoctrination. The Venceremos Brigade was, in fact, an arm of the DGI, which, by 1970, was under the control of the Soviet KGB.[101] The FBI has stated that DGI's purpose in creating the brigade was to recruit "individuals . . . who someday would provide the Cuban government with access to political, economic and military intelligence."[102]

Landau publicly participated in the World Communist Youth Festival held in Havana in 1978. Twenty thousand communist youths from one hundred forty nations attended the Soviet-organized festival. One of the main events was the Youth Accuse Imperialism Tribunal, a kangaroo court patterned after Stalin's show trials. For three days, "witnesses" such as Landau and CIA defector Philip Agee took the stand and lashed out against the United States and the West. On another occasion, Landau showed his solidarity with the Soviet front World Peace Council when he led the U.S. delegation to the WPC Conference on Solidarity with Chile.[103]

Landau's film *With Fidel* was followed in 1983 by *Target Nicaragua: Inside a Covert War*. In it Landau used footage supplied by Lenin Cerna, chief of

Sandinista State Security. The Sandinistas had captured an Argentine intelligence officer, Victor Frances, who under torture "confessed" that the CIA was behind the contras' crimes against the Nicaraguan people. (The footage was edited by Landau for the American TV audience.) After being tortured, Frances was executed, a fact that was tacitly admitted by Miguel D'Escoto to members of the U.S. House Intelligence Committee on a fact-finding mission to Nicaragua in 1983.[104]

Saul Landau, Cora Weiss, William Sloane Coffin, Robert Borosage, Peter Kornbluh, and Richard Barnet, all IPS luminaries, have always been welcomed in Nicaragua by the Sandinista hierarchy.[105] Tomas Borge, who works hand in glove with the Cuban DGI intelligence and is responsible for the execution of hundreds of political prisoners, has personally received IPS fellows, such as Richard Barnet and Peter Kornbluh, in his home in Managua.[106]

Conclusion

Some of those in the Latin network are naive global utopians; some simply oppose the Reagan administration, and by extension its policies; but others may be witting or unwitting agents of influence for hostile foreign powers.

Dissent and protest are guaranteed First Amendment rights. But, the question nags, Should organizations with tax-deferred status interfere with U.S. foreign affairs to promote revolutions not in the best interests of this nation? As we have seen, various groups and individuals in the Latin network are doing precisely this.

CHAPTER 15

Power and Influence on Capitol Hill
IPS and Congress

The prestige that IPS enjoys on Capitol Hill didn't just happen. Three years after its founding, the institute distributed a report on itself. Although he would later admit that it was "an extraordinary conceit," IPS cofounder Marcus Raskin boasted that IPS was called "to speak truth to power."[1] IPS members, the report stated, were "public scholars," who would attempt "to bridge the world of ideas and the world of affairs" and IPS fellows would "offer alternative frameworks for policy."[2]

While IPS is usually identified as a *liberal* institution by the major media, *Marxist* would be the more accurate term. In the institute's twentieth-anniversary publication, *First Harvest,* Raskin writes that "such positive social philosophies as Marxism are beginning to have a larger following. . . . We are all Marxists—either by using that analysis or playing out, as actors, the tragic role Marx foresaw."[3]

In his book *The Limits and Possibilities of Congress,* IPS fellow Philip Brenner would "help to bridge the gap between Marxist literature on the state and more traditional literature on the institutions of the United States government."[4] So many gaps, so many bridges to build. "The book," he continues, "addresses questions of importance to congressional scholars by means of an approach developed by Marxist scholars."[5]

Taking Aim: IPS Looks at Congress

IPS sought to proselytize Congress from the start. Seminars for congressmen and their staffs, often on Capitol Hill, were held regularly from 1963 to 1968 and more occasionally thereafter.[6] By 1978 IPS had institutionalized its outreach programs in lunch seminars and in its Washington School classes. Minor diversity exists among the fellows, but the views of founders Marcus Raskin and Richard Barnet reveal a great deal about the institute.

"In the modern-day United States," says Raskin, "neither a democracy nor a republic exists in operation. The state helps the powerful. The emergence of large-scale armed forces and corporate capitalism colonizes people into huge organizational structures."[7] As noted earlier, Raskin has skirted reality and conjured up a "national security state" on which to vent his animosity. He believes the United States really exists by "the maintenance of organized power in the hands of the state, its military and bureaucratic apparatus, and its corporate system"—what he calls a "modern tyranny."[8] The president cannot act in behalf of the poor without "doing battle with capitalism and imperialism," says Raskin. "He would be required, therefore, to fashion a new set of symbols from the American landscape of myths and dreams which would cause direct confrontation with the bloated genocide-preparing military system."[9] American-style democracy, he concludes, "menaces the freedom and well-being of its citizenry" and "poses a danger to world civilization."[10]

Barnet, usually more guarded than Raskin, distinguishes between "procedural" and "substantive" freedoms. The United States, he says, allows empty "procedural" freedoms of press, speech, and assembly, whereas the Soviet Union grants the more meaningful "substantive" freedoms—state-provided (and state-controlled) jobs, housing, and medical care.[11] In Barnet's eyes there is no substantial moral difference between the American and the Soviet systems. He expounds at length on their moral relativism in his latest books, *The Giants, Real Security,* and *The Alliance.*

In their book *The New Class War: Reagan's Attack on the Welfare State and Its Consequences,* which IPS promotes, associate fellow Frances Fox Piven and Richard A. Cloward argue that (1) class conflict centers around the state, and that (2) representational government is not democratic. Congressional elections are little more than a farce held for the benefit of the "moneyed interests," who, through control of the communications network, are responsible for "the manipulation, cooptation and coercion of public opinion."[12]

Philip Brenner sees Congress as the arena of class conflict. "Congress," he says, "provides essential services . . . for the private accumulation of wealth, accumulation that would not be possible in its present form without the intervention of the national government."[13] He accuses the members of Congress of trying "to serve property and people at the same time," which "creates an unrelieved tension . . . because the two efforts are contradictory."[14]

Democracy Redefined

Despite its disdain for the American system of government and private enterprise, IPS trumpets democracy, and even urges its expansion into economics, or rather, "economic democracy." IPS associate fellow Derek Shearer chose that term as a euphemism for the unpalatable word *socialism*. But in reality, economic democracy requires the abolition of private property.[15]

Shearer estimated that to implement "economic democracy" in America, the Left would need twenty to thirty governors, twenty to thirty big-city mayors, *ten or twenty senators, fifty House members*, three or four national union leaders, and a sympathetic president.[16] Given that IPS is supported by at least four major unions, a dozen mayors, and over sixty congressmen, Shearer's goal is well in sight. In the meantime, IPS patiently works on its short-term objectives, cajoling the "undemocratic" Congress even though, as Brenner says, "we should not expect that changing the personnel or the rules of Congress alone will enable it to do all the things we wish."[17]

Though the institute's 1979–80 annual report states that its fellows espouse decentralization, democracy, and spontaneity,[18] their writings and activities show quite the contradictory. Most have serious reservations about democracy as it exists in the United States and are forever advocating more government intervention. Associate fellow Michael Parenti declares, "I would call Cuba a democracy. . . . The governments in Eastern Europe actually expanded liberty for the people of that area," whereas in America the Founding Fathers believed in liberty only "for their own capitalist ruling class."[19]

Congress Looks at IPS

From the beginning disarmament was top priority for the institute. One of its first seminars was styled "National Security and Disarmament," and between 1964 and 1967, "Defense and Disarmament" seminars were held annually. The first two, chaired by a legislative assistant to Rep. William Fitts Ryan, hosted twenty-one and twenty-two congressional staffers respectively.

In 1974 IPS began holding seminars for freshman congressmen on foreign and domestic policy. The seminars, which *Barron's* called "ideological boot camp,"[20] were "designed to help the new legislators formulate an integrated national and international understanding," according to literature on the seminars distributed by IPS.[21] Senior Congressmen Kastenmeier, Conyers, and Rosenthal were on hand to lend an air of legitimacy. Fifty new congressmen participated in the 1976 seminar.[22]

IPS often asks congressmen to teach classes as an alternative to taking them. The radicals in the audience then ask questions, and so "educate" the congressmen.

Senators Abourezk (IPS trustee), Tsongas, and Hatfield and Congressmen Miller, Reuss, Dellums, and Conyers have all taught at IPS. In his course, Mark Hatfield addressed "the ultimate question, whether the legislative process is adequate for a reordering of national priorities." In March 1980 John Conyers organized a colloquium on the Hill with IPS fellows Richard Barnet and Mark Hertsgaard; it was titled "Energy and the Cold War: Roots of the International Crisis." And this only scratches the surface.

A Conyers aide, Neil G. Kotler, founded the Progressive House Staff Committee. Although Kotler has denied any formal relationship with IPS, associate fellow Gar Alperovitz spoke at the group's first forum, which attracted a hundred congressional aides. Alperovitz has been deeply involved with IPS since the early sixties; while a legislative assistant to Sen. Gaylord Nelson he became one of IPS's original eight "founding fellows."

Testifying before congressional hearings from time to time, IPS fellows influence the legislative process directly. Richard Barnet, for instance, testified before the Senate Committee on Foreign Relations on SALT II in 1979; Michael Moffitt spoke before the House and Senate Subcommittees on Banking and Finance in 1982; Elizabeth Schmidt testified before the House Subcommittee on Africa; and the ensuing years have seen much more of the same. In 1983 IPS fellow Michael Goldhaber testified before the House Science and Technology Committee on "Microelectronics and Developing Countries." In 1985 research associate David Chappell testified before the Subcommittee on Asian and Pacific Affairs of the House Foreign Affairs Committee on the "flawed content" of the Free Association Compact, an agreement on American and Micronesian rights in the Trust Territory.

IPS Admirers on Capitol Hill

On April 5, 1983, IPS threw a large twentieth-anniversary celebration to raise funds. On the committee were fourteen present and two former members of the House of Representatives and three present and six former senators.[23] Among the representatives then in office:

Les Aspin (D–Wis.), chairman of Economic Policy Task Force Subcommittee of the House Committee on Budget and the Subcommittee on Military Personnel and Compensation of the Committee on Armed Services (as of Ninety-ninth Congress, chairman of Armed Services Committee)

Ronald V. Dellums (D–Calif.), chairman of Subcommittee on Military Installations and Facilities of the House Committee on Armed Services

Don Edwards (D–Calif.), chairman of House Judiciary Committee's Subcommittee on Civil and Constitutional Rights, which oversees the Federal Bureau of Investigation

Richard L. Ottinger (D–N.Y.), chairman of Subcommittee on Energy Conservation and Power of the House Committee on Energy and Commerce

Leon E. Panetta (D–Calif.), chairman of Budget Process Task Force of the House Committee on Budget (chairman of Subcommittee on Police and Personnel, Ninety-ninth Congress)

Ted Weiss (D–N.Y.), chairman of Subcommittee on Intergovernmental Relations and Human Resources of the House Committee on Government Operations (as of Ninety-ninth Congress, member of Foreign Affairs Committee)

George E. Brown, Jr. (D–Calif.) (member of Select Committee on Intelligence, Ninety-ninth Congress)

Philip Burton (D–Calif.), now deceased

George Crockett (D–Mich.), member of Foreign Affairs Committee (chairman of Subcommittee on Western Hemisphere Affairs, 100th Congress)

Tom Harkin (D–Iowa), member of Committee on Science and Technology, now a senator

Robert Kastenmeier (D–Wis.), member of Subcommittee on FBI Oversight (member of Select Committee on Intelligence, Ninety-ninth Congress)

George Miller (D–Calif.), member of Budget Committee

Patricia Schroeder (D–Colo.), member of Committee on Armed Services and Committee on the Judiciary

John Seiberling (D–Ohio), member of Committee on the Judiciary

Also on the IPS committee was Henry Reuss, former representative, and chairman of the House Banking and Housing Affairs Committee and chairman of the Joint Economic Committee.

Among the senators then in office:

Christopher Dodd (D–Conn.), member of Committee on Foreign Relations

Gary Hart (D–Colo.), presidential candidate 1984, member of Committee on Armed Services

Mark O. Hatfield (R–Oreg.), member of Senate Rules Committee (chairman of Appropriations Committee, Ninety-ninth Congress)[24]

Senator Hatfield enthusiastically endorsed the institute: "I respect the often thoughtful and scholarly work of these individuals. I have no doubt that theirs is a legitimate and useful role in the formulation of national policy."[25] Congressmen Dellums and Kastenmeier and former Sen. George McGovern had the honor of "roasting" IPS cofounders Barnet and Raskin, and Congressman Conyers paid formal tribute to the institute.[26]

"Very Well Known, Very Highly Respected"

Special friends aside, IPS is almost universally known on Capitol Hill. As Sen. Robert Morgan (D–N.C.) put it in 1976, "This country is basically run by the legislative staffs"[27] of the Congress, and it is a measure of the prestige of IPS that so many aides, burdened with stacks of paper work, read its publications.

As Robert Dockery, legislative assistant to Senator Dodd, pointed out, "I can certainly get [information] faster from the Congressional Research Service [CRS] than from outside policy research groups." And CRS in turn uses IPS publications for its source material. CRS director Gilbert Gude, a former congressional member of the IPS-related Peace Through Law caucus, and his assistant, Elizabeth Yadlasky, introduced to CRS several papers on Cuba by IPS associate William LeoGrande, papers which favorably portrayed Castro and Cuban life.[28] Likewise, when Stanley Higinbotham, chief of the foreign affairs and national defense division of CRS, was formulating "some gross categorizations" for human rights violations as a standard for political analysis, he collaborated with Joe Eldridge of WOLA, a man skilled at rooting out human rights deficiencies in friendly countries but consistently sluggish about infractions in Cuba or Nicaragua.[29]

In an informal poll taken in early 1984 of eighty-four liberal House offices,[30] 74 percent of those interviewed said they read IPS materials or thought IPS a credible source of information. Nearly 50 percent had distinctly favorable opinions of IPS.

Of thirty-one interviews in liberal Senate offices, twenty-two, or 71 percent, said they read IPS material or thought it credible, and ten were quite favorable.

"They turn out quality work," said Diane Z. Stamm, legislative assistant to Mel Levine (D–Calif.).

"I've worked with them quite a bit over the years," said Dianna J. Baker, personal secretary and administrative aide to Tom Harkin, now senator from Iowa.

"These are the people who get very excited and have done the most work on human-rights-oriented thinking about El Salvador," said Doug Mashore, a House Foreign Operations Subcommittee staffer for Julian Dixon (D–Calif.).

"They're a good group," said Jeff Hertsbach, an aide to Bob Carr (D–Mich.).

Jeffrey Rosenberg, legislative assistant to Lane Evans (D–Ill.), said Evans "likes" IPS.

Lynn Perry, aide to Gus Savage (D–Ill.), said IPS had "considerable" influence in that office.

Suzanne Butcher, aide to Stephen J. Solarz (D–N.Y.), recommended IPS as a resource on human rights issues.

"We seek information from them a lot of times in terms of statistical information, as their statistical information is quite good," said Faye Johnson, legislative assistant to Sen. Mark Hatfield. IPS, she said, is "particularly useful in the area of defense spending," as its information "balances off with the State Department."

Several other aides working on arms-control issues echoed the praise. Robert M. Sherman, an arms-control expert working in three congressional offices as well as on the Defense Subcommittee of the House Committee on Appropriations, stated, "They're coming up. They used to be kind of flako left wing, but this recent *Nuclear Weapons Databook* they put out is excellent."

Bradford Penney, legislative assistant to the ranking minority member on the Senate Committee on Foreign Relations, Claiborne Pell (D–R.I.), said IPS is "very well known, very highly respected."

John H. Hess III, legislative assistant to the chairman of the Senate Committee on Rules and Administration, Charles Matthias (R–Md.), said, "I personally like their stuff. I take the time to read it."

Other favorable comments came from the House offices of Ronald V. Dellums (D–Calif.), Thomas Foglietta (D–Pa.), Wyche Fowler (D–Ga.), James M. Jeffords (D–Vt.), Mike Lowry (D–Wash.), Norman Y. Mineta (D–Calif.), and Timothy E. Wirth (D–Colo.), among others.

A Move Toward the Purse Strings

In one of its most sparkling achievements on Capitol Hill, the institute came out with an alternative budget. Speaking for forty-seven members of Congress, John Conyers (D–Mich.) asked IPS to prepare a study of President Ford's budget in 1975. The following year, fifty-five members asked IPS "to extend its excellent analysis of the Budget to include proposals on how federal spending should be redirected."[31] In 1978 fifty-four members signed Conyers' request for the budget study; in 1982, fifty-one; in 1983, sixty. (See Appendix 10.)

The essays for 1978, all designed in one way or another to socialize the United States, were compiled in a huge book, *The Federal Budget and Social Reconstruction*, edited by Marcus Raskin and published by IPS, and became an IPS institution. Characteristically, it urged slashes in military spending, massive increases in welfare spending, and the subsidizing of lagging industries.[32]

In 1983 IPS sponsored a day-long conference in the caucus room of the Cannon House Office Building to publicize its latest alternative budget. Congressman Harkin introduced Marcus Raskin as the featured speaker, John Conyers chaired the "Macroeconomic Policy" workshop, and Sam Gejdenson (D–Conn.) chaired the "Defense and Foreign Policy" workshop. Panel discussions on "Industrial Policy" and "Social Welfare" were chaired by Bob Edgar (D–Pa.) and Cardiss Collins (D–Ill.) respectively.

IPS, the Liberal Consensus, and the Death of Bipartisanship

The greatest success of IPS has been in the area of foreign policy. Since Vietnam, Congress has been split over how to deal with communist-backed revolutionary movements in the third world. In the early 1980s Congress debated whether or not to continue military and economic assistance to the El Salvadoran government under attack by the well-financed Marxist FMLN guerrillas. Similar debates ensued over support for anticommunist efforts in Angola, Afghanistan, Guatemala, and Nicaragua. And when Congress did approve aid, as in the cases of Afghanistan and Nicaragua, it was never enough.

The foreign aid bill reported out of the Democrat-controlled House Foreign Affairs Committee in early 1984 was typical of the anti-anticommunist mindset prevalent in the left wing of the Democratic party. The bill granted a certain amount of military and economic aid to El Salvador but bound it with tight conditions: the removal of all government and military personnel *alleged* to have ties with death squads; the cessation of U.S. training exercises in Honduras; a cap on the number of U.S. advisers in El Salvador; the prohibition of military aid to Guatemala; and the termination of the president's access to all special or emergency funds for El Salvador. It also mandated "unconditional" negotiations with the guerrillas and all parties to the conflict. And, finally, it demanded that once the president had certified that all the conditions had been met, Congress would have to pass a joint resolution of approval of the president's judgment before any funds could be released.

The restrictions were narrowly defeated in April 1984 by a 211–208 vote.

Secretary of State George P. Shultz was quoted in the *Washington Post* on March 29, 1984, as saying that the Reagan administration's foreign policy was "constantly undercut" by Congress. "There has to be a capacity for decisiveness under certain circumstances," Shultz said. "There has to be an ability to go along without being constantly undercut . . . or surrounded by so many conditions that you don't have much room for maneuver."[33]

On April 6, 1984, at Georgetown University, President Reagan asked for a renewal of the bipartisan consensus for U.S. foreign policy.

"We must restore America's honorable tradition of partisan politics stopping at the water's edge," the president said, noting that over a hundred prohibitions and restrictions had been imposed by Congress in the 1970s to limit the executive in the areas of trade, human rights, arms sales, foreign assistance, intelligence operations, and the dispatch of troops in times of crisis.

Too many in Congress, he said, seem to believe their only task is to be "vocal critics, not responsible partners" in foreign policy.

Bipartisanship can only work if both sides face up to real-world problems. I welcome a debate. But if it is to be productive, we must put aside mythology and uninformed rhetoric. Some, for example, insist that the root of regional violence is poverty, but not communism. . . . But economic aid alone cannot stop Cuban- and Soviet-sponsored guerrillas determined to terrorize, burn, bomb, and destroy everything from bridges and industries to electric power and transportation. And neither individual rights nor economic health can be advanced if stability is not secured.[34]

But certain congressmen take a different view of the "real-world problems." At a May 1982 forum on covert action against Nicaragua, sponsored by the Campaign for Political Rights in cooperation with IPS and other antiinterventionist groups, Rep. Matthew F. McHugh (D–N.Y.) stated that "if we are going to make progress in Central America, we simply must recognize that the changes that took place in Nicaragua were inevitable" and were "in some sense, pro- moted, not because it's the moral thing to do—although it is—but because it serves U.S. interests, because it is consistent with the realities of the world, with the realities of human nature and the inevitability of change."[35]

In the next three years, the Sandinistas tightened their totalitarian grip, in- creased repression, and became thoroughly militarized. Nevertheless, Congress- man McHugh maintained his earlier position, voting against any support for the contra freedom fighters, even after Daniel Ortega had secured $200 million in aid from Moscow in spring 1985.

More Miserable

Jeane Kirkpatrick, as U.S. ambassador to the United Nations, held a com- pletely different view of the moral imperatives of U.S. policy toward Central America. Qualifying her position by saying that she "does not . . . support 'moderately repressive regimes' in Central America or any place," Ambassador Kirkpatrick said:

> We must know why our concern for Central America and the Caribbean is morally acceptable and legitimate. The answer to this is crucial yet very easy. History, we know, demonstrates with a clarity that is irresistible, that no matter how ill-fed, ill-clothed, no matter how illiterate or how miserable people have been under their traditional governments, they will be *more* miserable under Communist governments. . . . It simply does not work as a human system. Everybody un- derstands that the number of refugees which pour out of Communist countries decade after decade proves the inhumanity of the system and its incompatibility with human survival and human realizations.
>
> The strength of the United States is inextricably and inevitably involved with the defense of freedom in our time. When we protect our own national security, we are, in fact, engaging in a morally acceptable enterprise.[36]

Such ideas meet with scorn at IPS. Indeed, to IPS the enemy is not the communists but those who share the opinions of Ambassador Kirkpatrick and President Reagan. The president had no sooner formed the bipartisan Kissinger Commission on Central America and the Caribbean than IPS set about opposing it.

In January 1984 the Kissinger Commission made public its recommendations that the United States send El Salvador economic aid to promote its democratic development and military aid to combat the Soviet-backed insurgency. IPS rushed to respond with a report, *Changing Course: Blueprint for Peace in Central America and the Caribbean.* Under the auspices of the Policy Alternatives for the Caribbean and Central America (PACCA), thirty people, including eleven from IPS, had a hand in the report. According to IPS, Jorge Sol, John Cavanagh, Cynthia Arnson, Saul Landau and Robert Borosage, all IPS and TNI fellows, "took the lead in drafting the PACCA report."[37]

"We intend this 'Blueprint' to be used as an action and organizing document for Congress," said the PACCA executive board in its introduction.[38] The main points of the "Program for Peace" are as follows:

Nicaragua: cease backing the anticommunist contras and support Contadora efforts to normalize relations between Nicaragua and its neighbors

El Salvador: cut off military aid and support a negotiated settlement with power-sharing among the contending forces

Honduras: dismantle the U.S. bases and withdraw U.S. troops and warships

Guatemala: express disapproval of the government's repressive policies toward indigenous people

Cuba: begin a process to achieve normal diplomatic and commercial relations[39]

No mention was made of the Nicaraguan government's repressive policies toward its own people—the Miskito, Sumo, Rama, and Misura Indians—nor of Cuba's and the Soviet Union's support of the unprecedented military buildup in Nicaragua, which in turn supported the FMLN insurgency in El Salvador.

After much congressional battling, El Salvador received a trickle of aid and the Nicaraguan contras were abandoned. To the extent that liberal congressmen took PACCA's recommendations seriously, no consensus with the administration over Central American policy was possible.

IPS and Congressional Foreign Policy

Even though IPS could not have caused the congressional rift in foreign policy by itself, the influence that it wields on the Hill is awesome.

Of the nine majority staffers on the House Foreign Affairs Committee who consented to be interviewed, six read IPS materials. The high percentage implies that IPS is taken fairly seriously. Victor Johnson, staff director of the Subcommittee on Western Hemisphere Affairs, which is responsible for Central America, admits that he works closely with Cynthia Arnson, an IPS associate fellow. Johnson says he doesn't even look at publications of the highly respected Center for Strategic and International Studies or the conservative Heritage Foundation.

Of the three Foreign Affairs Committee staff members who said they did not read IPS materials, only one commented negatively: "I do not view it as being an objective source of information." The same staffer also believed that the influence of IPS on the Hill was limited to those "who are predisposed to that ideological viewpoint," and that IPS was merely one of the "most egregious" examples of policy research too biased to take seriously.

"IPS just doesn't deal in the range of political opinion that people on the [Senate Foreign Relations] Committee really deal with," said one aide.

Special Friends in Congress

Certain "progressive" congressmen and legislative assistants have been especially sympathetic to the institute's attempt to have America abandon its commitment to resist communist expansionism.

Insofar as democracy is concerned, the progressive definition of it surfaced in the foreign policy debate over Central America. It is, for example, progressive to belittle El Salvador's attempts to establish constitutional government and equally progressive to defend the Sandinistas' "people's democracy."

Rep. George Miller (D–Calif.), demonstrated this "progressive" characteristic on the "MacNeil-Lehrer News Hour" the day after the March 25, 1984, Salvadoran presidential elections. He charged that elections were beside the point—no progress in human rights had been made by the Salvadorian government.

Asked to respond, the other guest on the program, Rep. Jack Kemp (R–N.Y.), said,

> Well, there has been progress, according to the archbishop. I realize George has his own source of information, but I think it's demonstrably progressive to see that country doing what it has done in the middle of a very serious conflict on the Left and the Right.

Whether Kemp had anyone in mind is not known, but Miller's aide on Central American policy is IPS stalwart Cynthia Arnson. Arnson is the author of two books on El Salvador, both published by IPS, both hostile to the Reagan administration's policy, both favorable to the Marxist Left in Central America.

Arnson and two others prepared the 1982 ACLU/Americas Watch report on human rights in El Salvador, widely used by congressional staff. She also co-authored, with IPS fellow Michael Klare, *Supplying Repression: U.S. Support for Authoritarian Regimes Abroad,* which criticized U.S. relations with some of its key third-world allies.

In March 1984 Arnson, an IPS associate fellow, drafted a letter addressed to the Speaker of the House for Miller's signature. The letter (see Appendix 11) demanded a cutoff of all military aid to El Salvador until Congress approved a joint resolution confirming that "changes have occurred in El Salvador regarding the death squads," that the government was negotiating with the Left, that the murders of U.S. citizens were being prosecuted, and that a functioning judicial system had been established. The letter, signed by sixty-eight congressmen, went on, "We are letting you know our views at this early date in order to avoid a divisive and acrimonious debate on this issue later in the year." The sixty-eight congressmen signing the letter hoped to force through the House, with as little debate as possible, a foreign aid bill minus military aid to El Salvador and the Nicaraguan contra freedom fighters.

Arms Control and Foreign Policy Caucus

At this time Congressman Miller chaired the Arms Control and Foreign Policy Caucus (ACFPC) task force on Latin America, an aggressively liberal in-house lobby numbering 13 senators and 119 representatives. Rep. Matthew McHugh (D–N.Y.), one of a handful on the radical fringe who voted against the Intelligence Agents Protection Act—which prohibits the exposure of American intelligence operatives—has been chairman of the caucus. Sen. Christopher Dodd (D–Conn.), a critic of the administration's foreign policy who fears American action in the Western Hemisphere more than the Soviet Union's, has served as vice chairman. On the ACFPC steering committee have been Senator Hatfield from Oregon and Congressman Seiberling from Ohio, both members of the IPS twentieth-anniversary committee. With offices in one of the House buildings, it has obvious advantages over outside policy research groups.

According to ACFPC's statement of purpose, the aims of the caucus can be summarized as "greater arms limitation, the development of a global economy, strengthening of the United Nations, and abolition of war." The caucus has opposed "virtually every new weapons system."[40] In point of fact, ACFPC is supposed to run a nonpartisan educational information source. Staff member Ken Sack privately elucidated the nature of ACFPC: "Our function is to provide timely research on issues of concern to members of the caucus. But between you and I [sic], what we really do is lobbying. We take sides, and we lobby for certain legislation."[41]

Certain congressmen have participated in the caucus and been involved with IPS since the 1960s. Three of the twelve who participated in a 1966 IPS seminar called "New Era of American Policy and Statecraft" were founding members of the caucus, which was originally known as Members of Congress for Peace Through Law.

In 1985, three of the original IPS seminar participants were still in office and still members of the caucus: John Conyers, Don Edwards, and Robert Kastenmeier. One of the original participants, Philip Burton, died in 1983, but his wife, Sala Burton, replaced him in Congress and on the caucus. Another of the original participants, Donald M. Fraser, left Congress to become the mayor of Minneapolis, where he hosted the Soviet delegation attending a 1983 IPS disarmament conference. The harmony of interests of IPS and ACFPC continues to the present. IPS associate fellow Cynthia Arnson is held in the highest regard by ACFPC staff. Caleb Rossitor, ACFPC staff director for human rights and foreign policy, says, "Cindy Arnson is one of the best staffers on the Hill."[42]

The current ACFPC executive director, Edith B. Wilkie, the moving force behind the caucus, has been involved since the 1970s with the Coalition for a New Foreign and Military Policy, a group IPS takes primary credit for organizing. Wilkie regularly attends Council for a Livable World's meeting of the Monday Lobby planning group at Stewart Mott's house on Capitol Hill, where she finds little on which to disagree with other participants, which include the Coalition for a New Foreign and Military Policy; the Committee for National Security, an IPS spinoff; SANE, a group directed by a former IPS fellow, David Cortright.

Whether or not the caucus is one of IPS's many spinoffs, there is certainly no ideological animosity between the two; for their objectives jibe—to form an activist liberal-left consensus in Congress. Fully 86 percent of the staff members interviewed in the offices of liberal representatives in early 1984 said they used ACFPC materials.

Of the twenty-three Democratic members of the House Foreign Affairs Committee, fourteen belong to ACFPC. The chairman of ACFPC, Jim Leach (R–Iowa), is on the committee, as is Joel Pritchard (R–Wash.). Thus, of the thirty-six members of the House Foreign Affairs Committee, sixteen of them are caucus members. ACFPC representation on certain key subcommittees is even greater. On the important Subcommittee on Human Rights and International Organizations, six of the nine subcommittee members belong to the caucus. Six of the ten members of the Subcommittee on Western Hemisphere Affairs, the major concern of which is Central America, are caucus members.

Of the sixty-eight congressmen who signed Cynthia Arnson's letter to the Speaker of the House, all but seven were ACFPC members. Most of the congressmen who signed requests for IPS alternative budget studies were caucus members. Also noteworthy, all of the members of Congress on the IPS anniversary committee were members, with the exception of Sen. Gary Hart, who was a member as late as 1977.

One of the congressmen on the IPS anniversary committee, John F. Seiberling, is president of the Board of Directors of the Peace Through Law Education Fund, which its letterhead says is "a private, non-profit organization which provides the Congress, its staff and the U.S. public a common ground of information and alternative approaches to the crucial problems of international cooperation, world security, and world peace. It works closely with the Arms Control and Foreign Policy Caucus of the U.S. Congress." Sen. Mark Hatfield, who gave a glowing endorsement of IPS on the occasion of its anniversary, is also a board member of the Peace Through Law Education Fund.

More Latin America Players

Robert Kurz was a legislative aide to Rep. Michael Barnes, chairman of the Subcommittee on Western Hemisphere Affairs of the 99th Congress, one of five staffers on that subcommittee. In March 1984 Kurz, with IPS senior fellow Jorge Sol, gave a seminar at IPS on Honduras, which was conducting joint maneuvers with the United States to deter the Sandinistas from exporting the revolution.

Cynthia Arnson, Wayne Smith, and William LeoGrande taught an IPS class, "Reagan's Central American Policy and Congress," in 1984. Both Smith and LeoGrande are for conciliation with Cuba. When LeoGrande worked in the office of Sen. Robert Byrd, he prepared a paper urging the United States to end intelligence surveillance of Cuba, accept paltry reparations for the property of U.S. citizens that was seized by Cuba, and surrender our naval base at Guantanamo, so that Cuba could have "breathing space to gradually loosen its relationship with the Soviet Union" just as Eastern European states such as Poland and Hungary were able to "distance themselves" from the Soviet Union.[43]

LeoGrande left Byrd's office to become director of the political science department at American University in Washington, D.C. In 1984 he returned to Capitol Hill as a staff member of the Senate Democratic Policy Committee. There he coauthored a position paper, "National Security Argument on Central America," with three colleagues at IPS: Robert Borosage, Saul Landau, and Richard Barnet.

Throughout the early years of the institute and into the 1970s, IPS associate fellow Richard Kaufman taught at the institute. Kaufman began as a legislative assistant to Rep. Henry Gonzalez (D–Tex.) and steadily rose in importance and seniority. No longer listed as part of the IPS community, he is now the most senior staff member on the Joint Economic Committee, where he prepares papers assessing Soviet economic and military capabilities. In 1973 Kaufman chaired a conference on "Strategy, Programs and Problems of an Alternative Political Economy" with Lee Webb, then a student at the Radical Studies Department of Goddard College and later founder of the IPS Conference on Alternative State and Local Public Policies; Derek Shearer, who would found the Campaign for Economic Democracy in California; IPS resident fellow Gar Alperovitz; and an assistant to Sen. Lee Metcalf.

During a lull in the Vietnam War in 1969, Kaufman kept busy by writing such articles as "We Must Guard Against Unwarranted Influence by the Military-Industrial Complex" (New York Times Magazine, June 22, 1969), "The Usury of War" (Nation, May 26, 1969), and "Billion Dollar Grab Bag" (Nation, March 17, 1969).

Another Joint Economic Committee staffer, deputy director James K. Galbraith, taught a course at the Washington School in 1982 titled "Rebuilding America: A Progressive Analysis of the American Economy," with Gar Alperovitz and David Smith, also a Joint Economic Committee economist and an economic policy adviser to Sen. Edward Kennedy. Smith later hosted a seminar at IPS on "Reagan's 1985 Budget: Politics of the Deficit" and pushed for wage controls and an industrial policy involving "substantially more planning."[44]

The Red and the Black: Sandinista Offensive on Capitol Hill

On April 22, 1983, three Sandinista officials—Alvaro Arguello, Carlos Nunez, and Humberto Lopez—briefed reporters and more than a hundred congressional staffers on Capitol Hill. Though all held important positions in the Nicaraguan government (general director of the Foreign Affairs Commission of the Council of State, first secretary of the Council of State, and president of the National University in Managua), the State Department had no knowledge of their presence in the United States. The Sandinistas "expressed their desire to put pressure on the administration by convincing members of Congress to take their part against current American policies in Nicaragua," according to one observer.

They appeared courtesy of the Progressive Hill Staff Group, launched by aides to Congressmen Conyers and Dellums, both known as IPS point men in Congress. Neil Kotler, an aide to Conyers, was the contact for the forum on Nicaragua.[45]

This behind-the-back maneuver was only one of a number of acts of unofficial diplomacy carried on by members of Congress. In 1983 and 1984 nearly a dozen groups ("fact-finding delegations") of the Latin network visited Central America. One such—sponsored by the Center for Development Policy's Commission on U.S.–Central American Relations and escorted by Janet Shenk of NACLA, Gino Lofredo of the commission, and Adam Hochschild of Mother Jones—included Rep. Edward F. Feighan (D–Ohio); Rep. Robert G. Torricelli (D–N.J.), member of the House Foreign Affairs Committee; Bernie Aronson, director of Policy for the Democratic National Committee; and Barbara Altman, legislative aide for the League of United Latin American Citizens. They returned to demand in Congress that all military and economic aid to El Salvador be stopped immediately.[46]

In April 1984 the Center for Development Policy sponsored another pilgrimage to Nicaragua, during which Rep. Berkley Bedell (D–Iowa) and Torricelli (D–N.J.) held a news conference in Managua to denounce Reagan's policy. Included in that delegation were Joseph Eldridge of WOLA, IPS associate fellows Cynthia Arnson and William LeoGrande, and chairman Peter Weiss. The president of the National Lawyers Guild, Michael Ratner, also went along. Ratner and Weiss were at the time suing President Reagan, charging that U.S. support for the contras was illegal. An American public-relations firm that works closely with IPS and the Latin network, Fenton Communications, was hired especially to sweeten the image of the Nicaraguan regime in the United States.

IPS and its friends on Capitol Hill promote the Sandinistas in other ways. When Magda Enriquez, head of Nicaragua's official women's organization, AMNLAE, came to the United States to gather support for the regime, she spoke at IPS. Enriquez is the Nicaraguan liaison for a women's "solidarity" group known as MADRE, which collects money in the United States to support the Sandinista regime in Nicaragua. IPS fellow Isabel Letelier sits on the board of MADRE, as do others on the faculty of the IPS Washington School, including the executive director of the Congressional Black Caucus Foundation, Francesca Farmer. The Washington, D.C., chapter of MADRE was organized by Robin Heart, an aide to Congressman Dellums, and another Dellums aide, Carlottia Scott, sits on the national board.

Human Rights and Wrongs: Left-Wing Democrats on Capitol Hill

Certain members of Congress have played prominent roles in the human rights campaigns against noncommunist governments. Tom Harkin's activism dates back to 1975, when a bill he introduced made a major impact on U.S. foreign policy. It amended the Foreign Assistance Act (Section 502B) so as to tie up foreign aid on the nebulous grounds of a human rights scorecard. His leadership in this area was unusual, for Harkin had never been a member of the Foreign Relations Committee, where most foreign policy legislation originates.

In early 1984 Harkin gave the introductory remarks at a reception hosted by IPS and PACCA in honor of the latter's policy recommendations on Central America.

> Now I am here to basically thank the Institute for Policy Studies and the people who have worked so hard over the last couple or three years. Many of you, I know, have been in my office a lot, and we've worked together with these things. Unless and until we understand . . . that those revolutions are coming, unless and until we're able to work in a spirit off cooperation, a spirit of understanding, we will never get the accommodation of the Third World countries.[47]

Harkin continued in his unusual style: "I think it's safe to say that the Reagan administration's policy is based upon a mistaken notion, in ideas, concepts, of what the revolution in Central America is all about.''[48] He went on to endorse the PACCA report:

We've got to do at least the following: number one, stop immediately all covert aid and activity. Secondly, we've got to pull our troops out of Honduras, unilaterally. . . . We've got to insist that government has to enter into real negotiations with the FDR and FMLN.[49]

Expressing his solidarity with IPS, Harkin predicted, ''It takes what's in this room—the information, the policies we've outlined . . . and if we're ready in November, not only with the policies but with the personalities . . . we can get on in the right place and start to make a change.''[50] And getting on the right place and making a change are what Harkin did. Marcus Raskin announced the congressman's candidacy for the Senate at the 1983 IPS Capitol Hill budget conference. With the help of the Left, Harkin won the race and took his ideology to the Senate.[51]

One of the most controversial unofficial diplomatic junkets ever taken was by Sens. Tom Harkin and John Kerry. They visited the Sandinista government on the eve of the April 14, 1985, congressional vote on a bill authorizing $14 million in aid to the contras. IPS fellow Peter Kornbluh arranged the trip, which helped sway the decision in Congress. Only after Sandinista President Daniel Ortega flew to Moscow and secured $200 million in aid did Congress reverse its earlier decision to deny aid to the contras.

Another special friend of IPS on Capitol Hill, Ted Weiss (D–N.Y.), declared in a speech at the Riverside Church on April 27, 1984, ''I spend more time at this institution than almost any other one. . . . You provide leadership and substance to people throughout the district.''[52] The church's numerous outreach programs have become a mouthpiece for IPS views since IPS's chief financial backer, Cora Weiss, became the director of the church's disarmament program. Congressman Weiss served on the IPS anniversary committee, participated in the Center for Cuban Studies symposium in September 1981, and was one of the six members of Congress to invite colleagues to meet with the WPC delegation in January 1978.

Don Edwards (D–Calif.) has been involved in IPS since the early 1960s. He attended the 1966 seminar for congressmen on ''The New Era of American Policy and Statecraft.'' As chairman of a House subcommittee that oversees the operations of the FBI, Edwards is one of the most powerful men in Congress. (Chapter 5 deals with Edwards's role in the mid-1970s drive to prevent the FBI from collecting intelligence on domestic groups and individuals having associations with hostile foreign powers.) In March 1984 Edwards sent IPS Washington School catalogues to his colleagues on Capitol Hill with a note: ''I know that many congressional staffers have benefitted from past lectures . . . I would appreciate very much your circulating the IPS spring 1984 catalog within your office.''[53]

When Saul Landau's film on Nicaragua was shown on Capitol Hill (in the hearing room of a committee chaired by Dellums), Edwards, together with Congressmen Leland and Kastenmeier, signed a letter addressed to congressmen and their staffs inviting them to attend the film.

Astonishing as it is that a congressman of Edwards's views should oversee the FBI, it is little short of stunning that the Democratic majority on Edwards's subcommittee shares his political views—Kastenmeier, Conyers, and Schroeder are all progressives who support IPS. Like Harkin, Schroeder finds IPS stimulating. "I don't agree with everything they do. . . ," she told a *New York Times* reporter, "but it's refreshing to have several points of view. The hardest thing to do in this town is to find time to think.''[54]

Special Friends in Congressional Black Caucus

Among the congressmen who have been especially friendly to IPS is Ronald V. Dellums (D–Calif.), chairman of the Subcommittee on Military Installations of the House Armed Services Committee.

In 1983 Dellums published *Defense Sense: The Search for a Rational Military Policy,* a collection of papers prepared for congressional ad hoc hearings, sponsored by Dellums, on an alternative military budget. The contributors included Richard Barnet, IPS fellow Michael Klare, David Cortright, and Marcus Raskin, whose paper was entitled, "US Foreign Policy: Imperialism and Military Power." Dellums' introduction stated: "Our nation's foreign policy is archaic and dangerous and in critical need of constructive reassessment to meet the real challenges of the modern world.''[55] In 1980 Dellums taught a Washington School course, "Political Paths in the '80s," with Raskin and Borosage.

Dellums unhesitatingly hosts officials of Soviet front groups. When World Peace Council delegations came to Capitol Hill in 1978 and 1981, Dellums invited his congressional colleagues to hear them.[56] When Farid Handal, brother of the head of the Salvadoran Communist party, toured the United States to raise support for the Salvadoran guerrillas, the Communist party, USA had no trouble arranging for him to meet Dellums on Capitol Hill.[57] And Dellums was one of the plaintiffs in a lawsuit to prohibit covert actions against the Sandinista regime in Nicaragua filed by the National Lawyers Guild.[58]

Dellums' administrative assistant, Carlottia Scott, was infatuated with Maurice Bishop, the Marxist prime minister of Grenada. Among the documents captured after the U.S. landing was a letter she had written to Bishop on Dellums' congressional stationery. "I love you madly," Scott said, noting also that "Ron [Dellums] has become truly committed to Grenada" and wants "to get all . . . his thoughts together in order as to how your interests can best be served.''[59] And get his thoughts together he did, for shortly thereafter Dellums condemned the U.S. action as a "war crime" in a press release to Radio Havana.[60] To rebut the evidence that the Pointe Salines airport was being prepared as a military base rather than a tourist airport as the Marxists maintained, Dellums sent an aide, Barbara Lee, to Grenada on a "fact-finding trip." Among the official documents captured by U.S. forces was a report by Barbara Lee which urged the Marxist Bishop government to make any necessary changes before she submitted the report to Congress.[61] So much for independent fact-finding.

Another long-time friend of IPS is Rep. George Crockett, who also met with the World Peace Council delegates in January 1978 and May 1981.[62] In March 1981 Congressman Crockett was keynote speaker at the First National Conference to End the U.S. Blockade Against Cuba, organized by the Center for Cuban Studies in cooperation with Jesus Jimenez Escobar. Escobar, former first secretary at the Cuban mission to the U.N., doubled as a DGI officer during his stay in the United States, acting as liaison between American militant groups and the Cuban dictatorship.[63] Among the members of the Conference Initiating Committee were the Venceremos Brigade, the Puerto Rican Socialist party, the National Lawyers Guild, and the National Conference of Black Lawyers.[64] Crockett blamed Cuba's Soviet-style government on the U.S. blockade against that country. And he said the ideas for his speech came from two congressmen, Ronald Dellums and Mickey Leland, whom he called "our unofficial ambassador to Cuba."[65] The conference leaders included Sandy Pollack, a Communist party leader and World Peace Council member who serves as National Solidarity Coordinator for the U.S. Peace Council, and Eva Cherto of the Trotskyist Socialist Workers party, who urged a national lobbying campaign in support of a bill introduced by Ted Weiss to repeal all U.S. sanctions against Cuba.[66]

Another conference on Cuba took place on September 23–24, 1981, in the House and Senate caucus rooms and drew even more congressmen. Dubbed "The U.S. and Cuba: Prospects for the '80's," the conference was, like the previous one, organized by the Center for Cuban Studies and sponsored by Reps. George Crockett, Ted Weiss, Mickey Leland, Stephen Solarz, and Mervyn Dymally; Sen. Lowell Weicker; and D.C. delegate Walter Fauntroy.[67] Stewart Mott gave a luncheon for conferees in his plush house a few blocks away at 122 Maryland Avenue.[68]

Congressmen Crockett and Weiss had just returned the week before from an Inter-Parliamentary Union Congress in Havana, where Crockett was reported to have charged the Reagan administration with "harboring fascist ideas."[69]

As with Dellums and Crockett, John Conyers and IPS go way back. The congressman taught "American Politics: Who Gets What, When and How" at the Washington School with IPS fellow Michael Parenti, and served as a moderator for the IPS budget conference on Capitol Hill, February 2, 1983. Considered an "IPS point man on the Hill," Conyers has no compunction about supporting the World Peace Council. He participated in its meeting in June 1982 with Rep. Gus Savage, and joined his colleagues in welcoming the 1978 and 1981 WPC delegations to Capitol Hill. Conyers also supported Maurice Bishop of Grenada, whom he invited to America to speak to the Congressional Black Caucus and others.[70]

It was Conyers who persuaded George Crockett to run for Congress. Crockett had been a member of the National Lawyers Guild since the late 1940s. Earlier in his legal career he was found guilty of criminal contempt of court and served a four-month prison term. At one point during his trial, he described the CPUSA as the "conscience of America."[71]

The executive director of the Congressional Black Caucus Foundation, Francesca Farmer, taught in 1983 a class at IPS on "Race and Poverty" with IPS senior fellow Roger Wilkins. One of Farmer's colleagues, Marsha Coleman, addressed a panel discussion on "South Africa and the Media" in 1984. She made it clear that the CBCF supports the Cuban-backed liberation movements in Africa.

George Crockett, who shares this view, is now chairman of the Subcommittee on Western Hemisphere Affairs. Anne Holloway, the staff director of the subcommittee on Africa, was the keynote speaker at an IPS seminar, "U.S. Policy in Southern Africa," exactly two weeks before Coleman. Cora and Peter Weiss had just returned from a trip to Southern Africa where they met with a number of Marxist liberation movement leaders. And in short order, Columbia University announced the appointment of Bishop Desmond Tutu to the Samuel Rubin Chair (a decision in which the Weisses, as the Samuel Rubin Chair benefactors, had considerable sway).

In her speech at IPS, Holloway revealed a great deal about how U.S. foreign policy is determined. "I would say that there are really two foreign policies that operate in the country, one is the informal one . . . and the other is the one that exists here in Washington in the sense of federal institutions," Holloway said. "In terms of the federal institutions of foreign policy we don't do as well with these as with the informal ones." She explained: "In terms of the non-governmental groups that the subcommittee works with . . . obviously we work with Jean Sindab and the Washington Office on Africa, TransAfrica, the Southern Africa Support Committee, and the American Committee on Africa."[72]

Given the audience, Holloway may have thought it unnecessary to mention that all these groups support the Cuban-backed Marxist liberation movements. Holloway also noted the important role that the Arms Control and Foreign Policy Caucus plays "inside the Congress." "We call on all of them when we have these kinds of legislative strategies to put together," she said.[73]

Black Caucus members generally do not hesitate to associate publicly with groups even other progressive congressmen shun. For example, in summer 1983 a demonstration opposing Reagan's Central America policy was held in Washington. The People's Anti-War Mobilization was dominated by members of the Workers World party, a Trotskyist organization that advocates the violent overthrow of the government.[74] IPS fellows Michael Parenti and Eqbal Ahmad and five Congressional Black Caucus members—George Crockett, Ronald Dellums, Mickey Leland, Parren Mitchell, and John Conyers—endorsed the movement. Communist party member Josephine Butler addressed the crowd, predicting that the U.S. is "not going to El Salvador to kill Communists, but to kill women and children."[75]

IPS's literature table at the demonstration was set up next to those of the Stalinist Bolshevik League, the Revolutionary Communist party, the Socialist Workers party, and *CounterSpy*. IPS flyers also touted IPS fellow Saul Landau's film *Target Nicaragua: Inside a Covert War*, which condemned U.S. support of the contras, and which was to be shown that evening at IPS headquarters.

WOLA: We Hear from Them a Lot

Among the liberal members of Congress, WOLA is the most respected Latin American policy group. Of those interviewed, 83 percent of the House offices and 71 percent of the Senate offices used WOLA materials. Only 9 percent were ignorant of WOLA.

"We hear from them a lot," said Michael Poloyac, an aide to Rep. Berkley Bedell.

"They are really good for general background information," said Kathy Gillie, aide to Rep. David Bonior of Michigan.

"I think they're about at a level with Georgetown," an aide to Senator Biden said. "They produce a lot of informative material on short notice. I think their stuff has reasonable credibility, given their point of view."

"Very credible," said Douglas Koelemay, an aide to Sen. Frank R. Lautenberg (D–N.J.).

WOLA director Joseph Eldridge's correspondence reveals that WOLA's connections on Capitol Hill are extraordinarily good. A personal letter from Edward Kennedy, dated August 23, 1978, reads, "Dear Joe, . . . I just wanted to express my thanks for your making last month's legislative conference on Chile the great success that it was. *As always,* WOLA was the key to this success" (emphasis added).[76] Another personal letter from the senator himself, dated October 17 of the same year, thanks Eldridge for helping to prepare a speech Kennedy gave in Miami. "I'm glad that it received such wide notice in Latin America," said the missive, which is signed "Ted" and bears the handwritten notation: "Thanks Joe—you are great."[77] Eldridge frequently testifies before Congress. A thank-you note from "Paul" (Sarbanes) to "Joe" thanks Eldridge for his statements, which Sarbanes says "were very helpful to me and the Subcommittee."[78]

Making Connections: Coalition for a New Foreign and Military Policy

In the campaign for his amendment to restrict foreign aid, Rep. Tom Harkin enjoyed the vigorous support of the Coalition for a New Foreign and Military Policy, which IPS credits itself with having helped found.

Sen. George McGovern and Harkin wrote personally to the coalition. "Many thanks for . . . the excellent help the Coalition provided on the human rights amendment," McGovern wrote. "I was aware of your effort, and I am certain it had a great deal to do with the acceptance of the amendment."[79] Harkin's letter noted that "the issue of human rights has become a central focus for those of us working to change American foreign policy. Your work, especially at the local level, in stimulating public concern and awareness of human rights legislation, is very important."[80]

The coalition's Human Rights Working Group, cochaired by Bruce Cameron, led the new campaign. Cameron would later work in Harkin's office. IPS's Cynthia Arnson participated in the strategy sessions of the group.

In September 1977 Harkin wrote a letter addressed to "Dear Coalition Friends" thanking them for their help in a legislative victory on human rights language in bank regulation. "I am convinced," wrote Harkin, "that the work of . . . the Coalition's grassroots network made the difference."[81] Senators Abourezk and Hatfield sponsored a similar bill in the Senate.

Abourezk, a trustee of IPS, worked closely with the coalition during his tenure on Capitol Hill. Expressing his gratitude, he wrote, "I wanted to write long before this to thank you and so many others for your impressive help with the Abourezk-Hatfield Amendment . . . it couldn't have been done without a lot of good work from you and so many others in the Human Rights Working Group."[82]

In 1978 the coalition called a press conference for Congressman Harkin to announce that he would work for drastic cuts in arms sales to countries run by dictators—Iran, Indonesia, the Philippines, and Nicaragua. The following year the pro-U.S. governments in Nicaragua and Iran fell to hostile parties.

In 1976 Harkin and Joe Eldridge, whose Washington Office on Latin America is also a member group of the coalition, visited Chile in search of human rights violations. Search as they did, the duo failed to unearth any hard evidence. Eldridge's friend William Sloane Coffin, of the Riverside Church in New York, voiced his concern in a letter. "Dear Brother Joe," he wrote. "Isn't it awful what they're turning up in Chile? The worst of it is, you find yourself wishing they'd recover more bodies to bring Pinochet down."[83] So much for compassion and human rights.

"We are a lobby working daily in the Congress, buttonholing Senators and Representatives, urging legislation, rallying votes, and bringing pressure," coalition literature says.[84] The coalition takes credit for stopping the deployment of ABMs in forty American cities, and the deployment of U.S. ground troops in Cambodia, and for cutting $5 billion from the Pentagon's 1973 budget. The CNFMP urged U.S. aid for the new communist regimes in Southeast Asia even after nearly a million boat people had fled Vietnam and the Pol Pot policies had wiped out two million Cambodians. Coalition literature also lists in its win column the ban on Rhodesian chrome imports (240–146 in the House); halt of the B-1 bomber program (234–182 in the House); halt of military aid to Chile (48–39 in the Senate); and passage of the Panama Canal Treaty (68–32 in the Senate).

A coalition advertisement boasted:

> We've helped ground the B-1 bomber. Cut off military aid to Nicaragua, Chile, Uruguay, Argentina, and reduced aid to the Philippines. Given the Transfer Amendment its first test-votes. Attached human rights guarantees to international lending bills. And restricted loans supporting South African apartheid. That's just the beginning.[85]

After funding for the antiballistic missile was almost halted by the Senate, Mark Hatfield remarked: "The Coalition mounted an extraordinary fight against the ABM. For the first time in my experience on the Hill, the military is being forced on the defensive."[86]

In 1982 the coalition's Disarmament Working Group played a key role in preparing for the U.N.'s special session on disarmament. Richard Barnet and IPS fellow Michael Klare were among those named to draft a "statement on substantive issues" to present to the U.S. coordinator of the session. CNFMP tried to influence selection of the U.S. delegates to the special session and also to arrange congressionally sponsored hearings on disarmament across the country.

The coalition's defense budget specialist, a former IPS fellow and research associate, Steve Daggett, has gained considerable respect on Capitol Hill. "Steve Daggett was quite helpful when we were going through the defense budget process," said an aide to Rep. Timothy E. Wirth (D–Colo.).[87] Daggett authored an IPS pamphlet titled *The New Generation of Nuclear Weapons*. David Cortright, another former IPS fellow/Ph.D. student and now executive director of SANE, has served on the Disarmament Working Group's steering committee.

The drive to transfer defense funds to welfare programs, often referred to as the "priorities" campaign, is an old refrain in the coalition's song, for which Sen. William Proxmire found praise, noting: "The Coalition . . . has become the most effective lobby for new priorities on Capitol Hill."[88]

The Congressional Black Caucus has been especially active in calling for such a transfer. In April 1978 the chairman of the Congressional Black Caucus, Parren Mitchell, represented the Coalition for a New Foreign and Military Policy at a press conference to announce his sponsorship of a coalition-inspired "transfer amendment," which would have slashed the defense budget in order to increase welfare spending. George McGovern was the Senate sponsor.

The amendment was not adopted. Mitchell wrote his friends at the coalition:

I personally want to thank you for what you did on the Transfer Amendment. There is no question that your presence was felt. There is no question that you had an impact in that organizing. Indeed you were effective.[89]

In 1979 Mitchell and McGovern tried again, and the effort continues. "We have brought 'new priorities' testimony before 10 Congressional Committees," coalition literature boasts, adding, "Coalition spokemen became the first 'outsiders' to testify before the Armed Services Committee of the House and Senate."[90]

In addition to its interest in Latin America, CNFMP seeks to prevent U.S. military intervention wherever it may occur, or end it where it exists. And when the coalition talks, Congress listens. Fifty percent of the liberal congressional offices interviewed use coalition materials.

Seventy-nine members of the House earned the dubious distinction of voting the straight coalition line in 1983. (See Appendix 12.) These representatives supported the nuclear freeze and opposed covert operations in Nicaragua, chemical weapons, MX missile funding, antisatellite weapons, the B-1 bomber, and the Cruise and Pershing missiles.

Eighteen senators, including presidential candidate Gary Hart, six of the eight Democratic members of the Senate Foreign Relations Committee, and the chairman of the Senate Appropriations Committee voted the straight coalition line in 1983. (See Appendix 13.)

CDI: Blaming America First

The Center for Defense Information (CDI) is another of the most respected foreign policy and special-interest groups on Capitol Hill. The CDI is supported by the Fund for Peace, whose leadership and funding interlocks with that of IPS. IPS fellow William Arkin, who gained notoriety after leaking classified information on U.S. nuclear defense plans, began his activist career at CDI.

Of the representatives and senators interviewed, 70 percent read the center's materials. A sample of the highly favorable comments: "very useful in providing information"; "very credible group, very well informed"; "very well respected." There were grumblers too: "CDI never has anything positive to say" about defense proposals, said one aide. "I'm sure that the Pentagon has had some good programs."

Even though the president and his ambassador to Moscow have difficulty in communicating with the Kremlin, Adm. Gene LaRoque (ret.), director of CDI, has no problem. Whenever the Soviets need American help to buttress their position, they can count on LaRoque, on whom they call frequently. Although LaRoque does travel to Moscow, from time to time, it's easier for the Soviets to drop into his office at CDI headquarters in Washington, where they can capture his amiable face for Soviet television. LaRoque, for instance, appeared on Moscow television on June 5, 1985, to say:

> It is the greatest honor to receive the answer from Secretary General Gorbachev. The content of the answer turned out to be even more exciting because he confirmed the USSR position speaking out against the arms race and for preventing the threat of nuclear war. He also clearly stated that, while the Soviet Union is striving for an accord in the field of arms control, the U.S. does not show such a desire.[91]

CLW and Congressional Campaigns: Targeting Peace Candidates

Another disarmament group active on Capitol Hill, the Council for a Livable World (CLW), was founded by onetime IPS associate fellow and trustee Leo Szilard and had Richard Barnet as an early board member. CLW's honorary chairman, Jerome Wiesner, was once an IPS trustee, and CLW board member Paul Warnke is a current IPS trustee. The oldest and perhaps most respected of the arms-control/disarmament groups, CLW is a registered lobby with a plain purpose: "The Council for a Livable World is dedicated to the promotion of stable and lasting security for our country. This is achieved only by working toward universal elimination of nuclear weapons. . . ."[92]

The council in its promotional literature takes credit for passing the Nuclear Test Ban Treaty, halting ABM, banning biological weapons, stopping chemical weapons production, defeating President Carter's proposed deployment of the MX missile, advancing the SALT process under four presidents, and slowing nuclear proliferation.

"The council also helps initiate and draft legislation, monitors appropriate committees, produces expert witness for important hearings and keeps accurate headcounts before crucial arms control votes are taken," says a CLW brochure.[93] Like the Coalition for a New Foreign and Military Policy, the council has a hotline updating members on the latest developments on Capitol Hill so it can apply pressure on key congressmen more effectively. In addition to its political action committee, the council "provides Senators with sophisticated technical and scientific information that helps them to make intelligent decisions about nuclear arms control and strategic weapons."[94]

Although the council calls itself "non-partisan," its beneficiaries are overwhelmingly Democratic. CLW has helped to elect sixty-five senators since 1962, the year of its founding, including Joseph Clark, one of the founders of Members of Congress for Peace Through Law. According to CLW literature, of the twenty-one senators in the Ninety-eighth Congress who were aided by the lobby, twelve voted the straight council line in 1983, and five voted the other way on only one of ten key votes.

CLW and its subsidiary, PeacePac, which targets House elections, spent $650,000 in the 1982 elections, targeting fifty-four House and eighteen Senate campaigns in which the freeze played an important part. Seventy percent of the candidates for the House won.

Senators also look to CLW. Bill Bradley (D–N.J.) said, "Those of us fighting in the Senate for the necessity of arms control need all the help we can get now. The council is providing that help in every important way." Alan Cranston (D–Calif.) remarked, "On such issues as arms control or military spending, it is hard to think of any more effective and resourceful organization than the Council for a Livable World."

CLW persists in trying to disarm the United States, even though, as Paul Warnke admitted, "procedures that would be necessary to verify a production freeze have not as yet been developed."

The extensive interlocking directorates of groups on the Left seem endless. For instance, Herbert Scoville, a board member of CLW, is also the president of the Arms Control Association, a ubiquitous speaker at leftist disarmament conferences, and a leading participant in CNFMP's Disarmament Working Group.

SANE: "On the Spot and Very Valuable"

After getting his "Ph.D." through an IPS program that has no accreditation, David Cortright began his career serving the cause of peace and disarmament by becoming director of the Committee for a Sane Nuclear Policy, known as SANE. SANE's promotional literature says that its purpose is to "disseminate information that Congress needs to make key policy decisions." Marcus Raskin is vice chairman of SANE, and former IPS trustee Jerome B. Wiesner sits on the board.

SANE gets high marks from Capitol Hill liberals. Of those interviewed, 78 percent of the House offices and 54 percent of the Senate offices read SANE's materials.

SANE has distinguished itself by sponsoring World Peace Council delegations on Capitol Hill. On May 5, 1981, Reps. John Conyers, Ronald Dellums, and Patricia Schroeder invited their congressional colleagues and staff to attend a two-hour briefing on "European Opposition to the New Generation of Nuclear Weapons." Speakers were Richard Barnet and the Italian communist Nino Pasti, a former NATO general and now a WPC member. The two warned against proceeding with the NATO decision to deploy Cruise and Pershing missiles in

Europe. The following day, Congressmen Conyers, Edwards, Dymally, Crockett, Weiss, and Leland invited their colleagues and staff to meet with WPC's president, Romesh Chandra, and six other WPC officials.[95]

The World Peace Council is, according to U.S. intelligence, "the largest and most active Soviet international front organization . . . one of the Soviet's major instruments for political actions and propaganda in the peace movement."[96] Not only does SANE sponsor World Peace Council delegations—its national treasurer is an active member of WPC. Despite these dubious ties, SANE has an excellent reputation among aides working on arms-control issues in liberal offices on Capitol Hill.

"Their newsletter is usually on the spot and very valuable," said an aide to Congressman Bedell of Iowa.

"They certainly have contributed a great deal to the [Senate Armed Services] Subcommittee," said an aide to a senior senator. "We hear from them very frequently."

"Very effective," said Sam Chapman, aide to Rep. Barbara Boxer of California.

"Fine group," said Jeff Hertsbach, aide to Rep. Bob Carr of Michigan.

Computer technology facilitates the Left in coordinating its activities. SANE cooperated with six other national organizations—the Council for a Livable World, the Coalition for a New Foreign and Military Policy, the Nuclear Weapons Freeze Campaign, Friends of the Earth, Physicians for Social Responsibility, and Greenpeace—in developing a "movement-wide" arms-control computer network. "It should provide the peace movement with an unprecedented degree of cooperation and technical sophistication," a report said.[97]

CNS: Redefining National Security

The Committee for National Security, yet another disarmament policy group, was created in 1980 as an IPS spinoff. The institute reports that Richard Barnet "played a major role in organizing the Committee for National Security, to mobilize broad support for détente to counter the voices calling for a return to confrontation and intervention."[98] In addition to Barnet, CNS includes IPS associate fellow Rustom Roy and Morton Halperin, director of the IPS spinoff Center for National Security Studies.

That CNS was intended simply to promote the well-known IPS position on national security may be seen from its own brochure:

A narrow policy that regards national security as solely the interest of the military/industrial complex is a self-fulfilling prophecy. National security is everyone's interest. . . . Recent events in Afghanistan and Iran—mirrored in Asia, Africa,

Latin America and Europe—present dangerous challenges to our national security. Although these crises frequently differ in nature, they illustrate a single simple truth—our world is changing and we must adapt to that change.[99]

To help Americans adapt to the changes, CNS, in the tradition of IPS, opts for "creative public education" to inculcate "a new, wider definition of national security that emphasizes international cooperation, development and social justice."[100]

The Bottom Line

IPS has garnered enormous support for its policies through all these and other groups covered elsewhere. As Appendices 10–13 illustrate, IPS positions enjoy the support of far more than a handful of fringe radicals. Nearly a majority of Democratic legislators have often swung behind the IPS agenda. Though no one can determine the extent to which IPS and its left-wing network have influenced the Democratic party, the implications for the country are far reaching. As IPS pointed out in a recent annual report, "The Institute's contribution to the public dialogue cannot be measured within the short-term boundaries of legislative calendars and presidential terms. IPS is engaged in a longer and deeper struggle, a struggle over the underlying principles and future direction of the political culture itself."[101]

The popularity of the nuclear freeze, despite the continuing Soviet buildup and treaty violations, and the de facto abandonment of the Monroe Doctrine with regard to Western Hemisphere security (just two examples) illustrate this change. What is even more serious, they represent the breakdown of a bipartisan consensus in U.S. foreign policy.

In politics, as in economics, marginal perceptions are often the deciding factors. This is particularly true in contemporary times, when special-interest groups heavily influence our policymaking. Thus, increasingly, left-wing groups that interlock variously with IPS wield a clout inordinately disproportionate to their actual numbers. They politicize and distort issues to such an extent that balanced debate is often made impossible.

Part VI

IPS, Religious Institutions,
and the Peace Movement

CHAPTER 16

Penetrating the Churches
Richard Barnet, World Peacemakers, and
Sojourners

The Institute for Policy Studies, radical though its visions are, never intended to operate on the sidelines of the American political scene. To affect legislation, IPS realized that public opinion must be guided. Appeals made in the environment of America's religious institutions, where the faithful seek to encounter their God, have a special force, for they not only touch the compassionate side of the human spirit but also call on authoritative moral reasoning. A forum that no one in America seeking political change can afford to overlook, the church provides an ideal vehicle to persuade the American people about any necessary change in national policies.

IPS founder Richard Barnet seems to grasp this. Although Jewish by birth, Barnet says he became a Christian in 1957. He began worshiping at the non-denominational Church of the Saviour in Washington, D.C., in 1962. Located right off Dupont Circle and only two blocks from the Institute for Policy Studies, the church is rather unusual. It was founded in 1947 by N. Gordon Cosby, a seemingly humble man with unconventional ideas about expressing his religious convictions. Under his tutelage, members of the church founded various mission groups, each enjoying considerable autonomy in pursuing its separate goals.

World Peacemakers was one of these groups, founded in 1978 by Gordon Cosby and Richard Barnet. Those familiar with its literature will recognize that it is Barnet who is the real inspiration behind this particular mission. Barnet does

277

not, however, steer his audience's mind along the usual evangelical lines. Rather he focuses on the wicked world in which the American government—Republican or Democratic—is the principal source of evil.

What prompted Barnet to venture into this rather unfamiliar terrain? The answer is suggested by a World Peacemakers newsletter, which asked, "What can we learn from Europe to nurture the American peace movement?" The response follows: American peace activists must "draw especially on the experience in the Netherlands and West Germany, where Christian communities form the vanguard of the European peace movement."[1]

By spring 1978, when World Peacemakers was founded, the European peace movement had scored a major victory; President Carter had canceled the neutron bomb. The antineutron bomb campaign was successful largely because Soviet front groups such as the World Peace Council and the Christian Peace Conference mobilized numerous religious people.[2] The religious contribution was indispensable, for it gave credibility to the campaign. The lesson was learned: from now on religious people must be "in the vanguard." World Peacemakers had its work cut out for itself.

The Dual Journey of Faith and Reason

In the brochure "Peacemakers: Our Call and Program," World Peacemakers stated that "to meet the coming crisis responsibly, Americans need to work and pray for world peace, especially within their church communities."[3] Christians at the local levels were encouraged to form "world peacemaker groups," which, with central leadership provided by the group around Barnet, would engage in the dual "journeys" of study and action. The action side would involve organizing at local, denominational, and regional levels, as well as at colleges and universities. The study would be based on a prayerful reading of the Scriptures, along with Barnet's book, *Real Security,* special "world peacepapers" and other material. The first five of twelve sources listed in the brochure "World Peace Papers and Other Resources" were authored by Barnet. And "Books and Booklets" lists the 1981 catalog of IPS publications.

A few passages from World Peacemakers publications give the flavor of the general message and allude to the central role the churches will play in the peace movement. For instance, in "A Time to Stop" Barnet writes:

> Is it possible for the church to play a prophetic role at this critical moment in human history by launching a massive public education campaign to help the American people to confront the moral bankruptcy of the policies and institutions that are providing them with the myth of security at the cost of sacrificing their most precious beliefs?

Could the church take the lead in organizing mayors and city officials, union people, congresspersons, and citizens from communities across the country to encourage the president to make an historic initiative for peace?

The point of the campaign [is] to set the stage for a long term, continuous public education campaign on national security.[4]

In a more recent World Peacemakers quarterly newsletter, Barnet is referred to as the "author of the first World Peace Paper which was the precursor to the Freeze,"[5] and the one who "urged the churches of the nation to back a bilateral nuclear freeze."[6]

Barnet's paper, "A Time to Stop," written in January 1978, demonstrated that he was "in the vanguard" of a movement that peaked four years later. Implicit also was the insight that in the United States, as in Europe, the churches would have to take the lead.

While Barnet provided the inspiration and guidance for the church-based disarmament movement, others busied themselves implementing it. The World Peacemakers study guide for Barnet's book *Real Security,* entitled *National Security and Christian Faith,* is the best example of the lengths to which some zealous World Peacemakers adherents will go. "Gathered together over Richard Barnet's analysis of international issues in the pages of *Real Security,*" the study guide states, "we listen to the Scriptures and pray together to know how we are to respond as faithful disciples who wish to help God bring real security to our time."[7]

The preface informs its readers to remember that "two things will be required. First, we will need to steep ourselves in our political reality. And second, we will need to be empowered to bring our faith to bear on that political reality."[8] This is what has been called the "dual journeys of study and action," the hallmark of the World Peacemakers peace educational program, a program that has become a model for hundreds of churches nationwide.

It goes on to point to Barnet's *Real Security* as meeting the first need, and to the study guide as meeting the second. The successive chapters are set up in two parts, "focusing" and "responding in faith," both built around Barnet's book. Barnet's book becomes, literally, the bible for peace education.

"Dehumanizing the Russians"

Another revealing example is the study guide section "Dehumanizing the Enemy," which deals with the "surrender" by President Carter to the militarist forces in the United States when he decided to strengthen American defenses following the Soviet invasion of Afghanistan. After an opening prayer in which the group is asked to envision "the Spirit of God descending as a dove on Jesus

at the start of his public ministry," Barnet's chapter is summarized, followed
by discussion questions, one of which inquires into "the American tendency to
dehumanize our major opponents and develop a 'devil image.' "[9]

"Responding in Faith" is the next section. It starts with the observation that
"sin in each of us separates us from others by naming them as 'enemies.' "[10]
Then comes a ten-minute period for spontaneous reflecting and writing about
some personal experience of "dehumanizing" another person. After that there
comes a group exercise in role playing: In an office situation, upon hearing of
the Soviet invasion of Afghanistan, only one person is against a "get-tough"
policy. He is pressured by the others to "surrender," that is, to "dehumanize
the Russians" as others are doing. But what do those others, meanwhile, discover
about themselves? Why, they are "dehumanizing" the one holdout by not recognizing as authentic his concerns, needs, and fears.

At the close of this sequence the Scriptures are consulted about "the treatment
of 'enemies,' both personal and national"—those, specifically, where Jesus
speaks of forgiving one's enemies and being one with them. And then on to
another week's session and another chapter according to Barnet.

Once the study guide and all its exercises—which Barnet himself helped
prepare—have been worked through by a local World Peacemaker group, the
members will be more nearly prepared "to bring their faith to bear on the political
reality," and can be counted upon as core activists for disarmament, IPS-style.

Focusing the Outward Journey and Pastor-Propheting

It is now time for "finding focus for the outward journey," as the *Handbook
for World Peacemaker Groups* calls it. Specific action is suggested: getting on
the editorial pages and on local radio and TV talk shows; visiting congressmen
and urging them "to take peacemaking positions on specific legislation such as
blocking appropriations for MX"; organizing means of public expression (prayer
vigils, rallies); working with other peace groups (in local campaigns to convert
military industries into "life-affirming" ones); developing programs of peace
education in schools and churches; and making the rounds in the community
with presentations and slide shows on the arms race.

Grassroots pressure on Congress is not overlooked, as a World Peacemakers
1983 newsletter points out: "Richard Barnet, World Peacemakers board president, urges persons to organize local public hearings with lawmakers in every
community. He suggests that every lawmaker be confronted with the moral
questions inherent in our present policies."[11]

In the election year of 1984 World Peacemakers made a special effort to
"increase the direct impact . . . on national affairs through the legislative and
electoral processes."[12] To that end a new outreach/lobbying method, pastor-

propheting, was created by Doug Tanner, a legislative assistant to Rep. Robin Britt (D–N.C.), who joined the World Peacemakers staff. A promotional brochure described the concept:

> Pastor-prophet is the name for a rare kind of personal relationship with a person whose work is formulating public policy. The pastor-prophet approaches elected officials in a way that combines pastoral caring and prophetic criticism. [He or she] takes the initiative to meet regularly with the policymaker to listen . . . and to help raise questions about the policymaker's work in light of the gospel.[13]

Not only elected officials, but their aides are also candidates, and the practice need not be restricted to Washington, D.C. "Rich interactions can occur particularly during the member's home visits," says World Peacemakers, "when groups are faithful pastor-prophets over a sufficient period of time."[14]

All this would indicate that World Peacemakers is intended as a formidable political force. The World Peacemakers essay "The American Churches Speak: We Are for Peace," issued in February 1984, is telling:

> Change has come through spontaneous actions throughout the churches at all levels, from those of individual members to denominational leadership . . . this peacemaking activity can barely be noticed by the person sitting in a pew of most churches, let alone by the public at large. . . .[15]

> [G]roups of committed Christians are centrally involved in awakening the American Churches to peace. Typically these communities are small, fewer than ten people who come together for fellowship, reflection and action.[16]

> A small group such as this can be the change agent which energizes an entire congregation or community, and through these local initiatives reach the entire nation.[17]

Myths and Metaphors

What is striking about the World Peacemakers is that no matter how far-fetched some of its approaches may seem, its leaders apply them to the political situation at hand. For instance, Barnet's World Peacemaker paper, "A Time to Stop," sets out to mobilize the churches of America and offers specific political advice for the nation's leaders. Barnet's article was reprinted in the March 1978 issue of the magazine *Sojourners*.

Sojourners was founded by Jim Wallis in 1976, the offspring of the *Post American*, which was published by a few radical theology students who banded together communal-style in Chicago in the late 1960s. Encouraged by Richard Barnet, Gordon Cosby, and others, Wallis decided to move his ragtag Christian hippie community to Washington. Barnet's influence was soon felt at *Sojourners,* for after Wallis moved the *Sojourners* commune to Washington and came in contact with IPS, the appearance of the magazine improved and its rhetoric was toned down. But when Wallis addresses his colleagues in the elite theological circles, he makes no effort to conceal his politics. He told *Mission Trends* in 1979, in the article "Liberation and Conformity," that he hoped "more Christians will come to view the world through Marxist eyes. . . ."[18]

The principal readership of *Sojourners* has always been the politicized clergy and activist laity. But *Sojourners* does not make random appeals to Christians. Instead, it focuses on evangelical bodies, because the mainstream Protestant churches and the Roman Catholic church are already under the influence of the like of the National Council of Churches, Clergy and Laity Concerned, Fellowship of Reconciliation, Maryknoll Missioner, and Pax Christi. *Sojourners* has taken on the last bastion of traditional Christian values.

In early 1977 Barnet wrote an article for *Sojourners,* "Race Without Reason," that dealt with the arms race. In it Barnet probed for a way to capture a Christian audience. He referred to "making, stockpiling and using nuclear weapons as a sin," and continued by stating that "if the protection of human rights is to have any meaning at all then these activities should also be understood as a crime. . . ."[19]

By the time "A Time to Stop" was reprinted in *Sojourners,* Barnet had made a few changes to allow for immediate action. At one point he called on the president to cease developing, testing, and deploying all nuclear weapons; to accept the "no first use" doctrine; to strive for a treaty outlawing nuclear weapons; and to initiate moves to convert military industries to civilian use. And he reminded him that the upcoming U.N. Special Session on Disarmament would be the right platform for taking the initiative. A little further on, where the earlier call for a massive Christian education campaign was issued, Barnet pointed out the urgency of the moment: "There are only a few weeks left between now and May"—yet another addition to the original text. In both instances, he called for immediate action. Barnet was coming into his own as a voice to tap religious energies for the cause of life, as against "imminent" death.

The First U.N. Special Session on Disarmament

It was just the right time for Barnet's debut on the religious scene. The U.N. Special Session on Disarmament of 1978 was to be an extravaganza for peace activists throughout the Western world. That was precisely what the whole enterprise was about, all solemn declarations about its ostensible purpose aside. The entire endeavor had been conceived and approved by the World Peace Council in 1975, based on the Soviets' perception of the "shift in correlation of forces" in their favor and their estimation of the power of public opinion in the West, as proved by the recent American defeat in Vietnam.

But again, the real significance of the occasion was that it was one stage of what Barnet had forecast as "a long-term, continuous public education campaign on national security." Never mind that nothing specific on disarmament resulted from the special session. What did emerge were some organizational vehicles for "the movement"—Mobilization for Survival, the Riverside Church Disarmament Program, World Peacemakers—all of which "IPS fellows were instrumental in organizing," as an IPS annual report pointed out.[20]

The Big Time: Richard Barnet and Billy Graham

The theme of the March 1978 *Sojourners* issue was in keeping with the campaign being promoted by World Peacemakers. Its front cover sounded the theme—"A Question of Survival, A Crisis of Faith." The back cover announced a future issue devoted to "The Nuclear Threat: A Study Guide for Churches," to which Barnet was a key contributor. Finally, in the May issue of *Sojourners*, Barnet's name appeared on the masthead as a contributing editor, where it remains.

With Barnet's place firmly established in the religious environment by that time, it is important to examine some of his specific messages, both in his *Sojourners* articles and elsewhere.

The August 1979 *Sojourners* was a very important issue. Rev. Billy Graham graced the front cover, accompanied by the caption: "Billy Graham: Preaching Against the Arms Race." *Sojourners* editors had interviewed the famous evangelist, and the ensuing article, "A Change of Heart," became a classic reprint for the religious disarmament movement. Graham made several points; on the one hand, "I have, I suppose, confused the kingdom of God with the American way of life," and on the other, "I especially was impressed with the concerns various Christians in these [Eastern European] countries expressed about peace. I believe . . . they have something to teach us here."[21]

Graham's interview was immediately followed by Barnet's feature article, "Lies Clearer Than Truth," in which he took "a look at the Russian threat." This piece too was reprinted a number of times. Among other things, he takes Graham's remorse a step further:

> The Soviet threat is the big lie of the arms race . . . a national myth used as the rationale for . . . a policy of U.S. military intervention over two generations.[22]

> The characteristic of sin is confusion. We become possessed by irrational fears. Our minds stop working. The Russians stop being people and become symbols.[23]

> To be obsessed by the Soviet threat . . . is, quite literally, to be blinded by hate.

Billy Graham's courageous confession . . . ought to force all of us to realize how often we fall into the same trap.[24]

Several years later Graham was invited to Moscow, where he proclaimed that he saw no evidence of religious persecution. It was another great propaganda coup for the Kremlin.

"Two Bumbling Giants"

The next Barnet contribution to *Sojourners* appeared in the February 1980 issue. As before, Barnet tailored his writing to the needs of the moment. "Two Bumbling Giants" was addressed primarily to those "ethicists" in the peace movement who were perhaps troubled by the Soviet invasion of Afghanistan the previous December.

After opining that "the world seems closer to a major war than at any time since the 1930s"—a staple in almost all of his articles, no matter the administration in power—Barnet appealed to the religious mind by evoking the apocalypse. In a neutral light, Barnet smoothed over the Soviets' action:

> The breakdown of order in the region was perceived by the Soviets as a threat rather than an opportunity. The Soviets moved in a spirit of insecurity and panic. . . .
> The ineptitude and butchery of the Amin regime had threatened to turn the whole country into a militant anti-communist state. . . .[25]

Having ignored Amin's self-styled communism, Barnet pointed to "a major escalation of the military budget by the U.S."; the dismissal of another Brezhnev offer to negotiate arms reductions; the further nuclearization of West Germany; and the prospect that the "U.S. military programs of the 1980s would restore an overwhelming nuclear superiority to the U.S. . . ."[26] as the chief reasons for the Soviet invasion of Afghanistan.

Upon sketching this kind of dangerous environment in which the Soviets must live, Barnet concluded that "the Soviets act out of weakness rather than strength."[27] Because Soviet actions were less of a threat to peace than the NATO missile deployment, Barnet exhorted:

> It is now more important than ever to offer an explicit, simple and comprehensive agreement for stopping the arms race and prohibiting the further deployment of military forces in other countries. . . .
> The U.S. does have an historical opportunity to help build a new world consensus to contain aggression. . . . To build a world consensus to condemn Soviet interventions, the U.S. must commit itself to cease further military interventions of its own.[28]

By now we are a long way from Afghanistan, which was the problem to begin with. People in the peace movement who might have been "confused" by what the Soviets had just done have been redirected.

If President Carter's liberalism had brought the world to crisis, the conservative Reagan administration could only gender catastrophe. Barnet's 1981 piece in *Sojourners* (a former sermon) thus appeared with the caption: "Battling This Present Darkness." Here Barnet argues: "No system in the world today has a very good answer . . . but in my view the idea that acquisition of money and property should be the central goal of either individual life or common life is a blasphemous and dangerous notion."[29] By contrast, a little further on, "The Russians are the supposed adversary, but if we look at the situation that we face around the world, the Russians are actually the metaphor . . . for those who I think are our society's real enemies."[30]

The real enemies, for Barnet, are the poor majority of mankind who make up the third world, for their rightful claims upon the redistribution of the earth's bounty are what we, the people living under capitalism, have reason to fear. That being the only real conflict in the world, the Russians, who are unburdened with the taint of capitalism, can be perceived as part of that threatening opposition—but only as a metaphor, for, Barnet reminds us, where fear and hatred demand an enemy, the identity hardly matters. Thus we arbitrarily settle for the Russians.

The U.S. would do better, Barnet thinks, not to waste its wealth on building "the massive threat of death," that is, a deterrent against Soviet aggression, but to work for "a different system for distributing the resources of the world."[31] Barnet's passion for the third world carries him so far as nearly to contradict his customary advocacy of peace:

> A new consciousness of liberation is at work all over the world, and, in part, that is the reason for so much violence [which] is of a different kind. [In the past, people felt] that some people are rich and some people are poor. But that kind of thinking about the world is changing, and that means that it is a very exciting time, a very dangerous time, but one . . . having the seeds of a very different kind of world order.[32]

Just what kind of world order does Barnet envision? In his 1969 book *The Economy of Death,* Barnet writes:

> . . . the U.S. has no alternative to offer the poor nations which is any better than revolution, which, for all its brutality, has had some spectacular success. The rapid modernization of backward Russia and her transformation into the world's second power, the end of massive starvation in China, and the great progress in literacy in Cuba are a few examples of what regimentation and the shake-up of an old corrupt order can do. We may not like it. . . . But what about the status quo in

many backward countries of the "Free World" where thousands starve. . . . It may be that revolution is the only answer to the physical survival of these societies. . . ."[33]

The continuity in Barnet's thought is striking. He endorses various Marxist liberation movements, and he finds Soviet-type systems of the Cuban and Nicaraguan variety fitting models for the third world.

Radical Scholar Turned Religious Prophet: Barnet on the Future of the Peace Movement

Toward the end of the "sermon" Barnet takes another turn, one that merits attention. Returning to some of those new things in the world that "cause the principalities and powers of the world to quake," Barnet praises the European peace movement and asks, "Would it not be possible now to have a revival in the churches in the U.S. . . which would cause people to move in ways we have never seen before?"[34] And then, immediately, and this well over a year before the fact, Barnet adds a specific appeal:

> Next spring at the United Nations there is going to be another special session on disarmament. Why would it not be possible to have a million people in the streets of New York to demonstrate. . . ?
> In the churches lies the power of the gospel message that it is possible to live without fear. That message could be that source of new and creative initiatives for peace.[35]

The first U.N. special session served as a catalyst for the creation of religious peace organizations. Three years later Barnet was drumming up support for the next round. Only the churches could mobilize the number of marchers in New York City on June 12, 1982—close to one million strong.

Taking Issue with Poland and the Euromissiles

By late 1981 the European peace movement was becoming increasingly influential all over the Continent, amassing huge crowds—250,000 in Bonn, 350,000 in Amsterdam, 400,000 in Madrid, and 200,000 in Athens—and grabbing TV and front-page attention. NATO's 1979 decision to deploy Pershing and Cruise missiles was shaken. President Reagan proposed Zero-Option as an alternative, offering to forgo U.S. deployment if the Soviets dismantled their arsenal of SS-20s.

As the Euromissile debate was brought home to the U.S., Barnet jumped in with a basic plan for the American peace movement. "For over 30 years the Western Alliance has been obsessed with combating an unlikely threat with an incredible defense," said Barnet, dismissing with one stroke the *raison d'être* for NATO.[36] "The Soviets pose a potential threat which seems increasingly implausible," Barnet continued, and particularly then, on the eve of the new NATO missile deployment.[37] Against this "ever implausible unlikely threat," President Reagan's Zero-Option appeared either cynical or silly. Barnet's alternative: we should "demonstrate our commitment to Europe by trading some of the cards we hold, such as forward bases, for the elimination of the Soviet nuclear threat to Europe . . . less one-sided proposals than the Reagan Administration offers."[38] If this were done, Banet argued, "the alliance might once again serve to unite Europeans and Americans."[39] Once again, when superpower relations come to public attention, Barnet so often manages to make the Soviet position more palatable.

December 1981 was the month of the infamous military crushing of Solidarity in Poland, an event that did not endear the Soviets to the West—the peace movement included. Appropriately, the March 1982 issue of *Sojourners* featured "The Polish Challenge," subtitled "Poland's meaning for the peace movement," written by Richard Barnet. Referring to the Polish situation as a "challenge to the international peace movement," Barnet forges ahead:

> Whether the Soviet Union [or the Polish communists themselves] directed the entire operation, as President Reagan has charged . . . is, morally speaking, beside the point. In either case it must be concluded that the Soviet Union could not tolerate an uncontrollable experiment in its backyard. . . .[40]

Not only does Barnet chide President Reagan for stating the self-evident, but he also carefully guides his readers to accept a new reality, the one imposed by the Soviets. Once the no-fault logic has been established, Barnet homes in on the matter of greatest concern to him:

> . . . peace activists in Europe as well as in the United States have been confused by the tragic turn of events in Poland. . . . Peacemaking . . . does demand that we seek moral clarity.
> . . . a peace movement that bows to the enormous social pressures in its own society to join the self-righteous chorus of anti-communism has lost its moral bearings.[41]

Arguing that "the Polish crackdown makes real negotiations to stop and reverse the arms race all the more urgent,"[42] Barnet works to get the peace movement back on track:

> A realism is growing in the United States about security: a recognition at last

by the major religious faiths that nuclear "defense" is morally and politically bankrupt. . . .

But until the U.S. peace movement joins its brothers and sisters . . . throughout the world in dramatizing a vision of a world that is freeing itself of both murderous weapons and murderous governments . . . it will not be able to challenge either the premises or the policies that are moving us closer to annihilation.[43]

In effect, Barnet provides moral justification for the Soviet empire, while asserting that U.S. defense efforts are morally and politically unsupportable.

A Glimpse into the Mind of Richard Barnet

A 1983 autobiographical sketch, "A Policy Analyst Connects His Faith with U.S. Nuclear Policy," in *Sojourners* reveals some valuable insights into Barnet's thinking. Reviewing his early days as an associate at Harvard's Russian Research Center, Barnet sums up his thoughts on U.S. and Soviet negotiating behavior in the early postwar period: "The Soviets, as the weaker power, evinced a greater self-interest in limiting nuclear arms than did the U.S."[44] Concerning his work at the Arms Control and Disarmament Agency during the Kennedy days, and the development, roughly simultaneous, of his Christian commitment, Barnet states:

I began to see that the way of the national security manager was . . . blasphemous. Ignorant men were taking delight in playing God . . . a profound spiritual sickness . . . had overtaken our country and much of the rest of the world. Yet it was in my country where the sickness was most advanced, for we alone had actually used the bomb, and we were the pacesetters in the arms race.[45]

Barnet's rejection of the United States and disdain for its leaders seem linked to his embrace of the socialist system. Barnet attributes the power of "playing God" to only two parties, and between them the sickness is more advanced in the U.S., since the Soviets evince greater interest in arms control. Moreover, for Barnet it is sinful to draw attention to the presence of the Soviet threat.

In July 1978 Richard Barnet and Marcus Raskin appeared in New York City to address an all-day seminar at the prestigious Riverside Church, which overlooks the Hudson River on the Upper West Side of the city. The event was the kickoff of a huge church-based peace program in the United States. Barnet's message was short and clear. It involved what he called "the four myths that underlie the nuclear arms race":[46] the "myth of national defense," the "myth of deterrence," the "myth of military power," the "myth of prosperity." "These are the myths that ordinary Americans believe about their security," Barnet said. "If we are going to change the system, we must go after these myths and reject them."[47]

With these themes—the Russian threat a metaphor, the need for a strong U.S. defense a myth—began IPS's peace activism that was to culminate in the 1980s.

CHAPTER 17

Radical Politics Under the Cloak of the Clergy
IPS and Riverside Church, 1977–81

A Mainline Church Goes Radical

Unusual things have been happening at the rich and prestigious Riverside Church on New York City's Upper West Side since 1977, when William Sloane Coffin became senior minister.

The church is interdenominational but has roots in the American Baptist church and the United Church of Christ. It has long been known as the Rockefeller church, for that legendary family built the edifice and endowed it with some $50 million in hopes that it would continue to embody their Protestant beliefs. The grandiose building overlooking the Hudson River expressed the self-confidence of the heyday of American Protestantism. For many years Harry Emerson Fosdick, a renowned Protestant preacher, was Riverside's senior minister and feared not to speak out from the pulpit on the great issues of the day.

In 1958 President Eisenhower laid the cornerstone for the new building of the National Council of Churches (NCC), an institution intended to provide ecumenical leadership for the riven Protestant faith. The building stands across the street from the Riverside Church, on Reinhold Niebuhr Place, named after the century's greatest American Protestant theologian, who taught just a block away at Union Theological Seminary. The NCC building and the Riverside Church are even connected by an underground tunnel, but the human bridges are more important, with numerous NCC staffers at all levels being active members in Riverside's congregation.

290

Fosdick, Niebuhr, and the National Council of Churches have stood firmly in the liberal political tradition. Thus it is not surprising that Riverside offers one of the country's preeminent liberal pulpits. When the congregation in 1976–77 was in search of a new senior minister, it was natural that some noteworthy preacher of liberal orientation would be chosen.

The traumatic decade that began in the mid-1960s left many institutions shaken by moral confusion. The affliction—a pervasive social and political radicalism of the times—did not leave the Riverside Church unscathed. Cora Weiss, daughter of former Communist Samuel Rubin and wife of IPS chairman Peter Weiss, managed to get her program aired on the Riverside Church's radio station, WRVR-FM, even before her friend William Sloane Coffin was selected as the new minister. At the time, Cora Weiss was working next door at the NCC's Church World Service. Through it she organized a program called Friendshipment to provide support for the new Soviet-backed occupation forces of North Vietnam, which she, Richard Barnet, Marcus Raskin, and William Sloane Coffin had enthusiastically backed even as American soldiers were dying to prevent just such a communist takeover. How curious that Cora Weiss, a woman who belonged to no church, whose family had long promoted an ideology implacably hostile to religion, now occupied positions in the heart of America's religious institutions. It surely illustrates how deeply the liberal malaise and moral confusion of those days had penetrated—how the radical Left had affected America's religious scene in its "long march through the institutions."

Cora Weiss Arrives at Riverside

Cora Weiss may have pulled some strings to have Riverside take another look at her good friend William Sloane Coffin for the position of senior minister. Once before, when the search for a new minister was being made, Coffin had been considered, and rejected. In the interim, moreover, his second marriage had broken up for reasons similar to those that led to his first divorce. A saying of his, "A family that demonstrates together stays together," did not work out for Coffin. In fact, his second wife protested in court that Coffin's political activism precluded his attending to his family responsibilities. This, in itself, should have clouded Coffin's chances of ministering to the congregation's spiritual needs. And, indeed, the chairman of the board of deacons had dropped Coffin's name early in the search. But after the candidate pool was narrowed down to a handful, Coffin's name mysteriously reappeared on the list. A month later, in the summer of 1977, when many members of the church were absent, Coffin was elected. Despite Coffin's rather shabby performance as a family man, it was hoped that he would prove flamboyant enough to bring in a full house on Sundays. There was also the hope that he could attract new members from the black and Hispanic community in nearby Harlem to Riverside's predominantly white flock.

Coffin was evidently anxious to get the position—his autobiography stated that he wanted to work in New York to advance a new "global vision"—and he hoped to strengthen his ties with old friends from the antiwar crusades of the 1960s. He remarked, "I always thought [Riverside] looked frosty and rather establishment—but my friends told me it was the one established church in New York City that could really make a difference."[1] Whatever Coffin may have meant when he told an interviewer that his invitation to Riverside "had been arranged through friends of his friends,"[2] he said at a disarmament meeting at the church that "without Cora Weiss we would not be here, any of us, myself, or any of you, for she is 'Mrs. Organization' herself."[3] The fact remains that when he arrived at Riverside in the summer of 1977, Coffin was the right man (Left activist) at the right place (America's foremost pulpit) at the right time (the beginning of the World Peace Council's peace campaign in the West). In an interview early in his career at Riverside, Coffin described how he viewed his work: "You change this country [not by going into politics but] by changing the climate so that decent politicians have room to maneuver. I see my role as trying to change the climate."[4]

But one looks in vain for an experience of Christian conversion in Coffin's autobiography (whose title, Once to Every Man, ironically, is derived from an antiwar event that was particularly meaningful to Coffin and not from the ancient hymn by that name). With a mission so defined, Coffin enthusiastically took over at Riverside Church, a place where, as his friend Richard Barnet pointed out, "the dictates of faith and rational politics could come together."[5]

No sooner did Coffin arrive than he invited Cora Weiss into the church's sanctuary. Though she never became a member, she would take charge of the disarmament program at Riverside. As such, she stood at the crossroads: a Soviet bloc demand for economic aid to communist Vietnam was being transmitted to a guilt-ridden West, where some were ready to step in with funds out of church coffers collected from unwitting churchgoers. This aid was indispensable to the communist government in Vietnam, given the disaster of the economy in the wake of its policies to create a new society—forced collectivization, resettlement programs, reeducation camps, the works.

In response to Joan Baez's change of heart and public condemnation of Vietnam's inhumane policies, Richard Barnet, Cora Weiss, and William Sloane Coffin endorsed an advertisement in the New York Times stating that "the present government of Vietnam should be hailed for its moderation and efforts at reconciliation among all its people."[6] Coffin was also a "comrade in arms" to Weiss and delivered a message to a Church World Service reception in January 1978 at the NCC headquarters before sending a shipload of aid to Vietnam.

Still, Coffin and Weiss could not limit their activism to such secondary projects while the peace movement at home remained stalled after the war. It was when their talents were joined that the peace "activism-ministry" at Riverside Church brought a certain fame to the renowned congregation.

Launching the Disarmament Program

In May 1978, some eight months after Coffin's arrival at Riverside, the Riverside Church Disarmament Program was officially launched. With Cora Weiss as director, it joined such groups as World Peacemakers and Mobilization for Survival. Weiss's interest in using religion as a political vehicle was demonstrated by her work with the Friendshipment program and Clergy and Laity Concerned (CALC), which she helped found back in the sixties. But also, curiously, the office of the Samuel Rubin Foundation, of which Cora Weiss is president, is located at 777 U.N. Plaza, which is the Church Center to the United Nations, though it is not listed in the building's directory or on the office door.

Since Cora Weiss does not have a personality that is attractive to churchgoers, Coffin's talents in that respect are fortunate. Weiss's gift is organizing—a "calm and efficiency one associates with wartime commanders,"[7] says Coffin—whereas Coffin's forte is his ability to frame the great political questions in religious terms. Through their antiwar activism, their journeys to North Vietnam, and their work with Clergy and Laity Concerned, the National Council of Churches, and Friendshipment, Weiss and Coffin have been linked by a special bond.

Disarming, the First Year at Riverside

From the outset Coffin and Weiss had major plans for the Riverside Church Disarmament Program. At its kickoff event in July 1978, Coffin offered a vision for the mission of Riverside:

> [S]omewhere in this country there should be a major effort to make peace the business of the establishment. . . .
>
> Other organizations could have done this . . . but they haven't. It is very right that the Church do it, so then why not Riverside? We have a certain legacy and a facility to make us the natural people to try this. . . .
>
> If we continue in this effort, I feel quite confident that we will be able to look back ten years from now and see that we were in the vanguard—like those in the anti-war movement in about the spring of '64.[8]

The disarmament program was a major strategic move.

From the pulpit of Riverside, Coffin rarely misses an opportunity to rail against the sins of the United States and to soften those of its chief adversaries. A recurring theme of his is the line, "If we are not one with the Soviets in love, at least we are one with them in sin—which is no mean bond, for it precludes the possibility of separation through judgment."[9] One "sin" that seems to preoccupy Coffin more than any other is ours alone—anticommunism—for "of all the world's ideologies" it is "the most potent, the one with the least questioned dogmas, the one with the most sacred slogans and symbols."[10]

Another theme frequently invoked by Coffin is what he calls his "lover's quarrel with this country," or with "patriotism." Coffin's problem, as he puts it, is "how to oppose the President in the name of the Presidency, the government in the name of the country, American policies in the name of American ideals."[11] But while he appears to champion what is best in the American tradition, Coffin espouses more marginal positions, as exemplified in this interview:

> I think that communism is a page torn out of the Bible . . . the social justice that's been achieved in China and North Vietnam . . . that's an achievement no "Christian Society" on that scale has ever achieved. That is a real indictment of Christians: that we are not able to do what they do. One could say that without a dictatorial approach to these things they couldn't have been accomplished.[12]

The inaugural at Riverside Church featured three IPS guests, Peter Weiss, husband of Cora, Richard Barnet, who delivered his "four myths" speech, and his partner, Marcus Raskin, who contributed a few opening remarks. "The weaponry which we have developed," Raskin said, ". . . must be judged and catalogued under war crimes and murder. . . ."[13] And he went on to emphasize that disarmament should become *the* core issue for activists.[14] Every other concern should be seen in relation to it.

Shortly thereafter, Cora Weiss's disarmament efforts at Riverside initiated the Cities and the Arms Race program. Designed to appeal to liberal sensibilities such as concern for the poor, the program demonstrated how the Pentagon robbed cities like New York of funds that could better be spent on housing and education in Harlem.

The churches must lead the way in "relating morality to politics," Raskin emphasized. "There is a distinction between war—just war, defensive war—and mass murder. And what is required at this point from the churches is some sort of moral definition of the limits of violence."[15] Raskin, a Jew by birth, like Barnet and Weiss, concluded by suggesting that Riverside lead other churches in the U.S. to expurgate the notion that deterrence is morally acceptable.

Here were the seeds of the Catholic Bishops' Pastoral Letter on Nuclear War. Its chief architect, Rev. Bryan Hehir, received the IPS Letelier-Moffitt Human Rights Award.

The churches would have their work cut out for them to create a new "political consensus" around disarmament. With almost prophetic foresight, Raskin understood back in 1978 the tremendous significance of the issue. At the inauguration of the Riverside Church Disarmament Program he stated:

> This is a government which is porous enough to be opened up and influenced by citizens groups and by the culture, and when I say "the culture," I mean churches, newspapers, universities—people who are laying out the guideposts as to what the do's and don'ts are for our future.[16]

Churches, newspapers, universities—IPS has its hands full in all of these.

Richard Barnet was on hand December 8, 1978, to open the first convocation of religious leaders under the auspices of the Riverside Church Disarmament Program with the speech "History of the Arms Race 1945–1978." He was joined by other movement people who had worked with IPS over the years—Rep. Ronald Dellums; William Winpisinger, president of the International Machinists Union; Randall Forsberg, future author of the first nuclear freeze proposal; IPS fellow Earl Ravenal; Seymour Melman of the Institute for World Order; and David Cortright of SANE. If this was an unusual assembly for religious leaders to break bread with, Cora Weiss and William Sloane Coffin had more in store. Announcing that "for the first time the Soviet government has responded affirmatively to an invitation to join an open forum on disarmament," Coffin introduced Yuri Kapralov, counselor at the Soviet embassy.[17] Kapralov was accompanied by Sergy Paramanov. Both of them were identified as KGB officers by U.S. intelligence.

Riverside Opens Its Doors to the Soviets

John Barron, a prominent expert on the KGB, said that Kapralov's duty in the United States was "to identify for the KGB, those Americans who, by whatever means, might be persuaded to propound Soviet views as their own."[18] But neither Kapralov nor Paramanov is the only Soviet official welcome at Riverside Church. Vladimir Shustov, a KGB officer who is a representative to the United Nations, has also frequented Riverside, addressing peace gatherings assembled there on at least three different occasions.[19] Another Soviet official suspected of being an intelligence officer, Sergey Divilkovsky, has also attended.[20]

Still more Soviet officials show up at the numerous public events at Riverside Church.[21] On October 31, 1982, Soviet U.N. attaché Sergey Belyaev attended a speech by a Riverside official on U.S.–Soviet relations.[22] Although some, like Kapralov and Shustov, are top Soviet officials, they are often accompanied by lower-level foot soldiers who can cultivate individuals behind the scenes. There are Soviet correspondents, for instance, from the like of TASS and *Pravda,* half of whom are likely to be involved in espionage activities. TASS correspondent Igor Ignatiev mixed with the crowd at the Riverside Conference on Central America on October 1–2, 1983; Vladimir Simonov of *Moscow News* attended the November 12–13, 1983, Riverside workshop on civil disobedience.[23] Anatoliy Manakov, New York bureau chief for Moscow's *Literary Gazette,* showed up with Soviet U.N. diplomat Igor Mishchenko at IPS fellow Eqbal Ahmad's speech at the Deadly Connections Conference, cosponsored by Mobilization for Survival and the Riverside Church, and held at the Cultural Center of the District 1199 Health Care and Hospital Workers, a union controlled by the Communist party.

When some of these Soviet connections were revealed by John Barron in the October 1982 issue of *Reader's Digest,* the church suffered a momentary blow and the Soviets became more cautious. Less than a year later, however, in September 1983, a small Soviet delegation was allowed into the country to attend a United Nations conference. A male and female in a car with New York plates registered to Peter Weiss were spotted picking up two members of the Soviet delegation, Sergey Plekhanov and Vasiliy Vlanikhin. Both Plekhanov and Vlanikhin were under surveillance by the FBI counterintelligence.

To many, questioning Soviet motives in frequenting Riverside Church or questioning Peter and Cora Weiss's comfortable relations with the Soviets may smack of modern-day McCarthyism. The peace movement feels so strongly about its agenda that it excoriates anyone calling attention to Soviet involvement in it. At the same time, the IPS and Riverside crowd shield the Soviets after such events as the invasion of Afghanistan, the persecution of Solidarity, and the downing of KAL flight 007.

As for "Americans propounding Soviet views as their own," Cora Weiss's disarmament program has performed quite well in this respect. Coffin said in October 1978 that the program was resolved "to provide the material and the faculty on a continuing basis" in order to "address groups around the country" in the "hope that the religious community of this country can begin to take the lead."[24]

The Riverside Church was to do just this in providing the requisite (IPS) education for the nation's religious institutions and anyone else who would listen. Several colleges, a group of New England prep school headmasters, Presbyterian and United Church of Christ leaders, church councils, and numerous local congregations, to name but a few, all wanted to draw upon Riverside's model for teaching.[25]

One of Riverside's most significant educational projects was the Peace Sabbath/Peace Sunday instituted by Weiss and Coffin and promoted to congregations throughout the country. As Weiss explained:

We can expect 1,000 pulpits in America to be giving the sermon [provided by

Riverside]. This has never happened before—a simultaneous appeal to a President of the United States for a reversal of the arms race.[26]

Disarming, the Second Year

Although 1979 was only the second year of the disarmament program, it was enormously successful. On top of providing the Peace Sabbath sermons for churches nationwide, Cora Weiss took credit for some sixty-seven meetings or "microconferences" patterned after Riverside's convocation.[27] In May 1979 she participated in an IPS Conference on U.S.–Soviet Relations, the purpose of which was to "debunk the myth of a new Soviet threat."[28] Speaking to the conferees, she said that Americans' fear of the Soviet threat was "but a hereditary disease transmitted over the past 60 years,"[29] but "as long as we give the meetings and people come to hear us, we will not see the essence of the fear of Soviets in this country."[30] In other words, Riverside and IPS (Cora spoke of them collectively as "we") were to be the "vanguard" in dispelling the perceived Soviet threat.

Autumn 1979, the eve of the Soviet invasion of Afghanistan, brought yet other affirmations of Riverside's growing prestige in the international "peace" community. In September Coffin joined a "peace delegation" to the Soviet Union, organized by Terry Provance, an official member of the Soviet front World Peace Council.[31] If Coffin harbored some doubts about where the fault lay before going to Moscow, he seemed to have few when he returned. "It just may be that on disarmament the Russians are more serious than we are," Coffin told a United Nations Day rally.[32] Coffin found the Soviets not only believable, but more trustworthy than his own government on the issues of arms control and disarmament.

Riverside launched its second national convocation in October 1979, along with a series of educational workshops, one of which was captioned "The Soviet Threat? How to Counter Fear of the Russians in Your Community." Other seminars included "How to Use the Structures of Religions" (for example, denominational programs) and "How to Teach Peace in Churches, Seminaries, Universities." Among the notables was Sen. Mark Hatfield, a familiar face at the IPS Washington School and a contributing editor of *Sojourners*. In all there were "some 900 delegates from 40 states." As Cora Weiss glowingly pointed out:

> The Pentagon has a lot to worry about now with a thousand determined, well-informed, committed organizers against the arms race. Each participant is already reporting back to churches and community groups and beginning to implement what was learned. The conference went beyond our wildest dreams in numbers and quality.[33]

At the end of the year the program's monthly newsletter, *Disarming Notes,* reported that 156 spinoff conferences had been held across the country. Peace Sabbath sermons had been sent out to five thousand clergymen nationwide. CBS-TV reported that "Riverside Church has played a major role in bringing the need for peace and disarmament to the attention of the nation."[34]

Coffin got yet more press coverage before the year was out by going to Tehran in behalf of the fifty-three Americans held hostage. On the day of his departure, Coffin remarked, "Though I am an American, I can appreciate that, to Iranians, their holding of my fellow Americans represents a reflection of decades of pain and anger."[35] The statement reveals why the Khomeini regime found Coffin acceptable to "help alleviate the misunderstanding."

When the Soviet Union invaded Afghanistan at the end of 1979, Riverside was embarrassed, particularly since Coffin and Weiss had repeatedly said that the Soviet threat was a myth. The duo responded by exhorting their disarmers to be patient, not to protest. Although a short expression of disapproval was forthcoming, the disarmament program stressed that "any form of U.S. intervention, escalation of a military presence or an increase in the defense budget is unnecessary and inappropriate . . . Russia's challenge continues to demand restraint, study and understanding. . . ."[36] The next issue of Riverside's *Disarming Notes* went even further:

> Since the 1930s the informal rules of the cold war allowed the U.S. freedom to dispatch forces outside its bloc. . . . The Soviet Union was not free to do the same outside its own turf. . . . The U.S. in this time span has intervened in other countries on an average of once every 18 months. . . . This is the first time the Soviet Union has sent troops outside of its bloc since World War II. Here we need to take stock of what has happened from the U.S. side to poison relations between the two superpowers.[37]

To assure its disarmers that events in Afghanistan should in no way cramp their style, *Disarming Notes* referred them to IPS works, such as those by Richard Barnet and Fred Halliday. And just how did they view Soviet intervention in Afghanistan? Barnet said that "a credible theory of what happened in Afghanistan is that the breakdown of order in the region was perceived by the Soviets as a threat rather than an opportunity. The Soviets moved in a spirit of insecurity and panic rather than overconfidence."[38] In his 1981 book *Real Security,* the primary educational vehicle of the World Peacemakers, Barnet justifies the invasion of Afghanistan by saying that the Soviet Union sensed "its own security slipping away."[39]

Fred Halliday argues that the Russians are not the main instigators of "instability,"[40] and that they are even playing a positive role in Afghanistan:

> The Soviet decision to rescue [the communist regime in Afghanistan] from collapse

cannot be compared with the invasion of Hungary or Czechoslovakia, where Russian troops were used to crush a popular movement towards a more democratic socialism. The guerrilla forces threatening to seize power in Afghanistan were feudal and clerical in ideology, fighting for a return to social conditions that have kept the Afghan people crouched in untold backwardness and misery.[41]

Riverside's *Disarming Notes* called the situation in Afghanistan "even more complex" than the one in Iran, but this much was clear:

The Soviet Union saw that matters were getting out of hand under President Amin. . . . Amin had resorted to military tactics and repression which only increased the spread of resistance. In order to eliminate Amin, who was well entrenched, the Soviets sent in troops.[42]

Amin was the villain of peace, with his "militarism" and "repression." The Soviets who invaded to dispose of him almost began to look good. Besides, peace activists must never forget that the main opponent to peace is the United States, as attested in that same issue of *Disarming Notes:*

So, friends, we have an "impossible" task that is going to take us a little longer. It is no time for wringing our hands. We need to let the White House know we oppose draft registration, and do all in our power to prevent it. We need to call the President to account on SALT II and detente . . . we need to let him know we know much of the hatred throughout the world for the U.S.A. can be laid at the door of C.I.A. covert activities.[43]

The words breathed the "vanguard" role of IPS and Riverside, as expressed by Cora Weiss.

Disarming, the Third Year

To reinforce the proper mindset, in January 1980 Riverside invited IPS fellow and Middle East specialist Eqbal Ahmad to give a presentation on "Afghanistan and Iran." Cora Weiss and Coffin were present (Coffin once said he consults frequently with Ahmad, an acknowledged nonbeliever).[44] Ahmad used the opportunity to convey his usual condemnation of Israeli imperialism and racism. As for the Afghanistan crisis, the Soviets invaded because, said Ahmad, "the U.S. had been unfaithful to détente," thus leaving the Soviets "defenseless" and in a "nightmare."[45] When one Russian émigré, General Grigorenko, attempted to speak his informed opinion, Coffin stepped in and stopped him. It was Ahmad's show.

Before closing the Riverside chapter on Afghanistan, a word about the Moscow pilgrimage undertaken in March 1980 by Cora Weiss's righthand man, Rev. Mike Clark. He went as a guest of the Soviet Peace Committee. On returning to the United States, Clark reported on his visit at a Riverside Church disarmament meeting. In his speech, "In the USSR After Afghanistan," he cited his fellow delegates' credentials (they had come from the U.S. Peace Council, the American Friends Service Committee, Mobilization for Survival, etc.—all the organizations that could be counted on to reciprocate their hosts' kindness once back in the U.S.). Then he turned to things of substance. "I think that what those of us here need to do is . . . come to as reasoned a judgment as possible," said Clark. "I think in doing that one comes to the position that essentially it [the Soviet invasion] is a defensive move."[46] Clark then referred to Barnet in decrying "the whole dynamic that now exists between the United States and the Soviet Union." He next turned to the business at hand:

> I have the sense that the U.S. response . . . is not an appropriate response to what has happened and in fact it will get us into even more difficulties. . . . I think we do not have much time in which to begin a very serious effort to blunt the reaction in this country that's being encouraged . . . by the Administration . . . and unless the kinds of efforts that we've been involved in are strengthened, we could be in for some very serious times.[47]

Not All Is Peace at Riverside

By this time the Riverside Church Disarmament Program and its national reputation had become such a thorn in the side off some of the congregation's long-time members that a few of them met with Coffin and Weiss to air their grievances. The immediate spark that led to the occasion was when a group of church members tried to display their own materials on disarmament at a church festival and Cora Weiss stepped in to inspect their literature in order to "interpret it correctly." Her threatening manner propelled representatives of the group to confront Weiss head-on—about her program's budget, its ideological thrust, and, last but not least, her religious affiliation and her authority (that is, from the board of deacons) to speak in the name of the Riverside Church to the outside world.

Nothing was resolved by the encounter. One member of the group was permitted to inspect Weiss's financial records, but only after he agreed not to divulge anything he learned. All that is known is that from a start in 1978 with $15,000 pledged by "church members and friends," to be supplemented if possible by contributions from foundations, by 1984 the church's portion of the program's budget had reached $148,000, which tells nothing about outside support.

The meeting did reveal that Weiss was not a member of Riverside. Asked point-blank where she did worship, she took refuge in her heritage, retorting,

"I am Jewish." When pressed further, she admitted that she belonged to no synagogue. But she did insist that her program had the full approval of the deacons, who, Coffin added, had also endorsed her appointment—at his suggestion. As for ideological balance, Coffin said he thought it neither necessary nor appropriate to dwell on the faults of the USSR.[48]

A little later, at a Sunday service the chairman of the board of deacons informed the congregation about the "serious charges" voiced by some members against their senior minister. He did not specify what these charges were—in fact, no charges had been expressed, only questions raised—but declared that the deacons unanimously supported Coffin, and Weiss, and the disarmament program. He then asked one and all to rise and applaud their minister. And that was the end of that. But, the question persists, Why can't church members inspect the books of a church program headed by a nonmember?

The disarmament program went full-steam ahead. The second Peace Sabbath/Peace Sunday was celebrated that spring in forty-six states. And illustrious speakers such as former British Communist party member E. P. Thompson, Prime Minister Olaf Palme of Sweden, and Archbishop Helder Camara of Brazil graced Riverside with their appearance.

Disarming, the Fourth Year

The year 1981 started with still further glory for Riverside Church. Rev. Mike Clark was invited to be a delegate from Riverside to the "World Forum of Youth and Students for Peace, Détente and Disarmament" in Helsinki, sponsored by the World Peace Council. Clark wrote in *Disarming Notes,* "More than 600 delegates gathered in Helsinki from around the world to discuss the international situation."[49] From around the world dignitaries gathered—the president of the Continental Organization of Latin American Students from Cuba, Fernando Remirez de Estenoz; a representative of the Ecumenical Youth Council of Europe from the USSR, Sergei Rasskazovsky; a representative of the Pioneer Organizations of Mongolia and the USSR from Mongolia, Khurelbater Otchir; a board member of the International Committee of Children's and Adolescents' Movements from the USSR, Elena Burmistova; the president of the International Union of Students from Czechoslovakia, Miroslav Stepan; the secretary general of the World Federation of Democratic Youth from Hungary, Miklos Barabas; and many others.[50] In a hall filled with these East bloc luminaries, the day before Ronald Reagan's inauguration, Mike Clark was introduced as the representative of the Riverside Church Disarmament Program. "I am honored to be with you here today. I bring you greetings from the United States," Clark said. He continued:

I bring you greetings from all Americans who are determined that the words spoken at tomorrow's inauguration are not the last words spoken about the life and death issue of war and peace. . . .

What we are here for this week is to find areas of commonality in that struggle. . . .

We hope that we can be a part of your campaigns, and we invite you to join us in ours.[51]

He did not have to wait very long for his invitation to bear fruit. The Riverside Church publication *Carillon* reported the following month that "a dozen visiting scientists and professionals from the Soviet Union . . . were treated to a tour of the Riverside Church tower and a luncheon following the morning service at which Coffin preached."[52] It added that their trip to the U.S. had been arranged by the American Friends Service Committee as a "reciprocal gesture following the invitation of the Soviet Peace Committee to a group of Americans including Helen Caldicott, and . . . Bill Coffin in September 1979."[53]

Another interesting event that year was the Conference in Solidarity with the Liberation Struggles of Southern Africa, which was held at Riverside in the fall. Some of the interesting characters to address the conference were Oliver Tambo, president of the African National Congress, and Sam Nujoma, leader of SWAPO, both prominent African members of the World Peace Council and, as such, supporters of Soviet foreign policy objectives.[54] (Since violence, which is deemed necessary by both ANC and SWAPO, and peace are contradictory, Coffin and Weiss may have decided not to list the conference as part of the disarmament program's activities for that year.) The Reverend Mr. Coffin was in attendance. He blessed the solemn event with an opening prayer, and apologized to any who might have taken offense at his invocation of the Deity. Coffin was being considerate of the feelings of those from the Soviet Union and the East bloc, and of the American communists. According to U.S. intelligence sources, the whole event had been run and chaired by members of the CPUSA, whose chairman, Henry Winston, appeared in person.[55]

The year 1981 featured yet another Peace Sabbath, the largest ever. It went beyond matters relating to nuclear confrontation, and celebrated the new consciousness of liberation at work all over the world.

By this time the burgeoning European peace movement was getting extensive media coverage at home. The protests against the deployment of American Pershing II and Cruise missiles were decidedly anti-American, although the Soviet Union had already deployed some seven hundred fifty SS-20 warheads targeted at Western Europe. A similar peace campaign in the United States would culminate in June 1982 at the U.N. Second Special Session on Disarmament. The meeting to launch the June rally—the biggest peace extravaganza in American history—was held on Halloween 1981 at the Riverside Church. James Avery, a representative of the U.N. Non-Governmental Organization (NGO) Special Committee on Disarmament, was there to bring a message from his

European peace colleagues. The Europeans, he said, were counting on them to mobilize an opposition to the arms race equal to that in Europe.

But Weiss, Coffin, and Barnet had greater expectations. The American peace movement would surpass anything Europe had ever put on! (See Appendix 8 for organizational chart of IPS and the peace movement.)

Along with Cora Weiss, organizers of the event included David McReynolds of the War Resisters League; Norma Becker, Leslie Cagan, and Tom DeLuca of Mobilization for Survival; and Connie Hogarth of the Women's International League for Peace and Freedom. The meeting itself, attended by some two hundred representatives from about seventy different organizations, solemnized the marriage, however incongruous, of religious and communist institutions.[56]

The fourth national convocation, in fall 1981, brought Barnet and Michael Klare back to Riverside. Fifteen hundred people attended. Klare and others from Riverside had just returned from Europe where they had met with leaders of the peace movement. Reporting their findings, *Disarming Notes* said, "It was inspiring to see the church-based bodies and the politically-based bodies working for the same goals—an uneasy alliance, but an alliance."[57]

Unintentionally, *Disarming Notes* had touched upon *the* problem that had from the outset plagued the European religious peace movement: the uneasy alliance between the genuinely religious elements in the peace movement and the communists. Interestingly and ironically, the reaction of both the World Peacemakers (Barnet) and the Riverside Church Disarmament Program (Weiss) was not to avoid the pitfalls of the European peace movement, but to go full-steam ahead.

Indeed, many Moscow-line and Trotskyist communist factions were there at Riverside to launch the Campaign for the Second Special Session on Disarmament. And a few months earlier Richard Barnet had joined Nino Pasti, an Italian communist and World Peace Council member, as a featured speaker at a SANE-sponsored Capitol Hill event, "Briefing on European Opposition to the New Generation of Theater Nuclear Weapons." Instead of distancing himself from the WPC position, Barnet agreed with Pasti that the Soviet proposals for a "nuclear moratorium" were commendable (the Soviets now had nearly three hundred intermediate-range ballistic missiles, NATO had none). Barnet pointed to the anti-NATO demonstrations sweeping Europe as further justification for going along with the Soviet proposals.[58]

Finally, the excitement of it all in Europe drew Coffin and Weiss there in November 1981. The World Council of Churches had organized an international hearing on nuclear weapons in Amsterdam. The duo were invited to testify. Coffin gave a familiar message, a derivative of his "If we're not one with the Soviets in love, at least we're one with them in sin" theme, and Weiss offered some specific recommendations:

It is in the Judeo-Christian tradition and in the tradition of the World Council of Churches to seek and enunciate prophetic vision . . . in the name of God and for the sake of all humanity, we should like to see the World Council of Churches call for an immediate stop to the production and start the reduction of all nuclear weapons. . . .

We should like to ask the World Council of Churches to implement this goal and demonstrate its approval by making legal and financial help available to religious movements actively building public opinion in support of these goals around the world.[59]

Finance the peace movement from the coffers of well-meaning unsuspecting churchgoers. So spoke Cora Weiss to the World Council of Churches.

CHAPTER 18

Peace and International Socialist Solidarity
IPS and Riverside Church, 1982–86

Disarming, the Fifth Year at Riverside

Entering its fifth year, the Riverside Church Disarmament Program found itself in an awkward position. The Soviet invasion of Afghanistan in December 1979 and General Jaruzelski's December 1981 crackdown in Poland, blessed by Moscow, stood in stark contrast to the benevolent picture William Sloane Coffin and Cora Weiss had painted of Soviet intentions.

Peace activism at Riverside, however, would not yield to such grim realities. Thus January 1982 brought a busy schedule of IPS visitors. Fellows Bill Arkin and Susan George spoke on "Poverty and Militarism" and Eqbal Ahmad addressed the curious subject "Interventionism in Libya." Sounding a dark warning about the aggressive "nuclear theology" of the Reagan administration, Arkin warned, "Let there be no illusion about it, the Soviet Union and its defensive plan will not stand for an attack upon the motherland and it will respond in kind."[1] Ahmad told his audience that "all this talk we hear about Libya is a farce."[2] After describing Libya as a tiny country of three million relatively backward people, surrounded by U.S. allies Egypt, Sudan, and Tunisia, Ahmad wondered, "76 million American-armed allies surround little Libya—not even including Israeli power at some further distance—so how the hell will Libya take on the U.S.?"[3]

Finally, in March 1982 *Disarming Notes* brought up the Polish tragedy. Ignoring the communists' responsibility for the repression, the article "Broken Dreams" castigated the United States: "We who were once the champions of the world's oppressed now are championing only the oppressed of Poland, while we support the oppressors in country after country where our vested interests are at stake."[4] That the unfolding events in Poland might reflect Soviet posture was not even considered. Only the United States was the cause of tensions between East and West. Furthermore, "sanctions are not likely to be of help to the situation in Poland," counseled *Disarming Notes*.[5] And that was it for Poland.

With the Polish problem disposed of, the disarmament program turned to the main business of the year—preparations for the U.N. Second Special Session on Disarmament in June. The organizers expected a crowd of a million thronging the streets of New York City—as proposed by Richard Barnet a year earlier—more than any European peace demonstration. In anticipation, the Riverside Church developed a "Learn to Disarm Course" to prepare for the tasks ahead.

Learning to Disarm

George Hunsinger, a young professor from the New Brunswick Theological Seminary, had served as "theologian in residence" at the Riverside Church Disarmament Program since 1978. He developed the course. In the preface to the second edition of the *Riverside Church Disarmament Reader*, subtitled *A Model Course for Disarmament Studies*, Hunsinger wrote that his syllabus and accompanying reader had been used on hundreds of campuses around the country (where his course could be taken for credit). Although the course purported to be educational, it was in fact designed to "equip students for taking more effective action."

But in what direction would the action be focused, or at whom? Hunsinger based his analysis on a typology comprising seven positions on the nuclear question, from nuclear superiority on the far right (model 1) to unilateral nuclear disarmament or abolition on the far left (model 7). Labeling the Reagan administration a proponent of model 1, Hunsinger declared that "the center of gravity in the syllabus falls somewhere around Model 5," which was best represented by the Institute for Policy Studies.[6] Hunsinger had done his homework poorly, for IPS has consistently advocated unilateral steps toward disarmament. In fact, both Richard Barnet and Marc Raskin have endorsed the abolitionist movement, which Hunsinger categorized as model 7.

Dale Aukerman, a radical religious activist, wrote the chief book for the course, *Darkening Valley*. Aukerman published an important article in the January 1984 *Sojourners*, subtitled "Giving the Russians Sanctuary," which the National Council of Churches used to prepare a delegation of 266 Americans who would take a peace tour of the Soviet Union that June. Says the article:

We do not leave them [the Russians] to their impending doom. We are ready to risk our lives in countering the [American nuclear] terror that presses upon them. . . . The most promising defense for them comes from communities of refuge here that disengage themselves from that base [of terror]. . . .[7]

A thesis of *Darkening Valley* is that the very possession of the American nuclear arsenal amounts to the recrucifixion of Christ. Hunsinger equated Americans who accepted statements by Reagan, Bush, and Haig about nuclear war survival with Germans who silently watched Hitler exterminate Jews.

Besides the Aukerman and Hunsinger challenges, Barnet's *Real Security* and Sidney Lens's *The Day Before Doomsday* raised more tangible questions, such as: Is there a Soviet threat? Is there reason for alarm at the Soviet military buildup? What is national security? What kind of country are we? The books, of course, provided the answers for students eager to join the numerous peace demonstrations.

Aukerman also depicted the nation/state as the ultimate evil of our time. To that graven image the American nuclear arsenal had been erected, and concepts like national security and national loyalty were actually evil deceptions for the unwitting Christian.

Aukerman implored his students to reject the "common sense" of providing for the national defense because nuclear weapons were biblically unjustifiable. The lesson of the last world war—the need to arm against evil—was no longer viable in the nuclear era, particularly since the advent of Reagan. Where Riverside was concerned, Christian and American ethics were quickly parting ways.

Mobilizing for June 12 Rally

If in 1978 people wondered whether the Soviet World Peace Council was behind the first U.N. Special Session on Disarmament, the communist involvement in the mass demonstrations of 1982 was apparent from the outset. Mobilization for Survival (MFS) organized the May 1978 demonstrations and took prime responsibility for the June 1982 activities.[8]

MFS was originally organized by Sidney Lens, Sidney Peck, Terry Provance, David McReynolds, Michael Klare, Norma Becker, and others before the 1978 special session. Lens had been involved with Communist party members in the Chicago Peace Council, a spinoff of the World Peace Council. Sidney Peck had been a member of the Wisconsin State Committee of the Communist party, USA.[9] Terry Provance was a member of the World Peace Council; and Norma Becker had been active in Communist party fronts.[10] IPS asserts in its 1979–80 annual report that its "Fellows were instrumental in organizing . . . Mobilization for Survival."[11]

The campaign organizers for the U.N. Second Special Session on Disarmament decided to have all events culminate in a mass demonstration in New York City on June 12. To ensure success—to influence public opinion through the media—MFS delegated the responsibilities initially to five groups: (1) the Cultural/Demonstration Taskforce; (2) the Civil Disobedience Taskforce; (3) the Public Education Taskforce; (4) the International Taskforce; and (5) the Religious Taskforce.

The June 12 event gave an unprecedented unity to "the movement" in New York City. For example, the New York Marxist School offered a lecture, "Building a Movement Against the Arms Race and Oppression," to elicit "discussion around the political issues and tactical questions raised in the Second Special Session on Disarmament campaign, and the long-term goals of the emerging movement."[12] Speakers included leaders of the MFS June 12 leadership: Norma Becker and Leslie Cagan, as well as Mike Clark of the Riverside Church Disarmament Program. Becker spoke at a conference at Riverside and implored her audience "to organize like we have never done before."[13]

MFS leaders decided to expand the organizational structure as activities geared up. Most of the responsibilities of the International Taskforce shifted to the newly created International Liaison Office at the Riverside Church, directed by Sidney Peck. The advisory board of the International Liaison Office included Cora Weiss and a number of people close to Soviet officials and front groups—Dwain Epps, Terry Provance, Paul Dinter (Catholic student chaplain at Columbia University), and Norma Becker. MFS also formed the Labor Taskforce, headed by Gil Green, a Communist party, USA Central Committee member.[14]

By this time the press had finally begun to wake up to the Communist role in the leadership of the peace movement and to ask probing questions, to which MFS members cried "McCarthyism"—and went right ahead. When MFS formed the June 12 Rally Committee, headed by Leslie Cagan, for the final activities, Communist party members were right at the center. In fact, Sandy Pollack, a Central Committee member of the Communist party, USA, whom the Cubans praised for her "militant solidarity," was at Cagan's right hand. Cagan commented that "Sandy was there for whatever work no matter how big or small, how public or behind the scenes the tasks were. . . . In fact, Sandy was one of the relatively small number of people who made June 12th the success it finally was."[15]

Though the Communist party has had but a marginal following in the United States, communists have often harnessed noncommunists to their causes. Lenin himself conceived of the "united front" as a way to enlarge the power base of a small "vanguard" party. Without its front organizations—variously referred to as united fronts, people's fronts, popular fronts, democratic fronts—the Communist party would almost be a "weaponless army." Fronts provide an ideal vehicle for coalition building, as Cagan attested in her tribute to Pollack:

[O]urs was a friendship that was born in work—all those unbelievable coalitions, and all that detailed planning for demonstrations . . . Sandy and I worked in what seemed to be an almost endless string of coalitions—each with their own unique and particular struggles and dynamics. . . . Sandy would zero right in on the problem and offer a way out of the muddle. Even if you disagreed with the particulars there was no way to miss the fact that Sandy was always moving the work ahead.[16]

Amidst all the preparations, Kenneth Briggs of the *New York Times* wrote an article, "Growing Role for Churches in Disarmament Drive," in which he noted: "In general, churches have done more than any other institution to carry the anti-nuclear campaign along, and their convictions seem to be deepening."[17] The next day the *Times* quoted William Sloane Coffin as having proclaimed from his Easter pulpit, "Thank God we have the beginning of an abolitionist movement."[18]

Indeed, the burning issue of peace—for men of goodwill and others—brought about a marriage between atheistic communists and religious activists, a relationship integral to the success of the European peace movement the previous year.

Converging on Biggest Peace Extravaganza Ever

A few days before the opening of the U.N. Second Special Session on Disarmament Peter Weiss, Marcus Raskin, and William Sloane Coffin spoke at the International Symposium on the Morality and Legality of Nuclear Weapons, along with luminaries like Lenin Peace Prize winner Sean MacBride.

Then there was the religious convocation for peace at the nearby Cathedral of St. John the Divine (whose dean, Rev. James Park Morton, was an IPS trustee) on the eve of the big day, followed by an all-night vigil at the U.N. The next day, June 12, nearly a million people were on hand, and later attended a huge rally in Central Park, where William Sloane Coffin gave his blessing-invocation.

The U.N.-sanctioned proceedings of the second special session unfolded quietly during the following month, and accomplished absolutely nothing.[19]

It hardly mattered. For action was secondary. Of primary importance was the political impact, the propaganda value of the demonstrations. And in that respect the event was an unqualified success: a huge crowd, skeleton costumes, buttons, T-shirts, balloons, streamers—and good footage aplenty for national TV.

Until then Americans, with memories still of the Soviet invasion of Afghanistan and the American hostage crisis in Iran, had not been particularly drawn to the nuclear freeze campaign. Now, less than a month after the June 12 demonstrations, the House of Representatives defeated a bill for a nuclear freeze by only two votes (204–202).

And this was only the beginning. Throughout 1982 and into 1983 the disarmament movement relentlessly lobbied Congress and staged teach-ins and other events that attracted considerable media coverage. The nuclear issue offered endless sensationalism, which translated into a steady drumbeat of fear—the imminence of nuclear war. Combined with the favorable results of the "freeze" and "jobs with peace" resolutions on many of the November 1982 ballots, the nuclear issue resulted in a bandwagon effect that swept a nuclear freeze resolution through the House of Representatives on May 4, 1983, by a wide margin (278–149). Indeed, despite the KAL 007 tragedy, gas warfare and genocide in Afghanistan, and Soviet ICBM superiority and treaty violations, one of the most frequent lines of the 1984 Democratic party presidential candidates was the need for a nuclear freeze.

Tours in the Spirit of Potemkin

When the tide of the peace demonstrations had ebbed, other related business sprang up at Riverside Church. Barbara Brianzeva, an active participant in the church's disarmament program, is an organizer of tours to the Soviet Union. Her company's leaflets advertising these "tours for peace" to "see Moscow, headquarters of the peace movement," can be found at some of the more private meetings for the active core group.

August brought one such tour for peace, cosponsored by an old Communist party front, the National Council for American-Soviet Friendship. Rev. Mike Clark of Riverside Church accompanied the tour and shared his impressions with *Disarming Notes* readers after he returned. In an article entitled "U.S.–Soviet Relations: The Burden Rests with Us," Clark said that his "unprecedented three-week trip" had afforded him the "opportunity to meet with peace committees . . . and individual citizens," and that a "Volga Peace Cruise" had introduced him to "four Soviet resource people,"[20] *Pravda,* the Institute for the Study of the USA and Canada, and the USA–USSR Friendship Society, all of which had "shared workshop leadership." Clark concluded:

> The Soviet government is waiting for the U.S. government to make the next moves. . . . Soviet officials point to a lengthy list of initiatives . . . that have, at best, been ignored, and, at worst, been rejected or ridiculed by the most recent U.S. administrations. . . .
> In an ideal world, those differences would not exist. . . . But we live in a real world. It is a real world that we are trying to disarm. In that real world of superpowers . . . it is our own government which stands now as the primary obstacle to real progress toward nuclear disarmament. . . .[21]

Cora Weiss, for her part, reported on her meeting in Paris with European and

American peace movement leaders. She specifically spoke of the independent peace groups that had sprung up and been harassed in Eastern Europe:

> . . . they [the independent groups] are careful not to jeopardize their ability to function by having Eastern governments accuse them of being funded or directed from the West . . . the most important way to cause those governments to relax . . . would be to achieve a concrete result in the West, such as a nuclear-free Holland.[22]

The day after the November 1982 elections, Cora Weiss presented a disarmament program, "If It's God's World, How Can We Help Preserve It?" Though she never got around to God, she did outline a "three point action agenda": (1) to monitor every congressman's stance on defense and make sure that those who were profreeze continued to vote "right"; (2) to link the cost of weapons to the state of the economy, especially as it concerned unemployment; and (3) to fight any increased expenditures for conventional weapons. "We must go from nuclear freeze to nuclear-free," she said, but "to defense-free" was clearly implied. For the freeze was only the first stage, and an educational stage. Next would come campaigns to close ports to naval vessels, close down military bases, establish nuclear-free zones.

IPS associate fellow Alan Wolfe came to Riverside later that month. Wolfe's book *America's Impasse* had just received rave reviews in the Soviet press, and excerpts from it have even been published by the Soviet Institute for Study of USA and Canada. At Riverside, Wolfe commended the organization for influencing the outcome of several races, particularly those in which candidates had "something of a progressive political orientation." Carl McCall, a New York politician, was also there that day to report on bringing minorities "along with others into huge coalitions that will be committed to changing national priorities," thus welding the disarmament movement into a potent political force.

In this spirit, Cora Weiss invited Roger Wilkins, a new senior fellow at IPS, and Dwain Epps of the NCC and WCC to address Riverside. Under the title "Racism and Militarism," Epps argued that militarism not only was evil, but had a racial basis:

> The present pattern of world-wide domination by the superpowers is racist in setting the framework for a world order based on the values and interests of the white world. . . Of the 140 or so wars fought during the period of the cold war and detente, virtually all have been fought in the non-white world. . . .[23]

Wilkins, who had just returned from an IPS-organized visit to the Soviet Union with the Episcopal bishop Paul Moore, Marcus Raskin, Richard Barnet, and others, said, "It is easier to deal with frustration and disappointment in one's own life when you can believe that the world is all fouled up because the

Soviets are evil and threatening and that blacks are inferior. . . ."[24] Linking racism, militarism, and anti-Sovietism was seen by Weiss and her IPS colleagues as a potent package for the disarmament cause.

At a convocation of preachers from around the country, Coffin instructed his colleagues: "We need to save our people from the self-serving delusions of a superpower,"[25] meaning the United States. Stressing the need for national self-criticism irrespective of the behavior of the other superpower, Coffin told the preachers, "If you're a good pastor to your people at all times, you can get away with anything in the pulpit."[26]

Disarming, the Sixth Year

April 1983 found Riverside hosting the fifth national conference on disarmament. Its theme, "Making Peace Possible," brought a number of celebrities, including Bianca Jagger; Ambassador Jarquin from Nicaragua; Ambassador Vladimir Shustov from the Soviet Union; and the international "Peace Child" chorus, complete with American boys and Soviet girls. Shustov's friend, Dwain Epps of the NCC and WCC, was also present, as were IPS chairman Peter Weiss, Marcus Raskin, Michael Klare, and various leaders from the European peace movement.

The gala celebration of peace was accompanied by hardheaded brainstorming on issues like redirecting federal budgetary priorities, tax resistance, and direct action (civil disobedience). An interesting sidelight came with the "chancel-side chat" between Coffin and Shustov, who appeared confident and jovial despite the embarrassing reports that had recently appeared in the media identifying him as a KGB agent.[27]

Shustov's Riverside audience was as acquiescent as ever, except for a few members of the Student Struggle for Soviet Jewry, who threatened the camaraderie by raising tough questions about the plight of Jews in the Soviet Union. Coffin saved the day, pointing out that the Jewish Defense League was not behaving at all sensibly before a Soviet guest. (A year later, Shustov returned to Riverside to brief the NCC delegation of 266 for its trip to the Soviet Union.)

In May over ten thousand Catholic, Protestant, and Jewish congregations honored the Peace Sabbath—not bad for a program conceived at Riverside a little over four years earlier.[28] Although these congregations were less active than the flagship church, they did circulate a brochure featuring the works of Richard Barnet.

At Riverside's own Peace Sunday, the focus was on Central America. Cora Weiss, on her return from Nicaragua and Honduras in early June, reported to the church on June 12—that historical anniversary. She described a foreboding storm, predicted a U.S.-made "graveyard" in Nicaragua before October, described death and torture, and blamed American allies who professed to be Christian. While the Nicaraguan government was "planting trees and building playgrounds" in Managua as a "gift to the people, the United States was supporting allies whose chief activity was inflicting torture." She assured her audience that the Sandinista regime was pluralistic and that it tolerated religious freedom. To make her point Mrs. Weiss quoted a little Nicaraguan girl who enjoyed religion classes because "Jesus was just as much for the poor as her own government." Earlier that year the IPS Washington School gave a course on liberation theology taught by Father Bryan Hehir entitled, "Matthew, Marx, Luke, and John," which focused on Nicaragua.

Minneapolis Dialogue with Soviets

In June 1983 Coffin and Weiss traveled to Minneapolis to participate in a disarmament conference jointly sponsored by IPS and the Soviet Institute for the Study of USA and Canada. With them was the Episcopal bishop Paul Moore. Although peace activism by the Episcopal church is not systematically linked to IPS, as in the case of Riverside Church, the denomination's major church, the Cathedral of St. John the Divine in New York City, a few blocks from Riverside, is shepherded by Rev. James Park Morton, a trustee of the Institute for Policy Studies.[29]

The Reverend Mr. Morton has made numerous attempts to launch peace activities from his cathedral, but has never succeeded in doing anything on the scale of Riverside Church. His decision to place a crucifix with a female figure of Christ ("Christa") near the high altar during Holy Week 1984 illustrates his general cynicism toward traditional Christian values.[30]

Throughout the years Morton has enjoyed the full support of Bishop Moore, who may owe his invitation to the annual exchanges with the Soviets to Moore's trusteeship at IPS. Robed in purple and with a matching purple totebag, Bishop Moore praised the gathering at the disarmament conference as "unofficial, co-sponsored by citizens of both countries acting in a private capacity." Further, he declared that "the only true and lasting security for the world lies in a just, international economy: Jesus Christ, the Prophets of the Old Testament, and Karl Marx would agree on this."[31]

It was Coffin, however, who made the greatest contribution to the Minneapolis meeting. Although Moore did apologize to the Soviet delegates for the protests over human rights going on outside the hall, Coffin took on the touchy issue about which the Soviets were so vulnerable. His strategy was to defuse the issue:

> You can be so indignant at what we would perceive to be real immorality that we become militaristic and raucous . . . but nothing must interfere with this central

issue because unless we solve the issue of the arms race, we won't be able to solve anything else. . . . So my own feeling is that those who want to support the human rights issue may be making a mistake.[32]

Randall Forsberg, a founder of the nuclear freeze movement and close friend of Richard Barnet, concurred: "I strongly believe that it is not necessary and probably not possible to have any significant convergence in Eastern and Western ideas of practices on human rights before we make very substantial progress in arms control, disarmament, and the sort of détente that is associated with arms control and disarmament."[33]

Cora Weiss summarized the conference in the June issue of *Disarming Notes* and echoed Bishop Moore's opinion that it was "one of a growing number of independent initiatives between citizens of the two countries trying to find some common ground."[34] Such statements, though perhaps comforting, are disingenuous. Weiss knew very well that the Soviet delegation was anything but independent of the Kremlin's party line. The IPS delegation, for its part, was opposed to the official U.S. position. The contrast between the Soviet and American delegations could not have been more pronounced.

Foreign Exchanges Reinforce Political Predilections

In a "spirit of friendly exchange" a ten-person delegation from the Soviet Union, representing the Komsomol (Young Communist League) and the Institute for the Study of USA and Canada, paid a visit to New York and was hosted by Cora Weiss at Riverside in early July 1983.

Meanwhile, William Sloane Coffin and Mike Clark were at that moment encamped in Nicaragua near the border of Honduras. It was not a gala tour of Nicaragua, but a somber vigil staged by Americans and sanctioned by the Sandinistas, a propaganda fest to safeguard against U.S. intervention. Clark said on his return, "What we do in the next weeks and months will determine not only whether the Nicaragua experiment continues, but also whether the U.S. finds itself once again on the wrong side of history."[35] Drawing the usual parallel to Vietnam, Clark did not hide the fact that he favored the triumph of communism in "the Nicaragua experiment" as in Vietnam, Laos, and Cambodia.

Clark and Coffin reported to the Riverside disarmers after their return and gave detailed instructions on how to contact congressmen, most particularly on the upcoming Boland-Zablocki amendment to the defense appropriations bill for Central America. Passage of the amendment would mean the end of all covert aid to the contra freedom fighters, given Senate approval. "We have ten days in which to stop the United States' covert war against Nicaragua,"[36] warned

Cora Weiss, urging her activists to blitzkrieg the United States Congress. Riverside's efforts, combined with those of groups of the Latin network closely associated with IPS, paid off. For in the end the House passed the Boland-Zablocki amendment 212–208. A *Wall Street Journal* editorial noted, "Today, as a result, the world is a little safer for communism."[37]

"The Victims of Flight 007 Deserve Better"

Summer came to a close with the tragedy of Korean Airlines (KAL) flight 007. The Soviets shot down the plane over the Sea of Japan, killing 269. They did so on the pretext that the flight was a cover for intelligence gathering by the United States. The Soviets, far from apologizing, warned that they would do it again, should any other plane violate their air space.

At Riverside Church, Coffin felt compelled to rise to the occasion: "I can think of no tragedy which elicited more uncalled-for responses. The Soviet leaders, of course, stand in need of forgiveness," he said, adding, "and the rest of us need forgiveness, at least those who, unwilling to give the Soviets the benefit of the doubt, preferred to believe that they knowingly took innocent lives." He concluded his sermon: "We secretly seem to be rejoicing at the occasion given us to revive that always horrendous dialectic—'us' versus 'them.' The American reaction to the Korean tragedy is emotionally satisfying and spiritually devastating. . . . The victims of flight 007 deserve better."[38]

D'Escoto's Amigos at Riverside Church and Direct Action

Having brushed off that question, Coffin turned his attention to a major conference of the Riverside Church Disarmament Program, "Nicaragua and Central America: Saying 'No' to Reagan's Wars." Speakers and honored guests included Miguel D'Escoto, once a Maryknoll priest, now the Sandinista foreign minister; Nicaragua's Ambassador Jarquin; and *New York Times* columnist Tom Wicker. In attendance were a host of Maryknollers, NCC staffers, and various radical activists. Saul Landau's film *Target Nicaragua* was shown; it contained footage supplied by Lenin Cerna, head of Sandinista internal security police, and depicted the contra freedom fighters as the villains.

Miguel D'Escoto was greeted with thunderous applause. He proceeded to proclaim that "American democracy is a farce that makes absolutely no difference to the people because they continue to play musical chairs in Washington."[39] Though he expressed pride in the motto of the fourth anniversary of the Sandinista victory, Arms to the People, D'Escoto reviled the United States for its "militaristic policies" and "repressive, hideous, interventionist crimes." Ironically, he boasted that Nicaragua was one of the few countries that "gives arms to all the people." And the final irony, "No other Latin American country has moved forward toward democracy in these last four years as Nicaragua has."[40]

A month later there was yet another conference at Riverside, "Direct Action: Your Next Step?" The conference was intended to steer the emotions aroused by the film *The Day After* in a politically desirable direction and prepare disarmers for extreme action, such as civil disobedience. Coffin tried to stir up his audience, invoking the specter of another Grenada, despite the public's support for the U.S. action. If the peace movement had lost on Grenada, Coffin and Weiss were determined to win on the issue of nuclear weapons deployment.

The Soviet Union found Riverside Church's activities congenial enough to merit coverage in one of its important propaganda organs, *Moscow News*.

> Activists from the Disarmament Programme at the Riverside Church in New York think there should be [other forms of protest]. Recently the Church held a conference—"Direct Action: Your Next Step?" The invitation, signed by Reverend Coffin, among others, says: "We have considered prayer, teach-ins, political action and demonstrations, the myriad ways to reverse the arms race. But the arms race has escalated beyond our worst nightmares. We believe it is time to consider yet another strategy."
> The idea is to use civil disobedience and "direct action."[41]

Moscow News saw civil disobedience in the U.S. as laudable, even though in the Soviet Union it is viewed—and harshly dealt with—as "anti-Soviet activity."

Disarming, the Seventh Year

The year 1984 was an important one. The disarmament movement desperately sought to defeat President Reagan. And it was time to take stock of what Riverside Church had already accomplished.

The January 1984 issue of *Disarming Notes* announced the departure of one of its core activists, Mike Clark, who had been there from the beginning. Clark reflected on the "good news of what we have done during these past few years":

> Five years ago made-for-T.V. movies about the aftereffects of nuclear war were not being made; the National Conference of Catholic Bishops had not issued a strong condemnation of nuclear weapons; nine states . . . had not passed nuclear-free referenda; 12,000 congregations had not celebrated Peace Sabbath on the same week-end; . . . and tens of thousands of conferences . . . had not taken place in every town and city in every state in the United States.[42]

It is a telling statement on the scope of the activities emanating from Riverside

Church, whose prestige was such that it shaped religious and popular culture nationwide. Coffin reiterated one of Clark's points a few months later when he told an interviewer that "the appearance of the Bishops' Pastoral Letter [on Nuclear War] is the most important event since we started our program."[43] IPS gave itself credit for influencing the pastoral letter and, in fact, awarded its friend Father Bryan Hehir with the 1983 Letelier-Moffitt Human Rights Award for his role in crafting it.

In early 1984 Cora Weiss was off to Nicaragua, part of a U.S. delegation, guests of the Sandinista government, to gauge the impact of the Kissinger Commission report.

Meanwhile, Coffin preached from his Riverside pulpit: "Love your enemies. . . . This certainly includes the Russians, who are our enemies in large part because we make them so. Love means positive Christianity, not negative anticommunism."[44] And moving to events in Latin America, Coffin continued:

> Shultz declared that we would never allow the Salvadoran rebels to "shoot their way into the government." Not only did his words cause Thomas Jefferson, Benjamin Franklin and George Washington to raise from the grave a collective eyebrow, but they mistakenly implied that peaceful methods in El Salvador today were synonymous with democracy, while the armed insurrection was somehow undemocratic. Clearly this is not the case; clearly, in that long-suffering country, peaceful methods are instruments of domination, repression and control.[45]

Coffin and Weiss were making ready for their major events: Central America Week in March, and Peace Sabbath–Peace with Justice Week in May. Peace Sabbath would be linked with the National Council of Churches Peace with Justice Week; Coffin and Weiss expected that some twenty thousand congregations would participate. The Moravian bishop John Wilson, from Nicaragua—supposedly a Miskito Indian, but in truth a Sandinista supporter —addressed leaders and activists at Riverside. Meanwhile, the disarmament program trained a small international group of "peace leaders," including Peter Zimmerman from East Germany and Bertalan Tomas from Hungary, to participate in the Peace with Justice Tour '84 around the United States.

NCC's Peace with Justice Tour

The tour's promotional brochure revealed what kind of peace these "leaders" had in mind:

> The purpose of the tour is to educate a wide cross section of the U.S. public. . . .
> The tour is especially relevant in this year of intense political debate. The leaders will directly address the effects of U.S. foreign and military policy on their areas

of the world . . . military conflict and injustice in these areas are sometimes directly related to U.S. policies.[46]

An East German, for example, told a congregation what misery the deployment of Cruise missiles in West Germany would bring to his country. No mention was made of the deployment of the Soviet SS-20s.

The NCC provided a Peace with Justice Week "Information Kit." In it one could read:

—the U.S. *invasion* of Grenada and a Soviet *presence* in Afghanistan

—the appeal to offer your church as a sanctuary to Salvadoran and Guatemalan refugees

—the U.S. as "part of a world order dominated by white European, Christian, imperialist nations," whose people are "turning away from God by making an idol of the nation-state and trusting in violence to protect us"

—U.S. troops engaging in exercises that "are often preparations for foreign intervention . . . far from U.S. borders and in areas where the Soviet Union has little or no presence," thus not at all legitimately defending anything but, "given the recent Korean Airline incident, engendering global dangers"

—the need to "discipline ourselves to live with a variety of political experiments in the Third World"

—a U.S. that was first to *use* nuclear weapons, and that "first developed and deployed eight of the eleven nuclear weapons and delivery systems which escalated the arms race, with the Soviet Union lagging from two to eight years behind"

—a U.S. strategy that "attempts to gain a military advantage through arms control treaties," while the Soviet Union is consigned to bitter criticism for its heavy reliance "on its land-based missiles which are more vulnerable to attack"

—a U.S. "reliance upon military force which far exceeds the requirements for national defense"

—a U.S. foreign policy that, "in part, represents the joining of domestic and international violence of people of color"[47]

And so on. The NCC's Peace with Justice Week "Information Kit" advertised the Institute for Policy Studies as a primary source to contact for further information.

The Reverend Mr. Coffin and the Democratic Party

By this time, Coffin's stature had earned him an invitation from the Democratic party to testify on foreign policy before the New York Democratic Platform

Committee. Coffin described the United States as "the fist shaking at everybody around the world" that cannot "accept or offer an extended hand." He was for the freeze and the test ban treaty, for cutting back on conventional arms, slashing the military budget, ending draft registration, normalizing relations with Cuba, and divesting from South Africa.

As for the Democratic candidates, Coffin had already made his choice, as indicated by his ringing endorsement on the brochure "Religious Leaders for Jesse Jackson." It comes as no surprise that IPS was already deeply involved in Jesse Jackson's campaign. IPS senior fellow Roger Wilkins had written Jackson's candidacy announcement speech, and both Wilkins and IPS director Robert Borosage served as political advisers to Jackson, the former on domestic issues and campaign strategy and the latter on foreign policy issues.[48]

Riverside Church Tower

Over the years the Riverside Church has supported and hosted numerous organizations, some short-lived, some long term. One such group, Educators for Social Responsibility/Metropolitan Area (ESR/MA), quietly opened up shop on the seventeenth floor of the Riverside Church tower in September 1983.

ESR/MA concentrates on infiltrating New York's schools with an antinuclear curriculum. Its success can be gauged by the fact that in spring 1984 the New York City Board of Education issued a shortened version of one of ESR's pamphlets to all of the city's public schools. ESR's Central American Committee circulates another curriculum favorable to the Sandinista regime. ESR has also put together a slide show depicting the good life in the Soviet Union and a videotape of Soviet children talking about nuclear war. In collaboration with the Soviet mission to the U.N. ESR initiated "pen pal relationships between American and Soviet youngsters," and during summer 1984 it sponsored two tours of the Soviet Union for educators and psychologists.

In July ESR/MA cosponsored a symposium, Education and the Arms Race, at Columbia University. It opened with a one-day lecture program, "What About the Russians?" IPS trustee Paul Warnke was scheduled to speak. Reading tables featured a reprint from *Soviet Military Review,* some copies of *Moscow News,* and, last but not least, an IPS brochure, "Books for Courses," offering teachers many institute titles.

On the eighteenth floor of the tower one can find Latinos at Riverside. When the organization hosted Cuban clergy in the church tower, a sizable gathering heard glowing accounts of religious life in Castro's paradise. In early July, Latinos at Riverside gained space in the Communist *Daily World* for cosponsoring with the Communist party's own Young Communist League a massive demonstration against President Reagan's policies in Central America.

Addressing the same rally was another radical churchman, Rev. David Garcia of the Episcopal Church of St. Marks. Under his clerical robes Garcia wears a coat of many colors. He is a cochairman of the National Alliance Against Racist and Political Repression, and serves on the executive committee of the National Emergency Civil Liberties Committee, both Communist party fronts. Garcia's church receives $15,000 annually from Cora Weiss's Samuel Rubin Foundation.[49]

Other interesting programs have also found a nest in the Riverside Church tower. The fifth floor houses the Sanctuary Commission, a leading organization in the sanctuary movement, which began in 1981 as an "underground railroad" for illegal aliens from El Salvador and Guatemala. Jim and Pat Corbett, two founders of the movement, received from IPS the Letelier-Moffitt Human Rights Award in September 1984.

The sanctuary movement helps people from El Salvador and Guatemala who enter the country illegally. Asserting that these are political refugees rather than illegal aliens, the movement seeks to circumvent the U.S. Immigration and Naturalization Service.

Sanctuary leaders not only provide haven for the oppressed of foreign lands, but are also active in efforts to change U.S. policies toward Latin America. Along with stating that "successful social revolution . . . in Nicaragua or El Salvador would be a beacon of hope," William Sloane Coffin told the first Inter-American Symposium on Sanctuary, held in January 1985, that "we must continue the sanctuary movement in its present form [and] we must plead with the Congress immediately to stop the funding of the contras and slow down, not to mention stop, rather than increase military aid to El Salvador, so that the military there will have to allow Duarte to negotiate an end to the conflict."[50]

Even though the number of illegal aliens helped by the sanctuary movement is small, there is concern that some of those seeking refuge in the United States may be connected with terrorism. If so, the movement may be laying the foundation for a revolutionary infrastructure in the United States.

1985: Expressions of International Socialist Solidarity

The extraordinary lengths to which the IPS community will go to express solidarity with socialism—often involving a de facto alliance with international communism—were poignantly demonstrated following the tragic death of Alexandra (Sandy) Pollack. Her Cubana Airlines flight crashed en route to Managua on January 19, 1985.

Pollack was a member of the Central Committee of the Communist party, USA, and a founding member of the U.S. Peace Council, an arm of the Soviet front World Peace Council. Although she was an avowed atheist, a memorial service was held for her on February 2, 1985, at Riverside Church. The Reverend Mr. Coffin opened the ceremony before a gathering of some six hundred party members, foreign diplomats, and others. Many wore red carnations.

"It is appropriate that we are all here, paying honor to Sandy," said Coffin. "She may not have believed in God, but God believed in Sandy . . . for she was a bridge builder."[51] (Coffin spoke from his own "bridge-building" experience for he frequently travels to communist countries to express one form of solidarity or another. He traveled to North Vietnam in 1970 to express solidarity with the communist Ho Chi Minh government. In his memoirs, *Once to Every Man,* Coffin recounts, "I was fascinated by the nationalities represented . . . East Germans, Russians, Cubans, Poles, Rumanians. . . ."[52] In 1984 and 1985 he made several trips to Nicaragua, where he expressed solidarity with various members of the Sandinista junta.)

IPS fellow Eliana Loveluck represented the Institute for Policy Studies community at Pollack's memorial service, and a message from senior fellow Isabel Letelier read, "We learned a tremendous amount from Sandy's commitment and the way she worked. . . . As Latin Americanists we know she will always be alive in our struggles and she will be with us in our victories."[53]

Sandy Pollack's loss was also deeply felt at the highest levels of the Communist party and Soviet bloc. Henry Winston, national chairman of the Communist party, USA, took the microphone from Coffin and told the solemn gathering, "Sandy . . . drank from the fountain of Marxism-Leninism, and was able to apply this science to everything she did." Johnetta Cole, a member of the World Peace Council, said that "Sandy's life touched all of us. She was an internationalist, so it shouldn't surprise us that her life also reached beyond us. Messages received from many countries reflect the strength of the bond Sandy committed herself to building and the respect and the affection she gained around the world."[54] And from around the world those messages poured.

The Middle East and Africa were well represented. Rabab Abdulhadi, of the Committee for a Democratic Palestine, showed up with a representative from the November 29 Committee for Palestine.[55] Also present was Zuri Terzi of the PLO, who said, "Sandy proved to be a very dear friend of the Palestine Liberation Organization . . . martyrs are immortals and on this occasion we say that Sandy is immortal. Victory to the revolution and immortality to its martyrs!"[56] The Iranian OIP Fadaian sent word, and the African National Congress was represented by a delegation of four, who commented, "We pledge never to rest until the course for which Sandy sacrificed emerges triumphant."[57]

A number of Soviets were present, and although those in attendance assumed a low profile, the ambassador to the U.N., Anatoly Dobrynin, sent his condolences.[58] Yuri Zhukov, the president of the Soviet Peace Committee, commented, "Her image as a restless fighter for peace and happiness for all peoples will forever be in our hearts."[59]

Representatives from East European satellite states were in attendance—Girolia Rava, second secretary from Czechoslovakia; Michael Putschke, third secretary from East Germany; and Dietmar Hucke, East German ambassador extraordinary and plenipotentiary. And Asian communist states such as North Korea and Vietnam were well represented.

But it was the Latin American communists who were most affected by her untimely death. The Sandinista directorate commandante, Bayardo Arce Castano, said, "The Sandinista National Liberation Front shares with you the pain caused by Sandy's departure, and we will keep alive the example that she left for us."[60] The Nicaraguan ambassador to the U.N., Carlos Tunnerman, told the Riverside gathering, "We have lost an exceedingly talented, and skillful leader, whose energies were devoted to peace and building solidarity with the peoples of Latin America."[61]

A member of the Central Committee of the Communist party of Cuba, Jesus Montane Oropesa, offered his tribute: "Her life was an example of revolutionary consistency and selfless devotion."[62]

Rene Mujica, first secretary of the Cuban Interests Section in Washington, was a keynote speaker at the memorial service. (Mujica's friendship with Saul Landau of IPS dates back to the 1960s. Landau was on the first Venceremos Brigade flight to Cuba on July 4, 1969,[63] along with Pollack, who was a founder of the national committee of the Brigade, which facilitated the travel of several thousand Americans to Cuba in defiance of the State Department ban on travel there.[64]) Mujica noted that "Sandy was always a soldier on many fronts, and there never was a moment that she was not present with all the power of her mind . . . in solidarity with our country." He continued, "It is because of . . . her particular love for and identification with the Cuban revolution, and because in so many ways she was indeed one of our own, that we feel her loss irreparably and painfully as also our own."[65] Appropriate for this occasion at Riverside, which drew so many from afar, Mujica described Pollack as the embodiment of socialist internationalism, and concluded by saying:

> There is virtually no significant process of progressive social change or struggle for national liberation any place in the world that did not receive support from her. . . . So extensive was her involvement that even many who knew her well and collaborated with her for years were able to acquire only a partial comprehension of her multiple talents and pursuits, of the important role she played in the common struggles.[66]

Nicaraguan Heads of State Revisit Riverside

In November 1985 Daniel Ortega, the Sandinista head of state, came to address the U.N. on the occasion of its fortieth anniversary. In addition to buying more than $3,500 worth of designer eyeglasses, charged on his American Express card, he took time to visit Riverside Church, where the Reverend Mr. Coffin and Cora Weiss had prepared a reception for him. Ortega was accompanied by an entourage—his ministers of trade and information, his ambassadors Carlos Tunnerman and Nora Astorga. (Astorga, recall, was the legendary Sandinista heroine who seduced one of Somoza's generals and lured him to his savage murder in her bed by her compañeros, who sprang from behind the curtains, armed with ice picks.)

Ortega dispelled any doubts about the state of emergency, which suspended the freedom of all Nicaraguans, that he had just imposed back home. "To protect the Nicaraguan people the Sandinista directorate declared a state of emergency because the U.S. is preparing for an invasion," said Ortega. "Ronald Reagan's U.N.-day speech yesterday was incompatible with the principles of international law." The responsibility for the lamentable state in Nicaragua lay with the United States. And the audience responded with thunderous applause.[67]

But things in Nicaragua got worse in 1986. The Sandinistas decided to close down the country's major newspaper, *La Prensa*, and get tougher on the Roman Catholic church. A number of church officials traveling abroad were denied reentry into Nicaragua. Bishop Vega was abducted and helicoptered out of the country with no more than the clothes on his back. What sympathy the Sandinistas had enjoyed was rapidly vanishing.

Daniel Ortega took his case before the U.N. Security Council and launched another public-relations effort to restore luster to the tarnished image of Sandinismo. William Coffin and Cora and Peter Weiss arranged a public forum for Ortega, his wife, Miguel D'Escoto, and Nora Astorga on July 28, 1986, once again under the bright lights of the media.

Physically embracing Coffin on the altar in the main sanctuary at Riverside, Ortega said, "It's natural that our encounters here in the United States have taken place in churches . . . for Nicaragua is a religious country. There is no such thing as religious persecution in Nicaragua."[68] Somberly, he went on, "Because of the $100 million aid decision by Congress we have been forced to take measures that we wish we did not have to. But these are legitimate measures taken in order to defend our revolution."

The Riverside audience again responded with thunderous applause.

"The U.S. needs a Trojan horse," continued Ortega. "That Trojan horse can be called *La Prensa* and others like Bishop Vega, financed by the CIA." Concluding his remarks under tight security provided by the U.S. Secret Service, he shouted, "We cannot afford to forget what happened in Chile." Coffin implored everyone to march on Washington and engage in civil disobedience and participate in a "people's filibuster." Meanwhile, Ortega's entourage was ushered out the side door to a waiting limousine that whisked it away.

Conclusion: The Long March Through the Institutions

In just eight years, by 1986, Cora Weiss and William Sloane Coffin had accomplished a great deal. While starting the disarmament program in 1978, she was also issuing grants to Columbia University and its Teachers College. In 1982 Cora Weiss and Peter Weiss contributed $1 million to Columbia to establish the Samuel Rubin Program for the Advancement of Liberty and Equality Through Law, which duly appointed Anthony Lewis of the *New York Times* as Samuel Rubin Fellow for the 1982–83 academic year. In fall 1984 IPS trustee Paul Warnke added another feather to his cap, becoming a trustee of Columbia University. Indeed, Cora Weiss and Bill Coffin not only accomplished a great deal within Riverside Church—hosting such groups as Latinos at Riverside, the Sanctuary Commission, and Educators for Social Responsibility—but also affected prominent neighboring institutions such as the National Council of Churches, Columbia University, Union Theological Seminary and the Cathedral of St. John the Divine.

The record certainly indicates that the ideas and organizational skills of Richard Barnet, Marcus Raskin, Cora and Peter Weiss, and William Sloane Coffin, manifest through the success and influence of IPS, World Peacemakers, and Riverside Church, and through those organizations' effect on other institutions, have altered the overall religious scene in the United States. They can be expected to continue writing, preaching, and organizing for some time to come. Elections come and go in the United States, but "the long march through the institutions continues."

Part VII

None Dares Call
It Treason

CHAPTER 19

Strange Encounters
East Bloc Diplomats Frequent the Institute

Sitting at the Café Rondo over a cup of coffee, I waited for the third session of the IPS Washington School class on "Talking with the Russians" to start. The class was being held at the St. Charles Hotel, a five-minute walk from IPS, down New Hampshire Avenue, right past the Nicaraguan embassy. It was dark out, and lights burned brightly on every floor of the IPS building across the street. People were busily going in and out, a small crowd was milling about the lobby.

In the first class IPS director Robert Borosage had recounted his version of the history of the cold war as background to the arms race. Like a few others in the class with some knowledge of history, I was unpersuaded that the United States was equally responsible for the cold war and felt that Borosage—like other revisionist historians associated with IPS, such as Richard Barnet, Gar Alperovitz, Gabriel Kolko, and Franz Schurmann—was manipulating history to make his case. It had been futile to challenge Borosage, however, for he deferred questions until the end of his three-hour presentation, when everyone was ready to go home.

The second class had been equally troubling, but for different reasons. Senior fellow Roger Wilkins and *Rolling Stone* editor William Greider had shared their impressions of the Soviet Union. Greider's admission that he was "largely ignorant about the Soviet Union . . . never having been there or really studied about it"[1] had disturbed a number of the students who had hoped to learn

327

something about the USSR. I couldn't understand why the institute had asked Greider to teach the class, except that he was a journalist and obviously a friendly one. Perhaps IPS found that the easiest way to gain influence in the major media was to pay big-name journalists to teach at the institute.

Wilkins had talked about the alternative arms-control dialogue between IPS and representatives of the Soviet Union. When he remarked that "probably one third of the Soviets are KGB [but it] doesn't really matter . . . because I'm sure that their minds are at the service of the Soviet government,"[2] it was disconcerting, because it was pretty clear that the views of IPS on arms control and foreign policy were closer to the Soviets' than to those of its own government.

But it was an incident before that second class, on November 27, 1983, that left a vivid impression in my memory, particularly in the context of Wilkins' remark. I had been sitting in the Rondo to kill time before class when I recognized Valeriy Lekarev, third secretary of the Department of Cultural Exchange at the Soviet embassy. Seeing him enter IPS this second time, I became curious and decided to follow him. Leaving some money on the table, I bolted across the street.

What would I say? I nervously groped for an excuse, a reason for bumping into him. It had been over a month since we had had our lengthy conversation on the first encounter with Michael Parenti. What if he has tried to contact me as he said he would? I thought, remembering that I'd given him the name and address of the friend with whom I was living, but not the unlisted phone number. But at the time I had no desire to have further contact with the smooth-talking Soviet diplomat, who had justified his government's actions in shooting down a civilian airliner, killing all passengers aboard, and threatening to do it again. I knew that Soviet embassy officials in Lekarev's position—those in cultural exchange—were generally in the employ of the KGB.

But curiosity outweighed whatever uneasiness I felt. I reminded myself that my interest in Lekarev and IPS was, after all, the subject of my freelance project. "Talking with the Russians" was the theme of the class, and now I was going to talk to a Russian.

I intuitively sensed that investigative reporting about whatever connection existed between IPS and hostile foreign powers would probably not be well received. If graduate school had taught me anything, it was that politics is dominated more by emotions than by reason, and when the need for illusion is deep, neither facts nor truth count for much.

As I entered the lobby of IPS, I glimpsed Lekarev and several others out the corner of my eye. I sat down behind the coffee table and picked up a copy of *In These Times* from the stack there. Lekarev was speaking Russian to someone who appeared to be his superior; next to him Marc Raskin was talking to a man who looked like Paul Warnke, the former director of the Arms Control and Disarmament Agency of the Department of State. After a fifth man walked in, they all began to leave. At that point, I got up. My eyes met Lekarev's, and I took the initiative.

"Valeriy? You remember me?" I asked, diffidently but in a friendly tone.

He hesitated for a split second, then smiled. "Rick, isn't it? We met here about a month ago," he replied in his perfect English. "I tried to call you, but. . . ."

"Well, I was moving, didn't I tell you?" I improvised, and remembered how angry my roommate had been for giving his name and address to some KGB agent. "Say, are you going to speak or participate in the class on 'Talking with the Russians?' "

"No, I can't afford $50, and they haven't invited me," he said jokingly.

"Oh, that's too bad. It's pretty worthwhile. Well, how have you been?" I said, trying to keep the conversation from stalling.

"Busy." And seeing that his colleagues were on their way down the street, he remarked, "Look, I've got to run." Taking out a business card and handing it to me, he said, "Give me a call, and we'll have lunch sometime."

I went back to the Rondo to kill another twenty minutes before the class. The waitress smiled at me. "Back so soon?" she asked.

She had been talkative and friendly, but when I asked her about IPS, she clammed up, after muttering something about "that place," and someone having been killed some years earlier. I assumed she was referring to Orlando Letelier, the Chilean Marxist who was assassinated on his way to work at IPS.

As I sat thinking over the incident, I got out my wallet and looked at Lekarev's business card. I was struck by his sense of humor and the fact that he knew exactly how much the tuition was for the IPS course. I thought, Where are they going, those Soviets, Marc Raskin, Paul Warnke? And what are they talking about?

In my subsequent research, I learned that Lekarev had been seen at IPS more than a dozen times in the previous year as had another Soviet diplomat, Viktor Taltz.

About a week later I was back at IPS to attend a talk by Robert Borosage and Saul Landau, who had just returned from Nicaragua and Cuba. I got there early. Among the people milling around, I noticed a tall, handsome, and impeccably dressed man with a mustache. He looked Slavic, although I could only see his profile as he was facing the wall, looking at some photographs. I sauntered over and asked casually where he thought the pictures were taken. He turned toward me, and in a distinct Russian accent said he thought that they represented native Latin American culture. He introduced himself as Viktor Taltz.

By now I was well into my writing project, which had grown considerably. There were too many things going on at IPS to limit myself to its "alternative arms-control talks."

I sat down next to Saul Landau and introduced myself and, while taking out my camera, told him I was "covering this story." Landau looked at me and seemed surprised by my open manner. I figured I had nothing to lose by documenting on film a few of the international personalities associated with IPS.

Borosage began his talk. "We were down there for a whole series of purposes," he announced. "One was to work on a project we have going in Europe to encourage European support for aid to Nicaragua to keep it from being isolated politically and economically, and to work with the eight ministries down there to make sure they had their projects in order to allow the Europeans to cooperate."[3]

After about five minutes Borosage turned the floor over to Landau. "Politically, it is very clear now that the Sandinistas have consolidated, that their organization has penetrated very deeply into the most remote parts of the country, and that consolidation is reflected in their confidence as well as in the obvious institutions that have been set up," Landau reported. "It is not only the bloc committees that defend the revolution, but the schools and the curriculum," and "along with this political consolidation has gone a police and a military consolidation."[4]

Taltz, who had taken a seat in the back, was jotting down a few notes. After the talk, he went over to talk with Borosage.

Borosage was visibly nervous about my picture-taking. I reminded him of my writing assignment, and told him that I also needed to interview him.

"When would be a good time to sit down for an hour or so?" I asked.

"Who did you say you were writing this for?" Borosage countered.

"I'm not altogether sure. The *Boston Phoenix* has expressed an interest in it, but I imagine I'll send it around to a few places. You know how freelancing is," I said.

The next encounter with foreign diplomats at IPS occurred about a month later, on January 19, 1984, to be precise, when the first secretary of the Cuban Interests Section, Rene J. Mujica, was the featured speaker following a showing of Saul Landau's film on life in Cuba, appropriately titled, *With Fidel*. Addressing the audience, Mujica said, "Saul and I are good friends. We first met when he came to Cuba to make this film."[5]

A month later, on the evening of February 22, 1984, a friend and I decided to attend a reception on the occasion of the release of the IPS publication *Changing Course: Blueprint for Peace in Central America and the Caribbean*.

The party was held at 122 Maryland Avenue on Capitol Hill in the building known as the Mott House, named after its owner, Stewart Mott, a generous funder of the American Left. The plush residence provides office space for the Center for National Security Studies, the IPS spinoff that led the campaign against the intelligence agencies in the mid-1970s, and is a convenient place for the Monday Group and others such as the Coalition for a New Foreign and Military Policy to meet with congressmen and their staffs.

On this particular evening, Tom Harkin (D–Iowa) and George Crockett (D–Calif.) showed up to express their support of IPS and *Changing Course,* a counterproposal to the findings of Henry Kissinger's Bipartisan Commission on Central America and the Caribbean. Unlike the Kissinger report, *Changing Course* made no mention of the Soviet military buildup under way in Nicaragua.

Congressman Harkin prefaced his statement by remarking, "I am here to basically thank the Institute for Policy Studies and the people who have worked so hard over the last couple or three years in putting together the terms for the debate which we are now having on Central America."[6]

Saul Landau, the master of ceremonies, proceeded to introduce other celebrities, such as Guadalupe Gonzales, a representative of the Salvadoran FDR/FMLN, and Nicaraguan diplomats William Vigil and Guillermo Morales. Another diplomat, though apparently invited, was not recognized—Viktor Taltz of the Soviet embassy.

Moving through the crowd, Taltz mixed and mingled without difficulty, though his Brooks Brothers suit stood out a bit amidst the disheveled dress of the rank-and-file Left, garbed in their usual proletarian style. "I read this book [*Changing Course*] last night," Taltz confided. "It was very good and accurate . . . and we are very grateful for IPS to be brave enough to tell the truth."[7]

Borosage, who saw that I had noticed Taltz, pretended not to see me. Landau and Borosage were clearly upset by my presence, my camera bag, tape recorder, and so on. Apparently Borosage had decided that I was an "unfriendly" reporter by the kind of questions I had asked in my interview with him two months earlier, in December. One question had particularly riled him. I had asked how he, as a member of the National Lawyers Guild, felt about the guild's affiliation with the International Association of Democratic Lawyers, a Soviet front.

My intuition that there was more to IPS than seminars and brown-bag lunches was increasingly confirmed by the response at IPS to my occasional visits to its public meetings. Word had apparently got out that I was an unfriendly reporter. It was quite interesting to see how attitudes turned around. Staff persons who had been friendly, engaged in revealing small talk, and shared information, were now cold and closed. Some evinced considerable signs of paranoia.

On March 23 I decided to drop in at IPS for a brown-bag lunch seminar featuring Alger Hiss, former aide to Franklin Delano Roosevelt and alleged spy for the Soviet Union who was convicted of perjury. Since Hiss was elderly, barely able to maintain a coherent train of thought, IPS's interest must have been in making a political statement rather than in providing a substantive public lecture. The message was essentially twofold: Alger Hiss was falsely accused and ought to be exonerated; and, anyway, concepts like espionage and treason are absurd creations of cold-war hysteria and should be dismissed as outdated and reactionary.

A month later, on April 21, 1984, IPS fellow Eqbal Ahmad was a featured speaker at the "Deadly Connections" conference held at the Cultural Center of District 1199 of the Union of Health Care and Hospital Workers in New York City, which is controlled by the Communist party. Two Soviet officials, Igor Mishchenko and Anatoliy Manakov, looked on with approval as the proceedings brought one denunciation after another of the United States. "Since 1945," said Ahmad, "there have been eighteen incidents involving nuclear technology that could have escalated into nuclear war. Seventeen [were created] by the United States and possibly one by the Soviet Union."[8]

On August 16, 1984, two officials from the Soviet embassy in Washington, Pavel Pavlov, a first secretary, and Vladimir I. Strokin, a third secretary and vice consul, appeared at an IPS seminar, "U.S. Policy in Southern Africa." After the conference, Strokin approached the panelists, Jean Sindab, adviser to IPS's Washington School and executive director of the Washington Office on Africa, and Anne Holloway, staff director of the U.S. House of Representatives Subcommittee on Africa, to arrange dates for a future meeting.

A month later, on September 13, Strokin showed up at another IPS seminar on South Africa, "South Africa and the Media." After the formal meeting was over, Strokin met with one of the panelists, Marsha Coleman, director of the Congressional Black Caucus Foundation. Coleman said that she had to defer any appointments until after the Black Caucus convention, scheduled for the next weekend. As Strokin showed an interest in attending, Coleman invited him and suggested they get together at that time.

Since all my IPS contacts had by this time dried up, I decided to approach some of the Soviets who frequented the institute.[9] I wrote a quick note to Lekarev and told him that I was back in town—"Would you have time to have lunch and discuss some of the things that I should be aware of in traveling in and writing about the Soviet Union?"

A few days later Lekarev called me on the phone and suggested that we have lunch at The Man in the Green Hat on the corner of Massachusetts Avenue and Third Avenue, N.E., near the offices of the U.S.–USSR Friendship Society and the Women's International League for Peace and Freedom. I got there early and took a table outside, with a good view. Shortly thereafter, I noticed Lekarev walking away from the restaurant. He appeared not lost, but as if he were concerned about being followed. Five minutes later he reappeared from the other direction, apparently having walked around the block.

We exchanged greetings and made small talk. I asked Lekarev how it was that he knew of this restaurant.

"I have been here before. My work representing the cultural interests of the Soviet Union has brought me in contact with a number of groups in this area," he responded.

Lekarev was quite interested in my background, where I came from, where I went to school, and my future plans. I wove a little Marxist rhetoric and analysis into my remarks. When I talked about the possibility of going into the foreign service or becoming a foreign correspondent he perked up.

"Tell me," he asked casually, "how did you come around to your way of thinking?"

"What do you mean?" I responded.

"You remember our meeting over at the Institute for Policy Studies. We had quite a long discussion after Michael Parenti's talk," he said, taking a deep drag on his cigarette. "We discussed the Korean Airlines incident. Understandably, you had a number of questions about it, but you seemed open-minded. I was particularly impressed that you could understand that we in the Soviet Union do not distinguish between the government and the people. That is generally hard for most Americans to grasp." he said.

"Well, most Americans' political consciousness is pretty low if it exists at all," I said.

"That's why I am curious to know how it is that you think the way you do . . . like Michael Parenti does."

"You mean how I think like a Marxist?" I asked frankly. "Well, I studied Marxism at the university. Marxism is in fashion on most campuses throughout the United States. Every school has its Marxist professors. I've attended four different schools in different parts of the country, and I would venture to say that it's impossible to go through college without being taught by professors who are favorably disposed to Marxism."

"That is interesting. I would never have assumed that to be the case," he said. "You know, I meet so few Americans who are open. When people learn that I represent the Soviet Union, their attitudes often change. Some even refuse to engage in social conversation."

"Well, I mentioned that I'm thinking about a career as a foreign correspondent. Of course it is the dream of every journalist to be stationed in Moscow, the capital of the United States' chief rival. Do you have any ideas what appropriate steps could be taken by an aspiring journalist like me?" I queried.

"Yes, but let's talk about your future at a later date. It is a serious career you are considering, and worthy of careful consideration," he said earnestly.

"Well, any advice would be appreciated," I said.

"Perhaps we can have lunch again. How about two weeks from today?" he asked.

"I don't think that I have any plans. That's okay," I replied.

"Fine, then. It was a pleasure. As you can imagine I do not have so many American friends, and I appreciate this opportunity," Lekarev said. "Shall we meet here two weeks from today at noon? We can go to another restaurant from here if you like. There are many around here. It is on me. I have to take advantage of the expense account provided by my generous government."

I was somewhat startled when Lekarev produced a wad of money to pay our modest bill. I had learned that most Soviet diplomats don't have the privilege of expense accounts—a sign of a diplomat's intelligence status is his cash supply or a credit card.

At that point we parted ways.

Two weeks later I was back at the Green Hat and took a seat outside to enjoy the pleasant weather. I arrived ten minutes early, prepared to wait. After fifteen minutes I began looking for Lekarev. A car parked nearby was occupied by someone reading a newspaper who seemed to take an interest in me. After half an hour or so I gave up and went ahead and ordered some lunch. Lekarev never did show.

I tried later that afternoon to call the Soviet embassy to reach Lekarev. However, no one even answered the telephone there. The next day I had to try half a dozen times before getting a secretary who knew virtually nothing. She said she would try to leave a message for Mr. Lekarev.

My frustration in dealing with the Soviet embassy is shared by others, who generally find the Soviets uninterested in unsolicited inquiries—they don't answer their phones because they don't care to.

IPS staffer John Mercer, who had dealt with Lekarev in making arrangements for the alternative arms-control talks which IPS was jointly sponsoring with the Soviet Institute for the Study of USA and Canada, said that the only time he could get through to the Soviet embassy was between eight and nine in the morning. "The best time to catch them is in the early morning before they go out for the day," Mercer said. "They operate differently than we do. That's just the way they are."[10]

I couldn't help wondering what keeps some one hundred thirty Soviet diplomats in Washington that busy all day. Moreover, I found it preposterous that the embassy of the country with the largest diplomatic presence in the United States is not set up to answer simple inquiries.

Several days later Lekarev called me from a pay phone and apologized for missing our lunch appointment, which he rescheduled for the coming week.

I was there at the appointed hour and again Lekarev was a few minutes late. Lekarev was extremely apologetic for having stood me up a week earlier. "Something came up unexpectedly," he said, "and I was unable to call. I hope it didn't cause you too much inconvenience." In the course of the ensuing small talk, he asked how my studies were going.

I was purposely carrying a book, *America's Impasse,* a Marxist analysis of the American economy written by IPS associate fellow Alan Wolfe. Lekarev picked it up and began thumbing through it.

"I think I know this book," said Lekarev. "When was it first published?" Turning to the copyright page, Lekarev said, "1981 . . . yes, parts of it were first published in the Soviet Union."

"You mean parts of it were published in the Soviet Union before coming out here? Where? Who published it?" I asked.

"The Institute for the Study of USA and Canada . . . the Arbatov Institute, I believe," he answered.

"Oh, really, that's interesting. I think Alan Wolfe is associated with the Institute for Policy Studies," I went on. "You've had some dealings with it. Do you think it's a good place to apply for an internship?"

"The place known as IPS. Well, it depends on what you want to do," Lekarev said somewhat circumspectly.

"The way I see it, having IPS on your credentials might hurt you if you were planning to go into the State Department. But for a career in journalism it might be a good thing," I suggested. "A lot of journalists seem to have close relations with IPS. Robert Kaiser of the *Washington Post* teaches over at IPS. I think he was stationed in Moscow for a few years. And the current *Post* correspondent in Moscow, Dusko Doder, has good rapport with IPS."

"IPS is certainly a reputable research center," said Lekarev. "But I cannot tell you what to do. That is for you to decide. I think it must take many years to establish enough seniority to get sent to Moscow as a correspondent," he added, a little fidgety.

"Maybe I'm too idealistic. I want to work for peace and better relations between your country and mine. Relations have been deteriorating," I said.

"That's the way it is, between your government and mine. It is a fact," Lekarev said bluntly, crushing his butt into the ashtray.

"These arms-control talks IPS is having with your government seem to offer some hope, some avenue of dialogue," I went on. "But why is your government willing to talk to people associated with IPS, but not with our government?"

"Well, the delegates of the Institute for USA and Canada Studies are not the Soviet government," he replied. "I don't know about the details of this exchange, but as you know the Reagan administration has been unresponsive to our overtures. Reagan is going ahead with the Cruise and Pershing missile deployment in Europe and he wants to take the arms race into space with Star Wars."

"I know, but from what I understand, the delegates of the Institute for the Study of USA and Canada express views no different from the official policies of the Soviet government," I said. "And most all of the Soviet delegates are chosen by your government precisely because they are good spokesmen. Take its leader, Georgi Arbatov—he always makes the U.S. look bad while masterfully defending your government's position."

Lekarev made no response, but he was obviously listening intently.

I realized that to reveal a great deal of knowledge about IPS or the Soviet system might alarm him. I decided to see what would emerge at future meetings.

As it turned out, that was to be my last encounter with Third Secretary Lekarev. Evidently, he concluded that I was not a good prospect for recruitment.

CHAPTER 20

IPS and the Soviets
Peace in Search of Makers

Frustrated with official U.S. channels that deal with arms control and disarmament, IPS initiated its own discussions with the Soviet Union when, in April 1982, senior fellow Marc Raskin led a delegation of ten people to Moscow. "The purpose of the meetings," Raskin said, "was to explore with the Soviets the notion of a series of discussions . . . to explore radical measures to reverse the arms race."[1] Valeriy Lekarev, third secretary at the Soviet embassy and in the employ of the KGB, served as liaison in making the necessary arrangements.

To break the deadlock in the talks in Geneva, Raskin said that IPS decided to "put together a new grouping of people who would be able to develop an alternative foreign policy in the United States and would have the political and intellectual strength to make that stick over the course of the next decade."[2] As Raskin told a group of potential funders of the enterprise, "We must take the intellectual and political leap of more comprehensive fundamental alternatives. . . ."[3]

The substantive meetings began a year later, in May 1983, when IPS hosted twenty-four Soviet officials associated with the Soviet Institute for the Study of USA and Canada for a five-day conference in Minneapolis. Rev. Paul Moore, Episcopal bishop of New York, in his purple garb, convened the proceedings. To avoid embarrassing the Soviets with the usual prayerful invocation, Bishop Moore gave an acceptable alternative: "The only true and lasting security for the world lies in a just, international economy: Jesus Christ, the Prophets of the

336

Old Testament, and Karl Marx would agree on this."[4] Next, Moore turned to a central theme of the conference: the need for trust. "I would ask our Russian colleagues to ask forgiveness for their individual and national sins," stated Moore. Then, gazing intently at his American colleagues, he continued, "Trust begins with forgiveness for our exploitation of other lands for economic gain . . . and for withholding our largess from the poor of the world."[5]

Richard Barnet of IPS elaborated on the same theme. He pointed out that the "American foreign policy elite, the relatively small circle of lawyers, industrialists, bankers, and strategists from universities and think tanks who have made the basic national security decisions over the past forty years, do not trust the Soviet Union,"[6] but that "since the very survival of both societies depends upon the establishment of a relationship of minimum trust, priorities must be reversed."[7]

But how could IPS hope to accomplish what U.S. officials had been unable to achieve over the years? And why would the Soviets respond to IPS fellows and not U.S. officials at Geneva?

Marc Raskin's call for a "new grouping of people" suggests an answer. Specifically, this new IPS grouping would include "people in the peace movement, people of the establishment, and people in the abolitionist movement"[8]—almost everyone, that is, from the Left on the political spectrum. IPS insists that its people are better equipped to deal with the Soviets than are U.S. officials. But Barnet's analysis of the fundamentals is flawed. For instance, "The dilemma for both superpowers," he says, "is that each talks to critical domestic audiences. . . ."[9] Now surely Barnet knows that the Soviet leadership does not face a critical domestic audience; does not face one that has the slightest influence on its foreign policy. Barnet's argument raises basic questions about the legitimacy of the whole enterprise.

The Soviets could hardly have picked a group of people more pliable and receptive to their proposals. IPS had succeeded in doing what the KGB could never have done—assembling a group of some of the most influential members of the American peace movement under the bright lights of the media.

And what of the "new grouping of people" from the Soviet side, the twenty-four members from the sponsoring Soviet Institute for the Study of USA and Canada (IUSAC)? To the untutored American peace enthusiast, IUSAC might well appear promising. IUSAC members are often more sophisticated than their counterparts in other Soviet fronts. They have left behind the stiff dowdy Soviet image and taken on a Western veneer; they dress well, command English with wit and colloquial adroitness, and have the ability to field questions spontaneously.

But IUSAC is by no means independent. It was established in the early 1960s in the reorganization effort by the International Department of the Central Committee of the Communist party to work with the KGB and more effectively influence academic circles in the United States. Although IUSAC does engage in scholarly research (of Western journals that are denied to Soviet citizens), it functions like all Soviet fronts. It operates in the service of the Soviet state and is answerable to the International Department of the Communist party, as well as to the KGB and the Ministry of Foreign Affairs. Ostensibly IUSAC has three main departments: one studies U.S. domestic and foreign policies; a second the U.S. economy; the third is more active and conducts meetings with Americans and Canadians. On such occasions, the Central Committee of the Communist party will use IUSAC to gather intelligence and as a mouthpiece.

A few words about the people who have been associated with IUSAC will reveal some interesting insights.

The head of the institute is Georgi Arbatov, a member of the Central Committee of the Communist party, whose skill as a propagandist is quite well known. Arbatov's articles and lectures are seemingly well-balanced mixtures of rational statements, intelligently contrived half truths, and skillfully covered omissions and distortions presented in calm, politically acceptable language. Henry Kissinger described Arbatov in his memoirs, *White House Years*, as "especially subtle in playing to the inexhaustible masochism of American intellectuals who took it as an article of faith that every difficulty in U.S.–Soviet relations had to be caused by American stupidity and intransigence."[10] Brezhnev relied heavily on Arbatov in selling détente to the United States; in 1973 Arbatov was a member of the entourage that came with Brezhnev to the United States; and in 1974 he accompanied Brezhnev to a meeting in Vladivostok with President Ford.[11] And today Mikhail Gorbachev relies heavily on the skills of Arbatov, who writes a good portion of Gorbachev's speeches directed at the United States.[12]

Radomir Bogdanov, Arbatov's most trusted assistant and IUSAC's deputy director, has long been affiliated with the KGB. In 1957 he began a ten-year tour of duty at the Soviet embassy in New Delhi, where he served as a senior KGB operations officer.[13] Under his command Indian Communist party member Romesh Chandra was groomed for active leadership. Later Chandra took charge of the World Peace Council.

From 1972 to 1974 Anatoliy Gromyko, son of the veteran Soviet foreign minister Andrei Gromyko, worked at IUSAC as a senior research fellow. Yuri Andropov's son Igor was a senior researcher at IUSAC the following two years, during which his father headed the KGB in Moscow.[14]

In addition to the strong KGB presence at IUSAC, many of the institute members have intelligence backgrounds in the Chief Intelligence Directorate (GRU) of the Ministry of Defense. So IUSAC is well equipped to collect intelligence for both personality assessment and scientific/military matters. A month before the IPS conference began in Minneapolis, one IUSAC "researcher," Aleksandr N. Mikheyev, was expelled from the United States for trying to obtain military secrets from Marc Zimmerman, an aide to Rep. Olympia Snowe (R–Maine) of the House Foreign Affairs Committee.

The International Department of the Central Committee and the KGB also use IUSAC for "active measures." These are generally geared to long-range goals, such as softening American political culture and changing the attitudes of the elites in the United States.

While the IPS delegation focused on the need to build more trust between the superpowers, the Soviets stressed quite different concerns. Their speeches were filled with grim descriptions of nuclear war. Nikolai Blokhin, associated with the International Physicians for the Prevention of Nuclear War, a Soviet peace front founded in 1981 with the help of Georgi Arbatov, harped on the disastrous biological effects of thermonuclear warfare.

Members of the Soviet delegation took their cues largely from Genrikh Trofimenko, IUSAC department chief, and Gen. Mikhail Milsteyn, a career GRU military intelligence officer presented as IUSAC's resident expert on disarmament issues. Trofimenko and Milsteyn are also both leaders of the Soviet Peace Committee. Early on, the Soviet delegation rallied around Trofimenko, who asserted that "the problem isn't the Soviet Union. The Soviet Union is for arms control . . . the problem is the United States."[15]

Milsteyn followed up, speaking with authority. "There's an opinion in some circles of the administration that the tougher you are with the Soviet Union, the more concessions you'll get from our country. That is a very dangerous conception," he warned. "You'll get concessions only by avoiding the new arms race."[16]

The IPS delegation offered little resistance to the propaganda offensive. The Soviets have long recognized that fear of nuclear war is one of the most effective weapons in their arsenal of political and psychological warfare. In short, obsessive fear of nuclear war has the potential to demoralize Western societies. The Soviets' goal is to encourage Western societies to turn against the very nuclear technologies and modernization that keep deterrence viable. Having pushed the issue of nuclear fear beginning in Europe in 1981, the Soviets could count on IPS to be a sounding board directed at the general American population.

The overriding issue at hand, which the Soviet delegation never lost sight of, was NATO's planned deployment of Pershing II and Tomahawk Cruise missiles. The thrust of the week-long discussions focused on ways to stall or prevent the deployment. There was, however, no significant discussion or protest of the Soviets' deployment of the SS-20s, which had caused the NATO response to begin with.

Randall Forsberg, author of the seminal statement calling for a nuclear freeze, even offered advice to the Soviet delegates on how they might coordinate their efforts to block the NATO deployment. "If the Soviet Union would cease any new deployments of SS-20s in the Far East and freeze SS-20s worldwide . . . and . . . dismantle some of the 250 old SS-4s and SS-5s," said Forsberg, it might be possible for the peace groups of the United States and

Europe and the political opposition to create "sufficient pressure on the conservative Reagan, Thatcher, and Kohl governments and sufficient division within their societies . . . that in fact they would be forced to delay the deployment."[17] Forsberg emphasized her point: "I want to make this statement very forcefully. I think that if all of these factors work together, the peace movements, the political leadership, and the Soviet government, in a very careful, focused, coordinated and clear way, the missiles can be stopped."[18] The Soviets listened carefully but did not commit themselves.

On balance, the first round of the alternative arms-control dialogue demonstrated that there was little common ground of agreement. The Soviet delegates were inflexible on every issue. But how could it have been otherwise? Unlike their American counterparts, the Russian delegates were not free to explore alternative approaches. Predictably, while the Soviets defended their government's military outlays (some 15 percent of the Soviet GNP), the IPS delegation roundly condemned the U.S. high defense expenditures (about 6 percent of our GNP).

What was striking about the whole show was that the Soviets' intransigence seemed not to faze the American delegates in the slightest. Nor did the American delegation's repeated failure to gain any concession from the Russians disabuse it of its notions about the Soviet Union. Nor was the IPS group troubled by the striking asymmetry of the exchange, or by Randall Forsberg's suggestion that the American peace movement coordinate with Soviet policies to block the deployment of NATO missiles.

Indeed, no sooner was the conference over than IPS director Borosage promoted unilateral disarmament (while denying he was doing so) in *Working Papers for a New Society*. Assuring his readers that "an independent or unilateral freeze is not unilateral disarmament," and that "support for an independent or unilateral freeze need not be predicated on trust of the Soviet Union," Borosage stated:

> In fact, bilateralism is naive, ignorant, or cynical about the institutional momentum behind the nuclear build-up. Unilateral initiatives are dismissed as either naive or treasonous; in fact they are a realistic way to counter the inertia of destruction. They may be our only hope. If the movement can impart this truth, it will have served a profound historic mission.[19]

The peculiar views and activities of IPS cannot help but baffle. If IPS were naive about the Soviet Union, one could attribute its unusual behavior to misguided utopianism. But it is not that simple. IPS staffers are the first to admit they know all about the people they are dealing with. Discussing the dialogue, Borosage stated, "Presumably some of them are active-duty KGB people. . . . It doesn't really matter even though you know who they are—they're kind of representing in this quasi-official way."[20] Senior fellow Roger Wilkins conceded, "Whether or not some of the Soviet delegates are KGB doesn't really matter . . . because I'm sure that their minds are at the service of the Soviet government."[21] And John Mercer, Marc Raskin's assistant, admitted that "probably one third of the people we dealt with were KGB, but that is what you simply have to put up with if you want to talk with the Soviets."[22]

The Soviets agreed to host the second conference, and in July 1984 a delegation of nineteen Americans made the pilgrimage to Moscow.

John Mercer was very disappointed with the results. "To be honest, the conference accomplished very little," he said. "The Soviets are very rigid; they don't bend at all. One thing—I certainly learned what the Soviet positions were. They're extremely smart. They come up with a predetermined agenda that they have all agreed upon and follow it. For instance, the Soviets were not interested in dismantling any of their nuclear weapons aimed at Europe, but they wanted to prevent the American deployment of Cruise and Pershing missiles."[23]

The second conference accomplished little, except indirectly to reveal something about the institute. Before the Moscow conference, Borosage was questioned about the worth of the enterprise. He said:

It's clear that one official benefit [the Soviets] see in these exchanges is to at least get the message to American liberals . . . that they [the Soviets] have all these good lines on traditional arms control. . . . The Reagan administration dominates the way Americans think about arms control. So clearly they [the Soviets] have a very large stake in having people [IPS] who are important in reminding others of all the important things to do, so that we can come back and repeat that.[24]

Borosage acknowledges that IPS serves as a mouthpiece for the Soviets. Undeniably, the institute's agenda reflects a certain sympathy and accord with positions of the ruling Soviet elite. "[A]lthough it is ignored in the American press," said Borosage before going to the Moscow conference, "I think the Russians have most of the good lines on traditional arms control."[25] Elaborating on this, he continued:

That is, the Russians are for the SALT II Treaty. The administration has not only refused to ratify it but the State Department indicated that it may be necessary to break both SALT I and SALT II by the end of 1985. The Russians are for the threshold test ban treaty which the United States refused to ratify. A comprehensive test ban treaty which was on the verge of being signed and the United States left the talks. [The Soviets] are for the freeze, which the Reagan Administration thinks is inequitable. They have announced a no-first-use position which the United States says is impossible for it and its allies. They're for a space ban which the United States is clearly against. . . .[26]

Curiously absent from both the May 1983 and July 1984 talks was any substantial discussion of the two most important concerns with regard to arms control: treaty compliance and verification. Political support for SALT II and détente was going nowhere in the early 1980s when IPS took up these exchanges with the Soviets, precisely because the Soviet Union was not complying with either the letter or the spirit of the ABM and the SALT I treaties.

At the dialogue in 1983, Barnet questioned whether the Soviets had actually violated SALT II limitations, though conceding that "they have been more interested in probing the limits of the agreement than in providing the extra margin of reassurance. . . ."[27] In the same breath, he accused the U.S. of taking "a similarly cavalier position with respect to arms control, particularly presidential statements about the ABM and space warfare."[28] Thus, Barnet dismissed Soviet *actions* indicating a breach of SALT II, but deplored American *statements* about the *possibility* that at some future time a space-based defense might make nuclear weapons and the ABM Treaty obsolete.

In January 1984, in answering a congressional mandate, the Reagan administration released a limited version of a report which documented seven cases of Soviet violations and probable violations of arms-control undertakings. For political reasons, the White House was reluctant to release the complete report.

In response, IPS accused the Reagan administration of souring the atmosphere for arms control, as if it were the discovery of Soviet violations that was reprehensible rather than the Soviets' breach of faith itself.

To be rid of the unsavory record for the future, Borosage had a proposal: "[In] line with the repeated position of the Soviet Union, however, perhaps [a] comprehensive step towards disarmament could merit greater flexibility on verification, making the latter a source of support for the process."[29] Raskin chimed in: "The inspection problem should not be seen as an insurmountable one. . . . We must inquire whether such inspections could involve Soviet citizens who would report violations to an international authority."[30]

While Raskin was exploring such novel ideas as monitoring the Soviets with Soviets, his youthful assistant, John Mercer, was doing a little exploring of his own. Frustrated with the stodgy uniformity of the Soviet delegates' thinking, Mercer decided to try to meet a few dissidents in Moscow. As he put it, "There were only two classes of people that we could talk to: Soviet officials and dissidents."[31]

"Dissidents, I would think those would be the last people you could meet. How were you able to do that?" Mercer was asked after his return to the United States.

A resourceful researcher, Mercer had obtained information on various dissidents from human rights monitoring groups like Helsinki Watch. "I had these names and addresses with me, and I would just hop in a cab and give the driver the name and address and we'd go out there," he said.

"Would you call first? Were they surprised to see you?"

"No, I'd just show up," Mercer said. "We thought they'd be surprised, but they weren't always. Their situation is so sad. They are being constantly harassed by the government. One guy whose door we showed up at even told us that he was expecting us.''

"How was that, if you didn't call him first?"

"Well, when his wife got home," recounted Mercer, "she told him that she had been followed home that day by the KGB, and so they knew that something was up. He frankly told us that the KGB is outside right now. And you know he was right, the KGB was outside."

No mention was ever made by IPS of Mercer's experience with dissidents in the Soviet Union. Obviously, calling attention to the Soviet government's callous treatment of its own citizens would expose the intellectual fraudulence of IPS overtures about trusting the Soviets.

Indeed neither events in the world nor personal experiences would deter the IPS community from hosting the Soviets for a third round of alternative talks on "radical proposals for disarmament."

The third IPS-IUSAC conference was held September 5–9, 1985, at the Sir Francis Drake Hotel in San Francisco. For the Soviets the conference was particularly important for it offered an important opportunity to help set the stage for the November summit between President Reagan and Secretary General Gorbachev in Geneva.

Walking into the Gold Ballroom at the Drake, I stopped by the literature table to pick up the packet of materials for the conference. I was struck by the piles of IPS literature stacked next to Soviet propaganda publications. The IPS/PACCA booklet *Changing Course: Blueprint for Peace in Central America and the Caribbean* was next to *Star Wars: Delusions and Dangers* of the Military Publishing House in Moscow; a pile of IPS Washington School course catalogues stood beside a little pamphlet from Novosti, *Keep Space Weapon-Free;* and a few copies of *Nuclear Battlefields* by IPS's William Arkin lay next to the Soviet apparatchik's Gennadi Gerasimov's *Disarmament: Who Is for and Who Is Against?*

Following a few pro forma remarks by IPS director Robert Borosage, IUSAC director Georgi Arbatov took the microphone. He wasted no time in setting the tone for the conference. "We are at a very dangerous point in our relations," said Arbatov, "but we have the opportunity to enter into negotiations and diminish the threat of war."[32]

Answering a question from a reporter about the Soviet reaction to Reagan's Strategic Defense Initiative (SDI), Arbatov said, "If the Americans take away this obstacle, Star Wars, there can be fruitful negotiations; otherwise the arms race and the threat of war will increase."[33]

It was clear from the format of the conference that the Soviets' chief goal was to stall or kill the Strategic Defense Initiative. IPS was, in short, hosting a major propaganda offensive against SDI.

After the opening plenary session, the American and Soviet delegates broke up into two groups to discuss different topics, such as "Star Wars/Earth Peace," "U.S.–Soviet Relations in the Third World," and "Ideology in the Modern World."

The "Ideology in the Modern World" panel was another attempt by IPS to portray the United States and the Soviet Union as morally equivalent, mirror images of each other. Taking the lead, Barnet said, "Anti-communist predisposition prevents the United States from conducting a pragmatic policy and . . . also reveals to our Soviet observers that we are less than rational in acting as a great power. . . ."[34]

Barnet continued, "The second ideological notion that I think is at the heart of the problem is projecting an ideological understanding and analysis of the direction of human history in extremely one-sided and self-serving terms. I see this most clearly on the Soviet side in the Brezhnev Doctrine . . . and it seems to me that the role that the United States played in Grenada was quite similar and justified very much in the same terms."[35]

Several of the Soviets listened to what Barnet had to say, but by and large they seemed preoccupied with their own agenda.

"And my final point was a point made by Georgi Arbatov yesterday," said Barnet looking at Arbatov. "I think the real ideological struggle that is going on is going on inside the two systems and that there is a very intense ideological struggle going on in both systems. And the more that the struggle can go on without hostile interference by the other, the better the relations can be."[36]

Barnet spoke of anticommunism as comparable to the American political system. But more troubling was his equating the Brezhnev doctrine and Afghanistan with U.S. policy and Grenada; it was illogical at best. The Soviet invasion of Afghanistan had already caused over a million deaths and driven four million more to seek refuge outside their country. Weren't U.S. troops out of Grenada, and didn't the Grenadans have an election?

Equally specious was another of Barnet's points. Yes, an open society such as the United States does experience ideological struggles, protests, and demonstrations. But where are these struggles found in the Soviet Union?

Although the small group sessions were not open to the public, the loose schedule afforded the opportunity to meet a number of the Soviet delegates. Several consented to being interviewed and they addressed the wider aspects of East-West relations as well as their perceptions of IPS. Spartak Beglov, a professor of journalism from Moscow State University and a senior commentator for Novosti Press Agency, was the first.

"If the goal of arms control is peace, then should it not be based on mutual respect of the status quo, not in trying to press one's advantage?" I asked.[37]

"Status quo does not apply to the competition between different ideologies and ways of life," responded Beglov. "Status quo is impossible in the context of the social development of mankind. To be for the status quo one must resign as a revolutionary. That is why we favor the separation of struggle over armaments from struggle over ideological matters," continued Beglov. "This is what we achieved in the SALT process—a limitation of arms, but a recognition that ideological struggle would continue."

"Well, the SALT process ended with the invasion of Afghanistan," I commented. "Given the deterioration of U.S.–Soviet relations and stalemate over official arms-control talks, do you think that dealing with the IPS citizens group offers a better channel for cooperation?"

"Yes, of course," Beglov responded. "In spite of differences between our governments there should be this mutual participation in areas of common interest, which may help influence the course of diplomacy."

"Do you see this dialogue with IPS as a more hopeful alternative than official state-to-state relations?"

"Yes, when an alternative to the present situation is formulated by the representatives of the two countries, then the two countries have a possibility to present alternatives to our politicians and governments to facilitate the course of affairs at the negotiating table," said Beglov.

"Like for the upcoming summit?"

"Yes, of course," Beglov replied.

"But there is a fundamental difference between the two delegations. The Soviet delegation faithfully represents its government's position, while IPS opposes the basic defense posture of the U.S."

"No, other than Georgi Arbatov and [Sergei Chetverikov] of the Foreign Ministry, the rest are representatives of the public," Beglov pointed out. "We are members of the Communist party, which is an avant-garde public force in formulating politics, and so in that sense we are representing the majority of the Soviet political spectrum."

"On the other hand, the Institute for Policy Studies does not represent the majority of American public opinion," I pointed out.

"Well in that case, how could you explain the opinion poll showing here that at least 85 percent of your people are in favor of accommodations with the Soviet Union, although the majority of your people do not approve, to put it mildly, of the Soviet system?" Beglov asked.

"Everyone is for peace, but the question is what kind of accommodation," I responded.

"But at least their instinct of preservation prompts them to favor accommodation on arms control and on prevention of nuclear war," Beglov said. "In this case, when you have people like IPS with their status, their papers, their projects and plans on a sane thinking, that means that they, irrespective of officials' views in the United States, reflect the majority of the American people."

"So you think that there is more accord between the Soviet delegation here and the IPS delegation than there is accord in state-to-state relations?" I asked.

"Yes, of course," said Beglov.

Edouard Batalov, chief of section, Department of American Ideology, IUSAC, was interviewed next.

"Professor Batalov, according to Marxist-Leninist ideology, capitalism fosters class conflict, while socialism promises to bring about a cessation of class conflict and class struggle. Why are so many socialist countries at war with each other?"

"We believe that socialism will put an end to all the wars," Batalov responded. "We have not arrived at that stage where all conflicts cease. But let me say, we don't want to impose our socialism on other nations, on other people."[38]

"What about the Prague spring of 1968, when the Czechoslovakian people wanted to assert independence from the Soviet Union and establish 'socialism with a human face'?" I asked. "The Czechs wanted to remain socialist, but become independent from the Soviet Union."

"Well," Batalov hesitated, "I suppose you can draw interpretations of those events."

"It is a matter of historical record that the Soviet Union would not tolerate the realization of a different kind of socialism—a so-called socialism with a human face."

"No, I cannot agree with that interpretation," Batalov flatly responded.

"Well, did Soviet troops intervene or didn't they?"

"No," Batalov flatly replied. "There was not intervention of Soviet troops, there was assistance, assistance as a result of responding to the needs of that government in their struggle against counterrevolution."

"It wasn't counterrevolution," I said. "It was the Czechoslovakian Communist party members and socialists who wanted to establish a different kind of socialism. It simply can't be understood as counterrevolution. They were progressive people who wanted to maintain socialism."

"Well, you see I suppose we have two different visions and two different pictures of one and the same event and maybe it is an illustration of what we spoke of before. You have one position and I have another position, but we can peacefully coexist." said Batalov.

"How do you feel about the scholarship of the Institute for Policy Studies?" I asked.

"Well we know them for a very long period of time as an institution with a good scholarly level," he replied. "We know some persons of IPS as very good specialists in the different fields of humanitarian and social sciences."

"The critics of IPS think that its views are in considerable accord with Soviet views," I pointed out. "Certainly IPS is not inclined to look very critically at the Soviet Union, even though there is no end to its criticism of the United States."

"Well, of course you will find some IPS positions which coincide with the perspectives of Soviet leaders," replied Batalov. "But this is not new. Some speeches of your leaders during the period of détente coincided with some Soviet positions. We are content to work with our American colleagues here."

I picked up a Soviet publication, *The Liberating Mission of the Soviet Union in the Second World War.* "IPS fellows have pointed out the progressive role that the Soviet Union plays in supporting national liberation movements. How is it that the Soviet Union is assisting countries in the third world by giving military aid, armaments, and advisers, or sending in troops as in the case of Afghanistan, and when the United States does the same thing it is considered intervention? The Soviet Union assists and the United States intervenes?"

"It seems to me that it is not one and the same thing," Batalov responded. "I should like first of all to remind you that revolution in Afghanistan was not made by the Soviet Union. The Afghanistan government asked several times for support, and as far as I know the course of events, it was not easy for us to answer those requests for assistance by the Afghanistan government. It was not easy for us to answer in the affirmative. And it was not an intervention for many reasons."

"But certainly most Afghans oppose the Soviet action. Who is to define intervention? You have your definition and I have mine. But can't the people of Afghanistan best determine this? Do the four million refugees from Afghanistan see the Soviet role as assistance?" I asked.

"The people of Afghanistan, as the people in many other countries, are not homogeneous," Batalov explained. "There are different groups, different classes, different strata in Afghanistan. And it is quite natural that after social revolution there are going to be some elements that rebel—it is quite natural. In Russia after the October revolution, many people were not content with the revolution, and as you know, there was a civil war in our country."

"But those people who are not content with the revolution, are not allowed to dissent. They are suppressed by force," I said.

"You see those people who are not content take machine guns and they use these weapons against the government of Afghanistan, against the Afghanistan army, against the legitimate government and the legitimate army," Batalov argued.

"But how is legitimacy determined?"

"It is a big problem, you see . . ." Batalov said, hesitating.

"How is legitimacy determined in the Soviet Union?" I asked.

"It is a big . . . uh . . . I'm not a lawyer, and I cannot give you a correct definition of legitimacy. So you must put your question before a lawyer," said Batalov. "But I want to answer your question in this way. The Afghanistan government came to power as a result, as an outcome of revolution made in Afghanistan by Afghanistan people. So in that case, I suppose the government that took to power in Afghanistan is a legitimate government."

"So what you are saying is that legitimacy is determined by force—whoever can seize power," I rejoined. "We don't need to go to a lawyer. . . . In our society, we look at political legitimacy not as seizure of power by force, but as something determined through democratic elections which involve free assembly and free speech."

"I'm not quite sure about that," protested Batalov. "What percent of the American people elected President Reagan? Less than 50 percent. There is a problem of political apathy, and we don't know really how many people in the United States support President Reagan."

"Insofar as there is considerable tension in the state-to-state relations between the Soviet Union and the United States, what do you think are the possibilities for this kind of alternative dialogue being sponsored by the Institute for Policy Studies?" I then asked.

"The members of the Institute for Policy Studies are part of what you would call the 'loyal opposition.' " Batalov replied. "They are quite legitimate and quite natural."

"Why are you raising this point?"

"They are doing their business in the normal framework of American politics, just as there are members of Congress, of the House, that understand the necessity of changing the relations between our two countries," Batalov said. "For example, to support the SDI program is an unreasonable position. . . . I mention SDI not occasionally because if the United States continues it will be disastrous and cause a new arms race, and there is a great possibility that we will approach the point of no return. SDI is a very good example of an unreasonable position."

"One of the main topics being discussed here is the SDI. How much common ground have you found with the IPS delegation on the issue of SDI?"

"It seems to me that members of IPS understand the great danger of SDI," Batalov said. "They were discussing it just as I left for this interview. But there is common ground, I can tell you that. There is common ground because members of the institute understand the great danger of this program and they understand that this can unleash a new stage in the arms race."

"Do you feel that one of the main purposes of this meeting is to raise the consciousness of the potential danger of SDI, particularly before the summit talk between President Reagan and Secretary General Gorbachev?" I asked.

"It is not only the purpose of this dialogue, but in my opinion every reasonable institution, particularly mass media in the United States, must come to understand the necessity of enlightening people about the danger of SDI," he said. "This is neither the first nor the last meeting between the Institute for Policy Studies and the Soviet representatives," said Batalov. "The truth about political problems doesn't lie on the surface. It must be excavated, and this kind of discussion is a form of excavating the truth."

"Why do these discussions with IPS provide a better opportunity to dig up the truth, as you say, than the arms-control forums like the Geneva talks?"

"I suppose one must not exclude the other," said Batalov. "We must meet at many levels, and one level will be an addition to the other level. Every level has its peculiarity and its function. One level cannot exclude the other level, and it is good that we shall soon have the summit meeting in Geneva. We don't know what kind of position Reagan will take with him to the summit. When we meet with members of the Institute for Policy Studies, it is of course different; they are not government officials or organizations, but our work is useful . . . not only in preparation for the summit directly, but in preparation of the atmosphere for the solutions of problems existing in the relations between the two countries."

"Do you think progressive Americans, like those from IPS, are better able to understand the solution to problems of the East-West conflict, the arms race, and the threat of nuclear war?" I asked.

"It seems to me," said Batalov, "that the people that cooperate with IPS in this, they understand their own people—the American people—better, and they express the wishes and aspirations of the American people."

"Well if that were the case, why are there not more people elected to public office who reflect these ideas? If the views expressed by the IPS delegation are so popular, why don't we have more representatives elected who express these views?

"Sometimes truth is not very popular," Batalov said.

"It does seem that there is an asymmetry here," I tried to demonstrate. "On the one hand, you and your colleagues represent official bodies of the Soviet government, and your views are in accord with the Soviet government. You support Gorbachev and his foreign policy goals. On the other hand, the American delegation from IPS is adamantly opposed to the foreign policy of its elected government."

"It is better to say that they do not support some elements, some steps of foreign policy," Batalov said.

"But in contrast to Soviet representatives who unquestionably support their government's defense policy and the deployment of new weapons systems, members of the IPS delegation do not support efforts to strengthen American defense. They even think that concepts like minimum deterrence are absurd."

"I told you they are reasonable," insisted Batalov, "and as I said, they are expressing the real, the genuine interests of American people. I am absolutely convinced that the SDI program is not in the interests of the American people, as well as the Soviet people. Thus, as the IPS delegation criticizes the SDI program they are expressing the real interest of the American nation," he said.

"Why aren't the common people allowed to organize in the Soviet Union?" I asked next. "The IPS delegates, with whom you are meeting, are in the forefront of peace activism and organizing here in the United States. Now there is no such independent peace movement in the Soviet Union. If you trust the people, as you say, why don't you allow them to organize?"

"Well, you see, our constitution guarantees the existence of non-governmental organizations," he responded. "It is not prohibited. I suppose the great majority of our people perceive the activities of the Soviet Peace Committee as adequate to their aspirations and expressing adequately their own desires for peace and security."

"But what about those Soviet citizens who have tried to organize independent peace groups?" I countered. "They have been arrested in the Soviet Union. This is quite well known."

"Yes, some people tried. But do you know what these people were?" Batalov asked. "To our great sorrow those people who called themselves watchers of Helsinki Accords, were actually those people who previously wanted to leave the Soviet Union."

"Well, what's wrong with that? Why can't they leave the Soviet Union?"

"People cannot leave who have national security secrets and information," Batalov responded. "Like any nation, we have to defend our national interests. Many of those Soviet people trying to organize were not actually peace fighters."

"But you don't allow for free emigration of those people who pose no national security threat; common people, a lot of Jewish people, are unable to leave the Soviet Union though they earnestly want to," I pointed out.

"I didn't specifically study this problem, and thus I can only express my own perceptions," he replied.

"American people in general are very suspicious of power," I noted. "We have a saying that power corrupts and absolute power corrupts absolutely. It seems to me that the Soviet elite constantly make an effort to rationalize everything within the Marxist-Leninist framework of analysis. But common sense would indicate that not everything fits according to any one model. I should think that Soviet spokesmen and policymakers would become quite cynical. Don't you ever feel frustrated having to repeat things you don't really believe?"

"It is a pity that you don't read Russian," said Batalov. "If you knew Russian I would send you some magazines and newspapers and you would be surprised to find articles that sharply criticize some actions of different authorities. There is no total rationalization as you point out."

Georgi Arbatov's assistant, Sergei Rogov, consented to a brief interview last. "Much is said about promoting democracy in the third world, particularly under the Reagan administration," I began. "Does the Soviet Union feel threatened by the movement toward democracy in the third world?"

"First of all . . . well, what is democracy for you and what is democracy for us . . . these are two different things," replied Rogov. "I don't think it is possible to discuss such an ideological issue in three or four minutes, because we have to analyze the factors which define democracy. Democracy involves first of all the role of the people, whether the voice of the people is heard, whether it is government for the people and all the people."[39]

"How do we know the needs of people if not by voting and if not by allowing private groups to express their views in the press and to organize and lobby?" I asked.

"Sure," replied Rogov. "But when you go through a revolution you have this enormous amount of change. . . . We have not reached the Marxist ideal, we have not reached the stage when our society corresponds to the communist ideal. We are a socialist country."

"Has the Soviet leadership renounced the Leninist theory and practice of the vanguard, whereby the Soviet Union supports and trains revolutionaries and national liberation movements?" I asked.

"Why should we repudiate this theory?" he asked indignantly. "I believe we should give an example and help others so that they can solve their social, economic, and political problems."

Before the conference was over Georgi Arbatov and Marcus Raskin addressed a public gathering at the Commonwealth Club. Their main subject was the question of trust between the superpowers.

"The first thing to understand is that we trust the Soviets whether they understand us or not," stated Raskin.[40]

"There will always be some amount of doubt, and this is just a fact of life," said Arbatov. "I can tell you a Russian story. . . . There was once a very suspicious husband and once he went away. This man wanted to check on his wife, and so he came home earlier than he said he would. He looked in the window and saw his wife with another man drinking and dancing. Then they went into the bedroom and undressed and then they put out the light and so in the end this man still had this tragic uncertainty."[41]

Still enjoying Arbatov's joke, the audience failed to notice that Raskin was dead serious when he stepped up to the microphone. "We have to understand that the nature of verification is enormously complex," said Raskin. "We may be in a very similar situation that the man was in Professor Arbatov's story . . . ultimately you're going to have to have a measure of trust, and in my view it's time that the people trust each other rather than trust the weapons [to which they have become hostage]."[42]

The San Francisco conference ended with much the same emphasis as the Minneapolis conference had two years earlier. There Barnet had argued, in his paper "A Question of Trust," that "to maintain the political climate to keep the arms race going requires painting the adversary as so threatening and so evil that political support for even such limited agreements cannot be maintained."[43]

But certainly the opposite is also true. To maintain the political climate to foster disarmament requires painting the Soviet Union as so benign that political support for a strong defense and deterrent cannot be maintained. And this has been one of the long-standing missions of IPS.

Earlier, at a 1979 IPS conference on U.S.–Soviet relations, Cora Weiss decried not anticommunism but "anti-Soviet communism" as "a hereditary disease transmitted over the past sixty years."[44] Associate fellow Alan Wolfe called for "a massive peace campaign . . . to try to take off the husk of the Soviet threat."[45] And at an IPS conference at the Transnational Institute in June 1981, fellow Fred Halliday said, "Much of the work of the Transnational Institute, and especially of the [IPS] Militarism and Disarmament Project, has been concerned with opposing and demystifying [the] claim . . . that there has been a fundamental shift in the balance between the East and the West over the past decade. . . ."[46]

To justify the IPS position, Barnet argues, "Leaders who urge the willing suspension of distrust . . . or call for unilateral acts of a conciliatory nature, risk having their loyalty called into question."[47] But the question won't go away: At what point should the loyalty of a group of American citizens be called into question if not when it consistently advocates the programs of its country's chief adversary?

CHAPTER 21

Soviet Objectives and IPS Objectives

As history has thrust upon the United States the responsibility of leadership in an increasingly dangerous world, the problems posed by the Institute for Policy Studies take on particular significance.

While carrying on its advocacy of public policy with the benefit of 501(c)(3) tax exemption from the IRS, IPS has in fact been anything but nonpartisan. It has consistently opposed the foreign policy of every administration, Republican or Democratic, and has often assisted the adversaries of the United States. IPS portrays the United States and the Soviet Union as being morally equivalent, but in practice its most virulent attacks are reserved for the U.S. position. And although they are not entirely uncritical of the Soviet Union, IPS fellows provide elaborate apologies for Soviet behavior.

To what end all these activities? According to the director, Robert Borosage, IPS is engaged in the "struggle over the underlying principles and future direction of the political culture itself." If so, the question must be asked, Whose side is IPS on?

Perhaps in earlier times, IPS would have been considered a subversive organization. Disloyalty has been a problem in the past, and has involved Americans on the right and the left—Alger Hiss, Ezra Pound, Eva Toguri (Tokyo Rose), Elizabeth Bentley, the Rosenbergs, to name but a few. Today, however, short of selling military secrets and technology to foreign agents, the concept of treason seems to have little relevance. Why? John Harington once said,

"Treason doth never prosper . . . for if it prosper, none dare call it treason." Operating in the open may well provide the best cover for pursuing subversive activities in a free society. IPS thrives. And few suspect it of seditious or disloyal behavior.

Time, circumstance, norms, and public opinion all play a role in defining disloyalty. The traitor is not always wrong, and the loyal individual not always right. George Washington was disloyal to his king, but his success in leading our revolutionary army made him a Founding Father of a new nation, one which gave birth to liberties heretofore unknown in the history of mankind. The real question then is: Loyalty to whom or what, and under what circumstances? Which values best merit allegiance? Having said this, it must be pointed out that loyalty is essential to the continuance of any nation, and disloyalty is a threat to national survival.

The framers of the Constitution of 1787 were familiar with the abuses of power. They knew that they faced charges of treason for even speaking out against British taxes. For this reason, once independence had been won, they were very careful about defining treason in the Constitution. In addition, the Bill of Rights was appended in 1790 to guarantee the inviolability of certain basic freedoms. The First Amendment guaranteed freedom of religion, speech, press, assembly, and provided for petitioning government; the Fourth, freedom from illegal search and seizure; and the Fifth, due process and protection from self-incrimination. Thus the citizen or group expressing diverse or unpopular views was protected by the government.

Similarly, the framers protected not only the disaffected but even the disloyal from charges of treason in Article III, Section 3, of the Constitution: "Treason against the United States shall consist only in levying war against them, or in adhering to their enemies, giving them aid and comfort."

But what did the framers mean by "levying war," "adhering to their enemies," and "giving them aid and comfort"?

George Washington himself knew that "foreign influence" and "foreign attachments" were "particularly alarming to the truly enlightened and independent patriot" as enunciated in his "Farewell Address of 1796," wherein he warned:

> How many opportunities do they afford to tamper with domestic factions, to practice the arts of seduction, to mislead public opinion, to influence or awe the public councils! . . . [T]he common and continual mischiefs of the spirit of party . . . open the door to foreign influence and corruption, which find a facilitated access to the government itself through the channels of party passion. Thus the policy and will of one country are subjected to the policy and will of another. . . . Against the insidious wiles of foreign influence (I conjure you to believe me, fellow citizens) the jealousy of a free people ought to be constantly awake, since history and experience prove that foreign influence is one of the most baneful foes of republican government.

Three years later (1799) Congress passed the Logan Act to prohibit relations between private citizens and foreign governments so as to protect the conduct of U.S. foreign policy from undue interference. In 1948 Congress reaffirmed the act, stating that it is illegal for

Any citizen of the United States, wherever he may be, who, without authority of the United States, directly or indirectly commences or carries on any correspondence or intercourse with any foreign government or any officer or agent thereof, with intent to influence the measures or conduct of any foreign government or of any disputes or controversies with the United States, or to defeat the measures of the United States . . .[2]

Can IPS activities and those of its fellows be considered treasonous as defined by Article III, Section 3, of the Constitution? Does IPS provide an avenue for foreign influence which interferes with the legislative process or with the public debate on policymaking? Do IPS fellows violate the Logan Act?

The evidence presented in this book indicates that IPS and its affiliates do indeed carry on intercourse with foreign parties and governments against the interests of the United States. IPS has worked and continues to work with foreign powers hostile to the United States, and with the explicit purpose of influencing debate in Congress. It has attempted to influence foreign governments to the detriment of the United States and to "defeat the measures of the United States."

It appears IPS violates IRS guidelines that limit tax-exempt organizations to nonpartisan research and educational programs and activities. But determining whether IPS activities are treasonous is much more problematic. Certainly the institute, its spinoffs, and fellows have given aid and comfort to enemies of the United States, during both a shooting war, as in the case of Vietnam, and an ideological war, as in the post-Vietnam period. But because wars are no longer declared, activities that support enemies of the United States cannot be unequivocally classified treasonous.

In 1787, when one nation wished to declare war on another, it sent its ambassador bearing a formal declaration of war to the foreign ministry of the other nation. American presidents asked Congress for and received declarations of war against Britain, Mexico, Spain, the Central Powers, and the Axis Powers. In the twentieth century the definition of war has transcended the antiquated notion of pitched battles of two or more clearly identified opponents. Moreover, since World War II, formal declarations of war have not been deemed necessary for countries to engage in war. Thus, during the Vietnam War there was no prosecution of Americans who collaborated with the communist government in Hanoi, whose army was even then killing American soldiers.

The problem of disloyalty has been exacerbated by the ascendance of transnational ideologies—fascism, communism, international socialism—and the development of mass communication. Developments before and during World War

II established a precedent that rendered concepts of national loyalty and treason less compelling and meaningful. As one nation after another surrendered to Nazi Germany, people sought an explanation; at first the submission of Austria and Czechoslovakia was thought to trace to the sickness or decay of those societies. But as more and more of the European continent was afflicted with this strange illness and decadence, there was a search for other explanations. After the war more than five hundred thousand Frenchmen were arrested under de Gaulle's administration on the alleged grounds of treason against France in collaborating with Nazi Germany. In Holland there were one hundred thirty thousand and in Belgium sixty thousand investigations of collaboration. In Europe, loyalty problems were a widespread and everyday occurrence, touching all strata of society.[3]

Herman Rauschning argued that the key to understanding Hitler's success lay in his ability to exploit factors that would induce the enemy to capitulate. This approach, based on what is called "informal penetration and attack," makes the psychology of the enemy the primary target rather than his objective situation. Instead of being concerned only with how to defeat the enemy, Hitler sought to induce a defeatist state of mind in the targeted society. As Hitler put it, "How to achieve the moral breakdown of the enemy before the war has started—that is the problem that interests me."[4]

Declared Hitler: "In the future, revolutionary propaganda [will] break down the enemy psychologically before the armies begin to function at all. The enemy people must be demoralized and ready to capitulate, driven to moral passivity, before military action can be thought of."[5] Elaborating on the importance of psychological warfare, Hitler said:

> When I wage war . . . in the midst of peace, troops will suddenly appear. . . .
> They will march through the streets in broad daylight. They will march to the
> headquarters of the General Staff. They will occupy the ministries, the Chamber
> of Deputies. Within a few minutes, France, Poland, Austria, Czechoslovakia, will
> be robbed of their leading men. . . . The confusion will be beyond belief. But I
> shall long have had relations with the men who will form a new government—a
> government to suit me.
>
> We shall find such men, we shall find them in every country. We shall not need
> to bribe them. They will come out of their own accord. . . . No Maginot Line will
> stop us. Our strategy . . . is to destroy the enemy from within, conquer him through
> himself.[6]

One of the hallmarks of the twentieth century is the emergence of totalitarianism and its fallout—the mass production of treason and disloyalty. National loyalty has declined in part because of fundamental factors like mass communication and increased interdependence. But the transnational reach of ideology combined with more sophisticated and extensive means of informal penetration has been equally influential. Whereas Nazi Germany successfully played on the psychology of the enemy, the Soviet Union, championing the cause of international socialism, has been immensely more successful in using political and ideological warfare to change the attitudes and loyalties of target populations.

From the beginning, Bolshevik leaders defined international politics as a continuing state of conflict or struggle. Soviet leaders reject the Western notion that world politics fluctuates between periods of war and peace. For them, war and politics are not distinct conditions but a continuum. Red Army Chief of Staff Boris Shaposhnikov argues that "if war is the continuation of politics by other means, then it is also true that peace, that is, politics, is the continuation of war by other means."[7] Boris Ponomarev, head of the International Department of the CPSU, said in 1975 that "an international peace is one which best allows the realization of the goals of Communism."[8] In 1976 Leonid Brezhnev told the Twenty-fifth Congress of the CPSU: "Peaceful coexistence . . . does not in the slightest abolish, and it cannot abolish or alter, the laws of class struggle."[9]

The central struggle of our time is between liberal democracies, led by the United States, and the international socialist order, led by the Soviet Union. From time to time a war of bullets breaks out on the peripheries of superpower confrontation, but the ongoing war is a *war of ideas*. And as the American experience in Vietnam revealed, wars are now waged with more force in the halls of Congress, on the streets, and in the media than on the battlefield.

The Soviet Union began in 1919 to extend its influence through informal penetration, primarily through the Comintern, Cominform, and party organizations and fronts. In the 1950s, Soviet leaders began to explore alternative means of informal penetration. Early Soviet propaganda efforts to advance the cause of world communism were clumsy and often failed. Soviet Foreign Minister Molotov recognized that the propaganda distributed via the local party newspapers and publishing houses had limited influence. Noting that only a few people who are already Communists read communist propaganda newspapers, Molotov said, "We don't need to propagandize them. We have to influence non-Communists if we want to make them Communists or if we want to fool them. . . . "So we have to try to infiltrate the big press, to influence millions of people, and not merely hundreds of thousands."[10]

But influencing the noncommunist world became more difficult as the promise of the Soviet model faded in the latter years of Stalin's rule. Khrushchev's revelations at the Twentieth Party Congress of 1956 thoroughly discredited Soviet communism and brought on a crisis within the Soviet system. As a result, the Communist party leadership mandated a reorganization to revitalize informal penetration and initiated what came to be known as "active measures," that is, overt and covert techniques for influencing policies and events in foreign countries.

In 1957 the Politburo established three major organs responsible for propaganda and for the planning and oversight of various active measures. They were the International Department (ID), the International Information Department (IID), and Department D of the KGB (later changed to Service A). Although the Soviets still relied on the KGB's operations with agents, underground cells, and the various active-measures programs, the International Department assumed responsibility for projecting Soviet influence in foreign countries through other means to achieve long-term goals.[11]

The International Department tries to influence third-world countries through the Communist party apparatus and revolutionary movements. But its strategy toward the first world, notably the United States, is broader. The Soviets continue to subsidize the Communist party in the United States, its publications, and support its active-measures campaigns, particularly demonstrations and mass protests. And the KGB continues to pursue its three highest priorities: (1) penetrating the government—to affect policymaking and gain access to national security secrets; (2) penetrating the media—to affect news reporting and public opinion; and (3) penetrating the scientific community and select industries—to obtain state-of-the-art technology.

But the International Department has increasingly put a high premium on religious institutions, think tanks, and foundations in the United States because of their increasing influence on public opinion and policymaking. According to Ladislav Bittman, a defector from the Czech STB intelligence service, the Soviet leadership "relies on the traditional compromised structure of front organizations primarily in developing countries, but in the United States, Canada, and Western Europe, it prefers to penetrate and manipulate legitimate foundations and well-established leftist organizations because this tactic is less risky, both politically and financially."[12]

The Soviets certainly appear interested in IPS, its spinoffs, and the network of groups supported by the Rubin Foundation. Their influence on the liberal political culture, the religious institutions, and the media is impressive. It is a misconception to assume that communist front groups and academic, advocacy, and alternative media organizations need to be financed from Moscow to serve Soviet interests.

IPS is strategically located in Washington with good access to policymakers and it has excellent relations with the country's two most influential newspapers, the *Washington Post* and the *New York Times*. In addition, IPS has close relations with: the American Federation of Government Employees (AFGE) and the American Federation of State, County and Municipal Employees (AFSCME), the two largest labor unions of government employees; the National Education Association (NEA), the largest teachers union; the United Auto Workers (UAW) and the International Association of Machinists and Aerospace Workers (IA-MAW), two major unions involved in high-technology industries.

The political ideology and anti-American bias of IPS and its network make them easy targets to penetrate. As noted throughout these pages, Soviet and East bloc personnel move freely in and out of IPS and its sister organization, the Riverside Church. Given the frequent and cordial relationships that exist between the Soviets and the Institute for Policy Studies, it is obvious that IPS provides an ideal environment for Soviet agents to identify and enlist people, either directly or indirectly: IPS is a haven for a wide range of people predisposed to recruitment, from the idealistic to the alienated, from the international socialists to the committed revolutionaries. Whether the Soviets have direct influence on or control over any IPS personnel is less relevant than that it is a matter of record that IPS activities frequently fall in line with Soviet active-measures campaigns conducted against the United States.

In the war of ideas, the Institute for Policy Studies and its network of spinoffs and affiliates have been of enormous assistance to adversaries of the United States. In addition to generating programs that support Soviet active-measures campaigns, the IPS network produces enormous volumes of literature presenting ideas on a full range of issues which often reflect the Soviet line, but which are written in contemporary terms and style that appeal to popular American sentiments. To suggest that IPS is, as one British conservative put it, "the perfect intellectual front for Soviet activities which would be resisted if they were to originate openly from the KGB,"[13] is a suggestion that evokes the cry of "McCarthyism." Is such a characterization appropriate here?

Sen. Joseph McCarthy was charged with lacking elementary ethics and incriminating individuals on the basis of their associations on often trumped-up charges that appealed more to emotion than to reason. McCarthy's charges succeeded in precipitating an hysteria that tended to see all liberal and socialist opinion as "un-American and communist." What McCarthy left in his wake were an overreaction and a residual reluctance to investigate or even discuss the problem of subversion and disloyalty.

Although the expansionist goals of Soviet foreign policy have changed very little, notwithstanding détente, glasnost, and periods of thaw, the character of liberal mainstream culture in the United States has changed considerably. There has been an erosion of the political center, vital for sustaining a bipartisan consensus on foreign policy. Anti-anticommunism is often more prevalent and respectable today than is anticommunism.

As a relatively unknown force, IPS has been working tirelessly to change the American political culture and bend public policy. While IPS finds no enemies on the Left, it considers anticommunism a dangerous ideology. IPS director Robert Borosage candidly admits that IPS hopes to "move the Democratic party's debate internally to the left by creating an invisible presence in the party."[14] There is a consistency between the way IPS operates and the revolutionary activity advocated by the Italian communist Antonio Gramsci. For both it is important to infiltrate autonomous institutions—schools, media, churches, public-interest groups—so as radically to transform the culture, which determines the environment in which political and economic policies are played out.

The purpose of this book has been not to castigate the personal lives of people associated with IPS, but to document the ideas and activities of the institute and its associates in the context of their bearing on the political culture, public opinion, and policymaking in the United States. And an ordered accounting of these reveals that much of what the institute does, for all intents and purposes, also serves the interests of the Soviet Union.

Soviet leaders do not feel constrained by conventional morality and often rely on deceit as a standard operating procedure. Soviet goals have remained fairly constant though particular themes may change to reflect the issues and events of the day. A wide variety of literature on Soviet propaganda and active measures from academic, congressional, State Department, and intelligence analysts suggests that Soviet leaders have consistently maintained the following seven specific aims:

1. To influence world and American public opinion against U.S. military and political programs by suggesting that they are the major cause of international conflict and crisis.
2. To demonstrate that the U.S. is an aggressive, "colonialist" and "imperialist" power, and demonstrate that its policies and goals are incompatible with the ambitions of the underdeveloped world.
3. To isolate the United States from its allies and friends and discredit those who cooperate with the U.S.
4. To discredit U.S. policies and representatives in the eyes of its citizens and the world by creating or exacerbating splits within the nation.
5. To discredit and weaken American intelligence services and expose their personnel.
6. To confuse world public opinion regarding the aggressive nature of Soviet policies.
7. To create a favorable environment for the execution of Soviet foreign policy.[15]

From its inception IPS, in its words and in its activities, has assisted the Soviet Union in attaining these seven objectives.

First: The Soviets wish "to influence world and American public opinion against U.S. military and political programs by suggesting that they are the major cause of international conflict." IPS and the affiliated groups in its disarmament network have never come out in favor of *any* American weapons system. IPS works for radically reduced military spending on Capitol Hill. IPS led in opposing the deployment of Pershing II and Tomahawk Cruise missiles in Europe (intended to counter Soviet SS-20s). IPS put together the PACCA report and a lobbying effort to counter the report of the Kissinger Bipartisan Commission on Central

America, which urged a two-track approach of economic and military aid to counter the Soviet and Cuban presence in the region. And whether it is intervention in the third world or the arms race, IPS focuses blame on the United States while playing down or ignoring Soviet policies and actions. IPS is presently involved in the campaign against the Strategic Defense Initiative, suggesting, as the Soviets do, that it is provocative. In addition, IPS attacks even benign educational efforts of the U.S. government, like Project Democracy, intended to clarify American political goals and values to people in third-world countries.

Second: The Soviets wish "to demonstrate that the U.S. is an aggressive, 'colonialist' and 'imperialist' power," and to "demonstrate that its policies and goals are incompatible with the ambitions of the underdeveloped world." IPS literature is rife with such insinuations. Rather blatant pronouncements come from many of the fellows associated with IPS's international arm, the Transnational Institute (TNI). The winter 1984 TNI quarterly, *Race and Class,* called the United States "the imperialist enemy." IPS chairman Peter Weiss states that a "categorical imperative is that we dispense, once and for all, with the utterly foolish notion that capitalism can bring about economic and social justice to the Third World."[16] Marcus Raskin refers to the United States as a "colonized society," and says, "The American imperium . . . is now viewed as the world's primary enemy by the poor and the young."[17] In addition, as noted, IPS has sponsored endless programs and activities through the Transnational Institute and its Transnational Information Exchange designed to turn third-world countries against the very corporations that might help them develop most rapidly.

In theory, IPS fellows champion some socialist alternative for the third world and oppose aid for private-sector development. In practice, they often support guerrilla insurgencies that are backed by the Soviet Union and dominated by Marxists. "Thus I would urge other people," says IPS fellow Susan George, "to give support to national liberation and minority political groups whose goal is to change the whole society. . . ."[18] She looks to Vietnam and Cuba as models for development, noting that "best of all, they do it without us."[19] IPS director Robert Borosage commends the Soviet Union for having spawned "interesting social experiments" such as "Yugoslavia, Hungary, Poland, Cuba, Nicaragua."[20] The IPS spinoff Institute for Food and Development Policy praises the policies of communist countries and supplies consulting services and assistance to Cuba, Nicaragua, Vietnam, and Mozambique—all allies of the Soviet Union.

Third: The Soviets wish "to isolate the United States from its allies and friends." As these pages testify, the writings of IPS fellows, notably founders Richard Barnet and Marcus Raskin, have time and again contributed to this longstanding Soviet objective. IPS has popularized the moral relativism of the two superpowers and the view that U.S. alliances are unnecessary burdens—"obsolete and dangerous," in the words of Barnet and Raskin.[21] "A peaceful democracy for American society," says Raskin, "is only possible by ending the American empire and discarding the concept of national security which buttresses that empire.''[22]

Over the years, IPS activities overseas have focused on undermining NATO by working directly with opposition parties and communists. In 1985 IPS fellow William Arkin leaked classified nuclear defense contingency plans that severely strained the NATO alliance, helped unravel the ANZUS alliance, and complicated relations with Japan. In the Middle East IPS worked for the fall of the shah of Iran, which precipitated the loss of Iran as a major ally against Soviet expansionism. In the Pacific IPS favors the neutralization of the Philippines and the closing of Subic Bay Naval Station and Clark Air Force Base. IPS chairman Peter Weiss wants to influence the fate of the Philippines by counseling the Aquino government, which has secured the legal services of the Center for Constitutional Rights, of which Weiss is vice president.

With regard to the rest—''discredit those who cooperate with the U.S.''—IPS and the Latin network have repeatedly reproached any governments in Latin America that cooperate with the United States. IPS has continually tried to discredit the democratically elected government of El Salvador and the Nicaraguan contras fighting for democracy even while it has assiduously sought support for the communist governments of Nicaragua and Cuba. IPS uses ''human rights'' as a political stick to beat the United States and its allies while ignoring any such abuses in the USSR and among its friends, the ''liberated'' third-world countries.

Fourth: The Soviets wish ''to discredit U.S. policies and representatives in the eyes of its citizens and the world by creating or exacerbating splits within the nation.'' IPS has worked against every major defense program of the United States, against America's role in NATO, and against U.S. policies in Latin America.

In addition tirelessly to portraying Ronald Reagan as the most contemptible president ever to occupy the White House, *Mother Jones*, IPS's West Coast spinoff publication, charged Secretary of State George Shultz and Defense Secretary Caspar Weinberger with bribery and impropriety in a cover story. Smear campaigns have surfaced in other IPS-related media outlets and magazines such as *In These Times* and *CounterSpy/National Reporter*, and are always aimed at public figures known for their resistance to the Soviet Union—Ambassador Jeane Kirkpatrick, CIA Director William Casey, Attorney General Edward Meese, Assistant Secretary of State Elliott Abrams, Ambassador Vernon Walters, to name only a few.

Fifth: The Soviets wish ''to discredit and weaken American intelligence services and expose their personnel.'' The IPS spinoff Center for National Security Studies took a leading role in the campaign against the intelligence agencies, working relentlessly to discredit the CIA, NSA, and FBI. IPS chairman Peter Weiss has helped instigate lawsuits against both the FBI and the CIA. IPS assisted

CIA defector Philip Agee in the startup of *CounterSpy* magazine and has supported his second magazine, *Covert Action Information Bulletin.* IPS fellows have written for both magazines, which explicitly state that their purpose is to expose U.S. intelligence agents and stop all U.S. intelligence operations. IPS also intervened to secure safe haven in Holland for Agee following his deportation from Great Britain as a security risk after repeated collaboration with Cuban agents. IPS fellow John Cavanagh and associate Walden Bello are advisory board members of *CounterSpy*'s successor, *National Reporter,* and IPS staffer Joy Hackel now serves as the production manager and keeps the magazine going.

Sixth: The Soviets wish "to confuse world public opinion regarding the aggressive nature of Soviet policies." As noted, IPS fellows, notably Barnet, Raskin, Kaldor, and Halliday, have continually suggested that the Soviet Union acts defensively and poses little threat to the U.S. or the world.

Barnet declares that "the Soviet threat is the big lie of the arms race,"[23] and Mary Kaldor supports the contention: "[T]he Soviet system emerged in opposition to capitalism and from its inception was involved in warfare to defend itself against the latter."[24] "It would be wrong to confuse the priority of war preparations with a tendency to wage war, to confuse militarism with imperialist expansion," insists Kaldor. "The Soviet system was developed in opposition to capitalism, and that is its *raison d'être.* The role of warfare is defensive, against capitalism."[25] Fred Halliday states that "no permanent overseas bases have been set up by the Soviet Union anywhere outside the Warsaw Pact itself."[26] And Raskin avers: "While Cuba has been a bone in the throat of American presidents since John F. Kennedy, it is no military threat to the United States."[27]

IPS fellows not only associate with and host officials of communist regimes—the USSR, Cuba, Nicaragua, and so on—but have also labored to raise funds for communist countries allied with the Soviet Union.

Seventh: The Soviets wish "to create a favorable environment for the execution of Soviet foreign policy." Again, as noted throughout the latter chapters, IPS has justified even the most brutal Soviet behavior. Numerous IPS publications promote the view that the Soviet threat is "dubious" or simply "a myth." "[A] credible theory for what happened in Afghanistan is that the breakdown of order in the region was perceived by the Soviets as a threat rather than an opportunity," Barnet says, and, "the Soviets moved in a spirit of insecurity and panic. . . ."[28] Senior fellow Saul Landau even apologizes for Soviet expansionism: "The Soviet Union has been the one insurance policy of successful [third-world] revolutions."[29]

The bilateral exchanges between IPS and the Soviet Union—at Minneapolis in 1983, Moscow in 1984, San Francisco in 1985, and Washington, D.C., in 1986—have done little more than provide a forum for the Soviets to attack U.S. policies, foster trust of their workers' utopia, and gain one more opportunity to vent their propaganda in our media.

It is, of course, possible that the high degree of correlation between Soviet and IPS objectives is merely coincidental. In any case, the Soviets do take a keen interest in what goes on in IPS. The Soviet press frequently cites IPS to buttress its positions in the international arena and to make its propaganda against the United States more effective. Repeatedly, Soviet intelligence personnel and diplomats appear at IPS functions. But irrespective of these associations and the correlation of objectives, the questions posed still remain: Loyalty to whom or what, and under what circumstances? Which values warrant allegiance? What is allegiance? What are the merits of the policy proposals IPS pushes?

In conclusion, we have seen how IPS has been remarkably successful in promoting a sweeping radical agenda by maintaining the facade of a liberal scholarly research center. That IPS has gained the respect of mainstream institutions—from the universities and the media to the U.S. Congress itself—is indicative of the moral and intellectual crisis facing our society. The institute could never have achieved the prominence and respectability that it has if it were not for the fact that contemporary times seem especially hospitable to the nostrums and illusions that IPS espouses.

In a free society fringe groups and extreme ideologies of all sorts can and do appear, and democracy has sufficient power of assimilation to withstand most contradictions and absurdities. And in times of fundamental faith, an organization like IPS—which openly states that its goal is the dismantling of all economic, political, social, and cultural institutions in the United States—would hardly be taken seriously, let alone have any influence on the country's domestic and foreign policies. In the end, the story told here may reveal as much about the leadership and judgment of the elites in the United States as about the Institute for Policy Studies itself.

Appendices

Partial Listing of IPS's Financial Backers (1964–86)

ARCA Foundation
Mary Reynolds Babcock Foundation
Smith Bagley
Bydale Foundation
Cummins Engine Foundation
DJB Foundation
Field Foundation
Fontaney Corporation
Ford Foundation
Funding Exchange
Janss Foundation
W. Alton Jones Foundation
Irving F. Laucks
J. Roderick MacArthur Foundation
Milbank Foundation
New World Foundation
Ottinger Charitable Trust
Max Palevsky
Palisades Foundation
Playboy Foundation
Robert Potter

Rabinowitz Foundation
Samuel Rubin Foundation*
San Francisco Foundation
Shalan Foundation
Sperry Family
Stern Fund
James P. Warburg and family
World Council of Churches
Youth Project
Jacob Ziskind Trust

*IPS receives the bulk of its funding ($400,000–$500,000 annually) from here.

Partial Listing of Organizations Receiving Support from the Samuel Rubin Foundation and the Fund for Tomorrow

Africa Fund
American Civil Liberties Union Foundation
Bay Area Institute
Breira, Inc.
CALC Foundation
Campaign for Political Rights
Capp Street Foundation
Center for Constitutional Rights, Inc.
Center for Cuban Studies
Center for Documentary Media
Center for International Policy
Center for Investigative Reporting
Center for Popular Economics
Columbia University
Corporate Data Exchange
Council for a Livable World Education Fund
Council for Economic Priorities, Inc.
Cuban Mission to the U.N.
Cultural Council, Inc.
District 1199 Cultural Center, Inc.
Environmental Policy Institute
Fellowship of Reconciliation
Film Fund

Foundation for National Progress
Foundation for Scientific Cooperation with Vietnam
Freedom of Information Act, Inc.
Fund for Constitutional Government
Fund for Peace, Inc.
Gray Panthers
Guild Hall
Hampshire College
Hudson Guild
Indochina Resource Center
Industrial States Policy Center
Institute for Democratic Socialism
Institute for Food and Development Policy, Inc.
Institute for Policy Studies*
Institute for Southern Studies, Inc.
Institute for World Order
International Physicians for Prevention of Nuclear War, Inc.
Interns for Peace
Investigative Resource Center
Lawyers' Committee on Nuclear Policy
MS. Foundation for Women
Nation Institute
National Council of Churches
National Emergency Civil Liberties Commitee Foundation
National SANE Education Fund
North American Congress on Latin America
N.O.W. Legal Defense and Education Fund, Inc.
Nuclear Information and Resource Service
OXFAM
Pacific Alliance
Pacific Studies Center
Pacifica Foundation
Physicians for Social Responsibility
Progressive Foundation
Promoting Enduring Peace
St. Mark's Church
Southeast Asia Resource Center
Survival International
Tides Foundation
Vietnam Mission to the U.N.
Washington Office on Latin America
Washington Peace Center
Youth Project
Yugoslavian Mission to the U.N.

*The bulk of the Rubin Foundation's annual funding goes to IPS.

IPS and the Campaign Against the Intelligence Agencies

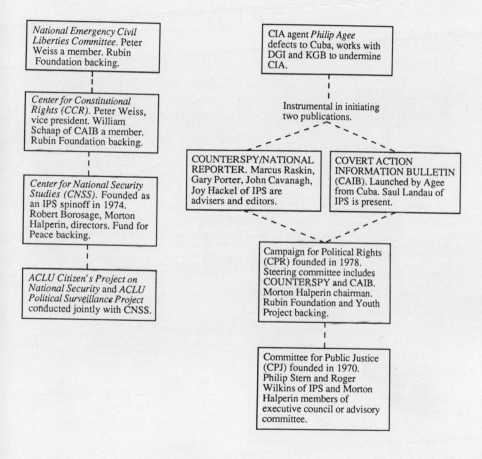

National Emergency Civil Liberties Committee. Peter Weiss a member. Rubin Foundation backing.

Center for Constitutional Rights (CCR). Peter Weiss, vice president. William Schaap of CAIB a member. Rubin Foundation backing.

Center for National Security Studies (CNSS). Founded as an IPS spinoff in 1974. Robert Borosage, Morton Halperin, directors. Fund for Peace backing.

ACLU Citizen's Project on National Security and *ACLU Political Surveillance Project* conducted jointly with CNSS.

CIA agent *Philip Agee* defects to Cuba, works with DGI and KGB to undermine CIA.

Instrumental in initiating two publications.

COUNTERSPY/NATIONAL REPORTER. Marcus Raskin, Gary Porter, John Cavanagh, Joy Hackel of IPS are advisers and editors.

COVERT ACTION INFORMATION BULLETIN (CAIB). Launched by Agee from Cuba. Saul Landau of IPS is present.

Campaign for Political Rights (CPR) founded in 1978. Steering committee includes COUNTERSPY and CAIB. Morton Halperin chairman. Rubin Foundation and Youth Project backing.

Committee for Public Justice (CPJ) founded in 1970. Philip Stern and Roger Wilkins of IPS and Morton Halperin members of executive council or advisory committee.

IPS and the Media

News and Wire Services

Liberation News Service founded 1967 with assistance from IPS.

Dispatch News Service founded 1969 by IPS chairman Philip Stern.

Pacific News Service founded 1970 as an IPS spin off. Richard Barnet, Michael Klare, John Dinges active.

Interlink Press Service founded 1981. Peter Weiss on board of directors. Rubin Foundation backing.

IPS Features founded 1985 as op-ed news service.

Journals and Periodicals

WORKING PAPERS FOR A NEW SOCIE-TY founded 1972 by Cambridge Institute, an IPS spinoff.

MOTHER JONES founded 1975 by Foundation for National Progress, an IPS spinoff.

IN THESE TIMES founded 1976. Published by IPS until 1982.

Middle East Information Project MERIP REPORTS founded 1971 by IPS fellow Joe Stork.

JOURNAL OF SOCIAL RECONSTRUCTION published by IPS and Hampshire College.

RACE AND CLASS published by TNI and Institute of Race Relations.

SOUTHERN EXPOSURE published by Institute for Southern Studies, an IPS spinoff.

COUNTER REPORTS published by Counter Information Services, an IPS/TNI spinoff.

WORLD POLICY JOURNAL edited by IPS fellows Richard Barnet and Mary Kaldor.

Rubin Foundation subsidizes the PROGRESSIVE and the NATION.

Investigative Reporting Organizations

Fund for Investigative Journalism founded by IPS chairman Philip Stern. Richard Barnet, Roger Wilkins advisers.

Center for Investigative Reporting, Project of Foundation for National Progress, an IPS spinoff. Rubin Foundation, ARCA Foundation, Shalan Foundation backing.

Investigative Resource Center. Rubin Foundation, Stern Fund, Shalan Foundation, ARCA Foundation backing.

Mother Jones Investigative Fund.

Radio Syndicates

In the Public Interest founded 1973. IPS trustee Philip Stern regular commentator. Fund for Peace backing.

SANE Radio founded 1975. IPS fellows commentators. Marcus Raskin vice chairman of SANE. Rubin Foundation backing.

IPS Air Express founded 1985 as radio commentary syndicate.

Africa News Service founded 1973. Fund for Tomorrow backing.

IPS and the Campaign Against the Corporation

Transnational Information Exchange (TIE) founded 1974 as IPS spinoff. Network of 130 organizations worldwide.

Pacific Studies Center (PSC) founded 1980. Fund for Tomorrow and Youth Project backing.

Government Accountability Project (GAP) founded 1975 as an IPS spinoff.

Counter Information Services (CIS); London-based TNI affiliate. IPS backing, promotion of Counter Reports.

Council on Economic Priorities (CEP) founded 1971. Richard Barnet, Cora Weiss, Philip Stern on board of directors. Rubin Foundation backing.

North American Congress on Latin America (NACLA) founded 1966. TIE affiliate. Rubin Foundation and Fund for Tomorrow backing.

Institute for Southern Studies (ISS) founded 1970. IPS spinoff. Rubin Foundation backing.

Data Center founded as NACLA spinoff. Rubin Foundation, Stern Fund, ARCA Foundation, Shalan Foundation backing.

Peoples Business Commission (PBC). Bydale Foundation

Interfaith Center on Corporate Responsibility (ICCR) TIE affiliate.

Corporate Data Exchange founded 1975 as NACLA spinoff. Rubin Foundation and IPS backing.

National Action/Research on the Military Industrial Complex (NARMIC). TIE affiliate.

Institute for Food and Development Policy (IFDP) founded by IPS fellow Joseph Collins. Rubin Foundation, Stern Fund, Ottinger Foundation, ARCA Foundation, Shalan Foundation, Ruth Mott Fund backing.

Infant Formula Coalition (INFACT). TIE affiliate.

Transnational Corporations Project founded 1983. Directed by IPS fellow John Cavanagh.

IPS and the Socialist Revolution in Stages

Conference on Alternative State and Local Policies (CASLP) founded 1974. IPS spinoff established by trustee Lee Webb. Serves as national clearinghouse for model legislation.

Foundation for National Progress (FNP) founded 1975 as IPS spinoff.

California Public Policy Center directed by FNP fellow Derek Shearer. Stern Fund backing through FNP.

National Center for Policy Alternatives founded 1982 as spinoff of CASLP.

Campaign for Economic Democracy (CED) founded 1977. FNP fellow Derek Shearer active. Stern Fund, ARCA Foundation, Youth Project backing.

National Center for Economic Alternatives founded 1982 by IPS fellow Gar Alperovitz.

Planners' Network. Directed by IPS fellow Chester Hartman.

Center for New Corporate Priorities, headed by Ruth Goldway, wife of FNP fellow Derek Shearer.

Community Ownership Organizing Project (COOP). Prominent member Ed Kirshner also FNP fellow. Youth Project, Stern Fund backing.

Progressive Alliance founded 1980. Marcus Raskin co chair of Issues Commission.

Project Democracy founded 1981. FNP fellow Derek Shearer is coordinator. ARCA Foundation backing.

New School for Democratic Management founded 1978 as a project of FNP. Youth Project backing.

Center for Study of Public Policy/Trusteeship Institute. Publishes Working Papers for a New Society, IPS spinoff.

IPS and the Latin Network

Policy Alternatives for the Caribbean and Central America (PACCA). Founded by IPS in 1983. Hub of Latin Network's effort to assist Sandinistas and thwart U.S. policies toward Central America.

Center for International Policy (CIP). Fund for Peace, Rubin Foundation, Stern Fund, Ruth Mott Fund backing. Participant in IPS PACCA Project.

Coalition for a New Foreign and Military Policy (CNFMP). Former IPS fellows Cynthia Washington and Steve Daggett active. Youth Project backing.

Center for Development Policy (CDP); Isabel Letelier, Michael Klare, Cynthia Arnson, Philip Stern members of CDP's Commission on U.S.-Central American Relations. ARCA Foundation, Bydale Foundation, Ottinger Foundation, Stern Fund, Youth Project backing

North American Congress on Latin America (NACLA). Rubin Foundation, Fund for Tomorrow, ARCA Foundation, Stern Fund backing. Participant in IPS PACCA project.

Committee in Solidarity with the People of El Salvador (CISPES). Isabel Letelier (IPS) and Robert Armstrong (NACLA) helped found.

Washington Office on Latin America (WOLA). Isabel Letelier adviser. WOLA Director Joe Eldridge on IPS Letelier-Moffitt Human Rights Award Committee. Stern Fund, Ottinger Foundation, Fund for Tomorrow, Bydale Foundation backing.

Central American Historical Institute (CAHI). Director Betsy Cohn active with IPS.

Institute for Food and Development Policy (IFDP) Founded by IPS fellow Joseph Collins. Rubin Foundation, Stern Fund, Ottinger Foundation, ARCA Foundation, Shalan Foundation, Ruth Mott Fund backing.

Americas Watch Committee (AWC). AWC Director Juan Mendez on IPS Letelier-Moffitt Human Rights Award Committee. Bydale Foundation backing.

Council on Hemispheric Affairs (COHA). IPS Trustees Roger Wilkins and Terry Herndon board members.

Sanctuary Movement. Richard Barnet's World Peacemakers and William Sloane Coffin's Riverside Church active. Sanctuary founders Jim and Pat Corbett recipients of IPS Letelier-Moffitt Human Rights Award.

IPS and the Peace Movement

SANE founded 1957. IPS Ph.D. student David Cortwright is executive Director, Marcus Raskin is Vice Chairman.

Coalition for a New Foreign and Military Policy founded 1975. Former IPS fellows Cynthia Washington and Steve Daggett active. Youth Project backing.

Women Strike for Peace (WSP) founded 1965. Cora Weiss leader.

Riverside Church Disarmament Program founded 1978. William Sloane Coffin and Rubin Foundation president Cora Weiss founders

Clergy and Laity Concerned (CALC) founded 1965. William Sloane Coffin and Cora Weiss leaders. Rubin Foundation, Fund for Tomorrow backing

Mobilization for Survival (MFS) founded 1977. IPS credits itself with helping found MFS. Close cooperation with Riverside Church Disarmament Program.

Physicians for Social Responsibility (PSR), founded 1961. Rubin Foundation, Fund for Tomorrow, W. Alton Jones Foundation backing.

World Peacemakers founded 1978 by Richard Barnet and Ned Crosby.

Council for a Livable World (CLW) founded 1962. Richard Barnet, Paul Warnke board members. CLW President Jerome Grossman participant in IPS dialogue with Soviet Union.

Committee for National Security founded 1980 by Richard Barnet and Paul Warnke.

Union of Concerned Scientists (UCS) founded 1969. IPS Fellow William Arkin writer for the *Bulletin of Concerned Scientists*. *Bulletin* editor Ruth Adams participant in IPS dialogue with Soviet Union.

European Nuclear Disarmament founded 1980. IPS fellows William Arkin, Mary Kaldor, Dan Smith active.

International Physicians for the Prevention of Nuclear War (IPPNW) founded 1981. Rubin Foundation, W. Alton Jones Foundation, Stern Fund backing.

Council on Economic Priorities (CEP) founded 1971. Rubin Foundation backing. Richard Barnet, Cora Weiss, Philip Stern board members.

Fellowship of Reconciliation (FOR). Rubin Foundation, Fund for Tomorrow backing.

Promoting Enduring Peace founded 1952. Rubin Foundation, Fund for Tomorrow backing. Director Howard Frazier participant in IPS dialogue with Soviet Union.

Nuclear Information Resource Service (NIRS) founded 1978. Rubin Foundation, ARCA Foundation, Stern Fund backing.

Lawyers Committee on Nuclear Policy (LCNP) founded 1981. Peter Weiss is cochairman. Rubin Foundation funding.

Institute for Defense and Disarmament Studies (IDDS) founded 1980. Director Randall Forsberg participant in IPS dialogue with Soviet Union.

Peace Links founded 1982. Chairman Betty Bumpers participant in IPS dialogue with Soviet Union.

Business Executives for National Security founded 1982. President Stanley Weiss is also IPS trustee.

Center for Defense Information (CDI) founded 1973. Fund for Peace project. IPS fellow William Arkin previously CDI researcher.

Institute for World Order (IWO). Rubin Foundation, Fund for Tomorrow backing. Richard Barnet, Richard Falk active.

Sojourners founded 1971. Richard Barnet is *Sojourners* editorial board member. *Sojourners* promotes IPS publications.

Rainbow Sign founded 1981. Director Arthur Waskow a founding fellow of IPS.

Educators for Social Responsibility/Metropolitan Area (ESR/MA) founded 1981. Headquartered in Riverside Church.

Peace Development Fund founded 1982. Fund for Tomorrow backing.

Coalition for a Nuclear Free Harbor founded 1984. Spin-off of Cora Weiss's Riverside Church Disarmament Program.

Tides Foundation, Rubin Foundation, Bydale Foundation, Shalan Foundation backing.

Arms control and foreign policy caucus (ACFP), founded 1966. IPS Associate fellow Cynthia Arason active.

Overview of TIE's European Organizations

Research Institute on Multinational Corporations

The Research Institute on Multinational Corporations (SOMO—a Dutch acronym for Stichting Onderzoek Multinationale Ondernemingen) was established in 1972 after the U.N.'s third UNCTAD conference. According to its literature, SOMO specializes in "counter-research and counter-information on multinational corporations at the request of and in conjunction with requests from the workers movements and action world."[1] Located at Paulus Potterstraat 20, in the Transnational Institute's headquarters building, SOMO is almost a subsidiary of the institute. Many of its activities are carried on in conjunction with TNI—a nice arrangement given the fact that much of SOMO's budget is directly subsidized by the Dutch government. Another group that SOMO works with is the Sjaloom Group in Odyk, an organization that has advocated sabotage and violent actions along with more traditional protests as viable means to bring about social change.

Institute for the Study of Military Problems

The Institute for the Study of Military Problems (STOMP—Studie Onderzoek Militaire Problemen) also shares TNI's premises. STOMP originated from the Bond voor Dienstplichtigen (White BVD Conscripts' Union), which organized the Anti-NATO '74 Congress. STOMP publishes information on strategic and technical developments in NATO to help the Left organize ways to counter them. Ben Dankbaar, an IPS associate fellow, is director of STOMP. Increasingly, STOMP has become involved in something known as "conversion," which seeks to mobilize workers collectively so as to coerce management of defense industries to "convert" their productive processes and output to "peaceful and social needs."

In November 1982 Ben Dankbaar and TNI fellow Mary Kaldor helped organize the Military Conversion Conference held at the TNI center in Amsterdam, where peace researchers and trade union representatives involved in the production of the joint Italian, West German, and British multirole combat aircraft Toronado got together. *TIE-Europe Bulletin* no. 13/14 reports that "representatives from British Aerospace and Rolls Royce in the United Kingdom, the Italian companies Aeritalia and Aeromacchi, and MBB and MTU in West Germany met to discuss the present position on the Toronado project, the future military requirements in Europe, and some of the problems involved in the conversion of the arms industries to other forms of production."[2]

Multinational Corporations in Latin America

Another member group of Transnational Information Exchange is Multinational Corporations in Latin America (MOL—Multinationale Ondernemingen Latijns Amerika), which focuses on research and publication of Dutch investments and corporations involved in Latin America.

World Information Service on Energy

The director of TNI, Basker Vashee, played a seminal role in forming the World Information Service on Energy (WISE) in 1978. Within a few short years, WISE became one of the leading antinuclear power lobbying groups in Europe. It says that it functions as "an international switchboard" for local and national antinuclear activists around the world "who want to exchange information and support one another." By 1982 WISE had relays in thirteen countries on four continents and a worldwide network of grassroots contacts.[3]

Research Group on Electronics

Another key organization in the Transnational Information Exchange, which coordinates TIE's Information Technology Task Force, is the Research Group on Electronics (SOBE—Stichting Onderzoek Bedrijfstak Elektrotechniek). SOBE compiles research on the worldwide electronics industry, but mainly focuses on the Philips Electronics Corporation, a Dutch-based corporation which is one of the world's three largest electronics firms. Philips employees have participated in SOBE conferences, some actively. Because of their employment in sensitive defense-related divisions at Philips, concern has been expressed about potential security breaches.

International Documentation on the Contemporary Church

IDOC, an acronym for International Documentation on the Contemporary Church, is another important participant in TIE. Although IDOC claims it was founded in 1962 to inform the Dutch Catholic bishops of Vatican II documentation, it has never had the sanction of the Roman Catholic church. The *Catholic Register*'s Paul Hallett describes IDOC as "an international apparatus to 'liberalize' the Catholic Church by spreading modernist and leftist views."[4] The Vatican found IDOC's influence so pernicious that it made a public statement condemning IDOC. The official Vatican daily, *L'Osservatore Romano*, reported on December 28, 1972, that IDOC had no competent ecclesiastical authority nor any official church standing. In the latter 1970s and 1980s, IDOC drifted further to the left, promoting doctrines from liberation theology and pro-Castro propaganda to attacks on multinational corporations. Increasingly, IDOC embraces the anticorporate agenda of the Transnational Institute and other IPS spinoffs.

End Loans to South Africa

Another important group in the Transnational Information Exchange is the London-based ELTSA (End Loans to South Africa), which has been headed by David Haslam and Pauline Webb. ELTSA has focused on mounting campaigns against Barclays Bank for its extension of credit to the South African government and corporations doing business in South Africa. ELTSA has cooperated closely with the Anti-Apartheid Movement, the leading British anti–South African pressure group, which has been accused of being controlled by the Communist party.

Members of Congress Requesting Budget Studies from IPS

1978 Budget Study

Herman Badillo (D–N.Y.)
Max Baucus (D–Mont.)
Berkley Bedell (D–Iowa)
Michael T. Blouin (D–Iowa)
David E. Bonior (D–Mich.)
William M. Brodhead (D–Mich.)
George E. Brown, Jr. (D–Calif.)
Yvonne Brathwaite Burke (D–Calif.)
Charles J. Carney (D–Ohio)
Bob Carr (D–Mich.)
Shirley Chisholm (D–N.Y.)
William Clay (D–Mo.)
Cardiss Collins (D–Ill.)
John Conyers, Jr. (D–Mich.)
Norman E. D'Amours (D–N.H.)
Ronald V. Dellums (D–Calif.)
Charles C. Diggs, Jr. (D–Mich.)
Robert F. Drinan (D–Mass.)
Robert W. Edgar (D–Pa.)

Don Edwards (D–Calif.)
Walter E. Fauntroy (D–D.C.)
Harold E. Ford (D–Tenn.)
Donald M. Fraser (D–Minn.)
Tom Harkin (D–Iowa)
Michael Harrington (D–Mass.)
Augustus F. Hawkins (D–Calif.)
Ken Hollard (D–S.C.)
Andrew Jacobs, Jr. (D–Ind.)
Martha Keys (D–Kans.)
John Krebs (D–Calif.)
Robert Krueger (D–Tex.)
Andrew Maguire (D–N.J.)
Ralph H. Metcalfe (D–Ill.)
Barbara A. Mikulski (D–Md.)
George Miller (D–Calif.)
Norman Y. Mineta (D–Calif.)
Parren J. Mitchell (D–Md.)
Anthony Toby Moffett (D–Conn.)
Stephen L. Neal (D–N.C.)
Robert N. C. Nix (D–Pa.)
Henry J. Nowak (D–N.Y.)
Richard L. Ottinger (D–N.Y.)
Jerry M. Patterson (D–Calif.)
Charles B. Rangel (D–N.Y.)
Henry S. Reuss (D–Wis.)
Frederick W. Richmond (D–N.Y.)
Peter W. Rodino, Jr. (D–N.J.)
Benjamin S. Rosenthal (D–N.Y.)
Edward R. Roybal (D–Calif.)
James H. Scheuer (D–N.Y.)
Paul Simon (D–Ill.)
Gladys Noon Spellman (D–Md.)
Fortney H. Stark (D–Calif.)
Bruce F. Vento (D–Minn.)

1982 Budget Study

Les Aspin (D–Wis.)
Michael Barnes (D–Md.)
Berkley Bedell (D–Iowa)
Jonathan A. Bingham (D–N.Y.)
David E. Bonior (D–Mich.)
William M. Brodhead (D–Mich.)

George E. Brown Jr. (D–Calif.)
John L. Burton (D–Calif.)
Shirley Chisholm (D–N.Y.)
William Clay (D–Mo.)
George W. Crockett, Jr. (D–Mich.)
Ronald V. Dellums (D–Calif.)
Julian Dixon (D–Calif.)
Bernard Dwyer (D–N.Y.)
Mervyn Dymally (D–Calif.)
Bob Edgar (D–Pa.)
Don Edwards (D–Calif.)
Walter E. Fauntroy (D–D.C.)
Hamilton Fish, Jr. (R–N.Y.)
Thomas Foglietta (D–Pa.)
Harold E. Ford (D–Tenn.)
William D. Ford (D–Mich.)
Wyche Fowler, Jr. (D–Ga.)
Robert Garcia (D–N.Y.)
William H. Gray (D–Pa.)
Tom Harkin (D–Iowa)
Andrew Jacobs, Jr. (D–Ind.)
Robert W. Kastenmeier (D–Wis.)
Mickey Leland (D–Tex.)
Mike Lowry (D–Wash.)
Robert T. Matsui (D–Calif.)
Barbara A. Mikulski (D–Md.)
George Miller (D–Calif.)
Norman Y. Mineta (D–Calif.)
Parren J. Mitchell (D–Md.)
Anthony Toby Moffett (D–Conn.)
Mary Rose Oakar (D–Ohio)
Richard L. Ottinger (D–N.Y.)
Charles B. Rangel (D–N.Y.)
Henry S. Reuss (D–Wis.)
Peter W. Rodino, Jr. (D–N.J.)
Benjamin S. Rosenthal (D–N.Y.)
Gus Savage (D–Ill.)
James H. Scheuer (D–N.Y.)
Patricia Schroeder (D–Colo.)
Charles E. Schumer (D–N.Y.)
John F. Seiberling (D–Ohio)
Gerry E. Studds (D–Mass.)
Morris K. Udall (D–Ariz.)
Bruce F. Vento (D–Minn.)
Ted Weiss (D–N.Y.)

APPENDIX 11

Letter on El Salvador to Tip O'Neill (Drafted by IPS Associate Fellow Cynthia Arnson)

March 6, 1984

The Honorable Thomas P. O'Neill, Jr.
Speaker of the House of Representatives
U.S. Capitol

Dear Mr. Speaker,

We are writing to express our deep concern about U.S. policy in El Salvador. We feel that Congress must act firmly to halt the dangerous direction of that policy.

The Administration has requested a tripling of our security assistance program in El Salvador (including military aid and cash transfers to the government), from under $200 million in Fiscal Year 1984 to over $600 million requested for Fiscal Year 1985 and a Fiscal Year 1984 Supplemental.

This new aid is being requested at a time when major unresolved questions remain about the efficacy of both our policy and previous aid programs in El Salvador. Over the past several weeks, U.S. government agencies—including the Government Accounting Office and A.I.D.'s Inspector General—have reported widespread corruption and waste in U.S. aid programs. There are also disturbing accounts of cover-ups by high Salvadoran officials in the investigation of the murders of four U.S. churchwomen, and of government complicity in death squad violence.

More importantly, the Reagan Administration has used U.S. aid to pursue a military victory in El Salvador rather than a negotiated settlement there.

384

We support last Thursday's action by the Western Hemisphere Subcommittee. It voted to provide security assistance *only* after the House and Senate have approved a joint resolution confirming that changes have occurred in El Salvador regarding the death squads; the government's willingness to enter into negotiations; the prosecution of the murderers of U.S. citizens; and the establishment of a functioning judicial system.

We are extremely reluctant to support any weaker measures on the floor of the House. We would also have serious reservations about approving any non-humanitarian aid for El Salvador until the results of the March and April presidential elections are known.

We are letting you know our views at this early date in order to avoid a divisive and acrimonious debate on this issue later in the year. We appreciate your leadership in the past on issues of vital foreign policy concern and look forward to working with you to chart a more reliable course in Central America.

Sincerely,

Gary L. Ackerman	Mike Lowry
Joseph Addabbo	Ed Markey
Les AuCoin	Robert T. Matsui
Berkley Bedell	Nick Mavroules
Howard L. Berman	Barbara A. Mikulski
David E. Bonior	George Miller
Barbara Boxer	Norman Mineta
Sala Burton	Parren J. Mitchell
Ronald Coleman	Joe Moakley
John Conyers	Jim Moody
William J. Coyne	Bruce A. Morrison
George W. Crockett	Bob Mrazek
Ronald Dellums	Henry J. Nowak
Byron L. Dorgan	Mary Rose Oakar
Tom Downey	James L. Oberster
Mervyn M. Dymally	Richard Ottinger
Bob Edgar	Leon Panetta
Don Edwards	Donald J. Pease
Lane Evans	Bill Ratchford
Walter E. Fauntroy	Bill Richardson
Vic Fazio	Martin O. Sabo
Edward F. Feighan	Gus Savage
Thomas M. Foglietta	Pat Schroeder
William D. Ford	John F. Seiberling
Barney Frank	Jim Shannon
Sam Gejdenson	Stephen J. Solarz
William H. Gray III	Esteban E. Torres
Tom Harkin	Bruce F. Vento
Dennis M. Hertel	Doug Walgren
Marcy Kaptur	Henry A. Waxman
Richard Lehman	Ted Weiss
Mickey Leland	Tim Wirth
Sander M. Levin	Howard Wolpe
Mel Levine	Ron Wyden

Members of House Voting Straight Coalition for New Foreign and Military Policy Line in 1983

Gary Ackerman (D–N.Y.)
Joseph Addabbo (D–N.Y.)
Les AuCoin (D–Oreg.)
Jim Bates (D–Calif.)
Berkley Bedell (D–Iowa)
Anthony Beilenson (D–Calif.)
Howard Berman (D–Calif.)
David Bonior (D–Mich.)
Donald Bonker (D–Wash.)
Barbara Boxer (D–Calif.)
Sala Burton (D–Calif.)
Robert Carr (D–Mich.)
William Clay (D–Mo.)
Cardiss Collins (D–Ill.)
John Conyers (D–Mich.)
William Coyne (D–Pa.)
Ronald Dellums (D–Calif.)
Tom Downey (D–N.Y.)
Joseph Early (D–Mass.)
Robert Edgar (D–Pa.)
Don Edwards (D–Calif.)

Lane Evans (D–Ill.)
Edward Feighan (D–Ohio)
Thomas Foglietta (D–Pa.)
Harold Ford (D–Tenn.)
William Ford (D–Mich.)
Wyche Fowler (D–Ga.)
Barney Frank (D–Mass.)
William Gray (D–Pa.)
Katie Hall (D–Ill.)
Tom Harkin (D–Iowa)
Andrew Jacobs (D–Ind.)
Marcy Kaptur (D–Ohio)
Robert Kastenmeier (D–Wis.)
Dale Kildee (D–Mich.)
Peter Kostmayer (D–Pa.)
John LaFalce (D–N.Y.)
Jim Leach (D–Iowa)
Richard Lehman (D–Fla.)
Mickey Leland (D–Tex.)
Mike Lowry (D–Wash.)
Edward Markey (D–Mass.)
Nick Mavroules (D–Mass.)
George Miller (D–Calif.)
Parren Mitchell (D–Md.)
John Moakley (D–Mass.)
Jim Moody (D–Wis.)
Henry Nowak (D–N.Y.)
James Oberster (D–Minn.)
Thomas O'Neill (D–Mass.)
Richard Ottinger (D–N.Y.)
Major Ownes (D–N.Y.)
Leon Panetta (D–Calif.)
Donald Pease (D–Ohio)
Charles Rangel (D–N.Y.)
Peter Rodino (D–N.J.)
Edward Roybal (D–Calif.)
Martin Sabo (D–Minn.)
Gus Savage (D–Ill.)
James Scheuer (D–N.Y.)
Claudine Schneider (R–R.I.)
Patricia Schroeder (D–Colo.)
Charles Schumer (D–N.Y.)
John Seiberling (D–Ohio)
James Shannon (D–Mass.)
Gerald Sikorski (D–Minn.)

Stephen Solarz (D–N.Y.)
Fortney Stark (D–Calif.)
Louis Stokes (D–Ohio)
Gerry Studds (D–Mass.)
Edolphus Towns (D–N.Y.)
Bruce Vento (D–Minn.)
Doug Walgren (D–Pa.)
Henry Waxman (D–Calif.)
Ted Weiss (D–N.Y.)
Alan Wheat (D–Mo.)
Timothy Wirth (D–Colo.)
Howard Wolpe (D–Mich.)
Sidney Yates (D–Ill.)

Members of Senate Voting Straight Coalition for New Foreign and Military Policy Line in 1983

Joseph Biden (D–Del.)
William Bradley (D–N.J.)
Alan Cranston (D–Calif.)
Christopher Dodd (D–Conn.)
Thomas Eagleton (D–Mo.)
Gary Hart (D–Colo.)
Mark Hatfield (R–Oreg.)
Ted Kennedy (D–Mass.)
Frank Lautenberg (D–N.J.)
Patrick Leahy (D–Vt.)
Carl Levin (D–Mich.)
Spark Matsunaga (D–Hawaii)
Claiborne Pell (D–R.I.)
William Proxmire (D–Wis.)
David Pryor (D–Ark.)
Donald Riegle (D–Mich.)
Paul Sarbanes (D–Md.)
Paul Tsongas (D–Mass.)

Notes

Chapter 2: In Washington but Not of It

1. IPS Annual Report, 1979–80, p. 5.
2. IPS Annual Report, 1983, p. 6.
3. Marcus G. Raskin, *Being and Doing*, Introduction, quoted in *First Harvest* (New York: Grove Press, 1983), p. 352.
4. Ibid., *Being and Doing*, quoted in *First Harvest*, pp. 354–55.
5. IPS Annual Report, 1979–80, p. 4.
6. Ibid., p. 3.
7. IPS Annual Report, 1983, p. 6.
8. IPS Ten Year Report, "Beginning the Decade, 1963–73."
9. IPS Three Year Report, "The First Three Years."
10. See, e.g., Egbal Ahmad, "On Arab Bankruptcy," *New York Times,* August 10, 1982, p. A25; Ahmad, in *Race and Class* 20, no. 3 (Winter 1979).
11. IPS 1981 catalogue, p. 15.
12. IPS prospectus, 1982–83.
13. IPS Annual Report, 1979–80, p. 14.
14. IPS-TNI, "The Link," February 1975.
15. Patrick Esmond-White described his strategy to manipulate the media in greater detail in an IPS seminar, January 17, 1984. For more details see Chapter 9.
16. Sue Goodwin, letter from Washington School, April 14, 1987.
17. IPS Annual Report, 1979–80, p. 12.
18. Joshua Muravchik, "Think Tank on the Left," *New York Times Sunday Magazine,* April 26, 1981, p. 122.
19. *In These Times*, November 4–10, 1981, p. 12C.

20. Ibid., p. 12B.
21. Frederik F. Clairmont and John Cavanagh, "Corporate Power in Selected Food Commodities," United Nations Conference on Trade and Development, Reprint Series no. 39, p. 2 (original article appeared in *Raw Materials Report*, vol. 1, no. 3).
22. Counter Information Services (CIS) is a project of the Institute for Policy Studies/Transnational Institute (IPS/TNI), which is supported by the World Council of Churches Program to Combat Racism. The Transnational Institute's multinational monitoring project also receives money from the World Council of Churches. Dwain Epps, the director of the World Council of Churches Office of Liaison for the United Nations, is a personal friend of Cora Weiss and participated in Riverside Church's Agenda 80's conference, cochaired by Cora Weiss. William Wipfler, director of the National Council of Churches (NCC) Office of Human Rights, is a close associate of IPS. IPS bestowed Wipfler with the Letelier-Moffitt Human Rights Award in 1981. Timothy Smith, director of the Interfaith Center on Corporate Responsibility, formerly a project of NCC—now separate, but still operating in the NCC building and still connected to NCC programs—has fairly close relations with IPS/TNI because of a shared commitment to anticorporate activism.

    Characteristic of modern Marxist revolutionaries and terrorists worldwide is their understanding of the value of the media and the importance of winning the political war in the United States; revolutionaries often calculate their actions for media effect and to maximize leverage in Washington.

    IPS annual reports and monthly calendars list representatives of communist governments and Marxist revolutionary movements that have been sponsored and hosted by IPS. That IPS has so many connections with third-world revolutionaries and parties hostile to the United States essentially means that they trust IPS as an agency to aid and advance their causes.
23. When Cora Weiss was confronted by Olga Hruby, a member of the Riverside Church for some twenty-five years, about her work in the church's disarmament program, Weiss admitted that she was neither a member of the Riverside Church nor a member of any other Christian church, explaining that she was of Jewish heritage. When Hruby pressed her further about her Jewish faith, Weiss would not admit to being a member of any temple. Before her arrival at Riverside, Weiss was involved with the National Council of Churches program Church World Service. Apparently, although not a Christian, Weiss finds the church a useful vehicle for carrying out political activity.
24. IPS Annual Report, 1979–80, p. 4.
25. Official Report to the Special Committee on Un-American Activities, 1936 General Election, New York City.
26. A. C. Fabergé, statement on family history, December 18, 1981.
27. Robert C. Williams, *Russian Art and American Money* (Cambridge: Harvard University Press, 1980), p. 199.
28. Fabergé, op. cit.
29. Ibid.
30. Philip Stern to IPS Staff, June 29, 1985.
31. *New York Times*, May 1, 1975, clipped article, no pagination.
32. Richard Neuhaus, interview, January 24, 1986.
33. Numerous attempts were made to obtain the audited financial statement of the Institute for Policy Studies in 1984 and 1985, which by law the institute must furnish to the public because of its 501(c)(3) tax-exempt status. IPS referred me to its auditor,

Larry Stokes, and Stokes referred me back to the institute. Both parties were clearly defensive, and found such a request very irregular.

34. IPS Annual Report, 1979–80, p. 27.
35. Ibid., p. 27.
36. IPS Annual Report, 1983, p. 3.
37. IPS Annual Report, 1979–80, p. 14.
38. See *Daily World*, February 9, 1977, pp. 1–2, *Pravda*, February 9, 10, 1977, as cited in *Foreign Broadcast Information Service*, Soviet Union Daily Report, vol. 3.
39. Committee for National Security promotional material, Public Affairs Council, 1220 Sixteenth Street, N.W., Washington, D.C.
40. Ibid.
41. Planners Network promotional literature, June 1985.
42. Ibid.
43. Cora Weiss, "Myths and Realities of the 'Soviet Threat,' " proceedings of IPS Conference on U.S.–Soviet Relations, May 14–15, 1979, p. 10.
44. Richard Barnet, "Lies Clearer Than Truth: A Look at the Russian Threat," *Waging Peace*, ed. Jim Wallis (San Francisco: Harper & Row, 1982), p. 57.
45. Center for National Security Studies promotional material, Public Affairs Council, 1220 Sixteenth Street, N.W., Washington, D.C.
46. These policy recommendations were made in Marcus G. Raskin, ed., *The Federal Budget and Social Reconstruction* (Washington: Institute for Policy Studies, 1978).
47. Arms Control and Foreign Policy Caucus statement of purpose, Public Affairs Council, 1220 Sixteenth Street, N.W., Washington, D.C.
48. Don Edwards, letter, "Dear Colleague," March 1, 1984.
49. Ted Weiss, address, at Riverside Church, New York City, April, 27, 1984.
50. Mark Hatfield, statement, April 5, 1983, at Twentieth Year Anniversary of Institute for Policy Studies.
51. Thomas Harkin, statement, February 22, 1984, at PACCA reception.
52. "Direct from Cuba," a service of *Prensa Latina*, Havana, September 30, 1981, p. 30.
53. IPS Annual Report, 1979–80, p. 14.
54. IPS Annual Report, 1983, p. 13.
55. IPS Publications Catalogue, 1982.
56. Karen DeYoung, statement at IPS Washington School course on "Foreign Reporting," spring 1980. Tape-recorded by journalist Cliff Kincaid.
57. In 1980, the *New York Times* carried twenty articles by IPS fellows, compared with nine articles by analysts from American Enterprise Institute and seven from Brookings Institution. In 1981, IPS fellows and associate fellows increased to thirty-seven, over three times more than the next policy research center.
58. IPS Annual Report, 1979–80, p. 3.
59. Leslie Gelb, "U.S. Tries to Fight Allied Resistance to Nuclear Arms," *New York Times*, February 14, 1985, p. 1.
60. See FBI Washington Field Office File #185-425; R. Bruce McColm, "The Letelier Killing," *National Catholic Register*, September 21, 1980, p. 10.
61. John Train, unpublished manuscript, February 1977.
62. Samuel Francis, staff, U.S. Senate Select Committee on Intelligence, verified identity of Joseph Slovo.
63. See IPS Annual Report, 1979–80; IPS Annual Report, 1983, "The Twentieth Year"; IPS Monthly Calendars.
64. IPS Annual Report, 1983, p. 39.

65. Ibid.
66. Robert Borosage, "Report from Nicaragua and Cuba," lecture and discussion at IPS, December 12, 1983.
67. See Institute for Food and Development, "Progress Report for Fiscal Year 1980," pp. 10–13; and funding proposal for fiscal year 1984, pp. 10–12.
68. Frances Moore Lappé and Joseph Collins, *Food First: Beyond the Myth of Scarcity* (New York: Ballantine Books, 1978), pp. 498–99.
69. Ibid., back cover.
70. IFDP, "Progress Report, Fiscal 1983," p. 8.
71. Robert Borosage, interview, December 19, 1983.
72. Michael Parenti, talk delivered at IPS seminar, October 12, 1983.

Chapter 3: Political Pilgrims Turn Militant

1. Garry Wills, "The Thinking of Positive Power," *Esquire*, March 1971.
2. Richard Barnet and Marcus Raskin, *After Twenty Years: The Decline of NATO and the Search for a New Policy in Europe* (New York: Vintage Books, 1966), p. 85.
3. FBI Report, WFO #100-46784, June 29, 1971, p. 20.
4. Ibid.
5. FBI Bureau File #100-447935, WFO #100-447735, vol. 3.
6. FBI Bureau File #100-447935, WFO #100-46784, March 15, 1973, p. 40.
7. *Examiner*, (Washington, D.C. weekly), September 24, 1967.
8. *Communism and the New Left* (Washington, D.C.: U.S. News & World Report, 1969), p. 74.
9. *Times Union* (Albany, N.Y.), December 9, 1966.
10. *Communism and the New Left* (Washington, D.C.: U.S. News & World Report, 1969). *Black Panther*, the official newspaper of the Black Panther party, regularly stated that the BPP advocates nothing short of the use of guns and guerrilla tactics in its revolutionary program to end oppression of the black people. Residents of the black community are urged to arm themselves against the police, who are consistently referred to as "pigs" that should be killed. In its September 7, 1968, issue, BPP's minister of education, George Murray, wrote an article that ended on the following note: "Black men. Black people, colored persons of America, revolt is everywhere! Arm yourselves. The only culture worth keeping is revolutionary culture. Change. Freedom everywhere. Dynamite! Black power. Use the gun. Kill the pigs everywhere." David Hilliard, BPP chief of staff, said in the BPP newspaper of December 13, 1969, "We advocate the very direct overthrow of the government by way of force and violence."
11. *Hatchet* (George Washington University student newspaper), May 4, 1970, p. 1.
12. FBI Bureau File #100-44935, WFO #100-46784, March 15, 1973, p. 35.
13. *Washington Post* (news clipping on funeral of Ralph Featherstone), March 15, 1970.
14. Carl Shoffler, interview, July 23, 1984.
15. *Hatchet*, April 16, 1970, p. 5.
16. Ibid.
17. WEB DuBois School of Marxist Studies, catalogue, Spring 1971.
18. Gerardo Peraza, U.S. Senate Subcommittee on Security and Terrorism, February 26, 1982, pp. 21–24.
19. *Militant*, February 27, 1967, pp. 1–3.
20. *Communism and the New Left* (Washington, D.C.: U.S. News & World Report,

1969), p. 54. The hidden agenda in nonviolent demonstrations and mass civil disobedience is to force the police to take action which precipitates physical confrontation. Demonstrators are often instructed to seek media attention which will portray law-enforcement authorities as repressive and brutal; and that, in turn, discredits the legitimacy of the government itself. In the name of the revolution it is acceptable for a demonstrator to be injured as long as the press sees the blood.

The Yippies believed that violence would help the cause of the movement. "What Chicago is going to do," said Rubin, "is dramatize that there are two sides and you can choose. It's not the Republicans and the Democrats, it's what America is doing and what it stands for . . . and when that becomes clear in every living room in the country, wow—our side's gonna win." In the end this strategy met with considerable success in the summer of 1968. In general, the media were inclined to condemn the actions of the police and security forces at the convention. For instance, Walter Cronkite's news commentary on CBS labeled the convention security forces "thugs."

21. Michael Rossman, as cited in David Armstrong, *A Trumpet to Arms: Alternative Media in America* (Los Angeles: J. P. Tarcher, 1981), p. 123.
22. Donald Janson, "Bronx Lawyer and Prosecutor Spar at Chicago March Trial," *New York Times*, March 18, 1969, p. 17.
23. FBI Bureau File #100-447935, undated report.
24. M. Stanton Evans, *Human Events*, November 7, 1981, p. 989.
25. Garry Wills, *Esquire*, March 1971.
26. Earl Ravenal, as cited in Joshua Muravchik, "Think Tank on the Left," *New York Times Sunday Magazine*, June 4, 1981, pp. 44–48.
27. FBI Bureau File #100-447935, July 8, 1971, p. 2.
28. Ibid., vol. 3, June 29, 1971, p. 15.
29. Raymond Mungo, *Famous Long Ago: My Life and Hard Times with Liberation News Service* (Boston: Beacon Press, 1970), p. 10.
30. Ibid., p. 17.
31. David Armstrong, *A Trumpet to Arms: Alternative Media in America*. (Los Angeles: J. P. Tarcher, 1981), p. 105.
32. Ibid., pp. 105–6.
33. Ibid., p. 107.
34. *Washington Star*, July 13, 1971.
35. Ibid.
36. Russ Braley, *Bad News: Foreign Policy of the New York Times* (Chicago: Regnery, Gateway, 1984), p. 340.
37. Shearer helped write Tom Hayden's platform for his 1976 bid for the U.S. Senate in California. Hayden and his wife Jane Fonda had cooperated with the Hanoi government in producing anti-American propaganda during the Vietnam War.
38. Armstrong, op. cit., p. 97.
39. *National Guardian*, October 9, 1965.
40. Braley, op. cit., pp. 238–39, 342–43.
41. U.S., Congress, Senate, Committee on the Judiciary, Subcommittee on Internal Security (SSIS) Hearings: November 3, 4, 5, 6, and 10, 1969.
42. FBI Bureau File #100-447935, June 29, 1971, vol. 3, p. 15.
43. Louis A. Fanning, *Betrayal in Vietnam* (New Rochelle, N.Y.: Arlington House, 1976), p. 30. Also, IPS Annual Report, "Beginning the Second Decade, 1963–1973," p. 13.
44. Fanning, op. cit., p. 30.
45. Ibid., p. 31.

46. Ibid., pp. 31–33.
47. U.S., Congress, House, Committee on Internal Security, *Annual Report for the Year 1970*, 91st Cong., 2d sess., reads: "Planning for the fall offensive reflected a consistent pattern of communist involvement. Meetings were held, among other localities, in Washington, D.C., Chicago, St. Louis, Philadelphia, and San Francisco. Evidence in the hearing record and in the committee staff study shows that the Communist Party, Socialist Workers Party, Young Socialist Alliance, and Student Mobilization Committee played leading roles in this planning and, to a large extent, have managed to dominate the New Mobilization Committee" (p. 130). The report goes on to identify a number of Communist party members as having key roles or "playing particularly active parts in organizing": Helen Gurewitz, an identified CPUSA member, a New Mobe staff employee, and a member of the New Mobe Washington Action Committee; Irving Sarnoff and Carlton Goodlett of the WPC; Arnold Johnson and Donald Gurewitz of the CPUSA; and Terence Hallinan, of the WEB DuBois Clubs of America (a CPUSA front) were all involved in the New Mobe leadership. IPS associate William Sloane Coffin claims in his memoirs, *Once to Every Man*, that "what was agitating the many doves in Congress . . . was the presence on the steering committee of one lone member of the Communist Party, Arnold Johnson."
48. U.S., Congress, House, Committee on Internal Security, 91st Cong., 2d sess., *Annual Report for the Year 1970*, p. 130.
49. William Sloane Coffin, Jr., *Once to Every Man* (New York: Atheneum, 1977), p. 297.
50. *Quicksilver Times*, December 8–18, 1969, p. 9. (*Quicksilver Times* was a Washington, D.C., underground weekly.)
51. Muravchik, op. cit., p. 42.
52. FBI Bureau File #447935-60, February 2, 1971, p. 6.
53. "Vietnam Bulletin," March 15, 1971.
54. Robert Elegant, "How to Lose a War: Reflections of a Foreign Correspondent," *Encounter* (London), August 1981, p. 76.
55. U.S., Congress, House, Committee on Internal Security, *Annual Report for the Year 1970*, 91st Cong., 2d sess., p. 149.
56. Liberation News Service, press release, March 14, 1970.
57. U.S., Congress, House Committee on Internal Security, *Annual Report for the Year 1973*, 93d Cong., 1st sess., January 24, 1974, p. 25.
58. Fred Halstead, *Out Now* (New York: Monad Press, 1979), p. 536.
59. Ibid., p. 547.
60. FBI Bureau File #447935-48, December 29, 1970, p. 2.
61. Fanning, op. cit., p. 87.
62. Sidney Blumenthal, "The Left Stuff: IPS and the Long Road Back," *Washington Post*, July 30, 1986, p. D2.
63. U.S., Congress, House, Subcommittee on Asian and Pacific Affairs of the Committee on Foreign Affairs, *Legislation on the Indochina War*, 92d Cong., 1st sess., 1971.
64. George McGovern was first elected with the help of a sizable monetary contribution from the Council for a Livable World, of which Richard Barnet was a board member. McGovern served as a vice president of MCPL. Mark Hatfield, also a member of MCPL, has since become a faculty member at the IPS Washington School.
65. The defense procurement bill that finally passed Congress did include specific restrictions on the commander in chief's ability to maneuver in the war in Indochina. Appropriations could not exceed of $2.8 billion for "the use of the Armed Forces

of the United States . . . to support (A) South Vietnamese and other free world forces in support of Vietnamese, (B) local forces in Laos and Thailand . . .'' (signed into Public Law 91-441 on October 7, 1970).

66. Lyndon B. Johnson, *The Vantage Point* (New York: Holt, Rinehart & Winston, 1971), p. 379.

67. Alvin Z. Rubinstein, *The Foreign Policy of the Soviet Union* (New York: Random House, 1972), p. 367.

68. Fanning, op. cit., p. 88.

69. Ibid., p. 89.

70. FBI Bureau File #447935, April 23, 1971, p. 15.

71. Ibid.

72. U.S., Congress, Senate, Committee on Foreign Relations, *Legislation on the Indochina War*, 92d Cong., 1st sess., 1971.

73. Sen. Vance Hartke (D-Ind.), Reps. Abner Mikva (D-Ill.), John Conyers (D-Mich.), Bella Abzug (D-N.Y.), and Herman Badillo (D-N.Y.). Meanwhile Sens. George McGovern (D-S. Dak.), Walter Mondale (D-Minn.), Philip Hart (D-Mich.), Edward Kennedy (D-Mass.), and Reps. Bella Abzug and Charles Vanik (D-Ohio) addressed a newly formed group known as the Vietnam Veterans against the War, which was participating in the PCPJ spring offensive.

Chapter 4: Machinations Behind the Scoop

1. Sanford J. Ungar, *The Papers and the Papers* (New York: E. P. Dutton, 1972), p. 19.

2. Ibid., p. 29.

3. Ibid., p. 56.

4. Ibid., p. 57. Ellsberg claims to have received this authorization from the assistant secretary of defense, Paul Warnke, although according to Ungar, "neither Leslie Gelb nor Paul Warnke remember any such arrangement."

5. United States Constitution, art. 1, sec. 6.

6. Harrison E. Salisbury, *Without Fear or Favor: An Uncompromising Look at the New York Times* (New York: Ballantine Books, 1980), p. 75.

   In spring 1970 FBI officer William McDermott approached Richard Best, Rand's top security official, about the possibility that Ellsberg had removed classified documents (namely, the Vietnam study papers) and reproduced them outside Rand. Rand's head, Dr. Harry Rowen, a close friend of Ellsberg's, told the FBI that an air force or Defense Department inquiry was going to be made into the matter, and the FBI dropped its investigation. Curiously, no investigation was ever undertaken. Ellsberg retained his security clearance at Rand and continued to work there intermittently, even copying other classified documents relating to the war.

7. Daniel Ellsberg, interview, October 16, 1978, as cited in Salisbury, op. cit., p. 88.

8. Ungar, op. cit., p. 78.

9. Salisbury, op. cit., pp. 85–86.

10. David Halberstam, *The Powers That Be* (New York: Alfred A. Knopf, 1979), p. 568.

11. Russ Braley, *Bad News: The Foreign Policy of the New York Times* (Chicago: Regnery, Gateway, 1984), p. 397.

12. FBI Bureau File WFO #100-447935, November 5, 1971, p. 4.

13. Ungar, op. cit., p. 131.

14. FBI Bureau File WFO #100-447935, November 5, 1971, p. 5.
15. The law firm of Rabinowitz and Boudin has served as chief legal counsel for Fidel Castro, Alger Hiss, and Soviet spy Judith Coplon. Incidentally, this is the Leonard Boudin whose daughter Kathy was a leader of the urban terrorist group Weather Underground, which took credit for bombing the U.S. Capitol, the Pentagon, the State Department, and two dozen other government buildings in the 1970s. Kathy was arrested and sentenced to twenty years for her part in the 1981 Brinks armored car holdup in Nyack, New York, an incident which left three people dead.
16. IPS Annual Report, "Beginning the Second Decade," 1973, p. 30.
17. Ungar, op. cit., p. 257.
18. *San Francisco Examiner*, March 19, 1968.
19. Ungar, op. cit., p. 268.
20. Edward Jay Epstein, *Legend: The Secret World of Lee Harvey Oswald* (New York: McGraw-Hill, 1978), pp. 260–65.
21. Gay Telese, back-cover endorsement of Salisbury, op. cit.
22. *Congressional Record*, February 8, 1977, p. E625.

Chapter 5: Blinding America

1. FBI Bureau File #100-447935; Report from the Los Angeles Field Office, November 27, 1970.
2. Richard J. Barnet, *The Economy of Death* (New York: Atheneum, 1969), p. 45.
3. Richard J. Barnet, "Dirty Tricks and the Underworld," *Transaction: Social Science and Modern Society*, vol. 12, no. 3, p. 57.
4. Ibid.
5. Barnet, *Economy of Death*, pp. 178–79.
6. Ibid., p. 179.
7. Ernest W. Lefever and Roy Godson, *The CIA and the American Ethic: An Unfinished Debate* (Washington, D.C.: Ethics and Public Policy Center, 1979), p. 75.
8. Paul Dickson, *Think Tanks* (New York: Atheneum, 1971), p. 283.
9. Notes of minutes of CNSS founding conference.
10. Barnet, "Dirty Tricks," p. 57.
11. Ibid.
12. Ibid.
13. IPS-Transnational Institute, *The Link*, February 1975.
14. *Congressional Record*, September 10, 1975, p. E4657.
15. Philip Abbott Luce, *Report on the Americas and the World* (Washington, D.C.: Council for Inter-American Security), vol. 4, no. 8, p. 1.
16. The interlocking relationships between the groups is well illustrated by the case of Peter Weiss, IPS chairman of the board. Weiss is also a prominent member of the National Lawyers Guild, the vice president of the Center for Constitutional Rights, a National Council member of the National Emergency Civil Liberties Committee, and an advisory committee member of the Center for National Security Studies.
17. Seymour Hersh, "CIA Is Linked to Strikes in Chile That Beset Allende," *New York Times*, September 20, 1974, p. 1.
18. Seymour Hersh, "Huge CIA Operation Reported in U.S. Against Antiwar Forces, Other Dissidents in Nixon Years," *New York Times*, December 22, 1974, p. 1.
19. U.S., Congress, Senate, Select Committee to Study the Governmental Operations

COVERT CADRE

with Respect to Intelligence Activities (henceforth referred to as the Church committee), *Final Report*, bk. 1, p. 7.
20. Lefever and Godson, op. cit., p. 35.
21. Church committee, *Final Report*, bk. 1, p. 7.
22. Frank Church, review of *Global Reach*, by Richard J. Barnet, *Washington Post Book World*, January 19, 1975.
23. In a *Washington Post* article of January 22, 1984, p. C7, Frank Church wrote: "Until we learn to live with revolution, we will continue to blunder, and it will work to the Soviets' advantage. It will put them on the winning side, while we put ourselves on the side of rotten, corrupt regimes that end up losing. And each time one of those regimes is overthrown, it feeds the paranoia in this country about the spread of communism. It furthers the premise of the national security state, which means more militarism, more censorship, more spending, more deficits—and more casualties."

   Such a perspective was in keeping with the IPS worldview. Church's analysis even applies a specific term in describing the United States—"the national security state"—a term coined by IPS.

   In another *Washington Post* commentary, in March 1984, p. C4, Church said: "We should stop exaggerating the threat of Marxist revolution in Third World countries. . . . The domino theory is no more valid in Central America than it was in Southeast Asia." Ironically, for most historians, the course of events that took place in Southeast Asia after the U.S. withdrew did more to vindicate than repudiate the domino theory.
24. *Village Voice*, cover story, February 16, 1976.
25. James L. Tyson, *Target America* (Chicago: Regnery, Gateway, 1981), p. 197.
26. William Colby has written that "every" new project subjected to the procedure of the Hughes-Ryan Act in 1975 was leaked. See William Colby, *Honorable Men* (New York: Simon and Schuster, 1978), p. 423.
27. Tyson, op. cit., p. 195.
28. Lefever and Godson, op. cit., p. 73. Also see *ACLU Annual Report*, 1970–71, p. 23.
29. U.S., Congress, House, Committee on Un-American Activities, *Annual Reports, 1957–1959*.
30. The strategy of the antiintelligence lobby was perhaps best paraphrased at a 1971 National Lawyers Guild convention in Boulder, Colorado, by one of the leaders present who proclaimed to his fellow guild members, "I am a double agent . . . and . . . I want to use the system to bring down the system."
31. There have been some twenty-five articles and books in English alone alleging that senior U.S. trade union officials have been CIA agents of one kind or another. Almost all of these publications cite as their sources publications of other authors. Only two people, Philip Agee and Tom Braden, claim firsthand knowledge of this relationship. Failing to produce any substantial documentary evidence of their own, writers have for the most part cited Agee and Braden again and again.
32. J. G. Heitink, "Philip Agee's Friends and the Forgotten Prisoners," *De Telegraf* (Amsterdam, Holland), June 4, 1977.
33. Philip Agee, "Rendezvous in Geneva," *CounterSpy*, vol. 3, no. 2, p. 18.
34. Heitink, op. cit.
35. Ibid.
36. Philip Agee, *Inside the Company: A CIA Diary* (Middlesex, England: Penguin Books, 1975), acknowledgments.

37. John M. Ashbrook, "A Report on the Impact of the Anti-Intelligence Lobby on the Foreign and Domestic Intelligence Capabilities of the United States," manuscript, p. 52.
38. "Trotskyism and Terrorism," *Congressional Record*, pts. 1–15, August 30, 31; September 1, 2, 8–10, 22, 23; October 1, 1976.
39. *Congressional Record*, Extensions of Remarks, May 28, 1980, p. E2619.
40. Robert Moss, *London Daily Telegraph*, December 4, 1978, p. 6.
41. Intercontinental Press, February 10, 1975, p. 177.
42. Ibid.
43. "Fifth Estate Update," *CounterSpy*, vol. 2, no. 1, p. 4.
44. Philip Agee, "Exposing the CIA," *CounterSpy*, Winter 1975, p. 20.
45. *CounterSpy*, Winter 1976, pp. 3–4.
46. "Richard S. Welch," *Washington Post*, December 29, 1975, p. A16.
47. Morton Halperin, "CIA News Management," *Washington Post*, January 23, 1977, p. C3.
48. U.S., Congress, Senate, Subcommittee to Investigate the Administration of the Internal Security Act and Other Internal Security Laws of the Committee on the Judiciary, Part I: *Organizing Committee for a Fifth Estate*, 94th Cong., 2d sess., March 26, 1976, pp. 24–25.
49. Ibid.
50. Ibid.
51. Paul Jacobs, "Who Is Richard Welch?" *CounterSpy*, Winter 1976, p. 29.
52. Ibid., pp. 3–4.
53. Philip Agee, "Why I Split the CIA and Spilled the Beans," *Esquire*, June 1975, p. 128.
54. Peter Studer, "Philip Agee—Turncoat CIA Agent," *Tages Anzeiger* (Zurich, Switzerland), March 1975 (undated clipping).
55. "Inside the CIA: An Interview with Philip Agee," *Intercontinental Press*, February 10, 1975, p. 173.
56. U.S., Congress, Senate, Committee on the Judiciary, Hearings before the Subcommittee to Investigate the Administration of the Internal Security Act and Other Internal Security Laws, *Subversion of Law Enforcement Intelligence Gathering Operations*, 94th Cong., 2d sess., March 26, 1976.
57. Ibid.
58. Ladislav Bittman, *The KGB and Soviet Disinformation* (New York: Pergamon-Brassey's International Defense Publishers, 1985), p. 190.
59. Ibid., p. 189.
60. J. G. Heitink, "The Netherlands: A Controversy Among the Allies," *De Telegraf*, April 27, 1977.
61. *Factsheet: IPS in the New York Times Magazine*, Institute for Policy Studies, Washington, D.C., May 5, 1981, p. 5.
62. Ashbrook, op. cit., p. 33.
63. *Covert Action Information Bulletin* (Premier Issue), July 1978, p. 3.
64. Moss, op. cit.
65. Cord Meyer, *Facing Reality: From World Federalism to the CIA* (New York: Harper & Row, 1980), p. 202.
66. For Seymour Hersh, see articles already cited; see also *New York Times*, September 11, 24; October 17, 1974. For William Greider, see "CIA Is Reported to Fear Links to Three Assassination Plots," *Washington Post*, June 3, 1975.
67. Church committee, *Final Report*, vol. 7.

68. Tyson, op. cit., p. 189.
69. "Documents: U.S. Nuclear War Plans for Europe," *CounterSpy*, March–May 1983, pp. 53–59.
70. William Preston, Jr., and Ellen Ray, "Disinformation and Mass Deception: Democracy as a Cover Story," *Covert Action Information Bulletin*, Spring–Summer 1983, p. 7.
71. Ibid., pp. 2, 5.
72. "Join the Campaign for Political Rights Network," Campaign for Political Rights, March 1982.
73. Francis J. McNamara, "FOIA: A Good Law That Must Be Changed," manuscript. See also *Human Events*, October 29, 1983, p. 12.
74. Ibid.
75. Ibid.
76. Ibid.
77. Ibid., p. 11.
78. Ibid.
79. Francis J. McNamara, *U.S. Counterintelligence Today* (Washington, D.C.: Nathan Hale Institute), pp. 71–72.
80. IPS 1981 Catalogue, p. 14.
81. *Congressional Record*, Extensions of Remarks, May 28, 1980, p. E2619.
82. Ibid.
83. Seymour Hersh, *New York Times*, December 22, 1974.
84. "Levi Guidelines for FBI Domestic Security Investigations," p. 1.
85. Raymond Wannell, former assistant director, FBI, Intelligence Division; interview, October 15, 1984.
86. FBI File WFO #185-425: "The Letelier Address Book."
87. American Civil Liberties Union, Annual Report, 1970–71.
88. Center for National Security Studies Annual Report, 1982.
89. See list of congressmen who endorsed this alternative budget study by IPS in Marcus G. Raskin, ed., *The Federal Budget and Social Reconstruction* (Washington, D.C.: Institute for Policy Studies, 1978), p. viii. Also, Don Edwards was one of the fifty-one congressmen who agreed to seek IPS for an alternative budget study in 1982.
90. Letter from Don Edwards, Congress of the United States, House of Representatives, Washington, D.C. 20515, June 1983.
91. "For the Record," *Washington Post*, July 27, 1980.
92. Ibid.
93. *Human Events*, April 10, 1982, p. 4.
94. Ronald Reagan, November 11, 1982.
95. Nat Hentoff, "The Passionate Congressman and the Wayward Press," *Village Voice*, December 14, 1982.
96. Edwards to William Webster, November 17, 1982.
97. Webster to Edwards, December 9, 1982.
98. Edwards to Webster, November 17, 1982.
99. The reader may find it peculiar that a Soviet front such as the World Peace Council could meet freely in the halls of the U.S. Congress, but in fact this privilege is encouraged by federal law. The statute prohibits the FBI from conducting intelligence activities in the Capitol or any of the congressional office buildings, without special authorization from a federal judge.
100. John M. Ashbrook, memorandum on World Peace Council, Institute for Policy Studies, and SANE, May 8, 1981.

101. "WPC Call from Washington" (World Peace Council, Helsinki, Finland), 1978, p. 4.
102. Federal Election Commission records, 1325 K Street, N.W., Washington, D.C.
103. *Human Events*, September 1, 1979, p. 1.
104. United States District Court for the District of Columbia, Civil Action 74-316: *Institute for Policy Studies, et al.* v. *John N. Mitchell, et al.* "Stipulated Settlement of Issues and Dismissal," par. 3.
105. IPS Annual Report, 1979–80, p. 3.
106. Robert Borosage, "Report from Nicaragua and Cuba," lecture and discussion at IPS, December 12, 1983.
107. *Human Events*, September 26, 1981.
108. Listed by Daniel Tsang, research librarian on the Alternatives Acquisitions Project, Temple University Libraries, Philadelphia, in "Anti-Surveillance Periodicals," *Library Journal*, December 1, 1979.
109. "A Summary of Its Functions and Activities," Center for National Security Studies brochure.
110. Barnet, "Dirty Tricks," p. 57.
111. Center for National Security Studies, Annual Report, 1982.
112. Edwards to William H. Webster, April 12, 1983.
113. Ray Wannell, interview, March 5, 1985.
114. William Webster, official text of speech delivered to American Newspaper Publishers Association, Atlanta, May 3, 1978, p. 7.
115. McNamara, *Counterintelligence*, p. 58.
116. Campaign for Political Rights, Annual Report, 1982, p. 19.
117. McNamara, "FOIA," p. 12.
118. McNamara, *Counterintelligence*, p. 72.
119. U.S., Congress, Senate, Subcommittee on Security and Terrorism, *FBI Oversight Hearings*, 97th Cong., 2d sess., February 4, 1982, p. 19.
120. "A Summary of Its Functions and Activities," Center for National Security Studies brochure, p. 4.
121. Michael Parenti, lecture, February 21, 1984, at IPS seminar, "Increasing FBI Domestic Activities."
122. Dan Schernber, lecture, February 21, 1984, at IPS seminar, "Increasing FBI Domestic Activities."
123. *Domestic Cover*, Center on Government Repression newsletter, Winter 1984; and handout, "When the FBI Comes."
124. Howard Aylesworth, *Domestic Cover*, Center on Government Repression newsletter, Winter 1984.

Chapter 6: Dividing American Alliances

1. Jeane Kirkpatrick, as quoted in *Washington Times*, June 26, 1985, p. D1.
2. Marcus Raskin, interview, December 15, 1983.
3. Earl C. Ravenal, "The Dialectic of Military Spending" from *The Federal Budget and Social Reconstruction*, ed. Marcus Raskin (Washington, D.C.: Institute for Policy Studies, 1978), p. 146.
4. Richard J. Barnet, "Lies Clearer Than Truth," *Waging Peace*, ed. Jim Wallis (San Francisco: Harper & Row, 1982).
5. Richard J. Barnet, *The Alliance* (New York: Simon and Schuster, 1983), p. 133.

6. Ibid., p. 431.
7. Barnet, *Alliance*, p. 133.
8. Ibid.
9. Marcus G. Raskin, *The Politics of National Security* (New Brunswick, N.J.: Transaction Books, 1979), p. 32.
10. Ibid., p. 34.
11. Marcus G. Raskin, *Being and Doing* (New York: Random House, 1971), pp. xii–xiii.
12. Raskin, *National Security*, p. 57.
13. Ibid., p. 58.
14. Richard J. Barnet, *The Giants: Russia and America* (New York: Simon and Schuster, 1977), p. 92.
15. Harry Rositzke, *The KGB: The Eyes of Russia* (Garden City, N.Y.: Doubleday, 1981), p. 79.
16. Barnet, *Giants*, p. 96.
17. Barnet, *Alliance*, p. 20.
18. Ibid., p. 22.
19. Ibid.
20. Ibid.
21. Richard J. Barnet, *Regional Security Systems*, p. 89.
22. Barnet, *Alliance*, p. 426.
23. Ibid., p. 428.
24. Ibid., p. 435.
25. Marcus Raskin, interview, December 15, 1983.
26. Richard J. Barnet and Marcus G. Raskin, *After 20 Years: Alternatives to Cold War in Europe* (New York: Random House, 1965), p. 63.
27. "Denmark Reevaluating Commitments to NATO," *Washington Post*, November 5, 1979.
28. Marcus Raskin, interview, December 15, 1983.
29. Cynthia Enloe in Wendy Chapkis, *Women in the Military* (Amsterdam: Transnational Institute, 1981), p. 51.
30. IPS Annual Report, 1983, pp. 10–11.
31. U.S., Congress, House, David Chappell, "Statement on the Strategic Context and Flawed Premises of the Proposed Compact of Free Association," before the Subcommittees on Asian and Pacific Affairs, International Operations and Human Rights, Foreign Affairs Committee, April 23, 1985.
32. Barnet, *Alliance*, p. 421.
33. TASS, December 23, 1984, on U.S. intentions toward Iceland.
34. John Lofton, "When 'the Public's Right to Know' Is More Important Than Survival," *Washington Times*, undated clipping.
35. William Steerman, interview, August 7, 1985.
36. Department of Defense News Briefing, June 13, 1985, 11:30 A.M., Michael I. Burch, ASD/PA.
37. Ibid.
38. IPS promotional literature for *Nuclear Battlefields*.
39. William M. Arkin and Richard W. Fieldhouse, *Nuclear Battlefields: Global Links in the Arms Race* (Cambridge, Mass.: Ballinger, 1985), p. 155.
40. Victor Suvorov, *Inside the Soviet Army* (New York: Macmillan, 1982), p. 20.

Chapter 7: From the Lawsuit Against the FBI to the Government Accountability Project

1. FBI Bureau File #44-56700, WFO #44-951, report of interview with Marcus Raskin, June 6, 1973.

2. FBI Bureau File #44-56700, WFO #44-951, Mitchell Rogovin to FBI Director William Ruckelshaus, May 25, 1973.
3. FBI Bureau File #44-56700, WFO #44-951, undated report.
4. FBI Bureau File #44-56700, WFO #44-951, Mitchell Rogovin to J. Stanley Pottinger, June 25, 1973.
5. Ibid.
6. FBI Bureau File #44-56700, WFO #44-951, AIRTEL, November 16, 1973, p. 4.
7. Ibid.
8. FBI Bureau File #44-56700, WFO #175-398, PLAINTEXT Teletype from FBI director to SAC, Detroit, May 27, 1976.
9. David H. White, counsel for FBI defendant, telephone interview, April 26, 1984.
10. U.S. District Court for the D.C., Civil Action No. 74-316: "Stipulated Settlement of Issues and Dismissal," filed October 3, 1979, James F. Davey, clerk.
11. When Ralph Stavins and George Pipkin were subpoenaed to testify before a grand jury about their involvement with the Pentagon Papers, both refused to make any statement.
12. FBI Bureau File #100-447935-2, report from Minneapolis field office, December 10, 1970.
13. Government Accountability Project promotional brochure.
14. FBI Bureau File #100-447935-45, report from Los Angeles field office, November 27, 1970.
15. Government Accountability Project promotional brochure.

Chapter 8: Fourth-Estate Interface

1. FBI File WFO#185-425 reveals that while Orlando Letelier was director of the Transnational Institute, the international arm of IPS, he was receiving funds from Cuba, disbursed by Beatriz Allende. In her youth in Santiago, Chile, Beatriz Allende acted as an intelligence courier for the Cuban DGI agent Luis Fernandez Ona, whom she later married. At the time of Mrs. Allende Ona's dealings with Letelier, her husband had risen to second in command of the Cuban DGI. It would have been unlikely, if not impossible, for Mrs. Allende Ona to be involved with Letelier without her husband's knowledge and approval. As there are no "private-sector" international monetary transactions allowed by the Cuban government, it is doubtful that Beatriz Allende Ona could have transferred funds to Letelier in the United States without the approval and cooperation of DGI. Inasmuch as the international operations of DGI are basically under Soviet control, it is also likely that the KGB was in on the Letelier case.
2. FBI File WFO #185-425 contains numerous items, such as Letelier's personal address book, which shows contacts with twenty-seven reporters and editors in major U.S. media institutions. Letelier worked closely with left-wing public-interest groups such as the Corporate Data Exchange, the Washington Office on Latin America (WOLA), North American Congress on Latin America (NACLA), the Center for International Policy (CIP), and the Council on Hemispheric Affairs (COHA)—all of which actively sought to influence the media. Letelier served on the advisory boards of CIP and COHA, while wife Isabel served on the advisory board of WOLA. CIP says in its statement of purpose that it "works towards its goals through a *network* of journalists, former diplomats, and international officials here and abroad."

The documents that the FBI recovered from Letelier's briefcase include statements of the activities and personal correspondence from the leaders of WOLA, CIP, COHA, and NACLA.

Why was Letelier carrying all this material in his briefcase? We know from the text of Saul Landau's letter to a Cuban friend, Pablo Armando Fernandez—"Since Orlando Letelier is going to Cuba I will give him a quick letter to bring to you"—that Letelier was on his way to Cuba. Letelier may have been carrying these documents because they would be of interest to Cuban intelligence.

3. Karen DeYoung and Milton Coleman, "Victim Denounced Policies of Junta," *Washington Post*, September 22, 1976, p. 1.

4. Lee Lescaze, "Letelier Briefcase Opened to the Press," *Washington Post*, February 17, 1977; and Saul Landau, "A Campaign to Smear Letelier," *Washington Post*, February 18, 1986.

5. *Washington Post*, September 22, 1976, editorial.

6. FBI File WFO #185-425; Saul Landau to Pablo Armando Fernandez.

7. Ibid.

8. Saul Landau's films on Cuba include *Fidel* (1972) and *Cuba and Fidel* (1975). Landau has also produced political propaganda films for pro-Soviet socialist governments such as Allende's Chile and Manley's Jamaica. One recent Landau film, *Paul Jacobs and the Nuclear Gang*, portraying the U.S. government as irresponsible in its nuclear research, won the Emmy Award in 1980. Landau's most recent film, *Target Nicaragua: Inside a Covert War*, is a pro-Sandinista film promoted by IPS. IPS also promotes an East German propaganda film, *The Dead Are Not Silent*, which stars IPS fellow Isabel Letelier.

9. Robert Lichter and Stanley Rothman, "The Media Elite: How Reporters Lean to the Left," *Public Opinion*, October 1981.

10. Irving Kristol, as cited in *Wall Street Journal*, October 14, 1982.

11. Leslie Gelb, *New York Times*, as cited in the IPS Annual Report, 1979–1980, p. 3.

12. On the occasion of U.S. intervention in Grenada, Secretary of State George Shultz explained why the media were initially excluded: "It seems as though reporters are always against us. They're always seeking to report something that's going to screw things up."

13. IPS Ten Year Report, "Beginning the Second Decade," p. 9.

14. In "The Power of the Press" (*Policy Review*, Fall 1978, p. 18), noted lawyer and distinguished ambassador Max Kampelman observes that "it is not easy and frequently not exciting for an intelligent person simply to report events. The tendency has been for imaginative and socially dedicated journalists to go beyond normal reporting in order to seek fuller expression of their talents or social values."

    In "Media Revolution" (*Washington Times*, October 25, 1983, p. C1), Ernest van den Haag, Fordham University professor and member of the U.S. National News Council, notes, "It would be naive to believe, as one might have in the past, that the media merely report on events such as revolutions. Today, more than ever, the media stimulate, magnify, spread, and even produce events."

15. Government Accountability Project promotional brochure.

16. Government Accountability Project Annual Report, 1982–1983.

17. Philip Agee announced the founding of *Covert Action Information Bulletin* in Havana in 1978 while participating in the Eleventh World Youth Festival, a major undertaking of two international Soviet CCP fronts, the Budapest-based World Federation of Democratic Youth (WFDY) and the Prague-based International Union of Students (IUS).

18. Philip Agee, as cited in *Human Events*, September 26, 1981.
19. Karen DeYoung, "Foreign Reporting," statement, IPS Washington School, summer 1980; tape-recorded by journalist Cliff Kincaid.
20. Karen DeYoung, *Washington Post*, October 16, 1978.
21. Ibid., July 6, 1979.
22. Ibid., July 23, 1979.
23. Ibid., "Share and Be Nice," *Washington Post*, July 29, 1979.
24. Miguel Bolanos Hunter, interview, July 27, 1983.
25. Karen DeYoung, *Washington Post*, interview with Miguel Bolanos Hunter, June 16–17, 1983.
26. Karen DeYoung, "The White Hand of Terror," *Mother Jones*, June 1981.
27. Ibid.
28. Alma Guillermoprieto was a paying guest at the 1984 Letelier-Moffitt Memorial Human Rights Award ceremony at the Capitol Hilton, September 21, 1984.
29. Joanne Omang, statement at IPS Washington School course, "Foreign Reporting," April 12, 1984.
30. Elizabeth Becker, as cited by James L. Tyson, *Target America* (Chicago: Regnery, Gateway, 1981), p. 262.
31. Ibid.
32. Elizabeth Becker, as cited by "Accuracy in Media Report," January 1979, no. 2.
33. Roger Wilkins, *New York Times*, July 12, 1983, p. A23.
34. "Accuracy in Media Report," vol. 8, no. 17, p. 3.
35. Teofilo Acosta, statement (tape-recorded), memorial service for Larry Stern, former *Washington Post* national news editor, August 14, 1979. Larry Stern was one of twenty-seven media contacts found in the address book of Orlando Letelier, "agent of influence" working with the Cuban DGI. Acosta was another of Letelier's frequent contacts in Washington.
36. I. F. Stone, statement (tape-recorded), memorial service for Larry Stern, former *Washington Post* national news editor, August 14, 1979.
37. Ibid.
38. Alexander Cockburn, *Village Voice*, September 10, 1979.
39. Ibid.
40. Peter Osnos, statement at IPS Washington School course, "Foreign Reporting," summer 1980; tape-recorded by journalist Cliff Kincaid.
41. Peter Osnos, *Washington Post*, March 11, 1979.
42. Robert Kaiser, *Washington Post*, June 9, 1981.
43. Most complete account of how the story was written appears in "Invisible Hand of Philip Agee," *Human Events*, July 11, 1981, pp. 5–6.
44. Howard Simon, statement, November 8, 1982, lecture, sponsored by the Commitee for Public Policy, University of Chicago.
45. At the IPS Washington School course, "Talking with the Russians," November 28, 1983, senior fellow Roger Wilkins said that "probably one-third of the Soviet delegates at the 'Minneapolis Dialogue' were KGB." He elaborated in a curious fashion: "Whether or not they are KGB doesn't really matter . . . because I'm sure that their minds are at the service of the Soviet government."
46. John Dinges, "Government Responsible for Violent Deaths," *Washington Post*, January 27, 1983.
47. John Dinges, *Progressive*, May 1982, p. 26.
48. John Dinges, statement, IPS Washington School class, April 5, 1984.
49. Ibid.

50. Shultz, op. cit.
51. Dinges, IPS Washington School class April 5, 1984.
52. Joanne Omang, statement, "The Cuban Revolution and the Media," Washington, D.C., November 17, 1984.
53. Stanford J. Ungar, *The Papers and the Papers* (New York: E. P. Dutton, 1972), p. 134. Also see FBI File WFO #100-447935, which makes reference to the people associated with Cambridge Institute, an IPS spinoff, helping Daniel Ellsberg while he was in hiding in Cambridge, Massachusetts.
54. M. S. Evans, "The Brethren: A Hatchet Job," *Human Events*, January 26, 1980, p. 11.
55. Sally Quinn Bradlee, *Washington Weekly*, August 16, 1979.
56. T. D. Allman, "U.S.–Backed Laos Troops Capture Two Rebel Areas," *New York Times*, September 18, 1969, p. 1.
57. Ibid.
58. John H. Maury, interview, August 16, 1981. See also U.S., Congress, House, Committee on Oversight of the Permanent Select Committee on Intelligence, "The CIA and the Media," 95th Cong., 1st and 2d sess. pp. 51–60.
59. Glenn MacDonald, *Report or Distort?* (Jericho, N.Y.: Exposition Press, 1973), p. 70.
60. David Armstrong, *A Trumpet to Arms: Alternative Media in America* (Los Angeles: J. P. Tarcher, 1981), p. 113.
61. Seymour Hersh, *New York Times*, September 7, 1974, pp. 1, 26.
62. Ibid., December 21, 1974, pp. 1, 26.
63. Seymour M. Hersh, "The Target Is Destroyed," *Atlantic Monthly*, September 1986, p. 46.
64. Seymour M. Hersh, *The Target Is Destroyed* (New York: Random House, 1986), p. 191.
65. Hersh, *Atlantic Monthly*, p. 47.
66. Thomas Powers, "Believing the Worst of Each Other," *New York Times Book Review*, September 21, 1986, p. 3.
67. Hersh, *Target Is Destroyed*, p. 269.
68. According to FBI Bureau File WFO #100-447935, November 5, 1971, p. 4, Ellsberg was staying at the Hotel Dupont Plaza, adjacent to IPS, at the time that Sheehan received his copy of the documents. The FBI report indicates that in all probability Ellsberg was staying there "to obtain the remainder of the study from IPS for Sheehan to Xerox in the early part of April 1971."
69. U.S., Congress, Senate, Committee on the Judiciary, Subcommittee on Internal Security (SSIS) Hearings, November 18, 1975; and SSIS Hearings, November 3–6, 10, 1969. See also *U.S. News & World Report*, February 27, 1967.
   While Salisbury admits in his book, *Behind Enemy Lines—Hanoi*, that he contacted "a number of Soviet newspapermen and other Communists, asking their assistance in gaining entry to North Vietnam," and that "some of them helped," he fails to credit Burchett explicitly as being the key facilitator. In writing the Introduction to Wilfred Burchett's memoirs, *At the Barricades*, published by the *New York Times*, Salisbury says, "Burchett has always possessed a gift for friendship. Few are the journalists who met and worked beside him in World War II in China and Burma or with the U.S. Fleet in the Pacific who did not become his enduring friends."
70. Virginia Prewett, interview, November 15, 1984.
71. Paul Hollander, *Political Pilgrims* (New York: Oxford University Press, 1980), p. 388.

72. Armstrong, op. cit., pp. 113–14.
73. Robert Kagan, "Realities and Myths of the Vietnam War," *Wall Street Journal*, April 1, 1982, editorial page.
74. MacDonald, op. cit., p. 61.
75. *U.S. News & World Report*, February 27, 1967.
76. Armstrong, op. cit.
77. Arnaud DeBorchgrave, interview, October 11, 1983.
78. Steve Munson, informal survey of the *New York Times* for 1980.
79. Lexis Noxis survey of the *New York Times* for 1981.
80. Ray Bonner, statement, IPS Washington School class, April 19, 1984.
81. Ibid.
82. Ibid., IPS lunch seminar, June 14, 1984.
83. Ibid., IPS Washington School class, April 19, 1984.
84. Ibid.
85. Ibid.
86. Monitoring of Radio Venceremos broadcasts by USIA has confirmed that the guerrillas claimed responsibility for deaths on many occasions in 1981, 1982, and 1983.
87. Daniel James, "Where Do Media Get Salvador Atrocity Stories," *Human Events*, March 6, 1982.
88. Ibid.
89. Ibid.
90. Karen DeYoung, statement, IPS Washington School course, "Foreign Reporting," summer 1980.
91. Ray Bonner, statement, IPS Washington School, April 19, 1984.
92. Carlucci to Rosenthal, February 19, 1982.
93. Ray Bonner, *New York Times*, June 4, 1982, p. 3.
94. *Center Magazine*, January/February 1982.
95. Ibid.
96. This was the perception of U.S. embassy officials in San Salvador at that time. Embassy source requested anonymity.
97. Ray Bonner, statement, IPS Washington School, April 19, 1984.
98. IPS Washington School catalogue, Spring 1984, p. 7.
99. David Burnham, *New York Times*, March 31, 1979, p. 1.
100. The City Voting Records of New York City for 1936 indicate that Samuel Rubin was registered as a Communist party member. The Office of Public Information at Columbia University describes the goals of the Rubin program as advancing "the ideals of [Samuel Rubin], an innovative philanthropist who was sensitive throughout his life to the needs and rights of the poor and defenseless and dedicated to the concern for universal human rights and the peaceful resolution of economic and social conflict." Further, Columbia describes Sam Rubin as the founder of Fabergé, Incorporated, and "a patron of the arts, medicine and education."

Normally, when an endowment is made to an institution, the donor vests the recipient institution with full responsibility and control over the funds and their application. However, Cora Rubin Weiss and Peter Weiss gave the funds to establish the Rubin Program for the Advancement of Liberty and Equality Through Law at Columbia with the precondition that the program "be directed by an advisory committee consisting of members of the Law School faculty, the Samuel Rubin Foundation and the public." Essentially, this means that the Weisses have a great deal to say about who participates and what curriculum is chosen for the program.
101. Anthony Lewis, *New York Times*, October 10, 1983, p. A25.

102. Ibid., September 11, 1983, p. A23.
103. It is estimated by Western counterintelligence analysts that at least 50 percent of all TASS representatives are actually intelligence officers working for the KGB. According to Thomas Schuman, a KGB defector who once worked for Novosti in Moscow, "Our main job was spying, subversion, recruiting agents, and sending reports back to Moscow . . . and at least 75 percent of Novosti staffers are KGB employees" (*Toronto Sunday Star*, February 26, 1978, p. B150).
104. Tom Wicker, *New York Times*, October 3, 1983, p. A23.
105. Herman H. Dinsmore, *All the News That Fits* (New Rochelle, N.Y.: Arlington House, 1969).
106. Flora Lewis, *New York Times*, March 6, 1981, p. A23.
107. Sam Donaldson, ABC White House correspondent, 9:00 A.M. "C-Span" call-in program, April 26, 1984.
108. Alice Widener, interview, October 5, 1970, manuscript.
109. *Saturday Evening Post*, October 9, 1965.
110. Robert Novak, interview, August 10, 1984.

Chapter 9: Transmission Belts to the Media

1. Franz Schurmann, *The Logic of World Power* (New York: Pantheon Books, 1974), p. 563.
2. Ibid., p. 564.
3. Ibid.
4. David Armstrong, *A Trumpet to Arms: Alternative Media in America* (Los Angeles: J. P. Tarcher, 1981), p. 349.
5. Ibid.
6. David Armstrong, "A Thinking Approach to the News," *Columbia Journalism Review* (September/October 1978): 62.
7. Mike Cooper, interview, September 23, 1983, as cited in Philip F. Lawler, *The Alternative Influence* (Lanham, Md.: University Press of America, 1984), p. 62.
8. Armstrong, "Thinking Approach," p. 62.
9. Pacific News Service prospectus entitled, "Delving into the Least Understood Side of the News," p. 2.
10. Ibid.
11. Schurmann, op. cit., p. xvii.
12. Foundation for National Progress, Financial Report, 1976.
13. Pacific News Service prospectus, "Delving," p. 5.
14. Sandy Close, telephone interview, October 31, 1984.
15. Michael Klare, "Is World War III Upon Us?" *Plain Dealer* (Cleveland), October 30, 1983, p. 1.
16. Fred Kaplan, who authored an IPS book on the Soviet military buildup, *Dubious Specter*, and who now writes for the *Boston Globe*, was also one of the first American journalists to pick up the Soviet line justifying the killing of 269 civilians by alleging that KAL flight 007 was engaged in a spy mission. In his *Globe* article of September 19, 1983, captioned "Korean Air Lines Linked to Nation's Intelligence Agency," Kaplan wrote that "Korean Air Lines, whose Boeing 747 was shot down by a Soviet fighter, also assembles military aircraft and has close ties to the Korean Central Intelligence Agency." Suggesting that the Korean government uses the Korean Airlines for intelligence gathering to bolster its relationship with the United States,

Kaplan asserted that "intelligence agencies of small nations [like Korea], occasionally at some risk, collect information they believe might be of value to the United States. . . ."

17. Michael Klare, "Why Soviet Paranoia Centers on the Northwest Pacific," Pacific News Service feature, September 9, 1983.
18. Pacific News Service prospectus, "Delving," p. 5.
19. Ibid., p. 2.
20. Paul L. Geopfert, "Managua Middle Class—Unsure About Sandinistas, but Far from Pro-Contra," Pacific News Service "Insight," September 25–October 1, 1983, p. 7.
21. James Ridgeway, "Thatcher Factor Worries Democrats," Pacific News Service feature, November 2, 1983.
22. Nelson Valdes, "For Cubans, Grenada Is a Symbolic Alamo," Pacific News Service feature, October 28, 1983, p. 2.
23. Ibid., p. 4.
24. Ibid., p. 5.
25. Percy Hintzen, "New U.S. Caribbean Role May Prove Complex, Costly," Pacific News Service feature, November 11, 1983, p. 6.
26. Ibid., p. 7.
27. IPS Annual Report, 1979–1980, p. 14.
28. IPS Washington School catalogue, Spring 1984, p. 7.
29. Rose Goldsen, "Assessing the Social Effects of Human Communications Systems," IPS seminar, March 20, 1984.
30. Patrick Esmond-White, "Electronic Media: A Guide for Public Interest Organizations," IPS seminar, January 17, 1984.
31. Arlen Slobodow, "Electronic Media: A Guide for Public Interest Organizations," IPS seminar, January 17, 1984.
32. Ibid.
33. Ibid.
34. Ibid.
35. IPS Annual Report, 1979–1980, p. 14.
36. FBI File WFO #185-425: "The Letelier Papers."
37. Frank Mankiewicz and Kirby Jones, *With Fidel* (New York: Ballantine Books, 1975), pp. 7–9.
38. Ibid., p. 9.
39. Betsy Cohn and Jim Angle, morning session of media workshop, Riverside Church conference on Central America, October 3, 1983.
40. IPS Washington School catalogue, Spring 1984, p. 7.
41. IPS Washington School course syllabus for "Foreign Reporting," April 5–May 10, 1984.
42. Bob Edwards, NPR "Morning Edition," March 27, 1984.
43. Robert K. Musil, telephone interview, November 15, 1984.
44. Miguel D'Escoto, SANE Radio, "Consider the Alternatives," tape no. 573, "Escalation in Central America."
45. IRS Records for Samuel Rubin Foundation for 1982, "Compensation to Officers and Directors, December 31, 1982."
46. Tom Harkin, "Tragedy in El Salvador," In the Public Interest (IPI), April 11–24, 1983, no. 295, p. 1.
47. Philip Stern, "Pushing Cuba into Russia's Arms," IPI, March 15–27, 1982, no. 267, p. 3.

48. Philip Stern, "Who's Repeating the 'Cuban Pattern'—We or the Communists?" IPI, May 10–22, 1982, no. 271, p. 6.
49. Philip Stern, "Haig and El Salvador: Refusing to Learn History's Lessons," IPI, March 29–April 10, 1982, no. 268, p. 3.
50. Corinna Gardner, "One of the Cold War's Hottest Trouble Spots," IPI, March 26–April 8, 1984, no. 320.
51. IPI promotional brochure.
52. Philip Stern, "Hostage to Bilateralism," IPI, July 18–31, 1983, no. 302, p. 1.
53. Ibid.
54. Philip Stern, "Making the World Safe for Democracy—and Others," IPI Nationwide Daily Radio Program and Press Service, August 1981, vol. 9, no. 3.
55. Philip Stern, "Fiddling with Linkage—While the World Burns," IPI, March 29–April 10, 1982, no. 268, p. 6.
56. Anne Cahn, "Bee Feces," IPI, December 5–18, 1983, no. 312, p. 2.
57. Edward P. Morgan, "Following Suit," IPI, December 19, 1983–January 1, 1984, no. 313.
58. Philip Stern, "Are the Soviets Really Superior," IPI, July 3–16, 1982, no. 275, p. 4.
59. Gene LaRoque, "How Much Is Security Worth?" IPI, April 12–24, 1982, no. 269, p. 2.
60. Gene LaRoque, "The Drums of War," IPI, April 26–May 7, 1982, no. 270, p. 5.
61. "Issues of Survival in the Modern World," Fund for Peace brochure, p. 9.
62. Ibid.
63. Robert Maslow, IPI producer and director, telephone interview, August 3, 1982.
64. Roberto Savio, transcript of 1980 interview obtained from Interlink Press Service, 777 U.N. Plaza, New York, N.Y.
65. Ibid.
66. Ibid.
67. FBI File WFO #185-425, "The Letelier Papers."
68. J. G. Heitink, "A Further Getting Acquainted with the 'New Order,' " De Telegraaf, June 22, 1977.
69. Ibid.
70. J. G. Heitink, "Pronk's Strange Ties to the Cubans," De Telegraaf, April 16, 1977, news clip.
71. Jim Lobe, IPS Washington School class, "Foreign Reporting," May 3, 1984.
72. Ibid.
73. Ibid.
74. Jim Lobe, telephone interview, March 28, 1984.
75. Claude Robinson, "United Nations: On the Slippery Legal Base of the Invasion," Inter Press Service feature, dateline New York, October 28, 1983.
76. Jim Lobe, "Grenada: U.S. Has No Plans to Complete Airport," Inter Press Service, dateline Washington, November 8, 1983.
77. Jim Lobe, "United States: Grenada Documents Don't Make Reagan's Case," Inter Press Service feature, dateline Washington, November 5, 1983.
78. Desmond Allen, "Grenada: The Airport at Point Salines," Inter Press Service feature, dateline Kingston, Jamaica, October 29, 1983.
79. Roger Boyer, Interlink Press Service, article in New York Times, February 9, 1982, p. A19.
80. Inter Press Service, factsheet.
81. Ibid.

82. Carol Skyrm, interview, July 12, 1982.
83. Although Interlink utilizes newsfeed from Rome-based Inter Press, Brennon Jones and Jim Lobe say they rely on information provided by a number of groups in the Latin network, such as the Washington Office on Latin America (WOLA), the Council on Hemispheric Affairs (COHA), the Center for International Policy (CIP), and the Coalition for a New Foreign and Military Policy (CNFMP), all of which support the revolutionary process in Latin America.
84. Sandy Close, editor-in-chief, Pacific News Service, telephone interview, October 31, 1984. Brennon Jones, interview, December 8, 1983.

Chapter 10: Bridging the Credibility Gap

1. Laurence Leamer, *The Paper Revolutionaries* (New York: Simon and Schuster, 1972), p. 83.
2. FBI File WFO #100-46784; Russ Braley, *The Foreign Policy of the New York Times* (Chicago: Regnery, Gateway, 1984), p. 160.
3. Francis M. Watson, *The Alternative Media* (Rockford, Ill.: Rockford College Institute, 1979), p. 8.
4. David Armstrong, *A Trumpet to Arms: Alternative Media in America* (Los Angeles: J. P. Tarcher, 1981), p. 183.
5. *Orpheus*, August 1968, as cited by Robert J. Glessing, *The Alternative Press in America* (Bloomington: Indiana University Press, 1971), p. 4.
6. Armstrong, op. cit.
7. Watson, op. cit., p. 13.
8. Ibid., p. 17.
9. Armstrong, op. cit., p. 24.
10. Ibid., p. 331.
11. Less than two years after *Mother Jones*'s first run in February 1976, the total paid circulation, it was claimed, was 275,500, equaling *Ramparts*' circulation at its height, according to Watson, op. cit., p. 37.
12. *Mother Jones*, February–March 1977, editorial.
13. Foundation for National Progress Annual Report, 1975.
14. Richard Reynolds, telephone interview, August 5, 1982.
15. Armstrong, op. cit., pp. 202–3.
16. Deidre English, "More Than Just a Pretty Face," *Mother Jones*, February–March 1982, p. 6.
17. Reynolds, op. cit.
18. Deidre English, *Mother Jones*, May 1982, editorial.
19. Ibid.
20. Armstrong, op. cit., p. 337.
21. James Weinstein, *Socialist Revolution*, July 1972, editorial.
22. Ibid., August 1972, p. 8.
23. *In These Times*, promotional literature, cited in Watson, op. cit., p. 34.
24. *In These Times*, December 6, 1972, p. 15.
25. Ibid., November 4–10, 1981, p. 12C.
26. Ibid., May 12–18, 1982, letter to editor.
27. A colleague of Joe Stork, who wishes to remain anonymous, shared this information with the author.

28. In 1983 and 1984, both *CounterSpy* editors, Johy Kelly and Konrad Ege, gave presentations and hosted seminars at IPS.
29. Konrad Ege, statement at IPS lecture, "Afghanistan: An Eyewitness Account," July 12, 1983.
30. IPS Annual Report, 1979–1980, p. 12.
31. *Journal of Social Reconstruction*, Statement of Purpose, undated publicity brochure.
32. Eqbal Amhad, "Memorial for an Exile: Rashed Hessein," *Race and Class* 20, no. 3 (Winter 1979): 289–93.
33. "Grenada: Tongues of the New Dawn," *Race and Class* 25, no. 3 (Winter 1984): 27.
34. IPS promotional literature.
35. Fund for Investigative Journalism List of Grants and Books, 1980.
36. List of CIR Investigative Reports; 1978, 1979, 1980, 1981.
37. IRC publicity brochure, "Corporate Profiles."
38. *The New Right: Issues and Analysis*, Fall 1981, preface.
39. Philip F. Lawler, *The Alternative Influence* (Lanham, Md.: University Press of America, 1984), p. 20.
40. IPS publicity brochure, undated.
41. Foundation for National Progress Articles of Incorporation filed with California secretary of state.
42. Fund for Investigative Journalism List of Grants and Books, 1978–1980.
43. *Mother Jones* masthead and various publicity brochures.
44. CIR Investigative Reports, 1978, 1979, 1980, 1981.
45. Ibid.
46. IRS Form 990, Schedule A, Part IV, 4.
47. Lawler, op. cit., p. 88.
48. Armstrong, op. cit., p. 335.
49. Mark Dowie, "Pinto Madness," *Mother Jones*, September–October 1977.
50. Ibid.
51. *New York Times*, May 6, 1976, editorial page.
52. Undated letter from People's Bicentennial Commission, signed "In the Spirit of '76 We Are the People's Bicentennial Commission."
53. Deidre English, "The Sleaze Thickens," *Mother Jones*, June 1984, p. 5.
54. Ibid.
55. Open Letter to *New York Times*, printed in *Covert Action Information Bulletin*, cited in *Human Events*, April 9, 1983, p. 318.
56. *Human Events*, April 9, 1983, p. 318.
57. Ibid.
58. Ibid., September 26, 1981.
59. Ibid., April 9, 1983, p. 318.
60. Ibid.
61. William Minter, *Africa News*, statement at IPS seminar, "South Africa and the Media," September 13, 1984.
62. Ibid.
63. Ibid.
64. Terry Pristin, "Cut Rate News," *Columbia Journalism Review* (May–June 1981): 42.
65. Criticism was expressed in various editorials and letters, one in particular circulated by the National Council of Churches, "The Gospel According to 60 Minutes."
66. Jonathan Kwitny, "Oh, What a Lovely War," *Mother Jones*, June 1984, p. 46.

67. Ibid.
68. Antonio Gramsci, *Selections from the Prison Notebooks*, ed. Q. Hoare and G. Nowell Smith (London, 1971), p. 57.
69. Armstrong, op. cit., p. 25.
70. Ibid., p. 24.
71. Jacques Ellul, *Propaganda: The Formation of Men's Attitudes*, trans. Jean Lerner (New York: Vintage Books, 1973), p. 25.
72. Ibid., p. 50.
73. Ibid., p. 121.
74. Ibid., p. 159.

Chapter 11: Laying Siege to the Corporate Castle

1. Staughton Lynd, "Attack War Contractors' Meetings," *Guardian*, November 16, 1969.
2. Peter L. Berger, *Ethics and the New Class* (Washington, D.C.: Ethics and Public Policy Center, 1982), pp. 3–5.
3. Joseph Schumpeter, *Capitalism, Socialism, and Democracy* (New York: Harper and Brothers, 1942), p. 147.
4. Benjamin Lambiotte, tape-recorded lecture at IPS seminar, "Breaking the Circle of Poison: Pesticide Misuse in the Third World," June 12, 1985.
5. Peter Weiss, "Human Rights and Vital Needs" (Washington, D.C.: Institute for Policy Studies, Issue Paper, 1977).
6. Marcus Raskin, *Notes on the Old System* (New York: David McKay, 1976), p. 13.
7. Richard Barnet, *Global Reach: The Power of the Multinational Corporations* (New York: Simon and Schuster, 1974), p. 104.
8. Ibid., p. 385.
9. Ibid., p. 257.
10. Richard Barnet, *The Crisis of the Corporation* (Washington, D.C.: Institute for Policy Studies, 1975).
11. Ibid., p. 13.
12. Ibid., p. 26.
13. Herman Nickel, "The Corporation Haters," *Fortune*, June 16, 1980.
14. David Vogel, *Lobbying the Corporation: Citizen Challenges to Business Authority* (New York: Basic Books, 1978), p. 73.
15. John Boland, "Nader Crusade," *Barron's*, October 12, 1981, p. 11.
16. *Multinational Monitor*, vol. 1, nos. 7–9, advertisement.
17. Ibid., February 1980, p. 14.
18. Lynd, op. cit.
19. Vogel, op. cit., p. 51.
20. Ibid.
21. *Research Methodology Guide*, North American Congress on Latin America, 1971, p. 1.
22. Ibid., inside cover.
23. Ibid., p. 2.
24. Ibid., pp. 2–3.
25. FBI File #100-447935; WFO File #100-61761, report of April 29, 1971, pp. 1–2.
26. Ibid., report of June 29, 1971, p. 9.
27. Ibid.

28. David Vogel, interview·with Alice Tepper Marlin, as cited in Vogel, *Lobbying the Corporation*, p. 134.
29. Ibid.
30. *Grapevine*, National Council of Churches, February 1971.
31. Religious News Service, June 3, 1971, p. 2.
32. Religious News Service, March 22, 1972, p. 5.
33. *Southern Africa*, June–July 1972, p. 41.
34. In November 1975 the Transnational Institute published a listing of "Activities, Fellows, Associates" which included a section devoted to a TNI "Multinational Project" which listed the Corporate Data Exchange as contributing to the project. A TNI activities summary, November 1975, also included a twenty-two-item "Political Economy" section, which included "project to compile a corporate stock directory of shareholders of 1,000 corporations; seminar on corporate power. (Michael Locker, Corporate Data Exchange.)"
35. Corporate Data Exchange, Inc., Annual Report, 1977, pp. 1–2.
36. Ibid., pp. 4–5.
37. Ibid., p. 2.
38. See *Southern Exposure*, quarterly of Institute for Southern Studies, 1976–81.
39. Corporate Data Exchange, Inc., Annual Report, 1977, p. 2.
40. John Train, "Transnational Institute" (unpublished manuscript, 1982).
41. Religious News Service, April 27, 1971, pp. 26–27.
42. Train, op. cit.
43. Ibid.
44. "Getting a Handle on Pesticides," *TIE-Europe Bulletin*, no. 15, p. 43.
45. According to *Meeting the Corporate Challenge: A Handbook on Corporate Campaigns*, Transnational Institute, affiliates of the Transnationals Information Exchange are located in Sweden, Denmark, Germany, France, Belgium, Austria, Switzerland, Spain, Italy, Mexico, Colombia, Peru, Brazil, Chile, Argentina, Japan, the Philippines, Malaysia, Thailand, India, Sri Lanka, Australia, and New Zealand.
46. For detailed explanation of the "new iron triangle," see Paul H. Weaver, "Regulation, Social Policy and Class Conflict," *Public Interest*, no. 50 (Winter 1978): 45–63.
47. Mark Dowie, Douglas Foster, Carolyn Marshall, David Weir, and Jonathan King, "The Illusion of Safety," Part I, *Mother Jones*, June 1982, p. 36.
48. Ibid.
49. Ibid., Part II, *Mother Jones*, July 1982, pp. 42–43.
50. John Cavanagh, "Fibers and Textiles," Part II, *Multinational Monitor*, August 1981, pp. 18–19; reprinted by Institute for Policy Studies.
51. John Cavanagh and Michael Goldhaber, "High on Technology," *Multinational Monitor*, March 1984, p. 6.
52. Jeremy Rifkin, "Age of Transition: The Impact of the Biotechnical and Computer Revolutions," IPS seminar, April 25, 1984.
53. Susan George, IPS Project on Transnational Corporations, June 9, 1984, tape recording.
54. Cavanagh and Goldhaber, op. cit.
55. Ibid.
56. A former member of the American Committee on Africa, who wishes not to be identified, stated that meetings with representatives of the African National Congress began in the 1960s and expanded thereafter.

57. IPS Annual Report, 1979–80, p. 14.
58. Samuel T. Francis, staff member, U.S. Senate Select Committee on Intelligence, interview, June 15, 1984.
59. Glenn Frankel, "South Africa's White Communist," *Washington Post*, July 14, 1985, p. B4.
60. Ibid.
61. Ibid.
62. Ibid.
63. Train, op. cit.
64. Ibid.
65. Carole Collins, "Opposition to South Africa Mounts in the U.S.," *In These Times*, April 6–12, 1983, p. 6.
66. Elizabeth Schmidt, *Decoding Corporate Camouflage* (Washington, D.C.: Institute for Policy Studies, 1980), p. 88.
67. Frances Moore Lappé and Joseph Collins, *Food First: Beyond the Myth of Scarcity* (New York: Ballantine Books, 1978), pp. 502–3.
68. Institute for Food and Development Policy, "Progress Report, Fiscal Year 1983."
69. Ibid.
70. Lappé and Collins, op. cit., p. 200.
71. Ibid., pp. 489–90.
72. Ibid., pp. 497–98.
73. Institute for Food and Development Policy, "Progress Report, Fiscal Year 1983," p. 4.
74. Institute for Food and Development Policy, "Funding Proposal, Fiscal Year 1984: July 1, 1983–June 30, 1984," p. 10.
75. Ibid., p. 11.
76. Institute for Food and Development Policy, "Progress Report, Fiscal Year 1983," p. 5.
77. Ibid.
78. Ibid.
79. David Weir and Mark Schapiro, *Circle of Poison* (San Francisco: Institute for Food and Development Policy, 1981), p. 69.
80. Ibid.
81. Ibid., p. 70.
82. Institute for Food and Development Policy, "Progress Report, Fiscal Year 1983," p. 8.
83. *TIE-Europe Bulletin*, no. 15, p. 25.
84. Ibid., p. 4.
85. Ibid., p. 26.
86. Louis Clark, interview, August 3, 1984.
87. Government Accountability Project, "Report for Fiscal Year 1982/1983."
88. Clark, op. cit.
89. Ibid.
90. IPS Report, 1983, "The Twentieth Year," p. 15.
91. Clark, op. cit.
92. Statement of representative of World Information Service on Energy, June 22, 1984, not for attribution.
93. Nuclear Information Resource Service Annual Report, 1982, p. 1.
94. IPS Report, 1983, "The Twentieth Year," p. 15.
95. Government Accountability Project, "Report for Fiscal Year 1982/1983," pp. 5–8.

See also Rael Jean Isaac, "Games Anti-Nukes Play," *American Spectator*, November 1985.

96. Ibid., p. 12.
97. See S. Robert Lichter and Stanley Rothman, "Risk and Nuclear Power," *Public Opinion*, August/September 1982.
98. The Government Accountability Project, "Report," op. cit., p. 6.
99. Failure to develop nuclear power makes the United States increasingly vulnerable to a crisis in the Middle East that would cut off oil supplies. If revolution sweeps South Africa and the African National Congress consolidates power and establishes a communist government, the United States could be cut off from its major source of certain strategic minerals. South Africa provides 80 percent of the world's reserves of chromium, essential for the production of jet aircraft engines. South Africa also provides 85 percent of the Western world's platinum group of metals, 80 percent of its diamonds, 70 percent of its gold, 50 percent of its manganese and vanadium, all used in high-technology and vital to the defense industry.
100. Martin Carnoy and Derek Shearer, *Economic Democracy: The Challenge of the 1980s* (White Plains, N.Y.: M. E. Sharpe, 1980).
101. Ibid.

Chapter 12: IPS and Economic Democracy

1. John Conyers, Jr., "Taking over America," *New York Times*, June 1, 1979.
2. Planners Network statement of purpose, newsletter, no. 52, June 17, 1985.
3. Ibid.
4. Chester Hartman and Michael Stone, "A Socialist Housing Program for the United States," *Urban and Regional Planning in an Age of Austerity*, ed. Pierre Clavel, John Forester, William Goldsmith (Elmsford, N.Y.: Pergamon Press, 1980), p. 239.
5. Ibid.
6. Ibid., p. 240.
7. Derek Shearer and Lee Webb, "How to Plan a Mixed Economy," *Nation*, October 11, 1975, p. 340.
8. Martin Carnoy and Derek Shearer, *Economic Democracy: The Challenge of the 1980s* (White Plains, N.Y.: M. E. Sharpe, 1980), p. 371.
9. Ibid., p. 371.
10. Ibid., p. 372. In 1977 the Exploratory Project on Economic Alternatives received a $300,000 grant from the Department of Housing and Urban Development to study the possibility of worker-community ownership for two Youngstown, Ohio, steel mills, which had been closed by its conglomerate owner. In 1978 the project became a permanent operation, the National Center on Economic Alternatives—"a kind of left-wing Brookings Institution" based in Washington, D.C.
11. Sidney Lens, *Unrepentant Radical* (Boston: Beacon Press, 1980), p. 25.
12. Ibid., p. 42.
13. Ibid.
14. Ibid., p. 404.
15. Ibid., p. 404–5.
16. Ibid., p. 407.
17. Sidney Lens, "What Socialists Can Do in 1984," *Nation*, July 21–28, 1984, p. 41.
18. Ibid., p. 42.
19. Paul Ciotti, "Socialism . . . On the Street Where You Live," *Reason*, April 1981.

20. Ibid.
21. Lee Webb, "Computerized Police Systems in the U.S.?" *Current*, September 1971, p. 17.
22. Ibid., p. 19.
23. Carnoy and Shearer, op. cit., p. 362.
24. Derek Shearer and Lee Webb, "How to Plan in a Mixed Economy," *Nation*, October 11, 1975, p. 339.
25. Ibid.
26. Barbara Bick, interview, *Communities*, February 1977.
27. Ibid., p. 23.
28. Ibid., p. 26.
29. *1975 Madison Conference Reader*.
30. Ibid.
31. Ibid.
32. Eve Bach, Thomas Brom, et al., *The Cities' Wealth: Programs for Community Economic Control* (Washington, D.C.: Conference on Alternative State and Local Policies, 1976).
33. Ibid.
34. The Community Ownership Organizing Project (COOP) has worked with the Campaign for Economic Democracy and prepared a paper, with Stern Foundation funding, on public ownership of telephone service in association with Gar Alperovitz's Exploratory Project for Economic Alternatives.
35. Ibid., p. 1.
36. Ibid., p. 45.
37. Ibid., p. 19.
38. Chester Hartman, "The Big Squeeze," *Politics Today*, May–June 1978, p. 60.
39. Bach and Brom, op. cit., p. 1.
40. Ciotti, op. cit.
41. Bick, op. cit.
42. "Nader Takes Charge," *WG Report*, vol. 1, no. 1, April 1980.
43. "Beyond Antitrust: Juicing Up Competition," *New Republic*, July 6–13, 1974.
44. A California CASLP conference was held in 1977 in Santa Barbara. The conference, known as the California Conference on Economic Democracy or the California Conference on Alternative Public Policy, used a handbook prepared by CPPC for its workshops. The book, *Working Papers on Economic Democracy*, was "meant . . . to lay the basis for further development of a state-wide perspective on Economic Democracy," and acknowledged the contribution of Tom Hayden, "who put considerable time into reading, editing and advising on each paper . . . and Derek Shearer, whose voluminous work has helped lay the theoretical basis for Economic Democracy."
45. *In These Times*, May 9, 1979. Carnoy and Shearer, op. cit., pp. 383–84, criticize CED: "At the outset, the CED held the potential to become a model for a statewide, multi-issue organization; perhaps because of its origin, however—one individual's campaign—it has not fulfilled the hopes of many initially associated with it. The organization has centered around one person, Tom Hayden, and its financial support has come mainly from his wife, actress Jane Fonda. While the CED has undertaken some innovative policy initiatives—most notably in its promotion of solar energy—it has not reached out to other activists and included them in the organization in a meaningful way." (Eventually Hayden was elected to the state senate with the help of Fonda, who contributed $600,000 to his campaign.)

46. Derek Shearer, as cited by Justin Raimondo, "Inside the CED," *Reason*, February 1982, p. 20.
47. Derek Shearer, "The North Moves Left," *Working Papers*, Spring 1974, p. 53; Carnoy and Shearer, op. cit., pp. 138, 139.
48. At a June 1984 IPS-sponsored conference, Meeting the Corporate Challenge, Bennett Harrison, an MIT economist often cited by Shearer, addressed the failure of France's socialist policies to help unemployment by explaining that socialism could not be implemented in just one country in order to be ultimately successful. From this it may be deduced that socialism will fail until implemented throughout the world.
49. Carnoy and Shearer, op. cit., p. 272.
50. Ibid. p. 21.
51. Ibid.
52. Ibid., p. 20.
53. Ibid., p. 385.
54. Ibid., p. 390.
55. Ibid., p. 396.
56. Martin Carnoy, Derek Shearer, and Russell Rumberger, *A New Social Contract: The Economy and Government After Reagan* (New York: Harper & Row, 1983), p. 47.
57. Ibid., p. 58.
58. Ibid., p. 159.
59. Ibid., p. 6.
60. Ibid.
61. Ibid., p. 8.
62. Ibid., p. 9.
63. Ibid., p. 159.
64. Ibid., pp. 114–15.
65. Ibid., p. 160.
66. Ibid.
67. Ibid., pp. 191–92.
68. Ibid., p. 196.
69. Ibid., p. 202.
70. Ibid.
71. Ibid., p. 203.
72. Ibid., p. 213.
73. Ibid.
74. David Bley, telephone interview, December 5, 1984.
75. NCEA promotional brochure.
76. Gar Alperovitz and Jeff Faux, *Rebuilding America* (New York: Pantheon Books, 1984), p. 55.
77. Ibid., p. 271.
78. Gar Alperovitz and Jeff Faux, "Forget Today's Fleeting Fashions—We Really Need More Government, Not Less," Outlook Section, *Washington Post*, October 7, 1984.
79. Ibid.
80. Alperovitz and Faux, *Rebuilding America*, p. 32.
81. Ibid., p. 279.
82. Ibid., p. 248.
83. Ibid., p. 122.
84. *The Cities' Wealth* on housing: "Radical groups in Berkeley have long emphasized housing programs as key to controlling the city's wealth. There are a number of sound strategic reasons for this. By far the largest portion of the city's private land

is used for housing. A substantial part of all personal income is spent on housing. Within the urban economy, the accruing capital of the community tends to be concentrated in the increasing values of land and real estate. Finally, housing can be controlled far more easily than other forms of wealth which are moveable and beyond the scope of legal regulation by the city.''

85. Alperovitz and Faux, p. 264.
86. Ibid., p. 263.

Chapter 13: Orlando Letelier

1. FBI Composite Report File #185-789-1079, "CHILBOM: Protection of Foreign Officials; Murder; Explosives and Incendiary Devices."
2. John Dinges and Saul Landau, *Assassination on Embassy Row* (New York: McGraw-Hill, 1980), p. 128.
3. Karen DeYoung and Milton Coleman, "Victim Denounced Policies of Junta," *Washington Post*, September 22, 1976.
4. Orlando Letelier to Beatriz (Tati) Allende, March 29, 1976, FBI File WFO #185-425.
5. FBI Composite Report File #185-789-1079, "CHILBOM," pp. 0708–10.
6. Ibid., p. 0730.
7. Ibid., pp. 0705–6; 0711–12.
8. Cord Meyer, *Facing Reality: From World Federalism to the CIA* (New York: Harper & Row, 1980), p. 188.
9. Ibid., p. 175.
10. Ibid.
11. Ibid.
12. FBI File #185-789-1079, op. cit., p. 0752.
13. Dinges and Landau, op. cit., p. 34.
14. Ibid.
15. James Whelan, *Allende: Death of a Marxist Dream* (Washington, D.C.: Council for Inter-American Security Educational Institute, 1981), p. 11.
16. R. Bruce McColm, "The Letelier Killing," *National Catholic Register*, September 21, 1980, p. 10.
17. Whelan, op. cit., p. 183.
18. Dinges and Landau, op. cit., p. 87.
19. Ibid.
20. Ibid.
21. DeYoung and Coleman, op. cit.
22. Letelier to Allende, op. cit.
23. Ibid.
24. Ibid.
25. Press release, Chile Committee for Human Rights, October 15, 1979.
26. Ibid.
27. Almeyda to Letelier, August 10, 1976, FBI File WFO #185-425.
28. Ibid.
29. Ibid.
30. Ibid.
31. "Registro Gastos Oficina Politica," FBI File WFO #185-425.
32. Bill from Linden Hill Hotel, FBI File WFO #185-425.

33. Handwritten notes, FBI File WFO #185-425.
34. Ibid.
35. Dinges and Landau, op. cit., p. 86.
36. "Viajes Pendientes," and handwritten notes, FBI File #185-425.
37. "The Letelier Diary," FBI File WFO #185-425.
38. McColm, op. cit., p. 10.
39. "Letelier Diary."
40. Orlando Letelier to Raul Roa (Ministro de Relaciones Exteriores del Gobierno Revolucionario de Cuba), August 23, 1976, FBI File WFO #185-425.
41. Valdes to Emilio Brito, September 14, 1976, FBI File WFO #185-425.
42. FBI File WFO #185-425. See also "FBI Files Expose Letelier," "Accuracy in Media Report," October 1, 1980, vol. 9, no. 19, p. 3.
43. Valdes to Brito, op. cit.
44. "Letelier Address Book," FBI File WFO #185-425.
45. Ibid.
46. Robert Moss, "The Letelier Papers," Foreign Report, March 22, 1977. See also "FBI Files Expose Letelier."
47. Rowland Evans and Robert Novak, "Letelier's Political Fund," Washington Post, February 16, 1977.
48. Saul Landau, "A Campaign to Smear Letelier," Washington Post, February 18, 1977.
49. Rowland Evans and Robert Novak, "Behind the Murder of Letelier," Indianapolis News, March 1, 1977.
50. Dinges and Landau, op. cit., p. 87.
51. Almeyda to Letelier, op. cit.
52. Ibid.
53. Robert Novak, interview, August 14, 1984. See also Moss, op. cit.
54. Beatriz Allende, "Letelier: What 'Strange Double Life'?" Washington Post, April 30, 1977.
55. "A Daughter of Allende Is a Suicide in Cuba," New York Times, October 13, 1977.
56. Isabel Letelier, "The Revival of 'Old Lies' About Orlando Letelier," New York Times, November 8, 1980, p. 22.
57. Allende to Letelier, op. cit.
58. Dinges and Landau, op. cit., p. 87.
59. Almeyda to Letelier, op. cit.
60. Ibid.
61. Dinges and Landau, op. cit., p. 16.
62. Landau, "Campaign to Smear Letelier."
63. Jeremiah O'Leary, "Chilean Exile's Murder: Many Mysteries, Few Clues," Washington Star, April 1, 1978.
64. Editorial, "Terror in Washington," New York Times, September 22, 1976.
65. "Remarks of Senator James Abourezk," Speeches and Writings by and About Orlando Letelier (New York: National Coordinating Center in Solidarity with Chile, 1976), p. 19.
66. Tim Wheeler, "131 in Congress Seek Full Probe," Daily World, September 23, 1976.
67. Mike Giocondo, "1,500 Mourners at UN Protest Letelier's Murder," Daily World, September 24, 1976.
68. Pablo Huneus, "Rebellion Replaces Apathy in Chile," Wall Street Journal, July 6, 1984.

Chapter 14: Lobbying

1. *The Southern Connection: Recommendations for a New Approach to Inter-American Relations*, report by the Ad-Hoc Working Group on Latin America (Washington, D.C.: Transnational Institute, February 1977), p. 3.
2. Zbigniew Brzezinski, *Between Two Ages: America's Role in the Technetronic Era* (New York: Viking Press, 1970), p. 289.
3. *The Americas in a Changing World*, report by the Commission on United States–Latin American Relations, Center for Inter-American Relations, October 1974, p. 2.
4. *Southern Connection*, pp. 3–6.
5. Ibid., p. 5.
6. FBI File WFO #185-425 contains copies of all the documents and contents that Orlando Letelier was carrying in his briefcase at the time of his assassination before his departure for Cuba in September 1976.
7. Jeane J. Kirkpatrick, *Dictatorships and Double Standards* (New York: Simon and Schuster, 1982), p. 60.
8. Jeane J. Kirkpatrick, cited by Alfonso Chardy, "Rights Groups' Lobby Targets Latin Policy," *Miami Herald*, May 8, 1982.
9. *Changing Course: Blueprint for Peace in Central America and the Caribbean* (Washington, D.C., 1984), p. 7.
10. Ibid.
11. Ibid., pp. 46, 64.
12. Tomas Borge, as cited in *Newsweek*, November 14, 1983.
13. See *Washington Post*, July 16, 1985, p. 12; *New York Times*, July 16, 1985, p. 6.
14. Father Luis Eduardo Pellecer, phone interview, November 5, 1984.
15. IPS Ten Year Report, "Beginning the Second Decade, 1963–1973," and IPS Annual Report, 1979–80. Cynthia Washington was an IPS fellow/trustee dating back to at least 1973. She has been a member of the Coalition for a New Foreign and Military Policy since 1979 and is now its publications director. Steve Daggett was an IPS research associate in 1978–79 before coming to CNFMP, of which he is now budget priorities director.
16. Coalition for a New Foreign and Military Policy promotional brochure distributed in 1983.
17. Terry Provance, listed as one of the speakers in "Speakers Brochure of the Coalition for a New Foreign and Military Policy," is identified as the national coordinator of U.S./USSR Relations for the Disarmament and Conversion Program of the American Friends Service Committee. Provance has also been a member of the World Peace Council, which lists him as the director of the Disarmament Program of the American Friends Service Committee. After some controversy about Provance's membership in and support of the WPC was raised, he left AFSC. However, Provance's name remains on the roster of the World Peace Council membership list as of the last printing of that list (1983).
18. SDS leader Carl Davidson characterized NACLA as "the intelligence-gathering arm of the New Left"; cited in *Congressional Record*, 97th Cong., vol. 128, no. 10, February 9, 1982, Senator Symms (R–Idaho), article, "The News from El Salvador: Slanted."
19. Draft statement on ideology by the North American Congress on Latin America, May 1976.

20. "Latins Getting Revolutionary Peace Corps," *Washington Post & Times Herald*, May 20, 1967.
21. Richard Shaull, as cited in Allan Brownfeld, *Washington Lobby on Latin America*, monograph (Washington, D.C.: Council on Inter-American Security, 1980), p. 5.
22. Draft statement on ideology by the North American Congress on Latin America, May 1967.
23. Helen Shapiro, *NACLA Report on the Americas*, September–October 1981, p. 47.
24. Ibid.
25. FBI File SF #100-66966, AIRTEL, dated August 10, 1972, pp. 4–5.
26. Ibid. See also FBI File NYFO #105-86160 on the North American Congress on Latin America.
27. Lindsay Mattison, interview, July 18, 1984.
28. Joseph Eldridge, telephone interview, November 15, 1984.
29. *Messenger*, magazine of Church of the Brethren, August 1977, p. 21.
30. Eldridge to Permanent Representative of the Republic of Cuba to the United Nations, January 10, 1979.
31. According to State Department documents, "Report of Farid Handel's Trip to the United States," recovered from a "safe house" in El Salvador, the Cuban mission to the UN recommended that Handel connect with Juan Ferreira of WOLA.
32. Hill to Mrs. Gale Bruce, September 28, 1978.
33. Eldridge to Harry and Cecelia Pollack, February 7, 1985.
34. WOLA, *Update*, November–December 1983, pp. 1, 7.
35. U.S. embassy cable, November 6, 1984, 7:50 P.M., "Nicaraguan Election Observers Comments."
36. Colletta Younger, WOLA intern, interview, July 23, 1982.
37. Stanley Higinbotham, Congressional Research Service, foreign affairs and national defense division, undated letter to Joe Eldridge.
38. Press release from the Washington Office on Latin America, November 4, 1984, "International Human Rights Law Group and the Washington Office on Latin America, Delegation Statement."
39. Washington Office on Latin America 1983 Annual Report, p. 6.
40. Americas Watch Committee and the American Civil Liberties Union, *Report on Human Rights in El Salvador* (New York: Vintage Books, 1982), pp. v–vi.
41. Aryeh Neier, "Abuses by Salvadoran Guerrillas," *New York Times*, July 26, 1985.
42. Americas Watch, Lawyers Committee for International Human Rights, Washington Office on Latin America, *Honduras: On the Brink* (Washington, D.C.: Washington Office on Latin America, 1984), p. 7.
43. Juan Mendez, interview, March 13, 1985.
44. *Human Rights in Nicaragua: Reagan, Rhetoric and Reality*, an Americas Watch Report, July 1985.
45. The Americas Watch and Washington Office on Latin America reports documenting alleged human rights abuses by the contras were cited in early March 1985 in most of the major press outlets, including CBS, ABC, NBC, the *New York Times*, *Washington Post*, *Los Angeles Times*, *Boston Globe*, *Newsweek*, and *Time*. The *Boston Globe* (from the *Los Angeles Times* wire) of March 10, 1985, p. 17, reads: "Democrats said that they will use the charges to fight the Administration's request for renewed U.S. aid for the *contras*."
46. *Human Rights in Nicaragua: Reagan, Rhetoric and Reality*, pp. 14–15.
47. Ibid., p. 86.
48. Ibid., p. 91.

49. Michael Massing, "The One-Man Band of the Human Rights Fight," *Politics Today*, January–February 1980, p. 52.

50. Laurence Birns, interview, March 5, 1977, cited in Council for Coordinated Action newsletter, June 1981.

51. Richard Allan White, "El Salvador Between Two Fires," *America*, November 1, 1980.

52. *Human Rights in Latin America, 1983*, report published by Council on Hemispheric Affairs, p. 54.

53. Ibid., p. 37.

54. Brownfeld, op. cit., p. 8.

55. Assistant Secretary of State Viron Vaky, as cited by Mark Falcoff of the American Enterprise Institute.

56. The document circulated by COHA identified as "Dissent Paper on El Salvador and Central America," §DOS 11/6/80, To: Dissent Channel, From: ESCATF/D, Re.: DM-ESCA #80-3† was identified by the State Department as a Soviet forgery.

57. Forged document, "Dissent Paper on El Salvador and Central America." p. 16.

58. "El Salvador's Elections: A 'Downright Phony' Event in a Country Without a Free Press and with 'Downright' Nasty Security Force," press release from Council on Hemispheric Affairs, April 2, 1984, p. 1.

59. Council on Hemispheric Affairs, "News and Analysis," October 31, 1984.

60. Council on Hemispheric Affairs, "News and Analysis," November 7, 1984.

61. Megan Ballard, spokesperson for Council on Hemispheric Affairs, telephone interview, November 12, 1984.

62. FBI File WFO #185-425, "The Letelier File."

63. Center for International Policy prospectus, "Provides an Independent Perspective on U.S. Foreign Policy."

64. Richard E. Feinberg, preface to William Biddle, "U.S.-Nicaragua Talks: Going Through the Motions," Center for International Policy report, December 1983.

65. W. Frick Curry, "Grenada: Force as a First Resort," Center for International Policy "International Policy Report," January 1984.

66. Center for International Policy prospectus, p. 2.

67. Edward Feighan, as quoted in Cleveland *Plain Dealer*, cited in Center for Development Policy publication, "El Salvador Report."

68. *USA Today*, October 28, 1982, as cited in Center for Development Policy publication, "Honduran Military Report."

69. Robert White, "Central America: The Problem That Won't Go Away," *New York Times Sunday Magazine*, July 18, 1982.

70. Philip Taubman, "Salvadoran Was Paid for Accusations," *New York Times*, March 21, 1984.

71. Lindsay Mattison, interview, April 16, 1984.

72. Virginia Prewett, "How We Came to Lose Either Way in Salvador Vote," *Wall Street Journal*, May 4, 1984, p. 27.

73. State Department documents recovered from a "safe house" in El Salvador, referred to as "Report of Farid Handel's Trip to the United States."

74. Ibid., p. 2.

75. Ibid., pp. 3–4.

76. Ibid.

77. Ibid., pp. 13, 20–21. (Farid Handel emphasized the need to present information "with its human features, without political language and, most importantly, without a political label." This was a strategy already utilized by other groups in the Latin

network. As already noted, the real success of IPS, WOLA, Coalition for a New Foreign and Military Policy, and other groups has largely resulted from their couching Marxist analysis in liberal terminology, a strategy which has been extremely successful with Congress and the media.)

78. Ibid., p. 12.
79. Ibid., p. 8.
80. Ibid., p. 9.
81. Ibid., pp. 12–13.
82. Ibid., p. 11.
83. *Congressional Record*, 97th Cong., 2d sess., vol. 128, no. 10, February 9, 1982, entry by Sen. Steven Symms, "The News from El Salvador: Slanted."
84. U.S. Committee in Solidarity with the People of El Salvador, First National Convention, program, Saturday, May 25, 1985, pp. 2–3.
85. *World Council of Churches 1983 Resource Sharing Book*, pp. 279–80.
86. Institute for Food and Development Policy "Progress Report, Fiscal Year 1983," p. 5.
87. Frances Moore Lappé and Joseph Collins, *Food First: Beyond the Myth of Scarcity* (New York: Ballantine Books, 1978), p. 200.
88. Ibid., pp. 489–90.
89. Institute for Food and Development Policy, "Progress Report, Fiscal Year 1983," p. 5.
90. Ibid., p. 11.
91. Ibid., p. 5.
92. Kit Miller, interview, March 3, 1986.
93. Ibid.
94. *In Contempt of Congress* (Washington, D.C.: Institute for Policy Studies, 1985), p. 70.
95. Daniel Siegal, Tom Spaulding, Peter Kornbluh, *Outcast Among Allies: The International Cost of Reagan's War Against Nicaragua* (Washington, D.C.: Institute for Policy Studies, 1985), p. 1.
96. Robert Borosage, IPS seminar, "Report from Nicaragua and Cuba," December 12, 1983.
97. FBI File WFO #185-425, "The Letelier File."
98. U.S., Congress, House, Select Committee on Intelligence, Hearings, Rep. Edward F. Boland, February 1980, Appendix III, "U.S. Peace Council Founding Conference, November 9–11, 1979, Philadelphia Conference Agenda."
99. Isabel Letelier, written statement read at Riverside Church, New York City, February 2, 1985.
100. Saul Landau, "Cuba: The Present Reality," *New Left Review*, May–June 1961, p. 22.
101. Gerardo Peraza, the highest-ranking DGI operative ever to defect, corroborated, in his testimony before the Senate Subcommittee on Security and Terrorism in 1982, that the Venceremos Brigade was used by the Cuban DGI to collect intelligence on the U.S. and recruit Americans for the cause of Cuba.
102. *New York Times*, October 9, 1977. See also *Situation Report*, Washington, D.C., Security and Intelligence Fund, March 1979.
103. J. A. Emerson Vermaat, "The Transnational Institute: The Cuban Connection," *Midstream*, February 1986.
104. Herbert Romerstein, former professional staff member of the U.S. House of Representatives Permanent Committee on Intelligence, interview, December 13, 1985.

105. Cora Weiss and Mike Clark reported to members of the Riverside Church Disarmament Program that they had met with various officials of the Sandinista government during their trip to Nicaragua in July 1983. Robert Borosage and Saul Landau told an IPS seminar on December 12, 1983, that they had met with key leaders of the Sandinista government: "We were there for a whole series of purposes . . . to work with the eight ministries down there to make sure they had their projects in order. . . ." Richard Barnet and Peter Kornbluh told an IPS seminar on February 7, 1984, that they had met with Thomas Borge, Sergio Ramirez, and Humberto Ortega in their January 1984 trip to Nicaragua.
106. Richard Barnet and Peter Kornbluh, IPS seminar, "Intervention and Revolution in Nicaragua," February 7, 1984.

Chapter 15: Power and Influence on Capitol Hill

1. IPS Annual Report, 1983, p. 2.
2. IPS Annual Report, 1979–80, p. 3.
3. John S. Friedman, ed., *First Harvest* (New York: Grove Press, 1983), p. 358.
4. Philip Brenner, *The Limits and Possibilities of Congress* (New York: St. Martin's Press, 1983), p. viii.
5. Ibid., p. viii.
6. Institute for Policy Studies, "Beginning the Second Decade," p. 27.
7. Marcus G. Raskin, *Notes on the Old System* (New York: David McKay, 1974), p. 4.
8. Ibid., p. 5.
9. Ibid., pp. 21–22.
10. Marcus G. Raskin, *The Politics of National Security* (New Brunswick, N.J.: Transaction Books, 1979), p. 31.
11. Richard J. Barnet, *The Giants* (New York: Simon and Schuster, 1977).
12. Frances Fox Piven and Richard A. Cloward, *The New Class War: Reagan's Attack on the Welfare State and Its Consequences* (New York: Pantheon, 1982), p. 146.
13. Brenner, op. cit., p. 188.
14. Ibid., p. 189.
15. *Reason*, April 1981, p. 25.
16. Ibid., p. 25.
17. Brenner, op. cit., p. vi.
18. IPS Annual Report, 1979–80.
19. Allan C. Brownfeld, "Defending Communism on a U.S. Campus," *Human Events*, November 14, 1981.
20. "Political Wreckers: A Radical Think Tank Is Out to Dismantle the System," *Barron's*, July 28, 1980.
21. Ibid.
22. John M. Ashbrook, memorandum on congressional relations with IPS, November 12, 1982.
23. "Twentieth Anniversary Committee," Institute for Policy Studies, March 22, 1983.
24. Ibid.
25. Mark O. Hatfield, statement, April 5, 1983.
26. Institute for Policy Studies Report, "The Twentieth Year," 1983, p. 1.
27. *Congressional Record*, September 8, 1976, p. 15432.

28. Dorles Moyano, Congressional Research Service, Hispanic division, interview, May 17, 1984.

29. Stanley Higinbotham, Congressional Research Service, foreign affairs and national defense division, undated letter to Joe Eldridge.

30. An attempt was made to interview someone on the staff of every member who: voted to impeach President Reagan; voted against the Intelligence Identities Protection Act, which made it a crime to publish the names of CIA agents; voted against covert aid to Nicaragua; voted against Radio Marti, which is a broadcast to Cuba along the same lines as Radio Free Europe; signed the request for the 1983 IPS budget study; or signed Cynthia Arnson's March 1984 letter to the Speaker of the House. Interviewees in the Senate were chosen on the basis of their Americans for Democratic Action Index rating.

31. Ashbrook, op. cit.

32. Ibid.

33. Associated Press, "Shultz Says Congress Undercuts Foreign Policy," *Washington Post*, March 29, 1984.

34. Text of remarks by president to National Leadership Forum, Center for Strategic and International Studies International Club, Washington, D.C., April 6, 1984.

35. Transcript of U.S. Covert Operations Against Nicaragua, A Public Forum, May 27, 1982, Dirksen Senate Office Building, Washington, D.C., Campaign for Political Rights (1982), p. 57.

36. Jeane Kirkpatrick, "America's Moral Imperative in Central America," *Guardian Eagle* 9, no. 1 (Spring 1984).

37. IPS Annual Report, 1983, p. 9.

38. PACCA, *Changing Course: Blueprint for Peace in Central America and the Caribbean* (Washington, D.C.: Institute for Policy Studies, 1984), inside cover.

39. Ibid.

40. "Members of Congress for Peace Through Law and Peace Through Law Education Fund," Heritage Foundation Institute Analysis (Washington, D.C.: Heritage Foundation, 1977), p. 1.

41. Ken Sack, Arms Control and Foreign Policy Caucus intern, interview, March 29, 1984.

42. Ibid.

43. Ashbrook, op. cit.

44. "Reagan's 1985 Budget I: Politics of the Deficit," IPS seminar given by David Smith, economic Policy adviser to Sen. Edward Kennedy and a staff member of the Joint Economic Committee, April 17, 1984.

45. "How Nicaraguan Regime Propagandizes the U.S.," *Human Events*, May 7, 1983.

46. Center for Development Policy pamphlet on El Salvador.

47. Thomas Harkin, comments at PACCA reception, February 22, 1984.

48. Ibid.

49. Ibid.

50. Ibid.

51. IPS 1983 Budget Conference Report on Capitol Hill, transcript, February 2, 1983.

52. Ted Weiss, speech at Riverside Church, New York City, April 27, 1984.

53. Edwards to "Dear Colleague," March 1, 1984.

54. Barbara Gamarekian, "20 Years of Decidedly Liberal Views," *New York Times*, April 22, 1983.

55. Ronald Dellums, *Defense Sense: The Search for a Rational Military Policy* (Boston: Ballinger Press, 1983), Introduction.

56. John Barron, *KGB Today: The Hidden Hand* (New York: Reader's Digest Press, 1983), pp. 271, 292.
57. Translation of Farid Handel report.
58. *Dellums* v. *Smith* was filed in July 1983 in the Northern District of California on behalf of Rep. Ronald Dellums. See Center for Constitutional Rights, Docket Report, 1983–84.
59. Lee Roderick, "Dellums Adviser on Grenada Tied to a Marxist Ruler," Scripps Newspapers, cited in *Washington Times*, October 22, 1984, p. 1.
60. Ronald Dellums, press release, October 26, 1983, as cited by Herbert Romerstein, USIA, interview, November 15, 1984.
61. Barbara Lee, aide to Ronald Dellums, letter, recovered in Grenada documents, as cited by Herbert Romerstein, interview, November 15, 1984.
62. Barron, op. cit.; John M. Ashbrook, file, "Briefing on European Opposition to the New Generation of Theatre Nuclear Weapons, May 5, 1981."
63. Cuba Blockade Conference was held on March 27–29, 1981, at George Washington University campus. Proceedings obtained from John M. Ashbrook, file, "Cuba Blockade Conference."
64. Ibid.
65. Ibid.
66. Ibid.
67. "Communists Are Claiming Special Privileges Under Election Law," *Conservative Digest*, March 1982, p. 28; *Human Events*, October 3, 1981, p. 4.
68. "Communists Are Claiming Special Privileges."
69. Ibid.; "Cuba: Interparliamentary Conference—United States," *Direct from Cuba*, September 30, 1981, no. 266, p. 30.
70. Maurice Bishop to John Conyers, June 7, 1983.
71. Ashbrook, file, "Cuba Blockade Conference."
72. Anne Holloway, staff director, House Foreign Affairs Subcommittee on Africa, statement, August 16, 1984.
73. Ibid.
74. "Liberal-Left Plans Anti-Reagan Rallies," *Human Events*, June 25, 1983, p. 5.
75. Ibid.
76. Kennedy to Eldridge, August 23, 1978.
77. Ibid., October 17, 1978.
78. Sarbanes to Eldridge, October 9, 1978.
79. Coalition for a New Foreign and Military Policy (CNFMP) promotional brochure.
80. Ibid.
81. Harkin to "Coalition Friends," September 30, 1977.
82. CNFMP promotional literature.
83. Coffin to Eldridge, December 11, 1978.
84. CNFMP promotional literature.
85. Ibid.
86. Ibid.
87. Interview, aide to Timothy Wirth, March 15, 1984 (not for attribution).
88. CNFMP promotional literature.
89. Ibid.
90. Ibid.
91. Gene LaRoque, Moscow Television Service, June 5, 1985.
92. Council for a Livable World promotional literature.
93. Ibid.

94. Ibid.
95. Ashbrook, file, "Briefing on European Opposition."
96. U.S., Congress, House, Permanent Select Committee on Intelligence, *Soviet Active Measure*, 97th Cong., 2d sess., July 14, 1982.
97. SANE, *Activities Report*, 1983.
98. "Washington's Movers and Shakers," *National Journal*, January 24, 1981, p. 132.
99. Committee for National Security promotional literature.
100. Ibid.
101. IPS Annual Report, 1983, p. 6.

Chapter 16: Penetrating the Churches

1. *World Peacemakers*, Spring 1982.
2. Deployment of the neutron bomb was considered a cost-effective way to neutralize Warsaw Pact tanks, which outnumbered NATO tanks three to one. To prevent NATO's deployment, the Soviets undertook a major "active-measures" campaign to mobilize Western public opinion against the neutron bomb.

   In January 1978 Brezhnev appealed to the Europeans to cancel deployment, asserting that the neutron bomb would "pose a grave threat to détente." A few weeks later, the presidential bureau of the World Peace Council (WPC) was received in Washington, D.C., to discuss the neutron bomb at the Dialogue for Disarmament and Détente Conference, cosponsored by Members of Congress for Peace Through Law (MCPL). During the next month the WPC brought together peace activists and leaders from the East and the West in Berlin and then again in Geneva under the auspices of the U.N.–related Special Nongovernmental Organizations Committee on Disarmament. Here plans were announced for the successful demonstrations, in major European cities, which followed. According to John McMahon, CIA deputy director, the Soviets spent over $100 million in the campaign to support "West European Communist parties" and other groups for "their activities and rallies, suborning of non-communists, contributions to common-cause-type affairs as quid pro quos for cooperative front activities, direct advertisements, travel of Soviet and East bloc lobbyists to the West, and of Western groups to the USSR." After President Carter decided to cancel the neutron bomb on April 7, 1978, the Kremlin decorated its ambassador to The Hague with a medal for his effective liaison with European leaders of the antineutron campaign.
3. "Peacemakers: Our Call and Program."
4. Richard Barnet, "A Time to Stop," *World Peace Paper #1*, 1978, p. 7.
5. *World Peacemakers*, Winter 1984, p. 5.
6. Henri Nouwen, "Christ of the Americas: Dying and Rising and Coming Again," *World Peace Paper #9*, p. 29.
7. Gayle Boss Koopman, William J. Price, and John Wagner, *National Security and Christian Faith* (Washington, D.C.: World Peacemakers, 1982), p. 3.
8. Ibid., p. i.
9. Ibid., p. 14 (paraphrased).
10. Ibid., p. 16.
11. *World Peacemakers*, Summer 1983, p. 7.
12. Ibid.
13. World Peacemakers and Central American Peace Institute of the Church of the Saviour, "Becoming a Pastor-Prophet: Bridging Faith and Politics," Spring 1984, p. 1.

14. Ibid., p. 5.
15. Bill Price, "The American Churches Speak: We Are for Peace" (World Peacemakers, 1984), p. 6.
16. Ibid., p. 5.
17. Ibid.
18. Jim Wallis, "Liberation and Conformity," *Mission Trends No. 4, Liberation Theologies in North America* (Grand Rapids: Eerdmans, 1979), pp. 54–55.
19. Richard Barnet, "Race Without Reason," *Sojourners*, February 1977, p. 9. Remember, these were the early days of the Carter administration, whose implementation of a "human rights foreign policy" largely resulted from the efforts of five people, Robert Pastor, Richard Fagen, Abraham Lowenthal, Guy Erb, and Riordan Roet, who jointly participated in the IPS Ad Hoc Working Committee on Latin America and the Linowitz Commission. The Linowitz Commission formed the basis for President Carter's human rights policies. Another IPS associate and human rights activist, Mark Schneider, friend to Orlando Letelier and assistant to Sen. Ted Kennedy, also helped as deputy assistant secretary of state for human rights under Patricia Derian, who has maintained a close relationship with IPS.
20. IPS Annual Report, 1977–80, p. 14.
21. Richard Barnet, "A Change of Heart—Billy Graham on the Nuclear Arms Race," *Sojourners*, February 1977, pp. 12–13.
22. Richard Barnet, "Lies Clearer Than Truth," *Sojourners*, August 1979, p. 16.
23. Ibid., p. 18.
24. Ibid.
25. Richard Barnet, "Two Bumbling Giants," *Sojourners*, February 1980, pp. 3–4.
26. Ibid.
27. Ibid.
28. Ibid., p. 5.
29. Richard Barnet, "The Spiritual Struggle of Peacemaking," *Sojourners*, October 1981, p. 14.
30. Ibid., p. 16.
31. Ibid.
32. Ibid.
33. Richard Barnet, *The Economy of Death* (New York: Atheneum, 1969), p. 45.
34. Barnet, "Spiritual Struggle of Peacemaking," p. 17.
35. Ibid.
36. Interfaith Center to Reverse the Arms Race, "Special Bulletin," December 1981, p. 1., citing Richard Barnet.
37. Ibid., p. 2.
38. Ibid., p. 3.
39. Ibid.
40. Richard Barnet, "The Polish Challenge," *Sojourners*, March 1982, p. 16.
41. Ibid., p. 18.
42. Ibid.
43. Ibid.
44. Richard Barnet, "Of Cables and Crises," *Sojourners*, February 1983, p. 18.
45. Ibid.
46. Riverside Church Disarmament Program, Blue Book Series, no. 1, July 11, 1978, p. 10.
47. Ibid., p. 16.

Chapter 17: Radical Politics Under the Cloak of the Clergy

1. William Sloane Coffin, "Speaking Out on Gay Rights," interview with James Saslow, *Advocate*, May 27, 1982.
2. Carol H. Wallace, "Religion's Man of Many Causes," *Dynamic Years*, January–February 1979, p. 37.
3. William Sloane Coffin, talk at opening session of Fifth Annual Disarmament Conference, Riverside Church, April 17, 1983.
4. Wallace, op. cit., p. 37.
5. Richard Barnet, sermon delivered at Church of the Saviour, April 26, 1981.
6. *New York Times*, January 30, 1977.
7. William Sloane Coffin, *Once to Every Man* (New York: Atheneum, 1977), p. 295.
8. William Sloane Coffin, Blue Book Series, no. 1, pp. 3–4.
9. William Sloane Coffin, frequent statement in sermons.
10. Coffin, *Once to Every Man*, p. 202.
11. Ibid., pp. 330–31.
12. William Sloane Coffin, interview with Josh Moron, *Columbia University Spectator*, December 1, 1977, pp. 9–10.
13. Riverside Church Disarmament Program, Blue Book Series, no. 1, p. 13.
14. Ibid., p. 51. Raskin said, "A political consensus can now be built in this country around those people who, over the last 20 years, have been committed . . . and . . . disarmament can be built up into the fundamental question of what a political program should be in this society. We will be 'caused' to death unless we can begin to see how . . . various individual issues [e.g., civil rights, human rights, environmental issues] relate to each other."
15. Ibid., p. 52.
16. Ibid., pp. 52–53.
17. William Sloane Coffin, statement, December 9, 1978.
18. John Barron, *KGB Today: The Hidden Hand* (New York: Reader's Digest Press, 1983), p. 280.
19. Vladimir Shustov spoke at the Riverside Church during Peace Sabbath, May 30, 1982; during Fifth Annual Disarmament Conference on April 18, 1983; and at the Orientation Program for 266 NCC-sponsored delegates before their departure for the USSR, June 5, 1984.
20. Barron, op. cit., p. 286.
21. A particular Soviet official approached Morton Halperin after the latter's speech at Riverside Church, July 26, 1981, and Ted Weiss's legislative aide at Riverside Church after her speech, February 25, 1982.
22. Belyaev attended this presentation at Riverside, October 31, 1982.
23. Igor Ignatiev attended the October 1–2, 1983, Riverside Church Disarmament Conference. Vladimir Simonov attended the November 12–13, 1983, Riverside Church Conference on Direct Action.
24. Riverside Church Disarmament Program, Blue Book Series, no. 2, p. 13.
25. Riverside Church, *Disarming Notes*, January 1980.
26. "Call to Reverse the Arms Race Crosses the Nation," *Carillon*, March 20, 1979, p. 1.
27. *Carillon*, March 20, 1979.
28. Institute for Policy Studies catalogue, p. 3.
29. Cora Weiss, as quoted in *Myths and Realities of the Soviet Threat*, proceedings of IPS conference on U.S.–Soviet relations, May 14–15, 1979, p. 4.

30. Ibid.
31. Riverside Church, *Disarming Notes*, September 1979; and *Carillon*, February 27, 1981, p. 3.
32. "Coffin Calls Disarmament 'Best Defense,' " *Presbyterian Journal*, November 21, 1979, p. 4.
33. "Second Disarmament Convocation Draws 900," *Carillon*, November 14, 1979, p. 2.
34. *Disarming Notes*, January 1980.
35. "Statement on Afghanistan by Disarmament Program" *Carillon*, January 28, 1980, p. 2., reprint of Coffin's February 23, 1979, sermon, the day of his departure for Iran.
36. Ibid., p. 4.
37. *Disarming Notes*, February 1980, p. 1.
38. Richard Barnet, "Two Bumbling Giants: The Superpowers' Outdated Policies in a Nuclear World," *Waging Peace*, ed. Jim Wallis (San Francisco: Harper & Row, 1982), p. 57.
39. Richard Barnet, *Real Security: Restoring American Power in a Dangerous Decade* (New York: Simon and Schuster, Touchstone, 1981), p. 110.
40. Fred Halliday, *Soviet Policy in the Arc of Crisis* (Washington, D.C.: Institute for Policy Studies, 1981), p. 111.
41. Fred Halliday, "The Sources of the New Cold War," *Exterminism and Cold War*, ed. *New Left Review* (London: Verso, 1982), p. 310.
42. *Disarming Notes*, February 1980, p. 2.
43. Ibid., p. 2.
44. Coffin, January 20, 1980, after praising Ahmad for the speech just given at Riverside, made this "consulting" reference, and once again during a discussion with church member William Peck in spring 1982.
45. "What's Behind the Crises in Iran and Afghanistan," Part II, transcript of talk given by Eqbal Ahmad at Riverside, January 20, 1980, pp. 2–3.
46. Mike Clark, "In the USSR After Afghanistan," Blue Book Series, no. 8, May 4, 1980, p. 8.
47. Ibid., p. 9.
48. Said by Coffin during a discussion held with some dissenting church members, July 17, 1980.
49. Mike Clark, in *Disarming Notes*, February 1981.
50. *For Peace, Détente, Disarmament*, the conference's official record, lists the delegates' names and affiliation, pp. 45–65.
51. Ibid., pp. 21–23.
52. "Russians Attend Service," *Carillon*, February 27, 1981, p. 3.
53. Ibid., p. 3.
54. Sam Nujoma and Oliver Tambo are listed in the World Peace Council membership for 1980–83.
55. Tim Edwards, interview, September 25, 1984.
56. Literature of these organizations was collected from tables at Riverside Church. Further identifications were derived from participants' introductions.
57. Mary Burton, in *Disarming Notes*, November–December 1981, p. 1.
58. *The Red Line*, newsletter of Cardinal Mindszenty Foundation, St. Louis, Mo. 63105; May and June 1981.
59. Cora Weiss, "The Challenge from a Local Congregation," *Before It's Too Late: The Complete Record of the Public Hearing on Nuclear Weapons and Disarmament*

Organized by the World Council of Churches, ed. Paul Abrecht (Geneva, 1982), pp. 361–62.

Chapter 18: Peace and International Socialist Solidarity

1. Riverside Church, *Disarming Notes*, March 1982, p. 2.
2. Eqbal Ahmad, "Interventionism in Libya," speech at Riverside Church, New York City, January 28, 1982.
3. Ibid.
4. "Broken Dreams," *Disarming Notes*, March 1982, p. 2.
5. Ibid.
6. George Hunsinger, ed., *The Riverside Church Disarmament Reader: A Model Course for Disarmament Studies*, preface.
7. Dale Aukerman, "City of Refuge," *Sojourners*, January 1984, p. 25.
8. Leslie Cagan, telephone interview, May 5, 1982.
9. U.S., Congress, House, Committee on Internal Security, 1970 Report. Sidney Peck was a former member of the Wisconsin State Committee of the Communist party, USA. Sidney Lens was a member of the Chicago Peace Council, a Communist party front.
10. Terry Provance is listed as a member of the World Peace Council in the WPC's official membership list for 1979–80 and for 1981–83. Norma Becker has been affiliated with the Women's International League for Peace and Freedom, a Communist party front organization.
11. IPS Annual Report, 1979–80, p. 14.
12. New York Marxist School publicity brochure.
13. Norma Becker, statement at Riverside Church, March 23, 1984.
14. Rael Jean and Eric Isaac, "The Counterfeit Peacemakers," vol. 15, no. 6, June 1982, p. 8.
15. Leslie Cagan, transcript, "Remarks at 2 February 1985 Memorial for Sandy Pollack."
16. Ibid.
17. Kenneth A. Briggs, "Growing Role for Churches in Disarmament Drive," *New York Times*, April 10, 1982.
18. Ibid.
19. The declaration of a WPC front, Generals for Peace and Disarmament, issued before the U.N. Second Special Session on Disarmament in June 1982, was distributed by Riverside Church for six months thereafter.
20. Mike Clark, "U.S.–Soviet Relations: The Burden Rests with Us," *Disarming Notes*, September 1982, p. 1.
21. Ibid., p. 2.
22. Cora Weiss, "Do Americans Know How Much We Fear the Cruise?" *Disarming Notes*, September 1982, p. 1.
23. "Militarism and Racism, Common Enemies—Common Dangers," *Disarming Notes*, November–December 1982, p. 2.
24. Ibid.
25. Charles Austin, "Ministers Seeking to Revitalize Preaching," *New York Times*, October 24, 1982.
26. Ibid.
27. John Barron, "The KGB's Magical War for 'Peace,' " *Reader's Digest*, October

1982; and John Barron, *KGB Today: The Hidden Hand* (New York: Reader's Digest Press, 1983).

28. *Fellowship*, monthly journal of the Fellowship of Reconciliation, April 1983, p. 9. The growth of Riverside's Peace Sabbath/Peace Sunday as a vehicle to link together and politically influence religious institutions was described in the April 1983 *Fellowship*: "Peace Sabbath began in 1979 as a project of the Riverside Church Disarmament Program in cooperation with the Religious Task Force/Mobilization for Survival. In 1980, Clergy and Laity Concerned became a co-sponsor; the FOR's formal sponsorship began in 1981. Last Year, two additional peace organizations, Pax Christi USA and Sojourners, joined in the broad-based effort. . . . In addition to the six organizations mentioned above, six others have joined in the planning and endorsing of Peace Sabbath/Peace Sunday 1983. These include: The *Baptist Peacemaker*, New Call to Peacemaking, Commission on Social Action of the Union of American Hebrew Congregations, the National Council of Churches, Evangelicals for Social Action and World Peacemakers. Together, these twelve endorsing organizations represent a broad religious constituency: Jews, Roman Catholics, mainline Protestants, Evangelical Christians, historic peace churches, and ecumenical and interfaith peace groups. . . . This May, the number of churches and synagogues participating is expected to exceed 20,000."

29. IPS Annual Report, 1979–83.

30. Rev. James Park Morton's positioning of a female Christ ("Christa") near the high altar in the Cathedral of St. John the Divine created such a flap that it was written up in the *New York Times*.

31. Paul Moore, statement, May 24, 1983, at sponsored bilateral exchange with representatives of the Soviet Institute of the Study of USA and Canada in Minneapolis.

32. William Sloan Coffin, statement, May 24, 1983.

33. Randall Forsberg, statement, May 24, 1983.

34. Cora Weiss, "Soviet and American Experts Confer," *Disarming Notes*, June 1983, p. 1.

35. Mike Clark, "Action for Peace in Nicaragua," *Disarming Notes*, July–August 1983, p. 2.

36. Cora Weiss, statement, to meeting of Riverside Church Disarmament Program, July 10, 1983.

37. "The Left's Victory," *Wall Street Journal*, editorial, August 1, 1983.

38. William Sloane Coffin, "Homecoming, Homeleaving," sermon on September 25, 1983.

39. Miguel D'Escoto, statement at Riverside Church, October 2, 1983, cited by S. Steven Powell, "Miguel D'Escoto's Amigos at Riverside Church," *Policy Review*, Winter 1984.

40. Ibid.

41. Vladimir Simonov, "From the Chicago River to the Elbe," *Moscow News Weekly*, no. 50, 1983.

42. "Mike Clark Leaving Disarmament Program," *Disarming Notes*, January 1984, p. 2.

43. William Sloane Coffin, "Peace in the Pulpit," *Disarming Notes*, March 1984, p. 1.

44. William Sloane Coffin, "Love Your Enemies," transcript of sermon, February 19, 1984, p. 4.

45. Ibid., p. 1.

46. Peace with Justice Tour '84 brochure, cosponsored by AFSC, CALC, FOR, RCDP, Riverside, and the NCC.

47 This analysis is taken from the various inserts in the NCC's resource packet for Peace with Justice Week 1984.

48. Leslie Gelb, "Charting a Course to Washington: The Advisors," *New York Times*, March 21, 1984.

49. Internal Revenue Service expenditure control reports, 1979, 1980, 1981, 1982; on file at Foundation Center, New York, N.Y.

50. William Sloane Coffin, as cited in Gary MacEoin, ed., *Sanctuary* (New York: Harper & Row, 1985), p. 181.

51. William Sloane Coffin, recorded statement at Riverside Church memorial service for Sandy Pollack, February 2, 1985.

52. William Sloane Coffin, *Once to Every Man* (New York: Atheneum, 1977).

53. Isabel Letelier, written statement, February 2, 1985.

54. Henry Winston and Johnetta Cole, statements, February 2, 1985.

55. National Steering Committee, November 29 Committee for Palestine, telegram, January 31, 1985.

56. Zuri Terzi, statement, February 2, 1985.

57. Iranian OIP Fadaian, written statement, January 28, 1985; Mfanafthi Makatini, African National Congress, telegram, January 30, 1985.

58. Anatoly Dobrynin, ambassador of the USSR, telegram, February 1, 1985.

59. Yuri Zhukov, president, Soviet Peace Committee, telegram, January 25, 1985.

60. Bayardo Arce Castano, member of the National Directorate of the FSLN, letter, January 21, 1985.

61. Carlos Tunnerman, ambassador, statement, February 2, 1985.

62. Jesus Montane Oropesa, member of Central Committee of Communist party of Cuba, undated letter.

63. Steve Baldwin, "Saul Landau: Castro's Top Propagandist," *SBA Issue Series* (Washington, D.C.: Students for a Better America, 1985), p. 2.

64. "Sandy Pollack: In Celebration of Her Life and Work," program of memorial service for Sandy Pollack, U.S. Peace Council, 7 East 15 Street, New York, N.Y. 10003, distributed at Riverside Church, February 2, 1985.

65. Rene Mujica, first secretary, Cuban Interests Section, recorded statement, February 2, 1985.

66. Ibid.

67. Tim Edwards, "Daniel in Coffin's Den," *National Review*, December 13, 1985, p. 16.

68. Daniel Ortega, statement, Riverside Church, July 28, 1986.

Chapter 19: Strange Encounters

1. William Greider, statement, November 28, 1983, at IPS Washington School class.

2. Roger Wilkins, statement, November 28, 1983, at IPS Washington School class.

3. Robert Borosage, statement, December 12, 1983, at IPS seminar, "Report from Nicaragua and Cuba."

4. Saul Landau, statement, December 12, 1983, at IPS seminar, "Report from Nicaragua and Cuba."

5. Rene J. Mujica, statement, January 19, 1984, at IPS after showing of Saul Landau's film, *With Fidel*.

6. Tom Harkin, statement, February 22, 1984, at reception for IPS's release of PACCA report, *Changing Course*.

7. Victor Taltz, attaché, embassy of USSR, statement, February 22, 1984, at IPS reception.
8. Eqbal Ahmad, statement, April 21, 1984, at "Deadly Connections" conference at Cultural Center of District 1199 of the Union of Health Care and Hospital Workers of New York City.
9. Although I tried to call most of the Soviet diplomats that frequented the institute to see what I could learn, it was my contact with the third secretary Valeriy Lekarev that proved most fruitful. The conversation constructed was taken from recorded statements made in informal conversations on July 11, 1984, and August 3, 1984.
10. John Mercer, IPS staff researcher, telephone interview, September 18, 1984.

Chapter 20: IPS and the Soviets

1. Marcus Raskin, interview, December 16, 1983.
2. Marcus Raskin, transcript of talk to informal meeting of foundations and individual funders concerned with nuclear arms control and peace issues, July 7, 1982, p. 2.
3. Ibid., p. 1.
4. Paul Moore, statement at bilateral exchange conference between IPS and IUSAC, Minneapolis, May 24, 1983.
5. Ibid.
6. Richard Barnet, "A Question of Trust," IPS report, U.S.–USSR Bilateral Exchange Conference, Minneapolis, May 24–29, 1983, p. 3.
7. Ibid., p. 11.
8. Raskin, transcript.
9. Barnet, op. cit., p. 5.
10. Henry Kissinger, *White House Years*, as cited by Carl Irving, *San Francisco Examiner*, September 9, 1985, p. A3.
11. U.S., Congress, House, Permanent Select Committee on Intelligence, *Soviet Active Measures*, 97th Cong., 2d sess., July 13, 14, 1982, p. 72.
12. *Time*, September 9, 1985, p. 22.
13. *Soviet Active Measures*, p. 70.
14. Ibid., p. 73.
15. "The Minneapolis Dialogue," Institute for Policy Studies report, July 29, 1983, p. 5.
16. Mikhail A. Milsteyn, statement at IPS-IUSAC conference, Minneapolis, May 24, 1983.
17. Randall Forsberg, statement, Minneapolis, May 25, 1983.
18. Ibid.; see also Riverside Church Disarmament Program, *Disarming Notes*, June 1983.
19. Robert Borosage, "The Bilateral Box," *Working Papers for a New Society*, Summer 1983, p. 40.
20. Robert Borosage, interview, December 21, 1983.
21. Roger Wilkins, statement, November 28, 1983, IPS Washington School class.
22. John Mercer, interview, December 19, 1984.
23. Ibid.
24. Robert Borosage, statement at IPS seminar, "The Chill and the Freeze," May 17, 1984.
25. Ibid.
26. Ibid.
27. Barnet, op. cit., p. 11.

28. Ibid.
29. Robert Borosage, "Reversing the Tide: Short-term Steps for Disarmament," IPS paper, July 1984, p. 7.
30. Marcus Raskin, "Security and General Disarmament," IPS paper, July 1984, pp. 3–4.
31. John Mercer, interview, December 19, 1984. Conversation taken from that interview.
32. Gorgi Arbatov, statement, September 5, 1985.
33. Ibid.
34. Richard Barnet, statement, September 5, 1986.
35. Ibid.
36. Ibid.
37. Spartak Beglov, interview, September 6, 1985. Conversation constructed from tape-recorded interview.
38. Edouard Batalov, interview, September 7, 1985. Conversation constructed from tape-recorded interview.
39. Sergei Rogov, interview, September 9, 1985. Conversation constructed from tape-recorded interview.
40. Marc Raskin, statement at Commonwealth Club, San Francisco, September 5, 1985.
41. George Arbatov, statement at Commonwealth Club, San Francisco, September 5, 1985.
42. Raskin, statement at Commonwealth Club.
43. Barnet, "Question of Trust," p. 2.
44. Cora Weiss, "Myths and Realities of the Soviet Threat," IPS publication of proceedings of IPS conference on U.S.–Soviet relations, May 14–15, 1979, p. 10.
45. Alan Wolfe, *The Rise and Fall of the Soviet Threat* (Washington, D.C.: Institute for Policy Studies, 1979), p. 87.
46. Fred Halliday, "Moscow and the Third World: Evolution of Soviet Policy," *Race and Class* (quarterly journal of Transnational Institute and Institute for Race Relations) 24, no. 2:138.
47 Barnet, "Question of Trust," pp. 3, 4.

Chapter 21: Soviet Objectives and IPS Objectives

1. George Washington, "Farewell Address of 1796," as cited in J. D. Richardson, ed., *Messages and Papers of the Presidents* (Washington, D.C., 1896), vol. 1, pp. 220–22.
2. The Logan Act was originally signed into law on January 30, 1799. Although there have been no prosecutions under the Logan Act, there have been a number of important judicial references to it, such as *United States* v. *Bryan* (1947); *United States* v. *Peace Information Center* (1951); *Martin* v. *Young* (1955); *Briehl* v. *Dulles* (1957); *United States* v. *Elliot* (1967).
3. Margaret Boveri, *Treason in the Twentieth Century* (New York: G. P. Putnam, 1963), p. 7.
4. Herman Rauschning, *The Voice of Destruction* (London: G. P. Putnam, 1940), pp. 9–10.
5. Ibid.
6. Ibid., pp. 7–8.
7. Boris M. Shaposhnikov, *The Brain of the Army* (Moscow, 1968), as cited in *Strategic*

Intentions of the Soviet Union (London: Institute for the Study of Conflict, 1978), p. 8.

8. Boris Ponomarev, as cited in Albert Weeks and William C. Bodie, *War and Peace: Soviet Russia Speaks* (New York: National Strategy Information Center, 1983), p. 20.

9. *Pravda*, October 19, 1973, cited in *Current Digest of the Soviet Press*, vol. 28, no. 8 (March 8, 1976), p. 14.

10. U.S., Congress, Senate, Internal Security Subcommittee Hearings, *Institute of Pacific Relations*, 1952, pt. 13, p. 4511.

11. Richard H. Shultz and Roy Godson, *Dezinformatsia* (New York: Pergamon-Brassey's International Defense Publishers, 1984), pp. 17–40.

12. Ladislav Bittman, *The KGB and Soviet Disinformation* (New York: Pergamon-Brassey's International Defense Publishers, 1985), p. 203.

13. Brian Crozier, "Power and National Sovereignty," *National Review*, February 2, 1979.

14. Robert Borosage, interview, December 19, 1983.

15. This literature is quite extensive and includes such works as Barghoorn, *Soviet Foreign Propaganda*; Clews, *Communist Propaganda Techniques*; Davison, *International Political Communication*; Ellul, *Propaganda*; Michael Gehlen, *The Politics of Coexistence: Soviet Methods and Motives*; Inkeles, *Social Change in Soviet Russia*; and Hearings of the House Subcommittee on Oversight of the Permanent Select Committee on Intelligence, 95th Cong., 1st and 2d sess., December 27–29, 1977; January 4–5 and April 20, 1978, *The CIA and the Media*; Hearings before the Permanent Select Committee on Intelligence of the House of Representatives, 97th Cong., 2d sess., July 13, 14, 1982.

16. Peter Weiss, *Human Rights and Vital Needs* (Washington, D.C.: Institute for Policy Studies, 1977).

17. Marcus G. Raskin, *Being and Doing* (New York: Random House, 1971).

18. Susan George, *How the Other Half Dies: The Real Reasons for World Hunger* (Montclair, N.J.: Allanheld, Osmun & Co., 1977), p. 261.

19. Ibid., p. 248.

20. Robert Borosage, as cited in Joshua Muravchik, *Commentary*, October 1986, p. 88.

21. Richard J. Barnet and Marcus G. Raskin, *After 20 Years: The Decline of NATO and the Search for a New Policy in Europe* (New York: Random House, 1966).

22. Marcus G. Raskin, *The Politics of National Security* (New Brunswick, N.J.: Transaction Books, 1979), p. 186.

23. Richard J. Barnet, "Lies Clearer Than Truth: A Look at the Russian Threat," *Waging Peace*, ed. Jim Wallis (New York: Harper & Row, 1982), p. 57.

24. Mary Kaldor, "Warfare and Capitalism," *Exterminism and the New Cold War*, ed. *New Left Review* (London: Verso, 1982), p. 279.

25. Ibid., p. 280.

26. Fred Halliday, "The Sources of the New Cold War," *Exterminism and the New Cold War*, p. 310.

27. Marcus G. Raskin, "Nuclear Extermination and the National Security State," *Exterminism and the New Cold War,* p. 211.

28. Richard Barnet, "Two Bumbling Giants: The Superpowers' Outdated Policies in a Nuclear World," *Waging Peace*, p. 66.

29. John Boland, "Peace, War and the Institute for Policy Studies," *Wall Street Journal*, February 5, 1982.

Appendix 9: Overview of TIE's European Organizations

1. Stichting Onderzoek Multinationale Ondernemingen (SOMO), promotional literature.
2. *TIE-Europe Bulletin*, no. 13/14, p. 73.
3. World Information Service on Energy, promotional literature.
4. Religious News Service, February 5, 1973, p. 2.

Index

454